English
Français
Deutsche
Italiano
Español
Português

www.forgottenbooks.com

Mythology Photography **Fiction**
Fishing Christianity **Art** Cooking
Essays Buddhism Freemasonry
Medicine **Biology** Music **Ancient**
Egypt Evolution Carpentry Physics
Dance Geology **Mathematics** Fitness
Shakespeare **Folklore** Yoga Marketing
Confidence Immortality Biographies
Poetry **Psychology** Witchcraft
Electronics Chemistry History **Law**
Accounting **Philosophy** Anthropology
Alchemy Drama Quantum Mechanics
Atheism Sexual Health **Ancient History**
Entrepreneurship Languages Sport
Paleontology Needlework Islam
Metaphysics Investment Archaeology
Parenting Statistics Criminology
Motivational

ISBN 978-0-266-06342-1
PIBN 10947797

THE PROCEEDINGS

RELATIVE TO

CALLING THE CONVENTIONS OF 1776 AND 1790.

THE

MINUTES OF THE CONVENTION

THAT FORMED THE PRESENT

Constitution of Pennsylvania,

TOGETHER WITH

THE CHARTER TO WILLIAM PENN,

THE

Constitutions of 1776 and 1790,

A VIEW OF THE PROCEEDINGS OF THE CONVENTION OF 1776,

AND

THE COUNCIL OF CENSORS.

HARRISBURG:

PRINTED BY JOHN S WIESTLING, MARKET STREET

1825.

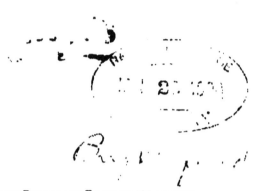

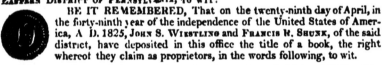

INDEX.

INTRODUCTION.

THE object of the compilers of this volume is to present to the people of Pennsylvania the constitutions of the province and the commonwealth, and the mode and manner in which the several changes in the frame of government were made—to effect this purpose, the following pages exhibit a view of all the official proceedings in relation to calling conventions in this state, the minutes of the conventions, and the frames of the proprietary and state governments.

Charles the second, on the 4th of March, 1681, granted to William Penn, proprietary and governor, a charter for the province of Pennsylvania. Under the powers delegated by this charter, the proprietary, with certain freemen of the province, adopted the first frame of government and certain laws, in England, on the 20th day of April, 1682, these were to be further explained and confirmed by the first provincial council, if they should see meet.

William Penn arrived in America, for the purpose of taking possession of the province, on the 24th of October, 1682. He landed at New Castle, now in the state of Delaware—the inhabitants on the Delaware then consisted of English, Dutch and Swedes; on the next day he convened the people at the court house, where after possession of the country was legally given to him, he made a speech to the old magistrates and the people, signifying to them the design of his coming, the nature and end of government in general, and particularly of that which he came to establish; assuring to them the full enjoyment of their spiritual and temporal rights, liberty of conscience and civil freedom; and recommending to them to live in sobriety and peace. After having renewed the magistrate's commissions, he proceeded to Upland, now called Chester, where, on the 4th day of December, 1682, he called an assembly of the people, which consisted of as many of the freemen of the province, and three lower counties, then called the territories, as thought proper to appear, according to the provisions of the 16th article of the frame of government. At this assembly an act of union was passed annexing the three lower counties (now the state of Delaware) to the province in legislation.

Among other laws, the act of settlement was passed, by which, with some alterations and additions, the frame of government agreed upon in England, was accepted and confirmed.* At this assembly all the laws agreed upon in England, were, with some alterations, passed in form, and the foreigners were naturalized. Nicholas Moore, was speaker of this assembly, which continued in session only three days.

In the latter part of the year 1682, the proprietary purchased the land whereon Philadelphia now stands, called by the natives Coaquannock, and with the assistance of his surveyor general, Thomas Holmes, laid out the city At this period the proprietor with the consent of the purchasers divided the province and territories, each, into three counties; those of the province were called Philadelphia, Bucks and Chester; and those of the territories, New Castle, Kent and Sussex; and having appointed sheriffs and other proper officers for each county, he issued writs for the election of members of council and assembly, according to the provisions of the frame of government

He met the council on the 10th day of March, 1683, O. S. at Philadelphia, and the assembly two days afterwards. There were three members of council, and nine members of assembly, returned for each county. The number of councillors and members of assembly returned, being deficient, the freemen of the counties prayed the proprietor that the number might be limited to three councillors and nine members of assembly for each county, and that their non-compliance with the terms

---

The act of settlement is not inserted in this work, because all the alterations which it introduced into the frame of 1682, are among others contained in the frame of 1683.

of the frame of government might not deprive them of it. The governor answered, " That they might amend, alter or add, for the public good, and that he was ready to settle such foundations as might be for their happiness, according to the powers vested in him."

This session continued twenty-two days. The principal business that was transacted, was the alteration of the frame of government. By the twenty-third section it was provided, that no law should be passed to alter, change or diminish the form or effect of the frame of government, or any part or clause thereof, or contrary to the true intent and meaning thereof, without the consent of the governor and six parts of seven of the freemen in provincial council and general assembly.

A conference was held between the governor and council and the general assembly, at which the council and assembly unanimously requested an alteration of the frame of government. Whereupon a committee was appointed by each house to amend the same, and include such alterations as had been agreed upon, and at a council held on the 2d of April, 1683, the frame, as amended, being prepared, was read, signed, sealed and delivered by the governor to a committee of the assembly, who returned to him the frame of 1682. The charter of 1683 continued to be the supreme law of the province until 1696.

William Penn continued in the province until the summer of the year 1684, when a dispute about the southern boundary of the province with Lord Baltimore, the proprietor of Maryland, and other important interests, called him home to England. Upon leaving the country, he empowered the provincial council to supply his place in the government. In the year 1686, the proprietary found that the executive part of the government was not well administered in consequence of being committed to so many hands, he therefore issued a new commission to five persons, constituting them commissioners of state, and vesting them with the executive power of government, with instructions to compel the attendance of the provincial council ; to suffer no intrenchment of the council or assembly upon the privileges and powers of the executive ; to inspect the proceedings of the legislature, the qualifications of the members, &c. Under the administration of the government by these commissioners, some difficulties occurred, particularly because of the dissatisfaction of the three lower counties ; and the proprietary was induced, in the year 1691, to submit to the choice of the council three different modes of administering the executive powers of government, viz. Either that of the council ; of five commissioners, or of a deputy governor. The council adopted the latter, and Thomas Lloyd was elected deputy. Owing to the disagreement between the province and territories, this election did not meet with the approbation of the latter, and the proprietary appointed William Markham, their governor.

It appears that William Penn, during the unfortunate reign of James II, was in favor at court : which, together with other circumstances, gave to his enemies an opportunity, after the revolution in 1688, of gaining over him a partial advantage.

In 1692 he was deprived, by William and Mary, of the government of the province and territories of Pennsylvania, and a commission was issued to Benjamin Fletcher, governor of New York, dated the 21st of October, 1692, authorising him to annex Pennsylvania to his jurisdiction. Governor Fletcher arrived at Philadelphia in April, 1693. The assembly met on the 16th May following, and resolved, that the laws of the province that were in force before the arrival of the new governor were still in force ; and that the assembly had a right to move for a continuance or confirmation thereof. They accordingly addressed the governor, acknowledged his power, and prayed that the legislative proceedings might be regulated according to the charter and laws of the province, and that the same might be confirmed to them.

The governor in his reply, stated that the late governor had been displaced because of the neglects and miscarriages of his administration, that the constitution of the government of the province, was in direct opposition to the government of England, and that their adherence to the former was proof of their opposition to the latter. These disputes between the governor and assembly arising from the assertion of rights on the one side, and the denial of them on the other, interrupted the harmony of the government. Several laws were however passed, whereupon governor Fletcher returned to New York, having appointed William Markham, lieutenant governor of Pennsylvania. The assembly again met in May and September, 1694, at which sessions several laws were passed, and here terminated the administration of governor Fletcher.

In November 1693, the friends of William Penn, at court, represented his case to the king, as oppressive; that the charges against him were urged by imposters, and that his political and private character were above reproach. This representation was well received by the sovereign, and the proprietor was reinstated in his government by letters patent, dated the 20th August, 1694; upon which he appointed William Markham his lieutenant governor, who convened the assembly on the 26th October, 1696; at this session the act of settlement or frame of 1696, was passed, which continued in force until the year 1701.

In August 1699, William Penn set sail from England for Pennsylvania, where he arrived early in December, the same year. During his stay he had various meetings with the general assembly, at which the business of the province was transacted with great harmony, and very much to the satisfaction of the people.

In May 1701, the former charter was surrendered into the hands of the proprietary and governor, by six parts in seven of the assembly. And on the 28th October 1701, the council, the assembly and several of the principal inhabitants of Philadelphia attending, the governor presented to them the last charter of privileges or frame of 1701. At the same time he established by letters patent, under the great seal, a council of state for the province and territories, to consult and assist the proprietary or his lieutenants with the best of their advice and counsel in public affairs and matters relating to the government, and to the peace, well being and safety of the people; and in the absence of the proprietary, or upon the lieutenants death or incapacity, to exercise all and singular the powers of government. And having appointed Andrew Hamilton, lieutenant governor of the province, he sailed for England.

The frame of 1701, continued the supreme law of the province during the residue of the proprietary government, and is inserted at large in the following pages. The first frame adopted in 1682 is also inserted, and the alterations and amendments made by the frames of 1683 and 1696, are annexed in notes. The last general assembly under the proprietary government was elected in October 1775, and adjourned on the 26th September 1776.

The origin and progress of the revolution which terminated in the establishment of the independence of the United States, is a matter of history well known to the people of Pennsylvania. It is only necessary here to state, that the continental congress, on the 15th May 1776, adopted a resolution recommending to the respective assemblies and conventions of the United Colonies, where no government sufficient to the exigencies of their affairs had been established, to adopt such government as should, in the opinion of the representatives of the people, best conduce to the happiness and safety of their constituents in particular, and America in general.[*] There was a diversity of opinion in the province, on the subject of this resolution. On the 21st May 1776, a protest was presented to the representatives in assembly, against the authority of the house to interfere in the premises. It was said that the chartered powers of the house were derived from the mortal enemy of the colonies, and the members were elected by such persons only as were in real or supposed allegiance to the king, that the house was in immediate intercourse with a governor bearing the king's commission, being his sworn representative, and by his oath obliged to hold official correspondence with his ministers. That the circumstances under which the members were elected, and their relation to, and connexion with the government of Great Britain, disqualified them to take into consideration the resolve of the congress. That they did not object to the house exercising the proper powers which it had hitherto enjoyed for the safety and convenience of the province, until such time as a new constitution originating from, and founded on the authority of the people, should be adopted by a provincial convention to be elected for that purpose, that an application would be made to the committee of inspection and observation of the city and liberties for calling a conference of committees of the several counties, to provide for the election of a convention for the purpose of carrying the resolve of congress into execution, and that they were fully convinced that their safety and happiness, next to the immediate providence of God, depended on their complying with, and supporting firmly the said resolve of congress.

This protest was answered by addresses to the assembly, from various parts of the state. It was urged by those of a contrary opinion, that the ground upon which the opposition to the arbitrary and oppressive measures of the British ministry was first made, was by these proceedings of the congress totally changed, that instead of forwarding a reconciliation with the parent state, on constitutional principle an object which all should have in view, a system of policy had been adopted tend.

---

* For this resolution and preamble see page 87 of this work.

ing immediately to the subversion of the constitution. It was said that if the inveterate enemies of the colonies should persist in their despotic measures, and drive them by violence to that last shift, a declaration of independence, all would then be united and strengthened by the conviction that the measure was absolutely necessary; that they had qualified themselves in military matters, and were exceeded by none in their exertions to terminate the oppression of their country, but it was with a determined resolution to defend their constitution against innovations—they advised the assembly to proceed in the weighty matters under their consideration with unanimity and firmness, and to look forward to a happy termination of difficulties in a constitutional reconciliation with ancient friends, to adhere religiously to the instructions given to the delegates in congress, by which they were enjoined to dissent from and utterly reject any propositions, should any such be made, that might lead to a separation from the mother country or a change of the form of government, and they prayed the assembly to oppose the changing or altering in any the least part, their invaluable constitution under which they had experienced so much happiness, and in support of which there was nothing just or reasonable, which they would not willingly undertake.

They also urged that the resolve of congress was a conditional recommendation, that the practice, had been, when assemblies and conventions were referred to by the congress, to commit the subject to the assemblies, as the ancient constitutional bodies in the respective colonies—that conventions were only resorted to in cases where arbitrary governors had dissolved the assemblies or had subverted their constitutions by abdicating their offices—that the assembly of this province could not be prorogued or dissolved, that it had not been exceeded in exertions in the common cause of liberty, that by the resolve of congress, the representatives of the people were the sole judges whether their governments were sufficient for the exigencies of their affairs or not—that by the charter, six parts in seven of the assembly were vested with the power of altering the constitution and that in times of confusion, changes should be cautiously adopted and only such should be made as were absolutely necessary.

The assembly took no measures in relation to the resolve of congress more than to appoint a committee to take the same into consideration, and to draft a memorial from the house, setting forth the different constructions and requesting an explanation from congress in definite terms. It does not appear that this committee made a report. These proceedings of the last provincial assembly took place in the latter part of May, 1776. After which time a quorum of members seldom appeared in the house, and they finally adjourned on the 26th September, following.

In order to carry into effect the said resolution of the congress, the committee of the city and liberties of Philadelphia addressed circular letters enclosing the resolve of congress, to the committees of the several counties, requesting them to appoint deputies to meet in provincial conference—the county committees complied with the request, and the conference met in Philadelphia on the 18th of June, 1776, and made provision for calling the convention which formed the constitution of 1776. Such proceedings of the conference and convention as relate to the constitution will be found in the following pages.

It appears that the constitution of 1776, did not meet the full approbation of the people, for in 1777, and in 1778, resolutions were adopted by the assembly for calling a convention,* but in 1779, upon the petitions of a very large number of citizens, the resolutions were rescinded.

By the 47th section of the constitution of 1776, the most important powers were delegated to the council of censors, which was to consist of two persons from each city and county, to be elected on the second Tuesday of October, 1783, and on the second Tuesday of the same month, in every seventh year thereafter,—the first and only council met upon the 10th of November 1783. The first session terminated on the 21st of January, 1784, the second session commenced on the 1st of June, 1784, and the council finally adjourned on the 25th of September, 1784.

Two detailed reports of the council, with reasons of assent and dissent to various parts are inserted in this volume,† they relate entirely to the constitution, and exhibit the opinions of the council upon that instrument and their construction of its several articles—The opinion of the council is quoted as a reason for the passage of the act of the 4th April, 1785, which see in note to page 101 of this vol.

* *See the resolution in note to page* [111 *of this volume.*
† *See page* 123.

INTRODUCTION.

It will be observed that at the first session a majority of the council was in favor of calling a convention for the purpose of altering the constitution, and at the second session the majority was opposed to a convention.

The following appear to have been the reasons for this difference in the sentiments of the majority.

George Bryan was elected in the room of Samuel Miles, resigned—James Potter was elected in the room of Samuel Hunter deceased, who had not attended, and James Read and Willian Montgomery, who were absent at the first, attended during the second session.

The proceedings relative to calling the convention, and the minutes of the convention that formed the present constitution, are inserted at large, together with the act of the 28th of March, 1825, for ascertaining the opinion of the people of the commonwealth relative to the call of a convention

August 3, 1825.

CONTENTS.

PART 1.

PART II.

PART III.

PART IV.

PART V.

Conventions

AND

CONSTITUTIONS

OF

PENNSYLVANIA.

PART I.

Chapter I.

The Royal Charter granted to William Penn, Esq. Proprietary and Governor of Pennsylvania

CHARLES the second, by the grace of God, king of England, Scotland, France and Ireland, defender of the faith, &c. To all to whom these presents shall come, Greeting:

Whereas our trusty and well beloved subject William Penn, Esq. son and heir of sir William Penn, deceased (out of a commendable desire to enlarge our English empire, and promote such useful commodities as may be of benefit to us and to our dominions, as also to reduce the savage natives by gentle and just manners to the love of civil society and christian religion) hath humbly besought leave of us to transport an ample colony unto a certain country hereinafter described, in the parts of America not yet cultivated and planted; and hath likewise humbly besought our royal majesty, to give, grant and confirm all the said country, with certain privileges and jurisdictions requisite for the good government and safety of the said country and colony, to him and his heirs for ever:

Section 1. Know ye, therefore, that we (favouring the petition and good purpose of the said William Penn, and having regard to the memory and merits of his late father in divers services, and particularly to his conduct, courage and discretion, under our dearest brother James duke of York, in that signal battle and victory fought and obtained against the Dutch fleet, commanded by the Heer Van Opdam, in the year 1665: In consideration thereof of our special grace, certain knowledge and

more motion) have given and granted, and by this our present charter,
for us our heirs and successors, do give and grant unto the said William
Penn, his heirs and assigns, all that tract or part of land in America
with all the islands therein contained, as the same is bounded on the
east by Delaware river, from twelve miles distance northwards of New
Castle town unto the three and fortieth degree of northern latitude, if
the said river doth extend so far northward: but if the said river shall
not extend so far northwards, then by the said river so far as it doth
extend; and from the head of the said river the eastern bounds are to
be determined by a meridian line, to be drawn from the head of the
said river unto the said three and fortieth degree. The said lands to
extend westwards five degrees in longitude, to be computed from the
said eastern bounds; and the said lands to be bounded on the north by
the beginning of the three and fortieth degree of northern latitude, and
on the south by a circle drawn at twelve miles distance from New
Castle northwards; and westwards unto the beginning of the fortieth
degree of northern latitude, and then by a straight line westwards to
the limits of longitude, above mentioned.

Sect. 2. We do also give and grant unto the said William Penn, his
heirs and assigns, the free and undisturbed use and continuance in,
and passage unto, and out of all and singular ports, harbours, bays,
waters, rivers, isles and inlets, belonging unto, or leading to and from
the country or islands aforesaid, and all the soil, lands, fields, woods,
underwoods, mountains, hills, fens, isles, lakes, rivers, waters, rivulets, bays and inlets, situate or being within, or belonging unto the
limits and bounds aforesaid, together with the fishing of all sorts of
fish, whales, sturgeons, and all royal and other fishes, in the seas, bays,
inlets, waters, or rivers, within the premises, and the fish therein taken;
and also all veins, mines and quarries, as well discovered as not discovered, of gold, silver, gems and precious stones, and all other whatsoever, be it stonse, metals or of any other thing or matter whatsoever,
found or to be found within the country, isles or limits aforesaid.

Sect. 3. And him the said William Penn, his heirs and assigns, we
do by this our royal charter, for us, our heirs and successors, make,
create and constitute the true and absolute proprietaries of the country aforesaid, and of all other the premises: Saving always to us, our
heirs and successors, the faith and allegiance of the said William Penn,
his heirs and assigns, and of all other the proprietaries' tenants and
inhabitants, that are or shall be within the territories and precincts
aforesaid; and saving always unto us, our heirs and successors, the
sovereignty of the aforesaid countries; to have, hold, possess and enjoy
the said tract of land, country, isles, inlets, and other the premises,
unto the said William Penn, his heirs and assigns, to the only proper
use and behoof of the said William Penn, his heirs and assigns for ever, to be holden of us, our heirs and successors, kings of England, as
of our castle of Windsor, in our county of Berks, in free and common
socage, by fealty only for all services, and not in capite, or by knights
service: Yielding and paying therefor to us, our heirs and successors,
two beaver skins, to be delivered at our said castle of Windsor, on the
first day of January in every year; and also the fifth part of all gold
and silver ore which shall from time to time happen to be found within the limits aforesaid, clear of all charges. And of our further grace,
certain knowledge, and mere motion, we have thought fit to erect, and
we do hereby erect the aforesaid country and islands into a province

and seignory, and do call it Pennsylvania, and so from henceforth we will have it called.

Sect. 4. And forasmuch as we have hereby made and ordained the aforesaid William Penn, his heirs and assigns, the true and absolute proprietaries of all the lands and dominions aforesaid, know ye, therefore, that we (reposing special trust and confidence in the fidelity, wisdom, justice and provident circumspection of the said William Penn) for us our heirs and successors, do grant free, full and absolute power, (by virtue of these presents) to him and his heirs, and to his and their deputies and lieutenants, for the good and happy government of the said country, to ordain, make and enact, and under his and their seals to publish any laws whatsoever, for the raising of money for the public use of the said province, or for any other end, appertaining either unto the public state, peace or safety of the said country, or unto the private utility of particular persons, according unto their best discretion, by and with the advice, assent and approbation of the freemen of the said country, or the greater part of them or of their delegates or deputies, whom for the enacting of the said laws, when and as often as need shall require, we will that the said William Penn, and his heirs, shall assemble in such sort and form, as to him and them shall seem best, and the same laws duly to execute, unto and upon all people within the said country and limits thereof.

Sect. 5. And we do likewise give and grant unto the said William Penn, and his heirs, and to his and their deputies and lieutenants, such power and authority to appoint and establish any judges and justices, magistrates and other officers whatsoever, for what causes soever (for the probates of wills, and for the granting of administrations within the precincts aforesaid) and with what power soever, and in such forms as to the said William Penn, or his heirs shall seem most convenient: Also to remit, release, pardon and abolish (whether before judgment or alter) all crimes and offences whatsoever, committed, within the said country against the said laws (treason and wilful and malicious murder only excepted, and in those cases to grant reprieves, until our pleasure may be known therein) and to do all and every other thing and things, which unto the complete establishment of justice unto courts and tribunals, forms of judicature, and manner of proceedings, do belong, although in these presents express mention be not made thereof; and by judges by them delegated, to award process, hold pleas, and determine in all the said courts and tribunals all actions, suits and causes whatsoever, as well criminal as civil, personal, real and mixed: which laws, so as aforesaid to be published, our pleasure is, and so we enjoin, require and command, shall be most absolute and available in law; and that all the liege people and subjects of us, our heirs and successors, do observe and keep the same inviolable in those parts, so far as they concern them, under the pain therein expressed, or to be expressed. Provided nevertheless, That the said laws be consonant to reason, and be not repugnant or contrary, but (as near as conveniently may be) agreeable to the laws, statutes and rights of this our kingdom of England; and saving and reserving to us, our heirs and successors, the receiving, hearing and determining of the appeal and appeals of all or any person or persons, of, in, or belonging to the territories aforesaid, or touching any judgment to be there made or given.

Sect. 6. And forasmuch as in the government of so great a country, sudden accidents do often happen, whereunto it will be necessary to apply a remedy, before the freeholders of the said province, or their delegates or deputies, can be assembled to the making of laws; neither will it be convenient that instantly, upon every such emergent occasion, so great a multitude should be called together: Therefore (for the better government of the said country) we will and ordain, and by these presents, for us, our heirs and successors, do grant unto the said William Penn, and his heirs, by themselves, or by their magistrates and officers, in that behalf duly to be ordained as aforesaid, to make and constitute fit and wholesome ordinances from time to time, within the said country to be kept and observed, as well for the preservation of the peace, as for the better government of the people there inhabiting; and publicly to notify the same to all persons, whom the same doth or any way may concern. Which ordinances, our will and pleasure is, shall be observed inviolably within the said province, under the pains therein to be expressed, so as the said ordinances be consonant to reason, and be not repugnant nor contrary, but (so far as conveniently may be) agreeable to the laws of our kingdom of England, and so as the said ordinances be not extended in any sort to bind, charge, or take away the right or interest of any person or persons, for or in their life, members, freehold, goods or chattles. And our further will and pleasure is, that the laws for regulating and governing of property within the said province, as well for the descent and enjoyment of lands, as likewise for the enjoyment and succession of goods and chattles, and likewise as to felonies, shall be and continue the same, as they shall be for the time being by the general course of the law in our kingdom of England, until the said laws shall be altered by the said William Penn, his heirs or assigns, and by the freemen of the said province, their delegates or deputies, or the greater part of them.

Sect. 7. And to the end that the said William Penn, or heirs, or other the planters, owners or inhabitants of the said province, may not at any time hereafter (by misconstruction of the powers aforesaid) through inadvertency or design, depart from that faith and due allegiance, which by the laws of this our realm of England, they and all our subjects, in our dominions and territories, always owe unto us, our heirs and successors, by colour of any extent or largeness of powers hereby given, or pretended to be given, or by force or colour of any laws hereafter to be made in the said province, by virtue of any such powers; our further will and pleasure is, that a transcript or duplicate of all laws, which shall be so as aforesaid made and published within the said province, shall within five years after the making thereof be transmitted and delivered to the privy council, for the time being, of us, our heirs and successors: And if any of the said laws, within the space of six months after that they shall be so transmitted and delivered, be declared by us, our heirs or successors, in our or their privy council, inconsistent with the sovereignty or lawful prerogative of us, our heirs or successors, or contrary to the faith and allegiance due to the legal government of this realm, from the said William Penn, or his heirs, or of the planters and inhabitants of the said province, and that thereupon any of the said laws shall be adjudged and declared to be void by us, our heirs or successors, under our or their privy seal, that then and from thenceforth, such laws, concerning which such judgment and declaration shall be made, shall become void:

Otherwise the said laws so transmitted shall remain and stand in full force, according to the true intent and meaning thereof.

Sect. 8. Furthermore, that this new colony may the more happily encrease, by the multitude of people resorting thither; therefore we, for us, our heirs and successors, do give and grant by these presents, power, licence and liberty unto all the liege people and subjects, both present and future, of us, our heirs and successors (excepting those who shall be especially forbidden) to transport themselves and families unto the said country, with such convenient shipping as by the laws of this our kingdom of England they ought to use, and with fitting provision, paying only the customs therefor due, and there to settle themselves, dwell and inhabit, and plant, for the public and their own private advantage.

Sect. 9. And furthermore, that our subjects may be the rather encouraged to undertake this expedition with ready and cheerful minds, know ye, that we, of our especial grace, certain knowledge, and mere motion, do give and grant, by virtue of these presents, as well unto the said William Penn, and his heirs, as to all others who shall from time to time repair unto the said country, with a purpose to inhabit there, or to trade with the natives of the said country, full licence to lade and freight in any ports whatsoever, of us, our heirs and successors according to the laws made or to be made within our kingdom of England, and into the said country, by them their servants or assigns, to transport all and singular their goods, wares and merchandises, as likewise all sorts of grain whatsoever, and all other things whatsoever, necessary for food or clothing, not prohibited by the laws and statutes of our kingdoms and dominions to be carried out of the said kingdoms, without any let or molestation of us, our heirs and successors; or of any the officers of us, our heirs and successors, saving always to us, our heirs and successors, the legal impositions, customs, and other duties and payments, for the said wares and merchandise, by any law or statute due or to be due to us, our heirs and successors.

Sect. 10. And we do further, for us, our heirs and successors, give and grant unto the said William Penn, his heirs and assigns, free and absolute power to divide the said country and islands into towns, hundreds and counties, and to erect and incorporate towns into boroughs, and boroughs into cities, and to make and constitute fairs and markets therein, with all other convenient privileges and immunities, according to the merit of the inhabitants, and the fitness of the places, and to do all and every other thing and things touching the premises, which to him or them shall seem requisite and meet, albeit they be such as of their own nature might otherwise require a more especial commandment and warrant than in these presents is expressed.

Sect. 11. We will also, and by these presents, for us, our heirs and successors, we do give and grant licence by this our charter, unto the said William Penn, his heirs and assigns, and to all the inhabitants and dwellers in the province aforesaid, both present and to come, to import or unlade, by themselves or their servants, factors or assigns, all merchandises and goods whatsoever, that shall arise of the fruits and commodities of the said province, either by land or sea, into any of the ports of us, our heirs or successors, in our kingdom of England, and not into any other country whatsoever: And we give him full power to dispose of the said goods in the said ports; and if need be, within one year next after the unlading of the same, to lade the said

merchandise and goods again into the same or other ships, and to
transport the same into any other countries either of our dominions
or foreign, according to law; provided always that they pay such customs and impositions, subsidies and duties for the same, to us, our heirs
and successors, as the rest of our subjects of our kingdom of England,
for the time being, shall be bound to pay, and do observe the acts of
navigation, and other laws in that behalf made.

Sect. 12. And furthermore, of our more ample and especial grace,
certain knowledge, and mere motion, we do for us, our heirs and successors, grant unto the said William Penn, his heirs and assigns, full
and absolute power and authority to make, erect and constitute, within the said province and the isles and inlets aforesaid, such and so many seaports, harbors, creeks, havens, keys, and other places for discharge and unlading of goods and merchandises out of the ships, boats
and other vessels, and lading them into such and so many places, and
with such rights, jurisdictions, liberties and privileges, unto the said
ports belonging, as to him and them shall seem most expedient; and
that all and singular the ships, boats and other vessels which shall
come for merchandise and trade unto the said province, or out of the
same, shall depart, shall be laden or unladen only at such ports as shall
be erected and constituted by the said William Penn, his heirs or
assigns, any use custom or other thing to the contrary notwithstanding: Provided, that the said William Penn, and his heirs, and the lieutenants and governors for the time being, shall admit and receive in
and about all such ports, havens, creeks and keys, all officers and their
deputies, who shall from time to time be appointed for that purpose by
the farmers or commissioners of our customs for the time being.

Sect. 13. And we do further appoint and ordain, and by these presents, for us our heirs and successors, we do grant unto the said William Penn, his heirs and assigns, that he the said William Penn,
his heirs and assigns, may from time to time for ever have and enjoy
the customs and subsidies, in the ports, harbours, and other creeks
and places aforesaid, within the province aforesaid, payable or due for
merchandises and wares there to be laded and unladed, the said customs and subsidies to be reasonably assessed upon any occasion, by
themselves and the people there as aforesaid to be assembled, to whom
we give power by these presents, for us, our heirs and successors, upon
just cause and in a due proportion, to assess and impose the same;
saving unto us, our heirs and successors, such impositions and customs,
as by act of parliament are and shall be appointed.

Sect. 14. And it is our farther will and pleasure, that the said
William Penn, his heirs and assigns, shall from time to time constitute and appoint an attorney or agent, to reside in or near our city of
London, who shall make known the place where he shall dwell, or may
be found, unto the clerks of our privy council for the time being, or one
of them, and shall be ready to appear in any of our courts at Westminster, to answer for any misdemeanors that shall be committed, or
by any wilful default or neglect permitted, by the said William Penn,
his heirs or assigns, against our laws of trade and navigation; and after it shall be ascertained in any of our said courts what damages we,
or our heirs or successors, shall have sustained by such default or neglect, the said William Penn, his heirs or assigns, shall pay the same
within one year after such taxation, and demand thereof from such attorney: Or in case there shall be no such attorney by the space of one

year, or such attorney shall not make payment of such damages within the space of one year, and answer such other forfeitures and penalties within the said time, as by the acts of parliament in England, are and shall be provided, according to the true intent and meaning of these presents, then it shall be lawful for us, our heirs and successors, to seize and resume the government of the said province or country, and the same to retain until payment shall be made thereof: But notwithstanding any such seizure or resumption of the government, nothing concerning the propriety or ownership of any lands, tenements or other hereditaments, or goods or chattels of any of the adventurers, planters or owners, other than the respective offenders there, shall any way be affected or molested thereby.

Sect. 15. Provided always, and our will and pleasure is, that neither the said William Penn, nor his heirs or any other the inhabitants of the said province, shall at any time hereafter have or maintain any correspondence with any other king, prince or state, or with any of their subjects, who shall then be in war against us, our heirs and successors; nor shall the said William Penn, or his heirs, or any other the inhabitants of the said province, make war, or do any act of hostility against any other king, prince or state, or any of their subjects, who shall then be in league or amity with us, our heirs or successors.

Sect. 16. And because in so remote a country, and situate near many barbarous nations, the incursions as well of the savages themselves as of other enemies, pirates and robbers, may probably be feared; therefore we have given, and for us, our heirs and successors, do give power by these presents unto the said William Penn, his heirs and assigns, by themselves or their captains or other their officers, to levy, muster and train all sorts of men, of what condition or wheresoever born, in the said province of Pennsylvania, for the time being, and to make war, and to pursue the enemies and robbers aforesaid, as well by sea as by land, yea even without the limits of the said province, and by God's assistance to vanquish and take them, and being taken to put them to death by the law of war, or to save them, at their pleasure, and to do all and every other act and thing which to the charge and office of a captain-general of an army belongeth or hath accustomed to belong, as fully and freely as any captain general of an army hath ever had the same.

Sect. 17. And furthermore, of our especial grace, and of our certain knowledge and mere motion, we have given and granted, and by these presents, for us, our heirs and successors, do give and grant unto the said William Penn, his heirs and assigns, full and absolute power, licence and authority, that he the said William Penn, his heirs and assigns, from time to time hereafter forever, at his or their will or pleasure, may assign, alien, grant, demise, or enfeoff of the premises so many and such parts and parcels, to him or them that shall be willing to purchase the same, as they shall think fit, to have and to hold to them, the said person or persons willing to take or purchase, their heirs and assigns, in fee-simple, or fee-tail, or for the term of life, or lives, or years, to be held of the said William Penn, his heirs and assigns, as of the said seniory of Windsor, by such services, customs and rents, as shall seem fit to the said William Penn, his heirs and assigns, and not immediately of us, our heirs or successors.

Sect. 18. And to the same person or persons, and to all and every of them, we do give and grant by these presents, for us our heirs and successors, licence, authority and power, that such person or persons may take the premises, or any parcel thereof, of the aforesaid William Penn, his heirs or assigns, and the same hold to themselves, their heirs and assigns, in what estate of inheritance soever, in fee-simple or in fee-tail, or otherwise, as to him the said William Penn, his heirs and assigns, shall seem expedient: The statute made in the parliament of Edward, son of king Henry, late king of England, our predecessor (commonly called *The statute quia emptores terrarum*, lately published in our kingdom of England) in anywise notwithstanding.

Sect. 19. And by these presents we give and grant licence unto the said William Penn, and his heirs, likewise to all and every such person and persons, to whom the said William Penn or his heirs, shall at any time hereafter grant any estate of inheritance as aforesaid, to erect any parcels of land within the province aforesaid into manors, by and with the licence to be first had and obtained for that purpose, under the hand and seal of the said William Penn, or his heirs; and in every of the said manors to have and to hold a court-baron, with all things whatsoever which to a court-baron do belong, and to have and to hold view of frank-pledge for the conservation of the peace and the better government of those parts, by themselves or their stewards, or by the lords for the time being of other manors, to be deputed when they shall be erected, and in the same to use all things belonging to the view of frank-pledge. And we do further grant license and authority, that every such person and persons, who shall erect any such manor or manors as aforesaid, shall or may grant all or any part of his said lands to any person or persons in fee-simple, or any other estate of inheritance, to be held of the said manors respectively, so as no further tenures shall be created; but that upon all further and other alienations thereafter to be made, the said lands so aliened shall be held of the same lord and his heirs, of whom the alienor did then before hold, and by the like rents and services which were before due and accustomed.

Sect. 20. And further our pleasure is, and by these presents, for us, our heirs and successors, we do covenant and grant to and with the said William Penn, his heirs and assigns, that we our heirs and successors shall at no time hereafter set or make, or cause to be set, any imposition, custom or other taxation, rate or contribution whatsoever, in and upon the dwellers and inhabitants of the aforesaid province, for their lands, tenements, goods or chattles within the said province, or in and upon any goods and merchandise within the said province, or to be laden or unladen within the ports or harbours of the said province, unless the same be with the consent of the proprietary, or chief governor and assembly, or by act of parliament in England.

Sect. 21. And our pleasure is, and for us, our heirs and successors, we charge and command, that this our declaration shall from henceforward be received and allowed, from time to time, in all our courts, and before all the judges of us, our heirs and successors for a sufficient and lawful discharge, payment and acquittance; commanding all and singular the officers and ministers of us, our heirs and successors, and enjoining them, upon pain of our highest displeasure, that they do not presume at any time to attempt any thing to the contrary of the premises, or that they do in any sort withstand the same, but that they be at all times aiding and assisting, as is fitting, unto the said William Penn, and his heirs, and to the inhabitants and merchants of the province aforesaid, their servants, ministers, factors and assigns, in the full use and fruition of the benefit of this our charter.

Sect. 22. And our further pleasure is, and we do hereby, for us, our heirs and successors charge and require, that if any of the inhabitants of the said province, to the number of twenty shall at any time hereafter be desirous, and shall by any writing, or by any person deputed for them, signify such their desire to the bishop of London, that any preacher or preachers, to be approved of by the said bishop, may be sent unto them for their instruction; that then such preacher or preachers shall and may be and reside within the said province, without any denial or molestation whatsoever.

Sect. 23. And if perchance hereafter any doubt or question should arise, concerning the true sense or meaning of any word, clause or sentence, contained in this our present charter, we will, ordain and command, that at all times and in all things, such interpretations be made thereof, and allowed in any of our courts whatsoever, as shall be adjudged most advantageous and favorable unto the said William Penn, his heirs and assigns: Provided always, no interpretation be admitted thereof, by which the allegiance due unto us, our heirs and successors, may suffer any prejudice or diminution; although express mention be not made in these presents of the true yearly value, or certainty of the premises, or of any part thereof, or of other gifts and grants made by us, our progenitors or predecessors unto the said William Penn; or any statute, act, ordinance, provision, proclamation, or restraint heretofore had, made, published, ordained or provided, or any other thing, cause or matter whatsoever, to the contrary thereof in anywise notwithstanding. In witness whereof we have caused these our letters to be made patents: Witness ourself, at Westminster, the fourth day of March, in the three and thirtieth year of our reign.

By writ of Privy Seal.

PIGOTT.

Chapter II.

PROPRIETARY FRAMES OF GOVERNMENT.

The frame of the government of the province of Pennsylvania, in America: together with certain laws agreed upon in England, by the Governor and divers freemen of the aforesaid province.

THE PREFACE.

When the great and wise God had made the world, of all his creatures, it pleased him to chose man his Deputy to rule it; and to fit him for so great a charge and trust, he did not only qualify him with skill and power, but with integrity to use them justly. This native goodness was equally his honour and his happiness; and whilst he stood

3

here, all went well; there was no need of coercive or compulsive means; the precept of divine love and truth, in his bosom, was the guide and keeper of his innocency. But lust prevailing against duty, made a lamentable breach upon it; and the law, that before had no power over him, took place upon him, and his disobedient posterity, that such as would not live conformable to the holy law within, should fall under the reproof and correction of the just law without, in a judicial administration.

This the Apostle teaches in divers of his epistles: "The law (says he) was added because of transgression:" In another place, "Knowing that the law was not made for the righteous man; but for the disobedient and ungodly, for sinners, for unholy and prophane, for murderers, for whoremongers, for them that defile themselves with mankind, and for manstealers, for lyers for perjured persons," &c. but this is not all, he opens and carries the matter of government a little further: "Let every soul be subject to the higher powers; for there is no power but of God. The powers that be are ordained of God: whosoever therefore resisteth the power, resisteth the ordinance of God. For rulers are not a terror to good works, but to evil: wilt thou then not be afraid of the power? do that which is good, and thou shalt have praise of the same." "He is the minister of God to thee for good." "Wherefore ye must needs be subject, not only for wrath, but for conscience sake."

This settles the divine right of government beyond exception, and that for two ends: first, to terrify evil doers; secondly, to cherish those that do well; which gives government a life beyond corruption, and makes it as durable in the world, as good men should be. So that government seems to me a part of religion itself, a thing sacred in its institution and end. For, if it does not directly remove the cause, it crushes the effects of evil, and is as such, (though a lower,) yet an emination of the same divine power, that is both author and object of pure religion; the difference lying here, that the one is more free and mental, the other more corporal and compulsive in its operations: but that is only to evil doers; government itself being otherwise as capable of kindness, goodness and charity, as a more private society. They weakly err, that think there is no other use of government, than correction, which is the coarsest part of it: daily experience tells us, that the care and regulation of many other affairs, more soft, and daily necessary, make up much the greatest part of government; and which must have followed the peopling of the world, had Adam never fell, and will continue among men, on earth, under the highest attainments they may arrive at, by the coming of the blessed *second Adam*, the *Jord*, from Heaven. Thus much of government in general, as to its rise and end.

For particular *frames* and *models*, it will become me to say little; and comparatively I will say nothing. My reasons are:—

First, That the age is too nice and difficult for it; there being nothing the wits of men are more busy and divided upon. It is true, they seem to agree to the end, to wit, happiness; but, in the means, they differ, as to divine so to this human felicity; and the cause is much the same, not always want of light and knowledge, but want of using them rightly. Men side with their passions against their reason, and their sinister interests have so strong a bias upon their minds, that they lean to them against the good of the things they know.

Secondly, I do not find a model in the world, that time, place, and some singular emergences have not necessarily altered; nor is it easy to frame a civil government, that shall serve all places alike.

Thirdly, I know what is said by the several admirers of *monarchy*, *aristocracy* and *democracy*, which are the rule of one, a few, and many, and are the three common ideas of government, when men discourse on the subject. But I chuse to solve the controversy with this small distinction, and it belongs to all three: *Any government is free to the people under it* (whatever be the frame) *where the laws rule, and the people are a party to those laws*, and more than this is tyranny, oligarchy, or confusion.

But, lastly, when all is said, there is hardly one frame of government in the world so ill designed by its first founders, that, in good hands, would not do well enough, and story tells us, the best, in ill ones, can do nothing that is great or good; witness the *Jewish* and *Roman* states. Governments like clocks, go from the motion men give them; and as governments are made and moved by men, so by them they are ruined too. Wherefore governments rather depend upon men, than men upon governments. Let men be good, and the government cannot be bad; if it be ill they will cure it. But, if men be bad, let the government be never so good, they will endeavour to warp and spoil it to their turn.

I know some say, let us have good laws, and no matter for the men that execute them: but let them consider, that though good laws do well, good men do better: for good laws may want good men, and be abolished or evaded by ill men; but good men will never want good laws, nor suffer ill ones. It is true, good laws have some awe upon ill ministers, but that is where they have not power to escape or abolish them, and the people are generally wise and good: but a loose and depraved people (which is to the question) love laws and an administration like themselves. That, therefore, which makes a good constitution must keep it, viz. men of wisdom and virtue, qualities, that because they descend not with worldly inheritances, must be carefully propagated by a virtuous education of youth; for which after ages will owe more to the care and prudence of founders, and the successive magistracy, than to their parents, for their private patrimonies.

These considerations of the weight of government, and the nice and various opinions about it, made it uneasy to me to think of publishing the ensuing frame and conditional laws, foreseeing both the censures, they will meet with, from men of differing humors and engagements, and the occasion they may give of discourse beyond my design.

But, next to the power of necessity, (which is a solicitor, that will take no denial) this induced me to a compliance, that we have (with reverence to God, and good conscience to men) to the best of our skill, contrived and composed the *frame* and *laws* of this government, to the great end of all government, viz. *To support power in reverence with the people, and to secure the people from the abuse of power;* that they may be free by their just obedience, and the magistrates honorable, for their just administration: for liberty without obedience is confusion, and obedience without liberty is slavery. To carry this evenness is partly owing to the constitution, and partly to the magistracy: where either of these fail, government will be subject to convulsions; but where both are wanting it must be totally subverted: then where both meet, the government is like to endure. Which I humbly pray and hope God will please to make the lot of this of *Pennsylvania.* Amen.

WILLIAM PENN.

THE FRAME, &c.

TO all people, to whom these presents shall come. WHEREAS king Charles the second, by his letters patents, under the great seal of *England,* for the consideration therein mentioned, hath been graciously pleased to give and grant unto me *William Penn* (by the name of *William Penn,* Esquire, son and heir of sir *William Penn* deceased) and to my heirs and assigns forever, all that tract of land, or province, called *Pennsylvania,* in *America,* with divers great powers, preeminences, royalties, jurisdictions, and authorities, necessary for the well being and government thereof: Now know ye, that for the well being and government of the said province, and for the encouragement of all the freemen and planters, that may be therein concerned, in pursuance of the powers aforementioned, I the said William Penn, have declared, granted and confirmed, and by these presents, for me, my heirs and assigns, do declare, grant and confirm unto all the freemen, planters and adventurers of, in and to the said province, these liberties, franchises and properties, to be held, enjoyed and kept by the freemen, planters and inhabitants of the said province of *Pennsylvania,* for ever.

Imprimis, That the government of this province shall, according to the powers of the patent, consist of the Governor and freemen of the said province, in form of a provincial council, and general assembly, by whom all laws shall be made, officers chosen, and public affairs transacted, as is hereafter respectively declared, that is to say—

II. That the freemen of the said province shall, on the twentieth day of the twelfth month, which shall be in this present year one thousand six hundred eighty and two, meet and assemble in some fit place, of which timely notice shall be before hand given by the governor or his deputy; and then, and there, shall choose out of themselves *seventy-two* persons of most note for their wisdom, virtue and ability, who shall meet, on the tenth day of the first month next ensuing, and always be called, and act as, the provincial council of the said province.*

III. That at the first choice of such provincial council, one-third part of the said provincial council shall be chosen to serve for three years then next ensuing; one-third part, for two years then next ensuing; and one-third part, for one year then next ensuing such election, and no longer; and that the said third part shall go out accordingly: and on the twentieth day of the twelfth month, as aforesaid, yearly for ever afterwards, the freemen of the said province shall, in like manner, meet and assemble together, and then choose twenty-four persons, being one third of the said number, to serve in provincial council for three years; it being intended, that one-third part of the whole pro-

---

* By the charter of 1683, the number of provincial councillors is reduced to 18, being three out of each county; and by Governor Markham's charter of 1696, the number of councillors is reduced to two out of each county.

vincial council (always consisting, and to consist, of seventy-two persons as aforesaid) falling off yearly, it shall be yearly supplied by such new yearly elections, as aforesaid; and that no one person shall continue therein longer than three years: and, in case any member shall decease before the last election during his time, that then at the next election ensuing his decease, another shall be chosen to supply his place, for the remaining time, he was to have served, and no longer.[*]

IV. That, after the first seven years, every one of the said third parts, that goeth yearly off, shall be uncapable of being chosen again for one whole year following: that so all may be fitted for government, and have experience of the care and burden of it.

V. That the provincial council, in all cases and matters of moment, as their arguing upon bills to be passed into laws, erecting courts of justice, giving judgment upon criminals impeached, and choice of officers, in such manner as is hereinafter mentioned; not less than two-thirds of the whole provincial council shall make a *quorum;* and that the consent and approbation of two thirds of such *quorum* shall be had in all such cases and matters of moment. And moreover that, in all cases and matters of lesser moment, twenty-four members of the said provincial council shall make a *quoram*, the majority of which twenty-four shall, and may, always determine in such cases and causes of lesser moment.[†]

VI. That in this provincial council, the governor, or his deputy, shall or may always preside, and have a treble voice; and the said provincial council shall always continue, and sit upon its own adjournments and committees.[‡]

VII. That the governor and provincial council shall prepare and propose to the general assembly, hereafter mentioned, all bills, which they shall, at any time, think fit to be passed into laws, within the said province; which bills shall be published and affixed to the most noted places, in the inhabited parts thereof, thirty days before the meeting of the general assembly, in order to the passing them into laws, or rejecting of them, as the general assembly shall see meet.

VIII. That the governor and provincial council shall take care, that all laws, statutes and ordinances, which shall at any time be made within the said province, be duly and diligently executed.

IX. That the governor and provincial council shall, at all times, have the care of the peace and safety of the province, and that nothing

---

[*] By the charter of 1683, the time of the election is changed to the tenth day of the first month [March]; and as three persons were chosen for every county, it is provided that the freemen shall meet on the aforesaid day of election, in every county, and choose one person, being one-third of the number to serve in provincial council for three years, it being intended that one-third of the whole provincial council, to consist of 18 persons falling off yearly, should be yearly supplied with such yearly elections, and that one person shall not continue in longer than three years.

[†] By the charter of 1683, the last clause of this article is so altered as that in matters of lesser moment, one third of the whole number shall make a quorum.

[‡] By the charter of 1683, the following appears to be substituted for this article, viz. That the governor or his deputy shall always preside in the provincial council, and that he shall at no time therein perform any public act of state whatsoever, that shall or may relate unto the justice, trade, treasury or safety of the province and territories aforesaid, but by and with the advice and consent of the provincial council thereof.

be by any person attempted to the subversion of this frame of government.

X. That the governor and provincial council shall, at all times, settle and order the situation of all cities, ports and market towns in every county, modelling therein all public buildings, streets and market places, and shall appoint all necessary roads, and highways in the province.

XI. That the governor and provincial council shall, at all times, have power to inspect the management of the public treasury, and punish those who shall convert any part thereof to any other use, than what hath been agreed upon by the governor, provincial council and general assembly.

XII. That the governor and provincial council, shall erect and order all public schools, and encourage and reward the authors of useful sciences and laudable inventions in the said province.

XIII. That, for the better management of the powers and trust aforesaid, the provincial council shall, from time to time, divide itself into four distinct and proper committees, for the more easy administration of the affairs of the province, which divides the seventy-two into four eighteens, every one of which eighteen shall consist of six out of each of the three orders, or yearly elections, each of which shall have a distinct portion of business, as followeth: *First*, a committee of plantations, to situate and settle cities, ports and market towns, and highways, and to hear and decide all suits and controversies relating to plantations. *Secondly*, A committee of justice and safety, to secure the peace of the province, and punish the mal-administration of those who subvert justice, to the prejudice of the public, or private interest. *Thirdly*, A committee of trade and treasury, who shall regulate all trade and commerce, according to law, encourage manufacture and country growth, and defray the public charge of the province. And, *Fourthly*, A committee of manners, education and arts, that all wicked and scandalous living may be prevented, and that youth may be successively trained up in virtue and useful knowledge and arts: the *quorum* of each of which committees being six, that is, two out of each of the three orders, or yearly elections, as aforesaid, make a constant and standing council of *twenty-four*, which will have the power of the provincial council, being the quorum of it, in all cases not excepted in the fifth article; and in the said committees, and standing council of the province, the governor, or his deputy, shall or may preside, as aforesaid; and in the absence of the governor, or his deputy, if no one is by either of them appointed, the said committees or council shall appoint a president for that time, and not otherwise; and what shall be resolved at such committees, shall be reported to the said council of the province, and shall be by them resolved and confirmed before the same shall be put in execution; and that these respective committees shall not sit at one and the same time, except in cases of necessity.*

* By the charter of 1683, the following appears to be substituted for this article, viz. One third part of the provincial council residing with the governor, from time to time shall, with the governor, have the care of the management of public affairs relating to the peace, justice, treasury and improvement of the province and territories, and to the good education of youth and sobriety of the manners of the inhabitants.

XIV. And, to the end that all laws prepared by the governor and provincial council aforesaid, may yet have the more full concurrence of the freemen of the province, it is declared, granted and confirmed, that at the time and place or places, for the choice of a provincial council, as aforesaid, the said freemen shall yearly choose members to serve in a general assembly, as their representatives, not exceeding two hundred persons, who shall yearly meet, on the twentieth day of the second month, which shall be in the year one thousand six hundred eighty and three following, in the capital town, or city, of the said province, where, during eight days, the several members may freely confer with one another; and if any of them see meet, with a committee of the provincial council (consisting of three out of each of the four committees aforesaid, being twelve in all) which shall be, at that time, purposely appointed to receive from any of them proposals, for the alterations or amendment of any of the said proposed and promulgated bills: and on the ninth day from their so meeting, the said general assembly, after reading over the proposed bills by the clerk of the provincial council, and the occasions and motives for them being opened by the governor or his deputy, shall give their affirmative or negative, which to them seemeth best, in such manner as herein after is expressed. But not less than two-thirds shall make a *quorum* in the passing of laws, and choice of such officers as are by them to be chosen.*

XV. That the laws so prepared and proposed, as aforesaid, that are assented to by the general assembly, shall be enrolled as laws of the province, with this stile: *By the governor, with the assent and approbation of the freemen in provincial council and general assembly.*

XVI. That for the establishment of the government and laws of this province, and to the end there may be an universal satisfaction in the laying of the fundamentals thereof; the general assembly shall, or may for the first year, consist of all the freemen of and in the said province; and ever after it shall be yearly chosen, as aforesaid; which number of two hundred shall be enlarged as the country shall increase in people, so as it do not exceed five hundred, at any time; the appointment and proportioning of which, as also the laying and methodizing of the choice of the provincial council and general assembly, in future times, most equally to the divisions of the hundreds and counties, which the country shall hereafter be divided into, shall be in the power of the provincial council to propose, and the general assembly to resolve.†

---

* By the charter of 1683, that part of this article which relates to the election of representatives, reads thus : 'The freemen of each county are to choose annually at the time and place of choosing councillors; six persons of most note for virtue, wisdom and ability to serve in assembly, as their representatives, who shall yearly meet on the 10th day of the third month, [May,] in the capital town or city of the said province, unless the governor and provincial council shall think fit to appoint another place to meet in, where during eight days, &c.

By Governor Markham's charter of 1696, the general assembly is to consist of four persons out of each county.

† By the charter of 1683, the following is substituted for the 16th article, viz. And that the representatives of the people in provincial council and assembly, may, in after ages, bear some proportion with the increase and multiplying of the people, the number of such representatives of the people may be from time to time increased and enlarged, so as at no time the number exceed seventy-two for the provincial council, and two hundred for the assembly; the appointment and propor-

XVII. That the governor and the provincial council shall erect, from time to time, standing courts of justice, in such places and number as they shall judge convenient for the good government of the said province. And that the provincial council shall, on the thirteenth day of the first month, yearly, elect and present to the Governor, or his deputy, a double number of persons to serve for judges, treasurers, masters of rolls, within the said province, for the year next ensuing; and the freemen of the said province, in the county courts, when they shall be erected, and till then, in the general assembly, shall, on the three and twentieth day of the second month, yearly, elect and present to the governor, or his deputy, a double number of persons, to serve for sheriffs, justices of the peace, and coroners, for the year next ensuing; out of which respective elections and presentments, the governor or his deputy shall nominate and commissionate the proper number for each office, the third day after the said presentments, or else the first named in such presentment, for each office, shall stand and serve for that office the year ensuing.*

XVIII. But forasmuch as the present condition of the province requires some immediate settlement, and admits not of so quick a revolution of officers; and to the end the said province may, with all convenient speed, be well ordered and settled, I *William Penn,* do therefore think fit to nominate and appoint such persons for judges, treasurers, masters of the rolls, sheriffs, justices of the peace, and coroners, as are most fitly qualified for those employments; to whom I shall make and grant commissions for the said offices, respectively, to hold to them, to whom the same shall be granted, for so long time as every such person shall well behave himself in the office, or place to him respectively granted, and no longer. And upon the decease or displacing of any of the said officers, the succeeding officer or officers shall be chosen as aforesaid.†

XIX. That the general assembly shall continue so long as may be needful to impeach criminals, fit to be there impeached, to pass bills into laws, that they shall think fit to pass into laws, and till such time as the governor and provincial council shall declare that they have nothing further to propose unto them, for their assent and approbation: and that declaration shall be a dismiss to the general assembly for that time; which general assembly shall be, notwithstanding, capable of assembling together upon the summons of the provincial council, at any time during that year, if the said provincial council shall see occasion for their so assembling.‡

XX. That all the elections of members, or representatives of the people, to serve in provincial council and general assembly, and all

---

tion of which number, as also the laying and methodizing of the choice of such representatives in future time, most equally to the division of the country or number of the inhabitants, is left to the governor and provincial council to propose, and the assembly to resolve, so that the order of proportion be strictly observed, both in the choice of the council and the respective committees thereof, viz. one-third to go off and come in yearly.

* By the charter of 1683, the judges, treasurers and masters of rolls, instead of holding their respective offices for one year, are to hold them so long as they shall well behave themselves in those capacities.

† This article is omitted in the charter of 1683.

‡ In the latter clause of this article, instead of the provincial council, the charter f 1683 requires the summons of the governor and provincial council.

questions to be determined by both, or either of them, that relate to passing of bills into laws, to the choice of officers, to impeachments by the general assembly, and judgment of criminals upon such impeachments by the provincial council, and to all other cases by them respectively judged of importance, shall be resolved and determined by the ballot; and unless on sudden and indispensible occasions, no business in provincial council, or its respective committees, shall be finally determined the same day that it is moved.*

XXI. That, at all times, when, and so often as it shall happen that the governor shall, or may, be an infant, under the age of one and twenty years, and no guardians, or commissioners, are appointed, in writing, by the father of the said infant, or that such guardians or commissioners, shall be deceased; that during such minority, the provincial council shall, from time to time, as they shall see meet, constitute and appoint guardians, or commissioners, not exceeding three; one of which three shall preside as deputy, and chief guardian, during such minority, and shall have and execute, with the consent of the other two, all the power of a governor, in all the public affairs and concerns of the said province.

XXII. That, as often as any day of the month, mentioned in any article of this charter, shall fall upon the first day of the week, commonly called the *Lord's Day*, the business appointed for that day, shall be deferred till the next day, unless in case of emergency.

XXIII. That no act, law, or ordinance whatsoever, shall at any time hereafter, be made or done by the governor of this province, his heirs or assigns, or by the freemen in the provincial council, or the general assembly, to alter, change, or diminish the form or effect, of this charter, or any part, or clause thereof, or contrary to the true intent and meaning thereof, without the consent of the governor, his heirs, or assigns, and six parts of seven of the said freemen in provincial council and general assembly.

XXIV. And lastly, that I, the said *William Penn*, for myself, my heirs and assigns, have solemnly declared, granted and confirmed, and do hereby solemnly declare, grant and confirm, that neither I, my heirs nor assigns, shall procure or do any thing or things, whereby the liberties, in this charter contained and expressed, shall be infringed or broken; and if any thing be procured by any person or persons contrary to these premises, it shall be held of no force or effect. In witness whereof, I, the said *William Penn*, have unto this present charter of liberties set my hand and broad seal, this five and twentieth day of the second month, vulgarly called April, in the year of our Lord one thousand six hundred and eighty two.

WILLIAM PENN.

The charter of 1683 contains the following new provisions.

And for the satisfaction and encouragement of all aliens, I do give and grant, that if any alien who is or shall be a purchaser, or who doth or shall inhabit in this province or territories thereof, shall decease at any time before he can well be natu-

---

* By the charter of 1683, the words "And unless on sudden and indispensible occasions, no business in provincial council, or its respective committees, shall be finally determined the same day that it is moved," are omitted, and the following words inserted, "And all things relating to the preparing and passing of bills into laws shall be openly declared and resolved by the vote.

ralized, his right and interest therein shall notwithstanding descend to his wife and children, or other his relations, be he testate or intestate, according to the laws of this province and territories thereof, in such cases provided in as free and ample a manner, to all intents and purposes, as if the said alien had been naturalized.

And that the inhabitants of this province and territories thereof may be accommodated with such food and sustenance as God, in his providence, hath freely afforded, I do also further grant to the inhabitants of this province and territories thereof, liberty to fowl and hunt upon the lands they hold, and all other lands therein not enclosed ; and to fish in all waters in the said lands, and in all rivers and rivulets in and belonging to this province and territories thereof, with liberty to draw his or their fish on shore, on any man's lands, so as it be not to the detriment or annoyance of the owner thereof, except such lands as do lie upon inland rivulets that are not boatable, or which are or may be hereafter erected into manors.

And that all the inhabitants of this province and territories thereof, whether purchasers or others, may have the last worldly pledge of my good and kind intentions to them and theirs, I do give, grant and confirm to all and every one of them full and quiet possession of their respective lands, to which they have any lawful or equitable claim, saving only such rents and services for the same as are or customarily ought to be reserved to me, my heirs or assigns.

The following provisions are contained in Governor Markham's charter of 1696.

No person shall be an elector, or be capable of being elected, unless they be free denizens, are of the age of 21 years, and have 50 acres of land, ten whereof being seated or cleared ; or be otherwise worth fifty pounds clear estate, and have been resident within this government two years next before such election.

All persons, who, for conscience sake, cannot take an oath, are permitted to make their solemn affirmation, attest or declaration.

All elections of representatives shall be free and voluntary. The electors who receive any reward or gift for giving a vote, shall forfeit their right to elect for that year ; and such persons as shall give or promise any such reward to be elected, or that shall offer to serve for nothing, or for less wages than the law prescribes, shall be rendered incapable to serve in Council or Assembly for that year. And the representatives so chosen in Council or Assembly shall yield their attendance accordingly, and be the sole judges of the regularity or irregularity of the elections of their respective members And in case of the death, absence or inability of any of the members so elected, the Governor, within ten days after knowledge of the same, shall issue his writ to the sheriff of the proper county, for holding an election to fill the vacancy.

The daily pay of Councillors and speaker of Assembly is fixed at five shillings, and of members of Assembly at four shillings, during their attendance, and two pence for each mile going to and returning from the place where the Assembly shall be held, which sums shall be paid out of the county levies, by the county receivers respectively.

All elections of representatives for Council and Assembly, and all questions to be determined by them, shall be by the major part of votes.

Chapter III.

LAWS AGREED UPON IN ENGLAND.

1. That the charter of liberties declared, granted and confirmed, the five-and-twentieth day of the second month, called April, 1682, before divers witnesses, by William Penn, Governor and chief proprietor of Pennsylvania, to all the freemen and planters of the said province, is hereby declared and approved, and shall be forever held for fundamental in the government thereof, according to the limitations mentioned in the said charter.

2. That every inhabitant in the said province, that is or shall be a purchaser of one hundred acres of land or upwards, his heirs and as-

signs, and every person who shall have paid his passage, and taken up one hundred acres of land, at one penny an acre, and have cultivated ten acres thereof, and every person that hath been a servant or bondsman, and is free by his service, that shall have taken up his fifty acres of land, and cultivated twenty thereof, and every inhabitant, artificer, or other resident in the said province, that pays scot and lot to the government, shall be deemed and accounted a freeman of the said province, and every such person shall and may be capable of electing, or being elected, representatives of the people in Provincial Council, or General Assembly, in the said province.

3. That all elections of members or representatives of the people and freemen of the province of Pennsylvania, to serve in Provincial Council, or General Assembly, to be held within the said province, shall be free and voluntary, and that the elector that shall receive any reward or gift, in meat, drink, monies, or otherwise, shall forfeit his right to elect; and such person as shall, directly or indirectly, give, promise or bestow any such reward as aforesaid, to be elected, shall forfeit his election, and be thereby incapable to serve as aforesaid. And the Provincial Council, and General Assembly, shall be the sole judges of the regularity or irregularity of the elections of their own respective members.

4. That no money or goods shall be raised upon or paid by any of the people of this province, by way of public tax, custom or contribution, but by a law for that purpose made, and whosoever shall levy, collect or pay any money or goods contrary thereunto, shall be held a public enemy to the province, and a betrayer of the liberties of the people thereof.

5. That all courts shall be open, and justice shall neither be sold, denied, nor delayed.

6. That in all courts all persons of all persuasions may freely appear in their own way, and according to their own manner; and there personally plead their own cause themselves, or, if unable, by their friend: And the first process shall be the exhibition of the complaint in court, fourteen days before the trial; and that the party complained against may be fitted for the same, he or she shall be summoned no less than ten days before, and a copy of the complaint delivered him or her, at his or her dwelling house. But before the complaint of any person be received, he shall solemnly declare in court, That he believes in his conscience his cause is just.

7. That all pleadings, processes and records in courts, shall be short and in English, and in an ordinary and plain character, that they may be understood, and justice speedily administered.

8. That all trials shall be by twelve men, and as near as may be, peers or equals, and of the neighborhood, and men without just exception. In cases of life there shall be first twenty-four returned by the sheriffs for a grand inquest, of whom twelve at least shall find the complaint to be true; and then the twelve men, or peers, to be likewise returned by the Sheriff, shall have the final judgment. But reasonable challenges shall be always admitted against the said twelve men, or any of them.

9. That all fees in all cases shall be moderate, and settled by the Provincial Council and General Assembly, and be hung up in a table in every respective court; and whosoever shall be convicted of taking

more, shall pay two-fold, and be dismissed his employment, one moiety of which shall go to the party wronged.

10. That all prisons shall be work-houses for felons, vagrants, and loose and idle persons; whereof one shall be in every county.

11. That all prisoners shall be bailable by sufficient sureties, unless for capital offences, where the proof is evident, or the presumption great.

12. That all persons wrongfully imprisoned or prosecuted at law shall have double damages against the informer or prosecutor.

13. That all prisons shall be free, as to fees, food and lodging.

14. That all lands and goods shall be liable to pay debts, except where there is legal issue, and then all the goods, and one-third of the land only.

15. That all wills in writing, attested by two witnesses, shall be of the same force as to lands, as other conveyances, being legally proved within forty days, either within or without the said province.

16. That seven years quiet possession shall give an unquestionable right, except in cases of infants, lunatics, married women, or persons beyond the seas.

17. That all briberies and extortions whatsoever shall be severely punished.

18. That all fines shall be moderate, and saving men's contencments, merchandise or wainage.

19. That all marriages, (not forbidden by the law of God, as to nearness of blood and affinity by marriage,) shall be encouraged; but the parents or guardians shall be first consulted, and the marriage shall be published before it be solemnized, and it shall be solemnized by taking one another as husband and wife, before credible witnesses, and a certificate of the whole, under the hands of the parties and witnesses, shall be brought to the proper register of that county, and shall be registered in his office.

20. And, to prevent frauds and vexatious suits within the said province, That all charters, gifts, grants and conveyances of land, (except leases for a year, or under) and all bills, bonds and specialties, above five pounds, and not under three pounds, made in the said province, shall be enrolled or registered in the public Enrolment-office of the said province, within the space of two months next after the making thereof, else to be void in law. And all deeds, grants and conveyances of land (except as aforesaid) within the said province, and made out of the said province, shall be enrolled and registered as aforesaid within six months next after the making thereof, and settling and constituting an Enrolment-office or Registry within the said province, else to be void in law against all persons whatsoever.

21. That all defacers or corrupters of charters, gifts, grants, bonds, bills, wills, contracts and conveyances, or that shall deface or falsify any enrolment, registry or record, within this province, shall make double satisfaction for the same, half whereof shall go to the party wronged; and they shall be dismissed of all places of trust, and be publicly disgraced as false men.

22. That there shall be a register for births, marriages, burials, wills, and letters of administration, distinct from the other registry.

23. That there shall be a register for all servants, where their names, time, wages and days of payment shall be registered.

24. That all lands and goods of felons shall be liable to make satisfaction to the party wronged twice the value ; and for want of lands or goods, the felons shall be bond-men, to work in the common prison or work-house, or otherwise, till the party injured be satisfied.

25. That the estates of capital offenders, as traitors and murderers, shall go, one-third to the next of kin to the sufferer, and the remainder to the next of kin to the criminal.

26. That all witnesses, coming or called to testify their knowledge in or to any matter or thing in any court, or before any lawful authority within the said province, shall there give or deliver in their evidence or testimony, by solemnly promising to speak the truth, the whole truth, and nothing but the truth, to the matter or thing in question. And in case any person so called to evidence, shall be convicted of wilful falsehood, such person shall suffer and undergo such damage or penalty, as the person or persons against whom he or she bore false witness did or should undergo; and shall also make satisfaction to the party wronged, and be publicly exposed as a false witness, never to be credited in any court or before any magistrate, in the said province.

27. And to the end that all officers chosen to serve within this province may with more care and diligence answer the trust reposed in them, it is agreed, That no such person shall enjoy more than one public office at one time.

28. That all children within this province, of the age of twelve years, shall be taught some useful trade or skill, to the end none may be idle, but the poor may work to live, and the rich, if they become poor, may not want.

29. That servants be not kept longer than their time, and such as are careful be both justly and kindly used in their service, and put in fitting equipage at the expiration thereof, according to custom.

30. That all scandalous and malicious reporters, backbiters, defamers, and spreaders of false news, whether against magistrates or private persons, shall be accordingly severely punished, as enemies to the peace and concord of this province.

31. That for the encouragement of the planters and traders in this province, who are incorporated into a society, the patent granted to them by William Penn, Governor of the said province; is hereby ratified and confirmed.

32. - - - - - - - - - - - -
- - - - - - - - - - - - -

33. That all factors or correspondents in the said province, wronging their employers, shall make satisfaction, and one-third over, to their said employers : And in case of the death of any such factor or correspondent, the committee of trade shall take care to secure so much of the deceased party's estate, as belongs to his said respective employers.

34. That all Treasurers, Judges, Masters of the Rolls, Sheriffs, Justices of the peace, and other officers and persons whatsoever relating to courts or trials of causes, or any other service in the government; and all members elected to serve in Provincial Council and General Assembly, and all that have right to elect such members, shall be such as profess faith in Jesus Christ, and that are not convicted of ill fame, or unsober and dishonest conversation, and that are of one and twenty years of age at least; and that all such, so qualified, shall be capable of the said several employments and privileges as aforesaid.

35. That all persons living in this province, who confess and acknowledge the one Almighty and eternal God to be the creator, upholder and ruler of the world, and that hold themselves obliged in conscience to live peaceably and justly in civil society, shall in no ways be molested or prejudiced for their religious persuasion or practice in matters of faith and worship, nor shall they be compelled at any time to frequent or maintain any religious worship-place or ministry whatever.

36. That, according to the good example of the primitive Christians, and for the ease of the creation, every first day of the week called the Lord's Day, people shall abstain from their common daily labour, that they may the better dispose themselves to worship God, according to their understandings.

37. That as careless and corrupt administration of justice draws the wrath of God upon magistrates, so the wildness and looseness of the people provoke the indignation of God against a country: Therefore, that all such offences against God, as swearing, cursing, lying, profane talking, drunkenness, drinking of healths, obscene words, incest, sodomy, rapes, whoredom, fornication and other uncleanness, not to be repeated; all treasons, misprisions, murders, duels, felonies, seditions, maims, forcible entries, and other violences to the persons and estates of the inhabitants within this province; all prizes, stage plays, cards, dice, may-games, masques, revels, bull-baitings, cock-fightings, bear-baitings, and the like, which excite the people to rudeness, cruelty, looseness and irreligion, shall be respectively discouraged, and severely punished, according to the appointment of the Governor and freemen in Provincial Council and General Assembly, as also all proceedings contrary to these laws that are not here made expressly penal.

38. That a copy of these laws shall be hung up in the Provincial Council, and in public courts of justice, and that they shall be read yearly, at the opening of every Provincial Council and General Assembly, and courts of justice, and their assent shall be testified by their standing up after the reading thereof.

39. That there shall be at no time any alteration of any of these laws, without the consent of the Governor, his heirs or assigns, and six parts of seven of the freemen, met in Provincial Council and General Assembly.

40. That all other matters and things not herein provided for, which shall and may concern the public justice, peace or safety of the said province, and the raising and imposing taxes, customs, duties, or other charges whatsoever, shall be and are hereby referred to the order, prudence and determination of the Governor and freemen in Provincial Council and General Assembly, to be held from time to time in the said province.

    Signed and sealed by the Governor and freemen aforesaid, the fifth day of the third month, called May, one thousand six hundred and eighty-two.

Chapter IV.

WILLIAM PENN, Proprietary and Governor of the province of Pennsylvania and territories therunto belonging, to all to whom these presents shall come, sendeth greeting—Whereas King Charles the second, by his letters patents, under the great seal of England, bearing date the fourth day of March, in the year one thousand six hundred and eighty, was graciously pleased to give and grant unto me, my heirs and assigns, for ever, this province of Pennsylvania, with divers great powers and jurisdictions for the well government thereof.

And whereas the King's dearest brother, James Duke of York and Albany, &c. by his deeds of feoffment, under his hand and seal duly perfected, bearing date the twenty-fourth day of August, one thousand six hundred eighty and two, did grant unto me, my heirs and assigns, all that tract of land, now called the territories of Pennsylvania, together with powers and jurisdictions for the good government thereof.

And whereas, for the encouragement of all the freemen and planters that might be concerned in the said province and territories, and for the good government thereof, I, the said William Penn, in the year one thousand six hundred eighty and three, for me, my heirs and assigns, did grant and confirm unto all the freemen, planters and adventurers therein, divers liberties, franchises and properties, as by the said grant, entituled, 'The frame of the government of the province of Pennsylvania, and territories thereunto belonging in America, may appear; which charter or frame being found, in some parts of it, not so suitable to the present circumstances of the inhabitants, was, in the third month, in the year one thousand seven hundred, delivered up to me, by six parts of seven of the freemen of this province and territories in General Assembly met, provision being made in the said charter for that end and purpose:

And whereas I was then pleased to promise, that I would restore the said charter to them again, with necessary alterations, or, in lieu thereof, give them another, better adapted to answer the present circumstances and conditions of the said inhabitants; which they have now, by their Representatives in General Assembly met at Philadelphia, requested me to grant.

KNOW ye therefore, that for the further well being and good government of the said province and territories, and in pursuance of the rights and powers before mentioned, I, the said William Penn, do declare, grant and confirm, unto all the freemen, planters and adventurers, and other inhabitants in this province and territories, these following liberties, franchises and privileges, so far as in me lieth, to be held, enjoyed and kept, by the freemen, planters and adventurers, and other inhabitants of and in the said province and territories thereunto annexed, forever.

First. Because no people can be truly happy, though under the greatest enjoyment of civil liberties, if abridged of the freedom of their consciences, as to their religious profession and worship: And Almighty God being the only Lord of conscience, father of lights and spirits, and the author as well as object of all divine knowledge, faith and worship, who only doth enlighten the mind, and persuade and convince the understandings of people, I do hereby grant and declare, that no person or persons, inhabiting in this province or territories, who shall confess and acknowledge one Almighty God, the creator, upholder and ruler of the world, and profess him or themselves obliged to live quietly under the civil government, shall be in any case molested or prejudiced in his or their person or estate, because of his or their conscientious persuasion or practice, nor be compelled to frequent or maintain any religious worship-place, or ministry, contrary to his or their mind, or to do or suffer any other act or thing, contrary to their religious persuasion.

And that all persons who also profess to believe in Jesus Christ, the Saviour of the world, shall be capable (notwithstanding their other persuasions and practices in point of conscience and religion) to serve this government in any capacity, both legislatively and executively, he or they solemnly promising, when lawfully required, allegiance to the king as sovereign, and fidelity to the proprietary and governor, and taking the attests, as now established by the law made at New-Castle, in the year one thousand seven hundred, entituled An Act directing the attests of several officers and ministers, as now amended and confirmed this present assembly.

Secondly. For the well governing of this province and territories, there shall be an Assembly yearly chosen, by the freemen thereof, to consist of four persons out of each county, of most note for virtue, wisdom and ability, (or of a greater number at any time, as the Governor and Assembly shall agree,) upon the first day of October for ever; and shall sit on the fourteenth day of the same month, in Philadelphia, unless the Governor and council for the time being shall see cause to appoint another place within the said province or territories; which Assembly shall have power to choose a speaker and other their officers; and shall be judges of the qualifications and elections of their own members; sit upon their own adjournments; appoint committees; prepare bills in order to pass into laws; impeach criminals, and redress grievances; and shall have all other powers and privileges of an Assembly, according to the rights of the free-born subjects of England, and as is usual in any of the King's plantations in America.

And if any county or counties shall refuse or neglect to choose their respective representatives as aforesaid, or, if chosen, do not meet to serve in Assembly, those who are so chosen and met shall have the full power of the Assembly, in as ample a manner as if all the representatives had been chosen and met, provided they are not less than two thirds of the whole number that ought to meet.

And that the qualifications of electors and elected, and all other matters and things relating to elections of representatives to serve in Assemblies, though not herein particularly expressed, shall be and remain as by a law of this government, made at New-Castle in the year one thousand seven hundred, entituled An Act to ascertain the number of members of Assembly, and to regulate the elections.

Thirdly. That the freemen in each respective county, at the time and place of meeting for electing their representatives to serve in Assembly, may, as often as there shall be occasion, choose a double number of persons to present to the Governor for sheriffs and coroners, to serve for three years, if they so long behave themselves well; out of which respective elections and presentments, the Governor shall nominate and commissionate one for each of the said offices, the third day after such presentment, or else the first named in such presentment, for each office as aforesaid, shall stand and serve in that office for the time before respectively limited; and in case of death or defaults, such vacancies shall be supplied by the Governor, to serve to the end of the said term.

Provided always, That if the said freemen shall at any time neglect or decline to choose a person or persons for either or both the aforesaid offices, then, and in such case, the persons that are or shall be in the respective offices of sheriff or coroner, at the time of election, shall remain therein, until they shall be removed by another election as aforesaid.

And that the justices of the respective counties shall or may nominate and present to the Governor three persons, to serve for clerk of the peace for the said county, when there is a vacancy, one of which the Governor shall commissionate within ten days after such presentment, or else the first nominated shall serve in the said office during good behaviour.

Fourthly. That the laws of this government shall be in this style, viz. By the Governor, with the consent and approbation of the freemen in General Assembly met; and shall be, after confirmation by the Governor, forthwith recorded in the rolls-office, and kept at Philadelphia, unless the Governor and Assembly shall agree to appoint another place.

Fifthly. That all criminals shall have the same privileges of witnesses and counsel as their prosecutors.

Sixthly. That no person or persons shall or may, at any time hereafter, be obliged to answer any complaint, matter or thing whatsoever, relating to property, before the Governor and Council, or in any other place but in the ordinary courts of justice, unless appeals thereunto shall be hereafter by law appointed.

Seventhly. That no person within the government shall be licensed by the Governor to keep an ordinary, tavern or house of public entertainment, but such who are first recommended to him, under the hands of the justices of the respective counties signed in open court; which justices are and shall be hereby empowered to suppress and forbid any person keeping such public house as aforesaid, upon their misbehaviour, on such penalties as the law doth or shall direct; and to recommend others from time to time, as they shall see occasion.

Eighthly. If any person, through temptation or melancholy, shall destroy himself, his estate, real and personal, shall notwithstanding descend to his wife and children, or relations, as if he had died a natural death; and if any person shall be destroyed or killed by casualty or accident, there shall be no forfeiture to the Governor by reason thereof.

And no act, law or ordinance whatsoever, shall at any time hereafter be made or done, to alter, change or diminish the form or effect of this charter, or of any part or clause therein, contrary to the true intent and meaning thereof, without the consent of the Governor for the time being, and six parts of seven of the Assembly met.

But because the happiness of mankind depends so much upon the enjoying of liberty of their consciences as aforesaid, I do hereby solemnly declare, promise and grant, for me, my heirs and assigns, that the first article of this charter, relating to liberty of conscience, and every part and clause therein, according to the true intent and meaning thereof, shall be kept and remain, without any alterations inviolably forever.

And lastly, I, the said William Penn, Proprietary and Governor of the province of Pennsylvania, and territories thereunto belonging, for myself, my heirs and assigns, have solemnly declared, granted and confirmed, and do hereby solemnly declare, grant and confirm, that neither I, my heirs or assigns, shall procure or do any thing or things, whereby the liberties in this charter contained and expressed, nor any part thereof, shall be infringed or broken: And if any thing shall be procured or done by any person or persons, contrary to these presents, it shall be held of no force or effect.

In witness whereof, I, the said William Penn, at Philadelphia, in Pennsylvania, have unto this present charter of liberties set my hand and broad seal, this twenty-eighth day of October, in the year of our Lord one thousand seven hundred and one, being the thirteenth year of the reign of king William the third over England, Scotland, France and Ireland, &c, and in the twenty-first year of my government.

And notwithstanding the closure and test of this present charter as aforesaid, I think fit to add this following proviso thereunto, as part of the same, that is to say: That notwithstanding any clause or clauses in the above mentioned charter, obliging the province and territories to join together in legislation, I am content, and do hereby declare, that if the representatives of the province and territories shall not hereafter agree to join together in legislation, and that the same shall be signified to me, or my deputy, in open assembly, or otherwise from under the hands and seals of the representatives, for the time being, of the province or territories, or the major part of either of them, any time within three years from the date hereof, that in such case the inhabitants of each of the three counties of this province shall not have less than eight persons to represent them in assembly for the province: and the inhabitants of the town of Philadelphia (when the said town is incorporated) two persons to represent them in assembly; and the inhabitants of each county in the territories shall have as many persons to represent them in distinct assembly for the territories, as shall be requested by them as aforesaid.

Notwithstanding which separation of the province and territories, in respect of legislation, I do hereby promise, grant and declare, That the inhabitants of both the province and territories shall separately enjoy all other liberties, privileges and benefits, granted jointly to them in this charter, any law, usage or custom of this government heretofore made and practised, or any law made and passed by this general assembly, to the contrary hereof notwithstanding.

WILLIAM PENN.

This Charter of Privileges being distinctly read in Assembly, and the whole and every part thereof being approved of and agreed to by us, we do thankfully receive the same from our Proprietary and Governor, at Philadelphia, this twenty-eighth day of October, one thousand seven hundred and one. Signed, on behalf and by order of the Assembly, per

JOSEPH GROWDEN, Speaker.

EDWARD SHIPPEN,
PHINEAS PEMBERTON,
SAMUEL CARPENTER,   } Proprietary and Governor's
GRIFFITH OWEN,   }   Council.
CALEB PUSEY,
THOMAS STORY,

Recorded in the Roll's-office in Phila-
delphia, in Patent Book A, vol. II,
page 125 to 129, the 31st of the
eighth month, 1701, by me,

THOMAS STORY, MASTER IDEM.

PART II.

Chapter I.

PROVINCIAL CONFERENCE.

Proceedings of the Provincial Conference of committees of the Province
of Pennsylvania, held at Carpenter's Hall, in Philadelphia, began
June 18th, and continued by adjournments to June 25th, 1776.

TUESDAY, June 18, 1776.

This day a number of gentlemen met at Carpenter's Hall, in Philadelphia, being deputed by the committees of several of the counties of this province, to join in provincial conference, in consequence of a circular letter from the committee of the city and liberties of Philadelphia, inclosing the resolution of the continental congress of the 15th of May last.

Col. M'Kean, as chairman of the city committee, declared the motives which had induced that committee to propose the holding of the present conference, and then laid on the table, a certificate of deputies appointed to attend on the part of said committee.

Returns were also given in, from the counties of Philadelphia, Bucks, Chester, Lancaster, Berks, Northampton, York, Cumberland, Bedford and Westmoreland, by the deputies of said counties, by which it appeared the following gentlemen were appointed, viz.§

For the committee of the city of Philadelphia.

*Dr. Benjamin Franklin,
Col. Thomas M'Kean,
Mr. Christopher Marshal, sen.
Major John Bayard,
Col. Timothy Matlack,
Col. Joseph Dean,
Cap. Francis Gurney,
Major William Coates,
Mr. George Schlosser,
Cap. George Goodwin,
Mr. Jacob Barge,
Mr. Samuel C. Morris,
Cap. Joseph Moulder,

Mr. William Lowman,
Dr. Benjamin Rush,
Mr. Christopher Ludwig,
Mr. Jacob Shriner,
Cap. Sharp Delaney,
Major John Cox,
Cap. Benjamin Loxley,
Cap. Samuel Brewster,
Cap. Joseph Blewer,
Mr. William Robinson,
Cap. Jonathan B. Smith,
Mr. James Milligen.

For the committee of Philadelphia county.

Col. Henry Hill,
Col. Robert Lewis,
Dr. Enoch Edwards,
*Col. William Hamilton,
Col. John Bull,
Col. Frederick Antis,

*Major James Potts,
Major Robert Loller,
Mr. Joseph Mather,
Mr. Matthew Brooks,
*Mr. Edward Bartholomew.

For the committee of Bucks county.

John Kidd, Esq.
Maj. Henry Wynkoop,
Mr. James Wallace,

Col. Joseph Hart,
Mr. Benjamin Segle.

For the committee of Chester county.

Col. Richard Thomas,
Maj. William Evans,
Col. Thomas Hockley,
Major Caleb Davis,
Elisha Price, Esq.
Mr. Samuel Fairlamb,
Col. William Montgomery,

Col. Hugh Loyd,
Richard Reiley, Esq.
Col. Evan Evans,
Col. Lewis Grono,
Major Sketchley Morton,
Cap. Thomas Levis.

For the committee of Lancaster county.

William Atlee, Esq.
Mr. Lodowick Lowman,
Col. Bartram Galbraith,
Col. Alexander Lowrey,
Cap. Andrew Graaf,

Mr. William Brown,
Mr. John Smiley,
Major James Cunningham,
Major David Jenkins.

For the committee of Berks county.

Col. Jacob Morgan,
Col. Henry Haller,
Col. Mark Bird,
Dr. Bodo Otto,
Mr. Benjamin Spiker,

Col. Daniel Hunter,
Col. Valentine Eakerd,
Col. Nicholas Lutz,
Cap. Joseph Hiester,
Mr. Charles Shoemaker.

For the committee of Northampton county.

Robert Levers, Esq.
Col. Neigal Gray,
John Weitzel, Esq.

Nicholas Depue, Esq.
Mr. David Deshler,
Mr. Benjamin Dupue.

For the committee of York county.

Col. James Smith,
Col. Robert M'Pherson,
Col. Richard M'Alister,
Col. David Kennedy,
Col. William Rankin,

Col. Henry Slagle,
Mr. James Egar,
*Mr. John Hay,
Cap. Joseph Read.

For the committee of Cumberland county.

Mr. James M'Lane,
*Col. John Allison,
John M'Clay, Esq.
William Elliot, Esq.
Col. William Clark,

Dr. John Colhoon,
Mr. John Creigh,
Mr. Hugh M'Cormick,
Mr. John Harris,
Mr. Hugh Alexander.

For the committee of Bedford county.

Col. David Espy,
Col. John Piper,

Samuel Davidson, Esq.

For the committee of Westmoreland county

Mr. Edward Cook,

Mr. James Perry.

§ All the members attended except those marked (*)

A quorum of the members from the above counties being met, ex.
cept that only two appeared from Chester county; proceeded to the
choice of a president, vice-president and two secretaries, and

Col. THOMAS M'KEAN, *was chosen president.*
Col. JOSEPH HART, *vice-president.*

JONATHAN B. SMITH, } *secretaries.*
SAMUEL C. MORRIS. }

WEDNESDAY, June 19, 1776.

The conference met, present; 12 committees, 97 members.
A return was delivered at the table, from Northumberland; and the
deputies attending, being

Col William Cook,   Mr. Robert Martin,
Alexander Hunter, Esq.   Mr. Matthew Brown.
Mr. John Heitzel,

As did those also from Chester.

On motion, it was resolved unanimously, That in taking the sense
of this conference, on any question which may come before them, the
city and counties respectively shall have one vote.

On motion, it was ordered, That the resolution of the continental
congress, of the 15th of May last, recommending the total suppres-
sion of all authority under the king of Great Britain, &c. be read—
and it was read accordingly, and is in the words following, viz.

IN CONGRESS, *May 15, 1776.*

Whereas, his Brittanic majesty, in conjunction with the lords and
commons of Great Britain, has by a late act of parliament, excluded
the inhabitants of these United Colonies from the protection of his
crown: And whereas, no answer whatever, to the humble petitions of
the colonies for redress of grievances and reconciliation with Great
Brittain, has been, or is likely to be given, but the whole force of that
kingdom, aided by foreign mercenaries, is to be exerted for the destruction of the good people of these colonies. And whereas, it appears absolutely irreconcilable to reason and good conscience, for the people
of these colonies, now to take the oaths and affirmations necessary for
the support of any government, under the crown of Great Britain; and
it is necessary, that the exercise of every kind of authority, under the
said crown should be totally suppressed, and all the powers of government exerted, under the authority of the people of the colonies, for the
preservation of internal peace, virtue and good order, as well as for the
defence of their lives, liberties and properties, against the hostile invasions and cruel depredations of their enemies. Therefore,

Resolved, That it be recommended to the respective assemblies and
conventions of the United Colonies, where no government sufficient to
the exigencies of their affairs, has been hitherto established, to adopt
such government as shall in the opinion of the representatives of the people, best conduce to the happiness and safety of their constituents in
particular, and America in general.

By order of the congress.
JOHN HANCOCK, *President.*

By special order, the same was read a second time, and after mature consideration,

Resolved unanimously, That the said resolution of congress, of the 15th of May last, is fully approved by this conference.

On motion, resolved unanimously, That the present government of this province is not competent to the exigencies of our affairs.

On motion, resolved unanimously, That it is necessary that a provincial convention be called by this conference, for the express purpose of forming a new government in this province, on the authority of the people only.

Resolved unanimously, That a committee be appointed to ascertain the number of members of which the convention ought to consist, and the proportion of representatives for the city and each county, and that two members from the city and each county, be appointed on said committee, except from Westmoreland, which can furnish but one, and the following gentlemen were appointed, viz.

Messrs. Bayard, Atlee, Hart, Gray, Weitzel, Creigh,
Bull, Bird, Levis, Smith, Cook, Piper,
Kidd, Matlack, Cunningham, M'Clean, Levis, Hunter.
Davis, Mather, Haller, Espy, M'Allister,

Resolved, That the committee now appointed, be instructed to fix upon some number, not less than ninety, nor more than one hundred and ten, for the whole province.

A petition from the German associators of the city and liberties of Philadelphia, was read, praying that all associators, who are taxables, may be entitled to vote.

On motion, resolved unanimously, that this conference will now enter into a consideration of the qualifications of electors, and of persons who may be elected.

THURSDAY, June 20, 1776.

Col. Hart, from the committee of the whole, reported, that they had come into two resolutions which he was ready to report, when the conferrence would receive them.

Ordered, That they be received forthwith; then the said resolutions being read and considered, were agreed to by the conference without one dissenting voice, and are as follow, viz.

Resolved, That every associator in the province shall be admitted to a vote for members of the convention, in the city or county in which he resides: Provided, such associator be of the age of 21 years, and shall have lived one year in this province immediately preceding the election, and shall have contributed at any time before the passing of this resolve, to the payment of either provincial or county taxes, or shall have been rated or assessed towards the same.

Resolved, That every person qualified by the laws of this province, to vote for representatives in assembly, shall be admitted to vote for members of the intended convention, provided he shall first take the following test on oath or affirmation, if thereunto required by any one of the judges or inspectors of the election, who are hereby empowered to administer the same.

I —— —— do declare, that I do not hold myself bound to bear allegiance to George the third, king of Great Britain, &c. and that I will not by any means, directly or indirectly oppose the establishment of a free government in this province, by the convention now to be chosen; nor the measures adopted by the congress against the tyranny attempted to be established in these colonies, by the court of Great Britin.

On motion, Resolved unanimously, That whereas the county of Westmoreland, hath been exempted from the payment of taxes for three years last past; and thereby many persons may be excluded from a vote at the ensuing election, in consequence of the foregoing regulations, contrary to the intention thereof; therefore, every person of 21 years of age, being a free man, residing in said county, shall be admitted to vote, he being an associator, and having lived one year in this province, next preceding the election, and taking the test aforesaid, if thereunto required.

Resolved unanimously, That the election shall be made by ballot, in the manner heretofore used in this province, at the general elections.

Resolved unanimously, That no person who has been published by any committee of inspection, or the committee of safety, in this province, as an enemy to the liberties of America, and has not been restored to the favor of his country, shall be permitted to vote at the election of members for said convention.

FRIDAY, June 21, 1776.

On motion, Resolved unanimously, That every voter at the proposed election shall be a free man, and if thereunto required by any of the judges or inspectors, shall before his vote is received, take the foregoing test.

Resolved unanimously, That any person qualified to vote for members of assembly, by the laws of this province, may be elected a member of convention, provided that he shall have resided at least one year immediately preceding the said election, in the city or county for which he shall be chosen, and shall before he takes his seat in convention, take the following oath or affirmation, viz.

I —— —— do declare, that I do not hold myself bound to bear allegiance to George the third, king of Great Britain, &c. and that I will steadily and firmly, at all times, promote the most effectual means, according to the best of my skill and knowledge, to oppose the tyrannical proceedings of the king and parliament of Great Britain, against the American Colonies; and to establish and support a government in this province, on the authority of the people only, &c. That I will oppose any measure that shall or may, in the least, interfere with or obstruct the religious principles or practices of any of the good people of this province, as heretofore enjoyed.

Also, Resolved, That no person elected to serve as a member of convention, shall take his seat or give his vote, until he shall have made and subscribed the following declaration.

I —— —— do profess faith in God, the father, and in Jesus Christ, his eternal son, the true God, and in the Holy Spirit, one God blessed for evermore; and do acknowledge the holy scriptures of the old and new testament, to be given by divine inspiration.

The committee appointed to ascertain the number and proportion of members to represent the province, and each particular city and county, in convention, made their report in the words following, viz.

The committee appointed for, &c. report, that your committee have conferred together, and endeavoured to obtain the best intelligence that can he had, find that full information respecting the number of taxables in each county, cannot now be had, and therefore cannot be adopted as a rule in fixing the number of representatives for the city and counties respectively. Your committee, however, are satisfied, that the number of taxables in the counties respectively, does not differ so much as to make it of any probable disadvantage to allow an equal representation from each county, especially as the convention will probably vote by city and counties, as in the preceding conventions, upon the questions which shall come before them.

We therefore recommend, that it be resolved, that eight representatives be sent by the city of Philadelphia, and eight by each county in the province, to the convention.

On motion, That the inhabitants of the city be divided from the county of Philadelphia, and that they' be not admitted to vote, or be voted for, in the elecion of the county members for the convention.

It was moved that the previous question be put, viz. Whether this question shall be now put? And it was put accordingly, and carried in the negative.

Resolved That this conference approve of the report of the committee.

SATURDAY, June 22, 1776.

On motion, Resolved unanimously, That the determinations of this conference, on the representation of the city and of the county of Philadelphia, shall not be drawn into precedent in future.

SUNDAY, June 23, 1776.

The committee appointed to consider of the proper time, &c. of holding the election, delivered their report at the table, which being read by order, was unanimously agreed to by the House.

The following is an abstract of the report.

1. They appoint Monday the 8th day of July next, for electing the said members of the convention.

2. They designate the places at which the elections shall be held, in the city and several counties.

3. They direct that the electors of the several wards, boroughs and townships, shall meet and choose their inspectors, on the 6th of July, and that each of the inspectors shall before he proceeds to take or receive any votes, take the following oath or affirmation.

    I —— —— do declare, that I will duly attend the ensuing election, during the continuance thereof, and will truly and faithfully assist the judges of said election, to prevent all frauds and deceits whatsoever, of electors or others, in carrying on the same, and in causing the poll or votes at such election to be marked off on the respective lists, and fairly cast up.

4. They direct that the deputies from the city and counties, shall appoint three discreet and able members of their respective committees, residing within the several districts, to be judges of the elec-

tion. And that the said judges and the inspectors shall appoint clerks.

5. They direct that the commissioners of the city and counties shall deliver to the judges of the election, duplicates of the taxables in the several districts. That the judges and inspectors of the several districts of such counties as are divided, shall cause certified accounts of the election, to be taken to the county town on the next day after the election, which shall be added together, and the eight highest numbers shall be the persons to represent such county in convention, and also, that the judges, or any two of them, for the city and counties respectively, shall certify under their hands and seals, to the convention, on the day appointed for their meeting, the names of the persons chosen.

6. They direct, that the persons so chosen, shall meet in convention at Philadelphia, on Monday the 15th of July next.

Ordered, That Dr. Rush, Col. Hill and Col. Smith, prepare a draft of an address to the inhabitants of the province, and report to the conference.

Resolved unanimously, That it be recommended to the said convention, to choose and appoint delegates or deputies, to represent this province, in the congress of the United Colonies; and, also, a council of safety, to exercise the whole of the executive powers of government, so far as relates to the military defence and safety of the province, and to make such allowance for the services of the said delegates, and council of safety respectively, as shall be reasonable, which said delegates and council of safety, are to continue for six months, unless a new government shall be formed within that time, in which case there appointment is to cease.

On motion, unanimously Ordered, That the chairman, Dr. Rush and Col. Smith, be a committee to draft a resolution, declaring the sense of the conference, with respect to an independence of the province, from the crown and parliament of Great Britain, and report to-morrow morning.

The gentlemen appointed to prepare a draft of an address, to the inhabitants of this province, delivered at the table, a draft, which was read.

By order, the same was read the second time, considered, amended and unanimously agreed to, in the following words,

The address of the deputies from the committees of Pennsylvania, assembled in provincial conference.

TO THE PEOPLE OF PENNSYLVANIA.

Friends and countrymen,

In obedience to the power we derived from you, we have fixed upon a mode of electing a convention, to form a government for the province of Pennsylvania, under the authority of the people.

Divine Providence is about to grant you a favor, which few people have ever enjoyed before, the privilege of choosing deputies to form a government under which you are to live. We need not inform you of the importance of the trust you are about to commit to them; your liberty, safety, happiness and every thing that posterity will hold dear to them to the end of time, will depend upon their deliberations. It becomes you, therefore, to choose such persons only, to act for you in the ensuing convention, as are distinguished for wisdom, integrity and a firm attachment to the liberties of this province, as well as to the liberties of the United Colonies in general.

In order that your deputies may know your sentiments as fully as possible, upon the subject of government, we beg that you would convey to them your wishes and opinions upon that head, immediately after their election.

We have experienced an unexpected unanimity in our councils, and we have the pleasure of observing a growing unanimity among the people of the province. We beg, that this brotherly spirit may be cultivated, and that you would remember that the present unsettled state of the province, requires that you should show forbearance, charity and moderation to each other. We beg that you would endeavour to remove the prejudices of the weak and ignorant, respecting the proposed change in our government, and assure them that it is absolutely necessary, to secure property, liberty and the sacred rights of conscience, to every individual in the province.

The season of the year, and the exigencies of our colony, require dispatch in the formation of a regular government. You will not therefore be surprised at our fixing the day for the election of deputies so early as the 8th of next July.

We wish you success in your attempts to establish and perpetuate your liberties, and pray God to take you under his special protection.

Signed by unanimous order of the conference.

THOMAS M'KEAN, *President.*

MONDAY, June 24, 1776.

The committee appointed for that purpose, brought in a draft, of a declaration, on the subject of the independence of this colony, of the crown of Great Britain, which was ordered to be read.

By special order, the same was read a second time, and being fully considered, it was with the greatest unanimity of all the members agreed to and adopted, and is in the words following, viz.

Whereas, George the third, king of Great Britain, &c. in violation of the principles of the British constitution, and of the laws of justice and humanity, hath by an accumulation of oppressions, unparralleled in history, excluded the inhabitants of this, with the other American Colonies, from his protection. And whereas, he hath paid no regard to any of our numerous and dutiful petitions for a redress of our complicated grievances, but hath lately purchased foreign troops to assist in enslaving us; and hath excited the savages of this country to carry on a war against us, as also the negroes to imbrue their hands in the blood of their masters, in a manner unpractised by civilized nations, and hath lately insulted our calamities, by declaring that he will shew us no mercy until he has reduced us. And whereas, the obligations of allegiance (being reciprocal between a king and his subjects) are now dissolved, on the side of the colonists, by the despotism of the said king, insomuch that it now appears that loyalty to him is treason against the good people of this country. And whereas, not only the parliament, but there is reason to believe, too many of the people of Great Britain, have concurred in the aforesaid arbitrary and unjust proceedings against us. And whereas, the public virtue of this colony (so essential to its liberty and happiness) must be endangered by a future political union with, or dependence upon a crown and nation so lost to justice, patriotism and magnanimity.

We the *Deputies of the people of Pennsylvania*, assembled in FULL PROVINCIAL CONFERENCE, for forming a plan for executing the resolve of congress, of the 15th May last, for suppressing all authority in this province, derived from the crown of Great Britain and for establishing a government upon the authority of the people only, now in this public manner, in behalf of ourselves, and with the approbation, consent and authority of our constituents, UNANIMOUSLY declare our willingness to concur in a vote of the congress, declaring the United Colonies free and independent states: Provided the forming the government, and the regulation of the internal police of this colony, be always reserved to the people of the said colony; and we do further call upon the nations of Europe, and appeal to the great arbiter and governor of the empires of the world, to witness for us, that this declaration did not originate in ambition, or in an impatience of lawful authority; but that we were driven to it in obedience to the first principles of nature, by the oppressions and cruelties of the aforesaid king and parliament of Great Britain; as the only possible measure that was left us, to preserve and establish our liberties, and to transmit them inviolate to posterity.

Ordered, That this declaration be signed at the table, and that the president deliver it in congress.

TUESDAY, June 25, 1776.

Resolved unanimously, That thanks be given to the president for his impartiality and close attention to the business of this conference.

Resolved unanimously, That the thanks of this conference be given to the committee of the city and liberties of Philadelphia, &c. for their unwearied endeavours in the public service, and particularly for their patriotic exertions in carrying into execution the resolve of congress, of May 15th, last, for suppressing all authority under the crown of Great Britain.

Then the conference dissolved itself.

THOMAS M'KEAN, *President.*

JONATHAN B. SMITH, } *Secretaries.*
SAMUEL C. MORRIS, }

The compilers have only included in their proceedings of the Provincial Conference, such of the transactions of that body as were connected with the proposed call of a convention; for the conference, during their session, which lasted from the 18th to the 25th of June, 1776, besides providing for the call of a convention, did, among other things, make provision for raising 4,500 militia, in obedience to resolutions of Congress of the 3d and 4th of June, 1776, for establishing a flying camp, to consist of 10,000 men, in the middle colonies. Although these proceedings are not connected with the immediate object which the compilers had in view when they undertook the publication of this volume, yet the address of the conference, on the subject of embodying the militia, in consequence of the resolutions of Congress, is such a master-piece of the kind, that it cannot be improper here to insert it.

On the 24th June, 1776, Messrs. Bayard, Rush and Smith were appointed a committee to draft an address to the associators of the province, on the subject of embodying 4,500 men. On the 25th of June they made report, which, by special order, was read a second time and agreed to unanimously, as follows :

The address of the deputies of the committees of Pennsylvania, assembled in provincial conference, at Philadelphia, June 25th, 1776.

TO THE ASSOCIATORS OF PENNSYLVANIA.

GENTLEMEN,

The only design of our meeting together was to put an end to our own power in the province, by fixing upon a plan for calling a convention, to form a government under the authority of the people. But the sudden and unexpected separation of the late assembly, has compelled us to undertake the execution of a resolve of Congress, for calling forth 4,500 of the militia of the province, to join the militia of the neighboring colonies, to form a camp for our immediate protection. We presume only to *recommend* the plan we have formed to you, trusting that in a case of so much consequence, your love of virtue and zeal for liberty will supply the want of authority delegated to us expressly for that purpose.

We need not remind you that you are now furnished with new motives to animate and support your courage. You are not about to contend against the power of Great Britain, in order to displace one set of villains to make room for another. Your arms will not be enervated in the day of battle with the reflection, that you are to risk your lives or shed your blood for a British tyrant; or that your posterity will have your work to do over again. You are about to contend for permanent freedom, to be supported by a government which will be derived from yourselves, and which will have for its object, not the emolument of one man or class of men only, but the safety, liberty and happiness of every individual in the community. We call upon you, therefore, by the respect and obedience which are due to the authority of the United Colonies, to concur in this important measure. The present campaign will probably decide the fate of America. It is now in your power to immortalize your names, by mingling your achievements with the events of the year 1776—a year which we hope will be famed in the annals of history to the end of time, for establishing upon a lasting foundation the liberties of one quarter of the globe.

Remember the honor of our colony is at stake. Should you desert the common cause at the present juncture, the glory you have acquired by your former exertions of strength and virtue, will be tarnished; and our friends and brethren, who are now acquiring laurels in the most remote parts of America, will reproach us and blush to own themselves natives or inhabitants of Pennsylvania.

But there are other motives before you. Your houses, your fields, the legacies of your ancestors, or the dear-bought fruits of your own industry, and your liberty, now urge you to the field. These cannot plead with you in vain, or we might point out to you further your wives, your children, your aged fathers and mothers, who now look up to you for aid, and hope for salvation in this day of calamity, only from the instrumentality of your swords.

Remember the name of Pennsylvania.—Think of your ancestors and of your posterity.

Signed by an unanimous order of the conference,

THOMAS M'KEAN, President.

June 25, 1776.

———

Chapter II.

CONVENTION OF 1776.

Minutes of the proceedings of the convention of the state of Pennsylvania, held at Philadelphia the 15th day of July, 1776, and continued by adjournments to the 28th September following.

At a meeting of the convention for the state of Pennsylvania, held in the city of Philadelphia, on the 15th day of July, in the year one thousand seven hundred and seventy-six.

MONDAY, July 15th, 1776. *P. M.*

The respective judges of the election of the city of Philadelphia and the several counties, made the returns as follow, viz.

For the city of Philadelphia.

Timothy Matlack,	James Cannon,
Benjamin Franklin,	George Clymer,
Frederick Kuhl,	George Schlosser,
Owen Biddle,	David Rittenhouse.

For the county of Philadelphia.

Frederick Antis,	John Bull,
Henry Hill,	Thomas Potts,
Robert Loller,	Edward Bartholomew,
Joseph Blewer,	William Coates.

For the county of Bucks.

Joseph Hart,	William Vanhorn,
John Wilkinson,	John Grier,
Samuel Smith,	Abraham Van Middleswarts,
John Keller,	Joseph Kirkbride.

For the county of Chester.

Benjamin Bartholomew,	Samuel Cunningham,
John Jacobs,	John Hart,
Thomas Strawbridge,	John Mackey,
Robert Smith,	John Flemming.

For the county of Lancaster.

George Ross,	Joseph Sherrer,
Philip Marsteller,	John Hubley,
Thomas Porter,	Henry Slaymaker,
Bartram Galbreath,	Alexander Lowrey.

For the county of York.

John Hay,	Francis Crazart,
James Edgar,	James Smith,

William Rankin,   Robert M'Pherson,
Henry Slagle,   Joseph Donaldson.
For the county of Cumberland.
John Harris,   William Duffield,
Jonathan Hoge,   James Brown,
William Clarke,   Hugh Alexander,
Robert Whitehill,   James M'Clean.
For the county of Berks.
Jacob Morgan,   Daniel Hunter,
Gabriel Hiester,   Valentine Eckert,
John Lesher,   Charles Shoemaker,
Benjamin Spyker,   Thomas Jones.
For the county of Northampton.
Simon Dresbach,   Jacob Stroud,
Jacob Arndt,   Neigal Gray,
Peter Buckholder,   Abraham Miller,
Peter Rhoads,   John Ralston.
For the county of Bedford.
Thomas Smith,   Joseph Powell,
John Wilkins,   Henry Rhoads,
Benjamin Elliot,   John Burd,
Thomas Coulter,   John Cessna.
For the county of Northumberland.
William Cooke,   Walter Clark,
James Potter,   John Kelley,
Robert Martin,   James Crawford,
Matthew Brown,   John Weitzell.
For the county of Westmoreland.
James Barr,   John Carmichael,
Edward Cook,   James Perry,
James Smith,   John M'Clellan,
John Moore,   Christopher Lavingair.

TUESDAY, July 16, 1776.

Dr. Benjamin Franklin was unanimously chosen President.
Col. George Ross was unanimously chosen Vice-President.
John Morris, Esq. was chosen Secretary.
Mr. Jacob Garrigues was chosen assistant clerk to the Secretary.
Mr. Morris not being in this city at present, Col. Matlack is re-
quested to perform the duty of Secretary till Mr. Morris may return.
The qualification and profession of faith recommended by the con-
ference of committees, held at Philadelphia on the 25th of June last,
were read, taken and subscribed by all the members now present, viz.

Benjamin Franklin,   Henry Hill,   William Vanhorn,
Timothy Matlack,   Robert Loller,   John Grier,
Frederick Kuhl,   Joseph Blewer,   Joseph Kirkbride,
Owen Biddle,   John Bull,   John Hart,
James Cannon,   Edward Bartholomew, Thomas Strawbridge,
George Clymer,   Joseph Hart,   Robert Smith,
George Schlosser,   John Wilkinson,   Samuel Cunningham,
David Rittenhouse,   Samuel Smith,   John Mackey,
Frederick Antis,   John Keller,   George Ross,

Bartram Galbreath,
Joseph Sherrer,
John Hubley,
Henry Slaymaker,
Alexander Lowrey,
John Hay,
James Edgar,
Francis Crazart,
James Smith,
Robert M'Pherson,
Joseph Donaldson,
John Harris,
Jonathan Hoge,
William Clarke,
William Duffield,

James Brown,
James M'Clean,
Jacob Morgan,
Gabriel Hiester,
John Lesher,
Benjamin Spyker,
Daniel Hunter,
Charles Shoemaker,
Thomas Jones,
Simon Dresbach,
Jacob Arndt,
Peter Buckholder,
Peter Rhoads,
Jacob Stroud,

Neigal Gray,
Abraham Miller,
John Ralston,
Thomas Smith,
John Wilkins,
Benjamin Elliot,
Thomas Coulter, .
Joseph Powell,
Henry Rhoads,
John Burd,
John Cessna,
Walter Clark,
John Kelley,
James Crawford.

William Sheed is appointed doorkeeper.

On motion, Resolved, That application be made to Gen. Roberdeau, requesting him to issue an order for permitting John Morris and Jacob Garrigues to return to this city, they being appointed to the offices of secretary and assistant clerk to this convention.

The convention then proceeded to the consideration of legislative business.

WEDNESDAY, July 17, 1776.

Upon motion, Resolved, That the Rev. Mr. William White, be requested to perform divine service to morrow morning before this convention, that we may jointly offer up our prayers to Almighty God, to afford us his divine grace and assistance in the important and arduous task committed to us, and to offer up our praises and thanksgivings for the manifold mercies and the peculiar interposition of his special providence, in behalf of these injured, oppressed and insulted United States.

Col. Matlack and Mr. Clymer are appointed to wait on the Rev. Mr. White, and furnish him with a copy of the foregoing resolve.

Mr. Matthias Brown, John Flemming, Philip Marsteller and Robert Whitehill appeared in the house for the first time, took the oaths, and made and signed the profession of faith required.

The convention then resumed the consideration of legislative and executive business,

THURSDAY, July 18th, 1776.

Mr. Morris, the Secretary, now attending, it was ordered, upon motion, that he should take the following affirmation, viz.

I, John Morris, do declare, that I do not hold myself bound to bear allegiance to George the third, king of Great Britain, and that I will steadily and firmly at all times promote the most effectual means, according to the best of my skill and knowledge, to oppose the tyrannical proceedings of the king and parliament of Great Britain, against the American colonies, and support a government in this state on the authority of the people only; and that as secretary of this convention. I will be faithful and make fair and just minutes of all their proceedings, according to the best of my abilities, and keep all such secrets as shall be directed to be kept by the convention.

Which he did accordingly.

Ordered, also, That the clerk, when he shall come, shall make a declaration to the like import.

The Rev. Mr. White attending, agreeably to the request of yesterday, and having performed divine service, and being withdrawn, it was

Ordered, on motion, That Mr. Matlack and Mr. Clymer wait upon that gentleman, with the thanks of the convention for his services.

Upon motion, and after debate, Resolved, That a committee be appointed to make an essay for a declaration of rights for this state.

Resolved also, That the said committee consist of eleven persons, viz. Mr. Biddle, Col. Bull, the Rev. Mr. Vanhorn, Mr. Jacobs, Col. Ross, Col. James Smith, Mr. Hoge, Mr. Morgan, Col. Stroud, Col. Thomas Smith and Mr. Martin.

Mr. Abraham Van Middleswarts, Mr. Robert Martin, Mr. John Weitzel and Mr. John Jacobs appeared in the house for the first time, took the oath or affirmation, and made and signed the profession of faith required.

The convention resumed the consideration of legislative and executive business.

FRIDAY, July 19, 1776.

Col. James Potter, one of the members from Northumberland, and Mr. William Rankin, one of the members for York county, appeared in the house for the first time, took the oaths and made and subscribed the profession of faith required.

The convention resumed the consideration of legislative and executive business.

SATURDAY, July 20, 1776.

The convention resumed the consideration of legislative and executive business.

MONDAY, July 22, 1776.

The following members from Westmoreland, viz. James Barr, Edward Cook, John Moore, John Carmichael, John M'Clellan, Christopher Lavingair and James Smith, now appeared in the house, took the oaths, and made and subscribed the profession of faith; as did also Hugh Alexander, of Cumberland, and Valentine Eckart, of Berks.

On motion, Ordered, That Mr. John Moore be added to the declaration of rights committee, and that the said committee have leave of absence.

The convention then resumed the consideration of legislative and executive business.

TUESDAY, July 23, 1776.

Mr. Benjamin Bartholomew and Mr. James Perry appeared in the house for the first time, took the oaths, and made and subscribed the profession of faith.

The convention then resumed the consideration of legislative and executive business.

WEDNESDAY, July 24, 1776.

Col. Henry Slagle appeared in the house for the first time, and took the oath, and made and subscribed the profession of faith.

On motion, Resolved, That the same gentlemen who are on the declaration of rights committee, be appointed to draw up an essay for a frame or system of government for this state.

On motion, Resolved, That Mr. John Lesher be one of the committee for essaying a frame of government, in the room of Mr. Jacob Morgan, who is absent with leave.

The convention resumed the consideration of legislative and executive business.

THURSDAY, July 25, 1776.

Mr. Thomas Porter appearing in the house for the first time, took the oath, and made and subscribed the profession of faith.

It was moved and Resolved, That this convention do agree to the following resolution and declaration, viz.

We, the representatives of the freemen of the state of Pennsylvania, in general convention assembled, taking into our most serious consideration the clear, strong and cogent reasons given by the honorable continental Congress, for the declaring this, as well as the other United States of America, FREE and INDEPENDENT, do thereupon resolve, and be it hereby resolved and declared, that we, in behalf of ourselves and our constituents, do unanimously approve of the said resolution and declaration of Congress of the 4th inst: And we do declare before God and the world, that we will support and maintain the freedom and independence of this and the other United States of America, at the utmost risk of our lives and fortunes.

The committtee for essaying a declaration of rights, reported a draft for that purpose, which being read, was ordered to lie on the table for further consideration.

On motion, Ordered, That Col. Matlack, Mr. Cannon, Col. Potter, Mr. Rittenhouse, Mr. Whitehill and Col. Galbreath, be added to the committee for bringing in an essay for a frame of government.

The convention resumed the consideration of legislative and executive business.

FRIDAY, July 26, 1776.

The report of the committee for the declaration of rights was again read, and a motion was made and seconded, that the same be recommitted, but the previous question being called for, it was thereupon

Resolved, That the question be not now put on the said motion.

Upon motion, Resolved, That the minutes of this convention be published weekly, in English and German, and that this house will appoint a committee to superintend the publication.

The convention resumed the consideration of the report of the declaration of rights, and after some considerable time spent thererein, it was,

Upon motion, Resolved, That the said report be recommitted to the committee who were originally appointed thereon.

5

The convention resumed the consideration of legislative and executive business.

SATURDAY, July 27, 1776.

The committee appointed to bring in an essay of the declaration of rights, and to whom the same was recommitted, reported a new draft thereof; which being in part read by paragraphs and debated upon for some time, was postponed for further consideration.

The convention resumed the consideration of legislative and executive business.

MONDAY, July 29, 1776.

The convention resumed the consideration of the draft of the declaration of rights, and went through the same by paragraphs. Whereupon it was

Ordered, That Col. Hill and Mr. Hubley procure to be printed 96 copies of the said draft, for the further consideration of the members of this house.

July 30, 31, and August 1, 1776.

The convention resumed the consideration of legislative and executive business, with this exception. On the 1st August,

On motion, Resolved, That this convention will to-morrow morning resolve itself into a committee of the whole, in order to take into consideration some important matters relative to the proposed new frame of government. Also

Ordered, That every member of this convention be punctual in his attendance at the house to-morrow morning.

FRIDAY, August 2, 1776.

A memorial from the inhabitants of Turkey-foot township, in Bedford county, setting forth their opinion respecting the intended new frame of government, was read, and

Ordered, To lie on the table.

The order of the day was then read, and the convention in consequence thereof resolved itself into a committee of the whole house; Col. Joseph Kirkbride was called to and assumed the chair.

After a very considerable time spent in deliberation, the president resumed the chair, and then Col. Kirkbride, the chairman of the committee, reported: That it was the opinion of the said committee, that the future legislature of this state shall consist of one branch only, under proper restrictions.

Wherupon, it was moved and resolved, That the future legislature of this state shall consist of one branch only, under proper restrictions.

August 5th, 6th, 7th, 8th, 9th, 10th and 12th, 1776.

The convention was occupied in the consideration of legislative and executive business.

On the 5th Jacob Garrigues, the assistant clerk, appearing, took the affirmation required by a former minute.

Aug. 7. William Cook appearing for the first time in the house, took the oath, and made and subscribed the profession of faith.

August 13*th*, 1776.

The convention in committee of the whole, made progress in the consideration of the bill of rights, and also resumed the consideration of legislative and executive business.

August 15, 1776.

According to the order of the day,
The convention resolved itself into a committee of the whole house; Col. Kirkbride was called to and assumed the chair. After some further deliberation on the declaration of rights, the president resumed the chair, and Col. Kirkbride, from the committee, reported that they had agreed to the report which he then delivered into the house, and being read, the further consideration thereof was postponed.

FRIDAY, August 16, 1776.

The convention resumed the consideration of the report of the committee respecting the declaration of rights, which being read by paragraphs, received the final assent of the convention.
[For declaration, &c. see page 55.]

SATURDAY, August 17, 1776.

The convention was occupied with the consideration of legislative and executive business.

MONDAY, August 19, 1776,

The convention appointed to essay a frame or plan for the future government of this state, brought in a draft for that purpose, which being read, was ordered for consideration on Wednesday next, the 21st inst.

TUESDAY, August 20, 1776.

The committee resumed the consideration of legislative and executive business.
WEDNESDAY, August 21, 1776.

The convention, according to the order of the day, resolved itself into a committee of the whole house, in order to take into consideration the frame of government—Mr. Rittenhouse was called to and assumed the chair. After a very considerable time spent in debating and deliberating, the president resumed the chair, and Mr. Rittenhouse reported from the committee, that they had made some progress in the business committed to them, and desired leave of the house to sit again to-morrow morning; which was given accordingly.

August 22*d and* 23*d*, 1776.

The committee reported further progress.

August 24, 26, 27 and 28, 1776.

The convention was occupied with the consideration of legislative and executive business.

August 29, 30 and 31, 1776.

The committee of the whole reported further progress in the consideration of the frame of government.

September 3d and 4th, 1776.

The convention, among other things, made progress in the committee of the whole in the consideration of the frame of government.

THURSDAY, September 5, 1776.

The convention resolved itself into a committee of the whole house, in order to resume the consideration of the frame of government. Mr. Rittenhouse was called to and assumed the chair; after some time the president resumed the chair, and Mr. Rittenhouse reported from the committee, that they had finished the business referred to them, and were ready to report thereon. Which report was read, and

Ordered, That the president, Mr. Rittenhouse and Mr. Vanhorn, be desired to revise the same, and make such alterations therein in method and stile, without affecting the sense, as they may think proper; and when that is done, to get 400 copies printed for public consideration.

The convention then resumed the consideration of legislative and executive business.

From the 5th to the 16th of September, 1776.

The convention was engaged in the consideration of legislative and executive business.

MONDAY, September 16, 1776.

The convention, agreeably to the order of the day, resumed the consideration of the frame of government.

It was moved by Col. Ross and seconded by Mr. Clymer, that the first and second sections of the proposed frame of government be debated upon and amended. Whereupon it was

Resolved, That the further debate on the second section is precluded, because it was fully debated and determined before, as appears by the minutes of the 1st and 2d of August last.

Moved and seconded that the yeas and nays on any question in the frame of government, shall be entered on the minutes, when it shall be required by any four members: But the previous question being put, it was determined that the question be not now put.

September 17, 18, 19, 20, 21, 23 *and* 24, 1776.

The convention was engaged in legislative and executive business, and in considering the frame of government.*

WEDNESDAY, *September* 25, 1776.

A letter from the Rev. Messrs. Duffield and Marshall, praying that the clergy of this state may be exempted from the burthen of civil offices, and setting forth their reasons for such exemption, was read, and ordered to lie on the table for consideration.

A letter from the Rev. Messrs. Muhlenberg and Weynberg, praying for an addition to the 47th article of the proposed frame of government., confirming the incorporations for promoting religious and charitable purposes, was read, and ordered to lie on the table.

The House resumed the consideration of the frame of government.

Ordered, That Mr. Cannon, Mr. Jacobs and Mr. Rittenhouse, be appointed to prepare a draft of a preamble to the declaration of rights and frame of government. and of the oaths of allegiance and office to be inserted in the said frame.

In the afternoon the gentlemen appointed to draw up a preamble to the declaration of rights and frame of government, reported an essay for that purpose, which was read and referred for further consideration.

They also reported an essay for the oaths and affirmations of allegiance and of office, which being read and amended, at the table, were approved of, and ordered to be inserted in the frame of government.

THURSDAY, *September* 26, 1776.

On the 23d September, Col. Matlack, Mr. Jacobs and Col. Thomas Smith, were appointed a committee to bring in a draft of a resolve, for settling and regulating the general election for the present year. On this day the committee reported a draft for that purpose, which was then read and amended: The following is an abstract of this resolution.

Whereas, it is not convenient to hold the next election throughout this state, for choosing the elective officers thereof, on the day on which it will be most convenient to the people to hold their elections for the future; and this convention being desirous that the freemen of this state may, as soon as possible, enjoy the advantages of a free and established government, it is therefore

Resolved, That the next election for representatives, &c. usually chosen on the 1st of October, shall be held for the city and counties respectively, on Tuesday the 5th day of November next.

Provision is made for the election of inspectors, and the appointment of judges and clerks, and making the returns of the election, &c.

Every elector before his vote shall be received, shall take the following oath or affirmation, in stead of that heretofore required, viz.

---

* No details are given of the proceedings of the convention in relation to the constitution. The journal only states on the several days, "That the house resumed the consideration of the frame of government, and after some time adjourned."

I ———— ——— do swear (or affirm) that I will be faithful and true to the commonwealth of Pennsylvania, and that I will not directly or indirectly do any act or thing prejudicial or injurious to the constitution or government thereof, as established by the convention.

And the judges and inspectors of the said elections, shall, besides the oaths prescribed in the law directing the choice of inspectors, take the oath of allegiance above recited.

Resolved, That the said general assembly, chosen in consequence of the foregoing resolves, shall meet at Philadelphia, on Tuesday the 19th day of November next.

The convention resumed the consideration of the draft of the preamble offered to them yesterday, and the same was agreed to.

The convention then resumed the consideration of other business.

FRIDAY, September 27, 1776.

On motion, Resolved, That it be recommended to the first general assembly of this state, to make a law similar to the *habeas corpus* act of England, for the security of the personal liberty of the inhabitants.

The convention resumed the consideration of other business.

SATURDAY, September 28, 1776.

THE frame or plan of government and preamble, being now fairly engrossed, were deliberately read and compared at the table, and being bound up with the declaration of rights, were passed and confirmed unanimously, in the words following, viz.

THE CONSTITUTION

Of the commonwealth of Pennsylvania, as established by the general convention elected for that purpose, and held at Philadelphia, July 15, 1776, and continued by adjournment, to September 28, 1776.

WHEREAS all government ought to be instituted and supported for the security and protection of the community as such, and to enable the individuals who compose it, to enjoy their natural rights, and the other blessings which the author of existence has bestowed upon man; and whenever these great ends of government are not obtained, the people have a right by common consent to change it, and take such measures as to them may appear necessary, to promote their safety and happiness. And whereas the inhabitants of this commonwealth have, in consideration of protection only, heretofore acknowledged allegience to the king of Great Britain, and the said king has not only withdrawn that protection, but commenced and still continues to carry on with unabated vengeance, a most cruel and unjust war against them, employing therein not only the troops of Great Britain, but foreign mercenaries, savages and slaves, for the avowed purpose of reducing them to a total and abject submission to the despotic domination of the British parliament (with many other acts of tyranny more fully set forth in the declaration of congress) whereby all allegiance and fealty to the said king and his successors are dissolved and at an end, and all power and authority derived from him ceased in these colonies. And whereas it is absolutely necessary for the welfare and safety of the inhabitants of said colonies, that they be henceforth free and independent states, and that just, permanent and proper forms of government exist in every part of them, derived from, and founded on the authority of the people only, agreeable to the directions of the honorable American congress. WE, the representatives of the free-men of Pennsylvania, in general convention met, for the express purpose of framing such a government, confessing the goodness of the great governor of the universe (who alone knows to what degree of earthly happiness mankind may attain by perfecting the arts of government) in permitting the people of this state, by common consent and without violence, deliberately to form for themselves, such just rules as they shall think best for governing their future society; and being fully convinced, that it is our indispensible duty to establish such original principles of government, as will best promote the general happiness of the people of this state and their posterity, and provide for future improvements, without partiality for, or prejudice against, any particular class, sect or denomination of men whatsoever, do, by virtue of the authority vested in us by our constituents, ordain, declare and establish the following *declaration of rights*, and *frame of government*, to be the constitution of this commonwealth, and to remain in force therein for ever unaltered, except in such articles as shall hereafter, on experience, be found to require improvement, and which shall by the same authority of the people, fairly delegated, as this frame of government directs, be amended or improved for the more effectual obtaining and securing the great end and design of all government, herein before mentioned.

CHAPTER I.

A declaration of the rights of the inhabitants of the commonwealth or state of Pennsylvania.

I. That all men are born equally free and independent, and have certain natural, inherent and unalienable rights, amongst which are the enjoying and defending life and liberty, acquiring, possessing and protecting property, and pursuing and obtaining happiness and safety.

II. That all men have a natural and unalienable right to worship Almighty God, according to the dictates of their own consciences and understanding, and that no man ought, or of right can be compelled to attend any religious worship, or erect or support any place of worship, or maintain any ministry, contrary to, or against his own free will and consent; nor can any man who acknowledges the being of a God, be justly deprived or abridged of any civil right as a citizen, on account of his religious sentiments, or peculiar mode of religious worship; and that no authority can, or ought to be vested in, or assumed by any power whatever, that shall in any case interfere with, or in any manner controul the right of conscience in the free exercise of religious worship.

III. That the people of this state have the sole, exclusive and inherent right of governing and regulating the internal police of the same.

IV. That all power being originally inherent in, and consequently derived from the people; therefore all officers of government, whether legislative or executive, are their trustees and servants, and at all times accountable to them.

V.. That government is, or ought to be, instituted for the common benefit, protection, and security of the people, nation or community; and not for the particular emolument or advantage of any single man, family, or set of men, who are a part only of that community; and that the community hath an indubitable, unalienable and indefeasible right to reform, alter or abolish government, in such manner as shall be by that community judged most conducive to the public weal.

VI. That those who are employed in the legislative and executive business of the state, may be restrained from oppression, the people have a right, at such periods as they may think proper, to reduce their public officers to a private station, and supply the vacancies by certain and regular elections.

VII. That all elections ought to be free, and that all free men, having a sufficient evident common interest with and attachment to the community, have a right to elect officers, or to be elected into office.

VIII. That every member of society hath a right to be protected in the enjoyment of life, liberty and property; and therefore is bound to contribute his proportion towards the expense of that protection, and yield his personal service when necessary, or an equivalent thereto; but no part of a man's property can be justly taken from him or applied to public uses, without his own consent or that of his legal representatives; nor can any man who is conscientiously scrupulous of bearing arms be justly compelled thereto if he will pay such equivalent; nor are the people bound by any laws but such as they have in like manner assented to, for their common good.

IX. That in all prosecutions for criminal offences, a man hath a right to be heard by himself and his council; to demand the cause and nature of his accusation; to be confronted with the witnesses, to call for evidence in his favor, and a speedy public trial by an impartial jury of the country, without the unanimous consent of which jury he cannot be found guilty; nor can he be compelled to give evidence against himself; nor can any man be justly deprived of his liberty, except by the laws of the land or the judgment of his peers.

X. That the people have a right to hold themselves, their houses, papers and possessions free from search and seizure; and therefore warrants, without oaths or affirmations first made, affording a sufficient foundation for them, and whereby any officer or messenger may be commanded or required to search suspected places, or to seize any person or persons, his or their property not particularly described, are contrary to that right, and ought not to be granted.

XI. That in controversies respecting property, and in suits between man and man, the parties have a right to trial by jury, which ought to be held sacred.

XII. That the people have a right to freedom of speech, and of writing and publishing their sentiments; therefore the freedom of the press ought not to be restrained.

XIII. That the people have a right to bear arms for the defence of themselves, and the state; and as standing armies in the time of peace, are dangerous to liberty, they ought not to be kept up: and that the military should be kept under strict subordination to, and governed by the civil power.

XIV. That a frequent recurrence to fundamental principles and a firm adherence to justice, moderation, temperence, industry and frugality, are absolutely necessary to preserve the blessings of liberty, and keep a government free. The people ought therefore to pay particular attention to these points in the choice of officers and representatives, and have a right to exact a due and constant regard to them from their legislatures and magistrates, in the making and executing such laws as are necessary for the good government of the state.

XV That all men have a natural inherent right to emigrate from one state to another that will receive them, or to form a new state in vacant countries, or in such countries as they can purchase, whenever they think that thereby they may promote their own happiness.

XVI. That the people have a right to assemble together to consult for their common good, to instruct their representatives, and to apply to the legislature for redress of grievances by address, petition or remonstrance.

CHAPTER II.

Plan or frame of government for the commonwealth or state of Pennsylvania.

Section 1. The commonwealth or state of Pennsylvania shall be governed hereafter by an assembly of the representatives of the freemen of the same, and a president and council, in manner and form following:—

Sect. 2. The supreme legislative power shall be vested in a house of representatives of the freemen of the commonwealth or state of Pennsylvania.

Sect. 3. The supreme executive power shall be vested in a president and council.

Sect. 4. Courts of justice shall be established in the city of Philadelphia, and in every county of this state.

Sect 5. The freemen of this commonwealth and their sons shall be trained and armed for its defence, under such regulations, restrictions and exceptions as the general assembly shall by law direct; preserving always to the people the right of choosing their colonels and all commissioned officers under that rank, in such manner, and as often as by the said laws shall be directed.

Sect. 6. Every freeman of the full age of twenty-one years, having resided in this state for the space of one whole year next before the day of election for representatives, and paid public taxes during that time, shall enjoy the right of an elector: Provided always, That sons of freeholders of the age of twenty-one years shall be entitled to vote, although they have not paid taxes.

Sect. 7 The house of representatives of the freemen of this commonwealth shall consist of persons most noted for wisdom and virtue, to be chosen by the freemen of every city and county of this commonwealth respectively, and no person shall be elected unless he has resided in the city or county for which he shall be chosen two years immediately before the said election, nor shall any member, while he continues such, hold any other office except in the militia.

Sect. 8. No person shall be capable of being elected a member to serve in the house of representatives of the freemen of this commonwealth more than four years in seven.

Section 9. The members of the house of representatives shall be chosen annually by ballot, by the freemen of the commonwealth, on the second Tuesday in October for ever (except this present year) and shall meet on the fourth Monday of the same month, and shall be stiled *The general assembly of the representatives of the freemen of Pennsylvania*, and shall have power to choose their speaker, the treasurer of the state, and their other officers; sit on their own adjournments; prepare bills and enact them into laws; judge of the elections and qualifications of their own members; they may expel a member, but not a second time for the same cause; they may administer oaths or affirmations on examination of witnesses; redress grievances; impeach state criminals; grant charters of incorporation; constitute towns, boroughs, cities and counties; and shall have all other powers necessary for the legislature of a free state or commonwealth; but they shall have no power to add to, alter, abolish or infringe any part of this constitution.

Sect. 10. A quorum of the house of representatives shall consist of two-thirds of the whole number of members elected, and having met and chosen their speaker, shall each of them, before they proceed to business, take and subscribe as well the oath or affirmation of fidelity and allegiance hereinafter directed, as the following oath or affirmation, viz.

I —— —— do swear (or affirm) that as a member of this assembly, I will not propose or assent to any bill, vote or resolution, which shall appear to me injurious to the people, nor do or consent to any act or thing whatever, that shall have a tendency to lessen or abridge their rights and privileges as declared in the constitution of this state, but will in all things conduct myself as a faithful honest representative and guardian of the people, according to the best of my judgment and abilities.

And each member, before he takes his seat, shall make and subscribe the following declaration, viz.

I do believe in one God, the creator and governor of the universe, the rewarder of the good and punisher of the wicked, and I do acknowledge the scriptures of the Old and New Testament to be given by Divine Inspiration.

And no further or other religious test shall ever hereafter be required of any civil officer or magistrate in this state.

Sect. 11. Delegates to represent this state in congress shall be chosen by ballot by the future general assembly at their first meeting, and annually for ever afterwards as long as such representation shall be necessary. Any delegate may be superseded at any time, by the general assembly appointing another in his stead. No man shall sit in congress longer than two years successively, nor be capable of re-election for three years afterwards; and no person who holds any office in the gift of the congress shall hereafter be elected to represent this commonwealth in congress.

Sect. 12. If any city or cities, county or counties, shall neglect or refuse to elect and send representatives to the general assembly, two-thirds of the members from the cities or counties that do elect and send representatives, provided they be a majority of the cities and counties of the whole state when met, shall have all the powers of the general assembly, as fully and amply as if the whole were present.

Sect. 13. The doors of the house in which the representatives of the freemen of this state shall sit in general assembly, shall be and remain open for the admission of all persons, who behave decently, except only when the welfare of this state may require the doors to be shut.

Sect. 14. The votes and proceedings of the general assembly shall be printed weekly, during their sitting, with the yeas and nays on any question, vote or resolution, where any two members require it, except when the vote is taken by ballot; and when the yeas and nays are so taken, every member shall have a right to insert the reasons of his vote upon the minutes, if he desires it.

Sect. 15. To the end that laws before they are enacted, may be more maturely considered, and the inconvenience of hasty determinations as much as possible prevented, all bills of a public nature shall be printed for the consideration of the people, before they are read in general assembly the last time for debate and amendment; and except on occasions of sudden necessity, shall not be passed into laws until the next session of assembly; and for the more perfect satisfaction of the public, the reasons and motives for making such laws shall be fully and clearly expressed in the preambles.

Sect. 16. The stile of the laws of this commonwealth shall be, *Be it enacted, and it is hereby enacted by the representatives of the freemen of the commonwealth of Pennsylvania, in General Assembly met, and by the authority of the same.* And the general assembly shall affix their seal to every bill, as soon as it is enacted into a law, which seal shall be kept by the assembly, and shall be called THE SEAL OF THE LAWS OF PENNSYLVANIA; and shall not be used for any other purpose.

Sect. 17. The city of Philadelphia and each county in this commonwealth respectively, shall on the first Tuesday of November in this present year, and on the second Tuesday of October, annually, for the two next succeeding years, viz. the year one thousand seven hundred and seventy-seven, and the year one thousand seven hundred and seventy-eight, choose six persons to represent them in general assembly. But as representation in proportion to the number of taxable inhabitants is the only principle which can at all times secure liberty and make the voice of a majority of the people the law of the land; therefore the general assembly shall cause complete lists of the taxable inhabitants in the city and each county in the commonwealth respectively, to be taken and returned to them on or before the last meeting of the assembly elected in the year one thousand seven hundred and seventy-eight, who shall appoint a representation to each in proportion to the number of taxables in such returns, which representation shall continue for the next seven years afterwards, at the end of which, a new return of the taxable inhabitants shall be made, and a representation agreeable thereto appointed by the said assembly, and so on septennially for ever. The wages of the representatatives in general assembly, and all other state charges shall be paid out of the state treasury.

Sect 18. In order that the freemen of this commonwealth may enjoy the benefit of election as equally as may be, until the representation shall commence, as directed in the foregoing section, each county, at its own choice, may be divided into districts, hold elections therein, and elect their representatives in the county and their other elective officers, as shall be hereafter regulated by the general assembly of this state: And no inhabitant of this state shall have more than one annual vote at the general election for representatives in assembly.

Sect. 19. For the present the supreme executive council of this state shall consist of twelve persons chosen in the following manner: The freemen of the city of Philadelphia, and of the counties of Philadelphia, Chester and Bucks respective'y, shall choose by ballot one person for the city and one for each county aforesaid, to serve for three years and no longer, at the time and place for electing representatives in general assembly. The freemen of the counties of Lancaster, York, Cumberland and Berks, shall in like manner elect one person for each county respectively, to serve as councillors for two years and no longer. And the counties of Northampton, Bedford, Northumberland and Westmoreland respectively, shall in like manner elect one person for each county, to serve as councillors for one year and no longer: And at the expiration of the time for which each councillor was chosen to serve, the freemen of the city of Philadelphia and of the several counties in this state respectively, shall elect one person to serve as councillor for three years and no longer, and so on every third year for ever. By this mode of election and continual rotation more men will be trained to public business, there will in every subsequent year be found in the council a number of persons acquainted with the proceedings of the foregoing years, whereby the business will be more consistently conducted, and moreover the danger of establishing an inconvenient aristocracy will be effectually prevented. All vacancies in the council that may happen by death, resignation or otherwise, shall be filled at the next general election for representatives in general assembly, unless a particular election for that purpose shall be sooner appointed by the president and council. No member of the general assembly or delegate in Congress, shall be chosen a member of the council. The president and vice-president shall be chosen annually by the joint ballot of the general assembly and council, of the members of the council. Any person having served as a councillor for three successive years, shall be incapable of holding that office for four years afterwards. Every member of the council shall be a justice of the peace for the whole commonwealth, by virtue of his office.

In case new additional counties shall hereafter be erected in this state, such county or counties shall elect a councillor, and such county or counties shall be annexed to the next neighbouring counties, and shall take rotation with such counties.

The council shall meet annually, at the same time and place with the general assembly.

The treasurer of the state, trustees of the loan-office, naval officers, collectors of customs or excise, judge of the admiralty, attornies-general, sheriffs and prothonotaries, shall not be capable of a seat in the general assembly, executive council or continental congress.

Sect. 20. The president, and in his absence the vice-president, with the council, five of whom shall be a quorum, shall have power to appoint and commissionate judges, naval officers, judge of the admiralty, attorney-general and all other officers, civil and military, except such as are chosen by the general assembly or the people, agreeable to this frame of government and the laws that may be made hereafter, and shall supply every vacancy, in any office, occasioned by death, resignation, removal or disqualification, until the office can be filled in the time and manner directed by law or this constitution. They are to correspond with other states, and transact business with the officers of government, civil and military, and to prepare such business as may appear to them necessary, to lay before the general assembly. They shall sit as judges, to hear and determine on impeachments, taking to their assistance, for advice only, the justices of the supreme court. And shall have power to grant pardons and remit fines in all cases whatsoever, except in cases of impeachment; and in cases of treason and murder shall have power to grant reprieves, but not to pardon, until the end of the next session of assembly, but there shall be no remission or mitigation of punishment on impeachments, except by act of the legislature; they are also to take care that the laws be faithfully executed; they are to expedite the execution of such measures as may be resolved upon by the general assembly; and they may draw upon the treasury for such sums as shall be appropriated by the house. They may also lay embargoes, or prohibit the exportation of any commodity, for any time, not exceeding thirty days, in the recess of the house only. They may grant such licences as shall be directed by law, and shall have power to call together the general assembly when necessary, before the day to which they shall stand adjourned. The president shall be commander in chief of the forces of the state, but shall not command in person, except advised thereto by the council, and then only so long as they shall approve thereof. The president and council shall have a secretary, and keep fair books of their proceedings, wherein any councillor may enter his dissent, with his reasons in support of it.

Sect. 21. All commissions shall be in the name, and by the authority of the freemen of the commonwealth of Pennsylvania, sealed with the state seal, signed by the president or vice-president, and attested by the secretary, which seal shall be kept by the council.

Sect. 22. Every officer of state, whether judicial or executive, shall be liable to be impeached by the general assembly, either when in office or after his resignation or removal for mal-administration. All impeachments shall be before the president or vice-president and council, who shall hear and determine the same.

Sect. 23. The judges of the supreme court of judicature shall have fixed salaries, be commissioned for seven years only, though capable of re-appointment at the end of that term, but removable for misbehaviour at any time by the general assembly; they shall not be allowed to sit as members in the continental congress, executive council or general assembly, nor to hold any other office, civil or military, nor take or receive fees or perquisites of any kind.

Sect. 24 The supreme court and the several courts of common pleas of this commonwealth shall, besides the powers usually exercised by such courts, have the powers of a court of chancery, so far as relates to the perpetuating testimony, obtaining evidence from places not within this state, and the care of the persons and estates of those who are *non compotes mentis*, and such other powers as may be found necessary by future general assemblies, not inconsistent with this constitution.

Sect. 25. Trials shall be by jury as heretofore, and it is recommended to the legislature of this state to provide by law against every corruption or partiality in the choice, return or appointment of juries.

Sect. 26. Courts of sessions, common pleas and orphans' courts shall be held quarterly in each city and county, and the legislature shall have power to establish all such other courts as they may judge for the good of the inhabitants of the state; all courts shall be open, and justice shall be impartially administered without corruption or unnecessary delay : All their officers shall be paid an adequate but moderate compensation for their services, and if any officer shall take greater or other fees than the laws allow him, either directly or indirectly, it shall ever after disqualify him from holding any office in this state.

Sect. 27. All prosecutions shall commence in the name and by the authority of the freemen of the commonwealth of Pennsylvania, and all indictments shall conclude with these words—*against the peace and dignity of the same.* The stile of all process hereafter in this state shall be *The commonwealth of Pennsylvania.*

Sect. 28. The person of a debtor, where there is not a strong presumption of fraud, shall not be continued in prison after delivering up, *bona fide,* all his estate real and personal for the use of his creditors, in such manner as shall be hereafter regulated by law. All prisoners shall be bailable by sufficient sureties, unless for capital offences, when the proof is evident or presumption great.

Sect. 29. Excessive bail shall not be exacted for bailable offences : And all fines shall be moderate.

Sect. 30. Justices of the peace shall be elected by the freeholders of each city and county respectively, that is to say, two or more persons may be chosen for each ward, township or district, as the law shall hereafter direct : And their names shall be returned to the president in council, who shall commissionate one or more of them for each ward, township or district, so returning for seven years, removeable for misconduct, by the general assembly ; but if any city or county, ward, township or district, in this commonwealth, shall hereafter incline to change the manner of appointing their justices of the peace as settled in this article, the general assembly may make laws to regulate the same, agreeable to the desire of a majority of the freeholders of the city or county, ward, township or district, so applying ; no justice of the peace shall sit in the general assembly, unless he first resign his commission, nor shall he be allowed to take any fees, nor any salary or allowance, except such as the future legislature may grant.

Sect. 31. Sheriffs and coroners shall be elected annually in each city and county by the freemen, that is to say, two persons for each office, one of whom for each, is to be commissioned by the president in council. No person shall continue in the office of sheriff more than three successive years, or be capable of being again elected during four years afterwards. The election shall be held at the same time and place appointed for the election of representatives : And the commissioners and assessors, and other officers chosen by the people, shall also be then and there elected, as has been usual heretofore, until altered or otherwise regulated by the future legislature of this state.

Sect. 32. All elections, whether by the people or in general assembly, shall be by ballot, free and voluntary : And any elector, who shall receive any gift or reward for his vote, in meat, drink, monies or otherwise, shall forfeit his right to elect for that time, and suffer such other penalty as future laws shall direct. And any person who shall directly or indirectly give, promise or bestow any such rewards to be elected, shall be thereby rendered incapable to serve for the ensuing year.

Sect. 33. All fees, license money, fines and forfeitures heretofore granted or paid to the governor or his deputies, for the support of government, shall hereafter be paid into the public treasury, unless altered or abolished by the future legislature.

Sect. 34. A register's office for the probate of wills and granting letters of administration, and an office for the recording of deeds, shall be kept in each city and county ; the officers to be appointed by the general assembly; removeable at their pleasure, and to be commissioned by the president in council.

Sect. 35. The printing presses shall be free to every person, who undertakes to examine the proceedings of the legislature, or any part of government.

Sect. 36. As every freeman, to preserve his independence, (if without a sufficient estate,) ought to have some profession, calling, trade or farm, whereby he may honestly subsist, there can be no necessity for nor use in establishing offices of profit, the usual effects of which are dependence and servility, unbecoming freemen, in the possessors and expectants, faction, contention, corruption, and disorder among the people : but if any man is called into public service to the prejudice of his private affairs, he has a right to a reasonable compensation : And whenever an office, through increase of fees, or otherwise becomes so profitable as to occasion many to apply for it, the profits ought to be lessened by the legislature.

Sect. 37. The future legislature of this state shall regulate entails in such manner as to prevent perpetuities.

Sect. 38. The penal laws as heretofore used, shall be reformed by the future legislature of this state, as soon as may be, and punishments made in some cases less sanguinary, and in general more proportionate to the crimes.

Sect. 39. To deter more effectually from the commission of crimes, by continued visible punishment of long duration, and to make sanguinary punishments less necessary, houses ought to be provided for punishing by hard labour, those who shall be convicted of crimes not capital; wherein the criminals shall be employed for the benefit of the public, or for reparation of injuries done to private persons. And all persons at proper times shall be admitted to see the prisoners at their labour.

Sect. 40. Every officer, whether judicial, executive or military, in authority under this commonwealth, shall take the following oath or affirmation of allegiance, and general oath of office before he enter on the execution of his office.

The oath or affirmation of allegiance.

I ———— ———— do swear (or affirm) that I will be true and faithful to the commonwealth of Pennsylvania : And that I will not directly or indirectly do any act or thing prejudicial or injurious to the constitution or government thereof as established by the convention.

The oath or affirmation of office.

I ———— ———— do swear (or affirm) that I will faithfully execute the office of ———— for the ———— of ———— and I will do equal right and justice to all men to the best of my judgment and abilities, according to law.

Sect. 41. No public tax, custom or contribution shall be imposed upon, or paid by the people of this state, except by a law for that purpose ; and before any law be made for raising it, the purpose for which any tax is to be raised, ought to appear clearly to the legislature to be of more service to the community than the money would be, if not collected, which being well observed, taxes can never be burthens.

Sect. 42. Every foreigner of good character, who comes to settle in this state, having first taken an oath or affirmation of allegiance to the same, may purchase, or by other just means acquire, hold and transfer land or other real estate, and after one year's residence, shall be deemed a free denizen thereof, and entitled to all the rights of a natural born subject of this state, except that he shall not be capable of being elected a representative until after two years' residence.

Sect. 43. The inhabitants of this state shall have liberty to fowl and hunt in seasonable times on the lands they hold, and on all other lands therein not inclosed, and in like manner to fish in all boatable waters and others not private property.

Sect. 44. A school or schools shall be established in each county by the legislature for the convenient instruction of youth, with such salaries to the masters paid by the public as may enable them to instruct youth at low prices: And all useful learning shall be duly encouraged and promoted in one or more universities.

Sect. 45. Laws for the encouragement of virtue, and prevention of vice and immorality, shall be made and constantly kept in force, and provision shall be made for their due execution: And all religious societies or bodies of men heretofore united or incorporated for the advancement of religion and learning, or for other pious and charitable purposes, shall be encouraged and protected in the enjoyment of the privileges, immunities and estates which they were accustomed to enjoy or could of right have enjoyed under the laws and former constitution of this state.

Sect 46. The declaration of rights is hereby declared to be a part of the constitution of this commonwealth, and ought never to be violated on any pretence whatever.

Sect. 47. In order that the freedom of this commonwealth may be preserved inviolate for ever, there shall be chosen, by ballot, by the freemen in each city and county respectively, on the second Tuesday in October, in the year one thousand seven hundred and eighty three, and on the second Tuesday in October, in every seventh year thereafter, two persons in each city and county of this state, to be called THE COUNCIL OF CENSORS, who shall meet together on the second Monday of November next ensuing their election; the majority of whom shall be a quorum in every case, except as to calling a convention, in which two-thirds of the whole number elected shall agree, and whose duty it shall be to enquire whether the constitution has been preserved inviolate in every part; and whether the legislative and executive branches of governemnt have performed their duty, as guardians of the people, or assumed to themselves or exercised other or greater powers than they are entitled to by the constitution; they are also to enquire whether the public taxes have been justly laid and collected in all parts of this commonwealth, in what manner the public monies have been disposed of, and whether the laws have been duly executed: For these purposes they shall have power to send for persons, papers and records; they shall have authority to pass public censures, to order impeachments, and to recommend to the legislature the repealing such laws as appear to them to have been enacted contrary to the principles of the constitution. These powers they shall continue to have for and during the space of one year, from the day of their election, and no longer. The said council of censors shall also have power to call a convention, to meet within two years after their sitting, if there appear to them an absolute necessity of amending any article of the constitution, which may be defective, explaining such as may be thought not clearly expressed, and of adding such as are necessary for the preservation of the rights and happiness of the people; but the articles to be amended, and the amendments proposed, and such articles as are proposed to be added or abolished, shall be promulgated at least six months before the day appointed for the election of such convention, for the previous consideration of the people, that they may have an opportunity of instructing their delegates on the subject.

On motion, Ordered, That the president and every member of this convention present, do sign the same, which was accordingly done, by the following members of the convention:

Philadelphia city.
Timothy Matlack,
Frederick Kuhl,
James Cannon,
George Schlosser,
David Rittenhouse.
Philadelphia county.
Robert Loller,
Joseph Blewer,
John Bull,
William Coates.
Bucks county.
John Wilkinson,
Samuel Smith,
John Keller,
William Vanhorn,
John Grier,
Abraham Van Middleswarts
Joseph Kirkbride.
Chester county.
Benjamin Bartholomew,
Thomas Strawbridge,
Robert Smith,
Samuel Cunningham,
John Mackey,
John Flemming.
Lancaster county.
Philip Marsteller,
Thomas Porter,
Bartram Galbreath,
John Hubley,
Alexander Lowrey.
York county.
James Edgar,
James Smith,
Cumberland county.
John Harris,
Jonathan Hoge,

William Clarke,
Robert Whitehill,
William Duffield,
James Brown,
Hugh Alexander,
James M'Clean.
Berks county.
Jacob Morgan,
Gabriel Hiester,
Benjamin Spyker,
Valentine Eckert,
Charles Shoemaker,
Thomas Jones, jr.
Northampton county.
Simon Driesbach,
Jacob Arndt,
Peter Burkholder,
Jacob Stroud,
Neigal Gray,
Abraham Miller,
John Ralston.
Bedford county.
Benjamin Elliot,
Thomas Coulter,
Joseph Powell,
John Burd,
John Cessna.
John Wilkins,
Thomas Smith,
Northumberland county.
William Cooke,
James Potter,
Robert Martin,
Matthew Brown,
Walter Clark,
John Kelley,
James Crawford,
John Weitzell.

Westmoreland county,   John Moore,
James Barr,   John Carmichael,
Edward Cook,   John M'Clellan,
James Smith,   Christopher Lavingair.

BENJAMIN FRANKLIN, *President.*

Attest—JOHN MORRIS, JR. *Secretary.*

Ordered, That the constitution of this commonwealth, as now agreed to and signed by the members of this convention, be committed to the charge of the council of safety, with directions to deliver the same to the general assembly of this state, at their first meeting, immediately after they shall have chosen their speaker.

On motion, Resolved, That Mr. Rittenhouse, Mr. Cannon and Mr. Matlack, be a committee to settle the incidental expenses of this convention.

On motion, Resolved, That the president of this convention be allowed the same wages as the speaker of the late house of assembly, and that the vice president draw an order on the state treasurer for the amount thereof.

On motion, Resolved, That Mr. Rittenhouse, Mr. Jacobs and Mr. Clymer, be a committee to prepare the seals for the future legislature and executive council of this state.

Resolved, That immediate public notice be given by the secretary, that the freemen of this state are empowered by the frame of government this day passed, to choose at their next election for representatives, in the city of Philadelphia, and each county, one person as a councillor of state.

Resolved, That Mr. Cannon, Mr. Rittenhouse, Col. Matlack and Col. Bull, be a committee to revise the minutes of this convention, and print 250 copies of the same, together with the constitution, ordinances, &c. (one hundred of which to be bound) for the use of the members of this House.

Resolved unanimously, That the thanks of this convention be given to the president, for the honor he has done it, by filling the chair during the debates on the most important parts of the bill of rights and frame of government, and for his able and disinterested advice thereon.

Then the convention rose.

PART III.

Chapter I.

COUNCIL OF CENSORS.

A view of the proceedings of the first session of the Council of Censors, convened at Philadelphia, on Monday the 10th day of November, one thousand seven hundred and eighty three.

MONDAY, November 10, 1783.

Pursuant to the 47th section of the constitution of this commonwealth, a number of gentlemen elected as censors for the city and several counties, met at the state house, in Philadelphia, but a quorum. not appearing, they adjourned from day to day, until

THURSDAY, November 13th, 1783.

The council met, and the returns of the elections held in the city of. Philadelphia, and the several counties of this state, were transmitted by the supreme executive council, and read, and it appeared that the following gentlemen were elected:

For the city of Philadelphia.

Samuel Miles,✪   Thomas Fitzsimons,

For the county of Philadelphia.

Frederick A. Muhlenburg,   Arthur St. Clair.

For the county of Bucks.

Joseph Hart,   Samuel Smith,

For the county of Bedford.

David Espy,   Samuel Davidson.

For the county of Chester.

Anthony Wayne,   John Evans.†,

For the county of Lancaster.

John Whitehill,   Stephen Chambers..

For the county of York.

Thomas Hartley,   Richard M'Allister.

For the county of Westmoreland.

John Smiley,   William Finley.

For the county of Cumberland.

James M'Lene,   William Irvine.

For the county of Berks.

James Read,   Baltzer Gehr,

For the county of Northampton.

John Arndt,   Simon Dreisbach.

For the county of Washington.

James Edgar,   John M'Dowell.

For the county of Northumberland.

Two different returns.—It was decided by the council, on the 26th November, 1783, that William Montgomery and Samuel Hunter,‡ were duly elected.

The council proceeded to the election of a president, and the ballots being taken, it appeared that the honorable Frederick Augustus Muhlenberg, Esq. was unanimously elected.

The council then proceeded to business; officers were elected, rules for conducting the business of the council were appointed, &c.

---

* Samuel Miles, resigned his seat on the 8th of June, 1784, and George Bryan was elected in his room, who took his seat June 24, 1784.

† James Moore, was elected in the room of John Evans, deceased, and took his seat on the 30th December, 1783.

‡ James Potter, was elected in the room of Samuel Hunter deceased, and took his seat on the 7th July, 1784.

WEDNESDAY, November 19, 1783.*

Ordered, That Mr. Fitzsimons, Mr. Wayne, Mr. Smiley, Mr. Irvine and Mr. Read, be a committee to enquire and report, whether the constitution has been preserved inviolate in every part.†

THURSDAY, December 4, 1783.

Resolved, That the council will on Monday the 15th instant, resolve itself into a committee of the whole, to consider whether there is a necessity for amending any article of the constitution, which may be defective; explaining such as may be thought not clearly expressed, and of adding such as are necessary for the preservation of the rights and happiness of the people.

WEDNESDAY, December 17, 1783.

Ordered, That the committee appointed November 19, to enquire whether the constitution has been preserved inviolate, in every part, be instructed to enquire, whether the legislative and executive branches of government have performed their duty, as guardians of the people, or assumed to themselves, or exercised other or greater powers than they are entitled to by the constitution.

THURSDAY, January 1, 1784.

The council resolved itself into a committee of the whole, Mr. M'-Allister in the chair, to consider whether the constitution of this state is perfect in all its parts, or whether the same requires any amendment or alteration.
After some time the president resumed the chair, and the chairman delivered in a report, which was read and laid on the table.

FRIDAY, January 2, 1784.

The report of the committee of the whole was read, and the following resolution was adopted.
Resolved, That some articles of the constitution of this commonwealth, are materially defective, and absolutely require alteration and amendment.

---

* On the 19th of November; two petitions signed by sundry inhabitants of the city and county of Philadelphia, were presented, setting forth that the freedom of election, and the laws and constitution of the commonwealth had been violated at the last election, and praying to be heard in support of the facts alleged, and that the election in the said city and county be declared null and void.
This petition was referred to a committee, on the 21st November, and the examination of the case occupied much of the time and attention of the council. On the 31st of December the report of the committee, that there appeared no just ground or legal cause for setting aside the election, was adopted.
† On the 20th January, 1784, Mr. M'Allister and Mr. Finley, were added to this committee —On the 24th June, 1784, Mr. Bryan and Mr Moore, were added to the committee.—On the 7th July, 1784, Mr. Potter was added to the committee.—On the 14th July, 1784, Mr. M'Lene was added to the committee.

On motion, Resolved, That a committee be appointed to report those articles of the constitution, which are materially defective and absolutely require alteration and amendment, agreeable to the foregoing resolution. The members chosen, were Mr. Miles, Mr. Fitzsimons, Mr. St. Clair, Mr. Hartley and Mr. Arndt.

SATURDAY, January 3, 1784.

Resolved, That it be an instruction to the committee appointed to report those articles of the constitution, which are materially defective, and absolutely require alteration and amendment, to report the alterations and amendments.

SATURDAY, January 17, 1784.

The committee appointed to enquire, whether the constitution has been preserved inviolate in every part, and whether the legislative and executive branches of government have performed their duty as guardians of the people, or assumed to themselves, or exercised other or greater powers than they are entitled to by the constitution, delivered in a report, in part, which was read and ordered to lie on the table.

The committee appointed the 2d instant, to report those articles of the constitution which are materially defective and absolutely require alteration and amendment, and who were instructed to report the alterations and amendments, delivered in a report, which was read and laid on the table.

MONDAY, January 19, 1784.

The council proceeded to consider the report of the committee on the defects and alterations of the constitution, and the same was read the second time, by paragraphs, considered, amended and adopted, and is in the following words, viz.[*]

Your committee, to whom it was referred to report those articles of the constitution which are defective and the alterations and amendments, beg leave to report,

That by the constitution of the state of Pennsylvania, the supreme legislative power is vested in one house of representatives, chosen by all those who pay public taxes. Your committee humbly conceive, the said constitution to be in this respect materially defective.

1. Because if it should happen that a prevailing faction in that one house was desirous of enacting unjust and tyrannical laws, there is no check upon their proceedings.

---

[*] The yeas and nays were taken upon the adoption of the several paragraphs, and the votes upon every question, were as follow:

YEAS.

Samuel Miles,	Arthur St. Clair,	Stephen Chambers	William Irvine,
Thomas Fitzsimons,	Anthony Wayne,	Thomas Hartley,	John Arndt,
Fredk A. Muhlenberg,	James Moore,	Richard M'Allister,	David Espy.

NAYS.

Joseph Hart,	Baltzer Gehr,	John Smiley,	James Edgar,
Samuel Smith,	Simon Dreisbach,	William Finley,	John M'Dowell.
John Whitehill,			

2. Because an uncontrolled power of legislation will always enable the body possessing it, to usurp both the judicial and the executive authority, in which case no remedy would remain to the people but by a revolution.

That by the said constitution the supreme executive power is delegated to a council. Your committee conceive the said constitution to be in this respect materially defective.

1. Because the constant sitting of a council is expensive and burthensome.

2. Because a numerous body of men, though possessed of wisdom necessary for deliberation, will never possess the decision necessary for action on sudden emergencies.

3. Because where a council act either weakly or wickedly, there is no individual so accountable to the public, as every man ought to be in such cases.

4. Because a single man would never be able of himself to do such acts as he may persuade a majority of his council to concur in, and support by their numbers.

5. Because the election of the president being by joint ballot of the council and assembly, if a prevailing faction should ever happen in the assembly, so as to lead a considerable majority, the president thus chosen, will have nothing to fear from the legislature, and by influencing the council, would possess exorbitant authority, without being properly accountable for the exercise of it.

That by the said constitution the judges of the supreme court are to be commissioned for seven years only, and are removable (for misbehaviour) at any time, by the general assembly. Your committee conceive the said constitution to be in this respect materially defective.

1. Not only because the lives and property of the citizens, must in a great degree depend upon the judges, but the liberties of the state are evidently connected with their independence.

2. Because if the assembly should pass an unconstitutional law, and the judges have virtue enough to refuse to obey it, the same assembly could instantly remove them.

3. Because at the close of seven years, the seats of the judges must depend on the will of the council; wherefore the judges will naturally be under an undue bias, in favor of those upon whose will their commissions are to depend.

That great care is taken by the said constitution to establish a rotation in sundry offices, which your committee humbly conceive to be improvident.

1. Because the hope of re appointment to office, is among the strongest incentives to the due execution of the trust it confers.

2. Because the state is thereby necessarily deprived of the service of useful men for a time, and compelled to make experiment of others, who may not prove equally wise and virtuous.

3. Because the check intended by such principle of rotation, can be of no good effect to repress inordinate ambition, unless it were extended so as to preclude a man from holding any office whatever.

4. Because the privilege of the people in elections, is so far infringed as they are thereby deprived of the right of choosing those persons whom they would prefer.

Your committee having thus briefly stated the leading objection to the constitution, proceed with all possible deference, to point out the articles they recommend to be struck out, and to propose the amendments. And first,

In the bill of rights, section 9; that there be added after the words, "judgment of his peers," *of the vicinage.* Because the verification of the facts in the vicinity where they happen, is one of the greatest securities to life, liberty and happiness.

That there is no clause in the bill of rights, to prevent retrospective laws being passed, your committee submit the following.

Laws made to punish for actions done before the existence of such laws, are unjust, tyrannical and oppressive, and inconsistent with the fundamental principles of a free government: nor ought any citizen in any case, to be declared guilty of treason or felony by the legislature.

That sections 1 and 2, of the constitution be left out, and the following substituted.

The supreme legislative power within this commonwealth, shall be vested in two separate and distinct bodies of men; the one to be called the legislative council, the other to be called the assembly of the commonwealth of Pennsylvania; who shall meet once, at least, in every year, for the despatch of public business, and shall be stiled the general assembly of Pennsylvania.

In lieu of section 3, we submit the following :

There shall be a principle executive magistrate, who shall be stiled the governor of the commonwealth of Pennsylvania.

That section 5 be altered and stand amended as follows,

The freemen of this commonwealth and their sons shall be trained and armed for its defence, under such regulations, restrictions and exceptions as the general assembly shall by law direct.

Because an uniformity in the constitution and discipline of the militia throughout the United States may be essential to its usefulness, and

Because the general assembly being the representatives of the people, will, in a point so essential to their security and happiness, make the law conformable to the opinion of their constituents, and to the interest of the commonwealth.

That in section 6, two years' residence be inserted instead of one year.

In the room of section 7, the following is submitted :

The general assembly of this commonwealth shall consist of persons most noted for wisdom and virtue, to be chosen by the freemen of every city and county therein respectively, and no person shall be elected unless he shall have resided in the city or county for which he shall be chosen, one year immediately before the said election : Nor shall any member, while he continues such, hold any other office, except in the militia.

Section 8 to be left out, for the reasons given on the principle of rotation.

The members of the general assembly shall be chosen annually, by ballot, by the freemen of this commonwealth, on the second Tuesday in October for ever, and shall meet on the fourth Monday of the same month. They shall be styled the assembly of the commonwealth of Pennsylvania; shall have power to choose their speaker, their other necessary officers, and the treasurer of the state; they shall judge of the elections and qualifications of their own members; may expel a member, but not a second time for the same cause; they may administer oaths or affirmations, on examination of witnesses ; impeach state criminals, and may prepare bills to be passed into laws. All money bills shall originate in the assembly only, but they shall not on any occasion annex to or blend with a money bill any matter, clause or thing, not immediately relating thereto, and necessary for imposing, assessing, levying or applying the taxes or supplies to be raised for the support of government, or the current expenses of the state, but shall have all other powers, necessary for one branch of the legislature of a free state or commonwealth.

In section 10, a quorum of the assembly shall consist of two-thirds of the whole number of members elected, but a smaller number shall have power to adjourn from day to day.

And add to the section the following clause,

The members of the legislative council and of the assembly, shall each of them (after they have chosen their president and speaker, and before they proceed to other business) take and subscribe the oath or affirmation of fidelity and allegiance, and the declaration directed to be taken by the members of assembly, in the 10th section of the constitution.

That section 11 stand amended as follows:

Delegates to represent this commonwealth in congress, shall be chosen by the joint ballot of the future general assembly, at their first meeting, annually, for ever. Any delegate may be superseded at any time by the general assembly, appointing another in his stead. No man shall sit in congress more than three years in any term of six years,; and no person, while he holds any office in the gift of congress, shall hereafter be elected to represent this commonwealth in congress.

Section 12, being provided for by section 10, to be left out.

Section 13, instead of " the doors of the house," to insert " the doors of each house."

That section 14 be altered, and stand amended as follows:

The votes and proceedings of the general assembly shall be printed weekly during their sitting, with the yeas and nays on any question, vote or resolution, when any two members require it, except when the vote is taken by ballot. We propose that the remainder of the section be left out.

Because we conceive the entering the dissent on the minutes, with reasons, only tends to foment party disputes, weaken the force of the laws, and impede their execution.

Section 15, we humbly conceive, was always delusory, and if a second branch is agreed to, will be rendered unnecesary.

That section 16 be altered and stand amended as follows:

The stile of the laws of this commonwealth shall be, Be it enacted, and it is hereby enacted by the general assembly of the commonwealth of Pennsylvania, and by the authority of the same.

That section 17 be altered as follows:

Whereas representation in proportion to the number of taxable male inhabitants, is the best principle which can at all times secure liberty, and make the voice of the people the law of the land: Therefore the general assembly shall cause complete lists of the taxable male inhabitants, in the city and each county of the commonwealth respectively, to be taken, and returned to them on or before the last meeting of the general assembly, which shall be elected in the year   , who shall in the year   appoint a representation in the general assembly, in proportion to the number of taxables in such returns, in the ratio of 1250 taxables for each representative in assembly, and of 2500 taxables for each representative in the legislative council, which representation shall continue for the ensuing seven years, at the end of which term a new return of the taxable male inhabitants shall be made, and a representation agreeably thereto appointed by the said general assembly, and in like manner septennially for ever.

And in order to prevent a too numerous representation, which would be expensive and burthensome, the representatives in assembly shall never exceed 100 in the whole; nor shall the representatives in the legislative council ever exceed 50; to prevent which, the ratio shall be altered from time to time, as the number of taxables increase, so as to preserve an equal representation in proportion to the taxable male inhabitants.

That section 18 be altered as follows:

In order that the freemen of this commonwealth may enjoy the benefit of election as equally as may be, they shall meet annually at such convenient place or places within the city and each county respectively, as the law may hereafter direct, and there choose their representatives and other elective officers; and no inhabitant of this state shall have more than one annual vote for representatives in the assembly and in the legislative council; nor shall any person be admitted to vote except in the city or county in which he shall be an inhabitant.

That section 19 be struck out, and the following substituted:

To the end that the blessings of free and equal government may be extended and secured to the good people of this commonwealth, and that the laws may be more maturely considered, there shall be a legislative council, which for the present and until a return is taken as heretofore directed, shall consist of twenty-nine persons, who shall be chosen by ballot and at the time and at the places appointed for holding the elections for members of assembly, and in the following proportions, that is to say.

The freemen of the city of Philadelphia shall elect 2 ⎫
            county of Philadelphia, 3 ⎪
                  Chester, 3 ⎬ persons.
                  Bucks, 2 ⎭

To serve for three years respectively.

The freemen of the county of Lancaster shall elect 4 ⎫
                  York, 3 ⎪
                  Cumberland, 3 ⎬ persons.
                  Berks, 2 ⎭

To serve for two years respectively.

The freemen of the county of Northampton shall elect 2 ⎫
                  Bedford, 1 ⎪
                  Northumberland, 1 ⎪
                  Westmoreland, 1 ⎬ persons.
                  Washington, 1 ⎪
                  Fayette, 1 ⎭

To serve for one year respectively.

And at the expiration of the time for which each councillor is chosen to serve, the freemen of the city of Philadelphia and of each county shall respectively elect the same number of councillors for the city and each county respectively, as is herein directed to serve for three years, and so on every third year. Provided, however, that the

general assembly shall not be precluded from altering the present
number of representatives, agreeably to the principle already laid down
in the constitution, with respect to the election of members of assembly, in proportion to the number of male taxables in the city and each
county. The legislative council shall be the first branch of the legislature; shall have power to choose a president, and their other necessary officers. The president shall have a casting vote on all questions in that body, but no other vote except when given by ballot. All
bills (except money bills) may originate in the legislative council or
assembly, and may be altered, amended or rejected by either. They
shall sit on their own adjournments, but neither the legislative council
or assembly shall have power to adjourn themselves for a longer time
than two days, unless by mutual consent. They shall judge of the
election and qualifications of their own members; may expel a member, but not a second time for the same cause. They shall be a court
with full authority to hear and determine all impeachments against
any officer or officers of the government, for misconduct or mal-administration in their offices, either when in office or otherwise, (provided the impeachment shall be prosecuted within one year after their
resignation or removal,) and shall take to their assistance (for advice
only) the judges of the supreme court; but previous to the trial of every impeachment, the members shall be respectively sworn, truly and
impartially to try and determine the cause, according to the evidence;
nor shall their judgment extend farther than to removal from office,
and disqualification from holding or enjoying any place of honor, trust
or profit under the commonwealth; but the party so convicted shall
nevertheless be liable to indictment, trial, judgment and punishment,
according to the laws of the land.

Not less than two-thirds of the legislative council shall be a quorum to do business, but a smaller number may adjourn from day to
day. All vacancies which may happen by death, resignation or otherwise, in the legislative council or assembly, shall be filled up by writ
from the president of the one and speaker of the other, directed to
the sheriff of the proper county or counties.

The legislative council shall meet at the same time and place with
the assembly, and shall have and enjoy all the powers necessary for
a distinct branch of a free legislature.

The treasurer of the state, trustees of the loan office, naval officers,
collectors of customs or excise, or any part of the public revenue,
judge of the admiralty, attorney-general, sheriffs and prothonotaries
shall not be capable of a seat in the general assembly or continental
congress.

That section 20 be left out, and the following inserted:
The governor shall be chosen annually by the freemen of this commonwealth, qualified as is required to entitle persons to vote for
members of assembly, at the same time and place or places, which
shall be directed for the choosing of their representatives in the general assembly, where they shall give in their votes by ballot, and elect
some fit person, who shall be a freeholder and shall have resided at
least seven years in the state next before the time of his election;
which votes shall be sorted, cast up and counted, and fair lists, containing the names of the persons voted for, and of the number of votes
for each, made by the sheriffs, judges and inspectors, in the same manner as is or may be directed by law for ascertaining the members

elected for the general assembly; which lists, signed and sealed by the said sheriffs, judges and inspectors shall be returned by the sheriffs into the office of the secretary of this commonwealth,
days at least before the time appointed by the constitution for the meeting of the general assembly, and the said secretary shall, on the first day of the session, lay before the general assembly the said returns, and the two branches together shall forthwith proceed to examine the said returns, and the person having the greatest number of votes shall be by them declared and published to be governor; but if no person shall have a majority of votes, the general assembly shall by joint ballot elect one person out of the two who had the highest number of votes, or if it should so happen that more than two persons had an equal and highest number of votes, then they shall elect one person from the whole of those that have such equal and highest number of votes, and the person so elected shall by them be declared and published to be the governor.

The governor shall be, in virtue of his office, general and commander in chief of the militia and all the forces of the commonwealth, and admiral of the navy of the same: He shall have power to convene the general assembly on extraordinary occasions, and, at his discretion, to grant reprieves and pardons to persons convicted of crimes, other than those that may be convicted on impeachment, or of treason or murder, in which cases he may suspend the execution of the sentence, until it shall be reported to the legislature at their subsequent meeting, and may direct him to pardon, grant further reprieves, or carry the sentence or sentences into execution: He shall have power to appoint and commissionate the judges of the supreme court and the judges of the courts of common pleas, naval officers, judge of the admiralty, the attorney general, and all other officers civil or military, except such as shall be appointed by the general assembly, or chosen by the people, agreeably to the constitution, whom he shall nevertheless commissionate.

It shall be his duty to inform the general assembly, at every session, of the condition of the commonwealth, as far as respects his department, and to recommend such matters to their consideration as he shall think conducive to its welfare. He shall correspond with the continental congress and with the other states, and transact the business of the state with the officers of government, civil and military. He shall take care that the laws be duly executed, and shall expedite such measures as may be resolved upon by the general assembly.

In case of absence, resignation, removal from office or death of the governor, the president of the legislative council shall execute all the powers vested in the governor, until another governor shall be chosen, or until the governor absent or impeached shall return or be acquitted; and in such case the legislative council shall choose by ballot one of their body to supply the place of the president during the time he shall exercise the authority of the governor.

All bills which have passed the legislative council and assembly shall, before they become laws, be presented to the governor for his revisal, and if, upon revision, he approves thereof, he shall signify his approbation by signing the same; but if he objects to the passing of such bill, he shall return it, together with his objections in writing, to the council or assembly in whichsoever it has originated, who shall enter the said objections at large upon their records, and proceed to reconsider the said bill. But if, after such reconsideration, two-thirds of the legislative council or assembly shall, notwithstanding the said objections, agree to pass the same, it shall, together with the objections, be sent to the other branch of the legislature, where it shall also be reconsidered, and if approved by two-thirds of the members present, it shall have the force of a law. but in all such cases, the votes of both houses shall be determined by yeas and nays, and the names of the persons voting for or against the said bill, shall be entered on their records; and in order to prevent unnecessary delays, if any bill shall not be returned by the governor within   days after it shall have been presented, the same shall be a law, unless the general assembly shall by an adjournment render a return within days impracticable, in which case the bill shall be returned on the first day of the meeting of the legislature, after the expiration of the said   days.

A secretary shall be elected by the joint ballot of the legislative council and assembly, and shall be commissioned by the governor for the time being. He shall be keeper of the seals of the state, and shall under the direction of a committee of both branches of the legislature, affix the seal to the laws when the same shall be enacted: He shall countersign all commissions signed by the governor, and all orders drawn by him on the treasury of the state, for monies appropriated, as well as all marriage and tavern licenses, and perform the other duties which may be enjoined on him by the constitution or laws of this commonwealth. He shall keep fair records of his proceedings, to be laid before either house of the legislature, when called for, and shall attend the governor or either house when required.

That section 21 be altered, and stand amended as follows:

All commissions shall be in the name of the commonwealth of Pennsylvania, sealed with the state seal, signed by the governor or the person exercising the powers of government for the time, and attested by the secretary.

That section 22 be altered as follows:

Every officer of this commonwealth, whether judicial or executive, shall be liable to impeachment by the assembly, either in office, or at any time within twelve months after removal or resignation, for maladministration; and all impeachments shall be before the legislative council, who shall hear and determine the same.

The judges of the supreme court and of the respective courts of common pleas, shall have fixed salaries; shall be appointed and commissioned by the governor, and shall hold their appointments and salaries during good behaviour; they may be removed by the governor, upon the address of the general assembly, provided that two thirds of each house agree to such address; they shall not be capable of sitting in the continental congress or general assembly, nor to hold any other office, civil or military, nor shall they take or receive any fees or perquisites of any kind.

That section 30 be altered as follows:

Justices of the peace shall be elected by the freeholders of each city and county respectively, that is say, two or more persons may be chosen for each ward, township or district, as the law shall hereafter direct, and their names shall be returned to the governor, who shall commissionate one or more of them for each ward, township or district so returning, for seven years, removable by the governor on the

address of the general assembly; but if any city or county, ward, town!
ship or district in this commonwealth, shall hereafter incline to change
the manner of appointing their justices of the peace, as settled in
this article, the general assembly may make laws to regulate the
same agreeable to the desire of a majority of the freeholders of the
city or county, ward, township or district so applying. No justice of
the peace shall sit in the general assembly, unless he first resign his
commission, nor shall he be allowed to take any fees nor any allowance or salary, except such as are or may hereafter be granted by
law.*

That in section 31 "*governor*" be inserted in the room of "*president and council.*"

That in section 33 the following words be struck out, "unless altered or abolished by the future legislature."

Because in our opinion the restriction should be absolute, and not
subject to the will of any future general assembly.

That in section 34, instead of "president and council," "*governor*"
be inserted.

That in section 40 the words "as established by the convention,"
be left out.

That section 42 be amended as follows:

Every foreigner of good character, who comes to settle in this state,
having first taken an oath or affirmation of allegiance to the same, may
purchase or by other just means acquire, hold and transfer land or
other real estate; and after two years' residence shall be deemed a
free denizen thereof, except that he shall not be capable of being
elected a representative in assembly or in the legislative council, or
of being elected or appointed to any office of trust until he has resided
in the state five years.

That section 47 be left out.

Your committee beg leave to add, that the confused manner in
which the constitution is thrown together, is justly exceptionable; at
the same time to remark, that their report will be liable to the same
objections, because they have thought it their duty to follow the constitution in the order in which it stands, and to propose the alterations
and amendments to each in the same order.

Dissentient.

1. Because the report is a manifest violation of the 47th section of
the constitution under which we are appointed. We think it a duty
we owe to ourselves and our constituents, to state fully and circum-
stantially the proceedings of this council, previously to the decision of
the present question, in order that our own characters may stand ac-

---

* In the report as made by the committee, the following was the proposed substitute for the 30th section:
"Justices of the peace shall be elected by the freeholders of each city and county
respectively, as the law shall hereafter direct, and their names shall be returned to
the governor, who shall commissionate one or more of them for each ward, town
or district so returning, for seven years, removable by the governor for misbehaviour in office, on the address of the general assembly. No justice of the peace shall
be allowed to take any fees, salary or allowance, except such as are granted by
law." This was negatived in council, and the above was agreed to.

quitted and that our constituents, whose happiness, together with our own, is so intimately connected with it, may be enabled to form a proper judgment.

On the 4th December last, the council resolved itself into a committee of the whole, to consider " whether there is a necessity of amending any article of the constitution, which may be defective, explaining such as may be thought not clearly expressed, and of adding such as are necessary for the preservation of the rights and happiness of the people." On the 1st of January, instant, the committee of the whole made report: " That some articles of the constitution of this commonwealth, are materially defective, and absolutely require amendment." Which was read the first time, and ordered to lie on the table. On the 2d of January, the above report was taken up for the second reading. when it was fully debated, and previously to the question being put on it, a member who voted against, and another who voted for the report, expressly and repeatedly declared (which the whole council acquiesced in) " That the decision of this question was to determine absolutely, whether a convention was to be called or not." Upon the question being put, it appeared that of all the members elected there were but twelve for adopting the report, and ten who were present, against it; and although the minutes of the council say it was carried in the affirmative, yet, as the constitution expressly requires two thirds at least, of all the censors elected, which is eighteen, to concur in proposing changes in the frame of government; we are warranted in saying, *it was determined by more than the number required*, that there does not exist a necessity of making any alterations. Therefore, we consider the appointment of a committee, after this, to bring in propositions for altering the form of government, and all the subsequent proceedings of the council on the subject, as factious, illegal and establishing an alarming precedent. We cannot suppose that an appeal to the people at large, is again intended, for this council is authorised to deliberate and determine upon the propriety of making changes. Besides, that appeal has been repeatedly made, and as often decided with unexampled unanimity in favor of the constitution. It is also inconsistent with the idea of representation, and subversive of all legal and orderly government. If however, this appeal be intended from the council to its constituents, we wish it to be so stated; if to the convention, we have already decided by the constitutional number, that no convention is to be called. Should good order and government be unhinged by this step, we persuade ourselves, that we have as little to fear as those who so violently urge the present measure.

2. Because we consider it as an essential principle in every constitution, that it shall not be lightly changed. Clogs and difficulties have therefore, with great wisdom been thrown in the way of all attempts to change fundamental principles. In ours, the spirit of the constitution requires, that in the course of seven years, faults of so alarming a tendency should be discovered, as to induce two thirds at least, of all the censors elected, to concur in propositions for a change. This we conceive to be a principle essential to the preservation of any constitution whatever; without it, we shall be subject to continual fluctuations, and we fear fall into anarchy or tyranny.

3. Because we are convinced, that the same departure from the rule, which is prescribed by the constitution, for the calling of a convention, will be perverted to authorise that convention, when

assembled (by whatever means) to proceed to further and more extravagant innovations (if possible) than any of those which have been hitherto proposed, or at least avowed. If we suffer ourselves to be carried away by the tide of the party prevailing in the place where we happen at present to convene, we fear that the state may be plunged into irretrievable destruction. We may be happy in the preservation of a free constitution; we tremble for the consequences of so wild a departure from the very principles which many of us have sworn to observe, and all of us profess to obey.

4. Because we recollect the present constitution was formed with great harmony, at the most auspicious period of time, when the flame of patriotism shone brightest, when the good people of the state were impressed with no other idea than that of acquiring and maintaining to themselves and their posterity, equal liberty, when no factions were formed with ambitious or mercenary motives. We have seen it support the safety and happiness of the state against a most formidable enemy without, with every embarrassment of a most indefatigable and insidious party within. We hoped, as the constitution had pointed out an orderly mode of reconsidering every part of our proceedings at the end of seven years, that peace and harmony would have prevailed in the review. If we are disappointed, we must ascribe it to those who have undertaken to propose articles for alteration, when no legal body is constituted for making those alterations, and when it has been already decided, upon the principles of the constitution, that a convention shall not be called.

5. Because the present constitution, with all the pretended aults and imperfections, which have been so industriously searched out and ascribed to it by men who wanted an excuse for real disaffection or factious views, has stood the test of the most arduous trial, at a time when vigor and energy were indispensably necessary in the execution of measures essential to our safety, among a people of whose purity, in some parts of the state, we cannot boast.

6. Because the alterations proposed will introduce a form of government much more expensive, burthensome and complicated. But what we dread more than expense and delay, they tend to introduce among the citizens new and aristocratic ranks, with a chief magistrate at their head, vested with powers exceeding those which fall to the ordinary lot of kings. We are sufficiently assured, that the good people of Pennsylvania, most ardently love equal liberty, and that they abhor all attempts to lift one class of citizens above the heads of the rest, and much more the elevating any one citizen to the throne of royalty; and herein we are confident we speak not only the language of our constituents, but that we proclaim also the voice of God and nature.

7. Because we have been taught to believe, that many free constitutions have been destroyed for want of the means of reducing them at fixed periods to their first principles. This has been constantly recommended by the greatest and best political writers, is fully established in the 14th section of our bill of rights, and has been wisely provided for by the 47th section of our frame of government. This salutary provision, among others, is now attempted to be destroyed, so that no guard may remain against innovations, no check may be left against the encroachments of power. Hereafter, if the present attempt should succeed, no constitutional mode can be appealed to, upon the most at-

trocious and alarming abuses of government.   Nothing will remain to the people, but the dreadful appeal to arms, to which so many before us have been reduced to the necessity of applying: An appeal frequently unsuccessful, and always dangerous; dangerous even in case of victory, because the conquerors, even under the standard of liberty have so often proved tyrants.   A legal mode is infinitely to be preferred, and we think ought always to be preserved.

Joseph Hart,   *John Smiley,*
Samuel Smith,   *William Finley,*
John Whitehill,   *James Edgar,*
Simon Dreisbach,   *John M'Dowell.*
Baltzer Gehr,

WEDNESDAY, January 21, 1784.

The following resolution was adopted, yeas 13, nays 9.

Whereas the dissentients to the report of the committee appointed to propose alterations and amendments in the constitution, have among other things, stated that on the 2d of January, when the report of a former committee on the constitution was under consideration, "A member who voted against, and another who voted for the report. expressly and repeatedly declared (which the council acquiesced in) that the descision of this question was to determine absolutely whether a convention was to be called or not."   Therefore,

Resolved, That the council did not then, nor at any time since, acquiesce or agree in the opinion, that the vote of the 2d of January, determined the question as to calling a convention.

The following address was then presented to the chair, and on motion, the same was read the second time and adopted, viz.

Friends and fellow citizens,

Agreeably to the trust reposed in us, we have met and seriously deliberated upon those matters submitted to our consideration, by the constitution of this state.

The most weighty subject that has come before us, is the constitution itself.   To that therefore, whilst we have not neglected the others, we have principally directed our attention.   We have examined it with candor; we have compared it with the constitutions of other states; we have discovered some of its defects; we have suggested the necessity of abolishing such parts of it as are expensive and burthensome, and dangerous to your liberties, and have with great deference thrown out, for your consideration, such alterations as appear to us to be best calculated to secure to you the blessings of free and equal government.

By the report of our committee which accompanies this address, you will perceive that though the majority of this council approve of the alterations, considering them essential to your existence as a free people, it has not yet met with the concurrence of two-thirds of our whole number, which the constitution has made necessary to enable us to call a convention.   We are strangers to the motives of the minority, for refusing to give you an opportunity to judge upon a matter, you and we, and all our posterity are so deeply interested in, while by their silence upon the subject of the report, they have confessed that the constitution wants amendment.   By refusing to indulge you in a convention for that purpose, they hold up consequences from that meeting that are dishonorable to freemen.   They have indeed had the power to prevent it for the present, in the manner pointed out by the constitution:—But their sullen *no* in this council cannot rob you of your birthright.

Is it that they were concerned in the framing of the constitution, and therefore cannot bear that any fault should be found with it? This fondness for the productions of the brain, is a weakness mankind is subject to But in so momentous a concern, passion and prejudice should, as far as human nature is capable of it, be laid aside, and the arguments offered, weighed with that cool deliberation the subject deserves.   Nor can it be in any case, much less in the intricate science of government, upon which so few have had either leisure or opportunity to turn their thoughts, an impeachment of any man's judgment, to say he is mistaken. If errors then have crept in, they ought to be corrected; if there are ambiguities, they should be explained, and if the. system itself is wrong it should be altered.

One cannot hesitate a moment in declaring that all these were naturally to be expected from the time and circumstances under which the present constitution was formed. Our political knowledge was in its infancy. The passions of the state were unusually agitated. A large body of militia were busy in preparing to march to another state to oppose the progress of the British army. Another body of citizens to the amount of five thousand were absent, on the same service, in the continental army. Amidst the din of arms and the dread of invasion, and when many wise and able men were necessarily absent, whose advice and assistance would have been of great use, was it reasonable to expect that a constitution could be formed proper for a great and growing state? And if an improper one was formed, which is our decided opinion, shall it not be altered or amended?

Let it not be said, that the constitution has carried us triumphantly through a perilous war; this is far from being the case. We owe all the exertions of Pennsylvania to the virtue of the people. In times of danger, it is well known, the constitution forsook us, and the will of our rulers became the only law. It is well known likewise, that a great part of the citizens of Pennsylvania, from a perfect conviction that political liberty could never long exist under such a frame of government, were opposed to the establishment of it, and that when they did submit to it, a solemn engagement was entered into by its then friends, that after seven years should be expired, and the enemy driven from our coasts, they would concur with them in making the wished for amendments. The seven years have elapsed, and our country now enjoys a peace, favorable to the most temperate deliberations on the subject of government; but a minority in this council, which by the absurdity of its constitution, can in this instance bind the majority, say it is unnecessary. We appeal to your common sense, whether such a conduct is calculated to restore order and mutual confidence. It may be proper here to remark, that this very minority, although near one half of the members present in this council, do not represent one third of you; so that the voice of more than two thirds of the people, if the majority speak your sense, is sunk entirely; and, contrary to all principles, the lesser number binds the greater. What do these men fear from a convention? are they afraid to trust you with the exercise of the inestimable power of choosing a government for yourselves? You cannot, you will not injure yourselves in this business. If the constitution in its present form is most agreeable, you have only to instruct your representatives in the convention to adopt it in all its parts. You are the sovereigns of Pennsylvania. All the power of the state is derived from your votes. Nothing can be obligatory on you which is contrary to your inclinations, or repugnant to your happiness. We do not quote any part of the bill of rights to prove to you that you may call a convention, when and in what manner you please. This privilege is your birth right and no power on earth can deprive you of it. We appeal to you therefore, to decide the great question, whether Pennsylvania shall continue unhappy and distracted under her present constitution, or whether by calling a convention, and amending it, you will restore harmony amongst yourselves and dignity to your government.

We recommend to your serious consideration, the report of our committee, which has been adopted by this council and has become one of its acts. Weigh the reasons upon which it is founded with coolness and deliberation, and suffer not yourselves to be imposed upon, or your passions inflamed by artful men, or by words without meaning. We can have no interest separate from yours; and as to our political principles, when you recollect that all have been the constant opposers of our British foes, and most of us have risked our lives and fortunes, during the whole of the contest, you can entertain no doubt about them. The proposed alterations are not experiments, but are founded on reason and the experience of our sister states. The future welfare of your country is in your hands. If you give her a good government she will be great and free. If you mistake in this point, the die will be cast, and you are sealed up to insignificance or misery.

We have not the most distant prospect, that the gentlemen in the minority will concur in calling a convention to amend the constitution, which we have thought, we hope not improperly, the most important part of our business; and it is that you might have an opportunity to instruct them on that subject, that we have at present suspended our deliberations.

On motion, that the president sign the address, and that it be published with the report, the yeas and nays were as follow:

YEAS.

Samuel Miles,	Arthur St. Clair,	Stephen Chambers	William Irvine,
Thomas Fitzsimons,	Anthony Wayne,	Thomas Hartley,	John Arndt,
Fredk. A. Muhlenberg,	James Moore,	Richard M'Allister,	David Espy.

NAYS.

Joseph Hart,	Baltzer Gehr,	John Smiley,	James Edgar,
Samuel Smith,	Simon Dreisbach,	William Finley,	John M'Dowell.
John Whitehill,	James Read,		

The convention then adjourned until 3 o'clock on Tuesday the 1st of June, next, P. M.

Chapter II.

A view of the proceedings of the second session of the council of censors, convened at Philadelphia, on the 1st of June, 1784.

TUESDAY, June 1, 1784.

A number of the members met pursuant to adjournment, but there not being a quorum present, they adjourned from day to day until Friday June 4th, 1784, when a quorum appearing, they proceeded to business, and were engaged until the 5th August following, in the consideration of other subjects than those connected with the constitution.

TURSDAY, August 5, 1784.

Resolved, That the powers of this council do extend to all abuses and deviations from the constitution, which happen as well during the existence of this council, as previous to its being constituted.

The committee appointed to enquire whether the constitution has been preserved inviolate in every part, and whether the legislative and executive branches of government have performed their duty, as guardians of the people, or assumed to themselves or exercised other or greater powers than they are entitled to by the constitution, delivered in a further report,* which was read and ordered to lie on the table.

WEDNESDAY, August 11, 1784.

It was resolved, that the council will on Monday the 16th instant, take up for a second reading the said report. Monday the 16th of August, the council proceeded to the consideration of the reports of the said committee, read the 17th of January and the 5th of August, and the same were considered by paragraphs, amended, and on the 3d of August adopted, in the words following, viz.

The committee appointed to enquire " whether the constitution has been preserved inviolate in every part, and whether the legislative or executive branches of government have performed their duty as guardians of the people, or assumed to themselves or exercised other or greater powers than they are entitled to by the constitution," beg leave to report:

That they have examined and investigated the proceedings of the legislative body of this state, and that they find various and multiplied instances of departure from the frame of government. But conceiving it to be the most important and at the same time the least disagreeable part of the duty of the council of censors to bring the administration back to its first principles, they have selected such and so many instances of deviation, as are necessary to illustrate and re-establish the several leading principles of the constitution. These, for perspicuity, they have arranged under the respective section, or clause of the section violated; together with the opinion of the committee

---

* The committee reported in part on the 17th January, 1783.

thereon, and their reasons for such opinion; and they now submit the whole to the council.

The journals of the general assembly and the laws passed since the revolution, have furnished all the cases referred to; because by the second statute of this commonwealth, in section 3, the acts of assembly of the late province of Pennsylvania, are revived and declared to be law within the state, so far only as they are not repugnant to, or inconsistent with the constitution.

In our enquiries we considered the constitution as a system, which, in establishing the natural rights of individuals, founds all civil power on the authority of the people only, in whom the sovereignty resides, and whose is that sovereignty in its several parts, as the same is delegated to different bodies of the citizens, as their trustees or servants. The exercise of power in the greatest articles of it, those of making laws, and carrying those laws into execution, is, by the three first sections of this grand bulwark of equal liberty, so honorable to the founders of it, and so invaluable to the citizens, by a most marked and decided distribution, assigned to two great branches. The legislative power is vested in the representatives of the people in general assembly, and the executive in a president and council; and from this last, for the greater security of the people, the judicial, of which it is a part, is again severed, and rendered independent of both. Thus wisely precluding an accumulation of power and influence, in the hands of one or of few, which the history of mankind evinces ever to have been subversive of all public justice and private right, and introductive of the capricious, unsteady domination of prejudice, party and self-interest, instead of the government of laws prescribed, promulgated and known.

The legislative, executive and judicial powers of the people being thus severally delegated to different bodies, the convention has carefully guarded against any encroachment of one on the proper authority of either of the other bodies, by making it a principal duty of a council of censors every seventh year to enquire, " Whether the constitution has been preserved inviolate, and whether the legislative and executive branches of government have assumed to themselves, or exercised other or greater powers than they are entitled to by the constitution."

These observations your committee premise to their report, as they are the clew by which they have been able to investigate the fabric.

The supposed doubts and difficulties, the contradictions and absurdities imputed to the constitution, which have been industriously and insidiously suggested to the people, as rendering it an impracticable system of administration, and as justifying acts of government in violation of it, have vanished before us as we proceeded. By thus recurring to the source of all authority, and recognising the distribution of powers, this frame of government, as established by the convention, appears to your committee to be clear in its principles, accurate in its form, consistent in its several parts, and worthy of the veneration of the good people of Pennsylvania, and of all the attachment they have formerly and during this session of the council of censors shewn to it.

Your committee beg leave further to suggest, that the checks and guards provided by the convention upon the proceedings of the legislative body, carry with them a very strong implied censure against the disposing of public money by vote; legislating for individuals, or in any case, by summary resolutions, which should be considered as no more than previous declarations of the sense of the house upon unfinished business; a foundation whereon to raise the superstructure of law, after mature deliberation, and clothed with the solemnities of enacting, which give weight and dignity, as well as public notoriety to the statute. This consideration is the more interesting, as the executive powers, being no longer opposed to the popular interest, and so restricted in this state that they cease to be objects of watchful jealousy.

We believe, with the illustrious Montesquieu, that the representative body is not fit for active resolutions, but for the enacting of laws, and to see whether the laws be duly executed. This latter duty of seeing whether the laws have been duly executed, the convention has assigned to the council of censors: thus wisely providing for a dispassionate review of so important an object, at a distance of time when animosities may have subsided, and calm reason may suffer the law of the land to resume its proper exercise. And we are of opinion with the great Locke, who, speaking of legislative power, lays it down as the fundamental law of all commonwealths, "that the legislative cannot assume to itself a power to rule by extemporary and arbitrary decrees, but is bound to dispense law and justice, and to decide the rights of the subject by promulgated, standing laws, and known authorised judges; and that men give up their natural independence to the society with this trust, that they shall be governed by known laws; otherwise their peace, quiet and property will be in the same uncertainty as in a state of nature."

This practice of entering into personal discussions and hasty votes, too often in contradiction to express laws, solemnly enacted, we fear, has been too much countenanced in some instances *from a determination that the people should experience, practically, what extravagancies a single legislature, unrestrained by the rules of the constitution, may be capable of committing.* And this while people were yet in some degree under the habits of the former vague, undefined and unsystematical proprietary government of the province; when every increase of power, obtained by their representatives from the executive, and every instance in which the force of law could be obtained to a resolve of the house, seemed at least to be favorable to the public interest, have not adverted to the dangerous effects arising to the community from such proceedings, in our present circumstances.

However irregular and inconsistent it may be, in well formed governments, for the representative body to legislate by a hasty vote, and to execute, or to appoint the officers who execute, yet every instance in which the representative body succeeded in such attempts, tended to restrict or counterbalance the enormous influence of a proprietor, having an interest opposed to that of the people; a negative on their orderly proceedings in legislation in his own person, and another within his influence; and having almost every officer (from the chief justice of the supreme court downwards) the creature of his power, and the servant of his will; every freeholder for his tenant. a rental from the quit rents, and a fixed revenue for his deputies, which made him and his governors independent of the people and their representatives; and millions of acres to dispose of, as his interest or ambition might suggest. Thus circumstanced, every opportunity was anxiously embraced of getting the public revenues into the disposition of the assembly or of officers appointed by them; and thus the same body who levied the money from the subject, expended it in some instances by their resolves, without control or accountability. However dangerous the powers of the proprietor may have been, yet your committee believe that these proceedings of the assembly were not the less irregular. They were however practised, and they have unfortunately acquired too great a sanction with the people from custom, and from the popular character of the last assembly before the revolution, and of the committees and council of safety since that period, who, having alone the exercise of every power of government, continued the practice of course.

From similar circumstances, and the continued opposition to the alarming influence of the proprietary power, arose and has been handed down, the usage in general assembly, through a committee of grievances, of extending their deliberations to the cases of individuals, who have been taught to consider an application to the legislature as a shorter and more certain mode of obtaining relief from hardships and losses, than the usual process of law. For as the erecting of a court of chancery would be adding to the weight of the proprietor, by giving him new jurisdiction, as well as the appointment of a new corps of officers, it was deemed expedient to retain the exercise of equitable power in the hands of the assembly ; and there is reason to think that favor and partiality have from the nature of public bodies of men, predominated in the distribution of this relief. These dangerous procedures have been too often recurred to since the revolution.

Your committee further observe, that from the peculiar circumstances attending the late struggle with great Britain, examples have been set, which it will be extremely dangerous, and in some cases derogatory to the sovereignty of the state, to suffer to pass into precedents. We are willing to leave the scale of depreciation and some other acts, *ex post-facto*, to be justified by the necessity of the case. But law is well defined to be "a rule prescribed or made before hand." Public monies ought to be appropriated before they are levied. The reward of services should be ascertained when they are prescribed, and neither increased nor diminished afterwards, from favor or prejudice to the party. Innocence and guilt, and all demands by or against the public, ought, in all instances, to be judged by the known and usual course of proceedings ; ever preserving, in case of doubts as to fact and law, the sacred right of trial by jury, and the proper tribunals ; jury trial being the only instance of judicial power which the people have reserved to themselves.

These considerations your committee offer to the council, to be recommended to the watchful attention of the citizens of the state, as a standing protest of this council of censors against the many violations of the constitution, which are now more generally hinted at, or hereinafter particularly noticed.

We flatter ourselves that by recurring to the line of duty prescribed to the several branches of government by the constitution, the expenses and burthensome length of the sessions of the legislature may be saved to the good people of Pennsylvania.

In some instances it is certainly true that the constitution has been invaded through necessity, in times of extreme danger, when this country was involved in a very unequal struggle for life and liberty, and when good men were induced to hazard all consequences, for the sake of preserving our existence as a people. Yet in a calm review of these proceedings, we think it proper to advert even to such breaches of the constitution, as have been occasioned by the extremest necessity, lest they should be brought into precedent when no such necessity shall exist.

BILL OF RIGHTS.

Section 8. "That every member of society hath a right to be protected in the enjoyment of life, liberty and property, and is therefore bound to contribute his proportion towards the expense of that protection, &c.

It is the opinion of this committee, that the acts of assembly, passed within this commonwealth since the revolution, for seizing and taking the goods of the inhabitants of this state, for the use of the army, and for setting prices thereon, are inconsistent with this article, and with the rights of property. See vol. 1, chap. 47, 48, 129, 170 and 178.

Some of the acts of assembly, made to prevent forestalling, were also unconstitutional invasions of the rights of property. See chapters 44, 62, 81, vol. I.

September 28, 1779, The general assembly resolve, " That the salt within the city and liberties, beyond the occasion of a private family, be taken from the proprietors, by the president and council, and that the price thereof be ascertained by council."

It is the opinion of this committee, that the attempts which have been made to regulate the prices of commodities, were absurd and impossible. They tended to produce the very opposite effects to those which they were designed to produce, and were invasions of the right of property. See vol. I, chap. 60.—Journals of assembly, Nov. 22, 1779 ; Dec. 16, 1777 ; Jan. 25 and Feb. 14, 1780.

Section 10. "The people have a right to hold themselves, their houses, papers and possessions free from search and seizure, and therefore warrants without oaths or affirmations first made, affording a sufficient foundation for them, and whereby any messenger or officer may be commanded or required to search suspected places, or to seize any person or his property, not particularly described, are contrary to that right, and ought not to be granted."

It is the opinion of this committee that the authority given by the act for county levies and other tax laws, and by the excise laws to the collectors of these taxes, to break open houses in the day time, without oath or affirmation first made, shewing a sufficient foundation for them, is inconsistent with the 10th section of the bill of rights.

Section 11. " That in all controversies respecting property, and in suits between man and man, the parties have a right to trial by jury, which ought to be held sacred."

In the third session of the present assembly, a law has been passed to vest in Isaac Austin a real estate in the city of Philadelphia, claimed and possessed by George Adam Baker, as his freehold. This extraordinary act of assembly moreover commands the sheriff to put Mr. Austin in possession.

It is remarkable that the bill depending on this occasion, was passed after it had been shewn to the house that an action of ejectment, concerning part of the premises, was depending in the court of common pleas of Philadelphia county; an attorney at law having appeared to the action for the defendant, Isaac Austin.

So flagrant an infringement of the sacred rights of a citizen to trial by jury, and so manifest, and withal so wanton a violation of the constitution of this commonwealth, calls for the severest censure of the people and of this council. To their respective constituents it belongs to enquire how their servants in assembly, individually, voted on this occasion. From the journals of the house they will derive full information on the subject.

THE CONSTITUTION.

Section 7, latter clause. "No member of the house of representatives, whilst he continues such, shall hold *any other office*, except in the militia."

It is the opinion of this committee, that members of the general assembly may not hold the office of county treasurer. There have been sundry instances of county treasurers sitting as members of the house of representatives, since the revolution.

Section 9. "The members of the house of representatives shall have power to prepare bills and enact them into laws."

It is the opinion of this committee, that acts of assembly to amend titles to land, which may be defective from the loss of deeds, and from the denial of deeds by the vendors, after the price has been paid, have been too frequently passed, and have too decidedly barred all other persons, who might have pretensions to the same; that the practice is dangerous, that it tempts to fraud, and that in either case they are seldom necessary, as the testimony upon which the house proceeds may now be perpetuated, under a clause of the constitution, as well in the courts of common pleas as in the supreme court, in order to have the effect it ought to have, and no greater. And perhaps it would be better to lodge a chancery power with proper judges, to compel the specific performance of bargains for lands in the latter case. See acts of assembly, vol. I, chap. 122, to confirm lands of T. Beans.—Chap. 123, to confirm lands of T. Summers.—Vol. II, chap. 94, to confirm lands of Percifor Frazer.

By these acts, all claims not made within one year after the passing of them, are for ever barred, saving only *femes covert, infants, &c.* Thus the loss of a deed becomes the advantage of the party, whilst, through mistake, others may be injured by the relief intended by the legislature to the applier, whose neglect in not recording his deeds, has given occasion to the interposition of the house.

It is the opinion of this committee, that the dissolving of the bands of marriage is another very improper exercise of legislative power, and an intrusion upon the judicial branch; and that instead of passing acts occasionally, there should be a power given to proper judges of determining on such applications.

It is the opinion of this committee that acts of assembly for vacating useless highways and roads, are also improper and unconstitutional. There should be an authority lodged with proper courts, to vacate useless roads.

Section 9. "The house of representatives shall have power to judge of the qualifications of their own members."

It is the opinion of this committee, that the general assembly has no right to expel one of its members, charged with crimes not committed as a member, but as a public officer or in his private capacity, until he shall be convicted thereof before his proper judges.

September 9, 1783, Mr. —— ——, a representative in the general assembly for —— county, is, first declared guilty of notorious frauds and other enormous crimes; secondly, he is expelled from his seat; thirdly, the attorney general is directed to institute actions against him for fraud and perjury. After such denunciations, would it be possible for the accused to obtain a fair trial? Suppose one of the members of the house were to kill a man, would it be just that the house should anticipate his sentence, and pronounce the homicide to be a malicious murder? Besides, after fixing such an odium on the unhappy manslayer, every member concerned would be interested against a fair hearing. But if, after all, the culprit should be acquitted by his peers, where would be the dignity of the legislature? Examples of this nature from the British house of commons will not serve for precedents in Pennsylvania. The proceedings against Sir Robert Walpole and Sir Richard Steele, in the reign of Queen Ann, and the expulsion of John Wilkes, in the days of George the third, for a libel, reflected dishonor on none but the authors of these violences. Mr. —— ——, whether guilty or not, was a citizen; the example which his case has set is dangerous to all.*

---

* To this paragraph the following reasons of dissent and assent were inserted upon the minutes of the council.

REASONS OF DISSENT.

We dissent, 1. Because the opinion of the committee, stated in the report, is contrary to the spirit and to the letter of the constitution. The 7th section directs, that "The house of representatives of this commonwealth shall consist of persons most noted for wisdom and virtue, to be chosen by the freemen of every city and county respectively." And the 9th section declares, that " the general assembly of the freemen of Pennsylvania, shall judge of the election and qualification of their own members; and " may expel" (that is, shall have power to expel) " a member, but not a second time for the same cause." To give meaning and effect to these clauses, we must suppose the first contains a general direction to the people, in the choice of their representatives, and that the second delegates a general power to the representative body, of judging in cases of election. But the power of judging, necessarily involves the power of enquiring into the facts; and for the assembly to remit that power to any inferior or other body, would be to betray the trust reposed in them by the people.

The tenth section requires an oath or affirmation of fidelity and allegiance to be taken, and a declaration of a certain religious belief to be made and subscribed by each member, before the general assembly proceed to business. The eighth section limits the time any member shall be capable of filling, successively, the office of a representative. These four sections, taken together, form the general system of election and representation. A restriction upon the power of expulsion is provided in the very act of creating that power; they may expel a member, but not a second time for the same cause. This is giving an appeal to the people, from the sentence of the assembly. If the expelled member is re-elected, it is a reversal of the sentence, and the power as to him ceases.

The only qualifications then for a seat in the general assembly, that are required by the constitution, are a general good reputation (for that is what must be understood by persons most noted for wisdom and virtue) the taking an oath or affirmation of allegiance, and a declaration of a religious nature. To judge of these is expressly referred to the general assembly for once and for once only, nor can they be enquired of elsewhere; neither, if they could be enquired of elsewhere, could that conviction, that is supposed necessary to direct the judgment of the assembly, be

Section 9. "The house of representatives may redress grievances."

It is the opinion of this committee that the general assembly, under reports of the committees of grievances, in some instances, has exercised powers inconsistent with the constitution.

---

had in some of the cases, in any of the courts of law, which are by the report supposed to be the proper judges.

2. Because, if it be allowed that the general assembly cannot expel a member, until he has been convicted in a court of law, of want of any of the qualifications required, the appeal to the people is defeated: For, from the regular and slow proceedings in these courts, and the delays that can be created, the term must necessarily be elapsed for which a person was elected, before it can be determined whether he was entitled to a seat in that body or not; yet all the time it is depending he retains his place, and exercises the greatest power that can be exercised, the power of making laws to bind the community. This would really be to render both the general assembly and the courts of justice, ridiculous. The sentence of the court is obtained, on which expulsion is to take place, but the year is out, and it can have no effect. The person may be returned again the succeeding year, and the same process is to be gone through, with the same ridiculous success. An explanation that would thus destroy the purposes of the constitution, we say, ought not to be admitted.

3. Because the proceedings of the general assembly, in the case of Mr. ———, which is an instance adduced to prove the impropriety of such a power being exercised by the general assembly, are not truly stated.

It is said in the report, " He was first declared guilty of notorious frauds and other enormous crimes. 2. He is expelled from his seat. 3. The attorney general is directed to prosecute him for fraud and perjury." A recurrence to the journals of the house, will shew that information had been given, that Mr. ——— ———, one of their members, and a public officer, had been guilty of forgery. On the 12th of February 1783, a letter from the comptroller general, enclosing divers depositions respecting the accounts and vouchers of Mr. ——— ———, was read, together with the said depositions. On the 18th they were read a second time, and referred to a committee. On the 20th the committee reported. The 21st the report was read a second time, and adopted in the following words; " The committee to whom was referred the report of the comptroller general, together with the depositions of John Cannon and others, relative to the conduct of Mr. ——— ———, late purchasing commissioner of ——— county, beg leave to report : That the charges set forth in the above mentioned depositions, and the report of the comptroller general, against the said Mr. ——— ———, respecting his passing forged receipts in settling his accounts, knowing them to be forged, are founded, in part, on the above depositions and his own confession." Whereupon, commissioners were appointed to make true enquiry into the matter, at the place where it happened, and to hear and examine such witnesses, on oath or affirmation, as ——— should produce in his defence, and to report to the comptroller general, on or before the first day of the ensuing session. It was further resolved, that ——— should be furnished with a copy of the above appointment, and the speaker was directed to command him to appear on the first day of the next session.

The 9th of September the business was again taken up, and the house expelled Mr.——— ——— by an unanimous vote, he having been guilty of frauds and other enormous crimes in the execution of his duty as commissioner, and the attorney general was directed to institute actions against him for fraud and perjury. Thus there was a regular chain of examination and enquiry, before the house proceeded to expulsion. Having confessed the facts, and being in contempt of the house, as the representatives of the people, it was their right and their duty to expel him. As guardians of the people, it was their duty to order the state officer to prosecute him.

As an unqualified and contemptuous member, Mr. ——— ———, was expelled; as an offender he was delivered over to the laws. It was the proper business of the judges of the courts to try the merits of the complaint, and to inflict the punishment.

The trial by jury was preserved in ———'s case, where it ought to be preserved; that is, in cases where the municipal laws were transgressed; and the right of the assembly was exerted, agreeably to the constitution: And it is with satisfaction we see the principles of the bill of rights and the frame of government are consistent.

April 7, 1781. The house took up the case of a militia fine, which, as it appears, the president and council had refused to remit. See the petition of Jane Smith.

---

but we cannot consider either, as paramount to the other They are parts of one whole viz. the constitution. The example which his case has set, is not dangerous to all, that if it be followed, as we hope it will be, it will effectually prevent persons of vile and profligate characters from imposing themselves upon the people, and secure to them at all times, a proper and virtuous representation.

Frederick A. Muhlenberg,	*John Arndt,*
Anthony Wayne,	*Richard M'Allister,*
James Moore,	*Arthur St. Clair,*
Thomas Fitzsimons,	*David Espy.*

REASONS OF ASSENT.

Lest there should be any misapprehension concerning the principles upon which we have proceeded, we give the reasons following, for our vote, in addition to those suggested in the report.

Because we hold that every citizen of this state, upon resigning his natural liberty to the community, and becoming subject to its laws, has, by the ninth section of the bill of rights, expressly stipulated for and reserved to himself, in case he be charged with crime, the inestimable privilege of trial by jury; or if he have taken an office under the state, the same privilege, or at least a fair and solemn trial before the president and council, upon specified and clear articles of impeachment; that he be confronted with the witnesses produced against him, be allowed to call for witnesses in his favor, and that he have the aid of council, if he think them necessary for his defence.

Because if we would admit of authority, in the general assembly, under pretence of purging the house of scandalous characters, to enquire of and determine upon such personal charges as those made against Mr. ———, previously to trial and conviction before the proper tribunal, such procedure would not only militate against the aforesaid indefeasible right of the citizen, but would also undermine the freedom of speech and independency of conduct of the members of the house, so essential to the representatives of a free people.

Because it will amply suffice to preserve the honor of the general assembly, if in these cases, the house adopt the wise and humane idea of the common law, that every man is to be treated as innocent, till he be pronounced guilty by his proper judges.

Because the house of assembly, alone possessing the legislative power, and feeling itself unconfined, is not only incompetent to such personal discussions, but would soon dishonor itself by prejudiced, partial and mistaken judgments; an evil to which large bodies of men are very liable: For the leaders of popular assemblies, less restrained than the members of standing tribunals, who are few, by the infamy which often attends upon wrong decisions, are sometimes tempted to give a loose to their passions, and even to their private resentments, whilst employed in the public business.

It is indeed with an heart felt satisfaction, that we embrace this opportunity of thus asserting and vindicating the principles of the bill of rights; that precious repository of the personal privileges of the freemen of the commonwealth, which we consider as paramount to the frame of government. If the people of England have suffered their *magna charta*, which was equally explicit and declaratory of the personal security of the people, to be undermined and defeated, by the assumed power of the house of commons to judge and punish arbitrarily, under pretence of undefined privilege; yet the good people of Pennsylvania, we trust, will never submit, that their representatives in general assembly, shall by a similar usurpation, so far pervert the constitution of this commonwealth.

George Bryan,	*James Edgar,*
John Smiley,	*John M'Dowell,*
Simon Dreisbach,	*John Whitehill,*
William Montgomery,	*Joseph Hart,*
James M'Lene,	*James Read,*
William Finley,	*Samuel Smith,*
Baltzer Gehr,	*James Potter.*

The assembly determine also that goods belonging to another, had in this case, been wrongfully distrained, and it is directed that they be returned.

April. 10, 1781. Upon the complaint of of Charles Wilpert, that he had been illegally condemned to pay a militia fine, the House remit the same. Here the legislature have assumed the business of the council, and of the courts of justice.

April 10, 1781. Isaac Austin sets up a claim to a forfeited estate, late his brother's, alleges that he tendered payment, by offering the president and council, a release of the demand of the administrators of his mother upon this estate, and the House declare that his claim ought to be allowed. It is plain, that if Isaac Austin had purchased, and tendered the price, he might have brought his ejectment; and upon equitable principles, which are admitted in our courts, he must have recovered the house and lot. The legislature ought not to have interposed.

Nov. 20, 1783. William Pollard complains of the verdict of a jury in the supreme court; the house refer his case to the commitee of grievances, who report "that he is aggrieved".

Whereupon the same being instantly read again, the house resolves "that the attorney general be desired to stop all law proceedings until the next sitting of the general assembly."

If complaints like these can be thus listened to, the laws of the land will be corrupted, and the house must sit every day in the year. And yet this summary relief would be in a great measure limited to such of the citizens of the state, as reside in the vicinity of the seat of government.

REMARK.

The word grievances seems to have changed its import. Fomerly the excesses and oppressive proceedings of the executive power, and of the courts of justice, were the grievances of England. Such as purveyance, or seizing in an arbitrary manner, provisions and other supplies for the use of the kings household; extorted benevolences to the crown; compositions of knighthood; ship money; levying taxes, after the laws which granted them were expired; monopolies; extrajudicial opinions of judges; denial of bail, where bail was of right; billeting of soldiers; suspending of law by prerogative; proclamations to alter the law; and such matters as, arising from the undue influence of the crown, could not be remedied without the interposition of parliament—not hardships which will always arise from the operation of general laws, nor even the misdeeds of particular officers, or private men, for which there is an easy and legal remedy; much less inconveniences, to which the negligence of the sufferer himself has subjected him.*

---

* To this paragraph the following reasons of dissent were entered upon the minutes of the council.

Although we agree with the report, that the general assembly, under reports of the committees of grievances, have in some instances exercised powers inconsistent with the constitution, yet we dissent from the report in some of the instances brought forward, and from the reasoning upon them. Because some of them were very proper objects for the interference of the legislature, no adequate remedy being to be had in any other way; and because it seems absurd to

Section 9th. "The general assembly may impeach state criminals."

It is the opinion of this committee, that the proceedings and sentence of the general assembly (5th March, 1783,) by which ⸺ the ⸺, late secretary of the supreme executive council, was declared "unworthy of public trust and confidence," were unconstitutional.

⸺ ⸺ was a public officer, holding at the pleasure of the president and council. He was liable, as other civil officers to an impeachment, and to trial (as an officer) for his misconduct, before the supreme executive council; he was also amenable in the ordinary course of justice. But the constitution of Pennsylvania countenances no undefined and arbitrary powers; such as the house assumed in his case; powers, that may be equally exerted to shelter a set of defaulters and peculators, and to destroy persons obnoxious to the predominant party. In Mr. ⸺ ⸺'s case there was neither summons, hearing, charge or trial. In short he was condemned unheard.

Section 9. "The house of representatives, shall have all other powers necessary for the legislature of a free commonwealth."

It appears to your committee that the act passed on the 21, January 1777, entitled "An act to enable a smaller number of the members of assembly, than a quorum to collect the absent members, and issue writs for filling vacancies occasiond by neglect or refusal" and the supplement thereto passed the 11 October, 1777, And the act "to amend the several acts of this commonwealth, directing the mode of electing members of the general assembly thereof," passed the 12th September 1782, are deviations from the 9th and 12th sections of the constitution, so far as respects the issuing writs for new elections, and subjecting the members to the payment of charges incurred by sending for absentees.

Section 10. "The members of the house of representatives shall, each of them, before they proceed to business, take and subscribe, as well the oath or affirmation of fidelity and allegiance hereinafter directed, as the following oath or affirmation." Then follows the oath of office.

---

say, that "If the complaints of the people are listened to by the legislature, the laws of the land will be corrupted; and that the relief would be limited, in any degree, to such of the citizens as reside in the vicinity of the seat of government, and the sessions of the assembly be lengthened to an immoderate degree." The assembly are chosen by the people to do their business, and they ought to sit as long as that business requires. But the inconveniences that arise to the individuals, from a long absence from their respective houses, will always induce them to shorten their sessions as much as possible, and, from the pressure of that inconveniency there is more danger of their being shortened too much; than of their being drawn out to an unnecessary length. It is of no importance what the word grievance meant, or means, in England or elsewhere, it is very well understood here; and here as well as in other countries, there may happen excesses, and oppressive proceedings of the executive power, and of the courts of justice. When they do happen, we trust the legislature will interfere and afford redress. But as it seems to be intended that all powers should be lodged in the hands of the executive, and, what the committee call, the judicial branch, it is a proper step to remove every thing that lies in the way of its being accomplished, and the interference of the legislature might be a troublesome restraint upon it. It is however the right of the people to be redressed in this way, and it is a security to them, we hope, they will not part with, nor suffer to be explained away.

Arthur St. Clair,	*David Espy,*
Fred. A. Muhlenberg,	*Thomas Hartly,*
John Arndt,	*Richard M'Allister,*
James Moore,	*Anthony Wayne.*

The oath or affirmation of allegiance is,

" I, A. B. do swear or affirm, that I will be true and faithful "to the commonwealth of Pennsylvania; and that I will not directly "or indirectly do any act or thing prejudicial or injurious to the com- "monwealth, or government thereof, as established by the convention." See section 40.

It appears by the journals of the general assembly that on the 5th day of November 1778, and on occasion of the first meeting of a new house, divers members "expressed some scruples with respect to taking the oath or affirmation of allegiance prescribed by the constitution, apprehending they would be thereby precluded from taking measures to obtain the sense of the people with respect to calling a convention &c."

Wherefore the next day, (November 6th,) it was "unanimously agreed that every member might take said oath, with a reservation of full liberty to himself to pursue such measures as he might judge necessary for collecting the sentiments of the people, on the subject of calling a new convention to revise, amend and confirm the constitution; and reserving also full liberty of co-operating, as well with his fellow citizens as with the said convention, if called."

It appears that twenty-five of the representatives in said assembly adopted the reservation above mentioned.

By information which your committee rely on, it appears that some of the members of the first assembly, after the revolution, were admitted to take the oath of allegiance (section 40,) without the words "as established by the constitution."

It is the opinion of this committee, that the admission of members of general assembly in the above instances, upon taking the oaths and affirmations required, with a reservation, were deviations from the constitution of this state.

Section. 11 "No person who holds any office in the gift of congress, shall hereafter be elected to represent this commonwealth in congress."

Benjamin Franklin Esq. one of the commissioners of congress, to the court of France, being on the 10th of December 1777, elected to represent Pennsylvania in congress, was a deviation from the above clause.

Section 15th. "To the end that laws, before they are enacted, may be more maturely considered, and the inconvenience of hasty determinations, as much as possible prevented, all bills of a public nature shall be published, and, except on occasions of sudden necessity, shall not be passed into laws until the next session of the general assembly."

Very many bills have been passed hastily, in the same session, in violation of this section.

Examples from a multitude.

Vol. 1. chap. 68, read the 1st time. 19 Aug. 1778, enacted the 31, of same month.

chap. 70, read.	19 Aug. 1778,	do.	31st.
chap. 184, read.	16 Sep. 1780,	do.	23.
chap 185, read.	22 May, 1780,	do.	30.
chap. 136, read,	3 Nov. 1772,	do	25.
chap. 207, read.	7 April. 1781,	do.	10.

chap. 130, rel. to apprehending suspected persons and increasing certain fines.

An act relative to navigation and trade passed, 10th of September, 1778.

Vol. 2. chap. 43, read.	6 Nov. 1782,	do.	22. same month.
chap. 84, read.	15 Sep. 1783,	do.	23.
chap. 74, read.	2 Sep. 1783,	do.	9.
chap. 77, resolved.	11 Sep. 1783,	do.	17.
chap. 96, resolved.	18 Sep. 1783,	do.	25.

Thus this important and essential restraint upon the proceedings of the legislature hath been laid aside in many instances, without any apparent necessity.

The postponing of bills to another sitting, is at length so much disregarded that of thirty nine acts of assembly, which were passed during the last session of the present house thirty one of them originated within the same sitting: and with respect to almost all these, so far from any sudden necessity existing for thus hastily passing them, there does not seem to be any considerable motives for thus precipitating more than two or three of them. If the act for regulating the choice of justices of the peace, had become immediately necessary, it was from the neglect of the house, to take up the business earlier.

It is the opinon of this committee, that the 15th section of the constitution, whereby the authority to legislate is laid under peculiar restraints, has been evaded, and in a great measure defeated, by the exercise of a power assumed by the general assembly to make laws, and to alter laws, and to appropriate the lands, goods and money, of the commonwealth, by resolve only; which, so far from being published for consideration, and deferred to the next session, is passed secretly, immediately.

Examples from a multitude.

Journals of general assembly, 12th October, 1777.— On motion resolved, that the salary of the vice president, instead of the sum of five hundred pounds, shall be at the rate of one thousand pounds per annum, to be computed from the time of his entering upon the business of his said office.

December 5th, 1778. It being represented to the house by sundry members that their necessary and unavoidable expenses greatly exceed their allowance, during their attendance on the business of the house.— Resolved, that each member of this house be allowed for his attendance during the session, forty five shillings per diem, and six pence per mile ; and that this house will, at their next sitting, make a law to provide for the same, and for the future wages of members of assembly.—By act of assembly passed, December 27th, 1777, Vol. 1 chapter 39th, the wages of the representatives in assembly, were fixed at twenty-five shillings per diem.

Journals general assembly, vol. 1 page 454, March 25th, 1778. The house resolve, that Mr. Bryan be allowed five hundred pounds for extra services rendered by him, during the recess, and present sitting of the house.

June 1st, 1780, page 502 resolved, that as this house have not time, at this sitting, to complete and enact the bill for the support of certain civil officers, the salaries and daily pay fixed by the resolve of February 28th, to the civil officers therein mentioned, be continued from the 9th of April last, to the end of the next sitting of assembly : and whereas the supreme executive council have appointed, and commissioned the honorable George Bryan, Esquire, as a third assistant judge, resolved that he be entitled to, and receive the same pay, as

the other assistant judges, to commence from the time of his appointment.

February 12, 1779, page 310. A letter from the president to the
speaker, setting forth, that in pursuance of a resolve of a former assembly, he had been applied to by council, to assist the attorney general in the prosecution of the state criminals, which services he had
faithfully performed, and assuring the house, that whatsoever sum they
should order him for his services, would be received by him with all
due respect, was read; and the house taking his important services into consideration, it was thereupon,

Ordered, That the speaker draw an order on the state treasurer, for
the sum of two thousand pounds, in consideration of the said services,
in favor of the president, which order was accordingly drawn and
signed at the table.

Note.—These services were performed previously to his being a
member of the supreme executive council.

Page 517, September 22, 1780. The committee appointed this morning, to consider the salaries of certain civil officers, and the wages of
the members of assembly. &c. made a report, which was read, and on
consideration, the following part thereof was adopted, viz.

Your committee, taking into consideration the great attention of his
excellency the president, to the affairs of this commonwealth, the small
allowance granted for his services, the variety of expenses he is necessarily exposed to, and the propriety of allowing him a compensation in some measure proportioned to his services, are of opinion, that
the sum of one thousand pounds, state money, or the exchange at sixty for one, be granted him as a gratuity, over and above the salary allowed him for the present year.

April 1, 1778. The general assembly resolve, that the president
and council draft the militia to fill up the Pennsylvania line, in the
army of the United States, and that the persons so drafted serve nine
months.

September 9, 1778. The general assembly resolve, that council place
chains across Chesnut street, (a public highway) in Philadelphia city,
whilst congress, &c. be sitting, to prevent the passing of carriages.

December 6, 1777. The general assembly, by resolve, set aside all
civil authority, and invest general Washington and the president and
council, with extraordinary and unconstitutional powers.

February 25, 1779. The fees of grand jurors are increased by vote.

April 5th, the rates of the city ferry over the Schuylkill, established
by act of assembly of the 30th March 1723, are increased by vote.

March 19, 1779. The wages of county commissioners, increased by
vote.

November 20, 1779. The house recommend to council to defer the
sale of a forfeited estate (late of the rev. Jacob Duche) and permit the
chief justice to reside therein.

December 20, 1780. Another resolution of the same import.

March 13, 1782. A salary of five hundred pounds per annum, is voted to the judge of the admiralty, inclusive of his fees as judge, to be
paid quarterly out of the treasury of the state.

May 26, 1780. Resolved, That Mrs. Ferguson hold Græme Park,
a forfeited estate, under the indulgence of the commonwealth, and free
of rent.

N. B. These forfeited estates, were by law, put under the direction of the president and council, and were to be let for any term not exceeding two years, for the highest rent.

October 9, 1779. Resolved, That one hundred barrels of flour, belonging to the state, be distributed among the distressed housekeepers, of the city of Philadelphia, giving preference to such as shall serve on the present expedition.

March 1, 1781. The house, by resolve, enable council to appoint additional auditors, to those who had been named in act of assembly, Vol. 1. Chap 183, for adjusting the depreciation of the military.

April 9, 1781. Resolved, That the property of a floating bridge, now lying in the Schuylkill, near George Gray's, be invested in the said Gray, upon his paying one hundred and fifty pounds (state money) into the treasury of the state.

September 18, 1783. Major Kennedy, late of the militia of Bucks county, being slain in taking burglers and robbers, and an act having passed soon after his death, to reward those who should apprehend these felons, and to recompense the families of such as mightbe killed in these exertions; the house, by vote resolve, that the widow and children of major Kennedy, receive three hundred pounds out of the public treasury.

September 1, 1783. The salary of the comptroller general, is by resolve, increased three hundred pounds per annum. By chap. 15. vol. 2. sect. 13, this officer's salary is fixed at five hundred pounds per annum.

Captain Ore, of the ship Grand D'Estaing, had complained to the house, that he was denied a drawback of the impost duty that he had paid on his goods, which he designs to export again.

September 11, 1783. The committee on the case of captain Ore, report, that the relief desired, cannot be given, unless by a new law; that to pass such a retrospective act would contradict the legislative principle; that his case is not singular, and that it would be unjust to relieve him only. Yet September 22, the house upon motion, resolve, that the naval officer refund the duties of such goods (being part of the original cargo of the ship Grand D'Estaing) which captain Ore shall export.

Sept. 24, 1783. Resolved, That the sum of fifteen hundred pounds be granted to the executors of the late president Thomas Wharton (including what is now due to them) for the use of his widow and children, to be divided equally among them. Same day, Resolved, That major general St. Clair, have a preference of right to about 5000 acres of land on the Chesnut Ridge, in Westmoreland county, (described in the journals) in consideration of his merits; subject to all prior claims, and to the purchase money to which the same may be liable.

December 2, 1783 The house appropriate by resolve, six hundred pounds of the public money, to defray the charge of a triumphal arch, and for providing illuminated paintings, to be exhibited in Market street, Philadelphia, on occasion of the definitive treaty of peace, between the United States of America and Great Britain.

November 21, 1783. Resolved, That the treasurer of this state, return to captain Walter Finney, the depreciation certificates, by him paid for land purchased; and that the comptroller general settle the interest due on such certificates, as though the said certificates had never been paid on account of the said purchase. Captain Finney purchased a forfeited real estate of the agents of council, and was allowed to return the same to the commonwealth.

April 1, 1784. The house by resolve, enable the supreme executive council to let out the barracks, &c. at Lancaster, and to appoint a superintendant of the same.

The house determine and declare, by resolve, which county collectors of taxes, &c. have been robbed of public money; and in like manner exonerate sundry of them of various sums, for which they were by law accountable.

Levi Doan, accused of burglary, is taken by John Shaw, and others; he breaks jail before trial. The house upon hearing adjudged to these men the reward of fifty pounds, which had been offered by proclamation in case of conviction. Journals 17th March 17:3.

March 13, 1781. The report of the committee appointed to confer with a committee of council, respecting Hog island, in the river Delaware, being again read, Resolved, that the supreme executive council be directed to prosecute the claims of this state to the said island, as part of the estate of Joseph Galloway, an attainted traitor. How unjustifiable was this interference of the legislative body! Must not such an enquiry and declaration of the house, against the pretensions of the possessors of this island, prejudice their cause with the court and jury.

August 25, 1783. The general assembly, by resolve, authorise the delegates in congress of Pennsylvania, to consent to an alteration of the great bond of union between the states of America.

The plan had been digested and proposed by congress. It purported an alteration in the mode of calculating the quotas of supplies of the states respectively, to the common treasury, by substituting estimates, derived from the number of inhabitants within each state, to valuations of improved lands and buildings. The change may perhaps be advantageous for Pennsylvania. But, to precipitate such business, and especially on a single resolve, to vest so important an authority in our delegates in congress, must alarm and astonish every citizen.

The president and council had transmitted this plan to the general assembly on the 18th of the same month, recommending it strongly. The house took it up on the 19th—On the 25th, the committee to whom it had been referred reported This report was read the second time immediately, and the general assembly, on the same day, unanimously adopted the proposition, and authorised their delegates in congress to establish it. Thus this great transaction was taken up and finished in the course of seven days, which could scarcely have happened, had the alteration received, as it ought, the sanction and ratification of an act of assembly.

September 25, 1783. The committee to whom the letter from the comptroller general, respecting the debt due to this state by Baynton, Wharton and Morgan, was referred, report: That after a due investigation of the matter, they find as follows:

First, That the sum mentioned by the comptroller general, £1407 4s. 7d. principal money, (besides interest,) is yet due to the state.

Second, That the commissioners of the late province of Pennsylvania, (appointed by act of assembly of the 8th of April, 1758, for preventing abuses in the Indian trade,) by an indenture under their hands, agreed to accept of the trust conveyed by Baynton, Wharton and Morgan; and three of the said commissioners, with Robert Morris. Esq. and others, are trustees in the deed of conveyance, made and duly executed by Baynton, Wharton and Morgan, for the sale af all the estates, and payment of all their debts, public and private. The commission- ers, therefore, acting in a public capacity, undoubtedly must be allow- ed to have knowledge that the estate was sufficient; otherwise they would not have accepted it, but have applied to the sureties, who were of acknowledged ability These considerations, therefore, induce the committee to offer the following resolution to the house:

Resolved, That the comptroller general be directed to proceed no further in the case of Baynton, Wharton and Morgan, the same being already under the care of trustees, in that case specially appointed.

The report was accordingly adopted by the assembly, on the second reading of it. The obligation by which the sureties of Baynton, Whar- ton and Morgan are bound, as above mentioned, is dated Aug. 2, 1765.

Many of these cases are of the most deserving nature; others of them applied strongly to the feelings and compassion of the house; but some of them would hardly have passed, in the usual course of publica- tion, to the third reading. This loose and summary manner, however, of appropriating the public estate by the legislative body, is very in- consistent with economy and safety. All these resolves were passed, if not in the face of law, yet *without* law. Every one of them is an in- fringement of the constitution, from the mode in which they have been adopted:*

* To this paragraph the following reasons of dissent were inserted upon the min- utes of the council.

Though we agree, that many laws have been brought in and passed in the same session, for which there may not now appear any necessity, yet we dissent from the opinion in the report upon this section. "That an important and essential re- straint upon the proceedings of the assembly, has been laid aside." For the section cited, does expressly give a power to the assembly to pass laws, in the same ses- sion in which they shall be first considered in the form of bills, on occasions of sud- den necessity. Of that necessity the assembly are, and from the nature of the case; must be the only judges; and for us to pretend to determine upon it, is arrogating a power we are incompetent to, and if we were competent, that is not vested in us by the constitution. But when we consider, of what very little use the publication of bills is; how very few of the people comparatively, ever see them, that it operates rather to deceive than inform them, and the heavy expense that attends it, we can- not help wishing this article was very materially altered But, alterations, neces- sary additions or explanations, can be made by a convention only.

We dissent from the second opinion upon this section of the constitution like- wise, because we think it goes to restraining the assembly from proceeding by re- solve in all cases. The power, however, to proceed in that manner, seems to have been clearly, in the view of the convention. as it is by the 20th section of the con- stitution, made the express duty of the executive council to forward the execution of their resolves. The words are, and they are remarkable, "They are to take care that the laws be duly executed, they are to expedite the execution of such meas- ures as may be resolved upon by the general assembly" There is in the same sen- tence a plain distinction taken betwixt laws and resolves; indeed, they are con- tra distinguished. The executive council are to execute the laws, they are to expedite the execution of measures resolved upon by the general assembly. The power of proceeding by resolve is then clearly acknowledged, and the council have a kind of concurrent power in the execution; or rather, they are to remove any difficulties that may lie in the way of their execution. But if no directions had been given to the executive council, the power of the assembly to proceed in that way might have, well enough, been inferred from the general words of the 9th sec- tion:—"They shall have all other powers necessary for the legislature of a free state or commonwealth." From the two together there remains not the shadow of a doubt. Had this committee been appointed to alter and amend the constitu- tion, which they seem all along to have thought their duty, we should have readily

Section 17, last clause. "The wages of the representatives in the general assembly, and all other state charges, shall be paid out of the state treasury."

As to the first part; the vote of Nov. 27th, 1779, whereby an estate, seized as forfeited, called Hale's stables, in Philadelphia, was appropriated and repaired for the reception of the horses of the members of assembly, and hay and oats provided, was a violation of this section, which directs that the representatives receive wages in money. See journals of the house, March 24, 1780; and the public accounts, particularly the drafts of the speaker of the house on the treasurer of the state, for these expenditures, in January, 1780.

Secondly, The act appointing commissioners to provide for the defence of the bay and river Delaware, (vol. 2, chap. 7, sect. 10,) enabled these commissioners to draw the monies appropriated to this service, from the naval officer who collected the same, without passing into the treasury of the state. This was a direct infringement of this 17th section of the constitution. And by vote of general assembly of September 22, 1783, the naval officer was constituted a sort of treasurer of the state extraordinary, for certain monies then in his hands, or to come to his hands. And the naval officer was subjected to drafts upon him, to be made by the president and council, partly for specified purposes, partly for general use.

Sections 17 and 18. By these it is provided that each county shall have representatives in the general assembly; and by the 19th section, clause 3, a councillor.

It is the opinion of this committee, that the setting off a new county, and restraining the same from electing representatives in assembly, a councillor and censors, at the then next ensuing election, was a breach of the constitution. See vol. II, chap. 101, passed 26th Sept. 1785, for erecting the county of Fayette.

Section 20. "The president, and in his absence the vice-president, with the council, five of whom shall be a quorum, shall have power to appoint and commissionate judges, naval officers, judge of the admiralty, attorney general, and all other officers civil and military (except such as are chosen by the general assembly or by the people,) agreeably to this frame of government, and the laws that may be made hereafter."

The constitution (sections 2 and 3) states two great depositories of the authority devolved by the people, through the medium of the convention. First, a supreme legislative, lodged with the general assembly;—a supreme executive, in the hands of a president and council.

---

agreed with them that this loose and summary method of legislating is very inconsistent with economy and safety, and that it ought in most cases to be abolished It is, however, a part of the constitution, and as such, it is no assumed power in the general assembly; neither were the resolves that have been detailed by the committee, passed, as it is said in the report, "if not in the face of the law, yet *without* law." The constitution is the law to govern the assembly, and they are consistent with the constitution. But this power likewise stands in the way of the exorbitant and unconstitutional powers intended for the executive council, and in that view it is a security for the people. It therefore became necessary to get rid of it one way or other.

Arthur St. Clair,   James Moore,
Fred A Muhlenberg,   David Espy,
Anthony Wayne,   Thomas It. Hey,
John Arndt,   Richard M'Allister.

All power, therefore, not placed out of its proper hands belongs to the legislative or the executive, according to its nature, but the appointment of officers is an executive prerogative, and belongs to the council in all cases, if it be not in express terms vested in the assembly or in the people: and all construction and interpretation of passages which may seem dubious, shall be favorable to the proper branch, and nothing beyond satisfying the words shall be intended, in case any authority be misplaced or put out of its natural hands.

We further say, that the words above recited give the nomination of all officers, civil and military, to council, unless in the reserved cases. That the expression, "except such as are chosen by the general assembly or by the people," ought to be considered as introduced by way of parenthesis, and that it refers to the officers assigned to the assembly or the people, in other sections of the constitution, of whom there are several; and that the following words, "agreeably to this frame of government and the laws that may be made hereafter," define the manner in which the appointments of council shall be made. Thus, for example, the judge of admiralty is by the constitution to be named by the president and council; but an act of assembly passed on the 8th of March, 1780, requires that his commission be "for seven years, in case he so long behave well." Council, therefore, must commissionate for seven years, agreeably to this law.

It is therefore the opinion of this committee, that the power of appointing revenue and other officers, not expressly assigned to the house of assembly or to the people, by the constitution, which has been exercised by the general assembly, is a deviation from the constitution.

The notoriety of appointments to offices by the house, in cases not expressly assigned to that body by the constitution, is too great to need instances thereof to be given. We offer, however, one or two, for example.

The first militia law, chap. 15, passed 17th March, 1777, assigned to the legislature the choice of county lieutenants and sub-lieutenants.

The act to revive and continue the laws for regulating sales by auction, in the city of Philadelphia and its vicinity, vol. 2, chap. 109, is remarkable for taking to the house the appointment of the vendue masters for once only. Future nominations remain with the president and council as before. And the nomination by act of assembly, of a collector of the port of Philadelphia. See acts of assembly, vol. II, chap. 122, sect. 8.°

---

* An act of assembly was passed on the 4th day of April, 1785, entitled "An act to declare and establish the right of the executive council of this commonwealth, to appoint all officers, civil and military, except in the cases reserved by the constitution to the general assembly, and to the people; and to repeal the laws whereby certain officers have been appointed contrary thereunto, &c."

The preamble of this law recites that part of the constitution, which delegates the appointing power to the supreme executive council; it also recites the opinion of the council of censors, that the appointment of revenue and all other officers, not expressly assigned to the house of assembly or to the people, by the constitution, which has been exercised by the general assembly, is a deviation from the constitution.

The act provides that the election of the speaker and of the clerks of the general assembly, the delegates to represent this state in Congress, the treasurer of the state, register of wills, recorders and trustees of the loan office, shall be reserv-

There was an act of assembly, vol. 1, chap. 35, by which divers extraordinary powers were vested in commissioners sent by congress into the western country. This was derogatory from the rights of the president and council, and of the commonwealth."*

---

ed to the general assembly; and that all other officers necessary for the execution of the laws, (except those that are directed by the constitution to be otherwise appointed,) are declared to lie in the nomination and appointment of the executive council.

The act also states that divers officers hold their offices by having their names inserted in the body of the acts of assembly, whereby the same offices have been constituted; that the said acts have been enacted in derogation of the rights of the executive council, and that the manner in which such officers hold their offices is deemed improper. The act repeals so much of the act of 13th April, 1782, as appoints John Nicholson to the office of comptroller general, and so much of the act of the 9th December, 1783, as authorises the house of assembly to appoint the auctioneers of the city of Philadelphia; and so much of the act for regulating the port of Philadelphia, as provides for the appointment of the wardens and collector; and so much of the act of the 15th March, 1784, as appoints Sharp Delany collector; and generally all other acts of assembly which derogate from the rights and privileges of the supreme executive council. The act also provides that the executive council shall make the appointments repealed within two months after the passage of the act, and that the officers appointed by the assembly shall hold their offices until others are appointed.

* To this paragraph of the report, touching the appointing power, the following reasons of dissent were inserted upon the minutes of the council:

We dissent also from the opinion and reasoning of the committee, as adopted by the council, upon this section of the constitution.

First—Because it seems to us to be more necessary that the executive branch should, in the appointment of officers, be strictly confined to those expressly assigned to them, than the legislature. The legislative body is the proper depository of all power not expressly placed elsewhere; for there, every man in the community is equally represented. In the executive council that is not the case; neither have the people the same control over them. They are permanent, and, notwithstanding the rotation established, encroachments can be easily reduced to system, and a majority to favor them, be ever found to exist. To the council is given the appointment of judges, naval officers, judge of the admiralty, attorney general, and all other officers, civil and military, except such as are chosen by the people, agreeably to the frame of government and the laws hereafter to be made. The appointment to certain offices is also given to the assembly. If this passage in the constitution appeared dark or doubtful, the committee ought to have so reported it, and left the explanation to a convention, who alone have that power. But it was going very much beside their duty to obtrude a construction that has the most dangerous tendency, and to introduce the parenthesis, which is not to be found in the original, to favor that construction. The clause stands fairly and intelligibly in the constitution. They are to appoint judges, naval officers, &c. and all other officers, civil and military. This is their general power, and a very extensive one it is. What follows is a limitation of that general power. "Except such as are chosen by the general assembly or the people, agreeably to the frame of government and the laws hereafter to be made." It requires indeed some ingenuity to mistake the sense and design of it, and they happily hit upon including a part of it in a parenthesis; but by altering and supplying in this manner, it is impossible that words can be so put together as that the plainest meaning may not be perverted.

The convention gave to the people, to the assembly and to the council, respectively, the appointment of certain officers. The creation of other offices that might be found necessary, and the appointment to those offices, when created, were left to the laws that were to be made. In the laws then creating them, it could be no infringement of the constitution to name the officers; because the power of appointing to them is, by the exception above mentioned, taken out of the general powers of the council, and placed no where else; and every power necessary for good government, not placed some where by the constitution, is vested in the as-

It is the opinion of this committee, that the act for erecting the county of Washington, as far as the same declares the justices of the peace of said county to be justices of the court of common pleas, is a deviation from the constitution.

Section 20. " The president and council shall supply every vacancy in any office, occasioned by death, removal or disqualification, until the office can be filled in the time and manner directed by law or this constitution."

It is the opinion of this committee, that chap. 24 of the 1st vol. of the state laws, No. 2, enabling the president alone to appoint the officers of the borough of Lancaster, in case the inhabitants neglect to elect them, is a deviation from the constitution.

Section 20. " The president and council are to prepare such business as shall appear to them necessary, to lay before the general assembly."

It is the opinion of this committee, that these words give a right to the president and council, and make it their duty, to lay forms of bills before the general assembly. Nevertheless, we do not suppose that the general assembly ought to admit of forms of money bills, prepared by the president and council.

The proper and peculiar business of the general assembly is to enact laws, therefore this clause of the 20th section, cannot otherwise have any meaning. " Business got ready before hand," as this passage imports, must be interpreted of sketches of bills; no less can be understood. To prepare business then for the general assembly is, we say, to frame drafts of bills. Not that the house is bound to adopt these drafts. No, they may commit, alter, amend or reject them on reading, at their pleasure.

Such a practice, if once established, would tend to despatch the legislative business, without lessening the right of the legislature to prepare bills, (section 9,) and very much shorten the sessions of the general assembly, the length of which is so justly complained of, for the great expense thereby incurred.

---

sembly, as the representatives of the people. It was the right of the assembly then, either by law to appoint those officers, or to empower the executive council to appoint them. In either way the constitution is satisfied, and there are many instances both ways. But we say, that as an increase of power in the hands of an executive council, permanent though rotatory, and so little responsible for the use of it as ours, is very dangerous to the community; and that those assemblies which reserved to themselves every appointment, where it was reconcilable to the constitution, have best adhered to its spirit, and shewed the greatest regard to the liberties and to the safety of the people.

Secondly—Because, as we think the executive council have no power to appoint to any offices besides those that are expressly named in the constitution, or given to them by law, if the meaning and construction pointed out by the committee should obtain, the executive would acquire a very undue influence upon the election of members of assembly; and we are the more alarmed at it from reflecting upon another part of the report of this committee, which would give them great influence on their deliberations. In short, it seems to be intended entirely to destroy the freedom of the assembly, and to throw into the hands of the executive branch the whole power of the state.

Thomas Hartley, *David Espy,*
Richard M'Allister, *Arthur St. Clair,*
Fred. A. Muhlenberg, *John Arndt.*
James Moore,

The president and council, on the 5th of February, 1779, and some days after, at a conference with the general assembly, proposed to furnish the form of a law, or heads of a bill, to the house, under the words of the 20th section, which authorises the board "to prepare such business as shall appear to them necessary to lay before the general assembly." These heads of a bill the assembly declined to receive.[*]

---

[*] To this paragraph of the report the following reasons of dissent were inserted upon the minutes of the council :

We dissent from the opinion upon this article, because it appears to us to be diametrically opposite to the 9th section of the constitution, whereby the power to prepare bills and enact them into laws, is expressly given to the assembly. In the report of the committee it is said that these words, "prepare business," give a right to the president and council, and make it their duty to lay forms of bills before the general assembly; nevertheless, say they, "we do not suppose that the general assembly ought to admit of forms of money bills, prepared by the president and council." If, under the words, "prepare business," the right and duty of the council to send bills to the general assembly can be supported, it is hard to account for the distinction taken betwixt money bills, and those of another nature. But when money bills are enacted, they must be attended with taxes; and these, however necessary they may be, are always odious. Let the representatives of the people become as odious as may be, no matter, but take care of the council; bye and bye it will not be so necessary. When once the people have submitted to the new system, the council can consider these as their right and duty, under the words, whenever they please. It would seem as if this had been the manner in which they reasoned, when they made up their opinion. The proper and peculiar business of the assembly is to enact laws; to prepare business is to frame drafts of bills, they say, "not that the assembly is bound to receive these drafts. No, they may commit, alter or amend them on the reading." Here then, the right and duty of the executive council to originate the laws of the state, is asserted unequivocally, and the duty of the legislature is pointed out, in a manner that cannot be mistaken. It is their proper and peculiar duty to enact laws. But if it be the right and duty of the executive council to prepare bills, which is, in other words, to originate laws, it must also be the duty of the assembly to receive them, and this they were perfectly sensible of, and have endeavoured to explain it away. But their "No, they may commit, alter or amend them," will impose upon nobody but those who are willing to be imposed upon. They cannot be cast aside, altered or amended on the reading, unless they have that reading. The assembly are therefore bound to receive them. Thus, by endeavouring to give a meaning to two words, which, from the revolution to the present time, (one instance alone excepted,) have been perfectly understood and acted under, the first formation of all laws, money bills excepted, is to be given to the executive council, and also a negative upon the laws before debate. For, this doctrine once established, it would soon be an open and avowed claim, that no law should pass that had not originated with the council; and if the assembly attempted it, they would not be executed; and they might be told, "Gentlemen, you have transgressed the bounds assigned you by the constitution,—you are to enact laws, but they must originate with us. This law, or these laws, we did not originate, it was business that was not prepared by us, and that you of yourselves could not take up. They want that essential quality; a prerequisite that cannot be dispensed with; they are not laws, and cannot be executed."

The power endeavoured to be given to the executive, to wit, the appointment to all offices; the originating all laws, and a negative before debate, by the strange explanation given to these two clauses of the 20th section of the constitution, we consider as of the most alarming and dangerous tendency, and, if acceded to, subversive of the liberties of the people; but we trust they are too much enlightened, and value them too much, to suffer themselves to be deprived of them by any arts, much less by a forced explanation of words and sentences. It is, however, a duty we owe to them, to warn them against the attempt, and to justify ourselves to the present generation and to posterity, to protest against it in the most solemn manner; and we have the greater reason to be alarmed, as we find an attempt of a simi-

Section 20. "The president and council shall have power to grant pardons and remit fines, in all cases whatsoever, except in cases of impeachment; and in case of treason and murder shall have power to grant reprieves, but not to pardon, till the end of the next session of assembly. But there shall be no remission or mitigation of punishments on impeachment, except by act of the legislature."

The very strong and extensive words by which this executive authority is secured to the council, exclude all interference therein, unless in the case excepted, viz. that of conviction on impeachment. The stay of pardon in treason and murder, might be intended to save the honor of the board from injury by hasty proceedings. The reference here made to the end of the next session of the assembly, rather than to a precise term, such as six months, might be with design that the representatives of the county, where the facts happened, coming to the seat of government, the council might have opportunity of information. But to suppose that the assembly have a right to intermeddle, would take away the responsibility of council with respect to pardons, (so very liable to abuse,) for the board would be apt to lean upon the legislative body, in odious and difficult instances of forgiveness.

It is indeed one of the great advantages of our frame of government, that there is in it a body so purely executive, that mercy can be extended in proper cases, without that solecism which must arise where those who make the laws, or those who judge, have the power of remission. Were the legislature to dispense remissions, it would tacitly condemn its own decrees. Were the persons who administer justice to undo their own sentences, such conduct would confound all right and wrong. The people would not be able to discover whether the prisoner was discharged for his innocence or through favor. Two powers, in the same state, granting pardons, would defeat the execution of the laws. The house of assembly, by vote, recommended the case of Mary Murray to the council. She had forfeited a hogshead of rum, under the excise laws. See journal 25th May, 1780.

It is the opinion of this committee, that the transmitting the petition of Matteo Bratelli, (who, with two other Italian seamen, had been convicted of murdering captain Pickles,) by the president and council to the assembly, on the 13th of November, 1783, in order that the house might allow of the immediate pardon of this murderer, and the consequent vote of the house, "that council do pardon Matteo Bratelli," were unauthorised proceedings, and infringements of the constitution. The pardon should have come from the council alone.

It appears by the journals of assembly of 22d March, 1783, that the house, by resolve, dismiss from imprisonment Thomas Hale, who was under execution by summary process, from the late auditors, for settling the public accounts.

---

lar nature was made by the executive council, at a time when the gentleman who drew up the report was vice-president, and warmly was contested with the assembly, doubtless for the purpose of establishing a precedent; but the assembly spurned at it with indignation, and asserted their rights, with which the happiness of the people was so intimately connected.

Arthur St. Clair,	*Thomas Hartly,*
John Arndt,	*Richard M'Allister,*
Fred. A. Muhlenberg,	*Anthony Wayne,*
David Espy,	*Thomas Fitzsimons.*
James Moore,	

The sheriff, by this proceeding of the general assembly, must have found himself in an irksome situation. On the one hand, should he disregard this irregular mandate of the legislature, he would probably have incurred the resentment of the members, who might perhaps, by another stretch of power, have made him fully sensible of their importance. On the other hand, in case he released Mr. Hale, he might, under the influence of another assembly of a different complexion, be considered as having acted without authority, and as liable for the demand of the state; for, though the release of the person of the creditor would operate as a full remission of the debt, yet the sheriff, in rigor might be made to answer for the money. Nothing less, we conceive, than a special act of insolvency was equal to this case. The prisoner might have been thereby released from confinement, and the demands of the commonwealth saved. That the house should, at the same time, they thus exonerate Thomas Hale, direct his accounts to be re-settled, is unintelligible.

Section 20. "The president and council are also to take care, that the laws be faithfully executed; they are to expedite the execution of such measures, as shall be resolved upon by the general assembly."

It is the opinion of this committee that the act of assembly for defending the Bay, and river Delaware, (vol. 2, chap. 7,) as to the powers given to the commissioners, was an infringement of the constitution.

The proper powers of council were, by this act, transferred to commissioners named by the house. These commissioners were authorised, to fit out what ships they saw fit; to continue them at their discretion, unless otherwise directed by the house. Duties on imports were appropriated to this service and subjected to the drafts of the commissioners on the officer who collected them; and lastly, the commissioners were authorised to borrow money on their funds, not exceeding 25,000 pounds, and directed to re-pay the same. To the council however, was reserved the nomination of the commander, and other officers employed in the naval armament.

Section 20, "The president and council may draw upon the treasurer, for such sums, as shall be appropriated by the house."

It is the opinion of this committee, that all appropriations of public money ought to be, by laws passed by the general assembly, and that all drafts on the treasurer of the state, ought to be made by the president and council.

The clause of section 20th last cited, is a limitation upon the proper authority of the executive branch to draw the public money. It is thereby confined to such money as shall be appropriated. The violations of this right of the council to draw the public money have been numerous. Drafts have been made by the house—by the auditors of public accounts,—by the justices of the supreme court and some others. The instance following is remarkable:

"Resolved that the treasurers of the several counties be empowered "and directed to draw on the state treasurer, for monies sufficient to "discharge the allowance made to wounded soldiers, and to the wid- "ows and orphans of officers killed in the public service; the same to be paid out of the one per centum impost by the act of December, 1780. Minutes of 28 December, 1783. *

---

* To this paragraph of the report the following reasons of dissent were entered, upon the minutes of the council.

Section 23. "The judges of the supreme court of judicature shall have fixed salaries."

_____

Although we agree that appropriations of public money ought, in general to be made by laws, yet we dissent from the opinion, that all drafts on the treasurer ought to be made by the president and council from the reasoning adduced in the report, in support of that opinion, we conceive an unnecessary power is intended to be lodged in the executive council, and, when this is taken into view with some other parts of the report, we think it a most dangerous power.

The report expresses that, "the clause of the section cited, is a limitation of the proper authority of council, to draw the public money." It is thereby confined. "To such money as shall be appropriated." The proper authority of the executive branch to draw for public money must be found in the constitution. But we find no authority given to them, for that purpose, in any part of it, except in the words of the 20th section. "They may draw for such sums as shall be appropriated by the house." The powers of the house, and of the council over money, are clearly contained in them, or to be deduced from them. For such sums of money as are appropriated, that is, set apart for particular purposes, the council are to draw on the treasurer. This is the sole power over money given to them by the constitution.—It is therefore their proper power ; and it is absurd to say that the power itself, is a limitation of the proper power. Such sums as are not appropriated, or set apart for particular purposes, remain in the treasury, subject to the orders of the house. The convention were the judges, what powers were proper to be entrusted with each branch of government. To the council they gave the power to draw for money appropriated only ; and to extend that power by construction, is to alter the constitution.— But to alter the constitution, is the sole exclusive business of a convention called for the purpose, and so, could not fall within the duty of the committee: this ought therefore to have made no part of the report.— It was necessary however, to the completion of the new system of government which would have been very inefficient without it. And as the introduction of that system, seems to have been a favorite object, we now draw the scattered parts of it, that lie up and down in the report, into one view, that the people may judge, whether there is really that danger to be apprehended from it, we have held forth; or that we have frightened ourselves with a phantom of our own raising.

The executive council are to appoint all officers, except the treasurer of the state a register of wills, a recorder of deeds, the sergeant at arms and a doorkeeper, These are left to the assembly.

The executive council are to originate all the laws. The assembly may indeed commit, alter or amend them, but they must have nothing to do with them in the first instances.— To prepare business is to form drafts of bills, but to form drafts of bills, is the right and duty of the executive council : therefore the assembly can have nothing to do with them, until they have been formed by the council.

The assembly, because in some instances they may have gone too far, are not to be allowed to redress grievances. The judicial branch, as it is called, is the proper body for that purpose.—They would keep the laws pure, which the assembly would corrupt, and do the business at less expense. The oppressions of executive and judicial authority, however, are the great grievances of every country. It can not be very consistent with liberty, or safety, to throw down that security, that fence against the abuse of power.

The executive council are, by the last mentioned section, to have the command of all the money also.— Even their own wages. the house of assembly, the legislature of Pennsylvania, will have to apply for, to the council, and if they have happened to be troublesome or refractory, may be told to call again.

If the committee really found this system to be the constitution of Pennsylvania, it is astonishing, that it has not been discovered earlier, for the administration of it has been, at times, in hands that were fond enough of power.— It is more astonishing still, that they should have bestowed so many encomiums upon it, Can it be believed that any reasonable creature, will think it the great bulwark of equal liberty ? is it not, what we have truly represented it ? the most complete system of aristocratic tyranny, that has appeared in the world. But in order to make it

The most important injunction of the convention has not been complied with as it ought. Permanent salaries should, without delay, be established by act of assembly, for the justices of the supreme court, for, and during their respective continuance in office. Judges should have nothing to hope or fear from any one."

Section 25th, "Trials shall be by jury as heretofore."

It is the opinion of this committee, that the act of the 16th of September, 1777, entitled, "An act to empower the supreme executive council of this commonwealth, to provide for the security thereof in special cases, where no provision is already made by law," and the act of January 2, 1778, to continue in force the former act, are deviations from the 9th, and 10th sections of the bill of rights, and the 9th, 10th, 20th, 25th and 40 sections of the frame of government.

It is the opinion of this committee, that the act of assembly passed on the 2nd of January, 1778, chapter 41, section 2, vol. 1, and that chapter 43, same vol. whereby persons charged with offences, might be tried out of the proper county, were unconstitutional.

The law passed in the province of Pennsylvania, after the fact, which declared Lazarus Stewart, and others, his confederates, to be guilty of treacherously murdering Nathan Ogden, and which directed that they be tried in the county of Philadelphia, ought to have no weight as a precedent.

Chapter 45, vol. 2, passed December 8, 1782, enabling the president and supreme executive council, to direct the trial of those, who should be charged with treasonably setting up a new and independent government within Pennsylvania, to be in an other county than that in which the facts were done, is unconstitutional.

The act of assembly constituting a council of safety, passed Oct. 13, 1777, in as much as it took away the right of trial by jury, and transferred the executive and legislative authority to the council of safety, were infringements of the 9th, and 10th, sections of the bill of rights, and of the 9th, 10th, 20th, 25th and 46th sections of the frame of government.

The summary jurisdiction, whereby the president and council have been authorised, to impose and levy fines, not exceeding five hundred

---

go down, it was necessary to speak favorably of it, and gull the people, that they might the more easily receive it. In other countries the government has been drawn from the popular, to the aristocratic form, by slow and almost insensible changes. The novelty of attempting to introduce an aristocracy, at one stroke of a pen, and to pursuade the people that they ought always to have been so governed—that it was the constitution they had chosen for themselves, was left for the first council of censors of Pennsylvania. But we trust the people are too enlightened to be so easily imposed upon, and too high spirited, and too fond of liberty, to suffer their representatives to be degraded to the mere registers of the mandates of their haughty and imperious masters. At any rate, foreseeing the evils attendant on this new system, to discharge the duty we owe to the people, and ourselves, we do again most solemnly protest against it.

When we consider, however, that on the committee who formed the report, there were two gentlemen, who had been vice presidents, and two who had been members of the executive council, it is not to be much wondered at, that a desire to increase its powers should have appeared. Yet we do them the justice to believe, that they had not all considered the extent of the plan, nor seen the fatal consequences that would inevitably follow from its being adopted.

Arthur St. Clair,   Anthony Wayne,   David Espy.
Frederick A. Muhlenberg,   John Arndt,   Thomas Hartley.
James Moore,   Thomas Fitzsimons,   Richard M'Allister.

pounds, on county commissioners, is neither the trial by jury, nor is it the trial on impeachment, directed by the constitution. It is a deviation from the constitution. See act of assembly, vol. 2, chapter 6, section 36, extended to the act for the federal supplies for 1783, vol. 2, chapter 66, section 7.

The acts for settling the public accounts of this state, as well by the late auditors, as that which constitutes the office of comptroller general of this state, do not give trial by jury upon the disputes concerning fact or law, which may arise in adjusting the public accounts, and are therefore unconstitutional.

Trial by jury is taken away, in the case of harboring deserters from the armies of the United States, and the offenders subjected to summary conviction and to whipping. Vol, 1, chapter 9, section 3.

The same is done in case of harboring deserters from the ships of war, of his most Christian Majesty. The offenders are liable to a fine of thirty pounds, on the summary judgment of two justices of the peace, and the certiorari denied vol. 2, chapter 59, section 2.

The jurisdiction of the court of admiralty, which proceeds without a jury, is brought upon the land, and extended to the demands of artificers who build or repair ships and vessels. Besides, it may with justice be apprehended, that this new embarrassment upon this kind of movable property, will deter foreigners from trusting their vessels into our port. Vol. 2. chapter 134.

Jury trial is denied in case of ships running foul of each other; and yet an action of debt, for the damages awarded, is supposed to be necessary, vol, 2, chapter 143, section 8.

Section 28, "All prisoner shall be bailable, by sufficient sureties, unless for capital offences, when the proof is evident and the presumption great."

It is the opinion of this committee, that the acts of assembly, which restrained, for a time, the full operation of the writ of habeas corpus, are infringements of the constitution.

These laws were intended to secure the persons, and restrain the traitorous practices of the disaffected, when legal evidence could not be obtained against them. See vol. 1, chapter 130 section 2 and 3, chapter 137, of the same vol. section 3.

Section 28. "The persons of a debtor, where there is not a strong presumption of fraud, shall not be continued in prison, after delivering up, bona fide all his estate real and personal for the use of his creditors, in such manner as shall be hereafter regulated by law."

The frequent interpositions of the legislature in behalf of particular persons, held in execution for debt, may all of them be justly branded with the appellation of laws after the fact; whereas this section calls for general regulations by a general law, which may be known before the contracts be made. These acts of mercy to individuals, too often dependent upon favor or prejudice, before large bodies of men, will probably bring us into discredit, if not into debates, with foreign nations. They ought to be abandoned immediately and a general law provided.

Section 30. "Justices of the peace, shall be elected by the freeholders of each city and county respectively; that is to say, two or more persons shall be chosen for each ward, township or district, as the laws shall hereafter direct; and their names shall be returned to the president in council, who shall commission one or more of them, "for each ward &c. so returning, for seven years; but if any city, "county, district &c. shall hereafter incline to change the manner of "appointing their justices of the peace, as settled by this article, the "general assembly may make laws to regulate the same, agreeable to "the desire of the majority &c. so applying."

It is the opinion of this committee that justices of the peace, otherwise constituted, than is set forth above, are not according to the constitution, unless the major number of the freeholders of the county, district or place, apply for another mode of appointing these magistrates, and the general assembly allow thereof by law.

The Burgesses of Bristol, Chester and Lancaster, have been declared justices of the peace, without such application. Vol. 1, chapter 4, section 7.

By chapter 14, section 7, 8, 9, of vol. 1, the council were enabled, on the application of twenty inhabitants of Chester, or other district, to appoint justices of the peace. Chapter 19th, authorised the president and council, to appoint five persons, not justices of the peace, to hold the court of quarter sessions, of the peace of the city of Philadelphia.

If the freeholders of Reading, or a majority of them, did apply for another mode of appointing justices of the peace, yet the term of seven years could not be altered. Such transitory magistrates, as the Burgesses of the borough of Reading, who are elected yearly, are too dependent to be the justices of the peace required by the constitution. See the act for incorporating the town of Reading, chapter 76, vol. 2, section 6, 7.

Section 30. "Justices of the peace shall be removable for misconduct, by the general assembly."

It is the opinion of this committee that the misconduct of justices of the peace, ought to be established elsewhere, before the general assembly can proceed to remove them.

According to the principles already stated, the legislative branch can exercise no judicial authority, that is not expressly given to it. These words can be fully satisfied, without supposing that the general assembly is vested with power to try justices of the peace. This enables us to say, that the house has no right to determine concerning their misconduct. Such authority would contradict the first principles of the constitution, and assign to the general assembly a jurisdiction, for which they are wholly incompetent, and would soon dishonor the house. For large bodies of men are so liable to be tainted by prejudice, favor and party, when employed in personal discussions, that justice is rarely attained by them. Resting therefore, on our principle that this is an executive power, put out of its proper place, we construe it literally, and carry it not beyond the words.— The solicitude shewn by the framers of the constitution, to render these magistrates permanent for seven years, will not admit that their misbehaviour be committed to a trial by sixty or seventy persons. See journals of assembly, Nov. 27, 1779. Feb. 26, 1783, and March 1, 1783.— But the 22d section has been adduced to support this claim of the general assembly, to try justices of the peace, as well as to remove them.— This section is as followeth viz. " Every officer of "government whether judicial or executive, shall be liable to be im-"peached, either when in office, or after his resignation, or removal "for mal-administration."

It has been contended from the words, "or removal for mal-administration," that the general assembly may remove justices of the peace, in order to impeach them, not considering that there is nothing in this section to give any power to the house. If such power were indeed designed at all, the council would take it, because it is executive business. But the difficulty here arises from the omission of a comma before mal-administration. Restore this, and the impeachment will be restrained, as it ought, to officers in their public capacity; and removal will apply to such civil officers as hold at pleasure, and who may be superseded ; and also to others, whose times expire ; as councillors and sheriffs, who, upon the erroneous construction which we reprobate, would not be liable to impeachment, if the malfeasances charged upon them should happen not to be prosecuted till after they were out of place.

Section 40. "Every officer whether judicial, executive or military, in authority, under this commonwealth, shall take the following oath or affirmation of allegiance, and general oath of office, before he enter on the execution of his office."

The oath or affirmation of allegiance.

" I, ———— ————, do swear (or affirm) that I will be true and faithful to the commonwealth of Pennsylvania; and that I will not directly or indirectly do any act or thing prejudicial or injurious to the constitution or government thereof, as established by the convention."

The oath or affirmation of office.

" I, ———— ————, do swear (or affirm) that I will faithfully execute the office of   for the   of   and I will do equal right and justice to all men, to the best of my judgment and abilities, according to law."

It is the opinion of this committee, that the act of 17th of March, 1777, entitled " An act to regulate the militia of the commonwealth of Pennsylvania," is a deviation from the 40th section of the constitution, as it dispenses with the oath therein prescribed.

Section 47. " The council of censors shall have power to call a convention to meet within two years after their sitting, if there appear to them an absolute necessity of amending any article in the constitution, which may be defective, explaining such as may be thought not clearly expressed, and of adding such as are necessary for the preservation of the rights and happiness of the people." But two thirds of the whole number of censors elected must agree to this call.

The resolves of assembly of 17th June 1777, for taking the sense of the people; and those for the like purpose of 28th November 1778, were violations of the constitution, yet we have no difficulty in declaring, that according to the 5th section of the bill of rights, the community have an indubitable, unalienable and indefeasible right to reform, alter or abolish government, in such manner as shall be by the community judged most conducive to the public weal.*

---

* By the resolve of 17th June 1777, it was directed that the freemen of every township, ward, &c. should at their elections of inspectors for the ensuing election, choose a respectable freeholder to be called a commissioner, whose duty it should be to go to the residence of every person entitled to vote for member of assembly, or take some other opportnity of meeting with them, and ask each and every of the said freemen whether he desired that a convention should be called. The answer was to be given in writing and put into a box or bag, to be provided for that

It is the opinion of this committee, that the general assembly of this state, in divers other instances, besides those already cited, have not acted as faithful guardians of the rights of the people. We give the following as examples thereof, viz.

It appears by the journals of the general assembly (December 29, 1777) that a committee was authorised by resolve, to open the chest of the loan office, wherein were deposited the bills of credit, brought in to

---

purpose, which box or bag the commissioner was to keep shut, and in his own possession, and return the same to the sheriff of the proper county, on or before the 10th day of November, then next. The sheriff and commissioners were to cast up the number of votes, an account of which, under their hands and seals, was to be returned to the next general assembly, at their first sitting. The resolve also provided a particular form of oath to be taken by the commissioners and the sheriffs.

The resolve of the 28th November 1778, states that certain resolutions which had theretofore been passed, for obtaining the sense and judgment of the people, in relation to the defects of the constitution, had not been carried into effect, because of the invasion of the state and other circumstances And then resolves unanimously, that the people qualified to vote, should meet at the usual places of holding elections, on the 25th of March, then next, and choose judges and inspectors, who should provide two boxes, &c. and that on the first Tuesday in April, the votes of the freemen should be received for and against a convention, which should be put in one of the boxes, in the other box the votes for members of the convention should be placed. The boxes were to be delivered to the assembly by the proper officers. The house was to count the votes, and if there should be a majority against a convention, then no further proceedings were to be had; but if a majority of votes should be for a convention, then the assembly was to proceed and open the boxes containing the names of the members of the convention voted for, and declare the six highest from each city and county to be the members to represent the same in the convention, and that the assembly should direct the convention to meet at Lancaster, on the 1st June, then next. The resolve then proceeds in the following words, viz.

" And the said convention having so met, shall judge of the qualifications of its members, and then proceed to determine on these points, viz.

1. Whether the legislative power of the state shall be vested, as at the present, in a single branch.

2. If the convention should be for a second branch of legislation, then how the same and the executive powers, for the administration of government, shall be constructed.

3. If the convention shall determine against a second branch of legislation, whether any provision shall be made for the revisal of laws (without any negative) before they receive their final sanction.

4. Whether the appointment of judges and field officers of the militia shall be vested in the executive powers of government.

5. Whether the council of censors shall be abolished.

6. Whether the president and vice president may not be eligible into council, so as to be capable of said offices after the expiration of three years, if their conduct shall render them worthy.

7. Whether the judges should not be made more independent by having their salaries fixed and certain.

8. Whether, agreeable to the articles of confederation of the United States, the delegates in congress may not be eligible, three years successively.

9. In case any alteration shall be made by the convention in the above parts, how the several oaths prescribed by the constitution, shall be adapted thereunto.

And the said convention having finished, they shall publish their proceedings and determinations, which shall be received and adopted by the inhabitants of this state, at and after the next general election, as part of the constitution by which, they are in future to be governed.

Upon the petitions of upwards of 13,000 inhabitants of the state, the resolve of 28th November 1778, was rescinded by the assembly on the 27th February 1779.— Yeas 47, Nays 7.

be cancelled according to law, to take thereout thirteen thousand pounds, and to deliver the same to the treasurer of the state, that they might be re-issued on order of the president and council. And by a subsequent entry of 27th February 1778, it appears that this resolve was executed. We consider this as a violation of public faith and confidence, that scarcely any necessity can excuse.

Another is taken from the laws. By the "act for funding and redeeming the bills of credit of the United States of America, &c " chap. 177, sect. 12, passed on the 1st June 1780, upon suspending the first tender law, it was enacted and declared " that from and after the passing of this act, all contracts hereafter to be made, shall take effect, and be payable according to the special nature of such contract, any law heretofore to the contrary notwithstanding." Yet the next house of assembly, in breach of this solemn assurance, made other bills of credit "a legal tender to all intents and purposes whatsoever, and in satisfaction of all debts, dues and demands." See chapters 1, 6, 169 and 204. vol. 1.

By the first section of the act of assembly to incorporate the bank of North America, passed the 1st of April 1782, the claim of congress to erect incorporations, is acknowledged. Yet there is no countenance given to this assumed authority, by the confederation. If it be necessary that the states severally should yield further powers to congress, they should do it professedly and in concert, not by such an indirect and dangerous implication as this. Vol. 2, chap 9, sect. 1.

The act for an additional impost of one and an half per centum, chap. 122, vol. 2, passed on the 15th of March 1784, has erected a new and as we apprehend, unnecessary and burthensome office, of great emolument. This business has been hitherto executed by the naval officer, without any complaint, as far as appears; but he is by the act in question, so completely divested of all attention to these duties on goods imported, that he is not suffered even to check the large sums which come to the hands of the new collector. But if a check in this case were necessary, surely it might be provided at a much cheaper rate than the erecting of this office, which loads so heavily the commerce of the commonwealth.

Here is a striking example of mischiefs, which would probably follow from the appointing to offices by the assembly, in other cases than those expressly assigned to the house by the constitution The bill for this purpose, as published, consisted of twenty-six lines only. It was read a second time on the 2 st of February last; read a third time on the 11th of March, when sundry new paragraphs were proposed. These were published as usual, on the 15th, and on the same day the bill was ordered to be engrossed, and it was enacted the 15th March. By these additional paragraphs, the collectorship of the port of Philadelphia, was first brought into view. They have swelled the act to more than two folio pages of the printed law books.

On the question, will the council adopt the report? the yeas and nays were as follow:

YEAS.

George Bryan,	James M'Lene,	William Montgomery,	William Finley,
Joseph Hart,	James Read,	James Potter,	James Edgar,
Samuel Smith,	Baltzer Gehr,	John Smiley,	John M'Dowell
John Whitehill,	Simon Dreisbach,		

NAYS.

Thomas Fitzsimons, Anthony Wayne, Thomas Hartley, John Arndt, Fred A. Muhlenberg, James Moore, Richard M'Allister, David Espy. Arthur St. Clair,

The following reasons for and against the adoption of the report were entered upon the minutes.

We dissent from the report of the committee as adopted by the council, generally; because, though there are some parts of it that meet our approbation, it is in a great measure made up of matters that were never submitted to them, and totally foreign to the nature and design of their appointment. Their duty was plain and simple, "To enquire whether the constitution had been preserved inviolate, in every part, and whether the legislative and executive branches of government, had assumed to themselves, or exercised other or greater powers than they are entitled to by the constitution." As this is a report in part only, and confined to the legislative branch, the journals of the assembly and the laws, fell properly under their notice, as it was from them only it could be discovered whether the legislative body had departed from their duty, or neglected the trust reposed in them. And had the committee contented themselves with pointing out, and reprobating in the strongest terms, the instances where these had happened, they would have met our hearty concurrence. But when we see explanations of many parts of the constitution introduced, which we think inconsistent with the liberty and safety of the people, and a labored commentary upon it, foisted into the report; it becomes a duty we owe to the people, to ourselves and to posterity, thus solemnly to protest against it in the gross, as big with mischief in itself, and forming a most dangerous precedent. If committees are at liberty to introduce into their reports, matters different from, and foreign to those submitted to them, public bodies may be surprised into a decission, on the most important subjects, unexpectedly, and unprepared for the discussion of them; or, as in the present case, into matters that do not at all belong to them. The greatest part of the report, which has taken up so much of the time of the council, being the proper and exclusive business of a convention.

This will fully appear, from the observations we have made upon the several parts which have received our negative. But in this place we cannot help observing, that by the explanations given to various parts of the constitution, the system of our government would be entirely changed, and the executive branch acquire such an increase of power and influence, as to make it easy for them to establish the most dreadful tyranny.

David Espy,   Arthur St. Clair,
Thomas Hartley,   Fred. A. Muhlenberg,
Richard M'Allister,   John Arndt,
Anthony Wayne.   James Moore.
Thomas Fitzsimons,

For adopting the report, we think proper to assign the following reasons, in addition to those placed upon particular parts of it, viz.

. We agree to the limit thereby set to the power of the house of representatives, as to their right to judge of the qualifications of their own members, viz. That the house has no right to expel one of them, who may be charged with a crime not committed in his official character, till he be convicted thereof by his proper judges; and we also adopt the strictures made on the case of —— ——. At the same time we reject, with indignation, all idea of sheltering persons guilty of peculation and fraud It was because the sacred rights of the citizens had been violated, through this culprit, that we mentioned him, and because we could not pass over such an enormous breach of the constitution in silence.

Because this construction of the power of the house over its members, allows of full scope to the general assembly, to determine concerning the legal and constitutional qualifications necessary, to entitle any person to sit therein; that is to say, whether the person returned by the sheriff, hath given the proper evidence of his attachment to, and interest in the community; in other words, whether he hath taken the test in due time, and paid taxes; whether he hath resided in the county he comes from two years before the election; whether he holds any office other than in the militia; or hath sitten in the representative body more than four years in seven, &c. This interpretation likewise admits of the sole right of the house to judge and determine, without appeal, of the merits of elections, and whether the person elected hath disabled himself for the year ensuing, by giving or promising any reward to be chosen into assembly. It is also consistent with the authority of the house, to decide concerning the behaviour of the members individually, and upon proper ground to expel any of them from his seat. But the house cannot enquire whether the persons fairly chosen by the people, be the " men most noted" in their respective counties " for wisdom and virtue," as called for by the 7th section of the frame of government. This requisition is merely directory to the electors. And the member expelled is capable of being immediately re-elected, unless he has been guilty of bribery at his former election.

On this point we harmonise with the assembly of the late province of Pennsylvania, of the year 1705, except perhaps as to the disabling of the expelled, who, by act for regulating elections, have stated the judicial authority of the house of representatives, in the words following, viz. " That no person shall be rejected or denied to sit, debate or act in the general assembly, who shall be willing to make and subscribe the declarations required by law; provided nevertheless, that nothing herein contained shall extend to debar or hinder the house of representatives to reject such persons as shall be unduly elected members of assembly, or such as the assembly shall see cause, from time to time, to expel or disable to sit there, by reason of ill practice in elections or misbehaviour in the house.

We say little of the right of assembly to punish for contempts, or to restrain breaches of privilege. The house is certainly invested with power to chastise those in a summery manner, who disturb or interrupt their proceedings. This is incident to every court of justice. We contend however, that the authority of the assembly to judge, in the cases stated above, was not given to them for their honor or advantage, but because it could not, consistently with the public welfare, be trusted in other hands. This, we say, is by no means the case in respect to criminal charges against an assemblyman, not concerning his official character. Here the freedom and independence of the house are not affected, and the right of the citizen to trial by his peers remains entire. He should therefore, be deemed innocent, till he be convicted by his proper judges.

And inasmuch as the proceedings of the late house, dated September 9, 1763, in the case of Mr. ———— ————, (one of the grounds upon which we have voted for this report) may not reach our constituents, we copy them here verbatim, from the printed journals of the general assembly, in order to shew that the proceedings in his case, have been candidly abstracted in the report.

"Whereas Mr. ———— ————, a member of this house, for the county of ————, and late a commissioner of purchases for the same, hath been guilty of notorious frauds, and other enormous crimes, in the execution of his duty aforesaid."

"Resolved therefore unanimously, That the said Mr. ———— ———— is hereby expelled this house, and that the attorney general be directed to institute actions against him for fraud and perjury."

And whereas, upon the express and clear words of the 15th section of the frame of government, the report in substance, states that all laws and alterations of laws, should be by bill, published for the consideration of the people, and, except in cases of sudden necessity, should not be enacted into laws till the next session of the general assembly; and that all appropriations of the lands, goods and monies of this commonwealth, by resolve, which is passed privately and immediately, are evasions of this 15th article, by which very peculiar restraints are imposed upon the power of legislating; yet a pretence hath been made for the house to proceed in this summary manner, from that part of the constitution (Sect. 20,) which, having enjoined that "the president and council shall take care that the laws be faithfully executed," declares that "they are to expedite the execution of such measures as may be resolved upon by the general assembly."

Upon this we remark, that the words last cited are manifestly introduced, to secure to the council the execution of such measures as shall be adopted by the legislature; and in order that the general assembly shall not, by nominating commissioners in their acts, or otherwise appointing officers, intercept this privilege of the board; but shall leave the executive part in every case, whether it be the levying of troops, the arming of ships of war, or other business whatever, to the proper and constitutional body.

This passage relates not at all to the mode of exerting the authority of the legislature. That had been too particularly and plainly described in the 15th section of the frame of government, to be unravelled and contradicted by the words used here for a very different purpose. Candour requires us to construe one part of the constitution by another, so as to understand the whole as a consistent system, if it can be done with fairness and justice; but forbids us to strain contradictions from general words. If it was indeed proper to state any distinction between "laws" and "measures resolved upon by the general assembly," the first might be referred to the standing laws of the state; the latter might intend business of a local and temporary nature; to be established however, by act of assembly, passed with the usual solemnities. In short, there is no countenance given by the 20th section, to legislating by hasty resolve.

It is stated in the report, that the second exception in the 20th section of the frame of government, viz. "Except such as are chosen by the general assembly, or by the people," ought to be considered as introduced there, by way of parenthesis. This interpretation, which solves every seeming difficulty, and gives operation and consistent sense to the whole sentence, has been reproached as adding to, or altering the constitution. But the charge is groundless. The constitution is still the same. We vote for the report, because nothing more is meant in this part of the report, than that the passage in question is to be read as if it were placed between the marks of a parenthesis; because similar interpositions of this nature occur in the frame of government, which are parentheses in sense, though they be not marked as such. Thus section 15, " Except on occasion of sudden necessity." Section 20, near the entrance " Five of whom shall be a quorum." Section 24, " Besides the powers usually exercised by such court," and section 28. " Where there is not a strong presumption of fraud," are instances of this kind. Far from being any strain on the words, this construction gives the natural sense of the passage. Lastly, we adopt the report, because the principles thereby established, tend to distinguish and sever the powers of government, and to prevent tyrannical exercises of them. The assumption of the judicial and executive, into the hands of the legislative branch, doth as certainly produce instances of bad government as any other unwarrantable accumulation of authority. It is only whilst these are distributed, and kept separate from each other, that liberty and safety can be expected.

We wish not to strip any of the branches of government, of the proper and constitutional powers belonging to it, nor to exalt any of them to the degradation of the rest; but persuaded as we are, that the transcendant authority of binding by law, together with the other clear rights of the representative body, are quite enough to be entrusted to any set of men, however qualified, we protest against the exercise of any other by the same persons. And we are decided, that the general assembly, for above seven years past, hath greatly invaded and dangerously usurped the business and powers of the other depositaries of the devolved sovereignty of the people of Pennsylvania.

George Bryan,   James Edgar,
Joseph Hart,   William Montgomery,
Samuel Smith,   John M'Dowell,
John Whitehill,   James Potter,
James M'Lene,   Boltzer Gehr,
William Finley,   John Smiley.

On the 16th of July, 1784, the petition of Thomas Mifflin and nine others was presented, stating that they are members of an ancient community, corporation and body politic, with continuance for ever, by the name of " The trustees of the college, academy, and charitable school of Philadelphia, in the province of Pennsylvania"; that they are entitled to certain estates, franchises, rights, &c. for the advancement of useful knowledge; that they conducted the seminary to the satisfaction of its benefactors, and to the advantage of the community, and that their rights were confirmed by the 45th section of the constitution of the state. That without any misdemeanor, offence, neglect of duty, or breach of trust, proved against them as a body corporate, they were disfranchised and deprived of their trust, immunities and estates in the said corporation, by a law of this commonwealth of the 27th November, 1779. That no legislature can have authority to divest them of their franchises, nor, without their consent, to take the fruits of their labor, as the foundation upon which to establish an university. They therefore pray the council of censors to take the premises under their wise consideratfon, and do therein as justice and equity shall direct.

In the original report, as made to the council by the committee appointed to enquire whether the constitution has been preserved inviolate in every part, &c. was contained the following paragraph, viz.

That the act passed on the 27th November, 1779, entitled 'An act to confirm the estates and interests of the college, academy and charitable school of the city of Philadelphia, and to amend and alter the charters thereof, conformably to the revolution and to the constitution and government of this commonwealth, and to erect the same into an university,' is a deviation from the constitution.

Upon the consideration of the report, the foregoing paragraph was negatived by the council of censors; and the following reasons for the votes given upon the question, were inserted upon the minutes;

Reasons of dissent from the decision of the Council.

1. Because charters granted to religious and charitable purposes, are carefully guarded by the 45th section of the frame of government, a clause introduced into the constitution, as is well known, with a particular view to the rights of this institution.

2. Because the suggestions in the act for seizing the charter of the college, that the trustees in the year 1764 had, by a bye law, narrowed the original broad and extensive plan of the institution, was not only without evidence, but against complete evidence, as has been shewn in council. We therefore consider this suggestion but as the specious colouring to a scene of pre-determined injustice, which the actors therein could not safely trust to a court of law, whose proceedings are conducted under the check and solemnity of oaths, administered to the occasion, and thus accounting why the proper tribunals were neglected, and resort had to the less scrupulous decisions of the legislature.

3. Because the supplementary suggestion of some in the council, that a forfeiture was, at a certain time subsequent to the revolution, incurred, from a deficiency of qualified persons to conduct the business of the institution, is frivolous and equally unsupported. We have full evidence, that at no time whatever, was there a want of qualified trustees, or of teachers; and accordingly, in their hands, until the war was brought immediately to their door, was the institution conducted with a degree of reputation which, with all the extravagant increase of endowment, and the imposing splendor of its new name, it has not been able under other management to emulate.

4. Because the law, in our opinion, is in itself, and independent of its immediate wrong, truly exceptionable. We consider the alteration in the mode of constituting the board of trustees, as materially for the worse. The care of education is best confined in private hands. Servants of government, and even ministers of religion, have been in all ages and in every country the interested tools and favorers of power. To make any of these trustees *ex officio*, is to create a dangerous alliance between the institution and the state, by which the dogmas of a slavish obedience may come gradually to displace the pure and exalted precept of liberty, and learning itself be made instrumental to the purposes of tyranny and oppression.

On the whole, we consider this 'act as a blind sacrifice to party, of the rights of individuals, (many of whom had eminently served the cause of this country in promoting our glorious revolution,) as an encouraging example to future attempts, against whatever may be imagined best secured and fenced by the highest legal sanctions; and as a bold infraction of a constitution, held up by the advocates of this injustice as a perfect model of political wisdom, and as such we protest against the act, and against every measure and proceeding tending to its support and confirmation.

Thomas Fitzsimons,	*John Arndt,*
Thomas Hartley,	*Richard M'Allister,*
David Espy,	*Arthur St. Clair,*
*James Read,	*Anthony Wayne.*

*Mr. Read would have it understood that he has sentiments as favorable to the constitution as those held by those from whom he here dissents.

Reasons for dismissing from the report of the committee appointed to enquire whether the constitution has been preserved inviolate, &c. the paragraph relative to the college, academy and charitable school of the city of Philadelphia.

1. Because the corporation named "The trustees of the college, academy and charitable school of the city of Philadelphia, in the province of Pennsylvania," constituted by two charters, granted by the late proprietors of Pennsylvania, the first bearing date the 13th of July, 1753, and the second on the 14th May, 1755, *had lost their activity,* and *were incapable of exercising their essential functions,* the power of appointing new trustees, and of appointing or discharging the provost, vice provost and professors, or any of them, being long lost before this act of assembly was made; and these integral and vital parts being *extinct,* the body corporate, if not dissolved, was so far *dead,* that it could not be *reanimated* or put again *in motion* by any power of its own. For at the time the act of assembly aforesaid was passed, there were but seven of the twenty-four persons named in the charter of 1755, who were not either dead, or who had not resigned their trusts, to wit: - - - - - - - - - - -
- - - - - - - - - - - - - - - :
the last of whom was civilly dead, he having been attainted of high treason; and upon a careful investigation of the minutes of the board, we find that there were never present at the election of a new trustee, from the date of the last charter, thirteen members, except on the 11th January, 1757, when Benjamin Chew, Esq. was chosen to be one of the trustees, so that with him there were but seven (were there no other objection) who were capable of doing any business.

By the last charter the trustees were enabled to fix the number capable of doing business at a meeting, which number so met shall by the majority of votes transact any *particular* affair or business, in as ample and effectual a manner as if all the said trustees were present; excepting always the nominating, constituting and discharging the provost, vice-provost, professors or any of them, in all and every of which acts there shall be *thirteen* members of the said corporation *present* and *consenting.* If therefore thirteen members were not only required to be present, but consenting to the nominating, constituting and discharging one of the professors, it seems reasonable to conclude that an equal number at least was requisite for the nominating and constituting a trustee. However, as to the number necessary for electing a trustee, the charter is silent, and therefore it appears to us, that this act must be done agreeably to the rule of the common law, which, in such case, always requires a majority of the whole society. But be that as it may, it is exceedingly clear that thirteen members were absolutely necessary to the appointing or removing the provost, vice-provost or a professor, and if there were not the number sufficient for these purposes, the *vital parts* of the body corporate were *extinct.*

On the 1st of June, 1778, the names of those who were said to be trustees, were, according to information from the minutes of the board and otherwise, twenty-one in number, of whom eleven were unable to execute the trust, by neglecting to take in due time the oath of allegiance and abjuration, and three others were civilly dead, they having been attainted of high treason; so that seven only remained who were capable of executing any part of the trust, and of these, three had remained with the British army in the city, and voluntarily put themselves under the power and dominion of the enemy.

The following remarkable entry appears in the minute book of these gentlemen, dated the 18th June, 1779; six members present:

"It was also resolved, that Mr. —— ——, not having for many years appeared at the board, and being now removed to New York, his place shall be supplied at this board by the choice of a new trustee."

On this we shall only observe, that these gentlemen well knew that —— ——, —— —— and —— —— had been attainted of treason long before, of which they take no notice, but on the contrary, resolve the place of —— —— shall be supplied, determining by implication, as far as they could, that the act of attainder was void and of no effect, and declaring, in the face of a law of their country, that his place as a trustee was full, till vacated by his removing to New York; for we find that by charter going to live five miles from Philadelphia city, vacated the seat of a trustee.

There appears another entry among the minutes of these persons, of the 28th of June, 1779, which is as followeth:

"Present eleven members. It being resolved, that the seats of —— —— and —— —— are vacant, it is agreed to choose two new trustees in their room on the third Tuesday in July, of which due notice is to be given to all the trustees as usual."

We remark on this proceeding that these gentlemen could not, nor could any corporation vacate the seat of a member by a bare resolve, but they did not choose to assign their attainder as a reason, and they were now afraid to assign any other; for this was done after the house of assembly had heard of their inimical disposition towards the American cause and the revolution, and had appointed a committee to enquire into their conduct and affairs.

2 Because no new trustee could be elected and take his seat at the board, without taking an oath of allegiance to the *king* of *Great Britain,* which was made a condition precedent by the charter.

3. Because the corporation passed a bye-law on the 14th day of June, 1764, whereby the provost was always to be a member of the church of England, and the vice-provost to be a person dissenting from that church; and *no person afterwards elected a trustee was to be permitted to take his seat at the board, until he subscribed the same.* By which the original plan and foundation of the seminary was narrowed,

an addition made to the charters, contrary to their spirit, and in the face of them; and the trustees were bound in an arbitrary manner, to support this bye-law. Viewing this bye-law in every light, and perceiving its tendency and operation, we conceive that it amounts to a forfeiture of the said charters.

4. Because the education of youth has been always considered by the greatest philosophers and lawgivers, as the most certain source of the tranquility and happiness both of private families and of states and empires. Youth are as the nursery of the state, and from among them magistrates, ministers, and all persons placed in authority and influence are taken; and it is evident that the good education of those who are one day to fill those places, will have a powerful effect on the whole body of the state, and stamp the spirit and general character of the whole nation. The republic is as much interested in the proper education of children as their parents, and therefore it behooves the state to take care that in public seminaries and schools, they be early inspired with a love of their country, respect for its laws, and a taste for the principles and maxims of the state wherein they are to spend their lives. The spirit and character of a republic is very different from that of a monarchy, and can only be imbibed by education. From these principles, we conceive it was the duty of the legislature of this commonwealth, as guardians of the rights of the people, (and we have no doubt of their power,) after so recent and great a revolution from monarchy, to take especial care of the education of the youth, in the first seminary of the state; to place it under the direction of gentlemen not only of education, but of known republican principles, and of tried virtue; and by all means in their power to prevent the commonwealth from receiving any detriment, either from the influence of men hostile to equal liberty, or inimical to the revolution and independence of this state, or from any other cause. We doubt not that it appeared to the assembly in 1779, which passed the act under consideration, as it doth to us, that the great majority of the late trustees of the college of Philadelphia were not only hostile to our independence, but abettors of the cause of the king of Great Britain, and totally disqualified for such a trust under our present government.

To remedy all these defects, incapacities, forfeitures and evils, legislative interposition became absolutely necessary. They accordingly reanimated the orphan seminary; gave it new guardians; secured its estate and interests, which were very near being lost; re-established the institution on its original broad bottom; provided it with new funds, and bestowed on it a new name and additional honors. In this the general assembly injured no man's property; they violated no part of the constitution of the college, but they added new strength to it. The qualified and worthy gentlemen among the former trustees, at any rate, had but a naked trust in the estates of the college, uncoupled with any interest whatsoever. And upon the whole, so far from censuring the assembly who passed the act referred to, they merit the warmest thanks of their constituents for their wisdom, virtue and just attention to the happiness of their country, displayed on this occasion.

5. Because, that although we highly reprobate all intermeddling of a general assembly with the estates, interests or misdeeds of individuals, who are by the bill of rights secured the privilege of trial by jury, unless the matter be strictly within the cognizance of the house, or be proceeded on by orderly impeachment, yet we have no

16

idea that corporations, which are the creatures of society, can, under the bill of rights, plead any exemption from legislative regulation. Cases may be supposed with the highest probablity, wherein, without breaking any law that may be devised, a body corporate might become not only a nuisance but dangerous; and therefore we cannot concede that a charter, obtained perhaps by fraud or imposition, or granted through the facility of our representatives, cannot be altered or repealed by any succeeding general assembly. Of this the university of Oxford, left improvidently in the reign of William the third of England, in the hands of the disaffected, is a striking proof If this doctrine were true, and verdicts ascertaining the abuse of charters were previously necessary, the extravagant inequality of representation in the English parliament could never be reduced to original principles; nor the rotten boroughs, as they are called, be deprived of their mischievous privileges. For it is plain, that this can only be cured by a law, which shall pass through all their charters. Nay, at this rate, should the bank of North America or any other corporation, become a monster of weight and influence, and be able to counteract and overrule our legislative proceedings, nothing less than a general rising of the people would be equal to the exigency.

We consider that these *imperia in imperio*, these governments within the government of the state, holding common estates of large value, and exercising the power of making bye-laws, as against the spirit and the policy of democracy, and only to be endured in order to obtain advantages which may greatly counterbalance the inconveniencies and dangers which accompany them. In Pennsylvania we have not a sole executive officer of permanency and weight, sufficient to restrain, and whose interest it is to keep those communities in awe; they may therefore gradually pro luce an indirect, yet firm aristocracy over the state, before we be aware of the mischief.

In England, a charter misused may be dissolved in a court of law upon the verdict of a jury; and if the king be deceived by false suggestions of the grantees, the court of chancery has authority to repeal the charter so obtained by fraud. But will it be said, that an act of incorporation passed here can be forfeited or repealed for imposition on the house, unless by the legislature? In fine, this doctrine, that the general assembly ought not to interfere with a corporate body, till a verdict of mis-user has been found against it, involves this absurdity, that one house of general assembly can enact a law that no succesor's general assembly can alter, amend or repeal without the consent of the corporators, who may be highly interested in opposing the interposition of the legislature.

By recurring to the journals of the general assembly, we find that on the 29th and 30th of September and 1st of October, 1779, the said trustees and pretended trustees were heard by counsel before the house; and that a bill for the purpose of confirming the estates and new modeling the seminary was afterwards ordered, brought in a read in assembly, but from want of time was recommended to the attention of the next house; and that the succeeding general assembly soon after its meeting, ordered a new bill to be framed for the same purpose, and that although they declined to hear counsel on this subject, they appointed a committee to procure the evidence, pap &c. necessary for the investigation thereof; and that Dr. Will

Smith furnished to the house all the information of which he was possessed.

George Bryan,	John Smiley,
Joseph Hart,	Simon Dreisbach,
James Potter,	James Edgar,
Samuel Smith,	William Montgomery,
James M'Lene,	John M'Dowell,
William Finley,	Baltzer Gehr.
John Whitehill,	

The preceding pages contain the reports &c. of the council of censors, made under the power delegated to them, to enquire whether the constitution had been preserved inviolate; and whether the legislative and executive branches had performed their duty as guardians of the people, or assumed to themselves or exercised other or greater powers than they were entitled to, by the constitution.— They embrace, it is apprehended, all the decisions of that body upon the constitution which can be of any interest to the public. There was a report adopted relative to such proceedings of the supreme executive council, as in the opinion of the council of censors were deviations from the frame of government, but, the details relate principally to proceedings of the executive council during the struggle for independence. Although the report contains many serious reflections, and cites a great many instances of deviations from the constitution, yet, as they can generally be traced to the particular situation of the state and nation at that period, it is believed the insertion of the report here, would not in any considerable degree serve to explain the powers of the executive branch of the government.

Under the authority delegated to the council, a committee was appointed to enquire whether the public taxes had been justly laid and collected in all parts of the commonwealth; also a committee to enquire in what manner the public monies had been disposed of, and whether the laws had been duly executed. These committees examined with great minuteness the subjects referred to them; their powers were extensive, and their duties required great labor and research; they severally made detailed reports which were apparently discussed very fully by the council, reasons for, and against various parts were entered upon the minutes, and the consideration occupied much time.

These reports are not inserted here for the reason above stated, they principally relate to transactions which sprung from the revolutionary war, and being predicated upon an extraordinary state of things, to which they almost exclusivly relate, their applicability is necessarily limited to similar circumstances.

It is true the same remark applies to a part of the reports which have been inserted, but it was believed it would be more satisfactory to the public to present these reports entire, though they do contain some matters of a local character, than to destroy their connexion by making partial extracts.—

During the second session of the council, remonstrances signed by upwards of 18,000 inhabitants of the state, against calling a convention were presented, the number of petitions did not amount to 300.

On the 16th of September 1784. The report of the committee of the whole read on the preceding day, was taken up for a second reading. viz. The committee of the whole report, that they have maturely considered the business referred to them, and having agreed to the following resolution they now submit the same to council viz.

Resolved that there does not appear to this council an absolute necessity to call a convention, to alter explain or amend the constitution.

On the question will the council adopt this resolution, the yeas and nays were as follow :

YEAS.

George Bryan,	James M'Lene,	William Montgomery,	William Finley.
Joseph Hart,	James Read,	James Potter,	James Edgar,
Samuel Smith,	Baltzer Gehr,	John Smiley,	John M'Dowell,
John Whitehill,	Simon Dreisbach,		

NAYS.

Thomas Fitzsimons,	Anthony Wayne,	Thomas Hartley,	John Arndt,
Fred. A. Muhlenberg,	James Moore,	Richard M'Allister.	David Espy,
Athur St. Clair,	Stephen Chambers,		

On the 24th of September 1784. The following draft of an address from the council to the freemen, of the commonwealth of Pennsylvania, was read the second time viz.

Having finished the period of our appointment, and having, as far as we are able, completed the new and important business assigned to us by the terms of the constitution, and the choice of the people, we are about to return to our private employments. Before we separate, we wish to address a few words to our constituents on this solemn and important occasion, when the guardianship of those sacred rights, which belong to us as freemen is again devolved on the community at large.

In the first place you perceive that we have determined not to hazard the calling of a convention, for the purpose of effecting any change in the frame of government, or bill of rights. To this determination the remonstrances of great numbers of freemen, against a plan of alteration, which had been proposed at our former sitting, not a little contributed. There is no human performance which might not be capable of amendment, and it would therefore be great presumption to say that our constitution is perfect ; but it certainly contains those great principles of equal liberty, which in our opinion ought never to be endangered. We have found also, that among the number of people who have been clamorous for alterations, very few could agree together what alterations were proper to be made : Some have proposed one thing, some another, and what one sett of them approved, another sett rejected with abhorrence. But, what is of greater importance, we found that some persons of high standing in life, and of great influence, among whom were a considerable proportion of our own body, had entertained ideas of government which they were struggling to carry into effect, in our opinion highly pernicious, and utterly inconsistent with liberty. We did not think it by any means consistent with our duty, for the sake of removing some pretended inconveniences, which are either imaginary, or have flown from abuse, and not from the constitution itself, to put to risk, at a time when such active and restless attempts were made to introduce an arbitrary government, the great fundamentals of our constitution, which hath hitherto proved, and we trust will long remain the palladium of liberty, In this opinion we have the happiness to believe, that we are supported by the sense o our constituents. We would add, that after all which has been said and written on the subject, we are firmly persuaded that the constitution of Pennsylvania needs only to be faithfully administered by men, who are honestly disposed to support it according to its true spirit and intention, to be the best system of government in the world.

Another great task enjoined upon us by the constitution, which indeed ought to have engaged our earliest attention, but which has been postponed to the last, was to enquire, " Whether the constitution has been preserved inviolate in every part, and whether the legislative and executive branches of government have performed their duty as guardians of the people, or have assumed to themselves or exercised other or greater powers than they are entitled to by the constitution." This arduous task we have undertaken and executed, we hope at least with impartiality. We know that our power is at an end ; that we are returning to the rank of private citizens, without any more interest in the concerns of the public than what belongs to every individual in a free state ; that for seven years to come, the censorial authority will be suspended; that during that period some of us in all probability will be numbered with the silent dead; and that few, perhaps none of us, will ever again sit in judgment upon the constitution of the state, and the administration of its servants. We known also, that the constitution has entrusted to us no power of enforcing our decisions. We can only give our opinion, we can only recommend. The good sense and virtue of the people are entrusted with the execution. We leave with you, therefore, our honest and well meant declarations, which for your own sakes we are confident you will seriously attend to. The last seven years which have elapsed since the formation of the constitution have been uncommonly tempestuous; we are sorry to say, but it is too obvious to be concealed, that although the storm has abated, yet the tossing of the waves has not subsided. The time we doubt not however is at hand, when our proceedings will be calmly considered, and fully attended to by the good people of Pennsylvania. They will then have that weight which the constitution requires them to have. They are not calculated for the passion of a day ; but for permanent regulation. We have freely censured deviations from the constitution, by whomsoever committed ; we have stated our sense of the true construction of different clauses of the constitution ; we have borne our testimony against the incroachments of one branch of government upon another, and have endeavored to restore that balance between the different branches which the constitution had wisely provided, and which is so highly essential to constitutional liberty, but which it was feared was in danger of being lost.

We are assured by the greatest writers on political law, and we firmly believe, that if all the different branches of power were to be centred in the hands of one body of men, liberty would be at an end.

It is unfortunately too true, that we have not been unanimous in our deliberations for the public good. It is well known that parties have for a long time run high on the question whether the constitution should be continued or altered ; whether a convention should be called or not. We apprehend that it is an unfortunate circumstance that this question, about which we were sure to differ, was first of all taken up, though it be the last proposed for our consideration in that section of the constitution which gives us our authoity and prescribes our duty. This unhappy question, which at different times has done so much mischief, kindled high debates in our council, consumed much of the time of our first session, and at last produced a direct appeal to the people at large during the adjournment. No wonder this transaction excited some considerable degree of animosity, especially in those who have been disappointed in the decision of a question so important in itself, and so eagerly contended This unhappy question, we are convinced, has lain at the bottom of all our disputes. Indeed this object has never been out of sight; for whilst one part of us has laboured to purge from the constitution the abuses that have crept in, others have never ceased to hold up the pretended necessity of a convention.

Our disputes have produced frequent appeals, in the form of reasons of assent and dissent, some of them too much in the stile of acrimony. Our fellow citizens we trust will be able to distinguish between the voice of reason and the language of disappointment. We should have been happy to have agreed with our brethren ; we were obliged to differ with them in opinion, especially on the great point so often mentioned.

One or two objections have been stated by the minority, which deserve a moment's cool attention. It is made an objection, that explanations of many parts of the constitution are introduced, which it is asserted is the exclusive business of the convention. The business of the convention, if a convention had been called, we apprehend would have been to establish and confirm such amendments, explanations and additions, as had been agreed upon by the council of censors, and promulgated at least six months before the election of the members of the convention. Our business was to examine "whether the constitution had been preserved inviolate in all its parts, and whether the legislative and executive branches of government had assumed to themselves other or greater powers than they were entitled to by the constitution." It was impossible to do this, without explaining what the constitution meant in the different passages which came under consideration upon these questions ; as impossible as it would be to determine whether a man had walked in the right path, without examining what the right path is. This is very different from altering the constitution ; as different as the duty of a judge is from that of a legislature. Judges in every part of the world explain and declare what the meaning of the law is ; but they cannot alter the law. We must have deserted a great, and perhaps the most important part of our duty, that of examining into the deviations from the constitution, if we had not undertaken to explain and understand what the constitution meant. More need not be added on this head.

Another objection is taken to our construction of the 20th section of the constitution, in that part which directs that the supreme executive council are to prepare such business as may appear to them necessary to lay before the general assembly. We have supposed, and have no doubt that this section, which directs the council to prepare such business as may appear to them necessary, directs them to prepare, among other things, sketches, or draughts of bills, which are a part of the business of the house, if on any occasion they should think such business, that is to say such draughts of bills, necessary. We apprehend no other construction can be put on the words. Yet it is asserted that this construction conveys a monstrous power to the coun-

cil, is an incroachment on the authority of the legislature, and a-
mounts to the power of originating all laws in the council. We trust
that candid and unprejudiced people will think otherwise, If indeed no
bills could be brought before the assembly, but those of which the
council prepared the draughts, it would be attended with the dangerous consequences which have been urged against us : But, on the
present construction, the legislature have the full power of bringing
in and rejecting what bills they please ; and as to any draughts which
may be prepared by council, the house, if they choose, may even refuse to suffer them to lie on the table. The house have the whole controul, the whole power. Council can only assist the house to expedite such
business as they choose to perform, and about which they are willing
to receive the assistance of council. There is no danger of any incroachment on the authority of the legislature. They are supreme
and sovereign in their own department, and wholly independent of
the council. On the other hand council in many instances, particularly
as to salaries and pay, are and ought to be dependent upon them. In
preparing business to lay before the general assembly, the council will
act in subordination to the pleasure of the house, without any authority to
controul the legislature. As well might a servant, who is bound to aid
and assist his master, be suspected to have it in his power to enslave him.

Other objections, in the heat of debate, have been urged and entered on our minutes against our proceedings, Amongst the rest we
are blamed for not approving of the power claimed by some persons
for the general assembly, of being at once the accusers and judges
of such as may be charged with misconduct in office· We think this
a power of an odious nature, which no assemblymen would wish to exercise; and that the only constitutional mode of trial for any supposed
crime is either by jury, or on impeachment by the assembly before the
council. We are confident that the people of Pennsylvania will never
be averse to the fairest and fullest opportunity of defence that can be
allowed to a supposed criminal, and will in ordinary cases prefer the
mode of trial by jury; in extraodinary, that of impeachment. We
think the constitution enjoins it.

But there would be no end to our address, if we were to go into all
the disputes that have taken place among us. Good men will judge
of our proceedings with candor: intelligent men will reflect and determine for themselves. The minutes of our proceedings are published
for the inspection of the world; and we wish them to be impartially examined. We have met with obstructions which we did not expect ;
but we wish not to inflame ; we wish the peace of Pennsylvania. It
would crown our days with joy; it would afford the most solid conso-
lation to our declining years (for the most of us have passed the meridian of life) should our endeavors contribute any thing towards re-
storing the peace and happiness of this distracted state. Should we be
disappointed, we shall still console ourselves with the reflection, that
we have used our best, our most honest endeavors. By you we were
appointed ; and into your hands we resign the sacred deposit of the
public welfare.

Before we take our final leave, however, we must intreat to be en-
dulged a few words more respecting the conduct which we conceive to
be necessary for the preservation of public liberty, and without which
the forms of all constitutions are vain. We have seen this state at
no very distant period, with her sister states, kindled into a flame of

patriotism, which enabled us to overlook mere personal considerations, and to consider the interests of the community as of more importance than our own.—That glorious principle seems much obscured; but we hope is not extinguished. If we could be induced to lay aside our personal animosities and party prejudices, we are persuaded that public spirit would revive, and the state would be happy.

The immediate effect of this spirit would be, that honest and able men, men of known fidelity, would be employed in the service of the public, and we should all be found promoting the good of each other, instead of quarrelling among ourselves, and hunting down and destroying some of the most faithful friends of the American cause. For seven years to come, the constitution cannot be changed ; it may be obstructed and opposed, abused and misapplied to bad purposes, as the best things often are, and always may be. Should this unhappily be the case, we shall continue to see days of tumult and confusion. But we hope for better things. It is certainly our interest and duty as a people to be at peace with each other, and not to be led away by persons who have private and selfish views, into scenes of discord and misery. If with heart and hand united, we will all combine to support the constitution, and apply its injunctions to the best use of society, we shall find it a sourse of the richest blessings. We would earnestly recommend this to you. Give it a fair and honest trial ; and if, after all, at the end of another seven years, it shall be found necessary or proper to introduce any changes, they may then be brought in, and established upon a full conviction of their usefulness, with harmony and good temper, without noise, tumult or violence.

May the God of harmony and love deeply impress these sentiments on all our minds—Farewell.

On the question will the council adopt the said address, the yeas and nays were as follow viz,

YEAS.

George Bryan,	John Whitehill,	William Montgomery,	William Finley,
Joseph Hart,	James M'Lene,	James Potter,	James Edgar,
Samuel Smith,	James Read,	John Smiley,	John M Dowell,

NAYS.

Thomas Fitzsimons,	Anthony Wayne,	Stephen Chambers,	Richard M, Allister,
Fred. A. Muhlenberg,	James Moore,	Thomas Hartley,	David Espy,
Arthur St. Clair,			

SEPTEMBER 25th, 1784.

The council adjourned till the day preceding the next general election.

PART IV.

Chapter I.

PROCEEDINGS RELATIVE TO CALLING THE CONVENTION OF 1789-90.

STATE OF PENNSYLVANIA.

IN GENERAL ASSEMBLY, March 24, 1789.

The motion made by Mr. Wynkoop, seconded by Mr. Schmyser, March 20th, containing an address on the subject of calling a convention for the purposes therein mentioned, was read the second time.

It was moved by Mr. Lewis, seconded by Mr. Clymer,

To postpone the same, in order to introduce the following resolutions in lieu thereof, viz.

Resolved, That in the opinion of this house, alterations and amendments of the constitution of this state are immediately necessary.

And whereas, by the declaration of independence, it is declared as a self-evident truth, "That all men are endowed by their Creator with certain unalienable rights; that among these are life, liberty, and the pursuit of happiness; that to secure these rights, governments are instituted among men, deriving their just powers from the consent of the governed; that whenever any form of government becomes destructive of these ends, it is the right of the people to alter or to abolish it, and to institute new government, laying its foundation on such principles, and organising its powers in such form, as to them shall seem most likely to effect their safety and happiness:" And whereas it is also declared by our own bill of rights, "That government is or ought to be instituted for the common benefit, protection and security of the people, nation or community, and not for the particular emolument or advantage of any single man, family or set of men, who are a part only of that community, and that the community hath an indubitable, unalienable and indefeasible right to reform, alter or abolish government, in such manner as shall be by that community judged most conducive to the public weal:" From all which, as well as from the nature of society and the principles of government, it manifestly appears, that the people have at all times an inherent right to alter and amend the form of government, in such manner as they shall think proper; and also that they are not and cannot be limited to any certain rule or mode of accomplishing the same, but may make choice of such method as to them may appear best adapted to the end proposed.

And whereas the burdens and expenses of the present form of government are with difficulty borne, and various instances occur wherein this form is contradictory to the constitution of the United States, which every member of the legislature and all executive and judicial officers must be bound by oath or affirmation to support—circumstances which will not admit of the delay of the mode prescribed in the constitution—It is, therefore, further

Resolved, That it be and it is hereby proposed and earnestly recommended by this house, in execution of their trust as faithful, honest

17

representatives and guardians of the people, to the citizens of this commonwealth, that they take this important subject into their serious consideration. And should they concur in opinion with this house, (it being the right of the people alone to determine on this interesting question,) that a convention, for the purposes of revising, altering and amending the constitution of the state, is necessary, it is hereby submitted to their decision, whether it will not be most convenient and proper for them to elect members of convention, of the same numbers and in the like proportions for the city of Philadelphia and the several counties with those of their representatives in assembly, on the day of the next general election, at the places and in the manner prescribed in cases of elections of members of assembly by the laws of the state.

That this house, on the pleasure of the people in the premises being signified to them at their next sitting, will provide by law for the expenses which will necessarily be incurred by the proposed convention, and will, if requested, appoint the time and place for the meeting thereof. And that the supreme executive council be, and they are hereby requested to promulgate this recommendation to the good people of this state, in such way and manner as to them shall seem most expedient for the purposes herein intended.

Which was carried in the affirmative.

And the said resolutions being by special order read the second time,

On the question,—"Will the house adopt the said resolutions?"— the yeas and nays were called by Mr. M Lene and Mr. Kennedy, and were as follow, viz.

YEAS.

George Clymer,	James Moore,	Peter Trexler, jr.
Thomas Fitzsimons,	Mark Wilcox,	Conrad Ihrie, jr.
Jacob Hiltzheimer,	John M'Dowell,	Stephen Balliot,
Lawrence Sickle,	Caleb James,	Jacob Saylor,
William Lewis,	Richard Downing, jr.	John White,
William M'Pherson,	Alexander Lowrey,	John Irwin,
John Salter,	James Cunningham,	Alexander Wright,
George Logan,	Henry Dering,	Robert Lollar,
Wm. Robinson, jr.	Thomas Clingan,	Jacob Reiff,
Gerardus Wynkoop,	Thomas Lilley,	Peter Richards,
John Chapman,	Michael Schmyser,	Jonathan Roberts,
Valentine Upp,	Henry Tyson,	John Carson,
Samuel Foulke,	Joseph Sands,	Obadiah Gore.
Richard Thomas,	Daniel Broadhead,	41

NAYS.

David Mitchell,	Samuel Maclay,	Theophilus Philips,
Thomas Kennedy,	James Barr,	James M'Lene,
Thomas Beale,	William Todd,	James Johnson,
Jonathan Hoge,	James Marshall,	Jacob Miley,
John Ludwig,	James Allison,	Adam Orth. 17
John Piper,	John Gilchreest,	

So it was carried in the affirmative, and the resolutions adopted.

Reasons for dissenting from the resolutions of the 24th March, respecting the calling a convention.

We dissent for the following reasons:—

1. For that the constitution of this state has wisely provided for a peaceable and orderly reformation of our government, if it shall be thought to require it, by a council of censors, who are to be elected once in every seven years, and whose stated time of election and meeting will be in the next year: and although we admit that in our government, as well as in all others, the community hath a right to reform, alter or abolish the government, in such manner as a majority of the people shall think right; yet the people themselves are sufficiently able to judge when the necessity of a revolution shall arrive; and we think it highly improper, to say no more, that the servants of the people, appointed under the constitution, for the purpose of maintaining, supporting and executing the constitution, who are bound by the solemnity of an oath to maintain the rights of the people, as declared in the constitution, should undertake a measure like the present, which is evidently calculated, as far as the power and influence of this house can extend, to subvert and destroy the constitution.

2. For that every government acquires respect and force from age, and the people are more disposed to obedience, more pleased and more happy. when, added to the authority of laws, their government has acquired the sanction of ancient examples, and the veneration which all men are disposed to pay to the opinions and practice of antiquity; and it is therefore of infinite consequence to form a good constitution in the beginning, and to adhere to it when formed. Frequent changes in government naturally destroy that respect which is so essential to its weight and energy; one change leads to another, and frequent changes are too apt to end in the contempt of laws, confusion and anarchy, even where they are effected in the most peaceable manner: but this is not all—the precedent established on this occasion will be introductory of a ruinous fluctuation in the principles of government; its consequences may be feuds and factions. As few revolutions are brought about without bitter and lasting animosities, contentions and violence, we cannot apprehend that anticipating one single year, or even two years, in the attempt to change the form of government, is worth the endangering the peace of the community, and the risk of bringing all government into irreparable contempt.

3. For that we cannot apprehend the present constitution of this state to be in any wise inconsistent with the new federal constitution. The government of the United States we know to be paramount to our own, and that our laws cannot be suffered to interfere with theirs: But we cannot conceive that our constitution is calculated to clash with that of the United States, any more than those of the other states in the Union; and we do not find that the other states have yet deemed it necessary to change their constitutions. Ours, as well as theirs, will be confined perhaps to fewer objects, and our laws will be more subject to controul than heretofore, but the constitution of the United States neither needs nor demands the alteration of the state constitutions. The constitutions of the individual states and that of the United States may move each in its own sphere, without clashing, for any thing we can discover to the contrary. The judges of Pennsylvania will not be empowered to contradict the laws of the United States, but judges of the separate states will be bound by the laws of the Uni-

ted States; and the judges of the United States will be sufficiently authorised by the express terms of their constitution, to prevent the interference of our laws with theirs: For by the sixth article of the federal constitution, that constitution and "the laws of the United States which shall be made in pursuance thereof, and all treaties made, or which shall be made, under the authority of the United States, shall be the supreme law of the land, and the judges in every state shall be a bound thereby, any thing in the constitution or laws of any state to the contrary notwithstanding." This reason therefore appears to us to be a mere pretence;—the fact is, that we are not authorised to judge of the extent of the powers and jurisdiction of the federal government; these are to be determined elsewhere, and nothing that one state alone can do, will either extend or abridge them; nor can we pretend to frame a government which shall quadrate with theirs. They will be bounded by no limits that we can prescribe, but will exercise their powers in their own way, and in whatever extent may appear necessary to them. Nothing less than the combined authority of all the states can set bounds to the powers of the federal government; and if a convention of this state were to attempt it, they might be found to vary from the opinion of the United States. Besides, it is by no means improbable that the federal government may yet receive very material amendments, and that speedily; so that if alterations were at all proper to be made in our government, in order to comply with the federal constitution, it would, even in that case, be our duty to wait the meeting of the new congress, and the result of the applications from different states for amendments.

4. For that we apprehend one part of the preamble to the second resolution, and that part which will probably excite the most attention, which declares "the burthen and expenses of the present form of government are with difficulty borne," is unfounded in fact. By the statement of the comptroller general, the expenses of government, including incidental expenses, is estimated at *twenty-eight thousand pounds per annum;* and this in future will be considerably lessened. The expenses of government in Virginia are annually upwards of *forty thousand pounds,* and in that of Massachusetts Bay upwards of *thirty thousand pounds;* in each of them considerably greater than that of Pennsylvania. And the true way of judging whether or not the present form of government is unfriendly to economy is, by comparing it with that of other states, of the same, or nearly the same extent and number of inhabitants: Nor can we conceive that creating another branch of the legislature (which is the avowed object of those who wish for an alteration of the constitution) by which two sets of men are to be maintained in the legislature instead of one, can lessen the expense of government. The defect in the former system of continental government consisted in the want of power in the United States, and not merely in the form of government. The states under the old confederation had denied to congress the power to fulfil its engagements either with foreigners or its own citizens; of collecting money, or regulating trade; in short, it was destitute of authority :—And if that authority, which was deficient in itself, had been divided into two or three branches, or into two or three and twenty, it never could have mended the matter. A body without strength would be weak with an hundred hands. If the expenses of government are too great, it is in the power of the legislature to lessen them, and there is no neces-

.sity for calling a convention for this purpose; nor can we conceive it to be a sufficient reason for tearing the government in pieces, and risking more important evils.

5. For that we are firmly persuaded the government and constitution of Pennsylvania has discovered as few faults upon trial as any on the continent. A number of people have watched from the beginning for every opportunity to decry it, and every mischief which they could possibly discover or occasion has been too often ascribed to the system. Under the present constitution, Pennsylvania has preserved her credit, and paid the interest of her debts, with more punctuality, and to a greater amount than any other state in the union; and has since the peace been able to sink a very considerable part of the aggregate debt accumulated by her in the course af the late war; besides all this, Pennsylvania is one of the foremost states in complying with the demands of the United States; she has paid her quotas of the requisitions of Congress fully to the year 1786, and hath advanced to the United States to the value of several millions of dollars in specie during the late war. A defect has undoubtedly existed in the federal plan of union; the constitutions of the states have been much less defective. Ours we believe to be one of the best. It may have defects, and those defects may be remedied in a constitutional way. But if we begin to tear up foundations, we are persuaded a much more dangerous system will be established in its stead.

Thomas Kennedy,	*William Todd,*
James Allison,	*James Marshall,*
John Ludwig,	*Thomas Beale,*
James Johnson,	*John Gilchreest,*
Jacob Miley,	*Theophilus Philips,*
James M'Lene,	*John Piper,*
Jonathan Hoge,	*Adam Orth,*
David Mitchell;	*James Barr.*

IN GENERAL ASSEMBLY, September 15, 1789.

THE committee of the whole, on the business referred to them respecting a convention to alter and amend the constitution of this state, report—

That having taken effectual measures for satisfying themselves of the sense of the good people of this commonwealth thereon, they are well assured, from the petitions referred to them, from enquiries made, and from information given by the several members, that a large majority of the citizens of this state are not only satisfied with the measures submitted to them by the house at their last session, but are desirous that the same should be carried into effect, in preference to the mode by the council of censors, which is not only unequal and unnecessarily expensive, but too dilatory to produce the speedy and necessary alterations, which the late change in the political union and the exigencies of the state require: And as the bill of rights declares it to be "An indubitable, unalienable and indefeasible right of the community, to reform, alter or abolish government, in such manner as shall be by that community judged most conducive to the public weal," so on this occasion your committee are perfectly satisfied, that a very great majority of them are desirous to exercise that right in the mode proposed.

The petitions in favor of the measure, though numerous and respectable, have not altogether influenced this opinion. The subject has engaged much of the public attention. Members have mixed with their constituents in all parts of the state, and have had full time and opportunity to learn their sentiments; they have, in a committee of the whole, severally communicated the knowledge which they had acquired, and the result has been, a full and thorough conviction that the voice of the great majority of the people calls for the measure, and that nothing but the slender opposition which it has met with, and an opinion of its being generally agreeable, has prevented more petitions in its favor.

The committee combine with these considerations a conviction that the measure is in itself right and necessary; that it will tend to promote the wishes of every good citizen, by settling a question which has long agitated the public mind, and thereby restore harmony, mutual confidence and good order, on the most solid foundations.

In addition to this, it is the fortunate season when all our citizens are on an equal footing to elect their members of convention, and are for the most part within the state, which was not the case when the constitution was framed. The convention too will possess every advantage which time and experience have unfolded, from the forms of government in other states, and the examples of improvement they have shewn, as well as from the excellent model, so far as it applies, exhibited in the constitution of the United States: The committee, therefore, in obedience to the wishes of the people, submit to the house the following resolutions, to wit.

Resolved, That, in the opinion of this house, it is expedient and proper for the good people of this commonwealth to choose a convention, for the purpose of reviewing, and, if they see occasion, altering and amending the constitution of this state; that in the opinion of this assembly, the said convention should consist of the like number of members from the city of Philadelphia, and the several counties in this commonwealth, as compose this house, and be chosen on the same day, in the same manner, by the same persons, at the same places, and under the same regulations, as are directed and appointed by the election laws of this state, save that the returns should be made to the convention so chosen; and that the said convention should meet at Philadelphia on the fourth Tuesday in November next.

Resolved, That, in the opinion of this house, a convention being chosen and met, it would be expedient, just and reasonable, that the convention should publish their amendments and alterations for the consideration of the people, and adjourn at least four months previous to confirmation.

Resolved, That it be and it is hereby recommended to the succeeding house of assembly, to provide, by law, for the expenses incurred by the said election and convention.

Ordered, That 7000 copies in the English, and 3000 in the German language, of the foregoing resolutions, be printed, and distributed for the information of the citizens of this state.

The resolution relative to publishing the amendments and alterations of the constitution for the consideration of the people, was moved as an amendment, and adopted with but one dissenting voice. Mr. Lewis, who voted in the negative, entered the following reasons upon the journal:

I dissent, because, although I admit, in the fullest extent, that it will be proper for the convention to submit to the consideration of the people the plan of government which may be formed, and although I fervently wish that sufficient time will be afforded them to deliberate thereon, I am so far from being satisfied of the right of this house to enter into any resolutions respecting it, that I cannot but consider them as unwarrantable assumptions of power. The resolution agreed to must be intended to have some weight and influence with the convention, or it would not have been proposed, and as that weight and influence, so far as they operate, must tend to prevent the unbiassed exercise of their own minds, in a matter submitted to them by the people, and not by this house, they must be highly improper. An adjournment by the convention is a thing in itself so desirable, that were its members to be appointed by this House, and to derive their authority from it, I should not only be for recommending, but directing the measure. But the convention must be chosen by the people, in whom alone the authority is lodged, and will derive all their powers from them. They will set, and they ought to act, both as to adjournments and in all other respects, independent of this house, and should not in the one case, any more than in others, be influenced by it. Being to be chosen by the same people with ourselves, it is rather assuming in us to suppose that their wisdom, virtue or discretion will be less than our own, and unless we distrust their prudent exercise thereof, it does not become us, to whom the business does not appertain, to dictate to those to whom it belongs. They will doubtless receive from their constituents, and duly respect, such instructions and recommendations as they may think proper to give, but ought not to receive any from us, who, as a body, have no right to interfere, and who, as individuals, will have a voice with other members of the community. The people may think that an adjournment of four months is too long or too short, and may recommend as they may think proper, but we have no right to think or to act for them. If we have a right to resolve that an adjournment is proper, we must have an equal right to resolve that it is improper, or that any matter in the formation of the government is right or wrong, according to the prevailing ideas in this house. In our resolution respecting the election, and the meeting of the convention, we are authorised by the wishes of the people, manifested to us, but we have no authority of our own, and are not warranted by them to proceeded further. When the convention meet, they will look to the source of their authority for instructions and recommendations, both as to adjourning and as to other matters, and act with a prudent discretion therein; and as that discretion ought not to be biassed by any supposed influence of this house, I dissent from the resolution, as being calculated to intrench on the rights of the people, and on the free deliberations of their representatives in convention, and have recorded my reasons, in justification of my conduct.

WM. LEWIS.

The yeas and nays on the adoption of the resolutions for calling a convention were as follow:

YEAS.

Jacob Hiltzheimer,	William M'Pherson,	Gerardus Wynkoop,
Lawrence Sickle,	John Salter,	John Chapman,
William Lewis,	William Robinson, jr.	Valentine Upp,

YEAS.

Samuel Fouke,
Richard Thomas,
James Moore,
Mark Wilcox,
John M'Dowell,
Caleb James,
Richard Downing, jr.
Alexander Lowrey,
Jacob Erb,
Henry Dearing,

Thomas Clingan,
Michael Schmyser,
Henry Tyson,
Joseph Read,
Joseph Sands,
Daniel Broadhead,
John Ludwig,
Peter Trexler,
Peter Ealer,
Conrad Ihrie, jr.

Stephen Balliot,
Jacob Saylor,
John White,
John Nevil,
Jacob Reiff,
Peter Richards,
Jonathan Roberts,
John Carson,
Obadiah Gore,
Hugh Davidson. — 39

NAYS.

George Logan,
David Mitchell,
Thomas Kennedy,
Thomas Beale,
Jonathan Hoge,
Gabriel Hiester,

John Piper,
James Barr,
John Irwin,
William Todd,
James Allison,
Alexander Wright,

John Gilchreest,
James M'Lene,
James Johnson,
Jacob Miley,
Adam Orth. — 17

Reasons of dissent from the measures for calling a convention.

We dissent from the measures adopted by this house for calling a convention,

1st. Because we are of opinion that this house is not competent to. the subject. We are delegated for the special purposes of legislation, agreeably to the constitution. Our authority is derived from it, and limited by it. We are bound by the sanction of our solemn oaths to do nothing injurious to it, and the good people of Pennsylvania have in the constitution declared the only mode in which they will exercise " the right of a community to reform, alter or abolish government," as being the manner most conducive to the public weal.

2d. Because we are of opinion that if this house were competent to the subject, they have not sufficient grounds for adopting this measure. It is clear to us that a majority of the good people of the state are averse to it. This house originated it from their own mere motion, without any application from their constituents, and invited the people to signify their assent. After an effort of several months, supported by the greatest exertions of legislative influence, and without any considerable interference to oppose them, this assent has been extorted from not more than (about) one seventh of the people; and this, we are authorised to assert from our own knowledge and the best information, was effected by the most deceptious means, and that in many instances the petitioners supposed the object of the application to this house was the obtaining amendments to the federal constitution, and for the lowering of the taxes in this state. These reasons, so far as they are grounded on the small number of petitioners, are strengthened by the information given in this house from, and of the most wealthy and populous parts of the state, that, since the petitions were signed, great changes have taken place in the wishes of the people on this subject.

3d. Because, when an attempt was lately made to effect the same measure, a majority of the good people of the state interposed, denying the right or power of their representatives to interfere, and gave a most decided and unambiguous evidence of their attachment to the present constitution.

4th. Because the supreme executive council have not been advised with nor had any concurrence in the measure proposed, but have given am unequivocal mark of their disapprobation, and yet they are equally interested, and equally representatives of the good people of the state.

5th. Because the time proposed to the people for electing members of the intended convention is too soon to admit of that general information and full consideration which so important a measure deserves. Sheriffs and coroners have been months canvassing for their comparatively trifling offices, and in a case of inconceivable importance to every member of the community and their posterity for ages, a knowledge of which should be carried to the doors of every house, but little more time is given than is sufficient to ride to the doors of the county court-houses of the state.

6th. Because this measure at once infringes the solemn compact entered into by the people of this state with each other, to be ruled by fixed principles; will render every form of government precarious and unstable; encourage factions, in their beginning contemptible for numbers, by a persevering opposition to any administration, to hope for success; and subject the lives and liberties of the good people of this commonwealth, and all law and government, to uncertainty; render every thing that is dear subject to the caprice of a factious and corrupt majority in the legislature; destroy all confidence in our government, and prevent foreigners from giving that preference to Pennsylvania, as an asylum from oppression, which we have hitherto experienced.

James M'Lene,	*John Gilchreest,*
John Piper,	*James Barr,*
Jonathan Hoge,	*James Allison,*
James Johnson,	*Thomas Beale,*
Alexander Wright,	*Thomas Kennedy.*

Chapter II.

MINUTES OF THE CONVENTION,

Of the commonwealth of Pennsylvania, commenced at Philadelphia, on Tuesday the twenty-fourth day of November, in the year of our Lord one thousand seven hundred and eighty-nine.

TUESDAY. *November* 24, 1789, *P. M.*

This being the day appointed by the legislature of this state for the meeting of the convention, a number of gentlemen, delegated for that purpose, met accordingly at the state house, but not being sufficient to constitute a quorum, they adjourned until three o'clock to-morrow, P. M.

WEDNESDAY, *November* 25, 1789, *P. M.*

A number of gentlemen, elected to serve in the convention, sufficient to constitute a quorum met, whereupon, on motion, the returns of the elections held for the city of Philadelphia, and the several coun- ties of this state, were read, by which it appeared that the following gentlemen were returned as delegates for the said city and counties respectively, viz.

For the city of Philadelphia.
James Wilson,
Hilary Baker,
George Roberts,
William Lewis,
Thomas M'Kean.

For the county of Philadelphia.
Thomas Mifflin,
George Gray,
William Robinson, junr.
Robert Hare,
Enoch Edwards.

For the county of Bucks.
Samuel Ogden,
Thomas Jenks,
John Barclay,
Abraham Stout.

For the county of Chester.
William Gibbons,
Thomas Bull,
Thomas Ross,
James Boyd.

For the county of Lancaster.
Edward Hand,
Robert Coleman,
Sebastian Graff,
William Atlee,
John Hubley,
John Breckbill.

For the county of York.
Henry Miller,
Henry Slegle,
William Reed,
Benjamin Tyson,
Benjamin Pedan,
Matthew Dill.

For the county of Cumberland.
Robert Whitehill,
William Irvine,
James Power.

For the county of Berks.
Joseph Hiester,

Christian Lower,
Abraham Lincoln,
Paul Groscop,
Baltzer Gehr.

For the county of Northampton.
Samuel Sitgreaves,
Thomas Mawhorter,
John Arndt,
Peter Rhoads.

For the county of Bedford.
Joseph Powell,
John Piper,

For the county of Westmoreland
William Findley,
William Todd,

For the county of Washington.
Alexander Addison,
John Hoge,
David Reddick,
James Ross.

For the county of Fayette.
John Smilie,
Albert Gallatin.

For the county of Franklin.
James N'Lene,
George Matthews.

For the county of Montgomery.
James Morris,
Samuel Potts,
Lindsay Coates,
Jonathan Shoemaker.

For the county of Dauphin.
John Gloninger,
William Brown,
Jacob Cook.

For the county of Luzerne.
Timothy Pickering.

For the county of Huntingdon.
Andrew Henderson.

For the county of Delaware.
John Sellers,
Henry Hale Graham.

NOTE.—No returns have been received from the counties of Northumberland and Allegheny.

The return from the county of Mifflin appearing to be double, was read as follows, viz.

MIFFLIN COUNTY, ss.

Agreeably to returns this day received from the following election districts in this county, viz. from an election held at this place, for the townships of Derry, Wayne and Armagh; from an election held at the house of Enoch Hastings, for the townships of Bald Eagle and Potter's, and from an election held at the house of Thomas Wilson, for the townships of Fermanagh and Milford, the undermentioned persons were highest in votes for members of convention, elected agreeably to a resolution of the general assembly of this state, passed September 15th, 1789.

William Brown, six hundred and ten votes,   610 votes.

Thomas Beale, five hundred and sixteen votes,   516

There were also received this day returns of elections held at the house of widow Stackhole, for the township of Lack, and at the house of Henry M'Connel, for Greenwood township, in this county, the legality of electing at these places being disputed by a part of the judges, the law authorising said elections not being present, we have thought proper to forward to your honorable body a statement of the election both with and without the returns from these townships of Greenwood and Lack; if the elections of these two townships are legal as to the place of holding the same, and their votes are admitted, the person highest in votes will be as follows, if not, it will be as above:

Thomas Beale, for convention, six hundred and fifty seven, 657 votes.

William Brown, for ditto, six hundred and ten,   610

We the subscribers, judges of the election afore-mentioned, do certify, that the above statement is just and true. Given under our hands and seals, at the house of Arthur Buchanan, in the county of Mifflin, this fifteenth day of October, 1789.

Samuel Osborne,	[L. S.]	Joseph Mender,	[L. S.]
William Corbet,	[L. S]	John Henderson Cnor,	[L. S.]
Thomas M'Ilroy,	[L. S.]	George Bratten, jr.	[L. S.]

MEMBERS PRESENT.

James Wilson,	John Breckbill,	John Piper,
Hilary Baker,	Henry Miller,	William Findley,
William Lewis,	Henry Slegle,	Alexander Addison,
Thomas M'Kean,	William Reed,	John Hoge,
Thomas Mifflin,	Benjamin Tyson,	David Reddick,
George Gray,	Benjamin Pedan,	James Ross,
William Robinson, jr.	Matthew Dill,	John Smilie,
Robert Hare,	Robert Whitehill,	James M'Lene,
Enoch Edwards,	James Power,	George Matthews,
Samuel Ogden,	Joseph Hiester,	James Morris,
Thomas Jenks,	Christian Lower,	Samuel Potts,
John Barclay,	Abraham Lincoln,	Lindsay Coates,
Abraham Stout,	Paul Groscop,	Jonathan Shoemaker,
James Boyd,	Samuel Sitgreaves,	John Gloninger,
Edward Hand,	Thomas Mawhorter,	Timothy Pickering,
Robert Coleman,	John Arndt,	Andrew Henderson,
Sebastian Gräff,	Peter Rhoads,	John Sellers,
John Hubley,	Joseph Powell,	Henry Hale Graham.

The convention proceeded to elect a president, and the ballots being taken, it appeared that his excellency Thomas Mifflin, Esquire, was duly elected.

A letter from Samuel Bayard, and a memorial from John Miller, were read, severally requesting to be appointed secretary to this convention.

Ordered to lie on the table.

Petitions from James Martin, Frederick Snyder and Nicholas Weaver, were read, severally praying to be appointed messenger to the convention.

Ordered to lie on the table.

A petition from Joseph Fry, was read, praying to be appointed door-keeper to the convention.

Ordered to lie on the table.

Petitions from Frederick Doublebower, John Dixon, William Reddiger, John George Lohrman, Christian Hubbart, Jacob Gideon and William Crispin, were read, severally praying the convention to grant them the appointment of messenger or door keeper.

Ordered to lie on the table.

On motion of Mr. M'Lene, seconded by Mr. Smilie, Resolved, That this convention will on Friday next, proceed to the election of a secretary, and that the nomination may continue, and applications be made, until the time of election.

Ordered, That Friday next be assigned for the election of a messenger and door keeper.

Adjourned until ten o'clock on Friday next, A. M.

FRIDAY, November 27, 1789, A. M.

The convention met pursuant to adjournment.

A member stated to the chair, a question upon which the opinion of the convention was requested, previous to taking the votes for a secretary, viz Whether the votes of a majority of all the members present should be essential to the choice?

The sense of the convention being taken upon the question, it was resolved in the affirmative.

Agreeably to the order of the day, the convention proceeded to the election of a secretary, and the ballots being taken, it appeared that Joseph Redman, Esq. was duly elected.

The convention then proceeded to the election of a messenger and doorkeeper, and the ballots being taken, it appeared that Frederick Snyder was duly elected messenger, and Joseph Fry duly elected door-keeper.

A motion was made by Mr. Hare, seconded by Mr. Ogden, that a committee be appointed to prepare a draft of rules and regulations for the government of this convention,

It was then moved by Mr. Smilie, seconded by Mr. Findley, to postpone the consideration of the said motion for the purpose of reading the resolutions, passed by the general assembly, on the 24th of March, 1789, and on the 15th of September, 1789, for calling a convention, which was carried in the affirmative, and the said resolutions were accordingly read.

On motion of Mr. M'Kean, seconded by Mr. Sitgreaves, ordered, that the resolves of the general assembly of the 24th day of March last, and of the 15th day of September, 1789, preface the minutes of the convention.

The motion made by Mr. Hare, seconded by Mr. Ogden, recurring, thereupon

Resolved, That a committee be appointed to prepare a draft of rules
regulations for conducting the business of the convention.

ered, That Mr. Wilson, Mr. Lewis, Mr. Hare, Mr. Hand and
hitehill, be a committee for the purposes contained in the fore-
resolution.

motion of Mr. Lewis, seconded by Mr. Wilson,

olved, That the general assembly be requested to furnish this
ention with two sets of the acts and minutes of the general assem-
, of this commonwealth, to be returned at the end of the present ses-
ion of the said convention; and also that they permit this convention
to have the use of the library during the said session.

On motion of Mr. M'Kean, seconded by Mr. M'Lene,

Resolved, That the doors of the convention shall be kept open, as
well in committee of the whole as in convention.

Adjourned until ten o'clock to-morrow, A. M.

SATURDAY, November 28, 1789. A. M.

The convention met pursuant to adjournment.

The committee appointed to draft rules and regulations for conducting the business of this convention made report, which was read, and
ordered to lie on the table.

On motion of Mr. Lewis, seconded by Mr. Wilson,

Resolved, That the president of this convention draw a warrant on
the state treasurer, for one hundred pounds, in favor of the secretary,
to be by him applied towards defraying the incidental expenses of
the said convention, and for which he shall account.

On motion of Mr. Sitgreaves, seconded by Mr. Thomas Ross, the
draft of rules and regulations for conducting the business of this
convention, was by special order, read the second time, as follows,
viz.

The committee appointed to report rules for conducting the business of the convention, beg leave to submit the following ones to the
consideration of the house:—

I. When the president assumes the chair, the members shall take
their seats.

II. At the opening of the convention each day, the minutes of the
preceding day shall be read, and shall then be in the power of the convention to be corrected.

III. A motion made and seconded shall be repeated by the president. A motion shall be reduced to writing if the president or any
member requires it. A motion may be withdrawn by the member
making it, before amendment or decision.

IV. Every motion, either in the house or in a committee of the whole
house, shall be entered on the journals, together with the names of the
members making and seconding it.

V. No member speaking shall be interrupted but by a call to order
by the president, or by a member through the president.

VI. No member shall be referred to in debate by name.

VII. The president himself, or by request, may call to order any
member who shall transgress the rules.

VIII. Every member attending the convention shall be in his place
at the time to which the convention stands adjourned, or within
half an hour of that time.

IX. The yeas and nays shall be called and entered on the minutes of the house, or of the committee of the whole house, when any *member requires* it.

X. The rules of proceedings in the house shall, so far as they may be applicable, be observed in committee of the whole.

And in debating the ninth section of the foregoing rules and regulations, it was moved by Mr. Lewis, seconded by Mr Boyd, to strike out the words " member requires," and in lieu thereof to insert the words " two members require."

On the question, will the convention agree to the amendment?

It was carried in the negative; and thereupon the rules and regulations, as reported by the committee, were adopted.

On motion of Mr. Lewis, seconded by Mr. M'Kean,

Resolved, That it be the order of the day for Tuesday next, to appoint a printer to this convention in the English, and an other in the German language.

On motion of Mr. Lewis, seconded by Mr. Smilie,

Resolved, That the secretary take measures to have this convention supplied with six sets of each of the public news-papers printed in this city, during the sitting of the convention.

On motion of Mr. M'Kean, seconded by Mr. Miller, the constitution of this commonwealth, was read. [For which see page 54 of this volume.]

A letter from the honorable the speaker of the general assembly, was read as follows, viz.

IN ASSEMBLY, November 28, 1789.

SIR,

I have the honor to enclose the resolution of the house of assembly, agreeing to the request of the convention on the subject of copies of the laws and minutes, and the use of the library.

I have the honor to be,

With great respect and esteem,

Your very obedient servant.

RICHARD PETERS.

His excellency, Thomas Mifflin,
President of the honorable convention of the state.

STATE OF PENNSYLVANIA.
In General Assembly, November 28, 1789.

A letter from his excellency the president of the state convention was read, with its enclosure, as follows, viz.

IN CONVENTION, Philadelphia, November 28, 1789.

SIR,

I have the honor to enclose to you a resolution of the convention of the twenty-seventh instant, which I request you to lay before the general assembly.

With great respect I have the honor to be sir,

Your most obedient and most humble servant,

THOMAS MIFFLIN.

Honorable Richard Peters, Esquire.
Speaker of the General Assembly.

STATE OF PENNSYLVANIA.

IN CONVENTION, November 27, 1789.

On motion of Mr. Lewis, seconded by Mr. Wilson,

Resolved, That the General Assembly be requested to furnish this convention with two sets of the acts and minutes of the general assembly of this commonwealth, to be returned at the end of the present session of the said convention; and also that they permit this convention to have the use of the library during the said session.

Extract from the minutes,
JOSEPH REDMAN, Secretary.

And on motion, and by special order, the same were read the second time, whereupon,

Resolved, That the request contained in the said resolution, be complied with.

Extract from the minutes,
PETER Z. LLOYD,
Clerk of the general assembly.

A letter from Hall and Sellers, was read, soliciting the appointment of printers to this convention. Ordered to lie on the table.

A motion was made by Mr. M'Kean, seconded by Mr. Hoge, in the words following, viz.

Resolved, That the convention will, on Monday next, resolve itself into a committee of the whole, to take into consideration that part of the constitution which relates to the department of legislation, and to report whether any or what alterations shall be made therein.

It was then moved by Mr. Sitgreaves, seconded by Mr. M'Kean, to strike out the words "that part of the constitution which relates to the department of legislation, and to report whether any or what alterations shall be made therein," and in lieu thereof to insert the following words, viz. " whether and wherein the constitution of this state requires alteration or amendment."

Which was carried in the affirmative, and the resolution as amended was adopted, viz.

Resolved, That this convention will on Monday next, resolve itself into a committee of the whole, to take into consideration, whether and wherein the constitution of this state requires alteration or amendment.

Adjourned until three o'clock on Monday next, P. M.

MONDAY, November 30, 1789, P. M.

The convention met pursuant to adjournment.

The returns of the elections held in the counties of Northumberland and Allegheny, for members to represent the said counties in this convention, were read, by which it appeared that Charles Smith and Simon Snyder, Esquires, were duly elected and returned for the said county of Northumberland, and John Gibson, Esquire, duly elected and returned for the county of Allegheny, aforesaid.

And the said members appearing in convention, were severally admitted to take their seats.

Petitions and letters from Pritchard and Hall, Zachariah Poulson, jr. Thomas Bradford and Francis Bailey, severally soliciting the appointment of printer to this convention, in the English language, were read and ordered to lie on the table.

A petition from Michael Steiner, was read, praying he may be appointed to print the business of this convention, in the German language. Ordered to lie on the table.

The order of the day being read, viz. the resolution adopted on the twenty-eighth instant, as follows:

Resolved, that this convention will, on Monday next, resolve itself into a committee of the whole, to take into consideration, whether and wherein the constitution of this state requires alteration or amendment.

It was moved by Mr. Hand, seconded by Mr. Irvine, to re-consider the said resolution, in order to introduce, in lieu thereof, the following, viz.

Resolved, that in the opinion of this convention it is expedient and proper to alter and amend the constitution of this state.

On the question—"Will the convention agree to re-consider the resolution for the aforesaid purpose ?" It was carried in the negative.

The order of the day then recurring—It was on motion of Mr. Smilie, seconded by Mr. Edwards, ordered that the same be postponed until to-morrow.

On motion of Mr. Lewis, seconded by Mr. Wilson, ordered, that the seats on the right and left of the chair be reserved for the members of congress, and of the legislature, supreme executive council and judges.

Adjourned until ten o'clock to-morrow, A. M.

TUESDAY, December 1st, 1789. A. M.

The convention met pursuant to adjournment,

A letter from James Pemberton was read as follows, viz.

Esteemed friend.

The Pennsylvania society for the abolition of slavery, &c. request the favour of the president to present to each member of the state convention a copy of the description of a slaves' ship lower deck, and of the address to the public, and plan annexed to it for the improvement of the condition of the free blacks, of each of which seventy copies are herewith sent.

I am, respectfully,
Thy real friend,
JAMES PEMBERTON.

Philadelphia. 1st. of twelfth month, 1789.

THOMAS MIFFLIN, *Esquire.*

The return of the election held in the county of Mifflin, for a member to represent said county in this convention, was again read, by which it appeared, that Thomas Beale, Esquire, was duly elected, who appearing in convention was admitted to take his seat.

Agreeably to the order of the day the convention proceeded to the election of a printer, in the English language, and the ballots being

taken it appeared that Zachariah Poulson, junior, was duly elected.

It was then, on motion of Mr. Edwards, seconded by Mr. Boyd,

Resolved, that Melchior Steiner be and is hereby appointed printer
to this convention in the german language.

Agreeably to the order of the day, the convention resolved itself into a committee of the whole, to take into consideration, whether and
and wherein the constitution of this state requires alteration or
amendment.

The president left the chair, and the honorable Mr. M'Kean, as
chairman, was placed therein.

After some time spent in discussing the business referred to them,
The chairman quitted the chair and the president resumed it.

The chairman then reported, that the committee had made some
progress in the business, but, not having completed the same, requested leave to sit again to morrow morning. Leave was accordingly granted.

Adjourned until ten o'clock to-morrow, A. M.

WEDNESDAY, December 2nd, 1789. A. M.

The committee of the whole reported further progress and obtained
leave to set again.

Adjourned until ten o'clock to-morrow, A. M,

THURSDAY, December 3rd, 1789. A. M.

The convention met pursuant to adjournment.

A motion was made by Mr. M'Kean, seconded by M. Lewis, to
re-consider the fourth rule for conducting the business of this convention, viz.

" Every motion, either in the house or in a committee of the whole
" house, shall be entered on the journals, together with the names of
" the members moving and seconding it,"

In order to introduce the following amendment, viz.

Every motion in the house shall be entered on the journals, together with the names of the members moving and seconding it.

And on the question—" Will the convention agree to re-consider
the fourth rule, to introduce the said amendment ?"—The yeas and
nays being called by Mr. Wilson, were as follow, viz.

YEAS.

Mr. Lewis	Mr. Boyd	Mr. Coates	Mr. Morris
M'Kean	Smilie		6

NAYS.

Mr. Wilson	Mr. Barclay	Mr. Graff	Mr. Pedan
Roberts	Stout	Hubley	Dill
Robinson,	Gibbons	Breckbill	Whitehill
Hare	Bull	Miller	Irvine
Edwards	T. Ross	Slegle	Power
Ogden	Hand	Reed	Hiester
Jenks	Coleman	Tyson	Lower

Mr. Lincoln	Mr. Powell	Mr. Hoge	Mr. Gloninger
Groscop	Piper	Redick	Brown
Gehr	Smith	J. Ross	Pickering
Sitgreaves	Snyder	M'Lene	Henderson
Mawhorter	Findley	Matthews	Gibson
Arndt	Todd	Potts	Beale
Rhoads	Addison	Shoemaker	Sellers
Graham			57

So it was determined in the negative.

On motion of Mr. M'Kean seconded by Mr. Lincoln, Ordered, that the journals of the committee of the whole be kept separate from those of the convention.

On motion of Mr. Ogden, seconded by Mr. Hand,

Resolved, that the secretary be impowered to employ a clerk.

Agreeably to the order of yesterday, the convention resolved itself into a committee of the whole. And after some time reported further progress and obtained leave to sit again,

Adjourned until ten o'clock to-morrow, A. M.

FRIDAY, December 4th, 1789. A. M.

The convention met pursuant to adjournment.

On motion of Mr. Thomas Ross, seconded by Mr. Gibbons, Resolved, that the printer to this convention, in the english language, be directed to strike two thousand copies of the minutes of the convention, and the like number of the minutes of the committee of the whole;—and that the printer in the german language be directed to strike one thousand copies of each of the minutes aforesaid.

On motion of Mr. Ogden, seconded by Mr. Hand, Resolved, that a committee be appointed to superintend the printing of the journals in the english language, and a committee to superintend the printing of the journals in the german.

Ordered that Mr. Hare, Mr. Smilie and Mr. Miller be a committee to superintend the printing of the journals in the english language; and Mr. Graff Mr. Gehr and Mr. Arndt be a committee to superintend the printing of the journals in the german language.

Agreeably to the order of yesterday, the convention resolved itself into a committee of the whole. And, after some time reported further progress and obtained leave to sit again.

Adjourned until ten o'clock to-morrow, A. M.

SATURDAY, December 5th, 1789. A. M.

The committee of the whole made further progress and obtained leave to sit again

Adjourned until three o'clock on Monday next, P. M.

MONDAY, December 7th, 1789. P. M.

The convention met pursuant to adjournment.

A motion was made by Mr. Gloninger, seconded by Mr. Brown, in the following words, viz.

Resolved, that it be recommended to the freemen of the county of

Dauphin, who are by the election laws of this commonwealth qualified to vote for members of the general assembly, to hold an election, at the same places and under the same rules and regulations prescribed by the said laws, on the first day of March next, for a member of this convention, to supply the vacancy occasioned by the death of Jacob Cook, Esquire.

Resolved, that it be recommended to the same officers and persons who conducted the last general election, to attend, conduct and regulate the election hereby recommended to be held for the purpose aforesaid, in like manner as is directed by the election laws of this state, and make return thereof to this convention; and in case of the death, absence or inability of any of the said officers or persons, that others be chosen or appointed in their stead, before the opening of the said election.

Resolved, that one hundred copies in the english, and seventy copies in the german language of the foregoing resolutions, be printed and distributed for the information of the citizens of the said county.

It was moved by Mr. M'Kean, seconded by Mr. Thomas Ross, to strike out the words "first day of March next," in the first of the foregoing resolutions, and in lieu thereof to insert "the seventeenth day of December," instant.

A motion was then made by Mr. Lewis, seconded by Mr. Brown, to postpone the consideration of the foregoing resolutions, together with the proposed amendment, until to-morrow.

On the question   Will the convention agree to the postponement?

It was carried in the affirmative.

Whereupon, agreeably to the order of the fifth of December, the convention resolved itself into a committee of the whole.

The president left the chair, and the chairman was placed therein.

After some time spent in the business before the committee, the chairman left the chair, and the president resumed it. The chairman then reported, that the committee had made further progress in the business committed to them, and requested leave to sit again to-morrow. Leave was accordingly granted.

A motion was made by Mr. Sitgreaves, seconded by Mr. Ogden, in the following words, viz.

A question of order, whether it shall arise in convention or committee of the whole, shall in the first instance, be determined from the chair—from which determination an appeal may be made, on the requisition of any one member, to the convention or committee of the whole; but on such appeal no argument shall be had.

Adjourned until ten o'clock to-morrow, A. M.

TUESDAY, December 8th, 1789. A. M.

The convention met pursuant to adjournmet.

And having resumed the consideration of the resolutions moved yesterday by Mr. Gloninger, seconded by Mr. Brown, together with the amendment proposed by Mr M'Kean and Mr. Thomas Ross, on the subject of holding an election for a member to represent the county of Dauphin in this convention, in the room of Jacob Cook, Esquire, deceased.

Mr. M'Kean withdrew his amendment and offered the following as a substitute, viz.

To strike out the words "first day of March next," and in lieu thereof to insert these words: " twenty-second day of December," instant.

Which was carried in the affirmative, and the resolutions, with the
amendment, adopted as follow, viz.

Resolved, that it be recommended to the freemen of the county of
Dauphin, who are by the election laws of this commonwealth qualified to vote for members of the general assembly, to hold an election,
at the same places and under the same rules and regulations prescribed by the said laws, on the twenty-second day of December, instant,
for a member of this convention to supply the vacancy occasioned by
the death of Jacob Cook, Esquire.

Resolved, that it be recommended to the same officers and persons
who conducted the last general election, to attend, conduct and regulate the election hereby recommended to be held for the purpose
aforesaid, in like manner as is directed by the election laws of this
state, and make return thereof to this convention ; and in case of the
death, absence or inability of any of the said officers or persons, that
others be chosen or appointed in their stead before the opening of the
said election.

Resolved, that one hundred copies in the english and seventy copies in the german language of the foregoing resolutions, be printed and
distributed for the information of the citizens of said county.

Mr. Sitgreaves called up his motion of yesterday, viz.

A question of order, whether it shall arise in convention or committee of the whole, shall, in the first instance, be determined from
the chair—from which determination an appeal may be made, on the
requisition of any one member, to the convention or committee of the
whole ; " but on such appeal no argument shall be had."

It was moved by Mr. Lewis, seconded by Mr. Smilie, to strike
out the words " but on such appeal no argument shall be had," and in
lieu thereof to insert these words : " but no debate shall be had without such appeal." Which was determined in the affirmative, and the
motion, as amended, was adopted, viz.

A question of order, whether it shall arise in convention or committee of the whole, shall, in the first instance, be determined from
the chair—from which determination an appeal may be made, on the
requisition of any one member, to the convention or committee of the
whole ; but no debate shall be had without such appeal.

A motion was made by Mr. Findley, seconded by Mr. Wilson, to
re consider the ninth rule for conducting the business of this convention, viz.

" The yeas and nays shall be called and entered on the minutes of
the house, or of the committee of the whole house, when any member requires it," for the purpose of amending the same, so as to read
as follows, viz.

The yeas and nays shall be called and entered on the minutes of
the house, " or of the committee of the whole house," if any member
shall require it before the house shall have been devided.

On the question, will the convention agree to the proposed amendment ?

It was determined in the affirmative.

It was then moved by Mr. Pickering, seconded by Mr. Smilie, to
strike out the words " or of the committee of the whole house," contained in the foregoing rule.

On the question. Shall those words be struck out.
The yeas and nays being called by Mr. Wilson, were as follow, viz.

YEAS.

Mr. Lewis	Mr. Lower	Mr. Findley	Mr. Coates
M'Kean	Lincoln	Hoge	Shoemaker
Gray	Groscop	Smilie	Gloninger
Robinson	Gehr	Gallatin	Brown
Edwards	Mawhorter	M'Lene	Pickering
Irvine	Powell	Matthews	Gibson
Power	Piper	Morris	Sellers
Hiester	Snyder	Potts	Graham 32

NAYS.

Mr. Wilson	Mr. Bull	Mr. Slegle	Mr. Rhoads
Roberts	T. Ross	Reed	Smith
Hare	Boyd	Tyson	Todd
Ogden	Coleman	Pedan	Addison
Jenks	Graff	Dill	Redick
Barclay	Hubley	Whitehill	J. Ross
Stout	Breckbill	Sitgreaves	Henderson
Gibbons	Miller	Arndt	Beale 32

And the votes appearing to be equal the president gave his casting vote in the negative.

Agreeably to the order of yesterday the convention resolved itself into a committee of the whole. And after some time reported further progress and obtained leave to sit again.

Adjourned until ten o'clock to-morrow, A. M.

WEDNESDAY, December 9th, 1789. *A. M.*

The convention met pursuant to adjournment.

Agreeably to the order of yesterday, the convention resolved itself into a committee of the whole.

The president quitted the chair, and the chairman was placed therein. The chairman after some time left the chair, and the president resumed it. The chairman then made the following report, viz.

I. That the legislative department of the constitution of this commonwealth requires alterations and amendments, so as to consist of more than one branch, and in such of the arrangements as may be necessary for the complete organization thereof.

II. That the executive department of the constitution of this commonwealth should be altered and amended, so as that the supreme executive power be vested in a single person, subject however to proper exceptions,

III. That the judicial department of the constitution of this commonwealth should be altered and amended, so as that the judges of the supreme court should hold their commissions during good behaviour, and be independent as to their salaries, subject however to such restrictions as may hereafter be thought proper.

IV. That the constitution of this commonwealth should be so ameded as that the supreme executive department should have a qualified negative upon the legislature.

V. That that part of the constitution of this commonwealth, called "A declaration of the rights of the inhabitants of the commonwealth or state of Pennsylvania," requires alterations and amendments, in such manner as that the rights of the people, reserved and excepted out of the general powers of government, may be more accurately defined and secured, and the same and such other alterations and amendments in the said constitution as may be agreed on, be made to correspond with each other.

Adjourned until ten o'clock to-morrow, A M.

THURSDAY, December 10th, 1789. A. M.

The convention met pursuant to adjournment.

The report of the committee of the whole read yesterday, was read the second time,

And on the question, Will the convention agree to the following resolution? viz.

"Resolved, that the legislative department of the constitution of this commonwealth requires alterations and amendments, so as to consist of more than one branch, and in such of the arrangements as may be necessary for the complete organization thereof."

The yeas and nays were called by Mr. Wilson, and were as follow, viz.

YEAS.

Mr. Wilson	Mr. T. Ross	Mr. Groscop	Mr. Gallatin
Baker	Boyd	Gehr	M'Lene
Roberts	Coleman	Sitgreaves	Matthews
Lewis	Graff	Mawhorter	Morris
M'Kean	Hubley	Arndt	Potts
Gray	Breckbill	Rhoads	Coates
Hare	Miller	Smith	Shoemaker
Edwards	Slegle	Snyder	Gloninger
Ogden	Reed	Findley	Brown
Jenks	Tyson	Addison	Pickering
Barclay	Pedan	Hoge	Henderson
Stout	Dill	Redick	Gibson
Gibbons	Irvine	J. Ross	Sellers
Bull	Lower	Smilie	Graham 56

NAYS.

Mr. Whitehill	Mr. Power	Mr. Piper	Mr. Beale
Lincoln			5

So it was determined in the affirmative.

And in debating the following resolution, viz.

Resolved, That the executive department of the constitution of this commonwealth should be altered and amended, so as that the supreme executive power be vested in a single person, subject however to proper exceptions.

On the question—Will the convention agree to the same?—The yeas and nays being called by Mr. Wilson, were as follow, viz.

YEAS.

Mr. Wilson	Mr. Boyd	Mr. Groscop	Mr. Smilie
Baker	Coleman	Gehr	Gallatin
Roberts	Graff	Sitgreaves	M'Lene
Lewis	Hubley	Mawhorter	Matthews
M'Kean	Breckbill	Arndt	Morris
Gray	Miller	Rhoads	Potts
Robinson	Slegle	Powell	Coates
Hare	Reed	Piper	Shoemaker
Edwards	Tyson	Smith	Gloninger
Ogden	Pedan	Snyder	Brown
Jenks	Dill	Findley	Pickering
Barclay	Whitehill	Todd	Henderson
Stout	Irvine	Addison	Gibson
Gibbons	Power	Hoge	Beale
Bull	Lower	Redick	Sellers
T. Ross	Lincoln	J. Ross	Graham 64

So it was unanimously determined in the affirmative.

And in debating the following resolution, viz.

Resolved, That the judicial department of the constitution of this commonwealth should be altered and amended, so as that the judges of the supreme court should hold their commissions during good behaviour and be independent as to their salaries, subject however to such restrictions as may hereafter be thought proper.

On the question—Will the convention adopt the resolution?—The yeas and nays were called by Mr. Sitgreaves, and were as follow, viz.

YEAS.

Mr. Wilson	Mr. Bull	Mr. Lower	Mr. Hoge
Baker	Coleman	Lincoln	J. Ross
Roberts	Graff	Groscop	Smilie
Lewis	Hubley	Gehr	Morris
M'Kean	Breckbill	Sitgreaves	Potts
Gray	Miller	Mawhorter	Coates
Robinson	Slegle	Arndt	Shoemaker
Hare	Reed	Rhoads	Gloninger
Edwards	Tyson	Powel	Brown
Ogden	Pedan	Smith	Pickering
Jenks	Dill	Snyder	Henderson
Barclay	Whitehill	Findley	Gibson
Stout	Irvine	Todd	Sellers
Gibbons	Power	Addison	Graham 56

NAYS.

Mr. T. Ross	Mr. Piper	Mr. Gallatin	Mr. Matthews
Boyd	Redick	M'Lene	Beale 8

So it was determined in the affirmative.

And in debating the following resolution, viz.

Resolved, That the constitution of this commonwealth should be so amended as that the supreme executive department should have a qualified negative on the legislature.

On the question—Will the convention adopt the resolution?—The yeas and nays were called by Mr. Wilson, and were as follow, viz.

YEAS.

Mr. Wilson	Mr. T. Ross	Mr. Groscop	Mr. Smilie
Baker	Boyd	Gehr	Gallatin
Roberts	Coleman	Sitgreaves	M'Lene
Lewis	Graff	Mawhorter	Matthews
M'Kean	Hubley	Arndt	Morris
Gray	Breckbill	Rhoads	Potts
Robinson	Miller	Powell	Coates
Hare	Slegle	Smith	Shoemaker
Edwards	Reed	Snyder	Gloninger
Ogden	Tyson	Findley	Brown
Jenks	Pedan	Todd	Pickering
Barclay	Dill	Addison	Henderson
Stout	Irvine	Hoge	Gibson
Gibbons	Lower	Redick	Sellers
Bull	Lincoln	J. Ross	Graham 60

NAYS.

Mr. Whitehill	Mr. Power	Mr. Piper	Mr. Beale 4

So it was determined in the affirmative.

And in debating the following resolution, viz.

Resolved, That that part of the constitution of this commonwealth, called *A declaration of the rights of the inhabitants of the commonwealth or state of Pennsylvania*, requires alterations and amendments, in such manner as that the rights of the people, reserved and excepted out of the general powers of government, may be more accurately defined and secured, and that the same and such other alterations and amendments in the said constitution as may be agreed on, be made to correspond with each other.

On the question, Will the convention adopt the resolution? The yeas and nays were called by Mr. Wilson, and were as follow, viz.

YEAS.

Mr. Wilson	Mr. Barclay	Mr. Slegle	Gehr
Baker	Stout	Reed	Sitgreaves
Roberts	Gibbons	Tyson	Mawhorter
Lewis	Bull	Pedan	Arndt
M'Kean	T. Ross	Dill	Rhoads
Gray	Boyd	Whitehill	Powell
Robinson	Coleman	Irvine	Piper
Hare	Graff	Power	Smith
Edwards	Hubley	Lower	Snyder
Ogden	Breckbill	Lincoln	Findley
Jenks	Miller	Groscop	Todd

YEAS.

Mr. Addison	Gallatin	Coates	Henderson
Hoge	M'Lene	Shoemaker	Gibson
Redick	Matthews	Gloninger	Beale
J. Ross	Morris	Brown	Sellers
Smilie	Potts	Pickering	Graham 64

And it was unanimously determined in the affirmative.

Whereupon, A motion was made by Mr. Lewis, seconded by Mr. Sitgreaves, viz.

Resolved, That a committee of nine members be chosen, by ballot, to take into consideration the constitution of this commonwealth, with such alterations and amendments as may be necessary therein ; and to report a draught of a proposed constitution, altered and amended as aforesaid, and that the resolutions reported by the committee of the whole, and adopted by the house, shall be instructions to the said committee so far as they extend.

It was then moved by Mr. Findley, seconded by Mr. Boyd, to postpone the consideration of the said resolution in order to introduce the following, viz.

Resolved that every freeman of the age of twenty-one years, having resided   years in the United States, or   years in this commonwealth, one of which at least in the county or district, next before the election where he claims his vote, and who hath been possessed, in freehold estate or other taxable property, to the value of   for the space of one whole year next before the election, and the sons of freeholders, qualified with respect to age and residence as is described above, shall have a right to vote for either branch of the legislature.

On the question, Will the convention agree to the postponement for the aforesaid purpose? The yeas and nays were called by Mr. Findley, and were as follow, viz.

YEAS.

Mr. Edwards	Mr. Gehr	Mr. Todd	Mr. Matthews
Gibbons	Mawhorter	Addison	Coates
T. Ross	Powell	Hoge	Shoemaker
Boyd	Piper	Redick	Gloninger
Whitehill	Smith	Smilie	Brown
Power	Snyder	Gallatin	Henderson
Lower	Findley	M'Lene	Beale
Lincoln			29

NAYS.

Mr. Wilson	Mr. Jenks	Mr. Slegle	Mr. Rhoads
Baker	Barclay	Reed	J. Ross
Roberts	Stout	Tyson	Morris
Lewis	Bull	Pedan	Potts
M'Kean	Coleman	Dill	Pickering
Gray	Graff	Groscop	Gibson
Robinson	Hubley	Sitgreaves	Sellers
Hare	Breckbill	Arndt	Graham
Ogden	Miller		34

So it was determined in the negative,

And the original resolution, made by Mr. Lewis, seconded by Mr. Sitgreaves, adopted.

Whereupon, On motion of Mr. Smilie, seconded by Mr. M'Kean, Ordered, That to-morrow be assigned for the election of a committee for the purposes contained in the said resolution, and that it be the order for that day.

Adjourned until ten o'clock to-morrow, A. M.

FRIDAY, December 11, 1789. *A. M.*

The convention met pursuant to adjournment.

Agreeably to the order of yesterday, the convention proceeded to the election of a committee " To take into consideration the constitution of this commonwealth, with such alterations and amendments as may be necessary therein, and to report a draught of a proposed constitution, altered and amended as aforesaid, &c. and that the resolutions reported by the committee of the whole, and adopted by the house, shall be instructions to the said committee so far as they extend," and the ballots being taken, it appeared that Mr. Findley, Mr. Hand, Mr. Miller, Mr. Wilson, Mr. Irvine, Mr. Lewis, Mr. James Ross, Mr. Smith and Mr. Addison, were duly elected.

Whereupon, On motion of Mr. Whitehill, seconded by Mr. Findley,

Adjourned until Tuesday next, three o'clock, P. M.

TUESDAY, December 15, 1789. *P. M.*

The convention met pursuant to adjournment.

The committee elected on the 11th instant, not being prepared to report, On motion,

Adjourned until Friday next, three o'clock, P. M.

FRIDAY, December 18, 1789. *P. M.*

The convention met pursuant to adjournment.

A letter from Samuel Sitgreaves, Esq. was read in excuse for his non-attendance. Ordered to lie on the table.

The chairman of the committee, appointed on the 11th of December, inst. to take into consideration the constitution of this commonwealth, &c. and report a draught of a proposed constitution, informed the convention, that they were not ready to report, and requested that the committee might be instructed to order a certain number of copies of their report, when complete, to be printed for the information of the members. Whereupon,

On motion of Mr. M'Lene, seconded by Mr. Irvine,

Resolved, That the said committee be instructed to have one hundred and thirty-eight copies of their report printed for the use of the members.

Adjourned until three o'clock on Monday next, P. M.

MONDAY, *December* 21, 1789. *P. M.*

The convention met pursuant to adjournment.

The committee appointed on the 11th of December, instant, to take into consideration the constitution of this commonwealth, &c. and report a draught of a proposed constitution, made report, in part, as follows, viz.

We, the people of the commonwealth of Pennsylvania, ordain and establish this constitution for its government.

ARTICLE I.

Section I. The legislative power of this commonwealth shall be vested in a general assembly, which shall consist of a Senate and House of Representatives.

II. The representatives shall be chosen annually by the citizens of the city of Philadelphia, and of each county in the state respectively, on the   Tuesday of October.

III. No person shall be a representative, who shall not, at the time of his election, have been, the three years next preceding, an inhabitant of the state, and one year next preceding an inhabitant of the city or county in which he shall be chosen.

IV. The representatives from the city of Philadelphia and the several counties shall be in proportion to the number of taxable inhabitants; provided that the number of representatives shall never be fewer than sixty nor more than one hundred: But each county shall have at least one representative. An enumeration of the taxable inhabitants shall be made within three years after the first meeting of the general assembly, and within every subsequent term of ten years, in such manner as they shall, by law, direct. Until such enumeration shall be made, the city of Philadelphia and the several counties of the state, shall be respectively entitled to choose the same number of representatives as is now prescribed by law.

V. The senate shall consist of not fewer than sixteen, nor more than thirty two members, chosen in districts, in proportion to the number of taxable inhabitants in each district.

VI. The city of Philadelphia and the several counties of this state, shall be formed into districts, containing each, as nearly as may be, such a number of taxable inhabitants as shall be entitled to elect one senator; but where that cannot be done, then such a number of adjoining counties shall be formed into one district, as shall be entitled to elect not more than three senators.

VII The citizens of the city of Philadelphia and of the several counties in this state, qualified to elect representatives, when assembled for that purpose, shall, if occasion require, at the same time, at the same places, and in the same manner, for every representative, elect two persons resident within their city or county respectively, as electors of the senator or senators of their district.

VIII. Within   days after their election, the electors of each district shall meet together at some convenient place within the district, and elect the senator or senators for their district.

IX. The senators shall be chosen for four years. But immediately after they shall be assembled in consequence of the first election, they shall be divided, as equally as may be, into four classes. The seats of the senators of the first class shall be vacated at the expiration of the first year; of the second class, at the expiration of the second year; of the third class, at the expiration of the third year; and of the fourth class, at the expiration of the fourth year: So that one-fourth may be chosen every year.

X. No person shall be elected a senator, who shall not have resided four years next before his election in the state, the last year whereof shall have been in the district for which he is chosen. No man shall be a senator who shall not have attained to the age of thirty years. And no elector shall be chosen a senator.

XI. No person shall be chosen an elector, who shall not have resided in the district three years next before his election. And no person shall be chosen an elector who is a member of the legislature, or who holds any office in the appointment of the executive department.

XII. Until the enumeration before mentioned shall be made, the number of senators shall be sixteen.

XIII. The general assembly shall meet at least once in every year; and such meeting shall be on the   Tuesday of November.

XIV. Each house shall choose its speaker and other officers; and the senate shall also choose a speaker *pro tempore,* when the speaker shall exercise the office of governor.

XV. Each house shall be the judge of elections, returns and qualifications of its own members; and a majority of each house shall constitute a quorum to do business; but a smaller number may adjourn from day to day, and may be authorised to compel the attendance of absent members, in such manner, and under such penalties as the house may provide.

XVI. Each house may determine the rules of its proceedings, punish its members for disorderly behaviour, and, with the concurrence of two-thirds, expel a member: And shall have all other powers necessary for either branch of a free legislature.

XVII. Each house shall keep a journal of its proceedings, and, from time to time, publish them, excepting such parts as may, in their judgment, require secrecy: And the yeas and nays of the members of either house, on any question, shall, at the desire of   , be entered on the journal.

XVIII. The doors of each house shall be open, unless when the business shall be such as, in their judgment, ought to be kept secret.

XIX Neither house shall, without the consent of the other, adjourn for more than three days, nor to any other place than that in which the two houses shall be sitting.

XX. The senators and representatives shall receive a compensation for their services, to be ascertained by law, and paid out of the treasury of the commonwealth. They shall, in all cases except treason, felony and breach of the peace, be privileged from arrest, during their attendance at the session of the respective houses, and in going to and returning from the same; and for any speech or debate in either house they shall not be questioned in any other place.

XXI. No senator or representative shall, during the time for which he was elected, be appointed to any civil office, under the authority of this commonwealth, which shall have been created, or the emoluments of which shall have been increased during such time: And no person holding any office, except in the militia, under this commonwealth or the United States, shall be a member of either house during his continuance in office.

XXII. When vacancies happen in either house, the speaker of that house shall issue writs of election to fill such vacancies.

XXIII. All bills for raising revenue shall originate in the house of representatives; but the senate may propose or concur with amendments, as in other bills.

XXIV. No money shall be drawn from the treasury, but in consequence of appropriations made by law.

XXV. Every bill which shall have passed the house of representatives and the senate, shall, before it become a law, be presented to the governor. If he approve, he shall sign it; but if he shall not approve it, he shall return it, with his objections, to that house in which it shall have originated, who shall enter the objections at large upon their journal, and proceed to re-consider it. If after such re-consideration, three-fifths of that house shall agree to pass the bill, it shall be sent together with the objections, to the other house, by which it shall likewise be re-considered, and if approved by three-fifths of that house, it shall become a law. But in all such cases, the votes of both houses shall be determined by yeas and nays, and the names of the persons voting for or against the bill shall be entered upon the journals of each house respectively. If any bill shall not be returned by the governor within ten days (Sundays excepted) after it shall be presented to him, the same shall be a law in like manner as if he had signed it, unless the general assembly, by their adjournment, prevent its return, in which case it shall not be a law.

XXVI. Every order, resolution or vote, to which the concurrence of the senate and house of representatives may be necessary (except on a question of adjournment) shall be presented to the governor, and before the same shall take effect, be approved by him; or, being disapproved by him, shall be re-passed by three-fifths of the senate and house of representatives, according to the rules and limitations prescribed in case of a bill.

ARTICLE II.

Section I. The supreme executive power of this commonwealth shall be vested in a governor.

II. He shall hold his office during the term of three years; and shall be chosen on the   Tuesday of October, in every third year, by the citizens throughout the commonwealth, at the places where they shall respectively vote for representatives.

III. He shall not be capable of holding his office longer than nine years successively; nor shall he be capable of being elected again till three years after the nine successive years shall have been expired.

IV. He must be, at least, thirty years of age; and he must have been an inhabitant of this state during seven years before his election.

V. No person shall be capable of exercising the office of governor who, at the same time, shall hold any other office under this state, or any office under the United States.

VI. The governor shall, at stated times, receive, for his services a compensation, which shall neither be increased or diminished during the period for which he shall have been elected.

VII. He shall be commander in chief of the army and navy of this commonwealth and of the militia, except when they shall be called into the actual service of the United States.

VIII. He shall appoint the chancellor, judges, prothonotaries, clerks, and all other officers of this commonwealth, whose offices are established by this constitution or shall be established by law, and whose appointments are not herein otherwise provided for; but no person shall be appointed to an office within any county who shall not have resided therein one year next before his appointment.

IX. The governor shall commission all the officers of this commonwealth.

X. He may require the opinion, in writing, of the officers in each of the executive departments upon any subject relating to the duties of their respective offices.

XI. He shall from time to time. give to the general assembly information of the state of the commonwealth, and recommend to their consideration such measures as he shall judge necessary or expedient.

XII. He may. on extraordinary occasions, convene both houses; and in case of disagreement between them with respect to the time of adjournment, he may adjourn them to such time as he shall think proper.

XIII. He shall take care that the laws be faithfully executed. .

XIV. In case of the removal of the governor from office, or of his death or resignation, it shall devolve on the speaker of the senate until the next annual election of representatives, when another governor shall be chosen in the manner hereinbefore mentioned.

XV. The state treasurer shall be appointed in the manner prescribed by the twenty-sixth section of the first article of this constitution: All subordinate officers in the treasury department, election officers, officers relating to the poor and highways, constables and other township officers shall be appointed in such manner as shall be directed by law. .

ARTICLE III.

Section I. In elections by the citizens every freeman of the age of twenty-one years, having resided in the state two years next before the days of the elections respectively, and paid taxes within that time, shall enjoy the rights of an elector. The sons of freeholders, of the age aforesaid, shall be entitled to vote, though they have not paid taxes. :

II. All elections shall be by ballot, except those by persons in their representative or public capacities, which shall be *viva voce*.

III. If elections are not properly attended; attendance on them shall be enforced by law. .

ARTICLE IV.

Section I. The house of representatives shall have the sole power of impeachment.

II. All impeachments shall be tried before the Senate; and the chancellor of the commonwealth shall preside therein. When sitting for that purpose, the senate shall be on oath or affirmation: No person shall be convicted without the concurrence of two-thirds of the members present.

III. Judgment in cases of impeachment shall not extend further than to removal from office, and disqualification to hold any office of honor, trust or profit under this commonwealth; but the party convicted shall nevertheless be liable to indictment, trial, judgment and punishment according to law.

ARTICLE V.

Section I. The judicial power of this commonwealth shall be vested in a high court of chancery and a supreme court, the jurisdiction of each of which shall extend over the state; in the courts of chancery and of oyer and terminer and general jail delivery, hereinafter mentioned; in a court of common pleas, orphans' court, register's court and court of quarter sessions for each county; and in such other courts as the legislature may, from time to time establish. But no special commission of oyer and terminer or jail delivery shall be issued.

II. The chancellor of the commonwealth, the judges of the supreme court, and the judges of the several courts of common pleas shall be commissioned and hold their offices during good behaviour; and shall, at stated times, receive for their services, a compensation, which shall not be diminished during their continuance in office: But the governor may remove any of them on the address of two-thirds of each branch of the legislature.

III. The chancellor, in addition to the other powers and duties of his office, shall cause to be tried, by a jury, such material facts as either party shall require to be so tried; provided a specification of the facts be made in writing.

IV. The supreme court and the several courts of common pleas shall, besides the powers usually exercised by such courts, have the powers of a court of chancery, so far as relates to the obtaining of evidence from places without the state.

V. Until it shall be otherwise directed by the legislature, the several courts of common pleas shall be established in the following manner: The state shall, by law, be divided into circuits, any of which shall include not more than   nor fewer than   counties: A president shall be appointed for the several courts in each circuit, who, during his continuance in office, shall reside within such circuit; and one judge shall be appointed from every county within such circuit, who, during his continuance in office, shall reside within such county: Such president and judges, or any three of them, shall be the judges who shall compose the several courts of common pleas.

VI. The judges of the courts of common pleas respectively, during their continuance in office, shall, the president being one of them, be justices of oyer and terminer and general jail delivery, for the trial of capital and other offenders, for each of the counties within the said circuits respectively: But they shall not hold a court of oyer and terminer and general jail delivery in any county when the judges of the supreme court, or some of them shall be sitting in the same county.

VII. The judges of the courts of common pleas respectively, shall during their continuance in office, be justices of the courts of quarter sessions for each of the counties within the said circuits respectively: And they shall, when sitting in a county, compose the orphans' court and register's court for that county: But the judge, who shall reside therein, and the register of wills may, at all other times, hold such courts, subject to the revision and decrees of the orphans' court upon appeal or otherwise.

VIII. The judges of the courts of common pleas shall have the like powers with the judges of the supreme court to issue writs of certiorari to the justices of the peace within the several counties respectively, and to cause their proceedings to be brought before them, and the like right and justice to be done.

IX. The judges of the courts of common pleas shall be conservators of the peace within the several counties of the circuits, in which they shall be empowered to hold courts.

X. A court of chancery shall be establishd within each of the said circuits, except that in which the high court of chancery shall be steadily held, and the president of the said courts of common pleas respectively, shall hold the same, and be stiled the chancellor of such circuit: He shall possess and exercise therein the like powers with the chancellor of the commonwealth, except the power of granting injunctions to stay the proceedings or suspend the judgments of any common law courts: The mode of proceeding shall be the same as shall be used in the high court of chancery. From any interlocutory or final decree in the chancery of any circuit, there shall be an appeal to the chancellor of the commonwealth.

XI. A competent number of justices of the peace for each county, shall from time to time, be ascertained by law; and the citizens of each county respectively, shall at the general election, choose double that number, or of the vacancies that may happen, and return their names to the governor, who shall appoint and commission, for   years, if so long they behave themselves well, half the number so elected and returned: But this mode of appointment may be altered as the legislature shall by law direct.

XII. A register's office for the probate of wills and granting letters of administration, and an office for the recording of deeds shall be kept in each county.

XIII. Prothonotaries, clerks of the peace and orphans' courts, recorders of deeds, registers of wills and sheriffs shall keep their offices in the county town of the county in which they respectively shall be officers. And circuit officers shall keep their offices in some county town within their circuits respectively.

XIV. The stile of all process shall be *The commonwealth of Pennsylvania:* All prosecutions shall be carried on in the name and by the authority of the commonwealth of Pennsylvania, and shall conclude, *Against the peace and dignity of the same.*

ARTICLE VI.

Section I. Sheriffs and coroners shall, at the places of the election of representatives, be chosen for three years, by the citizens of each county respectively; two persons shall be chosen for each office, one of whom for each shall be commissioned by the governor; no person shall continue in the office of sheriff more than three years successively.

II. The freemen of this commonwealth shall be armed and disciplined for its defence; the militia officers shall be appointed in such manner, and for such time as shall be by law directed.

ARTICLE VII.

All debts contracted and engagements entered into, before the establishment of this constitution, shall be as valid against the commonwealth, under this constitution, as they have been heretofore.

ARTICLE VIII.

Section I. A school or schools shall be established in each county for the instruction of youth, and the state shall pay to the masters such salaries as shall enable them to teach at low prices.

II. The arts, sciences and all useful learning shall be promoted in one or more universities.

III. Religious societies and corporate bodies shall be protected in their rights, immunities and estates.

Ordered to lie on the table.

Whereupon, on motion of Mr. Findley, seconded by Mr. James Ross, Ordered, That Wednesday next be assigned for the second reading of the said report, and that it be the order of that day.

Adjourned until Wednesday next, at ten o'clock, A. M.

WEDNESDAY, December 23, 1789. A. M.

The convention met pursuant to adjournment.

The committee appointed the eleventh of December, made a further report, which was read as follows, viz.

ARTICLE IX.

That the great and essential principles of liberty and free government may be recognised and unalterably established, **WE DECLARE,**

I. That all men are born equally free and independent, and have certain inherent and indefeasible rights, among which are those of enjoying and defending life and liberty, of acquiring, possessing and protecting property and reputation, and of pursuing their own happiness.

II. That all power being originally vested in is derived from the people, and all free governments originate from their will, are founded on their authority, and instituted for their common peace, safety and happiness; and for the advancement thereof, they have at all times, an unalienable and indefeasible right to alter, reform or abolish their government, in such manner as they may think proper.

III. That all men have a natural and indefeasible right to worship Almighty God according to the dictates of their own consciences, and that no man ought, or of right can be compelled to attend any religious worship, or to erect or support any place of worship, or to maintain any ministry against his free will and consent; and that no human authority can controul or interfere with the rights of conscience in any case whatever; nor shall any preference ever be given, by law, to any religious establishments or modes of worship.

IV. That no person who acknowledges the being of a God and a future state of rewards and punishments, shall, on account of his reli-

21

gious sentiments, be disqualified to hold any office or place of trust or profit under this commonwealth.

V. That elections shall be free and equal.

VI. That trial by jury shall be as heretofore, and the right thereof shall remain inviolate.

VII. That the printing presses shall be free'to every person who undertakes to examine the proceedings of the legislature or any branch of government, and no law shall ever be made restraining the right thereof. The free communication of thoughts and opinions is one of the most invaluable rights of man, and every citizen may freely speak, write and print, being responsible for the abuse of that liberty.

VIII. That the people shall be secure in their persons, houses, papers and possessions against unreasonable searches and seizures, and no warrant shall issue to search any place, or to seize any person or things, but on probable cause, supported by oath or affirmation, and describing them as nearly as may be.

IX. That in all criminal prosecutions the accused hath a right to be heard by himself and his counsel; to demand the cause and nature of the accusation; to meet the witnesses face to face; to have cumpulsory process for obtaining witnesses in his favor, and a speedy public trial by an impartial jury of the vicinage; nor can he be compelled to give evidence against himself; nor can any man be deprived of his life, liberty or property but by the judgment of his peers or the law of the land.

X. That no persons shall be proceeded against by information for any indictable offence, except in cases arising in the land or naval forces, or in the militia when in actual service in time of war or public danger; nor shall any person, for the same offence, be twice put in jeopardy of life or limb; nor shall any man's property be taken, or applied to public use, without the consent of his representatives, and on just compensation beii.g made.

XI. That all courts shall be open, and every freeman for an injury done him in his lands, goods, person or reputation, shall have remedy by the due course of the law, and right and justice administered to him without sale, denial or delay.

XII. That no power of suspending laws, or the execution thereof, shall be exercised, unless by the legislature or by the authority thereof.

XIII. That excessive bail shall not be required, nor excessive fines imposed, or cruel punishments inflicted.

XIV. That all prisoners shall be bailable by sufficient sureties, unless for capital offences, when the proof is evident or presumption great, and the privilege of the writ of habeas corpus shall not be suspended unless when, in cases of rebellion or invasion, the public safety may require it.

XV. That the person of a debtor, where there is not a strong presumption of fraud, shall not be continued in prison after delivering up all his estate for the benefit of his creditors, in such manner as shall be prescribed by law.

XVI. That no expost facto law, or law impairing contracts shall be made.

XVII. That no person shall be attainted of treason or felony by the legislature.

XVIII. That no attainder shall work corruption of blood or forfeiture of real estate, except during the life of the offender.

XIX. That the right of the citizens to bear arms in defence of themselves and the state, and to assemble peaceably together, and apply in a decent manner, to those invested with the powers of government, for redress of grievances or other proper purposes, shall not be questioned.

XX. That those who conscientiously scruple to bear arms shall not be compelled to do so, but shall pay an equivalent for personal service.

XXI. That no standing army shall, in time of peace, be kept up without the consent of the legislature, and the military shall, in all cases and at all times, be kept in strict subordination to the civil power.

XXII. That no soldier shall, in time of peace, be quartered in any house without the consent of the owner, nor in time of war, but in a manner to be prescribed by law.

XXIII. That the legislature shall, at no time, create any office the appointment to which shall be for a longer term than during good behaviour.

XXIV. That emigration from the state shall not be prohibited.

XXV. To guard against transgressions of the high powers which we have delegated, WE DECLARE, That every thing in this article expressed, is excepted out of the general powers of legislation, and shall for ever remain inviolate.

And on motion, and by special order, the same was read the second time, whereupon, on motion of Mr. Addison, seconded by Mr. Hare,

Resolved, That the convention resolve itself into a committee of the whole, to take into consideration the report of the said committee.

Whereupon the president left the chair, and Mr. M'Kean was placed therein.

After some time spent in the business referred to them, the chairman left the chair, and the president resumed it.

The chairman then reported, that the committee of the whole had made progress in the business referred to them, and requested leave to sit again to-morrow. Leave was accordingly granted.

Adjourned until ten o'clock, to-morrow, A. M.

On Thursday, December the 24th, Saturday the 26th, Monday the 28th, Tuesday the 29th, and on Wednesday the 30th, the convention in committee of the whole reported further progress in the business referred to them on the 23d.

THURSDAY, December 31, 1789. A. M.

The convention met pursuant to adjournment.

A return of an election held within the county of Dauphin, of a member to represent the said county in this convention, in the room of Jacob Cook, Esq. deceased, was presented to the chair and read, by which it appeared that Alexander Graydon, Esq. was duly elected, who appearing in the house was admitted to take his seat.

A letter from Jonas Phillips, in behalf of himself and others, Israelites, was read, and ordered to lie on the table.

Agreeably to the order of the day the convention resolved itself into a committee of the whole. And after some time the committee reported further progress and obtained leave to sit again.

Adjourned until ten o'clock to-morrow, A. M.

FRIDAY, January 1, 1790, *A. M.*

The convention met pursuant to adjournment.

A letter was presented to the chair from John Breckbill, Esq. a member of this convention for the county of Lancaster, in excuse for his non-attendance. Ordered to lie on the table.

Agreeably to the order of the day the convention resolved itself into a committee of the whole; and after some time the committee reported further progress and obtained leave to sit again.

Adjourned until ten o'clock to-morrow, A. M.

On Saturday, January 2d, 1790, Monday, January 4th, Tuesday, January 5th, Wednesday, January 6th, Thursday, January 7th, Friday, January 8th,* Saturday January 9th, Monday, January 11th, Tuesday, January 12th, Wednesday, January 13th, Thursday, January 14th, Friday, January 15th, Saturday, January 16th, Monday, January 18th, Tuesday, January 19th,† Wednesday, January 20th, Thursday, January 21st, and Friday, January 22d, the convention in committee of the whole, made further progress in the business referred to them on the 23d December.

SATURDAY, January 23, 1790. *A. M.*

The convention met pursuant to adjournment.

On motion of Mr. Findley, seconded by Mr. M'Kean,

Resolved, That a committeee be appointed to prepare a schedule for putting the government into operation.

Ordered that Mr. Wilson, Mr. Lewis, Mr. Hand, Mr. Findley and Mr. James Ross, be a committee for the purpose contained in the foregoing resolution.

Agreeably to the order of the day, the convention resolved itself into a committee of the whole, and after some time the committee reported further progress and obtained leave to sit again.

Adjourned until three o'clock on Monday next, P. M.

MONDAY, January 25, 1790, *P. M.*

The convention met pursuant to adjournment.

Agreeably to the order of the day the convention resolved itself into a committee of the whole, and after some time the committee reported further progress, and obtained leave to sit again.

On motion of Mr. Sellers, ordered, that Mr. Roberts, Mr. Gray, Mr. Gibbons, Mr. Thomas Ross and Mr. Sellers, be a committee to attend the funeral of Henry Hale Graham, Esq. deceased, late a member of this convention for the county of Delaware, to-morrow morning at eleven o'clock.

Adjourned until ten o'clock to-morrow, A. M.

---

* On the 8th, Mr. Wilson obtained leave of absence until Tuesday next.

† On the 19th, a letter from William Irvine, Esq. a member of the convention from the county of Cumberland, was read, in excuse for his non-attendance.

TUESDAY, January 26, 1790. A. M.

The convention met pursuant to adjournment.

Mr. M'Kean, chairman of the committee of the whole, informed the convention that business of a public nature would necessarily oblige him to be absent for a few days, and requested leave of absence; which was accordingly granted.

Agreeably to the order of the day the convention resolved itself into a committee of the whole; the president left the chair, and Mr. Hand was placed therein as chairman *pro tempore.*

After some time spent in the business referred to them, the president resumed the chair; the chairman then reported, that the committee had made further progress in the business referred to them, and requested leave to sit again to-morrow. Leave was accordingly granted.

Adjourned until ten o'clock to-morrow, A. M.

WEDNESDAY, January 27, 1790, A. M.

The convention met pursuant to adjournment.

Mr. Wilson informed the convention that business of a public nature would require his attendance at New York, and requested leave of absence; which was accordingly granted.

On motion, ordered, that Mr. Sitgreaves be added to the committee appointed on the 23d of January, instant, to prepare a schedule for putting the government into operation, in the room of Mr. Wilson.

Mr. Roberts of the committee appointed to attend the funeral of Henry Hale Graham, Esquire, reported, that they had performed that service.

Agreeably to the order of the day the convention resolved itself into a committee of the whole. And after some time the reported further progress, and obtained leave to sit again.

A motion was made by Mr. Sellers, seconded by Mr. Bull, and adopted as follows, viz.

Resolved, That it be recommended to the freemen of the county of Delaware, who are by the election laws of this commonwealth qualified to vote for members of the general assembly, to hold an election at the same places and under the same rules and regulations prescribed by the said laws, on Wednesday the third day of February next, for a member of this convention to supply the vacancy occasioned by the death of Henry Hale Graham, Esquire.

Resolved, that it be recommended to the same officers and persons who conducted the last general election, to attend, conduct and regulate the election hereby recommended to be held for the purpose aforesaid, in like manner as is directed by the election laws of this state, and make return thereof to this convention; and in case of the death, absence or inability of any of the said officers or persons, that others be chosen or appointed in their stead, before the opening of the said election.

Resolved, that one hundred copies of the foregoing resolutions be printed and distributed for the information of the citizens of the said county.

Adjourned until ten o'clock to-morrow, A. M.

The convention met pursuant to adjournment.

Mr. Hubley, a member of this convention for the county of Lancaster, asked leave of absence, which was accordingly granted,

Agreeably to the order of the day the convention resolved itself into a committee of the whole. And after some time the committee reported further progress, and obtained leave to sit again.

Ajourned until ten o'clock to-morrow, A. M.

The convention met pursuant to adjournment.

Mr. M'Kean, chairman of the committee of the whole, informed the house that the state of his health rendered it inconvenient for him to resume the chair.

Agreeably to the order of the day the convention resolved itself into a committee of the whole.

The president left the chair, and Mr. Hand was placed therein as chairman of the committee of the whole.

After some time spent in the business referred to them, the president resumed the chair.

The chairman then reported, that the committee had made further progress in the business referred to them, and requested leave to sit again to morrow. Leave was accordingly granted.

Adjourned until ten o'clock to-morrow. A. M.

On Saturday, January 30th, 1790, Monday, February 1st, Tuesday, February 2d, Wednesday, February 3d, and Thursday, February 4th, Convention, in the committee of the whole, made further progress in the business referred to them on the 23d December.

The convention met pursuant to adjournment.

Agreeably to the order of the day the convention resolved itself into a committee of the whole.

The president left the chair, and the chairman was placed therein.

After some time spent in the business referred to them, the president resumed the chair.

The chairman then reported, that the committee of the whole, to whom was referred the report of the committee of nine, had agreed to the following plan of government, which was presented to the chair and read, viz.

We, the people of Pennsylvania, having by our representatives, freely chosen and in convention met, altered and amended the constitution of this commonwealth, do ordain and establish as follows :—

ARTICLE I.

Section I. The legislative power of this commonwealth shall be vested in a general assembly, which shall consist of a senate and house of representatives.

Section II. The representatives shall be chosen annually by the citizens of the city of Philadelphia, and of each county respectively, on the second Tuesday of October.

Section III. No person shall be a representative who shall not have attained the age of twenty-one years, and have been, the three years next preceding his election, a citizen and inhabitant of the state, and the last year thereof an inhabitant of the city or county in which he shall be chosen.

Section IV. The number of representatives shall, at the several periods of making the enumeration in this section mentioned, be fixed by the legislature, and apportioned between the city of Philadelphia and the several counties, according to the number of taxable inhabitants in each, and shall never be less than sixty, nor more than one hundred; and that it shall be increased at the time of making each enumeration, except the first, in the same proportion which the increase of the number of taxables shall bear to the then number of representatives, until the same shall amount to one hundred. But each county shall have, at least, one representative; provided that no new county shall be entitled to a separate representation, until a sufficient number of taxable inhabitants shall be contained within the limits thereof, to entitle them to at least one representative, agreeably to the ratio which shall then be established for the city of Philadelphia and the several counties; an enumeration of the taxable inhabitants shall be made within three years after the first meeting of the general assembly and within every subsequent term of seven years, in such manner, as shall be, by law, directed. Until such enumeration shall be made, the city of Philadelphia and the several counties shall be respectively entitled to choose the same number of representatives as is now prescribed by law.

Section V. The senators shall be choosen for four years by the citizens of the city of Philadelphia and of each county respectively, at the same time, in the same manner and at the same places where they shall respectively vote for representatives.

Section VI. The number of senators shall, at the several periods of making the enumeration mentioned in the fourth section, be fixed by the legislature, and apportioned between the districts formed as hereinafter mentioned, according to the number of taxable inhabitants in each, and shall never be less than one-fourth, nor more than one-third of the number of representatives.

Section VII. The senators shall be chosen in districts, to be formed by the legislature, containing each, as nearly as may be, such a number of taxable inhabitants as shall be entitled to elect one senator; but where that cannot be done, then such number of adjoining counties shall be formed into one district as shall be entitled to elect not more than four senators: provided that neither the city of Philadelphia, nor any county, shall be divided in forming a district.

Section VIII. No person shall be a senator who shall not have attained to the age of twenty-five years, and who shall not have been a citizen and inhabitant of the state four years next before his election; the last year whereof shall have been in the district for which he shall be chosen.

Section IX. Immediately after the senators shall be assembled in consequence of the first election, they shall be divided, by lot, as equally as may be, into four classes. The seats of the senators of the first class, shall be vacated at the expiration of the first year; of the second class, at the expiration of the second year; of the third class, at the expiration of the third year; and of the fourth class, at the expiration of the fourth year; so that one-fourth may be chosen every year,

Section X. The general assembly shall meet at least once in every year; and such meeting shall be on the first Tuesday of December.

Section XI. Each house shall choose its speaker and other officers; and the senators shall also choose a speaker *pro tempore*, when the speaker shall exercise the office of governor.

Section XII. Each house shall be the judge of the qualifications of its own members; but in case of contested elections the same shall be judged of, and determined by a committee, to be selected from the house in such manner as shall be, by law, directed: and a majority of each house shall constitute a quorum to do business; but a smaller number may adjourn from day to day, and may be authorised to compel the attendance of absent members in such manner, and under such penalties, as the house may provide.

Section XIII. Each house may determine the rules of its proceedings, punish its members for disorderly behaviour, and, with the concurrence of two-thirds, expel a member, but not a second time for the same cause, and shall have all other powers necessary for either branch of the legislature of a free state.

Section XIV. Each house shall keep a journal of its proceedings, and publish them weekly, excepting such parts as may, in their judgment, require secrecy: and the yeas and nays of the members of either house, on any question, shall, at the desire of any two of them, be entered on the journals.

Section XV. The doors of each house shall be open, unless when the business shall be such as, in their judgment, ought to be kept secret.

Section XVI. Neither house shall, without the consent of the other, adjourn for more than three days, nor to any other place than that in which the two houses shall be sitting.

Section XVII. The senators and representatives shall receive a compensation for their services, to be ascertained by law, and paid out of the treasury of the commonwealth. They shall, in all cases, except treason, felony and breach of the peace, be privileged from arrest, during their attendance at the session of the respective houses, and in going to and returning from the same; and for any speech or debate in either house, they shall not be questioned in any other place.

Section XVIII. No senator or representative shall, during the time for which he was elected, be appointed to any civil office, under the authority of this commonwealth, which shall have been created, or the emoluments of which shall have been increased during such time: and no member of congress, or other person, holding any office, except in the militia, under this commonwealth or the United States, shall be a member of either house during his continuance in congress or in office.

Section XIX. When vacancies happen in either house the speaker of that house shall issue writs of election to fill such vacancies.

Section XX. All bills for raising revenue shall originate in the house of representatives; but the senate may propose or concur with amendments, as in other bills.

Section XXI. No money shall be drawn from the treasury, but in consequence of appropriations made by law.

Section XXII. Every bill, which shall have passed the house of representatives and the senate, shall, before it become a law, be presented to the governor. If he approve, he shall sign it, but if he shall not approve it he shall return it with his objections, to that house in which it shall have originated, who shall enter the objections at large upon their journals, and proceed to re-consider it. If, after such re-consideration, two-thirds of that house shall agree to pass the bill, it shall be sent, together with the objections, to the other house, by which it shall likewise be re-considered, and if approved by two-thirds of that house it shall become a law But in all such cases, the votes of both houses shall be determined by yeas and nays, and the names of the persons voting for or against the bill shall be entered on the journals of each house respectively. If any bill shall not be returned by the governor within ten days (Sundays excepted) after it shall be presented to him, the same shall be a law in like manner as if he had signed it, unless the general assembly, by their adjournment, prevent its return, in which case it shall be a law, unless sent back within three days after their next meeting

Section XXIII. Every order, resolution or vote, to which the concurrence of the senate and house of representatives may be necessary (except on a question of adjournment) shall be presented to the governor, and before the same shall take effect, be approved by him; or, being disapproved by him, shall be re-passed by two-thirds of the senate and house of representatives, according to the rules and limitations prescribed in case of a bill.

ARTICLE II.

Section I. The supreme executive power of this commonwealth shall be vested in a governor.

Section II. The governor shall be chosen on the second Tuesday of October, by the citizens throughout the commonwealth, at the places where they shall respectively vote for representatives. The returns of every election for governor shall be transmitted to the seat of government, directed to the speaker of the senate, who shall open and publish the same in the presence of both houses of the legislature. The person having the highest number of votes shall be governor; but if it should so happen that any two or more should be equal and highest in votes, the general assembly shall choose one of them for governor by the joint vote of both houses. In case of contested elections, the same shall be judged of and determined by a committee to be selected from both houses of the legislature, in such manner as shall be, by law, directed. During the trial of contested elections the speaker of the senate shall exercise the office of governor.

Section III. The governor shall hold his office during the term of three years from the third Tuesday of December next ensuing his election, and shall not be capable of holding his office longer than nine years in any term of twelve years.

Section IV. He must be, at least, thirty years of age; and must have been a citizen and inhabitant of this state seven years next before his election. Provided, that no person absent on public business of this state, or of the United States, shall thereby be disqualified.

Section V. No person shall be capable of exercising the office of governor who, at the same time, shall be a member of congress, or hold any other office under this state, or any office under the United States.

Section VI. The governor shall at stated times, receive for his services a compensation, which shall neither be increased nor diminished during the period for which he shall have been elected.

Section VII. He shall be commander in chief of the army and navy of this commonwealth and of the militia, except when they shall be called into the actual service of the United States.

Section VIII. He shall appoint all officers of this commonwealth, whose offices are established by this constitution, or shall be established by law, and whose appointments are not herein otherwise provided for; but no person shall be appointed to an office within any county, who shall not have resided therein one year next before his appointment. No member of congress from this state, nor any person holding or exercising any office of trust or profit under the United States, shall, at the same time, hold and exercise any office whatever, otherwise than in the militia, in this state.

Section IX, The governor shall commission all the officers of this commonwealth.

Section X. He shall have power to remit fines, and grant reprieves and pardons for crimes and offences, except in cases of impeachment.

Section XI. He may require the opinion, in writing, of the officers in each of the executive departments upon any subject relating to the duties of their respective offices.

Section XII. He shall, from time to time, give to the general assembly information of the state of the commonwealth, and recommend to their consideration such measures as he shall judge necessary or expedient.

Section XIII. He may on extraordinary occasions, convene the general assembly, and in case of disagreement between the two houses with respect to the time of adjournment, he may adjourn them to such time as he shall think proper, not exceeding four months.

Section XIV. He shall take care that the laws be faithfully executed.

Section XV. In case of the death or resignation of the governor, or of his removal from office, it shall devolve on the speaker of the senate until the next annual election of representatives, when another governor shall be chosen in the manner hereinbefore mentioned, and until such newly elected governor shall be duly qualified and commence the exercise of his office.

Section XVI. The state treasurer shall be appointed annually by the joint vote of both houses. All other officers in the treasury department, election officers, officers relating to taxes, to the poor and highways, constables and other township officers shall be appointed in such manner as is or shall be directed by law.

Section XVII. A secretary shall be appointed and commissioned by the governor. He shall be keeper of the seals of the state, and shall, under the direction of a committee of both branches of the legislature, affix the seal to the laws when the same shall be enacted. He shall countersign all commissions, charters of pardon, and patents for lands, signed by the governor, as well as marriage, tavern and other licences. He shall have the custody of all public acts, official documents and state papers which shall be addressed or belong to the executive department, to be laid before the governor or either house when called for. He shall attend the governor or either house when required, and shall perform all such other duties as shall be enjoined on him by future acts of the legislature.

ARTICLE III.

Section I. In elections by the citizens every freeman of the age of twenty-one years, having resided in the state two years next before the days of the elections respectively, and paid state or county taxes within that time, which tax shall have been assessed upon him at least six months before the election, shall enjoy the rights of an elector.

Section II. All elections shall be by ballot, except those by persons in their representative or public capacities, which shall be *viva voce*.

Section III. Electors shall be privileged from arrests in all cases except treason, felony and breach of the peace, during their attendance on elections and in going to and returning from the same.

ARTICLE IV.

Section I. The house of representatives shall have the sole power of impeachment.

Section II. All impeachments shall be tried by the senate; when sitting for that purpose, the senators shall be on oath or affirmation: no person shall be convicted without the concurrence of two-thirds of the members present.

Section III. Judgment in cases of impeachment shall not extend further than to removal from office, and disqualification to hold any office of honor, trust or profit under this commonwealth; but the party convicted shall nevertheless be liable to indictment, trial, judgment and punishment according to law.

ARTICLE V.

Section I. The judicial power of this commonwealth shall be vested in a supreme court, in courts of oyer and terminer and general goal delivery, in a court of common pleas, orphans' court, register's court, and court of quarter sessions for each county, in justices of the peace and in such other courts of law and equity as the legislature may, from time to time, establish.

Section II. The judges of the supreme court and the judges of the several courts of common pleas shall be commissioned and hold their offices during good behaviour; but the governor may remove any of them on the address of two-thirds of each branch of the legislature. The judges of the supreme court and the presidents of the several courts of common pleas shall, at stated times, receive for their services an adequate compensation, which shall not be diminished during their continuance in office: but they shall hold no other office of profit in this commonwealth.

Section III. The jurisdiction of the supreme court shall extend over the whole state. The judges of the same court shall, by virtue of their offices, be justices of oyer and terminer and general gaol deliv-

ery in the several counties. No special commission of oyer and terminer or gaol delivery shall be issued.

Section IV. The several courts of common pleas, for the present,
shall be established in the following manner : The governor shall appoint a number of judges in each county, not less than three and not
exceeding four, who, during their continuance in office, shall reside
within such county. The state shall, by law, be divided into circuits, any of which shall include not more than six, nor fewer than
three counties. A president shall be appointed for the several courts
in each circuit, who, during his continuance in office, shall reside
within such circuit. Such president and judges, or any two of them, shall
be the judges who shall compose the respective courts of common pleas.

Section V. The judges of the courts of common pleas in each county,
or any two of them—the president being one, shall be justices of oyer
and terminer and general gaol delivery for the trial of capital and
other offenders in their respective counties : but they shall not hold a
court of oyer and terminer and general gaol delivery in any county,
when the judges of the supreme court, or some of them, shall be sitting in the same county. But the parties accused, as well as the commonwealth, may remove the indictment and proceedings into the supreme court at any time before trial.

Section VI. The supreme court and the several courts of common pleas shall, beside the powers heretofore usually exercised by the
said courts, have the power of a court of chancery so far as relates to
the perpetuating testimony, obtaining evidence from places not within
the state, and the care of the persons and estates of those who are non
compotes mentis. And the legislature shall, as soon as conveniently
may be, after their first meeting under this constitution, vest in the
said courts such other powers to grant relief in equity in all cases to
which common law proceedings are not competent: and shall regulate the exercise thereof, and, from time to time, enlarge, diminish,
or vest the same in such other courts as they shall judge necessary for
the due administration of justice.

Section VII. The judges of the courts of common pleas shall compose the courts of quarter sessions and orphans' court in their respective counties, any two of whom shall be a quorum ; and the register
of wills, together with the said judges, or any two of them, shall compose the register's court in the respective counties.

Section VIII. The judges of the courts of common pleas shall have
the like powers with the judges of the supreme court to issue writs of
certiorari to the justices of the peace within the several counties respectively, and to cause their proceedings to be brought before them and
the like right and justice to be done.

Section IX, The president of the court of each circuit shall be conservator of the peace within such circuit ; and the judges of the court
of common pleas shall be conservators of the peace within their respective counties,

Section X. The governor shall appoint and commission a competent
number of justices of the peace in convenient districts in each county,
to be fixed in such manner as shall be, by law, directed. They shall
be commissioned during good behaviour ; but may be removed on conviction of misbehaviour in office or any infamous crime, or on the address of both houses of the legislature.

Section XI. A register's office for the probate of wills and granting letters of administration, and an office for the recording of deeds shall be kept in each county.

Section XII. Prothonotaries, clerks of the peace and orphans' courts, recorders of deeds, registers of wills and sheriffs shall keep their offices in the county town of the county in which they respectively shall be officers.

Section XIII. The stile of all process shall be *The commonwealth of Pennsylvania*: all prosecutions shall be carried on in the name and by the authority of the commonwealth of Pennsylvania, and shall conclude, *against the peace and dignity of the same.*

ARTICLE VI.

Section I. Sheriffs and coroners shall, at the places of the election of representatives, be chosen by the citizens of each county respectively; two persons shall be chosen for each office, one of whom for each shall be commissioned by the governor; they shall hold their offices for three years and until a successor be duly qualified. But no person shall be twice chosen or appointed sheriff in any term of six years.

Section II. The freemen of this commonwealth shall be armed and disciplined for its defence; the militia officers shall be appointed in such manner, and for such time, as shall be, by law, directed.

ARTICLE VII.

That the great and essential principles of liberty and free government may be recognized and unalterably established, WE DECLARE—

Section I. That all men are born equally free and independent, and have certain inherent and indefeasible rights, among which are those of enjoying and defending life and liberty, of acquiring, possessing and protecting property and reputation, and of pursuing their own happiness.

Section II. That all power being originally vested in, is derived from, the people, and all free governments originate from their will, are founded on their authority, and instituted for their common peace, safety and happiness; and for the advancement thereof, they have, at all times, an unalienable and indefeasible right to alter, reform or abolish their government, in such manner as they may think proper.

Section III. That all men have a natural and indefeasible right to worship Almighty God according to the dictates of their own consciences, and that no man can of right be compelled to attend any religious worship, or to erect or support any place of worship, or to maintain any ministry against his free will and consent; and that no human authority can controul or interfere with the rights of conscience in any case whatever; nor shall any preference ever be given, by law, to any religious establishment or modes of worship,

Section IV. That no person who acknowledges the being of a God and a future state of rewards and punishments, shall, on account of his religious sentiments, be disqualified to hold any office or place of trust or profit under this commonwealth.

Section V. That elections shall be free and equal.

Section VI. That trial by jury shall be as heretofore, and the right thereof shall remain inviolate.

Section VII. That the printing presses shall be free to every person who undertakes to examine the proceedings of the legislature or any branch of government, and no law shall ever be made restraining the right thereof. The free communication of thoughts and opinions is one of the invaluable rights of man, and every citizen may freely speak, write and print on any subject, being responsible for the abuse of that liberty. But upon indictments for the publication of papers investigating the conduct of individuals in their public capacity, or of those applying or canvassing for office, the truth of the facts may be given in evidence in justification upon the general issue.

Section VIII. That the people shall be secure in their persons, houses, papers and possessions, against unreasonable searches and seizures, and no warrant shall issue to search any place, or to seize any person or things, but on probable cause, supported by oath or affirmation, and describing them as nearly as may be.

Section IX. That in all prosecutions by indictment the accused hath a right to be heard by himself and his counsel; to demand the cause and nature of the accusation; to meet the witnesses face to face; to have compulsory process for obtaining witnesses in his favor, and a speedy public trial by an impartial jury of the vicinage; nor can he be compelled to give evidence against himself; nor can any man be deprived of his life, liberty or property but by the judgment of his peers or the law of the land.

Section X. That no person shall be proceeded against by information for any indictable offence, except in cases arising in the land or naval forces, or in the militia when in actual service in time of war or public danger; nor shall any person, for the same offence, be twice put in jeopardy of life or limb; nor shall any man's property be taken, or applied to public use, without the consent of his representatives, and on just compensation being made.

Section XI. That all courts shall be open, and every freeman for an injury done him in his lands, goods, person or reputation, shall have remedy by the due course of the law, and right and justice administered to him without sale, denial or delay.

Section XII. That no power of suspending laws, or the execution thereof, shall be exercised, unless by the legislature or by the authority thereof.

Section XIII. That excessive bail shall not be required, nor excessive fines imposed, or cruel punishments inflicted.

Section XIV. That all prisoners shall be bailable by sufficient sureties, unless for capital offences, when the proof is evident, or presumption great, and the privilege of the writ of habeas corpus shall not be suspended unless when, in cases of rebellion or invasion, the public safety may require it.

Section XV. That the person of a debtor, where there is not a strong presumption of fraud, shall not be continued in prison after delivering up all his estate for the benefit of his creditors, in such manner as shall be prescribed by law.

Section XVI. That no *expost facto* law, or law impairing contracts, shall be made.

Section XVII. That no person shall be attainted of treason or felony by the legislature.

Section XVIII. That no attainder shall work corruption of blood or forfeiture of estate to the commonwealth; the estates of such persons as shall destroy their own lives shall go as in the case of natural death. And if any person shall be killed by casualty or accident there shall be no forfeiture by reason thereof.

Section XIX. That the citizens have a right to assemble together in a peaceable manner for their common good, and to apply to those invested with the powers of government, for redress of grievances or other proper purposes, by petition, address or remonstrance.

Section XX. That the right of the citizens to bear arms in defence of themselves and the state shall not be questioned. But those who conscientiously scruple to bear arms shall not be compellable to do so, but shall pay an equivalent for personal service.

Section XXI. That no standing army shall, in time of peace, be kept up without the consent of the legislature, and the military shall, in all cases, and at all times, be kept in strict subordination to the civil power.

Section XXII. That no soldier shall, in time of peace, be quartered in any house without the consent of the owner, nor in time of war, but in a manner to be prescribed by law.

Section XXIII. That the legislature shall, at no time, grant any title of nobility or hereditary distinction, nor create any office the appointment to which shall be for a longer term than during good behaviour.

Section XXIV. That emigration from the state shall not be prohibited.

Section XXV. To guard against transgressions of the high powers which we have delegated, WE DECLARE, That every thing in this article expressed, is excepted out of the general powers of legislation, and shall for ever remain inviolate.

Whereupon, On motion of Mr. Smith, seconded by Mr. Smilie,

Ordered, That to-morrow be assigned for taking into consideration the said plan of government reported by the committee of the whole.

On motion of Mr. Miller, seconded by Mr. Henderson,

Ordered, That one hundred and fifty copies of the said plan of government be printed for the use of the members.

A return of an election held within the county of Delaware, of a member to represent the said county in this convention, in the room of Henry Hale Graham, Esquire, deceased, was presented to the chair and read, by which it appeared that Nathaniel Newlin, Esquire, was duly elected.

Adjourned until half past nine o'clock to-morrow, A. M.

SATURDAY, February 6th, 1790. A. M.

The convention met pursuant to adjournment.

A motion was made by Mr. Thomas Ross, seconded by Mr. Boyd, as follows, viz.

No member shall speak more than twice to the same question on the same day, without leave of the convention.

It was then moved by Mr. Smith, seconded by Mr. Power, to strike out the word "twice," and in lieu thereof, to insert the words "once, unless to explain."

Which was determined in the negative, and the motion of Mr. Thomas Ross, seconded by Mr. Boyd, adopted.

Agreeably to the order of the day, the convention proceeded to take into consideration the plan of government reported by the committee of the whole.

The first section of the first article of the said plan of government being under consideration, the same was adopted as follows, viz.

The legislative power of this commonwealth shall be vested in a general assembly, which shall consist of a senate and house of representatives.

The second section of the said first article being under consideration, viz.

The representatives shall be chosen annually by the citizens of the city of Philadelphia and of each county respectively, on the second Tuesday of October.

A motion was made by Mr. Pickering, seconded by Mr. Gray, to add the following words to the said section, viz. To serve for one year from the day preceding the first Tuesday of December next following their election.

On the question, Will the convention agree to the said amendment? It was determined in the negative.

It was then moved by Mr. Sitgreaves, seconded by Mr. Arndt, to strike out the word "second," and to insert in lieu thereof the word "first."

Which was determined in the negative, and the said second section, as reported by the committee of the whole, adopted.

The third section of the said first article being under consideration, the same was adopted as follows, viz.

No person shall be a representative who shall not have attained the age of twenty-one years, and have been, the three years next preceding his election, a citizen and inhabitant of the state, and the last year thereof an inhabitant of the city or county in which he shall be chosen.

The fourth section of the said first article being under consideration, viz.

The number of representatives shall, at the several periods of making the enumeration in this section mentioned, be fixed by the legislature, and apportioned between the city of Philadelphia and the several counties, according to the number of taxable inhabitants in each, and shall never be less than sixty, nor more than one hundred; and that it shall be increased at the time of making each enumertion, except the first, in the same proportion which the increase of the number of taxables shall bear to the then number of representatives, until the same shall amount to one hundred. But each county shall have at least one representative; provided that no new county shall be entitled to a separate representation, until a sufficient number of taxable inhabitants shall be contained within the limits thereof to entitle them to at least one representative, agreeably to the ratio which shall then be established for the city of Philadelphia and the several counties; an enumeration of the taxable inhabitants shall be made within three years after the first meeting of the general assembly, and within every subsequent term of seven years in such manner as shall be law, directed. Until such enumeration shall be made, the city of Philadelphia and the several counties shall be respectively entitled to choose the same number of representatives as is now prescribed by law.

A motion was made by Mr. Thomas Ross, seconded by Mr. Slegle, to strike out the word "sixty," and in lieu thereof, to insert the words "forty-five."

On the question, Will the convention agree to the same? The yeas and nays being called by Mr. Miller, were as follow, viz.

YEAS.

Mr. Roberts	Mr. Bull	Mr. Slegle	Mr. Potts	
Lewis	T. Ross	Reed	Coates	
M'Kean	Graff	Tyson	Graydon	
Gray	Breckbill	Sitgreaves	Sellers	
Barclay	Miller	Arndt	Newlin	
Stout				21

NAYS.

Mr. Baker	Mr. Hiester	Mr. Snyder	Mr. M'Lene	
Robinson	Lower	Findley	Matthews	
Hare	Lincoln	Todd	Shoemaker	
Boyd	Groscop	Addison	Gloninger	
Hand	Gehr	Hoge	Brown	
Atlee	Mawhorter	Redick	Pickering	
Pedan	Rhoads	J. Ross	Henderson	
Dill	Powell	Smilie	Gibson	
Whitebill	Piper	Gallatin	Beale	
Power	Smith			38

So it was determined in the negative.

It was moved by Mr. Gallatin, seconded by Mr. Smilie, to insert, after the words "shall amount to one hundred," the words "which number shall then be continued forever." Which was determined in the negative.

A motion was then made by Mr. Pickering, seconded by Mr. Miller, to strike out the words "except the first, in the same proportion which the increase of the number of taxables shall bear to the then number of representatives, until the same shall amount to one hundred." and in lieu thereof to insert the following, viz. "After the first, in such proportion to the increase of taxables that the next preceding ratio of representation, increased by twenty-five taxables, shall be the new ratio of representation, until the number of representatives shall amount to one hundred."

Adjourned until half past nine o'clock on Monday next, A. M.

MONDAY, February 8, 1790. A. M.

The convention met pursuant to adjournment.

The fourth section of the first article of the plan of government being under consideration, together with the amendment proposed by Mr. Pickering, seconded by Mr. Miller.

23

Mr. Pickering then withdrew his motion.

The original section, as reported by the commitee of the whole, recurring,

It was moved by Mr. Pickering, seconded by Mr. Brown, to strike out the words "and that it shall be increased at the time of making each enumeration, except the first, in the same proportion which the increase of the number of taxables shall bear to the then number of representatives, until the same shall amount to one hundred."

Which was unanimously determined in the affirmative.

A motion was then made by Mr. Pickering, seconded by Mr. Henderson, to strike out the word "new," and insert after the word "county," the words "hereafter erected."

Which was determined in the affirmative.

It was moved by Mr Henderson, seconded by Mr. Todd, to strike out the word "seven," and in lieu thereof, to insert the word "five."

On the question, Will the convention agree to the same? The yeas and nays being called by Mr. Smith, were as follow, viz.

YEAS.

Mr. Boyd	Mr. Powell	Mr. Hoge	Mr. M'Lene
Reed	Piper	Redick	Matthews
Dill	Snyder	J. Ross	Henderson
Whitehill	Findley	Smilie	Gibson
Power	Todd	Gallatin	Beale
Groscop	Addison		22

NAYS.

Mr. Roberts	Mr. Graff	Mr. Lower	Mr. Smith
Lewis	Atlee	Lincoln	Coates
M'Kean	Breckbill	Gehr	Gloninger
Robinson	Slegle	Sitgreaves	Graydon
Barclay	Tyson	Mawhorter	Brown
Stout	Pedan	Arndt	Pickering
Bull	Hiester	Rhoads	Sellers
Hand			29

So it was determined in the negative.

A motion was then made by Mr. James Ross, seconded by Mr. Smith, to strike out the following words from the said section, viz. "Until such enumeration shall be made, the city of Philadelphia and the several counties shall be respectively entitled to choose the same number of representatives as is now prescribed by law."

Which was determined in the affirmative, and the said fourth section adopted as follows, viz.

The number of representatives shall, at the several periods of making the enumeration in this section mentioned, be fixed by the legislature and apportioned between the city of Philadelphia and the several counties according to the number of taxable inhabitants in each, and shall never be less than sixty nor more than one hundred. But each county shall have at least one representative; provided that no county hereafter erected, shall be entitled to a separate representation until a sufficient number of taxable inhabitants shall be contained within the limits thereof to entitle them to at least one representative.

agreeably to the ratio which shall then be established for the city of Philadelphia and the several counties; an enumeration of the taxable inhabitants shall be made within three years after the first meeting of the general assembly, and within every subsequent term of seven years, in such manner as shall be, by law, directed.

The fifth section of the said first article being under consideration,

It was moved by Mr. M'Kean, seconded by Mr. Sellers, to adjourn the debates on the said section.

Which was determined in the negative, and the said section thereupon adopted as follows, viz.

The senators shall be chosen for four years by the citizens of the city of Philadelphia and of each county respectively, at the same time, in the same manner, and at the same places where they shall respectively vote for representatives.

The sixth section of the said first article being under consideration, the same was adopted as follows, viz.

The number of senators shall, at the several periods of making the enumeration mentioned in the fourth section, be fixed by the legislature and apportioned between the districts, formed as hereinafter mentioned, according to the number of taxable inhabitants in each, and shall never be less than one-fourth, nor more than one-third of the number of representatives.

The seventh section of the said first article being under consideration, the same was adopted as follows, viz.

The senators shall be chosen in districts to be formed by the legislature, containing each, as nearly as may be, such a number of taxable inhabitants as shall be entitled to elect one senator, but where that cannot be done, then such number of adjoining counties shall be formed into one district as shall be entitled to elect not more than four senators; provided that neither the city of Philadelphia, nor any county, shall be divided in forming a district.

The eighth section of the said first article being under consideration, it was moved by Mr. Lewis, seconded by Mr. M'Kean, to strike out the word "to." Which was determined in the negative.

A motion was then made by Mr. Pickering, seconded by Mr. Lewis, to strike out the words "whereof shall have been," and to insert after the word "election," the word "and," and in lieu of the words moved to be struck out, the following: "thereof a resident."

Which was determined in the negative. Whereupon,

On motion of Mr. Gallatin, seconded by Mr. M'Kean, the said eighth section was adopted as follows, viz.

No person shall be a senator who shall not have attained to the age of twenty-five years; and who shall not have been a citizen and inhabitant of the state four years next before his election, and the last year thereof an inhabitant of the district for which he shall be chosen.

A motion was made by Mr. M'Kean, seconded by Mr. Redick, to insert the following as the ninth section of the said first article, viz.

No person shall be capable of being chosen a senator who is not seized, in fee simple, of five hundred acres of land within this commonwealth, or possessed of real and personal estate to the value of five hundred pounds. Which was determined in the negative.

The ninth section of the first article of the said plan of government being under consideration, it was moved by Mr. Sitgreaves, seconded by Mr. Lewis, to amend the said section so as to read as follows, viz

Immediately after the senators shall be assembled in consequence of the first election subsequent to the first enumeration hereinbefore mentioned, they shall be divided, by lot, as equally as may be, into four classes. The seats of the senators of the first class shall be vacated at the expiration of the first year; of the second class, at the expiration of the second year; of the third class, at the expiration of the third year; and of the fourth class, at the expiration of the fourth year; so that one-fourth may be chosen every year.

Which was determined in the affirmative, and the said section, as amended, adopted.

The tenth section of the said first article being under consideration, it was moved by Mr. Pickering, seconded by Mr. Hare, to amend the said section so as to read as follows, viz.

The general assembly shall meet on the first Tuesday of December in every year, unless sooner convened by the governor.

Which was determined in the affirmative, and the said section, as amended, adopted.

The eleventh section of the said first article being under consideration, the same was adopted as follows, viz.

Each house shall choose its speaker and other officers ; and the senate shall also choose a speaker *pro tempore*, when the speaker shall exercise the office of governor.

The twelfth section of the said first article being under consideration, the same was adopted.

A motion was then made by Mr. M'Lene, seconded by Mr. M'Kean, to re-consider the said section, in order to amend the same so as to read as follows :

Each house shall be the judge of the qualifications of its own members ; but in case of contested elections the same shall be judged of and determined by a committee, to be selected from the house in such manner as shall be, by law, directed : And a majority of each house shall constitute a quorum to do business ; but a smaller number may adjourn from day to day, and may be authorised to compel the attendance of absent members in such manner, and under such penalties as may, by law, be provided.

Which was carried in the affirmative, and the said section, as amended, adopted.

The thirteenth section of the said first article being under consideration, it was moved by Mr. Smilie, seconded by Mr. Findley, to strike out the words "punish and" in order that the section may read as follows:

Each house may determine the rules of its proceedings, and may, with the concurrence of two-thirds, expel a member for disorderly behaviour, but not a second time for the same cause, and shall have all other powers necessary for either branch of the legislature of a free state.

On the question, Will the convention agree to the said section as amended?

The yeas and nays being called by Mr. Smilie, were as follow, viz.

YEAS.

Mr. Whitehill	Mr. Piper	Mr. Hoge	Mr. M'Lene
Power	Findley	Redick	Matthews
Lincoln	Todd	Smilie	Gloninger
Mawhorter	Addison	Gallatin	Beale
Powel			

17

NAYS.

Mr. Baker	Mr. Hand	Mr. Dill	Mr. J. Ross
Roberts	Graff	Hiester	Morris
Lewis	Atlee	Lower	Coates
M'Kean	Breckbill	Groscop	Brown
Gray	Miller	Gehr	Graydon
Hare	Slegle	Sitgreaves	Pickering
Barclay	Reed	Arndt	Henderson
Stout	Tyson	Rhoads	Gibson
Bull	Pedan	Smith	Sellers
Boyd			37

So it was determined in the negative.

And the thirteenth section adopted as follows, viz.

Each house may determine the rules of its proceedings, punish its members for disorderly behaviour, and may, with the concurrence of two-thirds, expel a member, but not a second time for the same cause, and shall have all other powers necessary for either branch of the legislature of a free state.

The fourteenth section of the said first article being under consideration, viz.

Each house shall keep a journal of its proceedings, and publish them weekly, excepting such parts as may, in their judgment, require secrecy: And the yeas and nays of the members of either house, on any question, shall, at the desire of any two of them, be entered on the journals.

It was moved by Mr. Lewis, seconded by Mr. M'Kean, to strike out the word "weekly," and in lieu thereof, to insert the words "at the end of each session."

Which was determined in the negative.

A motion was then made by Mr. Hare, seconded by Mr. Sitgreaves, to strike out the word "weekly," and in lieu thereof, to insert the following, viz. "as frequently as may be."

Which was determined in the negative, and thereupon the original section, as reported by the committee of the whole, adopted.

The fifteenth section of the said first article being under consideration, the same was adopted as follows, viz.

The doors of each house shall be open, unless when the business shall be such as, in their judgment, ought to be kept secret.

The sixteenth section of the said first article being under consideration, the same was adopted as follows, viz.

Neither house shall, without the consent of the other, adjourn for more than three days, nor to any other place than that in which the two houses shall be sitting.

The seventeenth section of the said first article being under consideration, the same was adopted as follows, viz.

The senators and representatives shall receive a compensation for their services, to be ascertained by law, and paid out of the treasury of the commonwealth. They shall, in all cases except treason, felony and breach of the peace, be privileged from arrest, during their attendance at the session of the respective houses, and in going to and returning from the same; and for any speech or debate in either house they shall not be questioned in any other place;

The eighteenth section of the said first article being under consideration, viz.

No senator or representative shall, during the time for which he was elected, be appointed to any civil office, under the authority of this commonwealth, which shall have been created, or the emoluments of which shall have been increased during such time: And no member of congress or other person holding any office, except in the militia, under this commonwealth or the United States, shall be a member of either house during his continuance in congress or in office.

A motion was made by Mr. Sitgreaves, seconded by Mr. Graydon, to strike out the words "member of congress, or other," as well as the words "in congress or"

Which was determined in the negative, and the said eighteenth section, as reported by the committeee of the whole, adopted.

The nineteenth section of the said first article being under consideration, the same was adopted as follows, viz.

When vacancies happen in either house, the speaker of that house shall issue writs of election to fill such vacancies.

The twentieth section of the said first article being under consideration, the same was adopted as follows, viz.

All bills for raising revenue shall originate in the house of representatives; but the senate may propose or concur with amendments, as in other bills.

The twenty-first section of the said first article being under consideration, the same was adopted as follows, viz.

No money shall be drawn from the treasury, but in consequence of appropriations made by law.

The twenty-second section of the said first article being under consideration, viz.

Every bill, which shall have passed the house of representatives and the senate, shall, before it become a law, be presented to the governor. If he approve, he shall sign it; but if he shall not approve it, he shall return it, with his objections, to that house in which it shall have originated, who shall enter the objections at large upon their journals, and proceed to re-consider it. If, after such re-consideration, two-thirds of that house shall agree to pass the bill, it shall be sent, together with the objections, to the other house, by which it shall likewise be re-considered, and if approved by two-thirds of that house, it shall become a law. But in all such cases, the votes of both houses shall be determined by yeas and nays, and the names of the persons voting for or against the bill shall be entered on the journals of each house respectively. If any bill shall not be returned by the governor within ten days (Sundays excepted) after it shall be presented to him, the same shall be a law in like manner as if he had signed it, unless the general assembly, by their adjournment, prevent its return, in which case it shall be a law, unless sent back within three days after their next meeting.

It was moved by Mr. Smith, seconded by Mr. Henderson, to strike out the words "in which case it shall be a law, unless sent back," and in lieu thereof to insert the following: "and in that case, if not sent back by the governor, with his objections thereto," and to add, after the words "next meeting," the words "of the legislature, it shall be a law in like manner as if he had signed it."

Which was determined in the negative.

A motion was then made by Mr. M'Lene, seconded by Mr. Brown, to strike out the words "enter the objections at large upon their journals."

Which was determined in the negative, and the said twenty-second section, as reported by the committee of the whole, adopted.

The twenty-third section of the said first article being under consideration, the same was adopted as follows, viz.

Every order, resolution or vote, to which the concurrence of the senate and house of representatives may be necessary (except on a question of adjournment) shall be presented to the governor, and before the same shall take effect, be approved by him; or, being disapproved by him, shall be re-passed by two-thirds of the senate and house of representatives, according to the rules and limitations prescribed in case of a bill.

The first section of the second article of the said plan of government being under consideration, the same was adopted as follows, viz.

The supreme executive power of this commonwealth shall be vested in a governor.

The second section of the said second article being under consideration, viz.

The governor shall be chosen on the second Tuesday of October, by the citizens throughout the commonwealth, at the places where they shall respectively vote for representatives. The returns of every election for governor shall be transmitted to the seat of government, directed to the speaker of the senate, who shall open and publish the same in the presence of both houses of the legislature. The person having the highest number of votes shall be governor; but if it should so happen that any two or more should be equal and highest in votes, the general assembly shall choose one of them for governor, by the joint vote of both houses. In case of contested elections, the same shall be judged of and determined by a committee to be selected from both houses of the legislature, in such manner as shall be, by law, directed. During the trial of contested elections, [the speaker of the senate, shall exercise the office of Governor.

It was moved by Mr. M'Kean, seconded by Mr. Smilie, to insert after the words " in the presence of " and after the words " by the joint vote of," respectively, the following: " the members of." Which was determined in the affirmative.

A motion was then made by Mr. Lewis, seconded by Mr. M'Kean, to amend the said section so as to read as follows, viz.

The governor shall be chosen on the second Tuesday of October, by the citizens throughout the commonwealth, at the places where they shall respectively vote for representatives. The returns of every election for governor shall be transmitted to the seat of government, directed to the speaker of the senate, who shall open and publish the same in the presence of the members of both houses of the legislature. The person having the highest number of votes shall be governor; but if two or more shall be equal and highest in votes, one of them shall be chosen governor by the joint vote of the members of both houses In case of contested elections, the same shall be judged of and determined by a committee to be selected from both houses of the legislature, in such manner as shall be, by law, directed.

Which was determined in the affirmative, and the said section as amended, adopted.

The third section of the said second article being under consideration, viz.

The governor shall hold his office during the term of three years from the third Tuesday of December next ensuing his election, and shall not be capable of holding his office longer than nine years in any term of twelve years.

It was moved by Mr. Findlay, seconded by Mr. Smilie, to strike out the words "nine" and "twelve," and to insert, in lieu of the former, the word "six," and in lieu of the latter, the word "nine."

On the question, Will the convention agree to the same?

The yeas and nays being called by Mr Power, were as follow, viz.

YEAS.

Robinson,	Mr. Hiester	Mr. Piper	Mr. Smilie
Hare	Lower	Findley	Gallatin
Stout	Lincoln	Todd	M'Lene
Boyd	Groscop	Addison	Matthews
Reed	Gehr	Hoge	Henderson
Whitehill	Mawhorter	Redick	Beale
Power	Powell		26

NAYS.

Mr. Baker	Mr. Graff	Mr. Sitgreaves	Mr. Coates
Roberts	Atlee	Arndt	Gloninger
Lewis	Breckbill	Rhoads	Brown
M'Kean	Miller	Smith	Graydon
Gray	Slegle	Snyder	Pickering
Barclay	Tyson	J. Ross	Gibson
Bull	Pedan	Morris	Sellers 30
Hand	Dill		

So it was determined in the negative.

Whereupon, on the question, will the convention agree to the said third section as reported by the committee of the whole?

The yeas and nays being called by Mr. Sitgreaves on the last clause, were as follow, viz.

YEAS.

Mr. Roberts	Mr. Reed	Mr. Rhoads	Mr. Smilie
Robinson	Tyson	Powell	Gallatin
Hare	Pedan	Piper	M'Lene
Barclay	Dill	Smith	Matthews
Stout	Whitehill	Snyder	Morris
Bull	Power	Findley	Coates
Boyd	Hiester	Todd	Gloninger
Hand	Lower	Addison	Brown
Graff	Lincoln	Hoge	Henderson
Breckbill	Groscop	Redick	Gibson
Miller	Gehr	J. Ross	Beale 45
Slegle			

NAYS.

Mr. Baker	Mr. Gray	Mr. Mawhorter	Mr. Pickering
Lewis	Atlee	Arndt	Sellers
M'Kean	Sitgreaves	Graydon	11

So it was determined in the affirmative, and the said section adopted.

The fourth section of the said second article being under consideration, a motion was made by Mr. Sitgreaves, seconded by Mr. James Ross, to amend the said section by striking out the word " thereby,'' and to add, after the words " be disqualified," the words " by reason of such absence."

It was then moved by Mr. Lewis, seconded by Mr. Whitehill, to amend the said section so as to read as follows, viz.

He must be, at least, thirty years of age; and must have been a citizen and inhabitant of this state seven years next before his election; but no person who shall have been absent from this state on the public business thereof, or of the United States, shall on account of such absence, be disqualified.

Which was determined in the affirmative, and the said section adopted.

The fifth section of the said second article being under consideration, viz.

No person shall be capable of exercising the office of governor, who at the same time, shall be a member of congress or hold any other office under this state, or any office under the United States.

It was moved by Mr. Robinson, seconded by Mr. Sitgreaves, to strike out the words "be a member of congress or," as well as the words "under this state, or any office under the United States."

Which was determined in the negative, and the original section, as reported by the committee of the whole, adopted.

The sixth section of the said second article being under consideration, the same was adopted as follows, viz.

The governor shall, at stated times, receive for his services a compensation, which shall neither be increased nor diminished during the period for which he shall have been elected.

The seventh section of the said second article being under consideration, the same was adopted as follows, viz.

He shall be commander in chief of the army and navy of this commonwealth, and of the militia, except when they shall be called into the actual service of the United States.

The eighth section of the said second article being under consideration, on motion,

Adjourned until half past nine o'clock to-morrow, A. M.

TUESDAY. February 9, 1790, A. M.

The convention met pursuant to adjournment.

The committee appointed on the 28d of January last, to prepare a schedule for putting the government into operation, made report, which was read as follows:

24

That no inconvenience may arise from the alterations and amendments in the constitution of this commonwealth, and in order to carry the same into complete operation, it is hereby declared and ordained,

1. That all laws of this commonwealth, in force at the time of making the said alterations and amendments in the said constitution, and not inconsistent therewith, and all rights, actions, prosecutions, claims and contracts, as well of individuals as of bodies corporate, shall continue as if the said alterations and amendments had not been made.

2. That all officers in the appointment of the executive department, shall continue in the exercise of the duties of their respective offices until the   day of   unless their commissions shall sooner expire by their own limitations, or the said offices become vacant by death or resignation, and no longer, unless re-appointed and commissioned by the governor. Except that the judges of the supreme court shall hold their offices for the terms in their commissions respectively expressed.

3. That justice shall be administered in. the several counties of the state, until the period aforesaid, by the same justices, in the same courts, and in the same manner as heretofore.

4. That the president and supreme executive council shall continue to exercise the executive authority of this commonwealth as heretofore, until the third Tuesday of December next; but no intermediate vacancies in the council shall be supplied by new elections.

5. That until the first enumeration shall be made, as directed in the fourth section of the first article of the constitution established by this convention, the city of Philadelphia and the several counties shall be respectively entitled to elect the same number of representatives as is now prescribed by law,

6 That the first senate shall consist of seventeen members, to be chosen in districts formed as follows, to wit: The city of Philadelphia, the county of Philadelphia, and the county of Delaware, shall be a district, and shall elect three senators; the county of Chester shall be a district, and shall elect one senator; the county of Bucks shall be a district, and shall elect one senator; the county of Montgomery shall be a district, and shall elect one senator; the county of Northampton shall be a district, and shall elect one senator; the counties of Lancaster and York shall be a district, and shall elect three senators; the counties of Berks and Dauphin shall be a district, and shall elect two senators; the counties of Cumberland and Huntingdon shall be a district, and shall elect one senator; the counties of Northumberland, Luzerne and Mifflin shall be a district, and shall elect one senator; the counties of Bedford and Franklin shall be a district, and shall elect one senator; the counties of Westmoreland, Fayette and Allegheny shall be a district, and shall elect one senator; and the county of Washington shall be a district, and shall elect one senator; which senators shall serve until the first enumeration before mentioned shall have been made, and the representation in both branches of the legislature shall be established by law, and chosen as in the constitution is directed. Any vacancies which shall happen in the senate within the said time, shall be supplied as prescribed in the nineteenth section of the first article.

7. That the elections of senators shall be conducted, and the returns thereof made to the senate, in the same manner as is prescribed by

the election laws of the state for conducting and making return of the elections of representatives. In those districts which consist of more than one county, the judges of the district elections within each county, after having formed a return of the whole election within that county, in such manner as is directed by law, shall send the same, by one or more of their number, to such place, hereinafter mentioned, within the district of which such county is a part; where the judges, so met, shall compare and cast up the several county returns, and execute, under their hands and seals, one general and true return for the whole district, that is to say, the judges of the district composed of the city of Philadelphia and of the counties of Philadelphia and Delaware, shall meet at the state house in the city of Philadelphia; the judges of the district composed of the counties of Lancaster and York, shall meet at   the judges of the district composed of the counties of Berks and Dauphin, shall meet at the judges of the district composed of the counties of Cumberland and Huntingdon, shall meet at   the judges of the district composed of the counties of Northumberland, Luzerne and Mifflin, shall meet at   the judges of the district composed of the counties of Bedford and Franklin, shall meet at   and the judges of the district composed of the counties of Westmoreland, Fayette and Allegheny, shall meet at   on the third Tuesday of October respectively, for the purpose aforesaid.

8. That the election of the governor shall be conducted in the several counties in the manner prescribed by the laws of the state for the elections of representatives, and the returns in each county shall be sealed up by the judges of the elections, and transmitted to the speaker of the senate as soon after the election as may be.

The eighth section of the said second article recurring, viz.

He shall appoint all officers of this commonwealth, whose offices are established by this constitution or shall be established by law, and whose appointments are not herein otherwise provided for; but no person shall be appointed to an office within any county who shall not have resided therein one year next before his appointment: No member of congress from this state, nor any person holding or exercising any office of trust or profit under the United States, shall, at the same time, hold and exercise any office whatever, otherwise than in the militia, in this state.

It was moved by Mr. Ogden, seconded by Mr. Brown, to strike out the word " resided," and, in lieu thereof to insert the following, "been a citizen and inhabitant." Which was determined in the affirmative.

A motion was made by Mr. Lewis, seconded by Mr. Hand, to strike out the words " of this commonwealth." Which was carried in the affirmative.

It was then moved by Mr. Lewis, seconded by Mr. Sitgreaves, to insert after the word " appointment," the following, viz. "If the county shall have been so long erected; but if it shall not have been so long erected, then within the limits of the county from which it shall have been taken."

A motion was made by Mr. M'Lene, seconded by Mr. Lower, to strike out from the said amendment, the words " from which it shall have been taken," and to insert, after the words " of the county," the words " so divided."

It was moved by Mr. James Ross, seconded by Mr. M'Lene, to strike out the remainder of the section after the words "hold and exercise," viz. " the office of sheriff, or any office in the gift of the governor other than in the militia or commission of the peace."

A motion was then made by Mr Robinson, seconded by Mr. Gallatin, to insert in the last amendment before the word "governor," the words " legislature or." Which was determined in the affirmative.

It was moved by Mr. Hand, seconded by Mr. Sitgreaves, to strike out from the amendment, moved by Mr James Ross, the words " the office of sheriff or." Which was determined in the negative.

A motion was made by Mr. M'Kean, seconded by Mr. Lewis, to add, after the word " peace," the words " notary public and sworn interpreter of languages." Which was determined in the affirmative.

It was moved by Mr. Ogden, seconded by Mr. Stout, to add the following words to the said amendment, viz. " Judges of the common pleas." Which was determined in the negative.

A motion was then made by Mr. Lewis, seconded by Mr. Sitgreaves, to insert after the words " interpreter of languages," the words " and wood rangers." Which was determined in the negative.

It was then moved by Mr. Pickering, seconded by Mr. Miller, to adjourn the debates on the said eighth section and amendments.

On the question, Will the convention agree to the same? The house being equally divided the president gave his casting vote in the affirmative.

The ninth section of the said second article being under consideration, viz.

The governor shall commission all the officers of this commonwealth.

On the question, Will the convention adopt the same? It was determined in the negative.

The tenth section of the said second article being under consideration, viz.

He shall have power to remit fines, and grant reprieves and pardons for crimes and offences, except in cases of impeachment.

It was moved by Mr Lewis, seconded by Mr. Thomas Ross, to insert after the word "fines," the words "and forfeitures."

Whereupon, on motion,

Adjourned until half past nine o'clock to-morrow, A. M.

WEDNESDAY, February 10, 1790. *A. M.*

The convention met pursuant to adjournment.

The tenth section of the said second article of the proposed plan of government, together with the amendment moved yesterday by Mr. Lewis, seconded by Mr. Thomas Ross, recurring, the same section, with the amendment, was adopted as follows, viz.

He shall have power to remit fines and forfeitures, and grant reprieves and pardons for crimes and offences, except in cases of impeachment.

The convention then resumed the consideration of the 8th section, postponed yesterday, as well as the several amendments.

A motion was made by Mr. Lewis, seconded by Mr. Edwards, to substitute the following in lieu of the amendment proposed by him and seconded by Mr. Sitgreaves, viz.

If it shall have been so long erected, but if that shall not be the case, then within the limits of the original county or counties out of which it shall have been taken.

Which was determined in the affirmative.

Whereupon, on the question, Will the convention agree to the following part of the said eighth section ? viz.

He shall appoint all officers whose offices are established by this constitution, or shall be established by law, and whose appointments are not herein otherwise provided for, but no person shall be appointed to an office within any county who shall not have been a citizen and inhabitant therein one year next before his appointment, if it shall have been so long erected, but if that shall not be the case, then within the limits of the original county or counties out of which it shall have been taken.

The yeas and nays being called by Mr. Sitgreaves, were as follow, viz.

YEAS.

Mr. Baker	Mr. Slegle	Mr. Powell	Mr. Matthews
Roberts	Tyson	Smith	Morris
Lewis	Whitehill	Snyder	Coates
Gray	Power	Findley	Shoemaker
Edwards	Hiester	Todd	Gloninger
Gibbons	Lower	Addison	Brown
Bull	Lincoln	Hoge	Graydon
T. Ross	Groscop	Redick	Pickering
Boyd	Gehr	J. Ross	Gibson
Hand	Sitgreaves	Smilie	Beale
Graff	Arndt	Gallatin	Sellers
Breckbill	Rhoads	M'Lene	Newlin
Miller			49

NAYS.

Mr. M'Kean	Mr. Barclay	Mr. Reed	Mr. Mawhorter
Robinson	Stout	Pedan	Piper
Ogden	Atlee	Dill	Henderson
Jenks			13

So it was determined in the affirmative.

A motion was made by Mr. Robinson, seconded by Mr. James Ross, to amend the motion made yesterday by Mr. James Ross, seconded by Mr. M'Lene, by adding after the word "governor," the words " nor shall hold and exercise any office in the department of the treasury, or any office relating to the revenue.

It was then moved by Mr. Pickering, seconded by Mr. M'Kean, to postpone the said amendments in order to introduce the following in lieu thereof:

No person holding an office or place of trust under the United States shall, at the same time, be a judge of the supreme court or other court of general jurisdiction, or president of any court of common pleas, or hold any other office under this state which any future legislature shall, by law, declare to be incompatible or improper to be held and exercised therewith.

On the question, Will the convention agree to the postponement for the aforesaid purpose?

The yeas and nays being called by Mr. Lewis, were as follow, viz.

YEAS.

Mr. Baker	Mr. Ogden	Mr. Atlee	Mr. Graydon
Roberts	Stout	Miller	Pickering
Lewis	Gibbons	Slegle	Henderson
M'Kean	T. Ross	Sitgreaves	Sellers
Gray	Graff	Arndt	Newlin 20

NAYS.

Mr. Robinson	Mr. Pedan	Mr. Powell	Mr. Gallatin
Hare	Dill	Piper	M'Lene
Edwards	Whitehill	Smith	Matthews
Jenks	Power	Snyder	Morris
Barclay	Hiester	Findley	Coates
Bull	Lower	Todd	Shoemaker
Boyd	Lincoln	Addison	Gloninger
Hand	Groscop	Hoge	Brown
Breckbill	Gehr	Redick	Gibson
Reed	Mawhorter	J. Ross	Beale
Tyson	Rhoads	Smilie	43

So it was determined in the negative, and the amendment moved by Mr. Robinson, seconded by Mr. James Ross, recurring,

On the question, Will the convention agree to the same? It was determined in the negative.

The motion made yesterday by Mr. James Ross, seconded by Mr. M'Lene, again recurring, the same was adopted.

And in debating the following part of the said eighth section as amended, viz.

No member of congress from this state, nor any person holding or exercising any office of trust or profit under the United States shall, at the same time, hold and exercise the office of sheriff, or any office in the gift of the governor, other than in the militia, or commission of the peace, notary public and sworn interpreter of languages in this state.

A motion was made by Mr. Sitgreaves, seconded by Mr. Ogden, to strike out the words " member of congress from this state nor any."

On the question, Will the convention agree to strike out the said words?

The yeas and nays being called by Mr. Sitgreaves, were as follow, viz.

YEAS.

Mr. Baker	Mr. Ogden	Mr. Miller	Mr. Graydon
Lewis	Stout	Sitgreaves	Pickering
M'Kean	Gibbons	Arndt	Henderson
Gray	Graff	Smith	Sellers
Hare	Atlee	Shoemaker	19

NAYS.

Mr. Roberts	Mr. Tyson	Mr. Rhoads	Mr. Smilie
Robinson	Pedan	Powell	Gallatin
Edwards	Dill	Piper	M'Lene
Jenks	Whitehill	Snyder	Matthews
Barclay	Power	Findley	Morris
Bull	Hiester	Todd	Coates
Boyd	Lower	Addison	Gloninger
Hand	Lincoln	Hoge	Brown
Breckbill	Groscop	Redick	Gibson
Slegle	Gehr	J. Ross	Beale
Reed	Mawhorter		42

So it was determined in the negative.

Whereupon, on the question, Will the convention agree to the latter part of the said section?

The yeas and nays being called by Mr. Lewis, were as follow, viz.

YEAS.

Mr. Robinson	Mr. Whitehill	Mr. Piper	Mr. M'Lene
Hare	Power	Snyder	Matthews
Edwards	Hiester	Findley	Morris
Jenks	Lower	Todd	Coates
Barclay	Lincoln	Addison	Gloninger
Boyd	Groscop	Hoge	Brown
Breckbill	Gehr	Redick	Gibson
Reed	Mawhorter	J. Ross	Beale
Pedan	Rhoads	Smilie	Newlin
Dill	Powell	Gallatin	39

NAYS.

Mr. Baker	Mr. Stout	Mr. Atlee	Mr. Smith
Roberts	Gibbons	Miller	Shoemaker
Lewis	Bull	Slegle	Graydon
M'Kean	T. Ross	Tyson	Pickering
Gray	Hand	Sitgreaves	Henderson
Ogden	Graff	Arndt	Sellers 24

So it was determined in the affirmative, and the said eighth section adopted as follows, viz.

He shall appoint all officers whose offices are established by this constitution or shall be established by law, and whose appointments are not herein otherwise provided for, but no person shall be appointed to an office within any county, who shall not have been a citizen and inhabitant therein one year next before his appointment, if it shall have been so long erected, but if that shall not be the case, then within the limits of the original county or counties out of which it shall have been taken. No member of congress from this state, nor any person holding or exercising any office of trust or profit under the United States, shall at the same time, hold and exercise the office of sheriff, or any office in the gift of the legislature or of the governor, other than in the militia, or commission of the peace, notary public and sworn interpreter of languages in this state.

A motion was made by Mr Thomas Ross, seconded by Mr. Smilie, to re-consider the ninth section of the said second article, viz.

The governor shall commission all the officers of this commonwealth. Which was determined in the affirmative.

It was moved by Mr. Ogden, seconded by Mr. Stout, to strike out the remainder of the said section, after the word " commission," and in lieu thereof, to insert "such officers of this commonwealth as he shall appoint under this constitution, or who shall be appointed by the laws of this state." Which was determined in the negative.

A motion was made by Mr. Sitgreaves, seconded by Mr. Tyson, to strike out the word " all." Which was determined in the negative.

A motion was then made by Mr. Smith, seconded by Mr. Addison, to amend the said ninth section so as to read as follows, viz.

All commissions shall be in the name and by the authority of the commonwealth of Pennsylvania, sealed with the state seal and signed by the governor. Which was carried in the affirmative.

It was moved by Mr. Pickering. seconded by Mr. Roberts, to insert the following as the eleventh section of the said second article, viz.

Every candidate applying for an office in the appointment of the governor, or of the legislature, or of either branch thereof, shall make his application only in writing; every application otherwise made, either by the candidate himself or any person for him, at his request, shall disqualify such candidate for the office requested.

Which was determined in the negative.

The eleventh section of the said second article being then under consideration, the same was, on motion of Mr. Sitgreaves, seconded by Mr. M'Lene, adopted as follows, viz.

He may require information, in writing, from the officers in the executive department upon any subject relating to the duties of their respective offices.

The twelfth section of the said second article being under consideration, the same was adopted as follows, viz.

He shall from time to time, give to the general assembly information of the state of the commonwealth, and recommend to their consideration, such measures as he shall judge necessary or expedient.

The thirteenth section of the said second article being under consideration, the same was adopted as follows, viz.

He may, on extraordinary occasions, convene the general assembly, and in case of disagreement between the two houses with respect to the time of adjournment, he may adjourn them to such time as he shall think proper, not exceeding four months.

The fourteenth section of the said second article being under consideration, the same was adopted as follows, viz.

He shall take care that the laws be faithfully executed.

The fifteenth section of the said second article being under consideration, the same was adopted as follows, viz.

In case of the death or resignation of the governor, or of his removal from office, it shall devolve on the speaker of the senate until the next annual election of representatives, when another governor shall be chosen in the manner hereinbefore mentioned, and until such newly elected governor shall be duly qualified and commence the exercise of his office.

On motion, ordered that Mr. James Ross have leave of absence.

Adjourned until nine o'clock to-morrow, A. M.

THURSDAY, February 11th, 1790. A. M.

The convention met pursuant to adjournment.

The sixteenth section of the second article of the proposed plan of government being under consideration,

It was moved by Mr. Pickering, seconded by Mr. M'Lene, to amend the same so as to read as follows, viz.

The state treasurer shall be appointed annually, by the joint vote of the members of both houses. All other officers in the treasury department, election officers, officers relating to taxes, to the poor and highways, constables and other township officers, shall be appointed in such manner as is or shall be directed by law.

On the question, Will the convention agree to the section as amended? It was determined in the affirmative.

The seventeenth section being under consideration, viz.

A secretary shall be appointed and commissioned by the governor. He shall be keeper of the seals of the state, and shall, under the direction of a committee of both branches of the legislature, affix the seal to the laws when the same shall be enacted. He shall countersign all commissions, charters of pardon, and patents for land, signed by the governor, as well as marriage, tavern and other licenses. He shall have the custody of all public acts, official documents and state papers, which shall be addressed or belong to the executive department, to be laid before the governor or either house when called for He shall attend the governor or either house when required, and shall perform all such other duties as shall be enjoined him by future acts of the legislature.

It was moved by Mr. Sitgreaves, seconded by Mr. Mawhorter, to insert after the word "appointed," the words "by the joint vote of the members of both houses of the legislature."

It was then moved by Mr. Lewis, seconded by Mr. Addison, to postpone the amendment offered, in order to introduce the following after the word "appointment," viz. "Who shall hold his commission during the governor's continuance in office, if he shall so long behave himself well." Which was determined in the affirmative.

It was then moved by Mr. Ogden, seconded by Mr. Hand, to postpone the amendment moved by Mr. Lewis, seconded by Mr. Addison, together with the seventeenth section, in order to introduce the following:

The governor shall keep fair and exact records of all his proceedings in the executive department, and shall lay the same before either house of the legislature when required, and shall deliver the same to his successor in office, complete.

And on the question, Will the house agree to postpone for the aforesaid purpose?

The yeas and nays being called by Mr. Gallatin, were as follow, viz.

YEAS.

Mr. Ogden	Mr. Boyd	Mr. Mawhorter	Mr. Snyder
Jenks	Hand	Arndt	Hoge
Barclay	Graff	Rhoads	Shoemaker
Stout	Breckbill	Smith	Henderson
Gibbons	Reed		

25   18

NAYS.

Mr. Baker	Mr. Slegle	Mr. Gehr	Mr. M'Lene
Roberts	Tyson	Sitgreaves	Matthews
Lewis	Pedan	Powell	Coates
M'Kean	Dill	Piper	Brown
Gray	Whitehill	Findley	Graydon
Robinson	Power	Todd	Pickering
Hare	Hiester	Addison	Gibson
Edwards	Lower	Redick	Beale
Bull	Lincoln	Smilie	Sellers
T. Ross	Groscop	Gallatin	Newlin
Atlee			41

So it was determined in the negative.

A motion was then mode by Mr. Sitgreaves, seconded by Mr. Lower, to amend the amendment offered by Mr. Lewis, by inserting after the word "appointed," the words "who shall hold his commission during good behaviour." Which was determined in the negative.

The original section, as first amended, then recurring, on the question, Will the house agree to the first clause thereof? viz.

A secretary shall be appointed, who shall hold his commission during the governor's continuance in office, if he shall so long behave himself well.

The yeas and nays were called by Mr. Lewis, and were as follow :

YEAS.

Mr. Baker	Mr. Slegle	Mr. Gehr	Mr. M'Lene
Roberts	Tyson	Powel	Matthews
Lewis	Pedan	Piper	Coates
M'Kean	Dill	Findley	Brown
Gray	Whitehill	Todd	Graydon
Edwards	Power	Addison	Pickering
Stout	Hiester	Redick	Beale
Bull	Lower	Smilie	Sellers
T. Ross	Lincoln	Gallatin	Newlin
Atlee	Groscop		38

NAYS.

Mr. Robinson	Mr. Boyd	Mr. Sitgreaves	Mr. Morris
Hare	Hand	Mawhorter	Shoemaker
Ogden	Graff	Arndt	Gloninger
Jenks	Breckbill	Rhoads	Henderson
Barclay	Miller	Snyder	Gibson
Gibbons	Reed	Hoge	23

So it was determined in the affirmative.

It was then moved by Mr. Lewis, seconded by Mr. Addison, to amend the second clause of the aforesaid section, by inserting, after the words "behave himself well," the following:

He shall be keeper of the great and lesser seals of the state, and shall affix the same as occasion may require, He shall keep a fair register of all the official acts and proceedings of the executive department, and shall when required, lay the same and all papers, minutes and vouchers relative thereto, before either branch of the legislature, and shall perform all such other duties as shall be enjoined him by law.

On the question, Will the House agree to the first part of the said amendment?

He shall be keeper of the great and lesser seals of the state, and shall affix the same as occasion may require. It was determined in the negative.

And the remainder of the said amendment being adopted, on the question, Will the convention agree to the clause as amended, viz.

A secretary shall be appointed who shall hold his commission during the governor's continuance in office, if he shall so long behave himself well: He shall keep a fair register of all the official acts and proceedings of the executive department, and shall, when required, lay the same and all papers, minutes and vouchers relative thereto, before either branch of the legislature, and shall perform all such other duties as shall be enjoined him by law.

The yeas and nays being called by Mr. Ogden, were as follow, viz.

YEAS.

Mr. Baker	Mr. Miller	Mr. Groscop	Mr. Gallatin
Roberts	Slegle	Gehr	M'Lene
Lewis	Tyson	Powell	Matthews
M'Kean	Pedan	Piper	Coates
Gray	Dill	Findley	Brown
Edwards	Whitehill	Todd	Graydon
Bull	Power	Addison	Pickering
T. Ross	Hiester	Redick	Beale
Atlee	Lower	Smilie	Sellers 36

NAYS.

Mr. Robinson	Mr. Gibbons	Mr. Sitgreaves	Mr. Morris
Hare	Boyd	Mawhorter	Shoemaker
Ogden	Hand	Rhoads	Gloninger
Jenks	Graff	Snyder	Henderson
Barclay	Breckbill	Hoge	Gibson
Stout	Reed		22

So it was determined in the affirmative.

A motion was made by Mr. M'Kean, seconded by Mr. Hoge, to add the following section to the said second article:

The governor and every person appointed or commissioned to any executive, judicial, military, or other office under the government, shall, before he enters on the discharge of the business of his place or office take and subscribe the following oaths or affirmations, viz.

I do swear, that I will be faithful and bear true allegiance to the commonwealth of Pennsylvania, as a free and independent state; and that I will not, at any time, willfully and knowingly do any matter or thing prejudicial or injurious to the freedom and independence thereof. So help me God.

I, A. B. do solemnly swear, that I will faithfully and impartially discharge and perform all the duties incumbent on me as according to the best of my abilities and understanding, agreeably to the rules and regulations of the constitution and the laws of this commonwealth. So help me God.

And if the persons aforesaid are not christians, the oaths shall be administered in the manner most usual and solemn among those of their religious persuasion. Any person who shall publicly declare, that he is conscientiously scrupulous of taking an oath in any case, shall take and subscribe his affirmation in the foregoing form, omitting the word swear and so help me God: and those who are now, by law, indulged to take an oath in any other form, may take the oaths aforesaid, in th words commonly used.

Adjourned until half past nine o'clock to-morrow, A M.

FRIDAY, February 12, 1790, A. M.

The convention met pursuant to adjournment.

The motion made yesterday by Mr. M'Kean, being withdrawn, it was moved by Mr. Lewis, seconded by Mr. Sitgreaves, to re-consider the fifteenth section of the second article, viz.

In case of the death or resignation of the governor, or of his removal from office, it shall devolve on the speaker of the senate until the next annual election of representatives, when another governor shall be chosen in the manner hereinbefore mentioned.

And to amend the same by inserting after the words " removal from office," the words " the speaker of the senate shall exercise the office of governor until the office shall be filled agreeably to this constitution.

Mr. Sitgreaves withdrew his seconding the motion made by Mr. Lewis, and Mr. Addison, in place thereof, seconded the motion.

On the question, Will the convention agree to re-consider the fifteenth section of the second article?

It was determined in the affirmative.

It was thereupon moved by Mr. Smith, seconded by Mr. M'Lene, to adjourn the debates on the motion of Mr. Lewis and Mr. Addison, in order to introduce the following, viz.

The speaker of the senate shall exercise the office of governor until a new governor, who shall in such case, be chosen at the next annual election, shall be duly qualified and commence the exercise of his office; and if the trial of a contested election shall continue longer than the third Tuesday in December, next ensuing the election of a governor, the speaker of the senate shall in like manner exercise the office until the determination of such contested election. Which was carried in the affirmative.

A motion was then made by Mr. Pickering, seconded by Mr. Lewis, to postpone the motion of Mr. Smith, and to insert, in lieu of the fifteenth section, the following :

During a vacancy in the office of governor the powers thereof shall be exercised by the speaker of the senate.

It was then moved by Mr. Hare, seconded by Mr. Hoge, to amend the said motion by adding the following words, viz.

But at such times he shall not be eligible to fill such office.

Which was determined in the negative.

The motion made by Mr. Pickering then recurring, on the question, Will the convention agree to the same? It was determined in the negative.

It was moved by Mr. Sitgreaves, seconded by Mr. Ogden, to amend the amendment offered by Mr. Smith, by inserting after the words " election of governor," the following:

The governor of the last year, or the speaker of the senate, which ever may be in the exercise of the executive authority, shall continue therein until the determination of such contested election, and until a governor shall be qualified as aforesaid.

A motion was then made by Mr. Edwards, seconded by Mr. Pickering, to adjourn the debates on the amendment as well as on the fifteenth section. Which was determined in the negative.

The amendment moved by Mr. Sitgreaves, seconded by Mr. Ogden, then recurring.

On the question, Will the convention agree to the same ?

The yeas and nays being called by Mr. Ogden, were as follow, viz

YEAS.

Mr. Baker	Mr. Reed	Mr. Mawhorter	Mr. Redick
Ogden	Pedan	Arndt	Smilie
Jenks	Dill	Rhoads	Gallatin
Barclay	Whitehill	Powell	M'Lene,
Stout	Power	Piper	Matthews
Gibbons	Lincoln	Snyder	Shoemaker
Bull	Groscop	Findley	Gloninger
T. Ross	Gehr	Todd	Brown
Boyd	Sitgreaves	Hoge	Beale 36

NAYS.

Mr. Roberts	Mr. Hand	Mr. Tyson	Mr. Graydon
Lewis	Graff	Hiester	Pickering
M'Kean	Atlee	Lower	Henderson
Gray	Hubley	Smith	Gibson
Robinson	Breckbill	Addison	Sellers
Hare	Miller	Morris	Newlin
Edwards	Slegle	Coates	27

So it was determined in the affirmative.

The amendment of Mr. Smith and Mr. M'Lene, as amended by Mr. Sitgreaves and Mr. Ogden, then recurring.

On the question, will the convention agree to the same?

The yeas and nays being called by Mr. Ogden, were as follow, viz.

YEAS.

Mr. Baker	Mr. Pedan	Mr. Mawhorter	Mr. Hoge
Roberts	Dill	Arndt	Redick
Ogden	Whitehill	Rhoads	Smilie
Jenks	Power	Powell	M'Lene
Barclay	Hiester	Piper	Matthews
Stout	Lincoln	Smith	Shoemaker
Gibbons	Groscop	Snyder	Gloninger
Bull	Gehr	Findley	Brown
Boyd	Sitgreaves	Todd	Beale
Reed			37

NAYS.

Mr. Lewis	Mr. Hand	Mr. Tyson	Mr. Graydon
M'Kean	Graff	Lower	Pickering
Gray	Atlee	Addison	Henderson
Robinson	Hubley	Gallatin	Gibson
Hare	Breckbill	Morris	Sellers
Edwards	Miller	Coates	Newlin
T. Ross	Slegle		26

So it was determined in the affirmative, and the section adopted as follows, viz.

In case of the death or resignation of the governor, or his removal from office, the speaker of the senate shall exercise the office of governor until a new governor, who shall, in such case, be chosen at the next annual election, shall be duly qualified and commence the exercise of his office. And if the trial of a contested election shall continue longer than the third Tuesday in December, next ensuing the election of a governor, the governor of the last year, or the speaker of the senate, whichever may be in the exercise of the executive authority, shall continue therein until the determination of such contested election, and until a governor shall be qualified as aforesaid.

A motion was made by Mr. Edwards, seconded by Mr. Gallatin, to re-consider the third section of the first article, in order to add the following words, viz.

But the inhabitants of the city of Philadelphia shall not be entitled to vote for or be elected members for the county of Philadelphia, neither shall the inhabitants of the county of Philadelphia, out of the limits of the said city, be entitled to vote for or be elected representatives for the said city.

The question being taken, it was agreed to re-consider.

It was then moved by Mr. Lewis, seconded by Mr. Sitgreaves, to postpone the said motion of Mr. Edwards.

Adjourned until half past nine o'clock to-morrow, A. M.

SATURDAY, February 13, 1790. *A. M.*

The convention met pursuant to adjournment.

Mr. Smith and Mr. Henderson, members of this convention, asked and obtained leave of absence.

The motion made yesterday by Mr. Edwards, seconded by Mr. Gallatin, recurring, as well as the motion for postponement, made by Mr. Lewis, seconded by Mr Sitgreaves.

On the question, Will the convention agree to postpone? It was determined in the negative.

The original motion made by Mr. Edwards, seconded by Mr. Gallatin, again recurring, and after some debate thereon,

It was moved by Mr. Lewis, seconded by Mr. Robinson, to postpone the consideration of the said motion until Tuesday next.

Which was determined in the affirmative.

The first section of the third article of the proposed plan of government being under consideration, viz.

In elections by the citizens every freeman of the age of twenty-one years, having resided in the state two years next before the days of the elections respectively, and paid state or county taxes within that time, which tax shall have been assessed upon him at least six months before the election, shall enjoy the rights of an elector.

It was moved by Mr. Lewis, seconded by Mr. Shoemaker, to strike out the word "tax."

Which was carried in the affirmative.

A motion was then made by Mr. Pickering seconded by Mr. Lewis, to amend the said section so as to read as follows, to wit.

In elections by the citizens every freeman of the age of twenty-one years, having resided in the state two years next before the days of the elections respectively, and within that time paid a state or county tax, which shall have been assessed upon him at least six months before the election, shall enjoy the rights of an elector.

Which was determined in the affirmative.

A motion was made by Mr. Sitgreaves, seconded by Mr. Mawhorter, to add the following proviso to the said section as amended, viz.

Provided that the sons of persons qualified as aforesaid, between the age of twenty-one and twenty-two years, shall be entitled to vote although they shall not have paid taxes.

It was then moved by Mr. Ogden, seconded by Mr. Hand, to amend the said proviso by striking out the word "persons," and in lieu thereof, to insert the word "freeholders."

And on the question, Will the convention agree to the same? The yeas and nays being called by Mr. Ogden, were as follow, viz,

YEAS.

Mr. Baker	Mr. Barclay	Mr. Gehr	Mr. Hoge
Ogden	Gibbons	Arndt	Redick
Jenks	Hiester	Rhoads	Shoemaker
			12

NAYS.

Mr. Roberts	Mr. Breckbill	Mr. Sitgreaves	Nr. Morris
Lewis	Miller	Mawhorter	Potts
M'Kean	Slegle	Powel	Coates
Gray	Reed	Piper	Gloninger
Hare	Tyson	Smith	Brown
Bull	Pedan	Snyder	Graydon
T. Ross	Dill	Todd	Pickering
Boyd	Whitehill	Smilie	Henderson
Hand	Power	Gallatin	Beale
Graff	Lower	M'Lene	Sellers
Atlee	Lincoln	Matthews	Newlin
Hubley	Groscop		46

So it was determined in the negative.

And the proviso moved by Mr. Sitgreaves, seconded by Mr. Mawhorter, recurring,

On the question, Will the convention agree to the same? The yeas and nays being called by Mr. Sitgreaves, were as follow, viz.

YEAS.

Mr. Gray	Mr. Dill	Mr. Mawhorter	Mr. Smilie
Boyd	Whitehill	Powel	M'Lene
Graff	Power	Piper	Matthews
Miller	Lower	Smith	Gloninger
Slegle	Lincoln	Snyder	Brown
Reed	Groscop	Todd	Henderson
Tyson	Gehr	Hoge	Gibson
Pedan	Sitgreaves	Redick	Beale 32

NAYS.

Mr. Baker	Mr. Jenks	Mr. Breckbill	Mr. Potts
Roberts	Barclay	Hiester	Coates
Lewis	Gibbons	Arndt	Shoemaker
M'Kean	Bull	Rhoads	Graydon
Robinson	T. Ross	Addison	Pickering
Hare	Hubley	Gallatin	Sellers
Edwards	Hand	Morris	Newlin
Ogden	Atlee		30

So it was determined in the affirmative.

A motion was then made by Mr. Lewis, seconded by Mr. Hubley, to strike out the words of the original section ' In elections by the citizens.'

Which was determined in the negative, and the said first section thereupon adopted with the amendments, as follows, viz.

In elections by the citizens every freeman of the age of twenty-one years, having resided in the state two years next before the days of the elections respectively, and within that time paid a state or county tax, which shall have been assessed upon him at least six months before the election, shall enjoy the rights of an elector; provided that the sons of persons qualified as aforesaid, between the age of twenty-one and twenty-two years, shall be entitled to vote although they shall not have paid taxes.

The second section of the said third article being under consideration, viz.

All elections shall be by ballot, except by persons in their representative or public capacities, which shall be *viva voce*.

It was moved by Mr. Lewis, seconded by Mr. Smilie, to insert after the words "which shall," the following, viz. " unless in the choice of committees and their own officers."

Which was determined in the affirmative, and the said section, as amended, adopted.

The third section of the said third article being under consideration, it was moved by Mr. Pickering, seconded by Mr. Lewis, to amend the said section so as to read as follows, viz.

Electors, during their attendance on elections, shall be privileged from arrests in all cases except treason, felony and breach of the peace, and in going to and returning from the same.

On the question, Will the convention agree to the same? It was determined in the negative, and the original section, as reported by the committee of the whole, adopted.

The first section of the fourth article of the proposed plan of government being under consideration,

On motion of Mr. Pickering, seconded by Mr. Jenks, the said section was adopted as follows, viz.

The house of representatives shall have the sole power of impeaching.

The second section of the said fourth article being under consideration, the same was adopted as follows, viz.

All impeachments shall be tried by the senate ; when sitting for that purpose, the senators shall be on oath or affirmation   No person shall be convicted without the concurrence of two-thirds of the members present.

The third section of the said fourth article being under consideration, it was moved by Mr. Lewis, seconded by Mr. M'Kean, to amend the same so as to read as follows, viz.

The governor and all civil officers under this commonwealth, shall be liable to be impeached for any misdemeanor in office, and, on conviction thereof, to be punished agreeably to law.

A division of the section being called, viz.

The governor and all civil officers under this commonwealth, shall be liable to be impeached for any misdemeanor in office.

On the question, Will the convention agree to that part of the said proposed section?   It was determined in the affirmative.

And the question being taken on the remainder of the said amendment, it was determined in the negative.

It was then moved by Mr. Addison, seconded by Mr. Miller to add the following to the said amendment, as adopted, viz.

But judgment on conviction thereof shall not extend further than to removal from office, and disqualification to hold any office of honor, trust or profit under this commonwealth ; but the party convicted shall nevertheless be liable to indictment, trial, judgment and punishment according to law.

A division of the said amendment being called for,

On the question, Will the convention agree to the first part thereof, viz.

But judgment on conviction thereof shall not extend further than to removal from office and disqualification to hold any office of honor, trust or profit under this commonwealth ?

It was determined in the affirmative.

And on the question, Will the convention agree to the latter part thereof, viz.

But the party convicted shall nevertheless be liable to indictment, trial, judgment, and punishment according to law ?

The yeas and nays being called by Mr. Lewis, were as follows, viz.

YEAS.

Mr. Roberts	Mr. Tyson	Mr. Mawhorter	Mr. Gallatin
Gray	Pedau	Rhoads	M'Lene
Robinson	Dill	Powell	Matthews
Hare	Whitehill	Piper	Brown
Jenks	Power	Smith	Pickering
Barclay	Hiester	Snyder	Henderson
Boyd	Lower	Findley	Gibson
Miller	Lincoln	Addison	Beale
Slegle	Groscop	Hoge	Sellers
Reed	Gehr	Smilie	Newlin 40

2R

NAYS.

Mr. Baker   Mr. Bull·   Mr. Atlee   Mr. Potts
   Lewis   T. Ross   Hubley   Shoemaker
   M'Kean   Hand   Breckbill   Gloninger
   Gibbons   Graff   Redick   15

So it was determined in the affirmative.

It was then moved by Mr. M'Kean, seconded by Mr. Shoemaker, to insert, after the words "in office," the words "within two years after the offence shall have been committed."

Which was determined in the negative, and thereupon the said third section, as amended, adopted as follows :

The governor and all civil officers under this commonwealth shall be liable to be impeached for any misdemeanor in office; but judgment, on conviction thereof, shall not extend further than to removal from office and disqualification to hold any office of honor, trust or profit under this commonwealth : the party convicted shall, nevertheless, be liable to indictment, trial, judgment and punishment according to law.

The first section of the fifth article of the proposed plan of government being under consideration, It was moved by Mr. Smilie, seconded by Mr. Findley, to strike out the words "of law and equity."

Which was carried in the affirmative.

Whereupon, on motion of Mr. Lewis, seconded by Mr. Thomas Ross, the said first section was adopted in the following words :

The judicial power of this commonwealth shall be vested in a supreme court, in courts of oyer and terminer and general gaol delivery, in a court of common pleas, orphans' court, register's court and a court of quarter sessions of the peace for each county, in justices of the peace, and in such other courts as the legislature may, from time time, establish.

The second section of the said fifth article being under consideration, viz.

The judges of the supreme court and *the judges* of the several courts of common pleas shall *be commissioned and* hold their offices during good behaviour; but the governor may remove any of them on the address of two-thirds of each branch of the legislature. The judges of the supreme court and the president of the several courts of common pleas shall, at stated times, receive for their services an edequate compensation, which shall not be diminished during their countinuance in office: but they shall hold no other office of profit in this commonwealth.

It was moved by Mr. Lewis, seconded by Mr. Thomas Ross, to strike out the words "the judges" after the word "and," as well as the words "be commissioned and."

Which was carried in the affirmative.

A motion was then made by Mr. Lewis, seconded by Mr. M'Kean, to strike out the word "but" after the words "continuance in office."

Which was determined in the affirmative.

It was moved by Mr. M'Lene, seconded by Mr. Smilie, to strike out the word "may" after the word "governor," and, in lieu thereof, to insert the word "shall."

Whereupon, On motion, Adjourned until half past nine o'clock on Monday next, A. M.

MONDAY, February 15th, 1790. A. M.

The convention met pursuant to adjournment.

The second section of the fifth article of the proposed constitution, as amended, being again under consideration, together with the amendment moved by Mr. M'Lene, seconded by Mr. Smilie, the thirteenth of February, instant, viz.

To strike out the word "may," and, in lieu thereof, to insert the word "shall."

Mr. M'Lene then withdrew his amendment.

A motion was made by Mr. Lewis, seconded by Mr. Pickering, to amend the said section so as to read as follows, viz,

The judges of the supreme court *and of the several courts of common pleas* shall hold their offices during good behaviour; but the government may, for any reasonable cause which shall not be sufficient ground of impeachment, remove any of them an the address of *two-thirds of each branch* of the *legislature*. The judges of the supreme court and the presidents of the several courts of common pleas shall, at stated times, receive for their services an adequate compensation, to be fixed by law, which shall not be diminished during their continuance in office; they shall hold no other office of profit in this commonwealth.

Which was determined in the affirmative.

A motion was then made by Mr. Findley, seconded by Mr. Gallatin, to strike out the words "two-thirds of each branch," and, in lieu thereof, to insert " both houses."

On the question, Will the convention agree to the same? The yeas and nays being called by Mr. Hubley, were as follow. viz.

YEAS.

Mr. Whitehill	Mr. Lincoln	Mr. Findley	Mr. Gallatin	
Power	Piper	Todd	Beale	8

NAYS.

Mr. Wilson	Mr. Bull	Mr. Dill	Mr. Redick	
Baker	T. Ross	Hiester	Smilie	
Roberts	Boyd	Lower	M'Lean	
Lewis	Hand	Groscop	Potts	
M,Kean	Graff	Gehr	Coates	
Gray	Atlee	Mawhorter	Shoemaker	
Robinson	Hubley	Arndt	Gloninger	
Hare	Breckbill	Rhoads	Brown	
Edwards	Miller	Powell	Grayden	
Jenks	Slegle	Snyder	Pickering	
Barclay	Reed	Addison	Gibson	
Stout	Tyson	Hoge	Newlin	
Gibbons	Pedan			50

So it was determined in the negative.

It was then moved by Mr. Whitehill, seconded by Mr. Findley, to strike out the words " and the president of the several courts of common pleas."

Which was determined in the negative.

A motion was made by Mr. Lewis, seconded by Mr, Edwards, to amend the said section so as to read as follows, viz.

The judges of the supreme court and of the several courts of common pleas shall hold their offices during good behaviour : but the governor may, for any reasonable cause which shall not be sufficient ground of impeachment, remove any of them on the address of two-thirds of each branch of the legislature. The judges of the supreme court and the presidents of the several courts of common pleas shall, at stated times, receive for their services an edequate compensation to be fixed by law, which shall not be diminished during their continuance in office: But they shall receive no fees or perquisites of office, nor hol l any other office of profit in this commonwealth.

On the question, Will the convention adopt the said section as amended ?

It was determined in the affirmative.

The third section of the fifth article of the said proposed plan of government being under consideration, viz.

The jurisdiction of the supreme court shall extend over the whole state, and the judges thereof shall, by virtue of their offices, be justices of oyer and terminer and general gaol delivery in the several counties. No special commission of oyer and terminer and gaol delivery shall be issued.

It was moved by Mr. Lewis, seconded by Mr. M'Kean, to amend the first part of the said section so as to read as follows :

The jurisdiction of the supreme court shall extend over the state, and the judges thereof shall, by virtue of their offices, be justices of oyer and terminer and general gaol delivery.

Which was determined in the affirmative.

And the latter part of the said section being under consideration, viz.

No special commission of oyer and terminer and gaol delivery shall be issued.

It was, on motion of Mr. Lewis, seconded by Mr. Pickering, Ordered, that the consideration thereof be postponed.

A motion was then made by Mr. Pickering, seconded by Mr. Lewis, to re consider the second section of the said fifth article in order to strike out the word "compensation," and, in lieu thereof, to insert the word " salaries.

On the question, Will the convention agree to re-consider ?

It was determined in the negative.

Adjourned until half past nine o'clock to-morrow, A. M.

TUESDAY, February 16th, 1790 *A. M.*

The convention met pursuant to adjournment.

Agreeably to the order of the day of the thirteenth instant, the motio made by Mr. Edwards, seconded by Mr. Gallatin, to amend the thir article, recurring.

It was moved by Mr. Lewis, seconded by Mr. Sitgreaves, to post pone the motion made by Mr. Edwards, in order to add the foll wi words to the said section, viz.

And no person residing within any city, town or borough, which shall be entitled to a separate representation, shall vote for, or be elect ed a member of any county; *nor shall any person residing without the li m* its of any such city, town or borough vote for or be elected a member thereof.

On the question, Will the convention agree to the postponement for the aforesaid purpose ?

It was determined in the affirmative.

A motion was then made by Mr. Gallatin, seconded by Mr. White-hill, to strike out the words "And no person residing within," as well as the words "residing without the limits of any," and, in lieu of the former insert "no inhabitant of," and of the latter the words "who is not an inhabitant of."

Which was determined in the negative, and Mr. Lewis' motion re-curring,

It was moved by Mr. Robinson, seconded by Mr. M'Lene, to post-pone the motion made by M. Lewis, in order to introduce the follow-ing, in lieu thereof, viz.

And no person shall represent a county, including any city, town or borough which may be entitled to a separate representation, un-less, during the year preceding such election, he shall have resided without the limits of such city, town or borough.

Mr. Lewis then withdrew his motion, and moved, seconded by Mr. Edwards, to amend the motion made by Mr. Robinson, by adding the following words, viz.

Nor shall any person represent any such city, town or borough un-less he shall have resided therein for the time aforesaid.

Which was determined in the negative, and on the question, Will the convention agree to the amendment moved by Mr. Robinson ?

It was determined in the negative, and the original section adopted.

The fourth section of the fifth article of the proposed plan of gov-ernment being under consideration, viz.

The several courts of common pleas, *for the present*, shall be es-tablished in the following manner : *The governor shall appoint a num-ber of judges in each county, not less than three and not exceeding four, who, during their continuance in office, shall reside within such county.* The state shall, by law, be divided into circuits, *any* of which shall include not more than six nor fewer than three counties. A pre-sident shall be appointed for the several courts in each circuit, who, during his continuance in office, shall reside within such circuit. Such president and judges, or any two of them, shall be the judges who shall compose the respective courts of common pleas.

The same being divided into propositions, and the first being under consideration, viz.

The several courts of common pleas, for the present, shall be estab-lished in the following manner : the governor shall appoint a number of judges in each county, not less than three nor exceeding four, who, during their continuance in office, shall reside within such county.

It was moved by Mr. Lewis, seconded by Mr. Addison, to amend the first part of the said proposition so as to read as follows :

Until it shall be otherwise directed by law, the several courts of common pleas shall be established in the following manner :

A motion was made by Mr. Sitgreaves, seconded by Mr. Ogden, to amend the motion of Mr, Lewis, so as to read as follows, viz.

The several courts of common pleas shall be established in the follow-ing manner:

Which was determined in the negative, And on the question, Will the convention agree to the amendment moved by Mr. Lewis?

It was determined in the affirmative.

The second part of the said first proposition being under consideration, it was moved by Mr. Lewis, seconded by Mr. Hubley, to amend the same so as to read as follows :

The governor shall appoint not fewer than three nor more than four judges in each county, who, during their continuance in office shall reside therein.

Which was carried in the affirmative.

A motion was made by Mr. Ogden, seconded by Mr. Jenks, to strike out the word "four," and, in lieu thereof, to insert the word "five."

Which was determined in the negative, and thereupon the said first proposition, as amended, adopted.

The second proposition being under consideration, viz.

The state shall, by law, be divided into circuits any of which shall include not more than six nor fewer than three counties.

It was moved by Mr. Lewis, seconded by Mr. Hubley, to strike out the word "any," and, in lieu thereof, to insert "none."

Which was determined in the affirmative, and the said proposition, as amended, adopted.

The third proposition being under consideration, viz

A president shall be appointed for the *several* courts in each circuit, who, during his continuance in office, shall reside within such circuit.

It was moved by Mr. Lewis, seconded by Mr. Pickering, to strike out the words " within such circuit," and in lieu thereof, to insert " therein."

Which was determined in the affirmative, and the said proposition, after striking out the word " several," as amended, adopted.

The fourth proposition being under consideration, viz.

Such president and judges, or any two of them, shall be the judges who shall compose the respective courts of common pleas.

It was moved by Mr. Sitgreaves, seconded by Mr. Wilson, to amend the same so as to read as follows :

Such president and judges shall compose the respective courts of common pleas, any two of whom shall be a quorum.

Which was determined in the affirmative.

And the said fourth section of the fifth article was adopted as follows, viz.

Until it shall be otherwise directed by law the several courts of common pleas shall be established in the following manner : The governor shall appoint not fewer than three nor more than four judges in each county, who, during their continuance in office, shall reside therein. The state shall, by law, be divided into circuits, none of which shall include more than six nor fewer than three counties. A president shall be appointed for the courts in each circuit, who, during his continuance in office, shall reside therein. Such president and judges shall compose the respective courts of common pleas, any two of whom shall be a quorum.

The fifth section of the said fifth article being under consideration, viz.

The judges of the courts of common pleas in each county, or any two of them, the president being one, shall be justices of oyer and terminer and general gaol delivery for the trial of capital and other offenders in their respective counties : but they shall not hold a court of oyer and terminer and general gaol delivery in any county, when the judges of the supreme court, or some of them, shall be sitting in the same county. But the parties accused, as well as the commonwealth, may remove the indictment and proceedings into the supreme court at any time before trial.

On motion of Mr. Sitgreaves,

Ordered, That the word "but," be struck out from the last clause.

It was moved by Mr. Lewis, seconded by Mr. Pickering, to strike out the words "the parties accused, as well as the commonwealth, may remove the indictment and proceedings into the supreme court at any time before trial."

A motion was then made by Mr. Pickering, seconded by Mr. Gray, to postpone the consideration of the said section and amendment.

Which was determined in the affirmative.

The sixth section of the said fifth article being under consideration, viz.

The supreme court and the several courts of common pleas shall, beside the powers heretofore usually exercised by the said courts, have the power of a court of chancery so far as relates to the perpetuating testimony, obtaining evidence from places not within the state, and the care of the persons and estates of those who are *non compotes mentis*. And the legislature shall, as soon as conveniently may be, after their first meeting under this constitution, vest in the said courts such other powers to grant relief in equity in all cases to which common law proceedings are not competent: and shall regulate the exercise thereof, and, from time to time, enlarge, diminish, or vest the same in such other courts as they shall judge necessary for the due administration of justice.

It was moved by Mr. Lewis, seconded by Mr. Pickering, to insert, after the words "in equity," the words " as shall be found necessary," and to strike out the words " shall regulate the exercise thereof, and," and the word " necessary," and in lieu of the former, to insert the word " may," and of the latter the word "proper," so as that the latter part of the said section read as follows, viz.

And may from time to time enlarge, diminish or vest the same in such other courts as they shall judge proper for the due administration of justice.

A division of the question on the latter part of the section, as far as the word necessary, being called for by Mr. Addison,

On the question, Will the convention agree to the same as amended by Mr. Lewis? It was determined in the affirmative.

It was then moved by Mr. Sitgreaves, seconded by Mr. Graydon, to re-consider the said amendments of Mr. Lewis, in order to restore the words " shall regulate the exercise thereof."

On the question, Will the convention agree to re-consider for the aforesaid purpose? It was determined in the negative.

A motion was made by Mr. Wilson, seconded by Mr. Boyd, to strike out the words " after their first meeting under this constitution."

Which was determined in the affirmative, and the said sixth section, as amended, adopted as follows, viz.

The supreme court and the several courts of common pleas shall, beside the powers heretofore usually exercised by the said courts, have the power of a court of chancery so far as relates to the perpetuating of testimony, obtaining evidence from places not within the state, and the care of the persons and estates of those who are *non compotes mentis*. And the legislature shall, as soon as conveniently may be, vest in the said courts such other powers to grant relief in equity as shall be found necessary: and may, from time time, enlarge, diminish or vest the same in such other courts as they shall judge proper for the due administration of justice.

Adjourned until half past nine o'clock to-morrow, A. M.

WEDNESDAY, February 17, 1790. *A. M.*

The convention met pursuant to adjournment.

The convention resumed the consideration of the fifth section of the fifth article of the proposed plan of government postponed yesterday, viz.

The judges of the courts of common pleas in each county, or any two of them, the president being one, shall be justices of oyer and terminer and general jail delivery, for the trial of capital and other offenders in their respective counties: But they shall not hold a court of oyer and terminer and general jail delivery in any county when the judges of the supreme court, or some of them, shall be sitting in the same county. The parties accused, as well as the commonwealth, may remove the indictment and proceedings into the supreme court at any time before trial.

It was moved by Mr. Pickering, seconded by Mr. Lewis, to amend the same by striking out the words "at any time before trial," and to add the following to the said section in lieu thereof, viz. "But no writ of removal presented by the party accused, shall be allowed by the court, where the indictment shall have been found, without the consent of the attorney general, or special cause shown, unless the same shall have been specially awarded by the supreme court or one of the justices thereof."

On the question, Will the convention agree to the said amendment? The yeas and nays being called by Mr. Boyd, were as follow viz.

YEAS.

| Mr. Lewis | Mr. M'Kean | Mr. Pickering | 3 |

NAYS.

Mr. Wilson	Mr. Hand	Mr. Gehr	Mr. Gallatin
Baker	Graff	Sitgreaves	M'Lene
Roberts	Atlee	Mawhorter	Matthews
Gray	Hubley	Arndt	Morris
Robinson,	Breckbill	Rhoads	Potts
Hare	Miller	Powell	Coates
Edwards	Slegle	Piper	Shoemaker
Ogden	Reed	Snyder	Gloninger
Jenks	Tyson	Findley	Brown
Barclay	Dill	Todd	Graydon
Stout	Whitehill	Addison	Gibson
Gibbons	Power	Hoge	Beale
Bull	Lower	Redick	Sellers
T. Ross	Lincoln	Smilie	Newlin
Boyd	Groscop		59

So it was determined in the negative.

A motion was made by Mr. Addison, seconded by Mr. Wilson, to amend the last clause of the said fifth section so as to read as follows, viz.

The parties accused, as well as the commonwealth, may, under such regulations as shall be prescribed by law, remove the indictment and proceedings into the supreme court.

Which was determined in the affirmative.

It was then moved by Mr. Lewis, seconded by Mr. Pickering, to insert after the word " proceedings," the words " or transcripts thereof." Which was determined in the affirmative.

A motion was made by Mr. Lewis, seconded by Mr. Pickering, to amend the two first clauses of the said fifth section so as to read as follows, viz.

The president of the courts of common pleas for each county, and such other justice thereof as shall be appointed and commissioned for that purpose, shall, during their continuance in office, be justices of oyer and terminer and jail delivery, for the trial of capital and other offenders therein ; but they shall not act as such when the justices of the supreme court or any of them shall be sitting in the same county ; nor shall any commission of oyer and terminer or jail delivery be issued to any other person.

On the question, Will the convention agree to the said amendment? It was determined in the negative.

And the said fifth section being then under consideration, as amended, viz.

The judges of the courts of common pleas in each county, the president being one, shall be justices of oyer and terminer and general jail delivery, for the trial of capital and other offenders in their respective counties; but they shall not hold a court of oyer and terminer and general jail delivery in any county when the judges of the supreme court, or some of them, shall be sitting in the same county. The party accused, as well as the commonwealth, may, under such regulations as shall be prescribed by law, remove the indictment and proceedings, or transcripts thereof, into the supreme court.

On the question, Will the convention adopt the same as the fifth section of the fifth article of the plan of government? The yeas and nays being called by Mr. Whitehill, were as follow, viz.

YEAS.

Mr. Wilson	Mr. Graff	Mr. Power	Mr. Potts
Baker	Atlee	Arndt	Gloninger
M'Kean	Hubley	Rhoads	Graydon
Gray	Breckbill	Findley	Pickering
Jenks	Miller	Todd	Gibson
Barclay	Slegle	Addison	Beale
Stout	Reed	Hoge	Sellers
T. Ross	Tyson	Redick	Newlin
Hand	Dill		34

NAYS.

Mr. Roberts	Mr. Robinson	Mr. Edwards	Mr. Gibbons
Lewis	Hare	Ogden	Boyd

27

NAYS.

Mr. Whitehill	Mr. Sitgreaves	Mr. Smilie	Mr. Morris
Lower	Mawhorter	Gallatin	Coates
Lincoln	Powell	M'Lene	Shoemaker
Groscop	Piper	Matthews	Brown
Gehr	Snyder		26

So it was determined in the affirmative.

The last clause of the third section of the said fifth article, postponed the 15th of February, recurring, viz.

No special commission of oyer and terminer or jail delivery shall be issued.

On the question, Will the convention agree to the same? It was determined in the negative, and the said third section adopted as follows:

The jurisdiction of the supreme court shall extend over the state, and the judges thereof shall, by virtue of their offices, be justices of oyer and terminer and general jail delivery in the several counties.

A motion was made by Mr. Sitgreaves seconded by Mr. Wilson, to re-consider the fifth section of the said fifth article, in order to amend the same so as to read as follows, viz.

The judges of the courts of common pleas in each county shall, by virtue of their offices, be justices of oyer and terminer and general jail delivery for the trial of capital and other offenders therein, any two of whom, the president being one, shall be a quorum; but they shall not hold a court of oyer and terminer and jail delivery in any county when the judges of the supreme court, or some of them, shall be sitting in the same county. The party accused, as well as the commonwealth, may, under such regulations as shall be prescribed by law, remove the indictment and proceedings, or transcripts thereof, into the supreme court. Which was determined in the affirmative.

The seventh section of the said fifth article being under consideration, a division of the said section was called by Mr. Addison, and the first proposition being under consideraton, viz.

The judges of the courts of common pleas shall compose the courts of quarter sessions and orphans' court in their respective counties, any two of whom shall be a quorum.

On motion of Mr. Lewis, Ordered, that the words "of the peace," be inserted after "quarter sessions."

It was moved by Mr. Sitgreaves, seconded by Mr. Arndt, to amend the same so as to read as follows, viz.

The judges of the court of common pleas in each county shall compose the courts of quarter sessions of the peace and orphans' court therein, any two of whom shall be a quorum.

Which was determined in the affirmative, and the second proposition being agreed to, the said seventh section was thereupon adopted as follows, viz.

The judges of the courts of common pleas in each county shall compose the court of quarter sessions of the peace and orphans' court therein, any two of whom shall be a quorum; and the register of wills, together with the said judges, or any two of them, shall compose the register's court in the respective county.

The eighth section of the said fifth article being under consideration,

It was moved by Mr. Lewis, seconded by Mr. Pickering, to amend the said section so as to read as follows, viz.

The judges of the courts of common pleas shall, within their respective counties, have the like powers with the judges of the supreme court to issue writs of certiorari to the justices of the peace, and to cause their proceedings to be brought before them and the like right and justice to be done.

It was moved by Mr. Pickering, seconded by Mr. Lewis, to add the word "therein" after "peace"

Which was determined in the negative.

On the question, Will the convention agree to the said amendment as the eighth section?

It was determined in the affirmative.

The ninth section of the said fifth article being under consideration,

A motion was made by Mr. Sitgreaves, seconded by Mr. Wilson, to amend the said section so as to read as follows, viz.

The president of the courts in each circuit, shall within such circuit, and the judges of the courts of common pleas shall, within their respective counties, be justices of the peace so far as relates to criminal causes.

On the question, Will the convention adopt the same as the ninth section of the said fifth article?

It was determined in the affirmative.

The tenth section of the said fifth article being under consideration, viz.

The governor shall appoint and commission a competent number of justices of the peace in convenient districts in each county, to be fixed in such manner as shall be, by law, directed. They shall be commissioned during good behaviour; but may be removed on conviction of misbehaviour in office or any infamous crime, or on the address of both houses of the legislature.

A motion was made by Mr. M'Kean, seconded by Mr. Arndt, to introduce the following as the tenth section, viz.

The judges of the supreme court and of the several county courts of common pleas, shall have the appointment of the prothonotaries or clerks of the said courts respectively, who shall hold and enjoy their said offices during their good behaviour.

On the question, Will the convention agree to the same?

It was determined in the negative.

It was moved by Mr. M'Lene, seconded by Mr. Piper, to substitute the following in lieu of the said tenth section, viz.

A competent number of justices of the peace for each county shall be ascertained by law, and elected by the citizens of each county qualified to vote for representatives. Each county shall, by the legislature, be divided into districts; two of the persons so elected to be inhabitants in the district for which they shall be chosen; the governor shall commission one of each two, who shall be a justice of the peace in the county.

A motion was made by Mr. Findley, seconded by Mr. M'Lene, to postpone the said section with the proposed substitute.

Which was determined in the negative.

Mr. M'Lene's motion then recurring,

On the question, Will the convention agree to the same? The yeas and nays being called by Mr. Gibbons, were as follow, viz.

YEAS.

Mr. Robinson	Mr. Rhoads	Mr. Smilie	Mr. Coates
Reed	Powell	Gallatin	Shoemaker
Whitehill	Piper	M'Lene	Gloninger
Power	Findley	Matthews	Brown
Mawhorter	Todd	Morris	Beale 20

NAYS.

Mr. Wilson	Mr. Barclay	Mr. Breckbill	Mr. Snyder
Baker	Stout	Miller	Addison
Roberts	Gibbons	Slegle	Hoge
Lewis	Bull	Tyson	Redick
M'Kean	T. Ross	Dill	Potts
Gray	Boyd	Lower	Graydon
Hare	Hand	Groscop	Pickering
Edwards	Graff	Gehr	Gibson
Ogden	Atlee	Sitgreaves	Sellers
Jenks	Hubley	Arndt	Newlin 40

So it was determined in the negative.

The original section again recurring, a division was called for.

And on the question, Will the convention agree to the first part thereof, viz.

The governor shall appoint and commission a competent number of justices of the peace in convenient districts in each county, to be fixed in such manner as shall be, by law, directed·

It was determined in the affirmative, and the second part of the said tenth section being under consideration, viz.

They shall be commissioned during good behaviour, but may be removed on conviction of misbehaviour in office, or any infamous crime, or on the address of both houses of the legislature.

It was moved by Mr. Sitgreaves, seconded by Mr. Hare, to strike out the words "during good behaviour," and in lieu thereof, to insert "for the term of   years."

On the question, Will the convention agree to the same?

The yeas and nays being called by Mr. Edwards, were as follows, viz.

YEAS.

Mr. Hare	Mr. Lower	Mr. Mawhorter	Mr. Piper
Edwards	Sitgreaves	Snyder	Gloninger
Jenks			9

NAYS.

Mr. Wilson	Mr. Barclay	Mr. Atlee	Mr. Whitehill
Baker	Stout	Hubley	Power
Roberts	Gibbons	Breckbill	Groscop
Lewis	Bull	Miller	Gehr
M'Kean	T. Ross	Slegle	Arndt
Gray	Boyd	Reed	Rhoads
Robinson	Hand	Tyson	Powell
Ogden	Graff	Dill	Findley

NAYS.

Mr. Todd	Mr. Gallatin	Mr. Coates	Mr. Gibson
Addison	M'Lene	Shoemaker	Beale
Hoge	Matthews	Brown	Sellers
Redick	Morris	Graydon	Newlin
Smilie	Potts	Pickering	51

So it was determined in the negative,

And the said tenth section of the fifth article, as reported by the committee of the whole, adopted.

On application of Zachariah Poulson, jr. it was on motion of Mr. Hare, seconded by Mr. M'Kean,

Resolved, That the president draw an order on the treasurer of the state in favor of Zachariah Poulson, jr. as printer to this convention, for the sum of one hundred pounds, he being accountable therefor in the settlement of his account.

Adjourned until half past nine o'clock to-morrow, A. M.

THURSDAY, February 18, 1790. *A. M.*

The convention met pursuant to adjournment.

The eleventh section of the fifth article of the proposed constitution being under consideration, the same was adopted as follows, viz.

A register's office for the probate of wills and granting letters of administration, and an office for the recording of deeds shall be kept in each county.

The twelfth section of the said fifth article being under consideration, viz.

Prothonotaries, clerks of the peace and orphans' courts, recorders of deeds, registers of wills and sheriffs shall keep their offices in the county town of the county in which they respectively shall be officers.

It was moved by Mr. Ogden, seconded by Mr. Shoemaker, to add the following proviso to the said section, viz. " Provided the county town shall have been established   years."

A motion was then made by Mr. Sitgreaves, seconded by Mr. Thomas Ross, to postpone the proviso moved by Mr. Ogden, and to strike out all the words in the original section after the words " shall keep their offices," and in lieu thereof, to insert the following words, viz.

" Within   of the court house or other place where the courts of the proper county shall be held, except when the governor shall, in special cases, dispense therewith."

On the question, Will the convention agree to the postponement?

It was determined in the affirmative.

Mr. Wilson then called for a division of the question on the said amendment.

And the question being taken on the first clause of the said amendment, viz.

Within   of the court house or other place where the courts of the proper county shall be held.

It was determined in the negative.

And the question being taken on the latter part of the said amendment, viz.

Except when the governor shall in special cases, dispense therewith.

It was determined in the affirmative.

It was then moved by Mr. Redick, seconded by Mr. Todd, to substitute the following in lieu of the twelfth section as amended, viz.

The legislature shall, as soon as conveniently may be, make provision by law for keeping all public county offices in the several county towns respectively; as also for the preservation of the papers and records belonging to such offices.

On the question, Will the convention agree to the same ?

It was determined in the negative.

A motion was then made by Mr. Pickering, seconded by Mr. Ogden, to add the following words to the second part of the amendment moved by Mr. Sitgreaves and adopted, viz.

During the term of   years after the town shall have been erected.

Which was determined in the negative.

Whereupon, on the question, Will the convention agree to the section as amended? viz.

Prothonotaries, clerks of the peace and orphans' courts, recorders of deeds, registers of wills, and sheriffs shall keep their offices in the county town of the county in which they respectively shall be officers, except when the governor shall, in special casers, dispense therewith.

The yeas and nays being called by Mr. Sitgreaves, were as follow:

YEAS.

Mr. Wilson	Mr. T. Ross	Mr. Miller	Mr. Hoge
Baker	Boyd	Slegle	Morris
Gray	Hand	Tyson	Potts
Hare	Graff	Gehr	Coates
Edwards	Atlee	Sitgreaves	Shoemaker
Gibbons	Hubley	Snyder	Pickering
Bull	Breckbill		26

NAYS.

Mr. Roberts	Mr. Dill	Mr. Rhoads	Mr. Gallatin
Lewis	Whitehill	Powell	M'Lene
M'Kean	Power	Piper	Matthews
Robinson	Hiester	Findley	Gloninger
Ogden	Lower	Todd	Brown
Jenks	Lincoln	Addison	Gibson
Barclay	Groscop	Redick	Beale
Stout	Mawhorter	Smilie	Newlin]
Reed	Arndt		31

So it was determined in the negative.

The thirteenth section of the said fifth article being under consideration, the same was adopted as follows, viz.

The stile of all process shall be *The commonwealth of Pennsylvania:* all prosecutions shall be carried on in the name and by the authority of the commonwealth of Pennsylvania, and shall conclude, *against the peace and dignity of the same.*

The first section of the sixth article being under consideration, viz.

Sheriffs and coroners shall, at the places of the election of representatives, be chosen by the citizens of each county respectively; two persons shall be chosen for each office, one of whom for each shall be commissioned by the governor; they shall hold their offices for three years and until a successor be duly qualified. But no person shall be twice chosen or appointed sheriff in any term of six years.

It was moved by Mr. Hubley, seconded by Mr. M'Lene, to strike out the word "three," and to insert after the words " representatives, be chosen," the word " annually."

Mr. M'Lene called for a division of the section, and the question being taken on the first clause, as amended by Mr. Hubley; it was determined in the negative.

A motion was then made by Mr. Addison, seconded by Mr. Brown, to insert after the word " respectively," the words "on the second Tuesday of October." Which was determined in the negative.

It was then moved by Mr. Findley, seconded by Mr. Beale, to add the following words to the said section, viz.

The sheriffs shall not enter upon the duties of their office sooner than three months after they shall be elected.

Which was determined in the negative, and the original section as reported by the committee of the whole, adopted.

A motion was made by Mr. Addison, seconded by Mr. M'Kean, to insert the following as the second section, viz.

Prothonotaries, clerks of the peace and clerks of orphans' courts, recorders of deeds and registers of wills, shall hold their commissions during good behaviour; they shall be removed on conviction of misbehaviour in office or any infamous crime, or may be removed for any other cause on the address of both houses of the legislature.

Whereupon, ordered, that the consideration of the said motion be postponed.

The second section of the said sixth article, reported by the committee of the whole, being under consideration, viz.

The freemen of this commonwealth shall be armed and disciplined for its defence; the militia officers shall be appointed in such manner and for such time as shall be by law directed.

A division of the section was called for by Mr. Ogden, and the question being taken on the clauses separately, they were agreed to.

Whereupon, on the question, Will the convention agree to the said second section as reported by the committee of the whole?

The yeas and nays being called by Mr. Roberts, were as follow, viz

YEAS.

Mr. Wilson	Mr. Graff	Mr. Groscop	Mr. Redick
Baker	Atlee	Gehr	Smilie
Lewis	Hubley	Sitgreaves	Gallatin
M'Kean	Miller	Mawhorter	M'Lene
Gray	Slegle	Rhoads	Matthews
Robinson	Reed	Powell	Morris
Hare	Tyson	Piper	Potts
Barclay	Dill	Snyder	Coates
Gibbons	Whitehill	Findley	Gloninger
Bull	Hiester	Todd	Pickering
T. Ross	Lower	Addison	Gibson
Boyd	Lincoln	Hoge	Beale
Hand			

49

NAYS.

Mr. Roberts	Mr. Jenks	Mr. Shoemaker	Mr. Sellers
Edwards'	Stout	Brown	Newlin
Ogden	Breckbill		10

So it was determined in the affirmative.

It was then moved by Mr. M'Kean, seconded by Mr. Gallatin, to connect the following with the sixth article of the proposed plan of government:

That such alterations and amendments in the foregoing system or form of government may be made in a regular and orderly way, so as to render it still more conducive to the security and happiness of the society, the general assembly, from time to time, when experience shall make it necessary, may, and they are hereby authorised and empowered to prepare and pass a bill for that purpose, specifying the parts or particulars proposed to be changed, altered or amended, and cause the same to be printed and published for the consideration of the people at least three months before a new election, and if the same shall be ratified and confirmed by five parts in seven of the whole number of the house of representatives, and six parts in seven of the senate, in the first session after such new election, the same shall become constitutionally obligatory upon the government and people of this commonwealth.

Ordered, That the consideration thereof be postponed.

It was moved by Mr. Robinson, seconded by Mr. Sitgreaves, to connect the following with the said sixth article, viz.

Members of the general assembly and all officers, executive and judicial, shall be bound by oath or affirmation to support the constitution of this commonwealth, and to perform the duties of their respective offices with fidelity.

Ordered, That the consideration thereof be postponed.

On motion, Ordered that Mr. Wilson, Mr. Lewis and Mr. Findley be a committee to revise and correct so much of the report of the committee of the whole as has been adopted by this convention.

Adjourned until half past nine o'clock to-morrow, A. M.

FRIDAY. February 19, 1790, *A. M.*

The convention met pursuant to adjournment.

On motion, ordered, that Mr. Thomas Ross, have leave of absence.

The first section of the bill of rights, reported by the committee of the whole, being under consideration, the same was adopted as follows, viz.

That all men are born equally free and independent, and have certain inherent and indefeasible rights, among which are those of enjoying and defending life and liberty, of acquiring, posessing and protecting property and reputation, and of pursuing their own happiness.

The second section of the said bill of rights, being under consideration.

It was moved by Mr. Roberts, seconded by Mr. Jenks, to amend the same so as to read as follows, viz.

That all power being originally vested in, is derived from the people, and all free governments are founded on their authority and instituted for their common peace, safety and happiness, the majority of whom have, at all times, an unalienable and indefeasible right to alter, reform or change their government in such manner as may be conducive to obtain those ends.

On the question, Will the convention agree to the said amendment? It was determined in the negative, and the second section, as reported, adopted as follows, viz.

That all power being originally vested in, is derived from, the people, and all free governments originate from their will, are founded on their authority, and instituted for their common peace, safety and happiness; and for the advancement thereof, they have, at all times, an unalienable and indefeasible right to alter, reform or abolish their government, in such manner as they may think proper.

The third section of the bill of rights being under consideration, the same was adopted as follows, viz.

That all men have a natural and indefeasible right to worship Almighty God according to the dictates of their own consciences, and that no man can of right be compelled to attend any religious worship, or to erect or support any place of worship, or to maintain any ministry against his free will and consent; and that no human authority can controul or interfere with the rights of conscience in any case whatever; nor shall any preference ever be given, by law, to any religious establishments or modes of worship.

The fourth section of the said bill of rights being under consideration, viz.

That no person who acknowledges the being of a God and a future state of rewards and punishments, shall, on account of his religious sentiments, be disqualified to hold any office or place of trust or profit under this commonwealth.

A motion was made by Mr. Robinson, seconded by Mr. Redick, to adopt the following as the fourth section, viz.

As civil society is instituted for the purposes of enforcing a discharge of the relative duties and preventing the violences of men towards each other, so the great author of their existence can alone determine the truths of religious opinions, therefore no power shall be assumed of depriving a citizen of the privilege of serving his country, in office, on account of his religious belief.

On the question, Will the convention agree to the same?

The yeas and nays being called by Mr. Robinson, were as follow, viz.

YEAS.

Mr. Robinson	Mr. Ogden	Mr. Iloge	Mr. Redick
Edwards	Sitgreaves		6

NAYS.

Mr. Wilson	Mr. M'Kean	Mr. Barclay	Mr. Boyd
Baker	Gray	Stout	Hand
Roberts	Hare	Gibbons	Graff
Lewis	Jenks	Bull	Atlee

NAYS.

Mr. Hubley	Mr. Lower	Mr. Findley	Mr. Shoemaker
Breckbill	Lincoln	Todd	Gloninger
Miller	Groscop	Addison	Brown
Slegle	Gehr	Smilie	Graydon
Reed	Mawhorter	Gallatin	Pickering
Tyson	Arndt	M'Lene	Gibson
Dill	Rhoads	Matthews	Beale
Whitehill	Powel	Morris	Sellers
Power	Piper	Potts	Newlin
Hiester	Snyder	Coates	55

So it was determined in the negative.

It was moved by Mr. Wilson, seconded by Mr. M'Kean, to strike out the words, in the original section, " of rewards and punishments."

A motion was then made by Mr. Roberts, seconded by Mr. Robinson, to postpone the said fourth section, together with the proposed amendment, in order to introduce the following as the fourth section:

No religious test shall ever be required as a qualification to any office or public trust under this constitution.

On the question, Will the convention agree to the postponement for the aforesaid purpose?

The yeas and nays being called by Mr. Roberts, were as follow:

YEAS.

Mr. Roberts	Mr. Hare	Mr. Breckbill	Mr. Redick
Gray	Edwards	Sitgreaves	Morris
Robinson	Ogden	Hoge	11

NAYS.

Mr. Wilson	Mr. Miller	Mr. Mawhorter	Mr. Matthews
Baker	Slegle	Arndt	Potts
Lewis	Reed	Rhoads	Coates
M'Kean	Tyson	Powell	Gloninger
Jenks	Dill	Piper	Brown
Barclay	Whitehill	Snyder	Graydon
Stout	Power	Findley	Pickering
Gibbons	Hiester	Todd	Gibson
Bull	Lower	Addison	Beale
Hand	Lincoln	Smilie	Sellers
Graff	Groscop	Gallatin	Newlin
Hubley	Gehr	M'Lene	47

So it was determined in the negative.

It was moved by Mr. Lewis, seconded by Mr. Potts, to postpone the amendment moved by Mr. Wilson, in order to insert after the word " God," the following: " the rewarder of the good and punisher of the wicked," and to strike out the words "and a future state of rewards and punishments." Which was determined in the negative.

A motion was then made by Mr. Sitgreaves, seconded by Mr. Ogden, to postpone the amendment of Mr. Wilson, in order to strike out the words "who acknowledges the being of a God and a future state of rewards and punishments."

On the question, Will the convention agree to postpone in order to strike out the said words?

It was determined in the negative, and the said fourth section as reported by the committee of the whole, adopted.

The fifth section of the said bill of rights being under consideration, the same was adopted as follows:

That elections shall be free and equal.

The sixth section of the said bill of rights being under consideration, the same was adopted as follows:

That trial by jury shall be as heretofore, and the right thereof shall remain inviolate.

The seventh section of the said bill of rights being under consideration, viz.

That the printing presses shall be free to every person who undertakes to examine the proceedings of the legislature or any branch of government, and no law shall ever be made restraining the right thereof. The free communication of thoughts and opinions is one of the invaluable rights of man, and every citizen may freely speak, write and print on any subject, being responsible for the abuse of that liberty. But upon indictments for the publication of papers investigating the conduct of individuals in their public capacity, or of those applying or canvassing for office, the truth of the facts may be given in evidence in justification upon the general issue.

A division of the section was called for by Mr. Ogden and Mr. Hare, and the question being taken on the several clauses as far as the word "liberty," it was determined in the affirmative.

A motion was made by Mr. M'Kean, seconded by Mr. Roberts, to strike out the words " or of those applying or canvassing for office," contained in the last clause of the said section.

A motion was then made by Mr. Edwards, seconded by Mr. Findley, to postpone the said clause and amendment in order to introduce the following as a substitute, viz.

But upon indictments for the publication of libels the truth of the facts may be given in evidence in justification upon the general issue.

Adjourned until half past nine o'clock to-morrow, A. M.

SATURDAY, February 20, 1790. A. M.

The convention met pursuant to adjournment.

The motion made by Mr. Edwards, seconded by Mr. Findley, on the nineteenth instant, recurring, viz.

To postpone the last clause of the seventh section of the bill of rights, together with the amendment offered thereto, in order to introduce the following in lieu thereof, viz.

But upon indictments for the publication of libels the truth of the facts may be given in evidence in justification upon the general issue.

After considerable debate thereon, on motion,

Adjourned until half past nine o'clock on Monday next, A. M.

MONDAY, February 22, 1790. A. M.

The convention met pursuant to adjournment.

Mr. Edwards withdrew his motion of the nineteenth instant to postpone.

A motion was made by Mr. Addison, seconded by Mr. M'Lene, to postpone the last clause of the seventh section, together with the amendment offered by Mr. Wilson, in order to introduce the following as a substitute, viz.

In prosecutions for libels their truth or design may be given in evidence on the general issue, and their nature and tendency, whether proper for public information or only for private ridicule or malice, be determined by the jury.

The yeas and nays, on postponing, being called by Mr. Ogden, were as follow, viz.

YEAS.

Mr. Wilson	Mr. Whitehill	Mr. Snyder	Mr. M'Lene
Hare	Power	Findley	Matthews
Edwards	Lower	Todd	Gloninger
Gibbons	Lincoln	Addison	Brown
Bull	Groscop	Hoge	Graydon
Boyd	Gehr	Redick	Gibson
Reed	Mawhorter	Smilie	Beale
Dill	Powell	Gallatin	31

NAYS.

Mr. Baker	Mr. Jenks	Mr. Breckbill	Mr. J. Ross
Roberts	Barclay	Miller	Potts
Lewis	Stout	Slegle	Coates
M'Kean	Hand	Tyson	Shoemaker
Gray	Graff	Sitgreaves	Pickering
Robinson	Atlee	Arndt	Newlin
Ogden	Hubley	Rhoads	27

So the question was determined in the affirmative.

A motion was then made by Mr. M'Kean, seconded by Mr. Atlee, to amend the substitute of Mr. Addison, by inserting after the words "for libels," the following: "against public officers respecting their official conduct," and after "jury," to insert "under the direction of the court as in other cases."

The yeas and nays being called, on the first part of the amendment, by Mr. Ogden, were as follow, viz.

YEAS.

Mr. Baker	Mr. Barclay	Mr. Hubley	Mr. J. Ross
Roberts	Stout	Breckbill	Potts
Lewis	Bull	Tyson	Coates
M'Kean	Hand	Sitgreaves	Shoemaker
Gray	Graff	Arndt	Pickering
Ogden	Atlee	Rhoads	Newlin
Jenks			25

NAYS.

Mr. Wilson	Mr. Edwards	Mr. Boyd	Mr. Reed
Hare	Gibbons	Slegle	Dill
Whitehill	Gehr	Addison	Matthews

NAYS.

Mr. Power	Mr. Mawhorter	Mr. Hoge	Mr. Gloninger	
Hiester	Powel	Redick	Brown	
Lower	Snyder	Smilie	Graydon	
Lincoln	Findley	Gallatin	Gibson	
Groscop	Todd	M'Lene	Beale	32

So it was determined in the negative, and the second part of the said amendment being under consideration.

On the question, Will the convention agree to the same?

The yeas and nays being called by Mr. M'Kean, were as follow, viz.

YEAS.

Mr. Wilson	Mr. Bull	Mr. Lower	Mr. J. Ross	
Baker	Hand	Lincoln	Gallatin	
Roberts	Graff	Groscop	M'Lene	
Lewis	Atlee	Gehr	Matthews	
M'Kean	Hubley	Sitgreaves	Potts	
Gray	Breckbill	Mawhorter	Coates	
Robinson	Miller	Arndt	Shoemaker	
Hare	Slegle	Rhoads	Gloninger	
Edwards	Reed	Powell	Brown	
Ogden	Tyson	Snyder	Graydon	
Jenks	Dill	Findley	Pickering	
Barclay	Whitehill	Todd	Gibson	
Stout	Power	Hoge	Beale	
Gibbons	Hiester	Redick	Newlin	56

NAYS.

Mr. Boyd	Mr. Addison	Mr Smilie	3

So it was determined in the affirmative.

Whereupon, on the question, Will the convention agree to the substitute as amended? viz.

In prosecutions for libels their truth or design may be given in evidence on the general issue, and their nature and tendency, whether proper for public information, or only for private ridicule or malice, be determined by the jury, under the direction of the court as in other cases.

The yeas and nays being called by Mr. Lewis, were as follow:

YEAS.

Mr. Wilson	Mr. Whitehill	Mr. Mawhorter	Mr. Gallatin	
Hare	Power	Snyder	M'Lene	
Edwards	Hiester	Findley	Matthews	
Gibbons	Lower	Todd	Gloninger	
Boyd	Lincoln	Addison	Brown	
Breckbill	Groscop	Hoge	Graydon	
Reed	Gehr	Redick	Gibson	
Dill	Powel	Smilie	Beale	32

NAYS.

Mr. Baker	Mr. Jenks	Mr. Hubley	Mr. J. Ross
Roberts	Barclay	Miller	Potts
Lewis	Stout	Slegle	Coates
M'Kean	Bull	Tyson	Shoemaker
Gray	Hand	Sitgreaves	Pickeiing
Robinson	Graff	Arndt	Newlin
Ogden	Atlee	Rhoads	27

So it was determined in the affirmative, and the seventh section of the bill of rights, as amended, was then adopted.

Adjourned until half past nine o'clock to-morrow, A. M.

TUESDAY, February 23, 1790. A. M.

The convention met pursuant to adjournment.

The eighth section of the seventh article of the proposed plan of government being under consideration, the same was adopted as follows, viz.

That the people shall be secure in their persons, houses, papers and possessions, against unreasonable searches and seizures, and no warrant shall issue to search any place, or to seize any person or things, but on probable cause, supported by oath or affirmation, and describing them as nearly as may be.

The ninth section of the said seventh article being under consideration, viz.

That in all prosecutions by indictment the accused hath a right to be heard by himself and his counsel; to demand the cause and nature of the accusation; to meet the witnesses face to face; to have compulsory process for obtaining witnesses in his favor, and a speedy public trial by an impartial jury of the vicinage; nor can he be compelled to give evidence against himself; nor can any man be deprived of his life, liberty or property but by the judgment of his peers or the law of the land.

It was moved by Mr. Lewis, seconded by Mr. James Ross, to insert the word "criminal" before the word prosecutions," and strike out the words "by indictment," and to insert after the words "favor and" the following: "in all proceedings by indictment to."

A division of the question on the said amendments was called for by Mr. Smilie, and the same being taken the amendments were adopted.

A motion was then made by Mr. Wilson seconded by Mr. Atlee, to re-consider the last of the said amendments, viz. "in all proceedings by indictment to," in order to strike out the words "all proceedings," and in lieu thereof to insert the word "prosecutions."

Which was determined in the affirmative, and the said ninth section thereupon adopted as follows:

That in all criminal prosecutions the accused hath a right to be heard by himself and his council; to demand the cause and nature of the accusation; to meet the witnesses face to face; to have compulsory process for obtaining witnesses in his favor, and in prosecutions by indictment to a speedy public trial by an impartial jury of the vicinage; nor can he be compelled to give evidence against himself; nor can any man be deprived of his life, liberty or property but by the judgment of his peers or the law of the land.

The tenth section of the said seventh article being under consideration, viz.

That no person shall be proceeded against by information for any indictable offence, except in cases arising in the land or naval forces, or in the militia when in actual service in time of war or public danger; nor shall any person, for the same offence, be twice put in jeopardy of life or limb; nor shall any man's property be taken, or applied to public use, without the consent of his representatives, and on just compensation being made.

A motion was made by Mr. M'Kean, seconded by Mr. Sitgreaves, to insert after the the words " by information," the words "ex officio."

Which was determined in the negative.

It was then moved by Mr. Lewis, seconded by Mr. Pickering, to strike out the words " for any indictable offence," and, in lieu thereof, to insert, after the word " except," the words "for specific penalties or forfeitures, or in matters merely civil, or."

Whereupon, on motion of Mr. M'Kean, seconded by Mr. Sitgreaves, Ordered, That the further consideration of the said section and amendment be postponed.

The eleventh section of the said seventh article being under consideration, viz.

That all courts shall be open, and every freeman for an injury done him in his lands, goods, person or reputation, shall have remedy by the due course of the law, and right and justice administered to him without sale, denial or delay.

It was moved by Mr. Wilson, seconded by Mr. Smilie, to strike out the word "freeman," and, in lieu thereof, to insert the word "man."

Which was determined in the affirmative, and the said section, as amended, adopted.

The twelfth section of the said seventh article being under consideration, the same was adopted as follows, viz.

That no power of suspending laws, or the execution thereof, shall be exercised, unless by the Legislature or by the authority thereof.

The thirteenth section of the said seventh article being under consideration, viz.

That excessive bail shall not be required, nor excessive fines imposed, or cruel punishments inflicted.

It was moved by Mr. Sitgreaves, seconded by Mr. Arndt, to strike out the word " or," and, in lieu thereof, to insert the word " nor."

Which was determined in the affirmative, and the said thirteenth section, as amended, adopted.

The fourteenth section of the said seventh article being under consideration, the same was adopted as follows, viz.

That all prisoners shall be bailable by sufficient sureties, unless for capital offences, when the proof is evident or presumption great, and the privilege of the writ of Habeas Corpus shall not be suspended unless when, in cases of rebellion or invasion, the public safety may require it.

A motion was made by Mr. Wilson, seconded by Mr. Power, to insert the following as the fifteenth section of the said seventh article, viz.

That no commission of oyer and terminer or gaol delivery shall be issued.

Which was determined in the affirmative.

The fifteenth section of the said seventh article, as reported by the committee of the whole, being under consideration, the same was adopted as the sixteenth section of the said article, as follows, viz.

That the person of a debtor, where there is not a strong presumption of fraud, shall not be continued in prison after delivering up all his estate for the benefit of his creditors, in such manner as shall be prescribed by law.

The sixteenth section of the said seventh article being under consideration, the same was adopted as the seventeenth section, viz.

That no *expost facto* law, or law impairing contracts shall be made.

The seventeenth section of the said seventh article being under consideration, the same was adopted as the eighteenth section, viz.

That no person shall be attainted of treason or felony by the Legislature

The eighteenth section of the said seventh article being under consideration, viz.

That no attainder shall work corruption of blood or forfeiture of estate, to the *commonwealth;* the estates of such persons as shall destroy their own lives shall go as in the case of natural death; and if any person shall be killed by casualty or accident there shall be no forfeiture by reason thereof.

It was moved by Mr Lewis, seconded by Mr. Boyd, to insert, after the word " commonwealth," the words " except during the life of the offender."

On the question, Will the convention agree to the amendment?

The yeas and nays being called by Mr. Wilson, were as follow, viz.

YEAS.

Mr. Lewis	Mr. Miller	Mr. Sitgreaves	Mr. Gallatin
Roberts	Slegle	Arndt	M'Lene
Gibbons	Reed	Rhoads	Matthews
Bull	Dill	Snyder	Coates
Boyd	Whitehill	Findley	Gloninger
Hand	Lower	Todd	Gibson
Graff	Lincoln	J. Ross	Beale
Atlee	Groscop		30

NAYS.

Mr. Wilson	Mr. Ogden	Mr. Hiester	Mr. Redick
Baker	Jenks	Gehr	Smilie
Roberts	Barclay	Mawhorter	Potts
M'Kean	Stout	Powell	Shoemaker
Gray	Hubley	Addison	Brown
Hare	Breckbill	Hoge	Graydon
Edwards	Power		26

So it was determined in the affirmative, and the same adopted as the ninteenth section of the said article.

The nineteenth section of the said article being under consideration,

The same was, on motion of Mr. Sitgreaves, seconded by Mr. Hare, adopted as the twentieth section, as follows, viz.

That the citizens have a right, in a peaceable manner, to assemble together for their common good, and to apply to those invested with the powers of government, for redress of grievances or other proper purposes, by petition, address or remonstrance.

The twentieth section of the seventh article being under consideration, viz.

That the right of the citizens to bear arms in defence of themselves and the state shall not be questioned. But those who conscientiously scruple to bear arms shall not be compellable to do so, but shall pay an equivalent for personal service.

It was moved by Mr. Ogden, seconded by Mr. Jenks, to strike out the remainder of the said second section after the words "shall not be questioned."

On the question, Will the convention agree to strike out the same? The yeas and nays being called by Mr. Roberts, were as follow, viz.

YEAS.

Mr. Roberts	Mr. Jenks	Mr. Breckbill	Mr. Shoemaker
Gray	Stout	Potts	Newlin
Ogden			9

NAYS.

Mr. Wilson	Mr. Hubley	Mr. Mawhorter	Mr. Smilie
M'Kean	Miller	Arndt	Gallatin
Robinson	Slegle	Rhoads	M'Lene
Hare	Reed	Powell	Matthews
Barclay	Dill	Snyder	Morris
Gibbons	Whitehill	Findley	Coates
Bull	Power	Todd	Gloninger
Boyd	Hiester	Addison	Brown
Hand	Lincoln	Redick	Beale
Graff	Groscop	J. Ross	Sellers
Atlee	Gehr		42

So it was determined in the negative, and the said section adopted as the twenty-first of the seventh article.

The twenty-first section of the said seventh article being under consideration, the same was adopted as the twenty second-section, viz.

That no standing army shall, in time of peace, be kept up without the consent of the legislature, and the military shall, in all cases, and at all times, be kept in strict subordination to the civil power.

The twenty-second section of the said article being under consideration, the same was adopted as the twenty-third section, as follows, viz.

That no soldier shall, in time of peace, be quartered in any house without the consent of the owner, nor in time of war, but in a manner to be prescribed by law.

The twenty-third section of the said article being under consideration, the same was adopted as the twenty-fourth section, as follows, viz.

That the legislature shall, at no time, grant any title of nobility or hereditary distinction, nor create any office the appointment to which shall be for a longer term than during good behaviour.

The twenty-fourth section of the said article being under consideration, the same was adopted as the twenty fifth section, as follows:

That emigration from the state shall not be prohibited.

The twenty-fifth section of the said article being under consideration, viz.

To guard against transgressions of the high powers which we have delegated, WE DECLARE—

That every thing in this article expressed, is excepted out of the general powers of legislation, and shall for ever remain inviolate.

It was moved by Mr. Wilson, seconded by Mr. Hare, to strike out the word "legislation," and, in lieu thereof, to insert the word "government." Which was carried in the affirmative, and the same as amended, adopted as the twenty sixth section of the said seventh article.

Mr. M'Kean renewed his motion, made the eighteenth instant, seconded by Mr. Gallatin, and the same being under consideration,

A motion was made by Mr. Findley, seconded by Mr. Gibbons, to postpone the consideration thereof until Thursday next.

It was then, on motion of Mr. Sitgreaves, seconded by Mr. Gallatin, Ordered, That the further consideration thereof be postponed until to-morrow.

The tenth section of the said seventh article being again under consideration, it was moved by Mr. Lewis, seconded by Mr. James Ross, to amend the same so as to read as follows:

That no person shall, for any indictable offence, be proceeded against criminally by information, except in cases arising in the land and naval forces, or in the militia when in actual service in time of war or public danger; nor shall any person for the same offence be twice put in jeopardy of life or limb; nor shall any man's property be taken, or applied to public use, without the consent of his representatives, and on just compensation being made.

And on the question, Will the convention agree to the same?

It was determined in the affirmative, and the said section adopted.

Mr. Addison withdrew his motion of the 18th instant, seconded by Mr. M'Kean.

Adjourned until half past nine o'clock to-morrow, A. M.

WEDNESDAY, February 24, 1790. A. M.

The convention met pursuant to adjournment.

A letter from Melchior Steiner, printer to this convention, in the German language, was read, praying a sum of money may be advanced him on account; and on motion, and by special order, the same was read the second time. Whereupon,

Resolved, That the president be directed to draw an order on the state treasurer, in favor of Melchior Steiner, for the sum of seventy-five pounds, he being accountable therefor.

The committee appointed the eighteenth of February, instant, to revise and correct the report of the committee of the whole, so far as the same has been amended and adopted in convention, made report of the following

PLAN OF GOVERNMENT.

ARTICLE I.

Section I. The legislative power of this commonwealth shall be vested in a general assembly, which shall consist of a senate and house of representatives.

Sect. II. The representatives shall be chosen annually, by the citizens of the city of Philadelphia, and of each county respectively, on the second Tuesday of October.

Sect. III. No person shall be a representative, who shall not have attained the age of twenty-one years, and have been a citizen and inhabitant of the state three years next preceding his election, and the last year thereof an inhabitant of the city or county in which he shall be chosen.

Sect IV. Within three years after the first meeting of the general assembly, and within every subsequent term of seven years, an enumeration of the taxable inhabitants shall be made, in such manner as shall be directed by law. The number of representatives shall, at the several periods of making such enumeration be fixed by the legislature and apportioned among the city of Philadelphia and the several counties according to the number of taxable inhabitants in each, and shall never be less than sixty nor more than one hundred. Each county shall have, at least, one representative; but no county hereafter erected, shall be entitled to a separate representation until a sufficient number of taxable inhabitants shall be contained within it, to entitle them to at least one representative, agreeably to the ratio which shall then be established.

Sect. V. The senators shall be chosen for four years by the citizens of Philadelphia and of each county respectively, at the same time, in the same manner, and at the same places where they shall vote for representatives.

Sect. VI. The number of senators shall, at the several periods of making the enumeration before mentioned, be fixed by the legislature, and apportioned among the districts, formed as hereinafter directed, according to the number of taxable inhabitants in each; and shall never be less than one-fourth, nor more than one-third of the number of representatives.

Sect. VII. The senators shall be chosen in districts to be formed by the legislature, each, containing as nearly as may be, such a number of taxable inhabitants as shall be entitled to elect one senator: Where that cannot be done, then such number of adjoining counties shall be formed into one district as shall be entitled to elect not more than four senators; but neither the city of Philadelphia, nor any county, shall be divided in forming a district.

Sect. VIII. No person shall be a senator who shall not have attained the age of twenty-five years; and have been a citizen and inhabitant of the state four years next before his election, and the last year thereof an inhabitant of the district for which he shall be chosen

Sect. IX. Immediately after the senators shall be assembled in consequence of the first election subsequent to the first enumeration, they shall be divided, by lot, as equally as may be, into four classes. The seats of the senators of the first class shall be vacated at the expiration of the first year; of the second class, at the expiration of the second year; of the third class, at the expiration of the third year; and of the fourth class, at the expiration of the fourth year; so that one-fourth may be chosen every year.

Sect. X. The general assembly shall meet on the first Tuesday of December in every year, unless sooner convened by the governor.

Sect. XI. Each house shall choose its speaker and other officers; and the senate shall also choose a speaker *pro tempore*, when the speaker shall exercise the office of governor.

Sect. XII. Each house shall judge of the qualifications of its own members; but contested elections shall be determined by a committee, to be selected in such manner as shall be directed by law: A majority of each house shall constitute a quorum to do business; but a smaller number may adjourn from day to day, and may be authorised, by law, to compel the attendance of absent members in such manner, and under such penalties, as may be provided.

Sect. XIII. Each house may determine the rules of its proceedings, punish its members for disorderly behaviour; and with the concurrence of two-thirds, expel a member, but not a second time for the same cause, and shall have all other powers necessary for either branch of the legislature of a free state.

Sect. XIV. Each house shall keep a journal of its proceedings, and publish them weekly, except such parts as may, in their judgment, require secrecy: And the yeas and nays of the members, on any question, shall, at the desire of any two of them, be entered on the journals.

Sect. XV. The doors of each house shall be open, unless when the business shall be such as, in their judgment, ought to be kept secret.

Sect. XVI. Neither house shall, without the consent of the other, adjourn for more than three days, nor to any other place than that in which the two houses shall be sitting.

Sect. XVII. The senators and representatives shall receive a compensation for their services, to be ascertained by law, and paid out of the treasury of the commonwealth. They shall, in all cases except treason, felony and breach of the peace, be privileged from arrest, during their attendance at the session of the respective houses, and in going to and returning from the same; and for any speech or debate in either house they shall not be questioned in any other place.

Sect. XVIII. No senator or representative shall, during the time for which he was elected, be appointed to any civil office, under the authority of this commonwealth, which shall have been created, or the emoluments of which shall have been increased during such time: And no member of congress or other person holding any office, except in the militia, under the United States or this commonwealth, shall be a member of either house during his continuance in congress or in office.

Sect. XIX. When vacancies happen in either house, the speaker of that house shall issue writs of election to fill such vacancies.

Sect. XX. All bills for raising revenue shall originate in the house of representatives; but the senate may propose or concur with amendments, as in other bills.

Sect. XXI. No money shall be drawn from the treasury, but in consequence of appropriations made by law.

Sect. XXII. Every bill, which shall have passed the house of representatives and the senate, shall, before it become a law, be presented to the governor. If he approve, he shall sign it; but if he shall not approve it, he shall return it, with his objections, to the house in which it shall have originated, who shall enter the objections at large upon their journals, and proceed to re-consider it. If, after such re-consideration, two-thirds of that house shall agree to pass the bill, it shall be sent, together with the objections, to the other house, by which it shall likewise be re-considered, and if approved by two-thirds of that house, it shall become a law. But in all such cases, the votes of both houses shall be determined by yeas and nays, and the names of the persons voting for or against the bill shall be entered on the journals of each house respectively. If any bill shall not be returned by the governor within ten days (Sundays excepted) after it shall have been presented to him, it shall be a law in like manner as if he had signed it; unless the general assembly, by their adjournment, prevent its return, in which case it shall be a law, unless sent back within three days after their next meeting.

Sect. XXIII. Every order, resolution or vote, to which the concurrence of the senate and house of representatives may be necessary (except on a question of adjournment) shall be presented to the governor, and before the same shall take effect, be approved by him: or, being disapproved shall be re-passed by two-thirds of the senate and house of representatives, according to the rules and limitations prescribed in case of a bill.

ARTICLE II.

Section I. The supreme executive power of this commonwealth shall be vested in a governor.

Sect. II. The governor shall be chosen on the second Tuesday of October, by the citizens throughout the commonwealth, at the places where they shall respectively vote for representatives. The returns of every election for governor shall be transmitted to the seat of government, directed to the speaker of the senate, who shall open and publish them in the presence of the members of both houses of the legislature. The person having the highest number of votes shall be governor; but if two or more shall be equal and highest in votes, one of them shall be chosen governor by the joint vote of the members of both houses. Contested elections shall be determined by a committee to be selected from both houses of the legislature, in such manner as shall be directed by law.

Sect. III. The governor shall hold his office during three years from the third Tuesday of December next ensuing his election, and shall not be capable of holding his office longer than nine in any term of twelve years.

Sect. IV. He shall be, at least, thirty years of age; and have been a citizen and inhabitant of this state seven years next before his election; unless he shall have been absent on the public business of the United States, or of this state.

Sect. V. No member of congress, or person holding any office under the United States or this state, shall be capable of exercising the office of governor.

Sect. VI. The governor shall, at stated times, receive for his services a compensation, which shall be neither increased nor diminished during the period for which he shall have been elected.

Sect. VII. He shall be commander in chief of the army and navy of this commonwealth, and of the militia, except when they shall be called into the actual service of the United States.

Sect. VIII. He shall appoint all officers whose offices are established by this constitution or shall be established by law, and whose appointments are not herein otherwise provided for; but no person shall be appointed to an office within any county, who shall not have been a citizen and inhabitant therein one year next before his appointment, if it shall have been so long erected, but if that shall not be the case, then within the limits of the original county or counties out of which it shall have been taken. No member of congress from this state, nor any person holding or exercising any office of trust or profit under the United States, shall at the same time, hold and exercise the office of sheriff, or any office in the gift of the legislature or of the governor, other than in the militia, or commission of the peace, notaries public and sworn interpreter of languages in this state.

Sect. IX. All commissions shall be in the name and by the authority of the commonwealth of Pennsylvania, and be sealed with the state seal, and signed by the governor.

Sect. X. He shall have power to remit fines and forfeitures, and grant reprieves and pardons, except in cases of impeachment.

Sect. XI. He may require information, in writing, from the officers in the executive department upon any subject relating to the duties of their respective offices.

Sect. XII. He shall from time to time, give to the general assembly information of the state of the commonwealth, and recommend to their consideration such measures as he shall judge necessary or expedient.

Sect. XIII. He may, on extraordinary occasions, convene the general assembly, and in case of disagreement between the two houses with respect to the time of adjournment, adjourn them to such time as he shall think proper, not exceeding four months.

Sect. XIV. He shall take care that the laws be faithfully executed.

Sect. XV. In case of the death or resignation of the governor, or of his removal from office, the speaker of the senate shall exercise the office of governor, until another governor, who shall in such case, be chosen at the next annual election, shall be duly qualified and commence the exercise of his office And if the trial of a contested election shall continue longer than until the third Tuesday in December next ensuing the election of a governor, the governor of the last year, or the speaker of the senate, who may be in the exercise of the executive authority, shall continue therein until the determination of such contested election, and until a governor shall be qualified as aforesaid.

Sect. XVI. The state treasurer shall be appointed annually, by the joint vote of the members of both houses. All other officers in the treasury department, election officers, officers relating to taxes, to the poor and highways, constables and other township officers, shall be appointed in such manner as is or shall be directed by law.

Sect. XVII. A secretary shall be appointed and commissioned during the governor's continuance in office, if he shall so long behave himself well. He shall keep a fair register of all the official acts and proceedings of the executive department, and shall, when required, lay tl

same and all papers, minutes and vouchers relative thereto, before either branch of the legis-ature, and shall perform such other duties as
shall be enjoined him by law.

ARTICLE III.

Section I. In elections by the citizens every freeman of the age of
twenty one years, having resided in the state two years next before the
days of the elections respectively, and within that time paid a state or
county tax, which shall have been assessed upon him at least six
months before the election, shall enjoy the rights of an elector; provided that the sons of persons qualified as aforesaid, between the age of
twenty-one and twenty-two years, shall be entitled to vote although
they shall not have paid taxes.

Sect. II. All elections shall be by ballot, except those by persons in
their representative or public capacities, who shall vote *viva voce*, unless in the choice of committees and their own officers.

Sect. III. Electors shall, in all cases, except treason, felony and
breach of the peace, be privileged from arrest during their attendance on elections, and in going to and returning from them.

ARTICLE IV.

Section I. The house of representatives shall have the sole power of
impeaching.

Sect. II. All impeachments shall be tried by the senate: When sitting for that purpose, the senators shall be on oath or affirmation. No
person shall be convicted without the concurrence of two-thirds of the
members present.

Sect. III. The governor and all other civil officers under this commonwealth shall be liable to impeachment for any misdemeanor in office; but judgment, in such cases, shall not extend further than to removal from office and disqualification to hold any office of honor, trust
or profit under this commonwealth: the party convicted shall, nevertheless, be liable to indictment, trial, judgment and punishment according to law.

ARTICLE V.

Section I. The judicial power of this commonwealth shall be vested
in a supreme court, in courts of oyer and terminer and general gaol delivery, in a court of common pleas, orphans' court, register's court and
a court of quarter sessions of the peace for each county, in justices of
the peace, and in such other courts as the legislature may, from time
time, establish.

Sect. II. The judges of the supreme court and of the several courts
of common pleas shall hold their offices during good behaviour: but for
any reasonable cause which shall not be sufficient ground of impeachment, the governor may remove any of them on the address of two-
thirds of each branch of the legislature. The judge of the supreme
court and the presidents of the several courts of common pleas shall,
at stated times, receive for their services an edequate compensation
to be fixed by law, which shall not be diminished during their continuance in office: But they shall receive no fees or perquisites of office
nor hold any other office of profit under this commonwealth.

Sect. III. The jurisdiction of the supreme court shall extend over the state, and the judges thereof shall, by virtue of their offices, be justices of oyer and terminer and general gaol delivery, in the several counties.

Sect. IV. Until it shall be otherwise directed by law, the several courts of common pleas shall be established in the following manner: The governor shall appoint, in each county, not fewer than three nor more than four judges, who, during their continuance in office, shall reside in such county: The state shall be, by law, divided into circuits, none of which shall include more than six nor fewer than three counties. A president shall be appointed of the courts in each circuit, who, during his continuance in office, shall reside therein. The president and judges aforesaid, any two of whom shall be a quorum, shall compose the respective courts of common pleas.

Sect. V. The judges of the court of common pleas in each county shall, by virtue of their offices, be justices of oyer and terminer and general jail delivery for the trial of capital and other offenders therein; and any two of whom, the president being one, shall be a quorum; but they shall not hold a court of oyer and terminer or jail delivery in any county when the judges of the supreme court, or any of them, shall be sitting in the same county. The party accused, as well as the commonwealth, may, under such regulations as shall be prescribed by law, remove the indictment and proceedings or a transcript thereof, into the supreme court.

Sect. VI. The supreme court and the several cour's of common pleas shall, beside the powers heretofore usually exercised by them, have the power of a court of chancery so far as relates to the perpetuating of testimony, the obtaining of evidence from places not within the state, and the care of the persons and estates of those who are *non compotes mentis*. And the legislature shall, as soon as conveniently may be, vest in the said courts such other powers to grant relief in equity as shall be found necessary: and may, from time time, enlarge or diminish those powers; or vest them in such other courts as they shall judge proper for the due administration of justice.

Sect. VII. The judges of the court of common pleas in each county, any two of whom shall be a quorum; shall compose the court of quarter sessions of the peace and orphans' court therein: And the register of wills, together with the said judges, or any two of them, shall compose the register's court in the respective counties.

Sect. VIII. The judges of the courts of common pleas shall, within their respective counties, have the like powers with the judges of the supreme court to issue writs of certiorari to the justices of the peace, and to cause their proceedings to be brought before them and the like right and justice to be done.

Sect. IX. The president of the courts in each circuit shall, within such circuit, and the judges of the courts of common pleas shall, within their respective counties, be justices of the peace so far as relates to criminal matters.

Sect. X. The governor shall appoint and commission a competent number of justices of the peace in convenient districts in each county, to be fixed in such manner as shall be directed by law. They shall be commissioned during good behaviour; but may be removed on conviction of misbehaviour in office or of any infamous crime, or on the address of both houses of the legislature.

Sect. XI. A register's office for the probate of wills and granting letters of administration, and an office for the recording of deeds shall be kept in each county.

Sect. XII. Prothonotaries, clerks of the peace and orphans' courts, recorders of deeds, registers of wills and sheriffs shall keep their offices in the county town of the county in which they respectively shall be officers.

Sect. XIII. The stile of all process shall be *The commonwealth of Pennsylvania*: all prosecutions shall be carried on in the name and by the authority of the commonwealth of Pennsylvania, and conclude, *against the peace and dignity of the same.*

ARTICLE VI.

Section I. Sheriffs and coroners shall, at the places of election of representatives, be chosen by the citizens of each county respectively. Two persons shall be chosen for each office, one of whom for each shall be commissioned by the governor. They shall hold their offices for three years and until a successor be duly qualified; but no person shall be twice chosen or appointed sheriff in any term of six years.

Sect. II. The freemen of this commonwealth shall be armed and disciplined for its defence: The militia officers shall be appointed in such manner and for such time as shall be directed by law.

It was moved by Mr. Lewis, seconded by Mr. Whitehill, to re-consider the fifteenth section of the said first article, in order to insert before the words "shall be open," the words "and of the place where they shall respectively sit in a committee of the whole."

Which was determined in the affirmative, and the said fifteenth section, as amended, adopted.

A motion was made by Mr. Lewis, seconded by Mr. Edwards, to re-consider the twenty-second section of the said first article, in order to amend the same so as to read as follows, viz.

Section XXII. Every bill, which shall have passed the house of representatives and the senate shall, before it become a law, be presented to the governor. If he approve, he shall sign it; but if he shall not approve it, he shall return it, with his objections, to that house in which it shall have originated, who shall proceed to re-consider it. If, after such re-consideration, two-thirds of that house shall agree to pass the bill, it shall be sent, together with the objections, to the other house, by which it shall likewise be re-considered: And, if approved by two-thirds of that house, it shall be again sent, with the reasons of both houses, to be agreed on by a joint committee from each of them, to the governor, who shall sign it if he approve of it; but if he does not approve of it, he shall again send it to the house in which it originated; and if it shall be approved of by two-thirds of each house, become a law. But in all such cases, the votes of both houses shall be determined by yeas and nays, and the names of the persons voting for or against the bill shall, together with the objections and reasons, be entered on the journals of each house respectively. If any bill shall not be returned by the governor within ten days (Sundays excepted) after it shall be presented to him, the same shall be a law in like manner as if he had signed it, unless the general assembly, by their adjournment, prevent its return, in which case it shall be a law, unless sent back within three days after their next meeting.

On the question, Will the convention agree to re-consider the said section for the aforesaid purpose? The yeas and nays being called by Mr. Lewis, were as follow, viz.

YEAS.

Mr. Lewis	Mr. Edwards	Mr. Mawhorter	Mr. M'Lene
M'Kean	Gibbons	Findley	Beale
Gray	Hiester	Redick	11

NAYS.

Mr. Wilson	Mr. Atlee	Mr. Gehr	Mr. Matthews
Baker	Hubley	Sitgreaves	Morris
Roberts	Breckbill	Arndt	Potts
Robinson	Miller	Rhoads	Coates
Hare	Slegle	Powell	Shoemaker
Ogden	Reed	Snyder	Gloninger
Jenks	Tyson	Todd	Brown
Barclay	Dill	Addison	Graydon
Stout	Whitehill	Hoge	Pickering
Bull	Power	J. Ross	Gibson
Boyd	Lower	Smilie	Sellers
Hand	Lincoln	Gallatin	Newlin
Graff	Groscop		50

So it was determined in the negative.

A motion was made by Mr. Pickering, seconded by Mr. Wilson, to adopt the following title to the plan of government, viz.

The constitution of the commonwealth of Pennsylvania, as altered and amended by the convention for that purpose freely chosen and assembled, and by them proposed for the consideration of their constituents. We, the people of the commonwealth of Pennsylvania, ordain and establish this constitution for its government.

On the question, Will the convention agree to the same? It was determined in the affirmative. Whereupon,

On motion of Mr. Lewis, seconded by Mr. Lower,

Resolved, That three thousand five hundred copies in the English, and one thousand five hundred in the German language, of the constitution of this commonwealth, as altered and amended, be printed for the information of the citizens and inhabitants of this state.

On motion, Ordered, That Mr. Wilson be added to the committee appointed to superintend the press.

It was moved by Mr. Wilson, seconded by Mr. Findley, to re-consider the second section of the second article of the said proposed plan of government, in order to insert, after the word " transmitted," the words " under seal." Which was determined in the affirmative.

On motion of Mr Addison, seconded by Mr. Hoge,

The order of the day for taking into consideration the motion of Mr. M'Kean, seconded by Mr. Gallatin, made the eighteenth instant, was postponed.

A motion was made by Mr. Wilson, seconded by Mr. Hubley, to transpose the twelfth section of the fifth article so as to institute it as the third section of the sixth article of the proposed plan of government, viz.

Prothonotaries, clerks of the peace and orphans' courts, recorders of deeds, registers of wills and sheriffs, shall keep their offices in the county town of the county in which they respectively shall be officers.

It was moved by Mr. Lewis, seconded by Mr. Pickering, to add the following clause to the said section, viz.

Unless when the governor shall, for special reasons, dispense therewith for any term not exceeding   years after the county shall have been erected.

A motion was then made by Mr. Robinson, seconded by Mr. Sitgreaves, to strike out the following words contained in the said amendment, viz. "for any term not exceeding   years after the county shall have been erected."

On the question, Will the convention agree to strike out the said words? It was determined in the negative, and the additional clause to the said section, proposed by Mr. Lewis, adopted

On motion of Mr. Shoemaker, Ordered, That the blank be filled with the word "five."

On the question, Will the convention agree to the section as amended, viz.

Prothonotaries, clerks of the peace and orphans' courts, recorders of deeds, registers of wills and sheriffs, shall keep their offices in the county town of the county in which they respectively shall be officers; unless when the governor shall, for special reasons, dispense therewith for any term not exceeding five years after the county shall have been erected?"

The yeas and days being called by Mr. Wilson, were as follow, viz.

YEAS.

Mr. Wilson	Mr. Stout	Mr. Slegle	Mr. Potts
Baker	Gibbons	Tyson	Coates
Roberts	Bull	Dill	Shoemaker
Lewis	Hand	Sitgreaves	Gloninger
Hare	Graff	Snyder	Graydon
Edwards	Atlee	Addison	Pickering
Ogden	Hubley	Hoge	Sellers
Jenks	Breckbill	J. Ross	Newlin
Barclay	Miller		34

NAYS.

Mr. M'Kean	Mr. Hiester	Mr. Rhoads	Mr. M'Lene
Gray	Lower	Powell	Matthews
Robinson,	Lincoln	Findley	Morris
Boyd	Groscop	Todd	Brown
Reed	Gehr	Redick	Gibson
Whitehill	Mawhorter	Smilie	Beale
Power	Arndt	Gallatin	27

So it was determined in the affirmative, and the same adopted as the third section of the said sixth article.

The convention then took into consideration the schedule, as reported by the committee of five, for putting the government into operation, and the first section being under consideration, the same was adopted as follows, viz.

I. That all laws of this commonwealth, in force at the time of ma-king the said alterations and amendments in the said constitution, and not inconsistent therewith, and all rights, actions, prosecutions, claims and contracts, as well of individuals as of bodies corporate, shall continue as if the said alterations and amendments had not been made.

The second section of the said schedule being under consideration, viz.,

II. That all officers in the appointment of the executive department, shall continue in the exercise of the duties of their respective offices until the   day of   unless their commissions shall sooner expire by their own limitations, or the said offices become vacant by death or resignation, and no longer, unless re-appointed and commissioned by the governor. Except that the judges of the supreme court shall hold their offices for the terms in their commissions respectively expressed.

It was moved by Mr. James Ross, seconded by Mr. Sitgreaves, to fill the blank with the word "first," and to add, after the words "day of," the following, "September, one thousand seven hundred and ninety-one."

Which was determined in the affirmative, and the said section, as amended, adopted.

The third section of the said schedule being under consideration, the same was adopted as follows, viz.

III. That justice shall be administered in the several counties of the state, until the period aforesaid, by the same justices, in the same courts, and in the same manner as heretofore.

The fourth section of the said schedule being under consideration, the same was adopted as follows, viz.

IV. That the president and supreme executive council shall continue to exercise the executive authority of this commonwealth as heretofore, until the third Tuesday of December next; but no intermediate vacancies in the council shall be supplied by new elections.

The fifth section of the said schedule being under consideration, the same was adopted as follows, viz.

V. That until the first enumeration shall be made, as directed in the fourth section of the first article of the constitution established by this convention, the city of Philadelphia and the several counties shall be respectively entitled to elect the same number of representatives as is now prescribed by law

The sixth section of the said schedule being under consideration, viz.

VI. That the first senate shall consist of seventeen members, to be chosen in districts formed as follows, to wit: The city of Philadelphia, the county of Philadelphia, and the county of Delaware, shall be a district, and shall elect three senators; the county of Chester shall be a district, and shall elect one senator; the county of Bucks shall be a district, and shall elect one senator; the county of Montgomery shall be a district, and shall elect one senator; the county of Northampton shall be a district, and shall elect one senator; the counties of Lancaster and York shall be a district, and shall elect three senators; the counties of Berks and Dauphin shall be a district, and shall elect two senators; the counties of Cumberland and Huntingdon shall be a district, and shall elect one senator; the counties of Northumberland, Luzerne and Mifflin shall be a district, and shall elect one senator; the counties of

Bedford and Franklin shall be a district, and shall elect one senator; the counties of Westmoreland, Fayette and Allegheny shall be a district, and shall elect one senator; and the county of Washington shall be a district, and shall elect one senator; which senators shall serve until the first enumeration before mentioned shall have been made, and the representation in both branches of the legislature shall be established by law, and chosen as in the constitution is directed. Any vacancies which shall happen in the senate within the said time, shall be supplied as prescribed in the nineteenth section of the first article.

It was moved by Mr. Gallatin, seconded by Mr. Matthews, to strike out the word "seventeen," and, in lieu thereof, to insert the words "twenty-three."

On the question, Will the convention agree to the same? The yeas and nays being called by Mr. Gallatin, were as follow, viz.

YEAS.

Mr. Reed	Mr. Groscop	Mr. Todd	Mr. Matthews
Dill	Gehr	Addison	Gloninger
Whitehill	Mawhorter	Redick	Brown
Hiester	Powell	Smilie	Gibson
Lower	Snyder	Gallatin	Beale
Lincoln	Findley	M'Lene	23

NAYS.

Mr. Wilson	Mr. Jenks	Mr. Hubley	Mr. J. Ross
Baker	Barclay	Breckbill	Morris
Roberts	Stout	Miller	Potts
Lewis	Gibbons	Slegle	Coates
M'Kean	Bull	Tyson	Shoemaker
Gray	Boyd	Power	Graydon
Robinson	Hand	Sitgreaves	Pickering
Hare	Graff	Arndt	Sellers
Ogden	Atlee	Rhoads	Newlin 36

So it was determined in the negative.

A motion was then made by Mr. Sitgreaves, seconded by Mr. Wilson, to strike out the word "seventeen," and, in lieu thereof, to insert the word "eighteen."

On the question, Will the convention agree to the same? The yeas and nays being called by Mr. Reed, were as follow, viz.

YEAS.

Mr. Wilson	Mr. Stout	Mr. Power	Mr. Hoge
Baker	Gibbons	Lower	Redick
Roberts	Boyd	Lincoln	J. Ross
M'Kean	Hand	Sitgreaves	Smilie
Gray	Atlee	Arndt	Gallatin
Robinson	Hubley	Rhoads	M'Lene
Hare	Breckbill	Powell	Morris
Edwards	Miller	Snyder	Coates
Ogden	Slegle	Todd	Graydon
Jenks	Tyson	Addison	Pickering
Barclay			41

NAYS.

Mr. Lewis	Mr. Whitehill	Mr. Findley	Mr. Gibson
Bull	Hiester	Matthews	Beale
Graff	Groscop	Shoemaker	Sellers
Reed	Gehr	Gloninger	Newlin 19
Dill	Mawhorter	Brown	

So it was determined in the affirmative.

It was moved by Mr. Sitgreaves, seconded by Mr. Graydon, to transpose the words "Mifflin" and "Huntingdon," in the said section.

Which was determined in the affirmative.

It was then moved by Mr. Sitgreaves, seconded by Mr, Ogden, to insert, after the word "Westmoreland," the word "Washington;" and, before the words "and the county of Washington," to strike out the words "one senator," and insert, in lieu thereof, "three senators;" and strike out the words "and the county of Washington shall be a district, and shall elect one senator" so as that the same should read "And the counties of Westmoreland, Washington, Fayette and Allegheny shall be a district, and shall elect three senators."

A motion was then made by Mr. James Ross, seconded by Mr Redick, to amend the said section by striking out the word "one," after the words "and the county of Washington shall be a district, and shall elect," and to insert, in lieu thereof, the word "two," and to transpose the word "Fayette" so as to read "Washington and Fayette."

Whereupon, on motion, Ordered that the further consideration of the said section and amendments, be postponed.

On motion, Ordered that Mr. Baker, Mr. Barclay ad Mr. Gloninger be a committee treasurer to settle and adjust the accounts of the accounts of the expenses of this convention.

Adjourned until half past nine o'clock to-morrow, A. M.

THURSDAY, February 25th, 1790. *A. M.*

The convention met pursuant to adjournment.

The schedule for the organization of the proposed government being under consideration.

It was moved by Mr. Wilson, seconded by Mr. M'Lene, to postpone the further consideration thereof.

Which was determined in the affirmative.

A motion was then made by Mr. James Ross, seconded by Mr. M'Kean, to re-consider the eighth section of the second article, in order to strike out the last clause thereof, and, in lieu thereof, to insert the following, viz,

No member of congress from this state, nor any person holding or exercising any office of trust or profit under the United States, shall, at the same time, hold or exercise the office of judge, secretary, treasurer, prothonotary, register of wills, recorder of deeds, sheriff, or any office in the state to which a salary is by law annexed, or any other office which future legislatures shall declare incompatible with offices or appointments under the United States.

On the question, Will the convention agree to re-consider for the aforesaid purpose?—The yeas and nays being called by Mr. Wilson, were as follow, viz.

YEAS.

Mr. Wilson	Mr. Stout	Mr. Reed	Mr. Gallatin
Baker	Gibbons	Tyson	M'Lene
Roberts	Bull	Dill	Potts
Lewis	Boyd	Sitgreaves	Coates
M'Kean	Hand	Snyder	Shoemaker
Gray	Graff	Findley	Gloninger
Robinson	Atlee	Todd	Brown
Edwards	Hubley	Addison	Graydon
Ogden	Breckbill	Hoge	Gibson
Jenks	Miller	Redick	Sellers
Barclay	Slegle	J. Ross	Newlin 44

NAYS.

Mr. Whitehill	Mr. Lincoln	Mr. Rhoads	Mr. Matthews
Power	Groscop	Powell	Morris
Hiester	Gehr	Piper	Beale 15
Lower	Arndt	Smilie	

So it was determined in the affirmative.

It was then moved by Mr. Wilson, seconded by Mr. M'Kean, to strike out the words contained in the amendment, viz. "Member of congress from this state, nor any."

Which was determined in the negative.

A motion was then made by M. Lewis, seconded by Mr. Edwards, to strike out the word "judge," and, in lieu thereof, to insert the words "jutices of any court."

Which was determined in the negative, and the said eighth section of the second article, as amended, adopted.

Whereupon, on motion of Mr. Sitgreaves, ordered, that the second article of the proposed plan of government be transcribed for the press.

On motion of Mr. Addison, seconded by Mr. Power, ordered, that the third, fourth, fifth, and sixth articles of the said plan of government be transcribed for the press.

The schedule for the organization of the proposed government, again recurring, and the sixth section thereof being under consideration, Mr. Sitgreaves withdrew his amendment proposed yesterday.

Whereupon, the amendment moved yesterday by Mr. James Ross, seconded by Mr. Redick, recurring, the same, with the section as amended, was adopted as follows, viz.

VI. That the first senate shall consist of eighteen members, to be chosen in districts formed as follows, viz. The city of Philadelphia, the county of Philadelphia, and the county of Delaware shall be a district, and shall elect three senators; the county of Chester shall be a district, and shall elect one senator; the county of Bucks shall be a district, and shall elect one senator; the county of Montgomery shall be a district and shall elect one senator; the county of Northampton shall be a district, and shall elect one senator; the counties of Lancaster and York shall be a district, and shall elect three senators; the counties of Berks and Dauphin shall be a district, and shall elect two senators; the counties of Cumberland and Huntingdon shall be a district, and elect one senator; the counties of Northumberland, Luzerne and Mifflin shall be a district, and shall elect one senator; the counties of Bedford and Franklin shall be a district, and shall elect one senator; the counties of Westmoreland and Allegheny shall be a district, and shall elect one senator; and the counties of Washington and Fayette shall be a district and shall elect two senators: which senators shall serve until the first enumeration before mentioned shall have been made, and the representation in both branches of the legislature shall be established by law, and chosen as in the constitution is directed. Any vacancies which shall happen in the senate within the said time, shall be supplied as prescribed in the nineteenth section of the first article.

The seventh section of the said schedule being under consideration, the same was adopted as follows:

VII. That the elections of senators shall be conducted, and the returns thereof made to the senate, in the same manner as is prescribed by the election laws of the state for conducting and making returns of the elections of representatives. In those districts which consist of more than one county, the judges of the district elections within each county after having formed a return of the whole election within that county, in such manner as is directed by law, shall send the same, by one or more of their number, to such place, herein after mentioned, within the district of which such county is a part; where the judges, so met, shall compare and cast up the several county returns, and execute, under their hands and seals, one general and true return for the whole district, *that is to say*, The judges of the district composed of the city of Philadelphia and of the counties of Philadelphia and Delaware shall meet at the state house in the city of Philadelphia; the judges of the district composed of the counties of Lancaster and York shall meet at the court house in the borough of Lancaster; the judges of the district composed of the counties of Berks and Dauphin shall meet at Middletown in the county of Berks; the judges of the district composed of the counties of Cumberland and Mifflin shall meet in Greenwood township, in the county of Cumberland, at the house now accupied by David Miller; the judges of the district composed of the counties of Northumberland, Luzerne and Huntingdon shall meet at the court house in the town of Sunbury; the judges of the district composed of the counties of Bedford and Franklin shall meet at the house now occupied by John Dickey, in Air township, Bedford county; the judges of the district composed of the counties of Westmoreland and Allegheny shall meet at the court house in the town of Greensborough, in Westmoreland county; and the judges of the district composed of the counties of Washington and Fayette shall meet at the court house in the town of Washington, in Washington county, on the third Tuesday of October respectivly, for the purpose aforesaid.

The eighth section of the said schedule being under consideration, it was moved by Mr. Hand, seconded by Mr. Sitgreaves, to amend the same so as to read as follows, viz.

VIII. That the election of the governor shall be conducted in the several counties in the manner prescribed by the laws of the state for the election of representatives, and the returns in each county shall be sealed up by the judges of the elections, and transmitted to the president of the supreme executive council, directed to the speaker of the senate as soon after the election as may be.

Which was determined in the affirmative, and the said section, as amended, adopted.

A motion was made by Mr Hubley, seconded by Mr. Addison, to insert the following as the fifth section of the said schedule, viz.

That no person now in commission as sheriff shall be eligible at the next election for a longer term than will, with the time which he shall have served in the said office, complete the term of three years.

Which was determined in the affirmative, and the said section adopted.

It was moved by Mr. Wilson, seconded by Mr. Hubley, to insert the following sections as the seventh article of the proposed plan of government, viz.

Section I. A school or schools shall be established in each county for the instruction of youth, and the state shall pay to the masters such salaries as shall enable them to teach at low prices.

Section II. The arts and sciences shall be promoted in one or more seminaries of learning.

Section III. Religious societies and corporate bodies shall be protected in their rights, privileges, immunities and estates.

On motion, Ordered, that the fourth section of the said schedule be transposed and placed as the second section therein.

A motion was made by Mr. James Ross, seconded by Mr. Sitgreaves, to re-consider the seventh section of the bill of rights in order to amend the same by striking out the last clause, viz.

In prosecutions for libels, their truth or design may be given in evidence on the general issue, and their nature and tendency, whether proper for public information, or only for private ridicule or malice, be determined by the jury. And to insert the following in lieu thereof :

" But upon indictments for the publication of papers investigating the conduct of individuals in their public capacity, or of those applying or canvassing for office, the truth of the facts may be given in evidence in justification upon the general issue, and the jury shall have the same right to determine thereon as in other cases."

On the question, Will the convention agree to re-consider for the aforesaid purpose? The yeas and nays being called by Mr. Ogden, were as follow, viz.

YEAS.

Mr, Baker	Mr. Jenks	Mr. Hubley	Mr. J. Ross
Roberts	Barclay	Miller	Morris
Lewis	Stout	Slegle	Coates
M'Kean	Bull	Tyson	Shoemaker
Gray	Hand	Sitgreaves	Pickering
Robinson	Graff	Arndt	Sellers
Hare	Atlee	Rhoads	Newlin 29
Ogden			

NAYS.

Mr, Wilson	Mr. Boyd	Mr. Dill	Mr. Heister
Edwards	Breckbill	Whitehill	Lower
Gibbons	Reed	Power	Lincoln

NAYS.

Mr. Groscop	Mr. Findley	Mr. Smilie	Mr. Brown
Gehr	Todd	Gallatin	Graydon
Powel	Addison	M'Lene	Gibson
Piper	Hoge	Matthews	Beale
Snyder	Redick	Gloninger	31

So it was determined in the negative.

A motion was made by Mr. James Ross, seconded by Mr. M'Kean, to re-consider the nineteenth section of the bill of rights, in order to amend the same so as to read as follows, viz.

That no attainder shall work corruption of blood or, except during the life of the offender, forfeiture of estate to the commonwealth.

Which was carried in the affirmative, and the said section adopted.

Adjourned until half past nine o'clock to-morrow, A. M.

FRIDAY, February 26th, 1790. *A. M,*

The convention met pursuant to adjournment.

The committee of three appointed for the purpose of revising and correcting the proposed plan of government, reported the declaration of rights, as amended, viz.

That the great and essential principles of liberty and free government may be recognized and unalterably established, WE DECLARE—

Section I. That all men are born equally free and independent, and have certain inherent and indefeasible rights, among which are those of enjoying and defending life and liberty, of acquiring, possessing and protecting property and reputation, and of pursuing their own happiness.

Section II. That all power is originally vested in the people, and all free governments are founded on their authority, and instituted for their peace, safety and happiness: For the advancement of those ends, they have, at all times, an unalienable and indefeasible right to alter, reform, or abolish their government, in such manner as they may think proper.

Section III. That all men have a natural and indefeasible right to worship Almighty God according to the dictates of their own consciences; that no man can, of right, be compelled to attend or erect, or support any place of worship, or to maintain any ministry against his consent; that no human authority can, in any case whatever, control or interfere with the rights of conscience; and that no preference shall ever be given, by law, to any religious establishments or modes of worship.

Section IV. That no person who acknowledges the being of a God and a future state of rewards and punishments, shall, on account of his religious sentiments, be disqualified to hold any office or place of trust or profit under this commonwealth.

Section V. That elections shall be free and equal.

Section VI. That trial by jury shall be as heretofore, and the right thereof shall remain inviolate.

Section VII. That the printing press shall be free to every person who undertakes to examine the proceedings of the legislature or any branch of government: And no law shall ever be made restraining the right thereof.

The free communication of thoughts and opinions is one of the invaluable rights of man, and every citizen may freely speak, write and print on any subject, being responsible for the abuse of that liberty. In prosecutions for libels, their truth or design may be given in evidence on the general issue, and their nature and tendency, whether proper for public information, or only for private ridicule or malice, be determined by the jury, under the direction of the court, as in other cases.

Section VIII. That the people shall be secure in their persons, houses, papers and possessions from unreasonable searches and seizures; and that no warrant to search any place, or to seize any person or things, shall issue without describing them as nearly as may be, nor without probable cause, supported by oath or affirmation.

Section IX. That in all criminal prosecutions the accused hath a right to be heard by himself and his council; to demand the nature and cause of the accusation against him ; to meet the witnesses face to face ; to have compulsory process for obtaining witnesses in his favor ; and, in prosecutions by indictment, a speedy public trial by an impartial jury of the vicinage ; that he cannot be compelled to give evidence against himself ; nor can he be deprived of his life, liberty or property, unless by the judgment of his peers, or the law of the land.

Section X. That no person shall, for any indictable offence, be proceeded against, criminally, by information ; except in cases arising in the land or naval forces, or in the militia when in actual service in time of war or public danger: Nor shall any person, for the same offence, be twice put in jeopardy of life or limb; nor shall any man s property be taken, or applied to public use, without the consent of his representatives, and without just compensation being made.

Section XI. That all courts shall be open, and every man for an injury done him in his lands, goods, person or reputation, shall have remedy by the due course of law, and right and justice administered without sale, denial, or delay.

Section XII. That no power of suspending laws, or the execution thereof, shall be exercised, unless by the legislature, or its authority.

Section XIII. That excessive bail shall not be required, nor excessive fines imposed, nor cruel punishments inflicted.

Section XIV. That all prisoners shall be bailable by sufficient sureties, unless for capital offences, when the proof is evident or presumption great: and the privilege of the writ of habeas corpus shall not be suspended, unless when, in cases of rebellion or invasion, the public safety may require it.

Section XV. That no commission of oyer and terminer or jail delivery shall be issued.

Section XVI. That the person of a debtor, where there is not a strong presumption of fraud, shall not be continued in prison after delivering up all his estate, for the benefit of his creditors, in such manner as shall be prescribed by law.

Section XVII. That no *expost facto* law, nor any law impairing contracts, shall be made.

Section XVIII. That no person shall be attainted of treason or felony by the legislature.

Section XIX. That no attainder shall work corruption of blood, nor, except during the life of the offender, forfeiture of estate to the commonwealth; that the estates of such persons as shall destroy their own lives shall go as in case of natural death; and if any person shall be killed by casualty or accident there shall be no forfeiture by reason thereof.

Section XX. That the citizens have a right, in a peaceable manner, to assemble together for their common good, and to apply to those invested with the powers of government, for redress of grievances or other proper purposes, by petition, address or remonstrance.

Section XXI. That the right of the citizens to bear arms in defence of themselves and the state shall not be questioned: But those who conscientiously scruple to bear arms, shall not be compelled to do so, but shall pay an equivalent for personal service.

Section XXII. That no standing army shall, in time of peace, be kept up without the consent of the legislature; and the military shall, in all cases, and, at all times, be kept in strict subordination to the civil power.

Section XXIII. That no soldier shall, in time of peace, be quartered in any house without the consent of the owner, nor in time of war, but in the manner to be prescribed by law.

Section XXIV. That the legislature shall not grant any title of nobility or hereditary distinction, nor create any office, the appointment to which shall be for a longer term than during good behaviour.

Section XXV. That emigration from the state shall not be prohibited.

Section XXVI. To guard against transgressions af the high powers which we have delegated, WE DECLARE, that every thing in this article, is excepted out of the general powers of government, and shall for ever remain inviolate.

A motion was made by Mr. M'Kean, seconded by Mr. Atlee, to insert the word "general" before the word "great," in the preamble to the said declaration of rights.

Which was determined in the affirmative.

And the report, as amended, was then adopted by this convention.

On motion, ordered, that Messrs. Dunlap and Claypoole be furnished with a transcript of the plan of government, together with the schedule, in order to publish seven hundred copies thereof, in their daily paper of to-morrow, for the use of the members of this convention.

The motion of Mr. Wilson, seconded by Mr. Hubley, on the twenty-fifth instant, recurring,

A motion was made by Mr. M'Kean, seconded by Mr. Findley, to insert at the end of the first section, *And the poor, gratis.*

It was then moved by Mr. Pickering, seconded by Mr. Edwards, to postpone the said section in order to introduce the following in lieu thereof:

The legislature shall provide, by law, for the establishment of schools throughout the state, in such manner that the poor may be taught gratis.

And the question on postponement being taken, it was determined in the affirmative.

A motion was then made by Mr. M'Lene seconded by Mr. Lincoln, to insert, after "legislature," the following : "As soon as convenient-ly may be."

Which was agreed to, and the section, as amended, adopted.

The second section, as moved by Mr. Wilson and Mr. Hubley, was then adopted as follows, viz.

The arts and sciences shall be promoted in one or more semin-aries of learning.

The third section, as moved by Mr. Wilson, being under consid-eration, a motion was made by Mr. Sitgreaves, seconded by Mr. Og-den, to insert the word "just," so as to read "protected in their just rights."

Which was determined in the negative.

It was moved by Mr. Lewis, seconded by Mr. Roberts, to amend the third section offered by Mr. Wilson, so as to read—the rights, privileges, immunities and estates of religious societies and corporate bodies shall remain as heretofore.

A motion was then made by Mr. Findley, seconded by Mr. M'Kean, to amend the amendment offered by Mr. Lewis, by striking out "as heretofore," and by inserting, after "remain" the following : "As if the constitution of this state had not been altered or amended."

Which was carried in the affirmative, and the section, as amended, adopted.

Whereupon, Ordered, that the three sections, as agreed to, be in-serted as the seventh article of the proposed constitution.

The motion made by Mr. Robinson, seconded by Mr. Sitgreaves, on the eighteenth instant, recurring, viz.

Members of the general assembly and all officers, executive and ju-dicial, shall be bound by oath or affirmation to support the constitu-tion of this commonwealth, and to perform the duties of their respec-tive offices with fidelity.

It was then moved by Mr. Lewis, seconded by Mr. Hare, to amend the motion of Mr. Robinson as follows, viz.

Members of the general assembly and other officers, executive and judicial, shall be bound by oath or affirmation to bear faith and true allegiance to the commonwealth of Pennsylvania, and to perform the duties of their respective offices with fidelity.

Which was determined in the negative.

And the motion of Mr. Robinson and Mr. Sitgreaves was adopted as the eighth article of the proposed plan of government.

Mr. M'Kean withdrew his motion of the 18th, instant, seconded by Mr. Gallatin.

The committee of accounts made the following report, viz.

That Zachariah Poulson, junior, printer to this convention, in the English language, has received the sum of one hundred pounds, and that Melchior Steiner, printer to this convention, in the German lan-guage, has received the sum of seventy-five pounds, on account of printing; but that the amount of their respective accounts cannot now be ascertained, therefore, as probably they may have occasion for further sums of money to enable them to expedite the printing of the minutes and the proposed constitution, your committee beg leave to submit the following resolution, viz.

Resolved, that the president draw an order, in favor of the secre-tary, on the state treasurer, for the sum of one hundred and fifty pounds, to be applied towards defraying the expenses of printing, and that he account for the same at the next sitting of this convention.

The committee further beg leave to report, that they have examined the accounts of Joseph Redman, Esquire, secretary, respecting the expenditure of the sum of one hundred pounds, drawn by him at the treasury, per order of this convention, for the purpose of defraying the contingent expenses, and find a balance in his hands of twenty-seven pounds, fifteen shillings and ten pence ; and beg leave to submit the following resolution, viz.

Resolved, that the president draw orders on the state treasurer as follows, viz.

In favor of Joseph Redman, Esquire, for the sum of sixty-seven pounds, four shillings and two pence, which, together with the above mentioned balance of twenty-seven pounds, fifteen shillings and ten pence (amounting in the whole to ninety five pounds) is the sum due to him for his services as secretary, during the sitting of the convention; and for the further sum of   pounds for his extra services, during the recess, in superinte ling the printing and distributing the minutes and proposed constituti on.

In favor of Jacob Shallus, Esquire, for the sum of ninety five pounds for his services as assistant secretary, during the sitting of the convention, and for the further sum of   pounds for services to be performed by him during the recess.

In favor of Frederick Snyder, messenger, for the sum of fifty pounds for his wages, including five days extra services.

In favor of Joseph Fry, door-keeper, for the sum of fifty pounds for his services, including five days extra service.

A motion was made by Mr. James Ross, seconded by Mr. Sitgreaves, to fill the first blank with "seventy-five."

Which was determined in the affirmative.

It was moved by Mr. Findley, seconded by Mr. Baker, to fill the second blank with "fifty."

Which was determined in the affirmative, and thereupon the report, as amended adopted.

A motion was made by Mr. Wilson, seconded by Mr. Findley, that the following question be taken, viz.

"Shall the constitution, as agreed to in convention, be published for the consideration of the good people of Pennsylvania?"

The names of the members being called over, it appeared that the question was unanimously determined in the affirmative.

On motion, Ordered, that Mr. Roberts and Mr. Baker be added to the committee appointed to superintend the press.

On motion of Mr. M'Kean, seconded by Mr. M'Lene, it was unanimously determined, that the thanks of this convention be given to his excellency Thomas Mifflin, Esquire, for his able and impartial conduct as president thereof.

The convention then adjourned to Monday, the ninth of August next, at three o'clock, P. M.

Chapter III.

MINUTES

Of the second session of the convention of the commonwealth of Pennsylvania, which commenced at Philadelphia, on Monday the ninth day of August, in the year of our Lord one thousand seven hundred and ninety.

MONDAY, August 9, 1790, P. M.

A number of members met pursuant to adjournment, but not being a quorum,
.   Adjourned until three o'clock to-morrow, P. M.

TUESDAY, August 10, 1790. P. M.

A number of members sufficient to constitute a quorum met pursuant to adjournment.
On motion of Mr. M'Kean, seconded by Mr. Whitehill,
Adjourned until three o'clock to-morrow, P. M.

WEDNESDAY, August 11, 1790, P. M.

The convention met pursuant to adjournment.
A letter from Samuel Ogden, Esq. in excuse for his non-attendance was read, and ordered to lie on the table.
On motion of Mr. M'Kean, seconded by Mr. Boyd, the first section of the first article of the constitution published for the consideration of the citizens of this commonwealth was read.
It was then moved by Mr. Smilie, seconded by Mr. Gallatin, to adjourn, which was carried in the affirmative.
Adjourned until ten o'clock to-morrow, A. M.

THURSDAY, August 12, 1790. A. M.

The convention met pursuant to adjournment.
A letter from Melchior Steiner, printer of the minutes in the German language, was read, in excuse for not having completed the business. Ordered to lie on the table.
The first section of the first article of the constitution published for the consideration of the citizens of this commonwealth recurring, the same was adopted as follows:
Section I. The legislative power of this commonwealth shall be vested in a general assembly, which shall consist of a senate and house of representatives.
The second section of the said first article being under consideration, the same was adopted as follows, viz.
Sect. II. The representatives shall be chosen annually, by the citizens of the city of Philadelphia, and of each county respectively, on the second Tuesday of October.

The third section of the said first article being under consideration, viz.

Sect. III. No person shall be a representative, who shall not have attained the age of twenty-one years, and have been a citizen and inhabitant of the state three years next preceding his election, and the last year thereof an inhabitant of the city or county in which he shall be chosen.

A motion was made by Mr. M'Kean, seconded by Mr. Lewis, to strike out the word " year," and in lieu thereof, to insert the words six " months." Which was determined in the negative.

A division of the section being called for by Mr. Sitgreaves and Mr. M'Kean, viz.

No person shall be a representative, who shall not have attained the age of twenty-one years, and have been a citizen and inhabitant of the state three years next preceding his election.

On the question, Will the convention agree to that part of the said section? It was determined in the affirmative.

And on the question, Will the convention agree to the remainder of the section, viz. And the last year thereof an inhabitant of the city or county in which he shall be chosen?

It was determined in the affirmative.

A motion was then made by Mr. Edwards, seconded by Mr. M'. Lene, to amend the said section by adding the following words, viz.

And no person residing within any city, town or borough which shall be entitled to a separate representation, shall vote for or be elected a member for any county; nor shall any person residing without the limits of any such city, town or borough vote for or be elected a member thereof.

It was then moved by Mr. Robinson, seconded by Mr. Harr, to strike out from the said amendment, the words " vote for or."

Which was determined in the affirmative.

And on the question, Will the convention agree to the motion of Mr. Edwards and Mr. M'Lene, as amended ?

The house being equally divided the president gave his casting vote in the affirmative, and the said section, with the amendment, was thereupon adopted as follows:

Section III. No person shall be a representative, who shall not have attained the age of twenty-one years, and have been a citizen and inhabitant of the state three years next preceding his election, and the last year thereof an inhabitant of the city or county, in which he shall be chosen; and no person residing within any city, town or borough, which shall be entitled to a separate representation, shall be elected a member for any county; nor shall any person residing without the limits of any such city, town or borough be elected a member thereof.

The fourth section of the said first article being under consideration, the same was adopted as follows, viz.

Sect. IV. Within three years after the first meeting of the general assembly, and within every subsequent term of seven years, an enumeration of the taxable inhabitants shall be made, in such manner as shall be directed by law. The number of representatives shall, at the several periods of making such enumeration, be fixed by the legislature and apportioned among the city of Philadelphia and the several counties according to the number of taxable inhabitants in each, and shall never be less than sixty nor more than one hundred.

Each county shall have, at least, one representative; but no county hereafter erected, shall be entitled to a separate representation until a sufficient number of taxable inhabitants shall be contained within it, to entitle them to at least one representative, agreeably to the ratio which shall then be established.

The fifth section of the said first article being under consideration, it was moved by Mr. M'Kean, seconded by Mr. Gray, to postpone the consideration of the same, together with the sixth, seventh, eighth and ninth sections of the said article, until Thursday next.

On the question, Will the convention agree to the postponement? It was determined in the affirmative.

The tenth section of the said first article being under consideration, viz.

Sect. X. The general assembly shall meet on the first Tuesday of December, in every year, unless sooner convened by the governor.

A motion was made by Mr. Gray, seconded by Mr. Coleman, to strike out the words " first Tuesday of December," and to insert in lieu thereof, " second Tuesday of November." Which was determined in the negative, and the original section adopted.

The eleventh section of the said first article being under consideration, the same was adopted as follows, viz.

Sect. XI. Each house shall choose its speaker and other officers; and the senate shall also choose a speaker *pro tempore*, when the speaker shall exercise the office of governor.

The twelfth section of the said first article being under consideration, the same was adopted as follows, viz.

Sect. XII. Each house shall judge of the qualifications of its own members; but contested elections shall be determined by a committee, to be selected in such manner as shall be directed by law: A majority of each house shall constitute a quorum to do business; but a smaller number may adjourn from day to day, and may be authorised, by law, to compel the attendance of absent members in such manner, and under such penalties, as may be provided.

The thirteenth section of the said first article being under consideration, the same was adopted as follows, viz.

Sect. XIII. Each house may determine the rules of its proceedings, punish its members for disorderly behaviour; and with the concurrence of two-thirds, expel a member, but not a second time for the same cause, and shall have all other powers necessary for either branch of the legislature of a free state.

The fourteenth section of the said first article being under consideration, the same was adopted as follows, viz.

Sect. XIV. Each house shall keep a journal of its proceedings, and publish them weekly, except such parts as may, in their judgment, require secrecy: And the yeas and nays of the members, on any question, shall, at the desire of any two of them, be entered on the journals.

The fifteenth section of the said first article being under consideration the same was adopted as follows, viz.

Sect. XV. The doors of each house of the places where they shall respectively sit in committee of the whole, shall be open, unless when the business shall be such as, in their judgment, ought to be kept secret.

The sixteenth section of the said first article being under consideration, the same was adopted as follows, viz.

32

Sect. XVI. Neither house shall, without the consent of the other, adjourn for more than three days, nor to any other place than that in which the two houses shall be sitting.
Adjourned until ten o'clock to-morrow, A. M.

FRIDAY. August 13, 1790, A. M.

The convention met pursuant to adjournment.
The seventeenth section of the first article of the constitution published for the consideration of the citizens of this commonwealth, being under consideration, the same was adopted as follows, viz.
Sect. XVII. The senators and representatives shall receive a compensation for their services, to be ascertained by law, and paid out of the treasury of the commonwealth. They shall in all cases, except treason, felony and breach of the peace, be privileged from arrest, during their attendance at the session of the respective houses, and in going to and returning from the same; and for any speech or debate in either house they shall not be questioned in any other place.
The eighteenth section of the said first article being under consideration the same was adopted as follows, viz.
Sect. XVIII. No senator or representative shall, during the time for which he was elected, be appointed to any civil office, under the authority of this commonwealth, which shall have been created, or the emoluments of which shall have been increased during such time: And no member of congress or other person holding any office, except in the militia, under the United States or this commonwealth, shall be a member of either house during his continuance in congress or in office.
The nineteenth section of the said first article being under consideration, the same was adopted as follows, viz.
Sect. XIX. When vacancies happen in either house, the speaker of that house shall issue writs of election to fill such vacancies.
The twentieth section of the said first article being under consideration, the same was adopted as follows, viz.
Sect. XX. All bills for raising revenue shall originate in the house of representatives; but the senate may propose or concur with amendments, as in other bills.
The twenty-first section of the said first article being under consideration, the same was adopted as follows, viz.
Sect. XXI. No money shall be drawn from the treasury, but in consequence of appropriations made by law.
The twenty-second section of the said first article being under consideration, the same was adopted as follows, viz.
Sect. XXII. Every bill, which shall have passed the house of representatives and the senate, shall, before it become a law, be presented to the governor. If he approve, he shall sign it; but if he shall not approve it, he shall return it, with his objections, to the house in which it shall have originated, who shall enter the objections at large upon their journals, and proceed to re-consider it. If, after such re-consideration, two-thirds of that house shall agree to pass the bill, it shall be sent, together with the objections, to the other house, by which it shall likewise be re-considered, and if approved by two-thirds of that house, it shall become a law. But in all such cases, the votes of both houses shall be determined by yeas and nays, and the names of the persons voting for or against the bill shall be entered on the journals of each house

respectively. If any bill shall not be returned by the governor within ten days (Sundays excepted) after it shall have been presented to him, it shall be a law in like manner as if he had signed it; unless the general assembly, by their adjournment, prevent its return, in which case it shall be a law, unless sent back within three days after their next meeting.

The twenty-third section of the said first article being under consideration, the same was adopted as follows, viz.

Sect. XXIII. Every order, resolution or vote, to which the concurrence of the senate and house of representatives may be necessary (except on a question of adjournment) shall be presented to the governor, and before the same shall take effect, be approved by him; or, being disapproved shall be re-passed by two-thirds of the senate and house of representatives, according to the rules and limitations prescribed in case of a bill.

The first section of the second article being under consideration, the same was adopted as follows, viz.·

Section I. The supreme executive power of this commonwealth shall be vested in a governor.

The second section of the said second article being under consideration, the same was adopted as follows: ·

Sect. II. The governor shall be chosen on the second Tuesday of October, by the citizens throughout the commonwealth, at the places where they shall respectively vote for representatives. The returns of every election for governor shall be transmitted, under seal, to the seat of government, directed to the speaker of the senate, who shall open and publish them in the presence of the members of both houses of the legislature. The person having the highest number of votes shall be governor; but if two or more shall be equal and highest in votes, one of them shall be chosen governor by the joint vote of the members of both houses. Contested elections shall be determined by a committee to be selected from both houses of the legislature, in such manner as shall be directed by law.

The third section of the said second article being under consideration, the same was adopted as follows: ·

Sect. III. The governor shall hold his office during three years from the third Tuesday of December next ensuing his election, and shall not be capable of holding his office longer than nine in any term of twelve years.

The fourth section of the said second article being under consideration, viz.

Sect. IV. He shall be, at least, thirty years of age; and have been a citizen and inhabitant of this state seven years next before his election; unless he shall have been absent on the public business of the United States, or of this state.

It was moved by Mr. Roberts, seconded by Mr. M'Kean, to amend the said section by adding the following words:

"And he shall be legally seized and possessed of a clear real and personal estate within this commonwealth of the value of four thousand dollars, six months previous to his election."

A motion was made by Mr. Hare, seconded by Mr. Edwards, to strike out from the said amendment the words " and personal" Which was determined in the affirmative.

It was moved by Mr. Pickering, seconded by Mr. Barclay, to strike out the word "six," and in lieu thereof to insert the word "twelve" Which was determined in the negative.

A motion was then made by Mr. Sitgreaves, seconded by Mr. M'. Kean, to strike out the words "and possessed." Which was determined in the affirmative.

It was moved by Mr. Wilson, seconded by Mr. Pickering, to postpone the consideration of the said fourth section, together with the amendment as amended.

On the question, Will the convention agree to the postponement? It was determined in the affirmative.

The fifth section of the said second article being under consideration, the same was adopted as follows, viz.

Sect. V. No member of congress, or person holding any office under the United States or this state, shall be capable of exercising the office of governor.

· The sixth section of the said second article being under consideration, the same was adopted as follows, viz.

Sect. VI. The governor shall, at stated times, receive for his services a compensation, which shall be neither increased nor diminished during the period for which he shall have been elected.

The seventh section of the said second article being under consideration, the same was adopted as follows:

Sect. VII. He shall be commander in chief of the army and navy of this commonwealth, and of the militia, except when they shall be called into the actual service of the United States.

· The eighth section of the said second article being under consideration, the same was adopted as follows:

Sect. VIII. He shall appoint all officers whose offices are established by this constitution or shall be established by law, and whose appointments are not herein otherwise provided for; but no person shall be appointed to an office within any county, who shall not have been a citizen and inhabitant therein one year next before his appointment, if the county shall have been so long erected, but if that shall not be the case, then within the limits of the original county or counties out of which it shall have been taken. No member of congress from this state, nor any person holding or exercising any office of trust or profit under the United States, shall at the same time, hold or exercise the office of judge, secretary, treasurer, prothonotary, register of wills, recorder of deeds, sheriff, or any office in this state, to which a salary is by law annexed; or any other office which future legislatures shall declare incompatible with offices or appointments under the United States.

The ninth section of the said second article being under consideration, viz.

Sect. IX. All commissions shall be in the name and by the authority of the commonwealth of Pennsylvania, and be sealed with the state seal, and signed by the governor.

A motion was made by Mr. M'Kean, seconded by Mr. Addison, to strike out the words "and by the authority." Which was determined in the negative, and the original section adopted.

The tenth section of the said second article being under consideration, the same was adopted as follows:

Sect. X. He shall have power to remit fines and forfeitures, and grant reprieves and pardons, except in cases of impeachment.

The eleventh section of the said second article being under consideration, the same was adopted as follows:

Sect. XI. He may require information, in writing, from the officers in the executive department upon any subject relating to the duties of their respective offices.

The twelfth section of the said second article being under consideration, the same was adopted as follows:

Sect. XII. He shall from time to time, give to the general assembly information of the state of the commonwealth, and recommend to their consideration such measures as he shall judge necessary or expedient.

The thirteenth section of the said second article being under consideration, the same was adopted as follows:

Sect XIII. He may, on extraordinary occasions, convene the general assembly, and in case of disagreement between the two houses with respect to the time of adjournment, adjourn them to such time as he shall think proper, not exceeding four months.

The fourteenth section of the said second article being under consideration, the same was adopted as follows:

Sect. XIV. He shall take care that the laws be faithfully executed.

The fifteenth section of the said second article being under consideration, the same was adopted as follows:

Sect. XV. In case of the death or resignation of the governor, or of his removal from office, the speaker of the senate shall exercise the office of governor, until another governor, who shall in such case, be chosen at the next annual election, shall be duly qualified and commence the exercise of his office. And if the trial of a contested election shall continue longer than until the third Tuesday in December next ensuing the election of a governor, the governor of the last year, or the speaker of the senate, who may be in the exercise of the executive authority, shall continue therein until the determination of such contested election, and until a governor shall be qualified as aforesaid.

The sixteenth section of the said second article being under consideration, the same was adopted as follows:

Sect. XVI. The state treasurer shall be appointed annually, by the joint vote of the members of both houses. All other officers in the treasury department, election officers, officers relating to taxes, to the poor and highways, constables and other township officers, shall be appointed in such manner as is or shall be directed by law.

The seventeenth section of the said second article being under consideration, a motion was made by Mr. Sitgreaves, seconded by Mr. Jenks, to postpone the consideration of the said section. Which was determined in the negative, and after some debate it was, on motion of Mr. Wilson and Mr. Coleman, ordered, that the debates on the said section be postponed.

The first section of the third article being under consideration, the same was adopted as follows, viz.

Section I. In elections by the citizens every freeman of the age of twenty-one years, having resided in the state two years next before the days of the elections respectively, and within that time paid a state or county tax, which shall have been assessed upon him at least six months before the election, shall enjoy the rights of an elector; provided that the sons of persons qualified as aforesaid, between the age of twenty-one and twenty-two years, shall be entitled to vote although they shall not have paid taxes.

The second section of the said third article being under consideration, viz.

Sect. II. All elections shall be by ballot, except those by persons in their representative or public capacities, who shall vote *viva voce*, unless in the choice of committees and their own officers.

Mr. Addison called for a division of the question on the said section to the word *viva voce* inclusive.

And on the question, Will the convention agree to the first part of the said section? It was determined in the affirmative.

The second part of the said section recurring, a motion was made by Mr. M'Kean, seconded by Mr. James Ross, to strike out the words " committees and." Which was determined in the affirmative.

And on the question, Will the convention agree to the second part of the said section as amended? It was determined in the negative.

The third section of the said third article being under consideration, the same was adopted as follows, viz.

Sect. III. Electors shall, in all cases, except treason, felony and breach of the peace, be privileged from arrest during their attendance on elections, and in going to and returning from them.

The first section of the fourth article being under consideration, the same was adopted as follows, viz.

Section I. The house of representatives shall have the sole power of impeaching.

The second section of the said fourth article being under consideration, viz.

Sect. II. All impeachments shall be tried by the senate : When sitting for that purpose, the senators shall be on oath or affirmation. No person shall be convicted without the concurrence of two-thirds of the members present.

A motion was made by Mr. Sitgreaves, seconded by Mr. M'Kean, to insert after the word " affirmation," the words " taking to their assistance, for advice only, the judges of the supreme court."

It was then on motion of Mr. M'Kean, seconded by Mr. Findley, Ordered, that the further consideration of the said section, together with the proposed amendment be postponed.

The third section of the said fourth article being under consideration, viz.

Sect. III. The governor and all other civil officers under this commonwealth shall be liable to impeachment for any misdemeanor in office ; but judgment, in such cases, shall not extend further than to removal from office and disqualification to hold any office of honor, trust or profit under this commonwealth : the party convicted shall, nevertheless, be liable to indictment, trial, judgment and punishment according to law.

A motion was made by Mr. Wilson, seconded by Mr. Addison, to amend the said section by inserting before the word " convicted," the word "whether," and after the word " convicted," the words " or acquitted." Which was carried in the affirmative, and the section as amended, adopted.

Adjourned until ten o'clock to-morrow, A. M.

SATURDAY, August 14, 1790.   A. M.

The convention met pursuant to adjournment.

A letter from Zachariah Poulson, jr. printer of the minutes, in the English language, to this convention, was read, requesting an additional sum of money.   Whereupon,

Resolved, that the president be authorised and raquested to draw an order in favor of Zachariah Poulson, jr. for the sum of two hundred pounds, on account.

A motion was made by Mr. M'Kean, seconded by Mr. Newlin, to re-consider the third section of the fourth article, adopted yesterday, in order to add the following amendment thereto, viz.

No impeachment shall be sustained against any person unless commenced within   years after the offence shall have been committed.

On motion of Mr. Sitgreaves, seconded by Mr. M'Kean, Ordered, That the further consideration of the said motion be postponed.

The first section of the fifth article of the constitution published for the consideration of the citizens of this commonwealth, being under consideration, the same was adopted as follows, viz.

Section I. The judicial power of this commonwealth shall be vested in a supreme court, in courts of oyer and terminer and general gaol delivery, in a court of common pleas, orphans' court, register's court and a court of quarter sessions of the peace for each county, in justices of the peace, and in such other courts as the legislature may, from time time, establish.

The second section of the said fifth article being under consideration, viz.

Sect. II. The judges of the supreme court and of the several courts of common pleas shall hold their offices during good behaviour: but for any reasonable cause which shall not be sufficient ground of impeachment, the governor may remove any of them on the address of two-thirds of each branch of the legislature. The judges of the supreme court and the presidents of the several courts of common pleas shall, at stated times, receive for their services an adequate compensation to be fixed by law, which shall not be diminished during their continuance in office: But they shall receive no fees or perquisites of office, nor hold any other office of profit under this commonwealth.

A motion was made by Mr James Ross, seconded by Mr. Redick, to strike out the words " receive no fees or perquisites of office, nor," and in lieu thereof to insert the word "not," in order that the section may read:

The judges of the supreme court and of the several courts of common pleas shall hold their offices during good behaviour: But, for any reasonable cause, which shall not be sufficient ground of impeachment, the governor may remove any of them on the address of two-thirds of each branch of the legislature. The judges of the supreme court and the presidents of the several courts of common pleas shall, at stated times, receive for their services, an adequate compensation, to be fixed by law; but they shall not hold any other office of profit under this commonwealth.

Adjourned until three o'clock on Monday next, P. M.

The convention met pursuant to adjournment.

The second section of the fifth article, with the amendment proposed on Saturday last by Mr. James Ross, seconded by Mr. Redick, recurring, Mr. Redick withdrew his seconding the motion, and thereupon the original section was adopted as follows:

Sect. II. The judges of the supreme court and of the several courts of common pleas shall hold their offices during good behaviour: But, for any reasonable cause, which shall not be sufficient ground of impeachment, the governor may remove any of them on the address of two-thirds of each branch of the legislature. The judges of the supreme court and the presidents of the several courts of common pleas, shall, at stated times, receive for their services, an adequate compensation, to be fixed by law; which shall not be diminished during their continuance in office; but they shall receive no fees or perquisites of office, nor hold any other office of profit under this commonwealth.

The third section of the fifth article being under consideration, the same was adopted as follows, viz.

Sect. III. The jurisdiction of the supreme court shall extend over the state, and the judges thereof shall, by virtue of their offices, be justices of oyer and terminer and general gaol delivery, in the several counties.

The fourth section of the fifth article being under consideration, the same was adopted as follows, viz.

Sect. IV. Until it shall be otherwise directed by law, the several courts of common pleas shall be established in the following manner: The governor shall appoint, in each county, not fewer than three nor more than four judges, who, during their continuance in office, shall reside in such county: The state shall be, by law, divided into circuits, none of which shall include more than six nor fewer than three counties. A president shall be appointed of the courts in each circuit, who, during his continuance in office, shall reside therein. The president and judges aforesaid, any two of whom shall be a quorum, shall compose the respective courts of common pleas.

The fifth section of the fifth article, being under consideration, the same was adopted as follows, viz.

Sect. V. The judges of the court of common pleas in each county shall, by virtue of their offices, be justices of oyer and terminer and general jail delivery for the trial of capital and other offenders therein; and any two of them, the president being one, shall be a quorum; but they shall not hold a court of oyer and terminer or jail delivery in any county when the judges of the supreme court, or any of them, shall be sitting in the same county. The party accused, as well as the commonwealth, may, under such regulations as shall be prescribed by law, remove the indictment and proceedings or a transcript thereof, into the supreme court.

The sixth section of the fifth article being under consideration, viz.

Sect. VI. The supreme court and the several courts of common pleas shall, beside the powers heretofore usually exercised by them, have the power of a court of chancery so far as relates to the perpetuating of testimony, the obtaining of evidence from places not within the state, and the care of the persons and estates of those who are *non compotes mentis.*

And the legislature shall, as soon as conveniently may be, vest in the said courts such other powers to grant relief in equity as shall be found necessary: and may, from time time, enlarge or diminish those powers; or vest them in such other courts as they shall judge proper for the due administration of justice.

A motion was made by Mr. Sitgreaves, seconded by Mr. Gallatin, to strike out the words " beside the powers heretofore usually exercised by them."

On the question, Will the convention agree to strike out the said words? It was determined in the negative, and the original section adopted.

The seventh section of the fifth article being under consideration, the same was adopted as follows, viz.

Sect. VII. The judges of the court of common pleas in each county, any two of whom shall be a quorum ; shall compose the court of quarter sessions of the peace and orphans' court therein : And the register of wills, together with the said judges, or any two of them, shall compose the register's court in the respective counties.

The eighth section of the fifth article being under consideration, the same was adopted as follows, viz.

Sect. VIII. The judges of the courts of common pleas shall, within their respective counties, have the like powers with the judges of the supreme court to issue writs of certiorari to the justices of the peace, and to cause their proceedings to be brought before them and the like right and justice to be done.

The ninth section of the fifth article being under consideration, viz.

Sect. IX. The president of the courts in each circuit shall, within such circuit, and the judges of the courts of common pleas shall, within their respective counties, be justices of the peace so far as relates to criminal matters.

A motion was made by Mr. Pickering, seconded by Mr. M'Kean, to amend the said section to read as follows:

The president of the courts in each circuit, within such circuit, and the judges of the courts of common pleas, within their respective counties, shall be justices of the peace, so far as relates to criminal matters.

On the question, Will the convention agree to the amendment? It was determined in the negative, and thereupon the original section adopted.

The tenth section of the said fifth article being under consideration, a motion was made by Mr. Addison, seconded by Mr. Henderson, to amend the section to read as follows:

Sect. X. The governor shall appoint a competent number of justices of the peace in such convenient districts in each county, as are, or shall be directed by law. They shall be commissioned during good behaviour; but may be removed on conviction of misbehaviour in office, or of any infamous crime, or on the address of both houses of the legislature.

On the question, Will the convention agree to the amendment? It was determined in the affirmative, and the said section as amended adopted.

The eleventh section of the fifth article being under consideration, the same was adopted as follows:

Sect. XI. A register's office for the probate of wills and granting letters of administration, and an office for the recording of deeds shall be kept in each county.

The twelfth section of the fifth article being under consideration, the same was adopted as follows:

Sect. XII. The stile of all process shall be *The commonwealth of Pennsylvania*: all prosecutions shall be carried on in the name and by the authority of the commonwealth of Pennsylvania, and conclude, *against the peace and dignity of the same.*

A motion was made by Mr. James Ross, seconded by Mr. Smith, to re-consider the second section of the fifth article in order to strike out the word "and," before the words "the presidents," and to insert after the word "presidents," the words "and judges."

It was moved by Mr. Addison, seconded by Mr. Smilie, to postpone the consideration of the said motion, whereupon, on motion,

Adjourned until ten o'clock to-morrow, A M.

TUESDAY, August 17, 1790. A. M.

The convention met pursuant to adjournment.

The motion made yesterday by Mr. James Ross, seconded by Mr. Smith, to re-consider the second section of the fifth article in order to amend the same, recurring.

On the question, Will the convention agree to re-consider the said section for the purpose contained in the said motion? It was determined in the negative.

The first section of the sixth article being under consideration, the same was adopted as follows, viz.

Section I. Sheriffs and coroners shall, at the places of election of representatives, be chosen by the citizens of each county respectively. Two persons shall be chosen for each office, one of whom, for each, shall be commissioned by the governor. They shall hold their offices for three years and until a successor be duly qualified; but no person shall be twice chosen or appointed sheriff in any term of six years.

The second section of the sixth article being under consideration, viz.

Sect. II. The freemen of this commonwealth shall be armed and disciplined for its defence: The militia officers shall be appointed in such manner and for such time as shall be directed by law.

A motion was made by Mr. Roberts, seconded by Mr. Shoemaker, to strike out after the word "commonwealth," the word "shall," and in lieu thereof to insert the word "may."

On the question, Will the convention agree to the amendment? It was determined in the negative, and the original section adopted.

The third section of the sixth article being under consideration, viz.

Section III. Prothonotaries, clerks of the peace and orphans' courts, recorders of deeds, registers of wills and sheriffs, shall keep their offices in the county town of the county in which they respectively shall be officers; unless when the governor shall, for special reasons, dispense therewith for any term not exceeding five years after the county shall have been erected.

A motion was made by Mr. Redick, seconded by Mr. Mawhorter, to insert after the words "register of wills," the words "county treasurers." Which was determined in the negative.

It was then moved by Mr. M'Kean, seconded by Mr, Henderson, to insert after the word "officers," the words " or within one mile thereof."

On the question, Will the convention agree to the said amendment? It was determined in the negative, and the original section adopted.

A motion was made by Mr. Addison, to re-consider the first section of the sixth article, as adopted, in order to annex the following amendment thereto, viz.

In case of a vacancy in the office of sheriff or coroner by death, resignation, removal or otherwise, the governor shall appoint one until a sheriff or coroner, who shall be chosen at the next general election, shall enter on the exercise of his office.

On the question, Will the convention agree to re-consider the said section for the aforesaid purpose? It was determined in the negative.

The first section of the seventh article being under consideration, the same was adopted as follows, viz.

Section I. The legislature shall, as soon as conveniently may be, provide by law for the establishment of schools throughout the state, in such manner that the poor may be taught gratis.

The second section of the seventh article being under consideration, the same was adopted as follows, viz.

Section II. The arts and sciences shall be promoted in one or more seminaries of learning.

A motion was made by Mr. Sitgreaves, seconded by Mr. Arndt, to insert the following as the third section of the said seventh article, viz.

The legislature shall, by law, regulate and ascertain the fees of the courts and public officers throughout the commonwealth; fees shall be adequate, but moderate

On the question, Will the convention adopt the same as the third section of the seventh article? It was determined in the negative.

The third section of the seventh article being under consideration, the same was adopted as follows:

Section III. The rights privileges, immunities and estates of religious societies and corporate bodies shall remain as if the constitution of this state had not been altered or amended.

The eighth article being under consideration the same was adopted as follows:

Members of the general assembly and all officers, executive and judicial, shall be bound by oath or affirmation to support the constitution of this commonwealth, and to perform the duties of their respective offices with fidelity.

The first section of the ninth article being under consideration the same was adopted as follows:

Section I. That all men are born equally free and independent, and have certain inherent and indefeasible rights, among which are those of enjoying and defending life and liberty, of acquiring, possessing and protecting property and reputation, and of pursuing their own happiness.

The second section of the ninth article being under consideration, the same was adopted as follows:

Section II. That all power is originally vested in the people, and all free governments are founded on their authority, and instituted for their peace, safety and happiness: For the advancement of those ends, they

have, at all times, an unalienable and indefeasible right to alter, reform, or abolish their government, in such manner as they may think
proper.

The third section of the ninth article being under consideration, the
same was adopted as follows:

Section III. That all men have a natural and indefeasible right to
worship Almighty God according to the dictates of their own consciences ; that no man can, of right, be compelled to attend or erect,
or support any place of worship, or to maintain any ministry against
his consent ; that no human authority can, in any case whatever, control or interfere with the rights of conscience ; and that no preference
shall ever be given, by law, to any religious establishments or modes
of worship,

The fourth section of the ninth article being under consideration,
the same was adopted as follows, viz.

Section IV. That no person who acknowledges the being of a God
and a future state of rewards and punishments, shall, on account of
his religious sentiments, be disqualified to hold any office or place of
trust or profit under this commonwealth.

The fifth section of the ninth article being under consideration, the
same was adopted as follows, viz.

Section V. That elections shall be free and equal.

The sixth section of the ninth article being under consideration, the
same was adopted as follows:

Section VI. That trial by jury shall be as heretofore, and the right
thereof shall remain inviolate.

The seventh section of the ninth article being under consideration,
it was moved by Mr. Lewis, seconded by Mr. Ogden, to postpone the
consideration thereof until Friday next.

On the question, Will the convention agree to the postponement? It
was determined in the affirmative.

The eighth section of the ninth article being under consideration, the
same was adopted as follows:

Section VIII. That the people shall be secure in their persons,
houses, papers and possessions from unreasonable searches and seizures; and that no warrant to search any place, or to seize any person or things, shall issue without describing them as nearly as may be,
nor without probable cause, supported by oath or affirmation.

The ninth section of the ninth article being under consideration, the
same was adopted as follows:

Section IX. That in all criminal prosecutions the accused hath a right
to be heard by himself and his council; to demand the nature and cause
of the accusation against him ; to meet the witnesses face to face ; to
have compulsory process for obtaining witnesses in his favor ; and, in
prosecutions by indictment, a speedy public trial by an impartial jury
of the vicinage ; that he cannot be compelled to give evidence against
himself; nor can he be deprived of his life, liberty or property, unless
by the judgment of his peers, or the law of the land.

The tenth section of the ninth article being under consideration, viz.

Section X. That no person shall, for any indictable offence, be
proceeded against, criminally, by information ; except in cases arising in the land or naval forces, or in the militia when in actual service in time of war or public danger: Nor shall any person, for the
same offence, be twice put in jeopardy of life or limb ; nor shall any

man's property be taken, or applied to public use, without the consent of his representatives, and without just compensation being made.

It was moved by Mr. Lewis, seconded by Mr. Sitgreaves, to amend the said section to read as follows:

Section X. That no person shall, for any indictable offence, be proceeded against criminally by information; except for oppression or misdemeanor in office, and in cases arising in the land or naval forces, or in the militia when in actual service in time of war or public danger; nor shall any person for the same offence be twice put in jeopardy of life or limb; nor shall any man's property be taken, or applied to public use, without the consent of his representatives, and without just compensation being made.

On the question, Will the convention agree to the amendment? It was determined in the affirmative, and the section as amended, adopted.

The eleventh section of the ninth article being under consideration, the same was adopted as follows:

Section XI. That all courts shall be open, and every man for an injury done him in his lands, goods, person or reputation, shall have remedy by the due course of law, and right and justice administered without sale, denial, or delay.

The twelfth section of the ninth article being under consideration, viz.

Section XII. That no power of suspending laws, or the execution thereof, shall be exercised, unless by the legislature, or its authority.

A motion was made by Mr. Addison, seconded by Mr. Smith, to strike out the words " or the execution thereof." Which was determined in the affirmative.

It was then moved by Mr. Smith, seconded by Mr. Ogden, to strike out the words "or its authority." Which was determined in the negative, and the said section as amended, adopted as follows:

Section XII. That no power of suspending laws shall be exercised, unless by the legislature, or its authority.

Adjourned until nine o'clock to-morrow, A. M.

WEDNESDAY, August 18, 1790. *A. M.*

The convention met pursuant to adjournment.

A motion was made by Mr. Wilson, seconded by Mr. Smith, to reconsider the tenth section of the ninth article adopted yesterday, and after some debate, it was, on motion of Mr. Wilson, seconded by Mr. M'Lene, ordered, that the further consideration of the said motion be postponed until Saturday next.

The thirteenth section of the ninth article being under consideration, the same was adopted as follows, viz.

Section XIII. That excessive bail shall not be required, nor excessive fines imposed, nor cruel punishments inflicted.

The fourteenth section of the ninth article being under consideration the same was adopted as follows, viz.

Section XIV. That all prisoners shall be bailable by sufficient sureties, unless for capital offences, when the proof is evident or presumption great: and the privilege of the writ of habeas corpus shall not be suspended, unless when, in cases of rebellion or invasion, the public safety may require it.

The fifteenth section of the ninth article being under cons deration, the same was adopted as follows, viz.

Section XV. That no commission of oyer and terminer or jail delivery shall be issued.

The sixteenth section of the ninth article being under consideration, the same was adopted as follows, viz.

Section XVI. That the person of a debtor, where there is not a strong presumption of fraud, shall not be continued in prison after delivering up all his estate, for the benefit of his creditors, in such manner as shall be prescribed by law.

The seventeenth section of the ninth article being under consideration, the same was adopted as follows, viz.

Section XVII. That no *ex post facto* law, nor any law impairing contracts, shall be made.

The eighteenth section of the ninth article being under consideration, the same was adopted as follows:

Section XVIII. That no person shall be attainted of treason or felony by the legislature.

The nineteenth section of the ninth article being under consideration, viz.

Section XIX. That no attainder shall work corruption of blood, nor, except during the life of the offender, forfeiture of estate to the commonwealth; that the estates of such persons as shall destroy their own lives shall go as in case of natural death; and if any person shall be killed by casualty or accident there shall be no forfeiture by reason thereof.

A motion was made by Mr. Smith, seconded by Mr. Lewis, to strike out the word "go," and insert in lieu thereof, the words "descend or vest." Which was determined in the affirmative.

It was moved by Mr. Pickering and Mr. M'Kean, to strike out the words "or accident."

Which was determined in the affirmative.

A motion was then made by Mr. Lewis, seconded by Mr. Sitgreaves, to insert, between the words "forfeiture of," and the word "estate," the word "real."

On the question, Will the convention agree to the said amendment? It was determined in the negative.

It was moved by Mr. Sitgreaves, seconded by Mr. Ogden, to amend the said section to read as follows:

'That no attainder shall work corruption of blood, nor, except in cases of treason, forfeiture of estate to the commonwealth, and then only during the life of the offender; that the estates of such persons as shall destroy their own lives shall descend or vest as in case of natural death; and if any person shall be killed by casualty there shall be no forfeiture by reason thereof.

On the question, Will the convention agree to the amendment?

It was determined in the negative, and the said nineteenth section, as amended, adopted as follows:

Section XIX. That no attainder shall work corruption of blood, nor, except during the life of the offender, forfeiture of estate to the commonwealth; that the estates of such persons as shall destroy their own lives shall descend or vest as in case of natural death; and if any person shall be killed by casualty there shall be no forfeiture by reason thereof.

The twentieth section of the ninth article being under consideration, the same was adopted as follows, viz.

Section XX. That the citizens have a right, in a peaceable manner, to assemble together for their common good, and to apply to those invested with the powers of government, for redress of grievances or other proper purposes, by petition, address or remonstrance.

The twenty-first section of the ninth article being under consideration, viz.

Section XXI. That the right of the citizens to bear arms in defence of themselves and the state shall not be questioned. But those who conscientiously scruple to bear arms shall not be compelled to do so, but shall pay an equivalent for personal service.

Mr. M'Kean called for a division of the question on the said section, to the word "questioned."

And on the question, Will the convention agree to the first part of the said section? It was determined in the affirmative.

The second part of the said section being under consideration, viz.

But those who conscientiously scruple to bear arms shall not be compelled to do so, but shall pay an equivalent for personal service.

A motion was made by Mr. Lewis, seconded by Mr. Ogden, to strike out, after the word "but," the word "shall," and insert, in lieu thereof, "may be obliged to." Which was determined in the negative.

. A division of the question on the said second part of the section being called for by Mr. Lewis, to the words "to do so."

On the question, Will the convention agree to that part of the said section? It was determined in the affirmative.

And on the question, Will the convention agree to the remainder of the said section, viz. But shall pay an equivalent for personal service? The yeas and nays being called by Mr. Roberts, were as follow, viz.

YEAS.

Mr. Wilson	Mr. Hubley	Mr. Gehr	Mr. J. Ross
Baker	Miller	Mawhorter	Smilie
Lewis	Slegle	Arndt	Gallatin
M'Kean	Reed	Rhoads	M'Lene
Gray	Tyson	Powell	Matthews
Robinson	Pedan	Piper	Morris
Hare	Dill	Smith	Coates
Edwards	Whitehill	Snyder	Gloninger
Barclay	Irvine	Findley	Brown
Bull	Power	Todd	Graydon
Boyd	Hiester	Addison	Pickering
Hand	Lower	Hoge	Henderson
Coleman	Lincoln	Redick	Gibson
Graff	Groscop		54

NAYS.

Mr. Roberts	Mr. Stout	Mr. Breckbill	Mr. Shoemaker
Ogden	T. Ross	Sitgreaves	Newlin 9
Jenks			

So it was determined in the affirmative, and the said section adopted as follows, viz.

Section XXI. That the right of the citizens to bear arms in defence of themselves and the state shall not be questioned: But those who conscientiously scruple to bear arms, shall not be compelled to do so, but shall pay an equivalent for personal service.

The twenty-second section of the ninth article being under consideration, the same was adopted as follows, viz.

Section XXII. That no standing army shall, in time of peace, be kept up without the consent of the legislature, and the military shall, in all cases, and at all times, be kept in strict subordination to the civil power.

The twenty-third section of the ninth article being under considertion, the same was adopted as follows, viz.

Section XXIII. That no soldier shall, in time of peace, be quartered in any house without the consent of the owner, nor in time of war, but in a manner to be prescribed by law.

The twenty fourth section of the ninth article being under consideration, the same was adopted as follows, viz.

Section XXIV. That the legislature shall not grant any title of nobility or hereditary distinction, nor create any office the appointment to which shall be for a longer term than during good behaviour.

The twenty-fifth section of the ninth article being under consideration, viz.

Section XXV. That emigration from the state shall not be prohibited.

A motion was made by Mr. M'Kean, seconded by Mr. Lewis, to amend the said section by adding the following words: "unless in time of war."

Which was determined in the negative, and the original section adopted.

The twenty-sixth section of the ninth article being under consideration, the same was adopted as follows, viz.

Section XXVI. To guard against transgressions of the high powers which we have delegated, WE DECLARE, that every thing in this article is excepted out of the general powers of government, and shall for ever remain inviolate.

Adjourned until nine o'clock to-morrow, A. M.

THURSDAY, August 25th, 1790. A. M.

The convention met pursuant to adjournment.

Agreeably to the order of the twelfth instant, the fifth section of the first article recurred, viz.

Sect. V. The senators shall be chosen for four years by the citizens of Philadelphia and of each county respectively, at the same time, in the same manner, and at the same places where they shall vote for representatives.

A motion was made by Mr. Hare, seconded by Mr. Shoemaker, to amend the said section by adding the following words, viz.

All the citizens of this commonwealth shall be entitled to vote in the election of each senator.

Ordered to lie on the table.

A motion was then made by Mr. M'Kean, seconded by Mr. Lewis, to substitute the following in lieu of the fifth section, viz.

The citizens of the city of Philadelphia and of the several counties of this state qualified to elect representatives, when assembled for that

purpose, shall, if occasion require, at the same time, at the same places, and in the same manner, for every representative, elect two persons resident within their said city or county respectively, as electors
of the senator or senators of their district.

On the question, Will the convention agree to the said substutite?
The yeas and nays being called by Mr. Wilson, were as follow, viz,

YEAS.

Mr. Roberts	Mr. Hare	Mr. Coleman	Mr. Smith
Lewis	Bull	Miller	J Ross
M'Kean	Hand	Slegle	Pickering
Gray			13

NAYS.

Mr. Wilson	Mr. Reed	Mr. Mawhorter	Mr. M'Lene
Baker	Tyson	Arndt	Matthews
Robinson	Pedan	Rhoads	Morris
Ogden	Dill	Powell	Coates
Jenks	Whitehill	Piper	Shoemaker
Barclay	Irvine	Snyder	Gloninger
Stout	Power	Findley	Brown
Gibbons	Hiester	Todd	Graydon
T. Ross	Lower	Addison	Henderson
Boyd	Lincoln	Hoge	Gibson
Graff	Groscop	Redick	Sellers
Hubley	Gehr	Smilie	Newlin
Breckbill	Sitgreaves	Gallatin	51

So it was determined in the negative.

And the original section, with the amendment moved by Mr. Hare
and Mr. Shoemaker, recurring, it was, on motion of Mr. Wilson and
Mr. Graydon,

Ordered, That the further consideration thereof be postponed until
to-morrow.

The sixth section of the first article, postponed the twelfth instant,
being under consideration, viz.

Section VI. The number of senators shall, at the several periods of
making the enumeration before mentioned, be fixed by the legislature,
and apportioned among the districts, formed as hereinafter directed,
according to the number of taxable inhabitants in each; and shall
never be less than one-fourth nor more than one-third of the number
of representatives.

A motion was made by Mr. M'Kean, seconded by Mr. Lewis, to
amend the said section so as to read as follows:

The number of senators shall, at the several periods of making the
enumeration before mentioned, be fixed by the legislature, and apportioned among the districts, formed as hereinafter directed, in a ratio
compounded of the number of taxable inhabitants in, and the quota of
state taxes assessed upon, each district, estimating the total amount of
the state taxation and the whole number of taxable inhabitants as equal
to each other, and shall never be less than one-fourth nor more than
one-third of the number of representatives.

On the question, Will the convention agree to the amendment?
The yeas and nays being called by Mr. M'Kean, were as follow;

YEAS.

Mr. Baker.	Mr. Ogden	Mr. Graff	Mr. Pickering
Lewis	Jenks	Hubley	Sellers
M'Kean	Stout	Morris	Newlin
Robinson	Bull	Shoemaker	15

NAYS.

Mr. Wilson	Mr. Dill	Mr. Arndt	Mr. J. Ross
Gibbons	Whitehill	Rhoads	Smilie
T. Ross	Irvine	Powell	Gallatin
Boyd	Power	Piper	M'Lene
Hand	Hiester	Smith	Matthews
Coleman	Lower	Snyder	Coates
Breckbill	Lincoln	Findley	Gloninger
Miller	Groscop	Todd	Brown
Slegle	Gehr	Addison	Graydon
Reed	Sitgreaves	Hoge	Henderson
Tyson	Mawhorter	Redick	Gibson
Pedan			45

So it was determined in the negative.

Adjourned until nine o'clock to-morrow, A. M.

FRIDAY, August 20, 1790. *A. M.*

The convention met pursuant to adjournment.

Agreeably to the order of the day, the fifth section of the first article, with the amendment proposed yesterday by Mr. Hare and Mr. Shoemaker, being under consideration,

A motion was made by Mr. Smith, seconded by Mr. Edwards, to postpone the consideration of the fifth as well as the sixth sections of the first article, in order to take into consideration the seventh section.

Mr. Hare withdrew his motion made yesterday.

On the question, Will the convention agree to the postponement moved by Mr. Smith and Mr. Edwards?

It was determined in the affirmative.

The seventh section of the first article being then under consideration, viz.

Sect. VII. The senators shall be chosen in districts to be formed by the legislature, each containing, as nearly as may be, such a number of taxable inhabitants as shall be entitled to elect one senator: Where that cannot be done, then such number of adjoining counties shall be formed into one district as shall be entitled to elect not more than four senators; but neither the city of Philadelphia, nor any county, shall be divided in forming a district.

A motion was made by Mr. Lewis, seconded by Mr. Sitgreaves, to amend the said section so as to read as follows, viz.

The senators shall be chosen in districts, not fewer than three nor more than six in number, to be formed of adjoining counties by the legislature, in such manner as that each shall contain, as nearly as may be, an equal number of taxables: But neither the city of Philadelphia nor any county shall be divided in forming a district.

And on the question, Will the convention agree to the amendment? The yeas and nays being called by Mr. Smilie, were as follow, viz.

YEAS.

Mr. Wilson	Mr. Edwards	Mr. Hubley	Mr. Coates
Baker	Ogden	Miller	Shoemaker
Roberts	Jenks	Slegle	Graydon
Lewis	Barclay	Tyson	Pickering
M'Kean	Stout	Sitgreaves	Henderson
Gray	Gibbons	Smith	Sellers
Robinson	Bull	Morris	Newlin
Hare	Graff		30

NAYS.

Mr. T. Ross	Mr. Irvine	Mr. Rhoads	Mr. J. Ross
Boyd	Power	Powell	Smilie
Hand	Hiester	Piper	Gallatin
Coleman	Lower	Snyder	M'Lene
Breckbill	Lincoln	Findley	Matthews
Reed	Groscop	Todd	Gloninger
Pedan	Gehr	Addison	Brown
Dill	Mawhorter	Hoge	Gibson
Whitehill	Arndt	Redick	35

So it was determined in the negative.

It was then moved by Mr. Gallatin, seconded by Mr. Hoge, to amend the said section to read as follows :

The senators shall be chosen in districts, to be formed of adjoining counties by the legislature, each containing such a number of taxable inhabitants as shall be entitled to elect not more than four senators : But neither the city of Philadelphia nor any county shall be divided in forming a district.

On the question, Will the convention agree to the section as amended? The yeas and nays being called by Mr. Sitgreaves, were as follow ·

YEAS.

Mr. Wilson	Mr. Bull	Mr. Irvine	Mr. Gallatin
Baker	Boyd	Sitgreaves	Morris
Roberts	Hand	Mawhorter	Coates
Lewis	Coleman	Arndt	Shoemaker
M'Kean	Graff	Powell	Brown
Gray	Hubley	Smith	Graydon
Robinson	Breckbill	Snyder	Pickering
Hare	Miller	Addison	Henderson
Ogden	Slegle	Hoge	Gibson
Jenks	Reed	Redick	Sellers
Barclay	Tyson	Smilie	Newlin
Stout	Pedan		46

NAYS.

Mr. Gibbons	Mr. Hiester	Mr. Gehr	Mr. J. Ross
T. Ross	Lower	Rhoads	M'Lene
Dill	Lincoln	Findley	Mathews
Whitehill	Groscop	Todd	Gloninger
Power			17

So it was determined in the affirmative, and the section, as amended, adopted.

The fifth section of the first article recurring, viz.

Section V. The senators shall be chosen for four years by the citizens of Philadelphia and of each county respectively, at the same time, in the same manner and at the same places where they shall vote for representatives.

A motion was made by Mr. Lewis, seconded by Mr. M'Kean, to strike out the word "four," and insert, in lieu thereof, the word "six."

On the question, Will the convention agree to the same? The yeas and nays being called by Mr. Lewis, were as follow:

YEAS.

Mr. Baker	Mr. Gray	Mr. Gibbons	Mr. Graff
Lewis	Hare	T. Ross	Newlin
M'Kean			9

NAYS.

Mr. Wilson	Mr. Miller	Mr. Sitgreaves	Mr. Smilie
Roberts	Slegle	Mawhorter	Gallatin
Robinson	Reed	Arndt	M'Lene
Edwards	Tyson	Rhoads	Matthews
Ogden	Pedan	Powell	Morris
Jenks	Dill	Piper	Coates
Barclay	Whitehill	Smith	Shoemaker
Stout	Irvine	Snyder	Gloninger
Bull	Power	Findley	Brown
Boyd	Hiester	Todd	Graydon
Hand	Lower	Addison	Pickering
Coleman	Lincoln	Hoge	Henderson
Hubley	Groscop	Redick	Gibson
Breckbill	Gehr	J. Ross	Sellers 56

So it was determined in the negative, and the original section adopted.

The sixth section of the first article recurring, the same was adopted as follows:

Sect. VI. The number of senators shall, at the several periods of making the enumeration before mentioned, be fixed by the legislature, and apportioned among the districts, formed as hereinafter directed, according to the number of taxable inhabitants in each; and shall never be less than one-fourth, nor more than one-third of the number of representatives.

The eighth section of the first article being under consideration, viz.

Sect VIII. No person shall be a senator who shall not have attained the age of twenty-five years, and have been a citizen and inhabitant of the state four years next before his election, and the last year thereof an inhabitant of the district for which he shall be chosen.

A motion was made by Mr. James Ross, seconded by Mr. Thomas Ross, to add the following words to the said section:

Unless he shall have been absent on the public business of the United States or of this state.

Which was determined in the affirmative.

It was moved by Mr. M'Kean, seconded by Mr. Sellers, to add the following words to the said section, viz.

Nor unless he shall be seized, in fee simple, at the time of his election, of five hundred acres of land within this commonwealth, or possessed of real and personal estate to the value of five hundred pounds.

On the question, Will the convention agree to the same?

The yeas and nays being called by Mr. M'Kean, were as follow, viz.

YEAS.

Mr. Baker	Mr. M'Kean	Mr. Slegle	Mr. Sellers
Roberts	Jenks	Morris	Newlin
Lewis			9

NAYS.

Mr. Wilson	Mr. Hubley	Mr. Gehr	Mr. Redick
Gray	Breckbill	Sitgreaves	J. Ross
Robinson	Miller	Mawhorter	Smilie
Edwards	Reed	Arndt	Gallatin
Barclay	Tyson	Rhoads	M'Lene
Stout	Pedan	Powell	Matthews
Gibbons	Dill	Piper	Coates
Bull	Hiester	Smith	Shoemaker
T. Ross	Whitehill	Snyder	Brown
Boyd	Irvine	Findley	Graydon
Hand	Lower	Todd	Pickering
Coleman	Lincoln	Addison	Henderson
Graff	Groscop	Hoge	Gibson 52

So it was determined in the negative.

A motion was made by Mr. Pickering, seconded by Mr. M'Kean, to add the following words to the said section, viz.

Nor unless he is seized of a clear real estate of the value of five hundred pounds.

Which was determined in the negative, and the said eighth section, as amended, adopted as follows:

Section VIII. No person shall be a senator, who shall not have attained the age of twenty-five years, and have been a citizen and inhabitant of the state four years next before his election, and the last year thereof an inhabitant of the district for which he shall be chosen, unless he shall have been absent on the public business of the United States or of this state.

Mr. M'Kean withdrew his seconding the motion of Mr. Roberts, made the thirteenth instant, to amend the fourth section of the second article.

The ninth section of the first article being under consideration, the same was adopted as follows, viz.

Sect. IX. Immediately after the senators shall be assembled in consequence of the first election subsequent to the first enumeration, they shall be divided, by lot, as equally as may be, into four classes. The seats of the senators of the first class shall be vacated at the expiration of the first year; of the second class, at the expiration of the second year; of the third class, at the expiration of the third year; and of the fourth class, at the expiration of the fourth year; so that one-fourth may be chosen every year.

A motion was made by Mr. James Ross, seconded by Mr. Thomas Ross, to re-consider the third section of the first article, viz.

Sect. III. No person shall be a representative, who shall not have attained the age of twenty-one years, and have been a citizen and inhabitant of the state three years next preceding his election, and the last year thereof an inhabitant of the city or county in which he shall be chosen ; and no person residing within any city, town or borough, which shall be entitled to a separate representation, shall be elected a member for any county; nor shall any person residing without the limits of any such city, town or borough, be elected a member thereof.

In order to insert, after the words " in which he shall be chosen," the words " unless he shall have been absent on the public business of the United States or of this state."

On the question, Will the convention agree to the amendment? It was determined in the affirmative, and the section, as amended, adopted.

Adjourned until nine o'clock to-morrow, A. M.

SATURDAY, August 21, 1790. A. M.

The convention met pursuant to adjournment.

A memorial from the religious society of people called **Quakers** was presented to the chair, and read as follows:

To the convention now sitting in Philadelphia:

The memorial of the people called Quakers,
Respectfully sheweth,

That ever since the establishment of our religious society we have professed and declared to the world our faith in a divine principle, which breathes peace on earth and good will to men, and have been thereby constrained to bear testimony against wars and bloodshed, for which our conscientious persuasion, we have suffered both by imprisonment and great spoiling of goods.

That our ancestors, who had deeply suffered in their native land, and well knew the inestimable value of liberty of conscience, encountered the dangers and difficulties of settling and improving, at their own expence, this then a wilderness country, in hopes of enjoying, without molestation, those immunities and privileges which they believed to be divinely authorised ; and, as a security therefor, our then worthy proprietor, William Penn, in his charter of privileges, declares and grants as follows :

" Because no people can be truly happy, though under the greatest enjoyment of civil liberties, if abridged of the freedom of their consciences, as to their religious profession and worship: And Almighty God being the only Lord of conscience, father of lights and spirits, and the author as well as object of all divine knowledge, faith and worship, who only doth enlighten the minds, and persuade and convince the understandings of people ; I do hereby grant and declare, That no person or persons, inhabiting in this province or territories, who shall confess and acknowledge one Almighty God, the creator, upholder and ruler of the world, and profess him or themselves obliged to live peaceably under the civil government, shall be in any case molested or prejudiced in his or their person or estate, because of his or their conscientious *persuasion* or *practice*, nor be compelled to frequent or maintain any religious worship, place or ministry, contrary to his or their mind, nor do or suffer any other act or thing, contrary to their religious persuasion."

With the sentiments expressed in this charter, the third section of the ninth article of your proposed constitution coincides; but, we apprehend, the twenty-first section of the same article materially affects our religious liberties, which proposes that those who conscientiously scruple to bear arms shall pay an equivalent for personal service; such an equivalent it is well known we cannot, consistent with our principles, voluntarily pay, and therefore become subjected either to distraint on our estates or imprisonment of our persons, so that under such a clause we are liable to suffer fine or imprisonment on account of our religious persuasion.

And as we believe there is a disposition in the convention to avoid and discourage persecution, we trust you will see the impropriety of retaining such a parapraph in the proposed constitution.

With desires that Divine Wisdom may direct you in the very weighty business on which you are convened,

We are your FRIENDS.

Signed in, and on behalf of, a meeting representing our religious society in Pennsylvania, &c. held in Philadelphia, the 20th day of the 8th month, 1790.

JAMES PEMBERTON, Clerk at this time.

Ordered to lie on the table.

The fourth section of the second article being under consideration, the same was adopted as follows, viz.

Sect. IV. He shall be, at least, thirty years of age; and have been a citizen and inhabitant of this state seven years next before his election; unless he shall have been absent on the public business of the United States or of this state.

The seventeenth section of the second article being under consideration, viz.

Sect. XVII. A secretary shall be appointed and commissioned during the governor's continuance in office, if he shall so long behave himself well. He shall keep a fair register of all the official acts and proceedings of the executive department, and shall, when required, lay the same and all papers, minutes and vouchers relative thereto, before either branch of the legisature, and shall perform such other duties as shall be enjoined him by law.

A motion was made by Mr. Wilson, seconded by Mr. Findley, to strike out the words "during the governor's continuance in office, if he shall so long behave himself well," and, in lieu thereof, to insert the words "by the governor."

Which was determined in the negative.

On the question, Will the convention adopt the original section? The yeas and nays being called by Mr. Ogden, were as follow:

YEAS.

Mr. Baker	Mr. M'Kean	Mr. Gibbons	Mr. Coleman
Roberts	Gray	T. Ross	Hubley
Lewis	Edwards	Hand	Miller

YEAS.

Mr. Slegle	Mr. Lincoln	Mr. Todd	Mr. Mortis
Tyson	Groscop	Addison	Coates
Pedan	Gehr	Redick	Shoemaker
Dill	Mawhorter;	J. Ross	Brown
Whitehill	Powel	Smilie	Graydon
Irvine	Piper	Gallatin	Pickering
Power	Smith	M'Lene	Gibson
Lower	Findley	Matthews	Newlin 44

NAYS.

Mr. Wilson'	Mr. Stout	Mr. Hiester	Mr. Snyder
Robinson	Bull	Sitgreaves	Hoge
Hare	Boyd	Arndt	Henderson
Ogden	Breckbill	Rhoads	Sellers
Barclay	Reed		18

So it was determined in the affirmative.

The convention resumed the consideration of the second section of the fourth article, with the amendment proposed by Mr. Sitgreaves, seconded by Mr. M'Kean, the 13th instant.

On the question, Will the convention agree to the proposed amendment? The yeas and nays being called by Mr. Lewis, were as follow:

YEAS.

Mr. Baker	Mr. Hand	Mr. Tyson	Mr. Redick
Lewis	Coleman	Sitgreaves	Coates
M'Kean	Hubley	Arndt	Shoemaker
Robinson	Miller	Rhoads	Brown
Gibbons	Slegle	Powell	Henderson
Bull			21

NAYS.

Mr. Wilson	Mr. Reed	Mr. Mawhorter	Mr. Gallatin
Roberts	Pedan	Piper	M'Lene
Gray	Dill	Smith	Matthews
Hare	Whitehill	Snyder	Morris
Edwards	Irvine	Findley	Gloninger
Ogden	Power	Todd	Graydon
Barclay	Hiester	Addison	Pickering
Stout	Lower	Hoge	Gibson
T. Ross	Lincoln	J. Ross	Sellers
Boyd	Groscop	Smilie	Newlin
Breckbill	Gehr		42

So it was determined in the negative, and the orignal section adopted as follows:

Section II. All impeachments shall be tried by the senate: When sitting for that purpose, the senators shall be on oath or affirmation. No person shall be convicted without the concurrence of two-thirds of the members present.

The convention resumed the consideration of the motion made by Mr M'Kean and Mr. Newlin, the fourteenth instant, to re-consider the third section of the fourth article, in order to add the following words thereto, viz.

No impeachment shall be sustained against any person unless com·menced within   years after the offence shall have been committed.

On the question, Will the convention agree to re-consider the said section for the aforesaid purpose?

It was determined in the negative.

A motion was made by Mr. Sitgreaves, seconded by Mr. Lewis, to re-consider the section, viz.

Section III. The governor, and all other civil officers under this commonwealth, shall be liable to impeachment for any misdemeanor in office. But judgment, in such cases, shall not extend further than to removal from office and disqualification to hold any office of honor, trust or profit under this commonwealth; the party, whether convicted or acquitted, shall, nevertheless, be liable to indictment, trial, judgment and punishment according to law.

In order to strike out the words "the party, whether convicted or acquitted, shall, nevertheless, be liable to indictment, trial, judgment and punishment according to law."

On the question, Will the convention agree to re-consider the section, for the aforesaid purpose? The yeas and nays being called by Mr. Sitgreaves, were as follow, viz.

YEAS.

Mr. Baker	Mr. Gray	Mr. Redick	Mr. Graydon
M'Kean	Sitgreaves	Morris	7

NAYS.

Mr. Wilson	Mr. Graff	Mr. Lower	Mr. Hoge
Roberts	Hubley	Lincoln	Smilie
Robinson	Breckbill	Groscop	Gallatin
Hare	Miller	Gehr	M'Lene
Edwards	Slegle	Mawhorter	Matthews
Barclay	Reed	Arndt	Coates
Stout	Tyson	Rhoads	Brown
Gibbons	Pedan	Powell	Pickering
Bull	Dill	Piper	Gibson
T. Ross	Whitehill	Smith	Henderson
Boyd	Irvine	Snyder	Sellers
Hand	Power	Findley	Newlin
Coleman	Hiester	Addison	51

So it was determined in the negative.

On motion, Ordered, That Mr. Wilson, Mr. Lewis, Mr. Smith, Mr. Findley and Mr. Addison, be a committee to revise, correct and arrange so much of the constitution for the government of this commonwealth as hath been adopted by this convention.

A motion was made by Mr. Findley, seconded by Mr. Gallatin, to re-consider the seventeenth section of the first article so far as the same relates to the privileges of the members of the senate and of the house of representatives. Whereupon,

On motion, Ordered, That the consideration of the said motion be postponed.

On motion of Mr. Smilie, seconded by Mr. Shoemaker,

Ordered, That Monday next be assigned for the second reading of the memorial of the religious society called Quakers.

Adjourned until three o'clock on Monday next, P. M.

MONDAY, August 23, 1790, *P. M.*

The convention met pursuant to adjournment.

Agreeably to the order of the day, the memorial of the religious society of the people called Quakers, was read the second time,

Whereupon, On motion,

Ordered, That the further consideration thereof be postponed.

A motion was made by Mr. Lewis, seconded by Mr. M'Kean. to re-consider the twenty-first section of the ninth article, viz.

Section XXI. That the right of the citizens to bear arms in defence of themselves and the state shall not be questioned: But those who conscientiously scruple to bear arms, shall not be compelled to do so, but shall pay an equivalent for personal service.

On the question, Will the convention agree to re-consider the said section? The yeas and nays being called by Mr. Redick, were as follow, viz.

YEAS.

Mr. Wilson	Mr. Robinson	Mr. Stout	Mr. Morris
Baker	Hare	T. Ross	Graydon
Roberts	Edwards	Graff	Pickering
Lewis	Ogden	Breckbill	Sellers
M'Kean	Jenks	Tyson	Newlin
Gray	Barclay	Sitgreaves	23

NAYS.

Mr. Bull	Mr. Whitehill	Mr. Powell	Mr. Gallatin
Boyd	Irvine	Piper	M'Lene
Hand	Power	Smith	Matthews
Coleman	Hiester	Snyder	Coates
Hubley	Lower	Findley	Gloninger
Miller	Lincoln	Addison	Brown
Slegle	Groscop	Hoge	Henderson
Reed	Gehr	Redick	Gibson
Pedan	Mawhorter	J. Ross	Beale
Dill	Rhoads	Smilie	39

So it was determined in the negative.

Adjourned until nine o'clock to-morrow, A. M.

TUESDAY, August 24, 1790. *A. M.*

The convention met pursuant to adjournment.

The seventh section of the ninth article being under consideration, viz.

Section VII. That the printing press shall be free to every person who undertakes to examine the proceedings of the legislature or any branch of government: And no law shall ever be made restraining the right thereof. The free communication of thoughts and opinions is one of the invaluable rights of man, and every citizen may freely speak, write and print on any subject, being responsible for the abuse of that liberty. In prosecutions for libels, their truth or design may be given in evidence on the general issue, and their nature and tendency, whether proper for public information, or only for private ridicule or malice, be determined by the jury, under the direction of the court, as in other cases.

A motion was made by Mr. Lewis, seconded by Mr. M'Kean, to strike out the remainder of the section after the words " for libels," and in lieu thereof, to insert " the jury shall have the same right to determine the law and the fact, under the direction of the court, as in other cases."

It was moved by Mr. Wilson, seconded by Mr. Gallatin, to amend the amendment by inserting, before the words " the jury," the words " their truth or design may be given in evidence on the general issue."

A motion was then made by Mr. Smith, seconded by Mr. M'Lene, to postpone the consideration of the said motions, in order to amend the said section to read as follows, viz.

Section VII. That the printing press shall be free to every person who undertakes to examine the proceedings of the legislature, or any branch of government: And no law shall ever be made restraining the right thereof. The free communication of thoughts and opinions is one of the invaluable rights of man, and every citizen may freely speak, write and print on any subject, being responsible for the abuse of that liberty. Upon indictments for the publication of papers investigating the conduct of individuals in their public capacity, or of those applying or canvassing for office, the truth of the facts alleged may be given in evidence on the general issue. And the jury shall have the same right to determine the law and the fact, under the direction of the court, as in other cases.

On the question, Will the convention agree to the postponement for the aforesaid purpose? The yeas and nays being called by Mr. Ogden, were as follow:

YEAS.

Mr. Baker	Mr. Stout	Mr. Sitgreaves	Mr. Morris
Lewis	Coleman	Arndt	Coates
M'Kean	Hand	Rhoads	Brown
Gray	Graff	Smith	Pickering
Robinson	Hubley	Redick	Gibson
Ogden	Breckbill	J. Ross	Sellers
Jenks	Miller	M'Lene	Newlin
Barclay	Tyson		30

NAYS.

Mr. Wilson	Mr. Reed	Mr. Lincoln	Mr. Todd
Roberts	Pedan	Groscop	Addison
Hare	Dill	Gehr	Hoge
Edwards	Whitehill	Mawhorter	Smilie
Bull	Irvine	Powell	Gallatin
T. Ross	Power	Piper	Matthews
Boyd	Hiester	Snyder	Gloninger
Slegle	Lower	Findley	Graydon 32

So it was determined in the negative.

The motion made by Mr. Wilson, seconded by Mr. Gallatin, then recurring,

On the question, Will the convention agree to the same? The yeas and nays being called by Mr. M'Kean, were as follow:

YEAS.

Mr. Wilson	Mr. Irvine	Mr. Piper	Mr. Gallatin
Hare	Power	Snyder	M'Lene
Edwards	Lower	Findley	Matthews
Boyd	Lincoln	Todd	Gloninger
Reed	Groscop	Addison	Brown
Pedan	Gehr	Hoge	Graydon
Dill	Mawhorter	Smilie	Beale
Whitehill	Powell		30

NAYS.

Mr. Baker	Mr. Barclay	Mr. Breckbill	Mr. Redick
Roberts	Stout	Slegle	J. Ross
Lewis	Bull	Miller	Morris
M'Kean	T. Ross	Tyson	Coates
Gray	Hand	Sitgreaves	Pickering
Robinson	Coleman	Arndt	Gibson
Ogden	Graff	Rhoads	Sellers
Jenks	Hubley	Smith	Newlin 32

So it was determined in the negative.

Adjourned until nine o'clock to-morrow, A. M.

WEDNESDAY, August 25, 1790, A. M.

The convention met pursuant to adjournment.

The seventh section of the ninth article, with the amendment moved yesterday by Mr. Lewis, seconded by Mr. M'Kean, recurring,

A motion was made by Mr. Redick, seconded by Mr. Reed, to postpone the consideration of Mr. Lewis and Mr. M'Kean's motion, in order to amend the section as follows, viz.

Section VII. That the printing press shall be free to every person who undertakes to examine the proceedings of the legislature or any branch of government: And no law shall ever be made restraining the right thereof. The free communication of thoughts and opinions is one of the invaluable rights of man, and every citizen may freely speak, write and print on any subject, being responsible for the abuse of that liberty. In prosecutions for libels, their truth may be given in evidence on the general issue, and their nature and tendency, whether proper for public and useful information, or whether calculated for ridicule or private malice, to be determined by the jury, under the direction of the court, as in other cases.

On the question, Will the house agree to the postponement for the aforesaid purpose? The yeas and nays being called by Mr. Lewis, were as follow:

YEAS.

Mr. Wilson	Mr. Hiester	Mr. Powell	Mr. Gallatin
Hare	Lower	Piper	M'Lene
Boyd	Lincoln	Addison	Matthews
Reed	Groscop	Redick	Graydon
Dill	Gehr	Smilie	Beale
Power			21

NAYS.

Mr. Baker	Mr. Bull	Mr. Whitehill	Mr. Morris
Roberts	T. Ross	Irvine	Coates
Lewis	Hand	Arndt	Shoemaker
M'Kean	Breckbill	Rhoads	Gloninger
Gray	Hubley	Smith	Brown
Robinson	Graff	Snyder	Pickering
Ogden	Miller	Findley	Henderson
Jenks	Slegle	Todd	Gibson
Barclay	Tyson	Hoge	Sellers
Stout	Pedan	J. Ross	Newlin 40

So it was determined in the negative, and thereupon the amendment moved yesterday by Mr. Lewis, seconded by Mr. M'Kean, adopted, viz.

To insert, after the words in the original section, "In prosecutions for libels," the words "the jury shall have the same right to determine the law and the facts, under the direction of the court, as in other cases."

A motion was made by Mr. Addison, seconded by Mr. Wilson, further to amend the last proposition as follows:

In prosecutions for the publication of papers investigating the conduct of officers or men in a public capacity, or where the matter published is necessary or proper for public information, the truth thereof may be given in evidence, in justification, on the general issue; and in all indictments for libels the jury shall have a right to determine the law and the facts, under the direction of the court, as in other cases.

It was moved by Mr. Lewis, seconded by Mr. M'Kean, to postpone the consideration of the said motion in order to introduce the following in lieu thereof, viz.

In indictments for the composing, making or publishing of papers investigating the conduct of individuals in their official capacity, the truth of the facts may be given in evidence; and in all prosecutions for libels the jury shall have a right to determine the law and the facts, under the direction of the court, as in other cases.

On the question, Will the convention agree to the postponement for the aforesaid purpose? The yeas and nays being called by Mr. Wilson, were as follow:

YEAS.

Mr. Baker	Mr. Jenks	Mr. Slegle	Mr. Coates
Roberts	Barclay	Sitgreaves	Shoemaker
Lewis	Stout	Arndt	Pickering
M'Kean	Coleman	Smith	Henderson
Gray	Graff	J. Ross	Sellers
Robinson	Hubley	Morris	Newlin
Ogden	Miller		24

NAYS.

Mr. Wilson	Mr. Boyd	Mr. Pedan	Mr. Hiester
Hare	Hand	Dill	Lower
Edwards	Breckbill	Whitehill	Lincoln
Bull	Reed	Irvine	Groscop
T. Ross	Tyson	Power	Gehr

NAYS.

Mr. Rhoads	Mr. Todd	Mr. Gallatin	Mr. Brown
Powell	Addison	M'Lene	Graydon
Piper	Hoge	Matthews	Gibson
Snyder	Redick	Gloninger	Beale
Findley	Smilie		38

So it was determined in the negative.

The motion made by Mr. Addison, seconded by Mr. Wilson, recurring, a motion was then made by Mr. Lewis, seconded by Mr. M'Kean, to insert the word "official" before the word "conduct."

Which was determined in the affirmative.

It was moved by Mr. Lewis, seconded by Mr. M'Kean, to strike out the words "on the general issue."

Which was determined in the affirmative.

A motion was made by Mr. Sitgreaves, seconded by Mr. Lewis, to strike out the words "in justification."

On the question, Will the convention agree to the same? The yeas and nays being called by Mr. Lewis, were as follow, viz.

YEAS.

Mr. Baker	Mr. Bull	Mr. Sitgreaves	Mr. Shoemaker
Roberts	T. Ross	Arndt	Brown
Lewis	Hand	Rhoads	Graydon
M'Kean	Coleman	Smith	Pickering
Gray	Graff	Todd	Henderson
Robinson	Hubley	Redick	Gibson
Ogden	Miller	J. Ross	Sellers
Jenks	Slegle	Morris	Newlin
Stout	Tyson	Coates	85

NAYS.

Mr. Wilson	Mr. Dill	Mr. Groscop	Mr. Hoge
Hare	Whitehill	Gehr	Smilie
Edwards	Irvine	Powell	Gallatin
Barclay	Power	Piper	M'Lene
Boyd	Hiester	Snyder	Matthews
Breckbill	Lower	Findley	Gloninger
Reed	Lincoln	Addison	Beale
Pedan			29

So it was determined in the affirmative.

On the question, Will the convention agree to the amendment moved by Mr. Addison, seconded by Mr. Wilson, as amended, viz.

In prosecutions for the publication of papers investigating the official conduct of officers or men in a public capacity, or where the matter published is necessary or proper for public information, the truth thereof may be given in evidence; and in all indictments for libels the jury shall have a right to determine the law and the facts under the direction of the court, as in other cases?"

The yeas and nays being called by Mr. Thomas Ross, were as follow, viz.

YEAS.

Mr. Wilson	Mr. Coleman	Mr. Groscop	Mr. Gallatin
Baker	Graff	Gehr	M'Lene
Roberts	Hubley	Arndt	Matthews
Lewis	Breckbill	Rhoads	Morris
M'Kean	Miller	Powell	Coates
Gray	Slegle	Piper	Shoemaker
Robinson	Reed .	Smith	Gloninger
Hare	Tyson	Snyder	Brown
Edwards	Pedan	Findley	Graydon
Jenks	Dill	Todd	Pickering
Barclay	Whitehill	Addison	Henderson
Stout	Irvine	Hoge	Gibson
Bull	Power	Redick	Beale
T. Ross	Hiester	J. Ross	Sellers
Boyd	Lower	Smilie	Newlin 62
Hand	Lincoln		

NAYS.

Mr. Ogden Mr Sitgreaves 2

So it was determined in the affirmative, and the seventh section of the ninth article adopted as follows, viz.

Section VII. That the printing presses shall be free to every person, who undertakes to examine the proceedings of the legislature or any branch of government: and no law shall ever be made restraining the right thereof. The free communication of thoughts and opinions is one of the invaluable rights of man; and every citizen may freely speak, write and print on any subject, being responsible for the abuse of that liberty. In prosecutions for the publication of papers, investigating the official conduct of officers, or men in a public capacity, or where the matter published is necessary or proper for public information, the truth thereof may be given in evidence; and, in all indictments for libels, the jury shall have a right to determine the law and the facts, under the direction of the court, as in other cases.

Adjourned until nine o'clock to-morrow, A M.

THURSDAY, August 26th, 1790. A. M.

The convention met pursuant to adjournment.

Agreeably to notice given the twenty-first instant, Mr. Findley moved to re-consider the seventeenth section of the first article, seconded by Mr. Gallatin. On the question, Will the convention agree to re-consider?

It was determined in the affirmative.

And the seventeenth section being under consideration, viz.

Section XVII The senators and representatives shall receive a compensation for their services to be ascertained by law, and paid out of the treasury of the commonwealth. They shall in all cases, except treason, felony and *breach of the peace*, be privileged from arrest during their attendance at the session of the respective houses, and in going to and returning from the same; and for any speech or debate in either house they shall not be questioned in any other place.

A motion was made by Mr. Findley, seconded by Mr. Gallatin, to amend the section by inserting after the word "breach," the words "or surety."

It was moved by Mr. Lewis, seconded by Mr. Bull, to postpone the consideration of the said motion in order to introduce the following amendment in lieu thereof, viz.

Breaches of the peace for which surety of the peace may be required.

On the question, Will the convention agree to the amendment of Mr. Lewis and Mr. Bull?

It was determined in the negative.

And thereupon the amendment moved by Mr. Findley, seconded by Mr. Gallatin, recurring, it was, on motion of Mr. Wilson, seconded by Mr. M'Lene, Ordered, that the further consideration thereof be postponed until to-morrow.

A letter from the Reverend William Smith, D. D. was read, together with an address enclosed, and ordered to lie on the table.

A motion was made by Mr. Wilson, seconded by Mr. Lewis to re-consider the tenth section of the ninth article, viz.

Section X. That no person shall, for any indictable offence, be proceeded against, criminally. by information ; except *for oppression or misdemeanor in office*, and in cases arising in the land or naval forces, or in the militia when in actual service in time of war or public danger ; nor shall any person, for the same offence, be twice put in jeopardy of life or limb ; nor shall any man's property be taken or applied to public use without the consent of his representatives, and, without just compensation being made.

Which was determined in the affirmative.

A motion was then made by Mr. Lewis, seconded by Mr. M'Kean, to amend the section to read as follows, viz.

Section X. That no person shall, for any indictable offence, be proceeded against, criminally, by information ; except in cases aris-ing in the land or naval forces, or in the militia when in actual ser-vice in time of war or public danger, or, by leave of the court, for oppression or misdemeanor in office : Nor shall any person, for the same offence, be twice put in jeopardy of life or limb ; nor shall any man's property be taken, or applied to public use, without the consent of his representatives, and without just compensation being made.

Which was determined in the affirmative.

It was moved by Mr. Wilson, seconded by Mr. Smith, to strike out the words "for oppression or misdemeanor in office."

On the question, Will the convention agree to strike out the words? The yeas and nays being called by Mr. Wilson, were as follow, viz.

YEAS.

Mr. Wilson	Mr. Piper	Mr. Addison	Mr. M'Lene
Stout	Smith	Hoge	Matthews
Whitehill	Snyder	Redick	Gloninger
Irvine	Findley	Smilie	Graydon
Power	Todd	Gallatin	Beale 21
Gehr			

NAYS.

Mr. Baker	Mr. M'Kean	Mr. Ogden	Mr. Gibbons
Roberts	Robinson	Jenks	Bull
Lewis	Edwards	Barclay	T. Ross

NAYS.

Mr. Boyd	Mr. Reed	Mr. Sitgreaves	Mr. Brown
Hand	Tyson	Rhoads	Pickering
Coleman	Pedan	Powell	Henderson
Graff	Dill	J. Ross	Gibson
Hubley	Hiester	Coates	Sellers
Breckbill	Groscop	Shoemaker	Newlin 36

So it was determined in the negative, and the section, as amended by Mr. Lewis and Mr. M'Kean, recurring, on the question, Will the convention adopt the same?

It was determined in the affirmative.

Adjourned until nine o'clock to-morrow, A. M.

FRIDAY, August 27, 1790, *A. M.*

The convention met pursuant to adjournment.

A letter from Michael Billmeyer was read as follows, viz.

SIR,

Having been informed that Melchior Steiner, who is appointed to print the minutes of the convention, in the German language, has it not in his power to accomplish the business so soon as the convention wish to have it done, I am willing (if the convention shall think proper to appoint me) to undertake the printing of the minutes of the committee of the whole, consisting of 101 pages, which I will engage to finish against the fifth day of October next, and to print the minutes of the present session (if they shall be ordered to be done) with an equal degree of expedition.

I have the honor to be, most respectfully,
SIR,
Your very humble servant,
MICHAEL BILLMEYER.

His excellency the president of the
convention of Pennsylvania now convened.

A motion was made by Mr. Ogden, seconded by Mr. Sitgreaves, as follows, viz.

Resolved, that Michael Billmeyer be appointed to print the minutes of the committee of the whole, of the last session, in the German language, and to do the future printing to the convention in the said language; and that the former resolution appointing Melchior Steiner, printer of the convention be rescinded so far as respects the business now assigned to Michael Billmeyer.

A motion was made by Mr. Redick, seconded by Mr. Smilie.

To postpone the resolution moved by Mr. Ogden and Mr. Sitgreaves, in order to introduce a motion, that the committee appointed to superintend the printing of the journals in the German language take order in the premises.

On the question, Will the convention agree to the postponement for the aforesaid purpose?

It was determined in the negative, and thereupon the motion of Mr. Ogden and Mr. Sitgreaves adopted.

A motion was made by Mr. Wilson, seconded by Mr. M'Kean, to re-consider the eleventh section of the ninth article, viz.

Section XI. That all courts shall be open, and every man for an injury done him in his lands, goods, person or reputation, shall have remedy by the due course of law, and right and justice administered without sale, denial, or delay.

In order to add the following amendment thereto, viz.

Suits may be brought against the commonwealth as well as against other bodies corporate and individuals.

On the question, Will the convention agree to the amendment ?

It was determined in the affirmative and the section, as amended, adopted as follows :

Section XI. That all courts shall be open, and every man for an injury done him in his lands, goods, person or reputation, shall have remedy by the due course of law, and right and justice administered without sale, denial or delay. Suits may be brought against the commonwealth as well as gainst other bodies corporate and individuals.

Agreeably to the order of the day the seventeenth section of the first article recurring, viz.

Sect XVII. The senators and representatives shall receive a compensation for their services, to be ascertained by law, and paid out of the treasury of the commonwealth. They shall in all cases, except treason, felony and breach of the peace, be privileged from arrest, during their attendance at the session of the respective houses, and in going to and returning from the same ; and for any speech or debate in either house they shall not be questioned in any other place.

Together with the amendment proposed by Mr. Findley and Mr. Gallatin, to insert, after the word "breach," the words "or surety."

On the question, Will the convention agree to the amendment? The yeas and nays being called by Mr. Henderson, were as follow: viz.

YEAS.

Mr. Wilson	Mr. Irvine	Mr. Piper	Mr. Matthews
Edwards	Power	Findley	Morris
Barclay	Heister	Todd	Coates
T. Ross	Lower	Addison	Gloninger
Boyd	Lincoln	Redick	Brown
Pedan	Groscop	Smilie	Graydon
Dill	Gehr	Gallatin	Gibson
Whitehill	Powell	M'Lene	Beale 32

NAYS.

Mr. Baker	Mr. Jenks	Mr. Miller	Mr. Hoge
Roberts	Stout	Tyson	J. Ross
Lewis	Gibbons	Reed	Shoemaker
M'Kean	Bull	Sitgreaves	Pickering
Gray	Hand	Arndt	Henderson
Robinson	Hubley	Rhoads	Sellers
Hare	Breckbill	Smith	Newlin 30
Ogden	Slegle		

So it was determined in the affirmative, and the section as amended, adopted.

A motion was made by Mr. Lewis, seconded by Mr. Redick, to re-consider the sixteenth section of the second article, viz.

Sect. XVI. The state treasurer shall be appointed annually, by the joint vote of the members of both houses. All other officers in the treasury department, election officers, officers relating to taxes, to the poor and highways, constables and other township officers, shall be appointed in such manner as is or shall be directed by law.

In order to amend the same by adding, after the word "department," the words "attornies at law."

On the question, Will the convention agree to the amendment?

It was determined in the affirmative, and the section, as amended, adopted as follows, viz.

Section XVI. The state treasurer shall be appointed, annually, by the joint vote of the members of both houses. All other officers in the treasury department, attornies at law, election officers, officers relating to taxes, to the poor and highways, constables and other township officers shall be appointed in such manner as is or shall be directed by law.

A motion was made by Mr. Edwards, seconded by Mr. Boyd, to reconsider the thirteenth section of the ninth article, viz.

Section XIII. That excessive bail shall not be required, nor excessive fines imposed, nor cruel punishments inflicted.

In order to add the following amendment thereto, viz.

And in all criminal prosecutions no person, if acquitted, shall pay costs.

On the question, Will the convention agree to re-consider the section for the aforesaid purpose?

It was determined in the negative.

A motion was made by Mr Smith, seconded by Mr. Lewis, to reconsider the ninth section of the ninth article, viz.

Section IX. That in all criminal prosecutions the accused hath a right to be heard by himself and his council; to demand the nature and cause of the accusation against him ; to meet the witnesses face to face ; to have compulsory process for obtaining witnesses in his favor ; and, in prosecutions by indictment, a speedy public trial by an impartial jury of the vicinage ; that he cannot be compelled to give evidence against himself; nor can he be deprived of his life, liberty or property, unless by the judgment of his peers, or the law of the land.

In order to insert, after the word "indictment," the words "or information."

On the question, Will the convention agree to re-consider for the aforesaid purpose?

It was determined in the affirmative, and the section, as amended, adopted as follows, viz.

Section IX. That, in all criminal prosecutions, the accused hath a right to be heard by himself and his council, to demand the nature and cause of the accusation against him, to meet the witnesses face to face, to have compulsory process for obtaining witnesses in his favor, and, in prosecutions by indictment or information, a speedy public trial by an impartial jury of the vicinage; that he cannot be compelled to give evidence against himself, nor can he be deprived of his life, liberty or property, unless by the judgment of his peers or the law of the land.

A motion was made by Mr. Lewis, seconded by Mr. M'Kean, to reconsider the sixteenth section of the ninth article, viz

Section XVI. That the person of a debtor, where there is not a strong presumption of fraud, shall not be continued in prison after delivering up all his estate for the benefit of his creditors in such manner as shall be prescribed by law.

In order to strike out the word "all."

Which was determined in the affirmative, and the section, as amended, adopted.

A motion was made by Mr. Lewis, seconded by Mr. Smilie, to reconsider the twelfth section of the first article, viz.

Sect. XII. Each house shall judge of the qualifications of its own members; but contested elections shall be determined by a committee, to be selected in such manner as shall be directed by law: A majority of each house shall constitute a quorum to do business; but a smaller number may adjourn from day to day, and may be authorised, by law, to compel the attendance of absent members in such manner, and under such penalties, as may be provided.

In order to insert, after the word " selected," the words " formed and regulated.

Which was determined in the affirmative, and the section, as amended, adopted.

A motion was made by Mr. Lewis, seconded by Mr. Smilie. to reconsider the second section of the second article, viz.

Sect. II. The governor shall be chosen on the second Tuesday of October, by the citizens throughout the commonwealth, at the places where they shall respectively vote for representatives. The returns of every election for governor shall be transmitted,under seal,to the seat of government, directed to the speaker of the senate, who shall open and publish them in the presence of the members of both houses of the legislature. The person having the highest number of votes shall be governor; but if two or more shall be equal and highest in votes, one of them shall be chosen governor by the joint vote of the members of both houses. Contested elections shall be determined by a committee to be selected from both houses of the legislature, in such manner as shall be directed by law.

In order to insert, after the words "from both houses of the legislature," the words "and formed and regulated."

On the question, Will the convention agree to re-consider for the aforesaid purpose?

It was determined in the affirmative, and the section with the amendment, adopted.

The first section of the schedule for the organization of the government of this commonwealth being under consideration, the same was adopted as follows, viz.

I. That all laws of this commonwealth, in force at the time of making the said alterations and amendments in the said constitution, and not inconsistent therewith, and all rights, actions, prosecutions, claims and contracts, as well of individuals as of bodies corporate, shall continue as if the said alterations and amendments had not been made.

The second section of the said schedule being under consideration, viz.

II. That the president and supreme executive council shall continue to exercise the executive authority of this commonwealth as heretofore, until the third Tuesday of December next; but no intermediate vacancies in the council shall be supplied by new elections.

A motion was made by Mr. Addison, seconded by Mr. Wilson, to strike out the words "the third Tuesday of December next," and, in lieu thereof, to insert the words "the governor, who shall be chosen at the next general election, shall enter upon the duties of his office."

Which was determined in the affirmative, and the section, as amended, adopted.

The third section of the schedule being under consideration, the same was adopted as follows, viz.

III. That all officers in the appointment of the executive department, shall continue in the exercise of the duties of their respective offices until the first day of September, one thousand seven hundred and ninety-one, unless their commissions shall sooner expire by their own limitations, or the said offices become vacant by death or resignation, and no longer, unless re-appointed and commissioned by the governor. Except that the judges of the supreme court shall hold their offices for the terms in their commissions respectively expressed.

The fourth section of the schedule being under consideration, the same was adopted as follows, viz.

IV. That justice shall be administered in the several counties of the state, until the period aforesaid, by the same justices, in the same courts, and in the same manner as heretofore.

The fifth section of the said schedule being under consideration, viz.

V. That no person now in commission as sheriff shall be eligible at the next election for a longer term than will, with the time, which he shall have served in the said office, complete the term of three years.

On motion of Mr. Findley and Mr. Todd, the further consideration was adjourned.

The sixth section of the said schedule being under consideration, the same was adopted as follows, viz.

VI. That until the first enumeration shall be made as directed in the fourth section of the first article of the constitution established by this convention, the city of Philadelphia and the several counties shall be respectively entitled to elect the same number of representatives as is now prescribed by law.

The seventh section of the said schedule being under consideration, viz.

VII. That the first senate shall consist of eighteen members, to be chosen in districts formed as follows, viz. The city of Philadelphia, the county of Philadelphia, and the county of Delaware shall be a district, and shall elect three senators ; the county of Chester shall be a district, and shall elect one senator ; the county of Bucks shall be a district, and shall elect one senator ; the county of Montgomery shall be a district and shall elect one senator ; the county of Northampton shall be a district, and shall elect one senator; the counties of Lancaster and York shall be a district, and shall elect three senators ; the counties of Berks and Dauphin shall be a district, and shall elect two senators ; the counties of Cumberland and Mifflin shall be a district, and shall elect one senator; the counties of Northumberland, Luzerne and Huntingdon shall be a district, and shall elect one senator ; the counties of Bedford and Franklin shall be a district, and shall elect one senator; the counties of Westmoreland and Allegheny shall be a district, and shall elect one senator ; and the counties of Washington and Fayette shall be a district and shall elect two senators : which senators shall serve until the first enumeration before mentioned shall be made, and the representation in both houses of the legislature shall be established by law, and chosen as in the constitution is directed. Any vacancies which shall happen in the senate within the said time, shall be supplied as prescribed in the nineteenth section of the first article.

A motion was made by Mr. Wilson, seconded by Mr. Hare, to postpone the consideration of the said section.

On motion, Adjourned until nine o'clock to-morrow, A. M.

SATURDAY, August 28, 1790. A. M.

The convention met pursuant to adjournment.

The seventh section of the schedule, under consideration yesterday, recurring.

A motion was made by Mr. Robinson, seconded by Mr. M'Kean, to amend the section by striking out the words " the county of Chester shall be a district and shall elect one senator; the county of Bucks shall be a district and shall elect one senator; the county of Montgomery shall be a district and shall elect one senator;" and in lieu thereof to insert " the counties of Chester, Bucks and Montgomery shall be a district and shall elect three senators."

A motion was made by Mr. Sitgreaves, seconded by Mr. Gallatin, to postpone the said section, with the amendment proposed by Mr. Robinson and Mr. M'Kean, in order to re-consider the seventh section of the first article, viz.

Sect. VII. The senators shall be chosen in districts, to be formed of adjoining counties by the legislature, each containing such a number of taxable inhabitants as shall be entitled to elect not more than four senators: But neither the city of Philadelphia nor any county shall be divided in forming a district.

In order to strike out the words " of adjoining counties," and to insert after the words " four senators," the following, "Where a district shall be composed of two or more counties they shall be adjoining."

On the question, Will the convention agree to re-consider for the aforesaid purpose?

It was determined in the affirmative, and the section, as amended, adopted as follows:

Sect. VII. The senators shall be chosen in districts, to be formed by the legislature; each containing such a number of taxable inhabitants as shall be entitled to elect not more than four senators: Where a district shall be composed of two or more counties, they shall be adjoining. But neither the city of Philadelphia nor any county shall be divided in forming a district.

The seventh section of the said schedule, with the amendment moved by Mr. Robinson, seconded by Mr. M'Kean, recurring,

On the question, Will the convention agree to the amendment? The yeas and nays being called by Mr. Ogden, were as follow, viz.

YEAS.

Mr. Wilson	Mr. Gray	Mr. Bull	Mr. Gloninger
Baker	Robinson	Hubley	Graydon
Roberts	Hare	Morris	Henderson
Lewis	Edwards	Coates	Sellers
M'Kean	Gibbons	Shoemaker	Newlin 20

NAYS.

Mr. Ogden	Mr. Reed	Mr. Gehr	Mr. Hoge
Jenks	Tyson	Sitgreaves	Redick
Barclay	Pedan	Arndt	J. Ross
Stout	Dill	Rhoads	Smilie
T. Ross	Whitehill	Powell	Gallatin
Boyd	Irvine	Piper	M'Lene
Hand	Power	Smith	Matthews
Coleman	Hiester	Snyder	Brown
Graff	Lower	Findley	Pickering
Breckbill	Lincoln	Todd	Gibson
Miller	Groscop	Addison	Beale
Slegle			45

So it was determined in the negative, and the original section adopted.

The eighth section of the said schedule being under consideration, viz.

VIII. That the election of senators shall be conducted, and the returns thereof made to the senate, in the same manner as is prescribed by the election laws of the state for conducting and making return of the election for representatives. In those districts which consist of more than one county, the judges of the district elections within each county after having formed a return of the whole election within that county, in such manner as is directed by law, shall send the same, by one or more of their number, to such place, hereinafter mentioned, within the district of which such county is a part; where the judges, so met, shall compare and cast up the several county returns, and execute, under their hands and seals, one general and true return for the whole district, *that is to say,* The judges of the district composed of the city of Philadelphia and the counties of Philadelphia and Delaware shall meet in the state house in the city of Philadelphia; the judges of the district composed the counties of Lancaster and York shall meet at the court house in the county of Lancaster; the judges of the district composed of the counties of Berks and Dauphin shall meet at Middletown in the county of Berks; the judges of the district composed of the counties of Cumberland and Mifflin shall meet in Greenwood township, county of Cumberland, at the house now occupied by David Miller; the judges of thedistrict composed of the counties of Northumberland, Luzerne and Huntingdon shall meet at the court house in the town of Sunbury; the judges of the district composed of the counties of Bedford and Franklin shall meet at the house now occupied by John Dickey, in Air township, Bedford county; the judges of the district composed of the counties of Westmoreland and Allegheny shall meet in Westmoreland county, at the court house in the town of Greensborough; and the judges of the district composed of the counties of Washington and Fayette shall meet at the court house in the town of Washington, in Washington county, on the third Tuesday in October respectively, for the purposes aforesaid.

A motion was made by Mr. Smith, seconded by Mr. Miller, to strike out the words "at the court house," after the words "Huntingdon shall meet."

On the question, Will the convention agree to strike out the words? It was determined in the affirmative, and the section, as amended, adopted.

The ninth section of the said schedule being under consideration, the same was adopted as follows, viz.

IX. That the election of the governor shall be conducted in the several counties in the manner prescribed by the laws of the state for the election of representatives, and the returns in each county shall be sealed by the judges of the elections, and transmitted to the president of the supreme executive council, directed to the speaker of the senate, as soon after the election as may be.

A motion was made by Mr. Wilson, seconded by Mr. Edwards, to amend the first section of the said schedule, viz.

I. That all laws of this commonwealth, in force at the time of making the said alterations and amendments in the said constitution, and not inconsistent therewith, and all rights, actions, prosecutions, claims and contracts, as well of individuals as of bodies corporate, shall continue as if the said alterations and amendments had not been made.

By adding the following words thereto, viz.

Nor shall any person, now a citizen of this commonwealth, who has resided in a city or county one year next preceding an election, be deprived, on account of the said alterations and amendments, of any right or privilege of electing or being elected into any office for the same to which he is entitled by the present constitution; except so far as is hereinbefore provided in the eighteenth section of the first article respecting members of congress and other persons holding any office under the United States or this state.

A motion was then made by Mr. M'Kean, seconded by Mr. Lewis, to amend the motion of Mr. Wilson, seconded by Mr. Edwards, by striking out the words "who has resided in a city or county one year next preceding an election, be deprived on account of the said alterations and amendments, of any right or privilege of electing or being elected into any office for the same, to which he is entitled by the present constitution," in order to insert the following words, in lieu thereof, viz. "be deprived, at the next general election, on account of the said alterations and amendments, of any right or privilege of electing or being elected into office."

On the question, Will the convention agree to the amendment moved by Mr. M'Kean and Mr. Lewis? It was determined in the negative.

And on the question, Will the convention agree to the amendment moved by Mr. Wilson and Mr. Edwards? It was determined in the negative, and the original section thereupon adopted.

The fifth section of the said schedule, postponed yesterday, being under consideration, viz.

V. That no person now in commission as sheriff shall be eligible at the next election for a longer term than will, with the time which he shall have served in the said office, complete the term of three years.

On the question, Will the convention agree to the same? The yeas and nays being called by Mr. Smith, were as follow, viz.

YEAS.

Mr. Jenks	Mr. Hubley	Mr. Pedan	Mr. Lower
Barclay	Breckbill	Dill	Lincoln
Stout	Miller	Irvine	Groscop
Gibbons	Slegle	Power	Gehr
Graff	Reed	Hiester	Sitgreaves

YEAS.

Mr. Arndt	Mr. Snyder	Mr. Smilie	Mr. Matthews
Powell	Addison	Gallatin	Gloninger
Piper	Hoge	M'Lene	Brown
Smith	Redick		34

NAYS.

Mr. Wilson	Mr. Hare	Mr. Tyson	Mr. Graydon
Baker	Edwards	Rhoads	Pickering
Roberts	Bull	Findley	Henderson
Lewis	T. Ross	Todd	Gibson
M'Kean	Boyd	Morris	Beale
Gray	Hand	Coates	Sellers
Robinson	Coleman	Shoemaker	Newlin 28

So it was determined in the affirmative, and the section adopted.

A motion was made by Mr. Sitgreaves, seconded by Mr. Henderson, to add the following section to the schedule, viz.

That persons now in commission as sheriffs and coroners, shall continue in the execution of the said offices until the governor shall be duly qualified and commence his administration.

On the question, Will the convention agree to the same? It was determined in the negative.

A motion was made by Mr. M'Kean, seconded by Mr. Pickering, to re-consider the eighteenth section of the first article, viz.

Sect. XVIII. No senator or representative shall, during the time for which he was elected, be appointed to any civil office, under the authority of this commonwealth, which shall have been created, or the emoluments of which shall have been increased during such time: And no member of congress or other person holding any office, (except in the militia,) under the United States or this commonwealth, shall be a member of either house during his continuance in congress or in office.

In order to insert, after the word "except," the words "attornies at law and corporation officers."

Mr. M'Lene called for a division on the amendment, on the words "attornies at law." Which was determined in the affirmative.

And on the question, Will the convention agree to the second part of the said amendment, viz. "and corporation officers?"

It was determined in the negative, and the section thereupon adopted as follows:

Sect. XVIII. No senator or representative shall, during the time for which he shall have been elected, be appointed to any civil office, under the authority of this commonwealth, which shall have been created, or the emoluments of which shall have been increased during such time; and no member of congress or other person holding any office (except attornies at law and officers in the militia) under the United States or this commonwealth, shall be a member of either house during his continuance in congress or in office.

Adjourned until three o'clock on Monday next, P.M.

MONDAY, August 30, 1790. P. M.

The convention met pursuant to adjournment.

The committee appointed the 1st instant to revise, correct and arrange so much of the constitution for the government of this commonwealth as hath been appointed by this convention, made report. And the several sections adopted, except the third section of the third article.

A motion was made by Mr. Sitgreaves, seconded by Mr. Hand, to postpone the consideration of the said third section, as reported by the committee of arrangement, in order to introduce a motion to re-consider the seventeenth section of the first article, to strike from it the words "for surety."

On the question, Will the convention agree to the postponement for the aforesaid purpose?

The yeas and nays being called by Mr. Hand, were as follow, viz.

YEAS.

Mr. Baker	Mr. Jenks	Mr. Slegle	Mr. Hoge
Roberts	Stout	Tyson	J. Ross
Lewis	Hand	Sitgreaves	Shoemaker
M'Kean	Coleman	Arndt	Pickering
Gray	Graff	Rhoads	Henderson
Robinson	Hubley	Smith	Sellers
Hare	Breckbill	Snyder	Newlin
Ogden	Miller		30

NAYS.

Mr. Wilson	Mr. Irvine	Mr. Piper	Mr. Matthews
Edwards	Power	Findley	Morris
Barclay	Hiester	Todd	Coates
Boyd	Lower	Addison	Gloninger
Reed	Lincoln	Redick	Brown
Pedan	Groscop	Smilie	Grayden
Dill	Gehr	Gallatin	Gibson
Whitehill	Powell	M'Lene	Beale 32

So it was determined in the negative.

A motion was then made by Mr. James Ross, seconded by Mr. Lew-is, to re-consider the said seventeenth section of the first article, in order to strike out the following words, viz. "They shall in all cases except treason, felony and breach of surety of the peace, be privileged from arrest during their attendance at the session of the respective houses and in going to and returning from the same.

On the question, Will the convention agree to re-consider for the aforesaid purpose?

The yeas and nays being called by Mr. Smilie, were as follow, viz.

YEAS.

Mr. Roberts	Mr. Ogden	Mr. Hubley	Mr. Shoemaker
Lewis	Jenks	Breckbill	Gloninger
M'Kean	Stout	Sitgreaves	Pickering
Gray	Coleman	J. Ross	Sellers
Robinson	Graff	Morris	Newlin 20

NAYS.

Mr. Wilson	Mr. Boyd	Mr. Tyson	Mr. Power
Baker	Hand	Pedan	Hiester
Hare	Miller	Dill	Lower
Edwards	Slegle	Whitehill	Lincoln
Barclay	Reed	Irvine	Groscop

NAYS.

Mr. Gehr	Mr. Addison	Mr. M'Lene	Mr. Findley
Arndt	Hoge	Matthews	Todd
Rhoads	Redick	Coates	Henderson
Powell	Smilie	Brown	Gibson
Piper	Gallatin	Graydon	Beale 40

So it was determined in the negative.

On motion of Mr. Wilson, seconded by Mr. Coleman, ordered, that the secretary be directed to have so much of the constitution transcribed as is passed by this convention.

Adjourned until ten o'clock to-morrow, A. M.

TUESDAY, August 31, 1790. A. M.

The convention met pursuant to adjournment.

A motion was made by Mr. James Ross, seconded by Mr. M'Lene, to re-consider the eleventh section of the ninth article, viz.

Section XI. That all courts shall be open, and every man for an injury done him in his lands, goods, person or reputation, shall have remedy by the due course of law, and right and justice administered without sale denial or delay. Suits may be brought against the commonwealth as well as against other bodies corporate and individuals.

In order to strike out the words " as well as against other bodies corporate and individuals," and in lieu thereof to insert the words " in such manner, in such courts and upon such contracts as the legislature shall, by law direct."

On the question, Will the convention agree to re-consider the said section? It was determined in the affirmative, and the amendment moved by Mr. James Ross, seconded by Mr. M'Lene, being under consideration.

A motion was made by Mr. Lewis, seconded by Mr. M'Kean, to postpone the consideration of the said amendment in order to substitute the following in lieu thereof, viz. " In such courts and under such regulations as shall be prescribed by law." Which was determined in the negative, and the amendment moved by Mr. James Ross, seconded by Mr. M'Lene, recurring.

It was moved by Mr. Lewis, seconded by Mr. Pickering, to strike out from the said amendment the words " upon such contracts," and in lieu thereof, to insert the words " in such cases." Which was determined in the affirmative.

On the question, Will the convention agree to the amendment as amended? viz.

In such manner, in such courts and in such cases as the legislature shall, by law, direct.

The yeas and nays being called by Mr. Wilson, were as follow, viz.

YEAS.

Mr. Roberts	Mr. Boyd	Mr. Tyson	Mr. Hiester
Lewis	Hand	Pedan	Lower
Hare	Hubley	Dill	Lincoln
Ogden	Miller	Whitehill	Groscop
Jenks	Slegle	Irvine	Gehr
Barclay	Reed	Power	Sitgreaves

YEAS.

Mr. Arndt	Mr. Todd	Mr. Gallatin	Mr. Gloninger
Rhoads	Addison	M'Lene	Brown
Powell	Hoge	Matthews	Henderson
Piper	Redick	Norris	Gibson
Smith	J. Ross	Coates	Beale
Snyder	Smilie	Shoemaker	47

NAYS.

Mr. Wilson	Mr. Gray	Mr. Stout	Mr. Pickering
Baker	Robinson	Breckbill	Sellers
M'Kean	Edwards	Graydon	Newlin 12

So it was determined in the affirmative, and the section adopted as follows, viz.

Section XI. That all courts shall be open, and every man, for an injury done him in his lands, goods, person or reputation, shall have remedy by the due course of law, and right and justice administered without sale, denial or delay. Suits may be brought against the commonwealth in such manner, in such courts and in such cases as the legislature shall, by law direct.

A motion was made by Mr. Lewis, seconded by Mr. Graydon, to reconsider the eighth section of the second article, viz.

Sect. VIII. He shall appoint all officers whose offices are established by this constitution, or shall be established by law, and whose appointments are not herein otherwise provided for; but no person shall be appointed to an office within any county, who shall not have been a citizen and inhabitant therein one year next before his appointment, if the county shall have been so long erected, but if it shall not have been so long erected, then within the limits of the county or counties out of which it shall have been taken. No member of congress from this state, nor any person holding or exercising any office of trust or profit under the United States, shall at the same time, hold or exercise the office of judge, secretary, treasurer, prothonotary, register of wills, recorder of deeds, sheriff, or any office in this state, to which a salary is by law annexed; or any other office which future legislatures shall declare incompatible with offices or appointments under the United States.

On the question, Will the convention agree to re-consider? The yeas and nays being called by Mr. Lewis, were as follow, viz.

YEAS.

Mr. Wilson	Mr. M'Kean	Mr. Sitgreaves	Mr. Pickering
Baker	Gray	Arndt	Henderson
Roberts	Hare	Shoemaker	Sellers
Lewis	Hubley	Graydon	Newlin 16

NAYS.

Mr. Robinson	Mr. Hand	Mr. Dill	Mr. Gehr
Edwards	Breckbill	Whitehill	Rhoads
Ogden	Miller	Irvine	Powell
Jenks	Slegle	Power	Piper
Barclay	Reed	Hiester	Snyder
Stout	Tyson	Lincoln	Findley
Boyd	Pedan	Groscop	Todd

NAYS.

Mr. Addison	Mr. Smilie	Mr. Mathews	Mr. Lower
Hoge	Gallatin	Gloninger	Gibson
Redick	M'Lene	Brown	Beale
J. Ross			41

So it was determined in the negative.

A motion was made by Mr. Addison, seconded by Mr. Hare, to reconsider the fourteenth section of the second article, viz.

Sect. XIV. In case of the death or resignation of the governor, or of his removal from office, the speaker of the senate shall exercise the office of governor, until another governor, who shall in such case, be chosen at the next annual election, shall be duly qualified And if the trial of a contested election shall continue longer than until the third Tuesday in December next ensuing the election of a governor, the governor of the last year, or the speaker of the senate, who may be in the exercise of the executive authority, shall continue therein until the determination of such contested election, and until a governor shall be qualified as aforesaid.

In order to strike out the words " who shall in such case be chosen at the next annual election."

On the question, Will the convention agree to re-consider for the aforesaid purpose?

It was determined in the affirmative, and the section as amended, adopted as follows.

Section XIV In case of the death or resignation of the governor, or of his removal from office, the speaker of the senate shall exercise the office of governor, until another governor shall be duly qualified. And if the trial of a contested election shall continue longer than until the third Tuesday in December, next ensuing the election of a governor; the governor of the last year, or the speaker of the senate, who may be in the exercise of the executive authority, shall continue therein, until the determination of such contested election, and until a governor shall be qualified as aforesaid.

The committee appointed the twenty first instant to revise, correct and arrange so much of the constitution for the government of this commonwealth, as hath been agreed to by this convention, made further report, in part, which was adopted.

[See article ninth of the constitution as adopted.]

A motion was made by Mr. Lewis, seconded by Mr. Smith, to reconsider the first section of the sixth article, viz.

Section I. Sheriffs and coroners shall, at the times and places of election of representatives, be chosen by the citizens of each county: Two persons shall be chosen for each office, one of whom for each respectively shall be appointed by the governor. They shall hold their offices for three years, if they shall so long behave themselves well, and until a successor shall be duly qualified; but no person shall be twice chosen or appointed sheriff in any term of six years.

In order to amend the same to read as follows. viz.

Section I. Sheriffs and coroners shall, at the time and places of election of representatives, be chosen by the citizens of each county: Two persons shall be chosen for each office, one of whom for each respectively shall be appointed by the governor. They shall hold their offices for three years, if they shall so long behave themselves well, and until a successor be duly qualified; but no person shall be twice chosen or appointed sheriff in any term of six years. Vacancies in either of the said offices, shall be filled by a new appointment to be made by the governor, to continue until the next general election, and until a successor shall be chosen and qualified as aforesaid.

On the question, Will the convention agree to re-consider for the aforesaid purpose?

It was determined in the affirmative, and the first section as amended, adopted.

A motion was made by Mr. Wilson, seconded by Mr. M'Lene, and adopted as follows, viz.

Resolved, That a committee be appointed to arrange the order of procession at the proclamation of the constitution.

Ordered, That Mr. Barclay, Mr. Miller and Mr. Sitgreaves, be a committee for the purpose contained in the foregoing resolution.

On motion, the convention agreed to re-consider the title of the constitution, viz.

The constitution of the commonwealth of Pennsylvania, as altered and amended by the convention for that purpose freely chosen and assembled.

A division of the question on the title being called for, viz. on the words " the constitution of the commonwealth of Pennsylvania."

On the question, Will the convention agree to the same? It was determined in the affirmative.

And on the question, Will the convention agree to the latter part of the said title? It was determined in the negative, and the title adopted as follows:

The constitution of the commonwealth of Pennsylvania.

Whereupon, ordered that the constitution as agreed to by this convention, be engrossed.

Adjourned until nine o'clock on Thursday next, A. M.

THURSDAY, September 2, 1790. A. M.

The convention met pursuant to adjournment.

A letter from John Arndt, Esq. a member for the county of Northampton, was read, stating the immediate necessity of leaving the convention on account of the indisposition of his family; and requesting the secretary or one of his colleagues may be permitted to sign the constitution of the commonwealth of Pennsylvania, as adopted, in his behalf.

On the question, Will the convention agree to the said request?

It was unanimously determined in the affirmative, and Mr. Sitgreaves directed to subscribe the name of Mr. Arndt, accordingly.

The constitution, as adopted by the convention, having been brought in engrossed, the same was compared at the table.

A motion was then made by Mr. Wilson as chairman of the committee of arrangement, that the following words be adopted as the concluding part of the constitution, viz.

DONE in convention, the second day of September, in the year of our Lord one thousand seven hundred and ninety, and of the independence of the United States of America, the fifteenth. IN TESTIMONY whereof we have hereunto subscribed our names.

On the question, Will the convention agree to annex the same to the constitution of the commonwealth of Pennsylvania? It was determined in the affirmative, and thereupon ordered, that the same be engrossed and annexed to the constitution already compared.

The committee appointed the thirty-first of August to arrange the order of procession for proclaiming the constitution of this commonwealth, made report, which was adopted as follows, viz.

Order of procession for the proclamation of the constitution of the commonwealth of Pennsylvania.

Constables with their staves;
Sub-Sheriffs with their wands;
High-Sheriff and Coroner with their wands;
Judges of the supreme court and Judges of the high court of errors and appeals;
Attorney General and Prothonotary of the supreme court;
Wardens of the port of Philadelphia;
Treasurer, Comptroller General and Register General;
Secretary of the Land Office;
Receiver General and Surveyor General;
Justices of the Peace;
Prothonotary of the court of common pleas, and Clerk of the court of quarter sessions;
Clerks of the Mayor's court and of the corporation;
Mayor, Recorder and Aldermen;
Common council;
Master of the Rolls and Register of Wills;
Register of German passengers, and Collector of excise of the city and county;
Messenger of the convention;
Secretary and Assistant Secretary of the convention;
President of the convention;
Members of the convention two and two;
Doorkeeper of the convention ;
Secretary and Assistant Secretary of council;
Vice president of the executive council;
Members of council two and two;
Doorkeeper of council;
Sergeant-at-arms with the mace;
Clerk of the general assembly;
Speaker of the general assembly ;
Members of the general assembly two and two;
Doorkeeper of the general assembly;
Provost and faculty of the university;
Provost and faculty of the college and academy of Philadelphia;
Officers of the militia.
Citizens.

The constitution, with the addition moved by Mr. Wilson, being before the convention.

On the question, Will the convention ratify the same as the constitution of the commonwealth of Pennsylvania?

The yeas and nays being called by Mr. Wilson, were as follow, viz:

YEAS.

Mr. Wilson	Mr. Coleman	Mr Groscop	Mr. Gallatin
Baker	Graff	Gehr	M'Lene
Lewis	Hubley	Sitgreaves	Matthews
M'Kean	Breckbill	Rhoads	Morris
Gray	Miller	Powell	Coates
Robinson	Slegle	Piper	Shoemaker
Hare	Reed	Smith	Gloninger
Edwards	Tyson	Snyder	Brown
Ogden	Pedan	Findley	Graydon
Jenks	Dill	Todd	Pickering
Barclay	Irvine	Addison	Henderson
Stout	Power	Hoge	Gibson
Gibbons	Hiester	Redick	Beale
Bull	Lower	J. Ross	Sellers
Boyd	Lincoln	Smilie	Newlin 61
Hand			

NAYS.

Mr. Roberts

So it was determined in the affirmative, and ratified and confirmed by the members present as follows, viz.

THE CONSTITUTION OF THE COMMONWEALTH OF PENNSYLVANIA.

We, the people of the commonwealth of Pennsylvania, ordain and establish this constitution for its government.

ARTICLE I.

Section I. The legislative power of this commonwealth shall be vested in a general assembly, which shall consist of a senate and house of representatives.

Section II. The representatives shall be chosen, annually, by the citizens of the city of Philadelphia, and of each county respectively, on the second Tuesday of October.

Section III. No person shall be a representative, who shall not have attained the age of twenty-one years, and have been a citizen and inhabitant of the state three years next preceding his election, and the last year thereof an inhabitant of the city or county in which he shall be chosen ; unless he shall have been absent on the public business of the United States or of this state. No person residing within any city, town or borough, which shall be entitled to a separate representation, shall be elected a member for any county; nor shall any person residing without the limits of any such city, town or borough, be elected a member thereof.

Section IV. Within three years after the first meeting of the general, assembly, and within every subsequent term of seven years, an enumeration of the taxable inhabitants shall be made, in such manner as shall be directed by law. The number of representatives shall, at the several periods of making such enumeration, be fixed by the legislature, and apportioned among the city of Philadelphia, and the several counties according to the number of taxable inhabitants in each;

and shall never be less than sixty, nor greater than one hundred. Each county shall have at least one representative; but no county hereafter erected, shall be entitled to a separate representation, until a sufficient number of taxable inhabitants shall be contained within it to entitle them to one representative, agreeable to the ratio which shall then be established.

Sect. V. The senators shall be chosen for four years by the citizens of Philadelphia and of the several counties, at the same time, in the same manner and at the same places where they shall vote for representatives.

Sect. VI. The number of senators shall, at the several periods of making the enumeration before mentioned, be fixed by the legislature, and apportioned among the districts, formed as hereinafter directed, according to the number of taxable inhabitants in each; and shall never be less than one-fourth, nor greater than one-third of the number of representatives.

Sect. VII. The senators shall be chosen in districts to be formed by the legislature, each district containing such a number of taxable inhabitants as shall be entitled to elect not more than four senators: When a district shall be composed of two or more counties they shall be adjoining. Neither the city of Philadelphia, nor any county, shall be divided in forming a district.

Sect. VIII. No person shall be a senator, who shall not have attained the age of twenty-five years, and have been a citizen and inhabitant of the state four years next before his election, and the last year thereof an inhabitant of the district for which he shall be chosen, unless he shall have been absent on the public business of the United States or of this state.

Sect. IX. Immediately after the senators shall be assembled in consequence of the first election subsequent to the first enumeration, they shall be divided, by lot, as equally as may be, into four classes. The seats of the senators of the first class shall be vacated at the expiration of the first year; of the second class, at the expiration of the second year; of the third class, at the expiration of the third year; and of the fourth class, at the expiration of the fourth year; so that one-fourth may be chosen every year.

Sect. X. The general assembly shall meet on the first Tuesday of December, in every year, unless sooner convened by the governor.

Sect. XI. Each house shall choose its speaker and other officers; and the senate shall also choose a speaker *pro tempore*, when the speaker shall exercise the office of governor.

Sect. XII. Each house shall judge of the qualifications of its members. Contested elections shall be determined by a committee to be selected, formed and regulated in such manner as shall be directed by law. A majority of each house shall constitute a quorum to do business; but a smaller number may adjourn from day to day, and may be authorised, by law, to compel the attendance of absent members in such manner and under such penalties as may be provided.

Sect. XIII. Each house may determine the rules of its proceedings, punish its members for disorderly behaviour; and with the concurrence of two-thirds, expel a member, but not a second time for the same cause, and shall have all other powers necessary for a branch of the legislature of a free state.

Sect. XIV. Each house shall keep a journal of its proceedings, and publish them weekly, except such parts as may require secrecy: And the yeas and nays of the members, on any question, shall, at the desire of any two of them, be entered on the journals.

Sect. XV. The doors of each house and of committees of the whole, shall be open, unless when the business shall be such as ought to be kept secret.

Sect. XVI. Neither house shall, without the consent of the other, adjourn for more than three days, nor to any other place than that in which the two houses shall be sitting.

Sect. XVII. The senators and representatives shall receive a compensation for their services to be ascertained by law, and paid out of the treasury of the commonwealth. They shall in all cases, except treason, felony and breach or surety of the peace be privileged from arrest during their attendance at the session of the respective houses, and in going to and returning from the same; and for any speech or debate in either house they shall not be questioned in any other place.

Sect. XVIII. No senator or representative shall, during the time for which he shall have been elected, be appointed to any civil office, under this commonwealth, which shall have been created, or the emoluments of which shall have been encreased, during such time; and no member of congress or other person holding any office (except of attorney at law and in the militia) under the United States or this commonwealth, shall be a member of either house during his continuance in congress or in office.

Sect. XIX. When vacancies happen in either house, the speaker shall issue writs of election to fill such vacancies.

Sect. XX. All bills for raising revenue shall originate in the house of representatives; but the senate may propose amendments, as in other bills.

Sect. XXI. No money shall be drawn from the treasury, but in consequence of appropriations made by law.

Sect. XXII. Every bill, which shall have passed both houses shall be presented to the governor. If he approve, he shall sign it; but if he shall not approve it, he shall return it, with his objections, to the house in which it shall have originated, who shall enter the objections at large upon their journals, and proceed to re-consider it. If, after such re-consideration, two-thirds of that house shall agree to pass the bill, it shall be sent, with the objections, to the other house, by which likewise it shall be re-considered, and if approved by two-thirds of that house, it shall be a law. But in such cases, the votes of both houses shall be determined by yeas and nays, and the names of the persons voting for or against the bill shall be entered on the journals of each house respectively. If any bill shall not be returned by the governor within ten days (Sundays excepted) after it shall have been presented to him, it shall be a law in like manner as if he had signed it; unless the general assembly, by their adjournment, prevent its return, in which case it shall be a law, unless sent back within three days after their next meeting.

Sect. XXIII. Every order, resolution or vote, to which the concurrence of both houses may be necessary (except on a question of adjournment) shall be presented to the governor, and before it shall take effect, be approved by him; or, being disapproved shall be re-passed by two-thirds of both houses, according to the rules and limitations prescribed in case of a bill.

ARTICLE II.

Section I. The supreme executive power of this commonwealth shall be vested in a governor.

Sect. II. The governor shall be chosen on the second Tuesday of October, by the citizens of the commonwealth, at the places where they shall respectively vote for representatives. The returns of every election for governor shall be sealed up and transmitted to the seat of government, directed to the speaker of the senate, who shall open and publish them in the presence of the members of both houses of the legislature. The person having the highest number of votes shall be governor. But if two or more shall be equal and highest in votes, one of them shall be chosen governor by the joint vote of the members of both houses. Contested elections shall be determined by a committee to be selected from both houses of the legislature, and formed and regulated in such manner as shall be directed by law.

Sect. III. The governor shall hold his office during three years from the third Tuesday of December next ensuing his election, and shall not be capable of holding it longer than nine in any term of twelve years.

Sect. IV. He shall be, at least, thirty years of age; and have been a citizen and inhabitant of this state seven years next before his election ; unless he shall have been absent on the public business of the United States, or of this state.

Sect. V. No member of congress, or person holding any office under the United States or this state, shall exercise the office of governor.

Sect. VI. The governor shall, at stated times, receive for his services a compensation, which shall be neither increased nor diminished during the period for which he shall have been elected.

Sect. VII. He shall be commander in chief of the army and navy of this commonwealth, and of the militia, except when they shall be called into the actual service of the United States.

Sect. VIII. He shall appoint all officers, whose offices are established by this constitution, or shall be established by law, and whose appointments are not herein otherwise provided for; but no person shall be appointed to an office within any county, who shall not have been a citizen and inhabitant therein one year next before his appointment, if the county shall have been so long erected; but if it shall not have been so long erected, then within the limits of the county or counties, out of which it shall have been taken. No member of congress from this state nor any person holding or exercising any office of trust or profit under the United States, shall at the same time, hold or exercise the office of judge, secretary, treasurer, prothonotary, register of wills and recorder of deeds, sheriff, or any office in this state, to which a salary is by law annexed, or any other office, which future legislatures shall declare incompatible with offices or appointments under the United States.

Sect. IX. He shall have power to remit fines and forfeitures, and grant reprieves and pardons, except in cases of impeachment.

Sect. X. He may require information, in writing, from the officers in the executive department upon any subject relating to the duties of their respective offices.

Sect. XI. He shall from time to time, give to the general assembly information of the state of the commonwealth, and recommend to their consideration such measures as he shall judge expedient.

Sect XII. He may, on extraordinary occasions, convene the general assembly, and in case of disagreement between the two houses with respect to the time of adjournment, adjourn them to such time as he shall think proper, not exceeding four months.

Sect. XIII. He shall take care that the laws be faithfully executed. ·

Sect. XIV. In case of the death or resignation of the governor, or of his removal from office, the speaker of the senate shall exercise the office of governor, until another governor shall be duly qualified. And if the trial of a contested election shall continue longer than until the third Tuesday in December next ensuing the election of a governor, the governor of the last year, or the speaker of the senate, who may be in the exercise of the executive authority, shall continue therein, until the determination of such contested election, and until a governor shall be qualified as aforesaid.

Sect. XV. A secretary shall be appointed and commissioned during the governor's continuance in office, if he shall so long behave himself well. He shall keep a fair register of all the official acts and proceedings of the governor, and shall, when required, lay the same and all papers, minutes and vouchers relative thereto, before either branch of the legislature, and shall perform such other duties as shall be enjoined him by law.

ARTICLE III.

Section I. In elections by the citizens every freeman of the age of twenty one years, having resided in the state two years next before the elections, and within that time paid a state or county tax, which shall have been assessed at least six months before the election, shall enjoy the rights of an elector; provided that the sons of persons qualified as aforesaid, between the age of twenty-one and twenty-two years, shall be entitled to vote although they shall not have paid taxes.

Sect. II. All elections shall be by ballot, except those by persons in their representative capacities, who shall vote *viva voce*.

Sect. III. Electors shall, in all cases, except treason, felony and breach of surety of the peace, be privileged from arrest during their attendance on elections, and in going to and returning from them.

ARTICLE IV.

Section I. The house of representatives shall have the sole power of impeaching.

Sect. II All impeachments shall be tried by the senate : When sitting for that purpose, the senators shall be upon oath or affirmation No person shall be convicted without the concurrence of two-thirds of the members present.

Sect. III. The governor and all other civil officers under this commonwealth shall be liable to impeachment for any misdemeanor in office ; but judgment, in such cases, shall not extend further than to removal from office and disqualification to hold any office of honor, trust or profit under this commonwealth : the party whether convicted or acquitted, shall nevertheless, be liable to indictment, trial, judgment and punishment according to law.

ARTICLE V.

Section I. The judicial power of this commonwealth shall be vested in a supreme court, in courts of oyer and terminer and general gaol delivery, in a court of common pleas, orphans' court, register's court and a court of quarter sessions of the peace for each county, in justices of the peace, and in such other courts as the legislature may, from time time establish.

Sect. II. The judges of the supreme court and of the several courts of common pleas shall hold their offices during good behaviour: But, for any reasonable cause, which shall not be sufficient ground of impeachment, the governor may remove any of them on the address of two-thirds of each branch of the legislature. The judges of the supreme court and the presidents of the several courts of common pleas, shall, at stated times, receive for their services, an adequate compensation, to be fixed by law; which shall not be diminished during their continuance in office; but they shall receive no fees or perquisites of office, nor hold any other office of profit under this commonwealth.

Sect. III. The jurisdiction of the supreme court shall extend over the state, and the judges thereof shall, by virtue of their offices, be justices of oyer and terminer and general gaol delivery, in the several counties.

Sect. IV. Until it shall be otherwise directed by law, the several courts of common pleas shall be established in the following manner : The governor shall appoint, in each county, not fewer than three nor more than four judges, who, during their continuance in office, shall reside in such county : The state shall be, by law, divided into circuits, none of which shall include more than six nor fewer than three counties. A president shall be appointed of the courts in each circuit, who, during his continuance in office, shall reside therein. The president and judges, any two of whom shall be a quorum, shall compose the respective courts of common pleas.

Sect. V. The judges of the court of common pleas in each county shall, by virtue of their offices, be justices of oyer and terminer and general jail delivery for the trial of capital and other offenders therein; any two of the said judges, the president being one, shall be a quorum; but they shall not hold a court of oyer and terminer or jail delivery in any county when the judges of the supreme court, or any of them, shall be sitting in the same county. The party accused, as well as the commonwealth, may, under such regulations as shall be prescribed by law, remove the indictment and proceedings or a transcript thereof, into the supreme court.

Sect. VI. The supreme court and the several courts of common pleas shall, beside the powers heretofore usually exercised by them, have the powers of a court of chancery so far as relates to the perpetuating of testimony, the obtaining of evidence from places not within the state, and the care of the persons and estates of those who are *non compotes mentis*. And the legislature shall vest in the said courts such other powers to grant relief in equity as shall be found necessary: and may, from time to time, enlarge or diminish those powers; or vest them in such other courts as they shall judge proper for the due administration of justice.

Sect. VII. The judges of the court of common pleas of each county, any two of whom shall be a quorum ; shall compose the court of quarter sessions of the peace and orphans' court thereof: And the register of wills, together with the said judges, or any two of them, shall compose the register's court of each county.

Sect. VIII. The judges of the courts of common pleas shall, within their respective counties, have the like powers with the judges of the supreme court to issue writs of certiorari to the justices of the peace, and to cause their proceedings to be brought before them and the like right and justice to be done.

Sect. IX. The president of the court in each circuit within such circuit, and the judges of the courts of common pleas within their respective counties, shall be justices of the peace so far as relates to criminal matters.

Sect. X. The governor shall appoint a competent number of justices of the peace in such convenient districts in each county, as are, or shall be directed by law. They shall be commissioned during good behaviour; but may be removed on conviction of misbehaviour in office, or of any infamous crime, or on the address of both houses of the legislature.

Sect. XI. A register's office for the probate of wills and granting letters of administration, and an office for the recording of deeds shall be kept in each county.

Sect. XII. The style of all process shall be *The commonwealth of Pennsylvania*: all prosecutions shall be carried on in the name and by the authority of the commonwealth of Pennsylvania, and conclude, *against the peace and dignity of the same.*

ARTICLE VI.

Section I. Sheriffs and coroners shall, at the times and places of election of representatives, be chosen by the citizens of each county. Two persons shall be chosen for each office, one of whom, for each, respectively, shall be appointed by the governor. They shall hold their offices for three years if they shall so long behave themselves well, and until a successor be duly qualified; but no person shall be twice chosen or appointed sheriff in any term of six years. Vacancies in either of the said offices, shall be filled by a new appointment to be made by the governor, to continue until the next general election and until a successor shall be chosen and qualified as aforesaid.

Sect. II. The freemen of this commonwealth shall be armed and disciplined for its defence: Those who conscientiously scruple to bear arms, shall not be compelled to do so, but shall pay an equivalent for personal service. The militia officers shall be appointed in such manner and for such time as shall be directed by law.

Sect. III. Prothonotaries, clerks of the peace and orphans' courts, recorders of deeds, registers of wills and sheriffs, shall keep their offices in the county town of the county in which they respectively shall be officers; unless when the governor shall, for special reasons, dispense therewith for any term not exceeding five years after the county shall have been erected.

Sect. IV. All commissions shall be in the name and by the authority of the commonwealth of Pennsylvania, and be sealed with the state seal, and signed by the governor.

Sect. V. The state treasurer shall be appointed annually, by the joint vote of the members of both houses. All other officers in the treasury department, attornies at law, election officers, officers relating to taxes, to the poor and highways, constables and other township officers shall be appointed in such manner as is or shall be directed by law.

ARTICLE VII.

Section I. The legislature shall, as soon as conveniently may be, provide by law for the establishment of schools throughout the state, in such manner that the poor may be taught gratis.

Sect. II. The arts and sciences shall be promoted in one or more seminaries of learning.

Sect. III. The rights, privileges, immunities and estates of religious societies and corporate bodies shall remain as if the constitution of this state had not been altered or amended.

ARTICLE VIII.

Members of the general assembly and all officers, executive and judicial, shall be bound by oath or affirmation to support the constitution of this commonwealth, and to perform the duties of their respective offices with fidelity.

ARTICLE IX.

That the general, great and essential principles of liberty and free government may be recognised and unalterably established, WE DECLARE,

Section I. That all men are born equally free and independent, and have certain inherent and indefeasible rights, among which are those of enjoying and defending life and liberty, of acquiring, possessing and protecting property and reputation, and of pursuing their own happiness.

Sect. II. That all power is inherent in the people, and all free governments are founded on their authority, and instituted for their peace, safety and happiness: For the advancement of those ends, they have, at all times, an unalienable and indefeasible right to alter, reform, or abolish their government, in such manner as they may think proper.

Sect. III. That all men have a natural and indefeasible right to worship Almighty God according to the dictates of their own consciences; that no man can, of right, be compelled to attend, erect, or support any place of worship, or to maintain any ministry against his consent; that no human authority can, in any case whatever, control or interfere with the rights of conscience; and that no preference shall ever be given, by law, to any religious establishments or modes of worship.

Sect. IV. That no person who acknowledges the being of a God and a future state of rewards and punishments, shall, on account of his religious sentiments, be disqualified to hold any office or place of trust or profit under this commonwealth.

Sect. V. That elections shall be free and equal.

Sect. VI. That trial, by jury shall be as heretofore, and the right thereof remain inviolate.

Sect. VII. That the printing presses shall be free to every person, who undertakes to examine the proceedings of the legislature or any branch of government: and no law shall ever be made to restrain the right thereof. The free communication of thoughts and opinions is one of the invaluable rights of man ; and every citizen may freely speak, write and print on any subject, being responsible for the abuse of that liberty. In prosecutions for the publication of papers, investigating the official conduct of officers, or men in a public capacity, or where the matter published is proper for public information, the truth thereof may be given in evidence ; and, in all indictments for libels, the jury shall have a right to determine the law and the facts, under the direction of the court, as in other cases.

Sect. VIII. That the people shall be secure in their persons, houses, papers and possessions from unreasonable searches and seizures; and that no warrant to search any place, or to seize any person or things, shall issue without describing them as nearly as may be, nor without probable cause, supported by oath or affirmation.

Sect. IX. That in all criminal prosecutions, the accused hath a right to be heard by himself and his council, to demand the nature and cause of the accusation against him, to meet the witnesses face to face, to have compulsory process for obtaining witnesses in his favor, and in prosecutions by indictment or information, a speedy public trial by an impartial jury of the vicinage: That he cannot be compelled to give evidence against himself, nor can he be deprived of his life, liberty or property, unless by the judgment of his peers or the law of the land.

Sect. X. That no person shall, for any indictable offence, be proceeded against criminally by information; except in cases arising in the land or naval forces, or in the militia when in actual service in time of war or public danger; or by leave of the court for oppression and misdemeanor in office. No person shall for the same offence be twice put in jeopardy of life or limb; nor shall any man's property be taken, or applied to public use, without the consent of his representatives, and without just compensation being made.

Sect. XI. That all courts shall be open, and every man for an injury done him in his lands, goods, person or reputation, shall have remedy by the due course of law, and right and justice administered without sale, denial or delay. Suits may be brought against the commonwealth in such manner, in such courts and in such cases as the legislature may, by law, direct.

Sect. XII. That no power of suspending laws shall be exercised, unless by the legislature, or its authority.

Sect. XIII. That excessive bail shall not be required, nor excessive fines imposed, nor cruel punishments inflicted.

Sect. XIV. That all prisoners shall be bailable by sufficient sureties, unless for capital offences, when the proof is evident or presumption great: and the privilege of the writ of habeas corpus shall not be suspended, unless when, in cases of rebellion or invasion, the public safety may require it.

Sect. XV. That no commission of oyer and terminer or jail delivery shall be issued.

Sect. XVI. That the person of a debtor, where there is not strong presumption of fraud, shall not be continued in prison after delivering up his estate, for the benefit of his creditors, in such manner as shall be prescribed by law.

Sect. XVII. That no ex post facto law, nor any law impairing contracts, shall be made.

Sect. XVIII. That no person shall be attainted of treason or felony by the legislature.

Sect. XIX. That no attainder shall work corruption of blood, nor, except during the life of the offender, forfeiture of estate to the commonwealth; that the estates of such persons as shall destroy their own lives shall descend or vest as in case of natural death; and if any person shall be killed by casualty there shall be no forfeiture by reason thereof.

Sect. XX. That the citizens have a right, in a peaceable manner, to assemble together for their common good, and to apply to those invested with the powers of government, for redress of grievances or other proper purposes, by petition, address or remonstrance.

Sect. XXI. That the right of the citizens to bear arms in defence of themselves and the state shall not be questioned.

Sect. XXII. That no standing army shall, in time of peace, be kept up without the consent of the legislature, and the military shall, in all cases, and at all times, be in strict subordination to the civil power.

Sect. XXIII. That no soldier shall, in time of peace, be buartered in any house without the consent of the owner, nor in time of war, but in a manner to be prescribed by law.

Sect. XXIV. That the legislature shall not grant any title of nobility or hereditary distinction, nor create any office the appointment to which shall be for a longer term than during good behaviour.

Sect. XXV. That emigration from the state shall not be prohibited.

Sect. XXVI. To guard against transgressions of the high powers which we have delegated, WE DECLARE, that every thing in this article is excepted out of the general powers of government, and shall for ever remain inviolate.

SCHEDULE.

That no inconvenience may arise from the alterations and amendments in the constitution of this commonwealth, and in order to carry the same into complete operation, it is hereby declared and ordained.

I. That all laws of this commonwealth, in force at the time of making the said alterations and amendments in the said constitution, and not inconsistent therewith, and all rights, actions, prosecutions, claims and contracts, as well of individuals as of bodies corporate, shall continue as if the said alterations and amendments had not been made.

II. That the president and supreme executive council shall continue to exercise the executive authority of this commonwealth as heretofore, until the third Tuesday of December next; but no intermediate vacancies in the council shall be supplied by new elections.

III. That all officers in the appointment of the executive department, shall continue in the exercise of the duties of their respective offices until the first day of September, one thousand seven hundred and ninety-one, unless their commissions shall sooner expire by their own limitations, or the said offices become vacant by death or resignation, and no longer, unless re-appointed and commissioned by the governor. Except that the judges of the supreme court shall hold their offices for the terms in their commissions respectively expressed.

IV. That justice shall be administered in the several counties of the state, until the period aforesaid, by the same justices, in the same courts, and in the same manner as heretofore.

V. That no person now in commission as sheriff shall be eligible at the next election for a longer term than will, with the time, which he shall have served in the said office, complete the term of three years.

VI. That until the first enumeration shall be made as directed in the fourth section of the first article of the constitution established by this convention, the city of Philadelphia and the several counties shall be respectively entitled to elect the same number of representatives as is now prescribed by law.

VII. That the first senate shall consist of eighteen members, to be chosen in districts formed as follows, viz. The city of Philadelphia, and the counties of Philadelphia and Delaware shall be a district, and elect three senators; the county of Chester shall be a district, and shall elect one senator; the county of Bucks shall be a district, and shall elect one senator; the county of Montgomery shall be a district and shall elect one senator; the county of Northampton shall be a district, and shall elect one senator; the counties of Lancaster and York shall be a district, and shall elect three senators; the counties of Berks and Dauphin shall be a district, and shall elect two senators; the counties of Cumberland and Mifflin shall be a district, and shall elect one senator; the counties of Northumberland, Luzerne and Huntingdon shall be a district, and shall elect one senator; the counties of Bedford and Franklin shall be a district, and shall elect one senator; the counties of Westmoreland and Allegheny shall be a district, and shall elect one senator; and the counties of Washington and Fayette shall be a district and shall elect two senators: which senators shall serve until the first enumeration before mentioned shall be made, and the representation in both houses of the legislature shall be established by law, and chosen as in the constitution is directed. Any vacancies which shall happen in the senate within the said time, shall be supplied as prescribed in the nineteenth section of the first article.

VIII. That the elections of senators shall be conducted, and the returns thereof made to the senate, in the same manner as is prescribed by the election laws of the state for conducting and making return of the election of representatives. In those districts which consist of more than one county, the judges of the district elections within each county, after having formed a return of the whole election within that county, in such manner as is directed by law, shall send the same, by one or more of their number, to the place hereinafter mentioned, within the district of which such county is a part; where the judges, so met, shall compare and cast up the several county returns, and execute, under their hands and seals, one general and true return for the whole district, *that is to say,* The judges of the district composed of the city of Philadelphia and the counties of

Philadelphia and Delaware, shall meet in the state house in the city of Philadelphia; the judges of the district composed of the counties of Lancaster and York, shall meet at the court house in the county of Lancaster; the judges of the district composed of the counties of Berks and Dauphin, shall meet at Middletown, in the county of Berks; the judges of the district composed of the counties of Cumberland and Mifflin, shall meet in Greenwood township, county of Cumberland, at the house now occupied by David Miller; the judges of the district composed of the counties of Northumberland, Luzerne and Huntingdon, shall meet in the town of Sunbury; the judges of the district composed of the counties of Bedford and Franklin, shall meet at the house now occupied by John Dickey, in Air township, Bedford county; the judges of the district composed of the counties of Westmoreland and Allegheny, shall meet in Westmoreland county, at the court house in the town of Greensborough; and the judges of the district composed of the counties of Washington and Fayette, shall meet at the court house in the town of Washington, in Washington county, on the third Tuesday in October respectively, for the purposes aforesaid.

IX. That the election of the governor shall be conducted in the several counties in the manner prescribed by the laws of the state for the election of representatives, and the returns in each county shall be sealed by the judges of the elections, and transmitted to the president of the supreme executive council, directed to the speaker of the senate, as soon after the election as may be.

DONE in convention, the second day of September, in the year of our Lord one thousand seven hundred and ninety, and of the independence of the United States of America, the fifteenth. IN TESTIMONY whereof we have hereunto subscribed our names.

THOMAS MIFFLIN, President.

James Wilson,	Henry Slegle,	Alexander Addison,
Hilary Baker,	William Reed,	John Hoge,
William Lewis,	Benjamin Tyson,	David Redick,
Thomas M'Kean	Benjamin Pedan,	James Ross,
George Gray,	Matthew Dill,	John Smilie,
William Robinson, jr.	William Irvine,	Albert Gallatin,
Robert Hare,	James Power,	James M'Lene,
Enoch Edwards,	Joseph Hiester,	George Matthews,
Samuel Ogden,	Christian Lower,	James Morris,
Thomas Jenks,	Abraham Lincoln,	Lindsay Coates,
John Barclay,	Paul Groscop,	Jonathan Shoemaker,
Abraham Stout,	Baltzer Gehr,	John Gloninger,
William Gibbons,	Samuel Sitgreaves,	William Brown,
Thomas Bull,	John Arndt,	Alexander Graydon,
James Boyd,	Peter Rhoads,	Timothy Pickering,
Edward Hand,	Joseph Powell,	Andrew Henderson,
Robert Coleman,	John Piper,	John Gibson,
Sebastian Graff,	Charles Smith,	Thomas Beale,
John Hubley,	Simon Snyder,	John Sellers,
John Breckbill,	William Findley,	Nathaniel Newlin.
Henry Miller,	William Todd.	

ATTEST—JOSEPH REDMAN, *Secretary.*
JACOB SHALLUS, *Assistant Secretary.*

On motion, ordered, that three thousand five hundred copies of the said constitution be printed in the English language, and one thousand five hundred of the same in the German language, for the information of the citizens of this state.

The convention then, agreeably to the order of procession, proceeded to the court house in Market street, to make proclamation of the constitution, and having returned to their chamber, it was on motion, ordered, that the secretary be directed to deliver the engrossed copy of the constitution of the commonwealth of Pennsylvania, to the master of the rolls, in order that the same may be recorded.

Which was accordingly done in the presence of the convention.

Whereupon, on motion of Mr. Lewis, seconded by Mr. Miller,

Resolved, That the thanks of this convention be presented to his excellency the president for his able and upright discharge of the duties of his station.

The convention then rose *sine die.*

Chapter IV.

MINUTES

Of the grand committee of the whole convention of the commonwealth of Pennsylvania, which commenced at Philadelphia, on Tuesday the twenty fourth day of November, in the year of our Lord, one thousand seven hundred and eighty-nine.

TUESDAY, December, 1, 1789. A. M.

The honorable Mr. M·Kean in the chair.

A motion was made by Mr. Hare, seconded by Mr. Edwards, in the following words, viz.

Resolved, That in the opinion of this committee it is expedient that the constitution of this state be altered.

It was then moved by Mr. Robinson, seconded by Mr. Smilie, to postpone the consideration of the said resolution.

On the question, "Will the committee agree to the postponement?" It was carried in the affirmative.

It was moved by Mr. Lewis, seconded by Mr. M·Lene, that the committee rise, report progress and ask leave to sit again to-morrow; which was carried in the affirmative.

The committee rose, and the chairman reported, that the committee had made some progress in the business referred to them, but, not having completed the same, requested leave to sit again to-morrow.

Which was agreed to.

WEDNESDAY, December 2, 1789. A. M.

A motion was made by Mr. Wilson, seconded by Mr. Hand, in the following words, viz.

Resolved, as the opinion of this committee, that the legislature of this state should consist of more than one branch.

And after some debate, it was moved by Mr. Addison, seconded by Mr. Smilie, to postpone the proposed resolution, in order to introduce the following, viz.

Whether that part of the constitution which relates to the legislative part of the government ought to be altered?

A motion was made by Mr. M'Lene, seconded by Mr. Smilie, that the committee rise, report progress and ask leave to sit again; which was determined in the negative.

And on the question "Will the committee agree to the postponement for the aforesaid purpose?"

It was determined in the negative.

Whereupon, a motion was made by Mr. Thomas Ross, seconded by Mr. Sitgreaves,

Resolved, That the committee rise, report progress in the business committed to them, and request leave to sit again to-morrow.

Which was accordingly done.

THURSDAY, December 3, 1789. A. M.

The motion made yesterday by Mr. Wilson, seconded by Mr. Hand, recurring, it was moved by Mr. Thomas Ross, seconded by Mr. Coates, to postpone the consideration thereof, in order to introduce the following, viz.

Resolved, That the constitution be read by articles and sections, and the sense of this committee be taken on each article and section, whether it be necessary to make any alteration and amendment therein, and what.

And on the question—"Will the committee agree to postpone for the purpose above mentioned?" It was determined in the negative.

It was then moved by Mr. Lewis, seconded by Mr. Edwards, to postpone the motion of Mr. Wilson, in order to introduce the following in lieu thereof, to wit.

Resolved, That in the opinion of this committee the legislative department of the constitution of this commonwealth requires alterations and amendments, so as to consist of more than one branch, and in such of the arrangements as may be necessary for the complete organization thereof; which was carried in the affirmative.

And on the question—"Will the committee agree to the proposed resolution?"—The yeas and nays being called by Mr. Lewis, were as follow, viz.

YEAS.

Mr. Wilson	Mr. Ross	Mr. Lower	Mr. Smilie
Roberts	Boyd	Groscop,	M'Lene
Lewis	Hand	Gehr	Matthews
M'Kean	Coleman	Sitgreaves	Morris
Mifflin	Graff	Mawhorter	Potts
Gray	Breckbill	Arndt	Coates
Robinson	Miller	Rhoads	Shoemaker
Hare	Slegle	Smith	Gloninger
Edwards	Reed	Snyder	Brown
Ogden	Tyson	Findley	Pickering
Jenks	Pedan	Todd	Henderson
Barclay	Dill	Addison	Gibson
Stout	Irvine	Hoge	Beale
Gibbons	Power	Redick	Sellers
Bull	Heister	J. Ross	Graham—60

NAYS.

Mr. Whitehill   Mr. Lincoln   Mr. Powell   Mr. Piper—4.

So it was determined in the affirmative.

On motion, ordered, that the committee rise, report progress and request leave to sit again to-morrow. Which was done.

FRIDAY, December 4, 1789. A. M.

On motion of Mr. Wilson, seconded by Mr. Sitgreaves,

Resolved, unanimously, That in the opinon of this committee the executive department of the constitution of this commonwealth should be altered and amended, so as that the supreme executive power be vested in a single person; subject however to proper exceptions.

A motion was made by Mr. Wilson, seconded by Mr. Pickering, in the following words, viz.

Resolved, That in the opinion of this committee the judicial department of the constitution of this commonwealth should be altered and amended, so as that the judges of the supreme court hold their commissions during good behaviour and be independent as to their salaries.

The committee then rose, reported progress and asked leave to sit to-morrow.

Which was accordingly granted.

SATURDAY, December 8, 1789.

The motion made yesterday by Mr. Wilson, seconded by Mr. Pickering, recurring, viz.

Resolved, That in the opinion of this committee the judicial department of the constitution of this commonwealth should be altered and amended, so as that the judges of the supreme court hold their commissions during good behaviour and be independent as to their salaries.

It was moved by Mr. Thomas Ross, seconded by Mr. Lewis, that the following words be added to the said motion, viz.

Subject however to such restrictions as may hereafter be thought proper.

Which was carried in the affirmative.

A motion was then made by Mr. Smilie, seconded by Mr. Findley, to postpone the consideration of the resolution, as amended, in order to introduce the following, viz.

Resolved, that in the opinion of this committee the judicial department of the constitution of this commonwealth should be altered and amended, so as that the judges of the supreme court be rendered more independent.

On the question "Will the committee agree to the postponement for the aforesaid purpose? It was determined in the negative.

And the original resolution, as amended, adopted, viz.

Resolved, That in the opinion of this committee the judicial department of the constitution of this commonwealth should be altered and amended, so as that the judges of the supreme court hold their commissions during good behaviour and be independent as to their salaries, subject however to such restrictions as may hereafter be thought proper.

A motion was made by Mr. Wilson, seconded by Mr. Hare, in the following words, viz.

Resolved, That in the opinion of this committee the supreme executive department should have a qualified negative on the legislature. The committee then rose, reported progress and asked leave to sit again on Monday. Which was accordingly granted.

MONDAY, December 7, 1789. P. M.

The motion made by Mr. Wilson, seconded by Mr. Hare, December 5, recurring, and the same having been amended, so as to read as follows, viz.

Resolved, That in the opinion of this committee the constitution of this commonwealth should be so amended as that the supreme executive department should have a qualified negative on the legislature.

On the question—"Will the committee agree to the resolution as amended?" The yeas and nays were called by Mr. Wilson, and were as follows, viz.

YEAS.

Mr. Wilson	Mr. T. Ross	Mr. Lincoln	Mr. J. Ross
Baker	Boyd	Groscop	Smilie
Roberts	Hand	Gehr	Gallatin
Lewis	Coleman	Sitgreaves	M'Lene
M'Kean	Graff	Mawhorter	Matthews
Mifflin	Hubley	Arndt	Morris
Gray	Breckbill	Rhoads	Potts
Robinson	Miller	Powell	Coates
Hare	Slegle	Piper	Shoemaker
Edwards	Reed	Smith	Gloninger
Ogden	Tyson	Snyder	Brown
Jenks	Pedan	Findley	Pickering
Barclay,	Dill	Todd	Henderson
Stout	Irvine	Addison	Gibson
Gibbons	Hiester	Hoge	Sellers
Bull	Lower	Redick	Graham 64

NAYS.

Mr. Whitehill   Mr. Power   Mr. Beale   3.

So it was determined in the affirmative.

The committee then rose, reported progress and asked leave to sit to-morrow.

Which was accordingly granted.

TUESDAY, December 8, 1789. A. M.

It was moved by Mr. Sitgreaves, seconded by Mr. Ogden, that the committee rise and make report of their proceedings to the convention.

A motion was then made by Mr. Findley, seconded by Mr. Smilie, to postpone the motion of Mr. Sitgreaves, in order to introduce the following, viz.

Resolved, That the bill of rights be now taken up for the consideration of the committee.

The committee then rose, reported progress and asked leave to sit again to-morrow.   Which was accordingly granted.

WEDNESDAY, December 9, 1789. A. M.

˒ The motion made yesterday by Mr. Sitgreaves, seconded by Mr. Ogden, *viz.* That the committee rise and make report of their proceedings to the convention, recurring,

A motion was then made by Mr. James Ross, seconded by Mr. Pickering, to postpone the consideration of the said motion, in order to introduce the following resolution, viz.

Resolved, That that part of the constitution of this commonwealth, called A *declaration of the rights of the inhabitants of the commonwealth or state of Pennsylvania*, requires alterations and amendments, in such manner as that the rights of the people, reserved and excepted out of the general powers of government, may be more accurately defined and secured, and the same and such other alterations and amendments as may be made in the said constitution, be made to correspond with each other.

On the question, Will the committee agree to the postponement for the aforesaid purpose ?

It was carried in the affirmative, and the proposed resolution unanimously adopted.

The motion made by Mr. Sitgreaves, seconded by Mr. Ogden, again recurring, that the committee rise and make report of their proceedings to the convention.

It was carried in the affirmative.

And the report of the committee of the whole agreed to as follows, viz.

I. That, in the opinion of this committee, the legislative department of the constitution of this commonwealth requires alterations and amendments, so as to consist of more than one branch, and in such of the arrangements as may be necessary for the complete organization thereof.

II. That, in the opinion of this committee, the executive department of the constitution of this commonwealth should be altered and amended, so as that the supreme executive power be vested in a single person, subject however to proper exceptions.

III. That, in the opinion of this committee, the judicial department of the constitution of this commonwealth should be altered and amended, so as that the judges of the supreme court hold their commissions during good behaviour, and be independent as to their salaries, subject however to such restrictions as may hereafter be thought proper.

IV. That, in the opinion of this committee, the constitution of this commonwealth should be so amended as that the supreme executive department should have a qualified negative upon the legislature.

V. That in the opinion of this committee, that part of the constitution of this commonwealth, called a declaration of the rights of the inhabitants of the commonwealth or state of Pennsylvania, requires alterations and amendments, in such manner as that the rights of the people, reserved and excepted out of the general powers of government, may be more accurately defined and secured, and the same and such alterations and amendments in the said constitution as may be agreed on, be made to correspond with each other.

The committee of the whole then rose for the purpose of making the said report.

WEDNESDAY, December 23, 1789. A. M.

The honorable Mr. M'Kean in the chair.

The committee of the whole proceeded to take into consideration the draft of a proposed constitution, as reported by the committee appointed on the eleventh day of December, instant, for that purpose.

And after debating the first section of the first article of the proposed constitution, On the question, Will the committee agree to the same ?

It was determined in the affirmative.

And in debating the second section of the first article of the proposed constitution, viz.

II. The representatives shall be chosen annually, by the citizens of the city of Philadelphia, and of each county in the state respectively, on the   Tuesday of October.

It was moved by Mr. Irvine, seconded by Mr. Smith, to fill the blank with the word "second."

Which was carried in the affirmative, and the section unanimously adopted.

And in debating the third section of the first article of the proposed constitution, viz.

III. No person shall be a representative, who shall not, at the time of his election, have been, the three years next preceding, an inhabitant of the state, and one year next preceding an inhabitant of the city or county in which he shall be chosen.

It was moved by Mr Lewis, seconded by Mr. Piper, to strike out the words "one year next preceding," and in lieu thereof to insert the words "at the time of his election."

And on the question, Will the convention agree to strike out the words for the aforesaid purpose ?

The yeas and nays were called by Mr. Coleman, and were as follow, viz.

YEAS.

Mr. Wilson	Mr. Roberts	Mr. M'Kean	Mr. Robinson 7
Baker	Lewis	Gray	

NAYS.

Mr. Mifflin	Mr. Hubley	Mr. Gehr	Mr. M'Lene
Hare	Breckbill	Mawhorter	Matthews
Edwards	Miller	Powell	Morris
Ogden	Slegle	Piper	Potts
Jenks	Reed	Smith	Coates
Barclay	Tyson	Snyder	Shoemaker
Stout	Pedan	Findley	Gloninger
Gibbons	Dill	Todd	Brown
Bull	Whitehill	Addison	Pickerin
T. Ross	Irvine	Hoge	Henderson
Boyd	Power	Redick	Gibson
Hand	Hiester	J. Ross	Beale
Coleman	Lower	Smilie	Sellers
Graff	Lincoln	Gallatin	Graham 58
Atlee	Groscop		

So it was determined in the negative.

40

It was then moved by Mr. Lewis, seconded by Mr. Pickering, to amend the said resolution, so as to read as follows, viz.

III No person shall be a representative who shall not have attained the age of twenty-one years, and have been three years next preceding his election a citizen and inhabitant of the state, and the last year thereof an inhabitant of the city or county in which he shall be chosen.

It was thereupon moved by Mr. Ogden, seconded by Mr. Edwards, to add the following words to the said section, viz. "and shall hold, in his own right, a freehold estate of the value of one hundred pounds."

The committee then rose in order to report, that they had made some progress in the business committed to them, and to ask leave to sit again.

Which was accordingly done.

THURSDAY, December 24, 1789. *A. M.*

The third section of the first article of the proposed constitution for the government of this commonwealth, together with the several amendments made thereto, again recurring, viz.

No person shall be a representative who shall not have attained the age of twenty-one years, and have been, three years next preceding his election, a citizen and inhabitant of the state, and the last year thereof an inhabitant of the city or county in which he shall be chosen, and shall hold, in his own right, a freehold estate of the value of one hundred pounds.

Mr. Ogden withdrew his amendment, proposed yesterday, in the the following words:

"And shall hold, in his own right, a freehold estate of the value of one hundred pounds."

It was moved by Mr. Henderson, seconded by Mr. Boyd, to add after the word "chosen," the following: "Nor shall he be capable of serving as a representative longer than   years in any term of years."

On the question, Will the committee agree to the proposed amendment?—The yeas and nays being called by Mr. Ogden, were as follow, viz.

YEAS.

Mr. Gibbons	Mr. Lower	Mr. Powell	Mr. Redick
Boyd	Lincoln	Piper	Smilie
Breckbill	Groscop	Findley	M'Lene
Whitehill	Gehr	Addison	Matthews
Power	Mawhorter	Hoge	Henderson
Hiester			21

NAYS.

Mr. Wilson	Mr. Edwards	Mr. Graff	Mr. Irvine
Baker	Ogden	Atlee	Smith
Roberts	Jenks	Hubley	Snyder
Lewis	Barclay	Miller	Todd
M'Kean	Stout	Slegle	J. Ross
Mifflin	Bull	Reed	Gallatin
Gray	T. Ross	Tyson	Morris
Robinson	Hand	Pedan	Potts
Hare	Coleman	Dill	Coates

NAYS.

Mr. Shoemaker	Mr. Brown	Mr. Gibson	Mr. Graham
Gloninger	Pickering	Sellers	43

So it was determined in the negative.

And thereupon, the third section of the first article of the said proposed constitution, as amended, was unanimously agreed to as follows, viz.

III. No person shall be a representative who shall not have attained the age of twenty-one years, and have been, three years next preceding his election, a citizen and inhabitant of the state, and the last year thereof an inhabitant of the city or county in which he shall be chosen.

The fourth section of the first article of the proposed constitution having been read.

The committee rose in order to report further progress in the business referred to them, and to request leave to sit again.

SATURDAY, December 26, 1789. A. M.

The fourth section of the first article of the proposed constitution, recurring, viz.

IV. The representatives from the city of Philadelphia and the several counties shall be in proportion to the number of taxable inhabitants; provided that the number of representativts shall never be fewer than sixty, nor more than one hundred : But each county shall have, at least, one representative. An enumeration of the taxable inhabitants shall be made within three years after the first meeting of the general assembly, and within every subsequent term of ten years, in such manner as they shall, by law, direct Until such enumeration shall be made, the city of Philadelphia and the several counties of the state, shall be, respectively, entitled to choose the same number of representatives as is now prescribed by law.

A motion was made by Mr. Addison, seconded by Mr. Matthews, to strike out the word "ten" in order to insert the word "five."

It was then moved by Mr. Smith, seconded by Mr. Miller, to postpone the consideration of the said motion in order to introduce the following amendment, viz.

After the words "general assembly, and" to add the words "within every seven years afterwards, until the term of twenty-one years shall have elapsed, and then."

On the question, Will the committee agree to the postponement for the aforesaid purpose ?

It was determined in the negative.

The original motion then recurring, On the question, Shall the word "ten" be struck out ?—The yeas and nays being called by Mr. Smith, were as follow, viz.

YEAS.

Mr. M'Kean	Mr. Atlee	Mr. Dill	Mr. Lower
T. Ross	Miller	Whitehill	Groscop
Boyd	Reed	Irvine	Lincoln
Hand	Tyson	Power	Gehr
Coleman	Pedan	Hiester	Mawhorter

YEAS.

Mr. Powell	Mr. Addison	Mr. Gallatin	Mr. Gloninger
Piper	Hoge	M'Lene	Brown
Smith	Redick	Matthews	Pickering
Snyder	J. Ross	Coates	Henderson
Findley	Smilie	Shoemaker	Gibson
Todd			41

NAYS.

Mr. Wilson	Mr. Gray	Mr. Barclay	Mr. Hubley
Baker	Robinson	Stout	Slegle
Roberts	Hare	Bull	Sellers
Lewis	Ogden	Graff	Graham
Mifflin	Jenks		18

So it was carried in the affirmative.

A motion was then made by Mr. Pickering, seconded by Mr. Wilson, to postpone the question for filling up the blank in order to introduce the following amendment: to strike out the words "and within every subsequent term of   years," and in lieu thereof to insert the words "and afterwards as often as once in ten years and not oftener than once in five years."

On the question, Will the committee agree to the postponement for the aforesaid purpose?

The yeas and nays being called by Mr. Wilson, were as follow, viz.

YEAS.

Mr. Wilson	Mr. T. Ross	Mr. Pickering	Mr. Sellers

NAYS.

Mr. Baker	Mr. Hand	Mr. Hiester	Mr. Redick
Roberts	Coleman	Lower	J. Ross
Lewis	Graff	Lincoln	Smilie
M'Kean	Atlee	Groscop	Gallatin
Mifflin	Hubley	Gehr	M'Lene
Gray	Miller	Mawhorter	Matthews
Robinson	Slegle	Powel	Coates
Hare	Reed	Piper	Shoemaker
Ogden	Tyson	Smith	Gloninger
Jenks	Pedan	Snyder	Brown
Barclay	Dill	Findley	Henderson
Stout	Whitehill	Todd	Gibson
Bull	Irvine	Addison	Graham
Boyd	Power	Hoge	55

So it was determined in the negative.

It was moved by Mr. Miller, seconded by Mr. Coleman, to fill the blank in the foregoing resolution with the word "seven."

Whereupon, a question was taken, viz. "Shall the vote be taken on the word "five" previous to the word "seven?"

Which was carried in the affirmative.

The original motion then recurring, to fill the blank with "five."

On the question, Will the convention agree to the same? The yeas and nays being called by Mr. Wilson, were as follow, viz.

YEAS.

Mr. M'Kean	Mr. Lower	Mr. Snyder	Mr. Smilie
T. Ross	Lincoln	Findley	Gallatin
Boyd	Groscop	Todd	M'Lene
Reed	Gehr	Addison	Matthews
Pedan	Mawhorter	Hoge	Gloninger
Dill	Powell	Redick	Henderson
Whitchill	Piper	J. Ross	Gibson
Power			29

NAYS.

Mr. Wilson	Mr. Ogden	Mr. Atlee	Mr. Smith
Baker	Jenks	Hubley	Coates
Roberts	Barclay	Miller	Shoemaker
Lewis	Stout	Slegle	Brown
Mifflin	Bull	Tyson	Pickering
Gray	Hand	Irvine	Sellers
Robinson	Coleman	Hiester	Graham
Hare	Graff		30

So it was determined in the negative.

The motion made by Mr Miller then recurring, viz. shall the blank be filled with the word "seven?"

It was unanimously carried in the affirmative.

A motion was thereupon made by Mr. Lewis seconded by Mr. Miller, to strike out the word "sixty" and the words "one hundred," and to insert instead of the word "sixty" the words "forty-five," and in lieu of the words "one hundred" the word "ninety."

The committee then rose, reported progress and asked leave to sit again.

MONDAY, December 28th, 1789. *A. M.*

Mr. Lewis withdrew his motion made on Saturday last, viz. to strike out of the fourth section of the first article of the proposed constitution the words "sixty" and "one hundred," and in lieu thereof to insert the words "forty-five" and "ninety."

The fourth section again recurring, with the proposed amendments, it was moved by Mr. Lewis, seconded by Mr. Wilson, to amend the section so as to read as follows, viz.

The number of representatives shall, at the several periods of making the enumeration in this section mentioned, be fixed by the legislature, and apportioned between the city of Philadelphia and the several counties, according to the number of taxable inhabitants in each; and shall never be less than sixty, nor more than one hundred: But each county already established shall, during its continuance, have, at least one representative. An enumeration of the taxable inhabitants shall be made within three years after the first meeting of the general assembly, and within every subsequent term of seven years, in such manner as shall be, by law, directed. Until such enumeration shall be made, the city of Philadelphia and the several counties shall be, respectively, entitled to choose the same number of representatives as is now prescribed by law.

A motion was then made by Mr. Irvine, seconded by Mr. M'Lene, to insert in the said proposed section, after the words "at least one representative," the words "provided that no new county shall be established unless there be   taxable inhabitants therein."

It was moved by Mr. Pickering, seconded by Mr. Thomas Ross, to amend the said section by inserting after the words "at least one representative," the following, viz. "but no county, hereafter erected, shall be entitled to a separate representation until it contains such a number of taxable inhabitants as constitutes the ratio by which representatives are apportioned in the counties already established."

Mr. Lewis then moved, seconded by Mr. Irvine, to strike out the words contained in the section proposed by him this forenoon, viz. "already established shall, during its continuance," in order to insert the following proviso, after the word "representative." Provided, that no new county shall be erected until a sufficient number of taxable inhabitants shall be contained within the limits thereof, to entitle them to at least one representative, agreeably to the ratio which shall then be established for the city of Philadelphia and the several counties."

It was then moved by Mr. Wilson, seconded by Mr. Irvine, to add the words in the said section proposed by Mr. Lewis, viz. " already established and during their continuance."

Thereupon, On motion of Mr. Findley, seconded by Mr. Wilson, Ordered, that the further consideration of the said section, together with the several amendments, be postponed.

The fifth section of the first article of the proposed constitution coming under the consideration of the committee, viz.

V. The senate shall consist of not fewer than sixteen, nor more than thirty-two members, chosen in districts, in proportion to the number of taxable inhabitants in each district.

It was moved by Mr. Hare, seconded by Mr. Redick, to strike out the words " not fewer than sixteen, nor more than thirty-two."

A motion for an amendment was then made by Mr. Findley, seconded by Mr. M'Lene, to strike out the words contained in the said section, viz. "the senate shall consist of not fewer than sixteen, nor more than thirty-two members," and in lieu thereof to insert the following words, "the number of senators shall be in the proportion of one senator to every three representatives.

Whereupon, it was moved by Mr. Pickering, seconded by Mr Thomas Ross, to postpone the consideration of the said section, together with the several amendments proposed, in order to introduce the following as a substitute for the section under consideration, as well as the sixth section of the first article of the said proposed constitution, viz.

The number of senators shall not be less than one-fourth, nor more than one-third of the number of representatives, and chosen in districts into which the commonwealth shall, from time to time, be divided by the legislature; and the number of senators assigned to each district shall be in proportion, as nearly as may be, to its quota of public taxes; provided that no district shall be so large as to be entitled to choose more than   senators.

A motion was made by Mr. Hare, seconded by Mr. Ogden, that the committee rise, report progress in the business referred to them, and ask leave to sit again.

On the question, Will the committee agree to the motion ?

It was determined in the negative.

After a considerable debate—the same motion was renewed by Mr. Wilson, seconded by Mr. Gray.

On the question, Shall the committee now rise, report further progress in the business referred to them, and ask leave to sit again?

The members appearing to be equally divided—the chairman gave his casting vote in the affirmative, and the committee accordingly rose, reported progress and asked leave to sit again.

TUESDAY, December 29th, 1789. A. M.

The committee resumed the consideration of the fourth section of the first article of the proposed constitution, with the several amendments, postponed yesterday, and adopted the proviso moved by Mr. Lewis and Mr. Irvine, so that the said section read as follows, viz.

The number of representatives shall, at the several periods of making the enumeration in this section mentioned, be fixed by the legislature, and apportioned between the city of Philadelphia and the several counties according to the number of taxable inhabitants in each, and shall never be less than sixty, nor more than one hundred : But each county shall have, at least, one representative; provided that no new county shall be erected until a sufficient number of taxable inhabitants shall be contained within the limits thereof, to entitle them to at least one representative, agreeably to the ratio which shall then be established for the city of Philadelphia and the several counties. An enumeration of the taxable inhabitants shall be made within three years after the first meeting of the general assembly, and within every subsequent term of seven years, in such manner as shall be, by law, directed. Until such enumeration shall be made, the city of Philadelphia and the several counties shall be, respectively, entitled to choose the same number of representatives as is now prescribed by law.

Whereupon, A motion was made by Mr. Gallatin, seconded by Mr. Smilie, to re-consider the said section, as amended, in order to strike out the words "and shall never be less than sixty, nor more than one hundred :" and in lieu thereof to insert the following, viz. allowing one representative for every   taxable inhabitant, "until the whole number of representatives amounts to   which number shall then be kept forever."

On the question, Will the committee agree to re consider for the aforesaid purpose ?

It was determined in the affirmative.

It was then moved by Mr. Gallatin, seconded by Mr. Findley, to fill the blank in the said amendment with the words "twelve hundred," and to fill the second blank in the said amendment with the words "one hundred and twenty."

On motion of Mr. Lewis, seconded by Mr. Smilie, Ordered, that the further consideration of the said section, together with the several amendments, be postponed.

The fifth section of the first article of the proposed constitution, with the several amendments, recurring,

On the question, Will the committee agree to the postponement moved yesterday by Mr. Pickering, seconded by Mr. Thomas Ross, in order to take into consideration the following, as a substitute for the fifth and sixth sections of the first article of the proposed constitution, viz,

The number of senators shall not be less than one-fourth, nor more than one-third of the number of representatives, and chosen in districts into which the commonwealth shall, from time to time, be divided by the legislature; and the number of senators assigned to each district shall be in proportion, as nearly as may be, to its quota of public taxes; provided that no district shall be so large as to be entitled to choose more than   senators."

And the yeas and nays being called by Mr. Whitehill, were as follow, viz.

YEAS.

Mr. Robinson   Mr. Pickering

NAYS.

Mr. Wilson	Mr. Boyd	Mr. Hiester	Mr. J. Ross
Baker	Hand	Lower	Smilie
Roberts	Coleman	Lincoln	Gallatin
Lewis	Graff	Groscop	M'Lene
M'Kean	Atlee	Gehr	Matthews
Mifflin	Hubley	Mawhorter	Morris
Gray	Miller	Powell	Potts
Hare	Slegle	Piper	Coates
Edwards	Reed	Smith	Shoemaker
Ogden	Tyson	Snyder	Glouinger
Jenks	Pedan	Findley	Brown
Barclay	Dill	Todd	Henderson
Stout	Whitehill	Addison	Gibson
Gibbons	Irvine	Hoge	Sellers
Bull	Power	Redick	Graham 60

So it was determined in the negative.

The motion made by Mr. Findley, seconded by Mr. M'Lene, then recurring, viz.

To strike out the words "the senate shall consist of not fewer than sixteen, nor more than thirty-two members," and in lieu thereof to insert the following, viz. "the number of senators shall be in the proportion of one senator to every three representatives."

After some debate the committee rose in order to report further progress and ask leave to sit again.

WEDNESDAY, December 30, 1789. A. M.

The fourth section of the first article of the proposed constitution, as amended, together with the amendment moved yesterday by Mr. Gallatin, seconded by Mr. Smilie, recurring.

It was moved by Mr. Lewis, seconded by Mr. Potts, to insert after the words "one hundred," these words ; "and that it shall be increased at the time of making each enumeration, except the first, in the same proportion which the increase of the number of taxables shall bear to the number of representatives, until the same shall amount to one hundred."

A question was then taken, whether the committee will agree that the number of representatives shall not be fewer than sixty?

It was unanimously carried in the affirmative.

A question was taken, Shall the words "one hundred" be struck

out for the purpose of inserting the words "one hundred and twenty?"
And the yeas and nays being called by Mr. Ogden, were as follow,
viz.

YEAS.

Mr. Whitehill	Mr. Lincoln	Mr. Todd	Mr. Gallatin
Power	Piper	Addison	M'Lene
Lower	Findley	Smilie	Matthews
			12

NAYS.

Mr. Wilson	Mr. Gibbons	Mr. Dill	Mr. Morris
Baker	Bull	Irvine	Potts
Roberts	Boyd	Hiester	Coates
Lewis	Hand	Groscop	Shoemaker
M'Kean	Coleman	Gehr	Gloninger
Mifflin	Graff	Mawhorter	Brown
Gray	Atlee	Powell	Pickering
Robinson	Hubley	Smith	Henderson
Edwards	Miller	Snyder	Gibson
Ogden	Slegle	Hoge	Beale
Jenks	Reed	Redick	Sellers
Barclay	Tyson	J. Ross	Graham
Stout	Pedan		50

So it was determined in the negative.

The amendment moved by Mr. Lewis, seconded by Mr. Potts, recurring, the same was unanimously adopted.

It was then moved by Mr. Ogden, seconded by Mr. James Ross, to strike out the word "erected," in the amendment of Mr. Lewis and Mr. Irvine, of the twenty-eighth instant, and in lieu thereof to insert the following words, viz. "entitled to a separate representation."

Which was carried in the affirmative.

And thereupon, the said fourth section, as amended, agreed to as follows, viz.

Sect. IV. The number of representatives shall, at the several periods of making the enumeration in this section mentioned, be fixed by the legislature, and apportioned between the city of Philadelphia and the several counties, according to the number of taxable inhabitants in each, and shall never be less than sixty nor more than one hundred; and that it shall be increased at the time of making each enumeration, except the first, in the same proportion which the increase of the number of taxables shall bear to the then number of representatives, until the same shall amount to one hundred. But each county shall have at least one representative; provided that no new county shall be entitled to a separate representation, until a sufficient number of taxable inhabitants shall be contained within the limits thereof, to entitle them to at least one representative, agreeably to the ratio which shall then be established for the city of Philadelphia and the several counties; an enumeration of the taxable inhabitants shall be made within three years after the first meeting of the general assembly, and within every subsequent term of seven years in such manner as shall be, by law, directed. Until such enumeration shall be made, the city of Philadelphia and the several counties shall be respectively entitled to choose the same number of representatives as is now prescribed by law.

The fifth section of the first article recurring, together with the amendment proposed by Mr. Findley, seconded by Mr. M'Lene, the twenty-eighth instant.

It was moved by Mr. Smith, seconded by Mr. Miller, to postpone the consideration of the said section and the several amendments, in order to introduce the following as a substitute, viz.

That the senators shall be chosen in districts, in proportion to the number of taxable inhabitants in each district, and shall consist of members until the first enumeration, before mentioned, shall be made, when, and at the several periods of making the enumeration thereafter, the number of senators shall be fixed by the legislature, and shall never be less than one-fourth nor more than one-third of the number of representatives.

It was moved by Mr. Wilson, seconded by Mr. Findley, to postpone the further consideration of the said fifth section with the several amendments, as well as the substitute proposed by Mr. Smith and Mr. Miller, together with the sixth section of the first article of the said proposed constitution, in order to take into consideration that part of the said proposed constitution which declares "That the senators shall be chosen by electors."

On the question to agree to the postponement for the aforesaid purpose—It was determined in the negative.

And the substitute proposed by Mr. Smith, seconded by Mr. Miller, was agreed to.

The sixth section of the first article of the proposed constitution being next in order before the committee, viz.

The city of Philadelphia and the several counties shall be formed into districts, containing each, as nearly as may be, such a number of taxable inhabitants as shall be entitled to elect one senator; but where that cannot be done, then such a number of adjoining counties shall be formed into one district as shall be entitled to elect not more than three senators.

It was moved by Mr. Smilie, seconded by Mr. M'Lene, to strike out the word "three" from the said section.

Which was carried in the affirmative. And thereupon the sixth section adopted.

The seventh section of the first article of the said proposed constitution being the next in order before the committee, viz.

The citizens of the city of Philadelphia and of the several counties, qualified to elect representatives, when assembled for that purpose, shall, if occasion require, at the same time, at the same places, and in the same manner, for every representative elect two persons, resident within their city or county respectively, as electors of the senator or senators of their district.

A motion was made by Mr. James Ross, seconded by Mr. Pickering, to postpone the consideration of the seventh section in order to re-consider the sixth.

Which was carried in the affirmative.

It was then moved by Mr. Smith, seconded by Mr. Lewis, to amend the sixth section so as to read as follows, viz.

The city of Philadelphia and the several counties shall be divided into districts, any of which shall contain such a number of taxable inhabitants as shall be entitled to choose any number of senators not exceeding four; but the city or any county shall not be divided in forming such districts.

A motion was made by Mr. Hand, seconded by Mr. Boyd, to postpone the consideration of the said amendment in order to add to the said section the following words, viz. Provided that neither the city of Philadelphia nor any county shall be divided in forming such districts.

On the question, Will the committee agree to the postponement for the aforesaid purpose?

It was carried in the affirmative, and the sixth section, with the amendments, adopted as follows, viz.

The city of Philadelphia and the several counties shall be formed into districts, containing each, as nearly as may be, such a number of taxable inhabitants as shall be entitled to elect one senator; but where that cannot be done, then such a number of adjoining counties shall be formed into one district as shall be entitled to elect not more than   senators; provided that neither the city of Philadelphia nor any county shall be divided in forming a district.

The seventh section then recurring, the following motion was made by Mr. Wilson, seconded by Mr. M'Lene, viz.

Resolved, That the senators be chosen by the citizens qualified to elect representatives.

The committee then rose in order to report further progress and ask leave to sit again.

THURSDAY, December 31, 1789. A. M.

The motion made yesterday by Mr. Wilson, seconded by Mr. M'Lene, recurring, viz.

To postpone the consideration of the seventh section of the first article of the proposed constitution, in order to introduce the following resolution:

Resolved, That the senators be chosen by the citizens qualified to elect representatives.

After considerable debate thereon, the committee rose, in order to report further progress and ask leave to sit again.

FRIDAY, January 1, 1790. A. M.

Mr. Wilson's motion of the thirtieth of December, again recurring, viz.

That the senators be chosen by the citizens qualified to elect representatives.

It was thereupon moved by Mr. Wilson, seconded by Mr. Smilie, to re-consider the fifth and sixth sections of the first article of the proposed constitution, as adopted by this committee.

After considerable debate the committee rose, reported progress and obtained leave to sit again to-morrow.

SATURDAY, January 2, 1790. A. M.

The motion made yesterday by Mr. Wilson, seconded by Mr. Smilie, to re-consider the fifth and sixth sections of the first article of the proposed constitution, as adopted by this committee, again recurring.

On the question, Will the committee agree to re-consider the said fifth and sixth sections? The yeas and nays being called by Mr. Wilson, were as follow:

YEAS.

Mr. Wilson	Mr. Pedan	Mr. Mawhorter	Mr. Gallatin
Baker	Dill	Arndt	M'Lene
Gray	Whitehill	Powell	Matthews
Robinson	Power	Piper	Coates
Ogden	Hiester	Findley	Shoemaker
Jenks	Lower	Todd	Gloninger
Stout	Lincoln	Addison	Brown
Gibbons	Groscop	Hoge	Graydon
Boyd	Gehr	Redick	Henderson
Hubley	Sitgreaves	Smilie	Gibson
Reed			41

NAYS.

Mr. Roberts	Mr. T. Ross	Mr. Slegle	Mr. Morris
Lewis	Hand	Tyson	Potts
M'Kean	Coleman	Irvine	Pickering
Mifflin	Graff	Smith	Sellers
Hare	Atlee	Snyder	Graham
Bull	Miller	J. Ross	23

So it was carried in the affirmative.

Whereupon, it was moved by Mr. Wilson, seconded by Mr. Hubley, to substitute in lieu of the fifth, sixth, seventh, eighth, ninth, tenth and eleventh sections of the first article of the proposed constitution, the following, viz.

V. The senators shall be chosen for four years by the citizens of the city of Philadelphia and of each county respectively, at the same places where they shall respectively vote for representatives.

VI. The number of senators shall, at the several periods of making the enumeration mentioned in the fourth section, be fixed by the legislature, and apportioned between the districts hereinafter mentioned, and shall never be less than one-fourth, nor more than one-third; and that it shall be increased at the time of making each enumeration, except the first, in the same proportion which the increase of the number of taxables shall bear to the then number of senators, until the same shall amount to .

VII. The senators shall be chosen in districts, to be formed by the legislature; in such a manner as that the citizens of each district shall be entitled to choose   and not more than senators.   In forming districts, neither the city of Philadelphia nor any county shall be divided.

VIII. No person shall be a senator, who shall not have attained to the age of thirty years, and shall not have resided four years next before his election in the state; the last year whereof shall have been in the district for which he shall be chosen.

IX. Immediately after the senators shall be assembled in consequence of the first election, they shall be divided, as equally as may be, into four classes. The seats of the senators of the first class shall be vacated at the expiration of the first year; of the second class, at the expiration of the second year; of the third class, at the expiration of the third year; and of the fourth class, at the expiration of the fourth year; so that one-fourth may be chosen every year.

X. Until the enumeration before mentioned shall be made the number of senators shall be

The committee then rose in order to report, That they had made further progress in the business referred to them, and request leave to sit again.

MONDAY, January 4, 1790. A. M.

The fifth section of the proposed substitutes offered by Mr. Wilson, and seconded by Mr. Hubley, recurring—

It was moved by Mr. M'Lene, seconded by Mr. Thomas Ross, to amend the said section so as to read as follows, viz.

Sect. V. The senators shall be chosen for four years by the citizens of the city of Philadelphia and of each county respectively, at the same time, in the same manner and at the same places where they shall respectively vote for representatives.

A motion was then made by Mr. Lewis, seconded by Mr. Ogden, to postpone the consideration of the said section, with the proposed amendments, in order to introduce the following in lieu thereof, viz.

The number of senators shall never be less than   nor more than   and be chosen in districts into which the commonwealth shall, from time to time, be divided by the legislature; and the number of senators assigned to each district shall be, as nearly as may be, in the compound ratio of its number of taxable inhabitants and quota of public taxes; provided that no district shall be so large as to be entitled to choose more than   senators.

On the question, Will the committee agree to the postponement for the aforesaid purpose? The yeas and nays being called by Mr. Wilson, were as follow, viz.

YEAS.

Mr. Roberts	M.. Ogden	Mr. Graff	Mr. J. Ross
Lewis	Stout	Atlee	Potts
M'Kean	Bull	Miller	Pickering
Gray	Hand	Slegle	Sellers
Hare	Coleman	Smith	19

NAYS.

Mr. Wilson	Mr. Power	Mr. Piper	Mr. M'Lene
Mifflin	Hiester	Snyder	Matthews
Robinson	Lower	Findley	Coates
Edwards	Lincoln	Todd	Gloninger
T. Ross	Groscop	Addison	Brown
Boyd	Gehr	Hoge	Graydon
Hubley	Sitgreaves	Redick	Henderson
Reed	Mawhorter	Smilie	Gibson
Dill	Arndt	Gallatin	Beale
Whitehill	Powell		58

So it was determined in the negative.

The fifth section, as amended by Mr. M'Lene and Mr. Thomas Ross, recurring,

On the question, Will the committee agree to the same?

The yeas and nays being called by Mr. Thomas Ross, were as follow, viz.

YEAS.

Mr. Wilson	Mr. Whitehill	Mr. Powell	Mr. M'Lene
Baker	Power	Piper	Matthews
Robinson	Hiester	Findley	Coates
Edwards	Lower	Todd	Gloninger
T. Ross	Lincoln	Addison	Brown
Boyd	Groscop	Hoge	Graydon
Graff	Gehr	Redick	Henderson
Hubley	Sitgreaves	Smilie	Gibson
Reed	Mawhorter	Gallatin	Beale
Dill	Arndt		38

NAYS.

Mr. Roberts	Mr. Ogden	Mr. Atlee	Mr. Smith
Lewis	Stout	Miller	Snyder
M'Kean	Bull	Slegle	J. Ross
Mifflin	Hand	Tyson	Potts
Gray	Coleman	Irvine	Pickering
Hare			21

So it was carried in the affirmative.

The sixth section proposed by Mr. Wilson, seconded by Mr. Hubley, thereupon being under the consideration of the committee,

It was moved by Mr. Sitgreaves, seconded by Mr. Ogden, to postpone the consideration of the said sixth section in order to amend the same so as to read as follows, viz.

The number of senators shall, at the several periods of making the enumeration hereinbefore mentioned, be fixed by the legislature, and apportioned between the districts formed as hereinafter directed, in a ratio compounded of the number of taxable inhabitants in, and the quota of the state taxes assessed upon each district, estimating the total amount of the state taxation and the whole number of taxable inhabitants as equal to each other. Provided that the number of senators shall never exceed one-third, nor be less than one-fourth of the number of representatives.

Whereupon, On motion, the committee rose in order to report, That they had made further progress in the business referred to them, and ask leave to sit again.

TUESDAY, January 5, 1790. A. M.

The motion made yesterday by Mr. Sitgreaves, seconded by Mr. Ogden, recurring,

After considerable debate thereon, the committee rose in order to report, That they had made further progress in the business referred to them, and ask leave to sit again.

WEDNESDAY, January 6, 1790. A. M.

The motion made on the fourth day of January instant, by Mr. Sitgreaves, seconded by Mr. Ogden, again recurring,

After considerable debate thereon, the committee rose in order to report, That they had made further progress in the business referred to them, and ask leave to sit again to morrow.

THURSDAY, January 7, 1790. A. M.

The motion made on the fourth day of January, instant, by Mr. Sitgreaves, seconded by Mr. Ogden, again recurring,

After considerable debate,

On the question, Will the committee agree to the postponement ? The yeas and nays being called by Mr. Sitgreaves, were as follow, viz.

YEAS.

Mr. Baker	Mr. Edwards	Mr. Graff	Mr. Sitgreaves
Roberts	Ogden	Atlee	Potts
Lewis	Jenks	Hubley	Shoemaker
M'Kean	Stout	Miller	Pickering
Gray	Bull	Slegle	Sellers
Robinson	Hand	Tyson	Graham
Hare	Coleman		26

NAYS.

Mr. Wilson	Mr Hiester	Mr. Smith	Mr. Matthews
Mifflin	Lower	Snyder	Morris
Gibbons	Lincoln	Findley	Coates
T. Ross	Groscop	Todd	Gloninger
Boyd	Gehr	Addison	Brown
Reed	Mawhorter	Hoge	Graydon
Dill	Arndt	Redick	Henderson
Whitehill	Rhoads	Smilie	Gibson
Irvine	Powell	Gallatin	Beale
Power	Piper	M'Lene	39

So it was determined in the negative.

Whereupon, On motion, the committee rose in order to report, That they had made further progress in the business referred to them, and ask leave to sit again.

FRIDAY, January 8, 1790. A. M.

The sixth section of the substitutes moved by Mr. Wilson, seconded by Mr. M'Lene, recurring, viz.

VI. The number of senators shall, at the several periods of making the enumeration mentioned in the fourth section, be fixed by the legislature, and apportioned between the districts formed as hereinafter mentioned, and shall never be less than one-fourth nor more than one-third of the number of representatives ; and that it shall be increased at the time of making each enumeration, except the first, in the same proportion which the increase of the number of taxable inhabitants shall bear to the then number of senators.

A motion was made by Mr. Lewis, seconded by Mr. Smilie, to strike out the remainder of the said section after the word "representatives."

Which was then carried in the affirmative.

It was then moved by Mr. Gallatin, seconded by Mr. Smilie, to insert after the words "hereinafter mentioned," the following, viz. "according to the number of taxables in each."

On the question, Will the committee agree to the proposed amendment? The yeas and nays being called by Mr. Lewis, were as follow, viz.

YEAS.

Mr. Wilson	Mr. Reed	Mr. Arndt	Mr. Gallatin
Mifflin	Dill	Rhoads	M'Lene
Gibbons	Whitehill	Piper	Mathews
T. Ross	Irvine	Smith	Morris
Boyd	Power	Snyder	Potts
Hand	Hiester	Findley	Coates
Coleman	Lower	Todd	Gloninger
Graff	Lincoln	Addison	Brown
Atlee	Groscop	Hoge	Graydon
Hubley	Gehr	Redick	Henderson
Miller	Sitgreaves	J. Ross	Gibson
Slegle	Mawhorter	Smilie	Beale 48

NAYS.

Mr. Roberts	Mr. Gray	Mr. Jenks	Mr. Sellers
Lewis	Robinson	Tyson	Garham
M'Kean	Edwards	Pickering	11

So it was carried in the affirmative.

It was thereupon ordered, That the remainder of the said section be struck out.

A motion was then made by Mr. Gallatin, seconded by Mr. Smilie, to insert the following words in lieu thereof:

Provided that the number of senators shall never be less than thirty after the number of representatives shall have arisen to one hundred.

On the question, Will the committee agree to the amendment?

It was determined in the negative. and the sixth section adopted as follows, viz.

Sect. VI. The number of senators shall, at the several periods of making the enumeration mentioned in the fourth section, be fixed by the legislature, and apportioned between the districts formed as hereinafter mentioned, according to the number of taxable inhabitants in each, and shall never be less than one-fourth nor more than one-third of the number of representatives.

The seventh section coming under the consideration of the committee, it was moved by Mr. Wilson, seconded by Mr. Hand, to amend the same so as to read as follows, viz.

The senators shall be chosen from districts to be formed by the legislature in such a manner as that each district shall contain and not more than senators. In forming districts neither the city of Philadelphia nor any county shall be divided.

On the question, Will the committee agree to the same? The yeas and nays being called by Mr. Coleman, were as follow, viz.

YEAS.

Mr. Wilson	Mr. Hare	Mr. Atlee	Mr. Potts
Baker	Edwards	Hubley	Shoemaker
Roberts	Jenks	Miller	Graydon
Lewis	Gibbons	Slegle	Pickering
M'Kean	Hand	Tyson	Sellers
Mifflin	Coleman	Morris	Graham
Gray	Graff		26

NAYS.

Mr. Robinson	Mr. Lower	Mr. Smith	Mr. Gallatin
T. Ross	Lincoln	Snyder	M'Lene
Boyd	Groscop	Findley	Matthews
Reed	Gehr	Todd	Coates
Dill	Sitgreaves	Addison	Gloninger
Whitehill	Mawhorter	Hoge	Brown
Irvine	Arndt	Redick	Henderson
Power	Rhoads	J. Ross	Gibson
Hiester	Piper	Smilie	Beale 36

So it was determined in the negative.

The committee then rose in order to report, That they had made further progress in the business referred to them, and request leave to sit again.

SATURDAY, January 9, 1790. A. M.

The seventh section proposed by Mr. Wilson, seconded by Mr. M'Lene, recurring, viz.

The senators shall be chosen in districts to be formed by the legislature, in such a manner as that the citizens of each district shall be entitled to choose   and not more than   senators. In forming districts, neither the city of Philadelphia nor any county shall be divided.

It was moved by Mr. Robinson, seconded by Mr. Lewis, to strike out the words "and not more than," and in lieu thereof to insert the words "and not more than one-third nor less than one-eighth of the whole number of".

On the question, Will the committee agree to the amendment? The yeas and nays being called by Mr. Robinson, were as follow, viz.

YEAS.

Mr. Baker	Mr. Gray	Mr. Slegle	Mr. Graydon
Roberts	Robinson	Gallatin	Pickering
Lewis	Hare	Morris	Sellers
M'Kean	Edwards	Coates	Graham
Mifflin	Jenks	Shoemaker	19

NAYS.

Mr. Gibbons	Mr. Atlee	Mr. Irvine	Mr. Groscop
T. Ross	Hubley	Power	Gehr
Boyd	Reed	Heister	Sitgreaves
Hand	Dill	Lower	Arndt
Graff	Whitehill	Lincoln	Rhoads

42

NAYS.

Mr. Piper	Mr. Addison	Mr. Smilie	Mr. Brown
Smith	Hoge	M'Lene	Henderson
Snyder	Redick	Matthews	Gibson
Findley	J. Ross	Gloninger	Beale
Todd			37

So it was determined in the negative.

The original section, moved by Mr. Wilson, seconded by Mr. M'Lene, again recurring—

It was moved by Mr. M'Lene, seconded by Mr. Brown, to fill the first blank with the word "one," and the second with the word "four."

A motion was then made by Mr. Gallatin, seconded by Mr. Robinson, to fill the first blank with the word "two."

Which was determined in the negative.

And the motion made by Mr. M'Lene, seconded by Mr. Brown, adopted.

It was then moved by Mr. James Ross, seconded by Mr. Smith, to amend the said seventh section so as to read as follows, viz.

Sect. VII. The senate shall be cho-en in districts to be formed by the legislature, containing each, as nearly as may be, such a number of taxable inhabitants as shall be entitled to elect one senator; but where that cannot be done, then such number of adjoining counties shall be formed into one district as shall be entitled to elect not more than four senators: Provided that neither the city of Philadelphia, nor any county, shall be divided in forming a district.

On the question, Will the committee agree to the section, as amended? The yeas and nays being called by Mr. Thomas Ross, were as follow, viz.

YEAS.

Mr. T. Ross	Mr. Dill	Mr. Sitgreaves	Mr. Hoge
Boyd	Whitehill	Arndt	J. Ross
Haad	Irvine	Rhoads	Smilie
Coleman	Power	Piper	M'Lene
Graff	Hiester	Smith	Matthews
Atlee	Lower	Snyder	Gloninger
Hubley	Lincoln	Findley	Brown
Slegle	Groscop	Todd	Gibson
Reed	Gehr	Addison	Beale
Tyson			87

NAYS.

Mr. Baker	Mr. Gray	Mr. Gallatin	Mr. Pickering
Roberts	Robinson	Morris	Henderson
Lewis	Hare	Coates	Sellers
M'Kean	Jenks	Shoemaker	Graham
Mifflin	Gibbons	Graydon	19

So it was determined in the affirmative, and the seventh section, as amended, adopted.

The eighth section, proposed by Mr. Wilson, and seconded by Mr. M'Lene, coming under the consideration of the committee, viz.

No person shall be a senator who shall not have attained to the age of thirty years, and who shall not have resided four years next before his election in the state; the last year whereof shall have been in the district for which he shall be chosen.

It was moved by Mr. Smilie, seconded by Mr. Hand, to strike out the word "thirty," and in lieu thereof to insert the words "twenty-one."

A motion was then made Mr. Hand, seconded by Mr. Smith, to insert the words "twenty-five."

Which was carried in the affirmative.

It was thereupon moved by Mr. Hare, seconded by Mr. Graydon, to amend the said section so as to read as follows, viz.

No person shall be a senator who shall not have attained to the age of twenty five years, and who shall not have resided four years in the state within seven years next before his election.

Which was determined in the negative.

It was then moved by Mr. Henderson, seconded by Mr. Piper, to amend the said section so as to read as follows, viz.

No person shall be a senator who shall not have attained to the age of twenty five years, and have been four years a citizen of this state, and have resided four years next before his election in the United States; the last year whereof shall have been within the district for which he shall be chosen.

Which was determined in the negative.

A motion was then made by Mr. Smith, seconded by Mr. Thomas Ross, to amend the eighth section so as to read as follows, viz.

No person shall be a senator who shall not have attained to the age of twenty-five years, and have been a citizen of this state four years next before his election; the last year whereof he shall have been resident in the district for which he shall be chosen.

Which was determined in the negative, and the eighth section, as amended, adopted as follows, viz.

Sect. VIII. No person shall be a senator who shall not have attained to the age of twenty-five years, and who shall not have been a citizen and inhabitant of the state four years next before his election; the last year whereof shall have been in the district for which he shall be chosen.

The ninth section proposed by Mr. Wilson coming under the consideration of the committee, the same was adopted as follows, viz.

Sect IX. Immediately after the senators shall be assembled in consequence of the first election, they shall be divided by lot, as equally as may be, into four classes. The seats of the senators of the first class shall be vacated at the expiration of the first year; of the second class, at the expiration of the second year; of the third class, at the expiration of the third year; and of the fourth class, at the expiration of the fourth year; so that one fourth may be chosen every year.

The tenth section proposed by Mr. Wilson coming under the consideration of the committee, viz.

Until the enumeration before mentioned shall be made, the number of senators shall be

It was moved by Mr. Sitgreaves, seconded by Mr. Addison, to fill the blank with the words "twenty-three." Whereupon, On motion,

Ordered, That the further consideration of the said tenth section be postponed.

The thirteenth section of the constitution reported by the committee of nine coming under the consideration of this committee, viz.

The general assembly shall meet at least once in every year, d such meeting shall be on the   Tuesday of November.

It was moved by Mr. Findley, seconded by Mr. Smith, to   e out the words " Tuesday of November," and to insert the   ʺ first Tuesday of December."

Which was carried in the affirmative.

A motion was then made by Mr. Lewis, seconded by Mr. Tl ....as Ross, to add the following words, viz. " until the same shall be altered by the legislature."

Which was determined in the negative.

And the said section was adopted by this committee as the eleventh section of the first article of the said proposed constitution, as follows, viz.

Sect. XI. The general assembly shall meet at least once in every year; and such meeting shall be on the first Tuesday of December.

The fourteenth section of the first article of the said proposed constitution coming under consideration, the same was adopted as the twelfth section, as follows, viz.

Sect. XII. Each house shall choose its speaker and other officers;. and the senate shall also choose a speaker *pro tempore*, when the speaker shall exercise the office of governor.

The committee then rose in order to report, That they had made further progress in the business referred to them, and ask leave to sit again.

MONDAY, January 11, 1790. *A. M.*

The fifteenth section of the proposed constitution, as reported by the committee of nine, being under the consideration of this committee, it was moved by Mr. Lewis, seconded by Mr. M'Lene, to amend the same so as to read as follows, viz.

Sect. XIII. Each house shall be the judge of the qualifications of its own members; but in case of contested elections the same shall be judged of and determined by a committee, to be selected from the house in such manner as shall be, by law, directed. And a majority of each house shall constitute a quorum to do business; but a smaller number may adjourn from day to day, and may be authorised to compel the attendance of absent members in such manner, and under such penalties, as the house may provide.

On the question, Will the committee agree to the said amendment? It was carried in the affirmative, and the said section adopted as the thirteenth section of the first article of the said proposed constitution.

The sixteenth section of the first article of the proposed constitution, as reported by the committee of nine, coming under the consideration of this committee, viz.

Each house may determine the rules of its proceedings, punish its members for disorderly behaviour, and, with the concurrence of two-thirds, expel a member; and shall have all other powers necessary for either branch of a free legislature.

It was moved by Mr. Gallatin, seconded by Mr. Smilie, to strike out the words " and with the concurrence of two-thirds, expel a member," and in lieu thereof to insert the following words, viz. " either by censure or expulsion; provided that no member be expelled without the concurrence of two-thirds."

Whereupon, on motion of Mr. Smilie, seconded by Mr. Findley, Ordered, That the further consideration of the said section, together with the proposed amendment, be postponed.

The committee then rose in order to report, that they had made further progress in the business referred to them, and ask leave to sit again to-morrow.

TUESDAY, January 12, 1790. A. M.

' The sixteenth section of the constitution reported by the committee of nine, together with the amendment proposed by Mr. Gallatin, seconded by Mr. Smilie, recurring

It was moved by Mr. M'Lene, seconded by Mr. Gallatin, to insert after the words " expel a member, " " but not a second time for the same cause." Which was carried in the affirmative.

The section, with the amendment proposed yesterday, then recurring, a division of the question on the amendment was called for and agreed to.

Whereupon, on the question, Will the committee agree to the first part of the amendment proposed by Mr. Gallatin and Mr. Smilie, viz. " either by censure or expulsion?"

The yeas and nays being called by Mr. Gallatin, were as follow, viz.

YEAS.

Mr. Edwards	Mr. Lincoln	Mr. Todd	Mr. Gallatin
Boyd	Powell	Addison	M'Lene
Whitehill	Piper	Hoge	Matthews
Power	Findley	Smilie	Gloninger 16

NAYS.

Mr. Wilson	Mr. Hand	Mr. Irvine	Mr. J. Ross
Baker	Coleman	Hiester	Morris
Roberts	Graff	Lower	Coates
Lewis	Atlee	Groscop	Shoemaker
M'Kean	Hubley	Gehr	Brown
Mifflin	Breckbill	Sitgreaves	Graydon
Gray	Miller	Arndt	Pickering
Robinson	Slegle	Rhoads	Henderson
Hare	Reed	Smith	Gibson
Stout	Tyson	Snyder	Sellers
Gibbons	Dill	Redick	Graham
T. Ross			45

So it was determined in the negative.

The original section reported by the committee of nine, then recurring as amended.

It was moved by Mr. Sitgreaves, seconded by Mr. Lewis, to insert after the word " members," the words following, viz. " and others for breach of privilege or."

On the question, Will the committee agree to the amendment? It was determined in the negative.

A motion was then made by Mr. Findley, seconded by Mr. Whitehill, to strike out the words " punish its members for disorderly behaviour." Which was determined in the negative.

It was moved by Mr. Hare, seconded by Mr. Wilson, to amend the said section so as to read as follows, viz.

Sect. XIV. Each house may determine the rules of its proceedings, punish its members for disorderly behaviour; and with the concurrence of two-thirds, expel a member, but not a second time for the same cause, and shall have all other powers necessary for either branch of the legislature of a free state.

Which was carried in the affirmative.

On the question, Will the committee adopt the same as the fourteenth section of the first article of the proposed constitution?

The yeas and nays being called by Mr. Smilie, were as follow, viz.

YEAS.

Mr. Wilson	Mr. Boyd	Mr. Hiester	Mr. Redick
Baker	Hand	Lower	J. Ross
Roberts	Coleman	Lincoln	Morris
Lewis	Graff	Groscop	Coates
M'Kean	Atlee	Gehr	Shoemaker
Mifflin	Hubley	Arndt	Gloninger
Gray	Breckbill	Rhoads	Brown
Robinson	Miller	Powell	Graydon
Hare	Slegle	Smith	Pickering
Edwards	Reed	Snyder	Henderson
Stout	Tyson	Todd	Gibson
Gibbons	Dill	Addison	Sellers
T. Ross	Irvine	Hoge	Graham 52

NAYS.

Mr. Whitehill	Mr. Piper	Mr. Smilie	Mr. M'Lene
Power	Findley	Gallatin	Matthews
Sitgreaves			9

So it was carried in the affirmative.

The seventeenth section of the first article of the proposed constitution, as reported by the committee of nine, being under the consideration of this committee, viz.

Each house shall keep a journal of its proceedings, and from time to time publish them, excepting such parts as may in their judgment, require secrecy: and the yeas and nays of the members of either house, on any question, shall at the desire of   be entered on the journal.

It was moved by Mr. Sitgreaves, seconded by Mr. Boyd, to fill the blank with the words " any five of them in the representatives and two in the senate." Which was determined in the negative.

A motion was then made by Mr. Lewis, seconded by Mr. Whitehill, to fill the blank with the words "any two of them."

On the question, Will the committee agree to the same? It was carried in the affirmative.

It was moved by Mr. Addison, seconded by Mr. Hoge, to strike out the word "their," and in lieu thereof to insert the word " the," and after the word " judgment," to insert the words " of both." Which was determined in the negative.

A motion was then made by Mr. M'Lene, seconded by Mr. Smilie, to add the following words to the said section, viz. " with their reasons at large."

On the question, Will the committee agree to the same?
The yeas and nays being called by Mr, Wilson, were as follow, viz.

YEAS.

Mr. Lewis	Mr. Lincoln	Mr. Findley	Mr. Gallatin
Edwards	Groscop	Todd	M'Lene
Whitehill	Powell	Smilie	Matthews
Lower	Piper		14

NAYS.

Mr. Wilson	Mr. Hand	Mr. Power	Mr. Morris
Baker	Coleman	Gehr	Coates
Roberts	Graff	Sitgreaves	Shoemaker
M'Kean	Atlee	Arndt	Gloninger
Mifflin	Hubley	Rhoads	Brown
Gray	Breckbill	Smith	Graydon
Robinson	Miller	Snyder	Pickering
Hare	Slegle	Addison	Henderson
Stout	Reed	Hoge	Gibson
Gibbons	Tyson	Redick	Sellers
T. Ross	Dill	J. Ross	Graham
Boyd	Irvine		46

So it was determined in the negative.

It was moved by Mr. Edwards, seconded by Mr. Smilie, to strike out the words " from time to time," and in lieu thereof to insert the word "and," and to insert after the words " publish them," the word " weekly." Which was determined in the affirmative.

The seventeenth section, as reported by the committee of nine, was then adopted as the fifteenth section of the first article of the proposed constitution, as follows, viz.

Sect. XV. Each house shall keep a journal of its proceedings, and publish them weekly, excepting such parts as may, in their judgment, require secrecy: And the yeas and nays of the members, of either house, on any question, shall, at the desire of any two of them, be entered on the journal.

The eighteenth section, reported by the committee of nine, coming under the consideration of this committee, the same was adopted as the sixteenth section of the first article of the said proposed constitution, as follows, viz.

Sect. XVI. The doors of each house shall be open, unless when the business shall be such, as in their judgment, ought to be kept secret.

The nineteenth section of the first article of the proposed constitution, reported by the committee of nine, being under the consideration of this committee, the same was adopted as the seventeenth section of the said first article, as follows, viz.

Sect. XVII. Neither house shall, without the consent of the other, adjourn for more than three days, nor to any other place than that in which the two houses shall be sitting.

The twentieth section of the first article of the said proposed constitution being under consideration, the same was adopted as the eighteenth section of the said article, viz.

Sect. XVIII. The senators and representatives shall receive a compensation for their services to be ascertained by law, and paid out of the treasury of the commonwealth. They shall in all cases, except treason, felony and breach of the peace be privileged from arrest during their attendance at the session of the respective houses, and in going to and returning from the same; and for any speech or debate in either house they shall not be questioned in any other place.

The twenty first section reported by the committee of nine, being then under consideration, it was moved by Mr. James Ross, seconded by Mr. Findley, to amend the said section so as to read as follows, viz.

Sect. XIX. No senator or representative shall, during the time for which he was elected, be appointed to any civil office, under the authority of this commonwealth, which shall have been created, or the emoluments of which shall have been increased, during such time; and no member of congress or other person holding any office, except in the militia, under this commonwealth, or the United States, shall be a member of either house during his continuance in congress or in office.

On the question, Will the committee agree to the amendment? It was carried in the affirmative, and, with the amendment, adopted as the ninteenth section of the first article of the said proposed constitution.

The twenty-second section of the said first article, reported by the committee of nine, coming under the consideration of this committee, the same was adopted as the twentieth section of the said article, viz.

Sect. XX. When vacancies happen in either house, the speaker of that house shall issue writs of election to fill such vacancies.

It was then moved by Mr. Sitgreaves, seconded by Mr. Edwards, to re-consider the eighteenth section of the first article adopted by this committee, in order to introduce the following amendment; to insert after the words "and paid," the following, viz. " to the representatives out of the treasury of the city or proper county, and to the senators by a rateable contribution from the treasuries of the counties which form the districts by which they are respectively chosen, except the travelling charges which shall be paid."

On the question, Will the committee agree to re-consider for the aforesaid purpose?

The yeas and nays being called by Mr. Sitgreaves, were as follow, viz.

YEAS.

Mr. Roberts	Mr. Stout	Mr. Arndt	Mr. Brown
Gray	Graff	Morris	Sellers
Hare	Breckbill	Shoemaker	Graham
Edwards	Sitgreaves	Gloninger	15

NAYS.

Mr. Wilson	Mr. Hand	Mr. Whitehill	Mr. Powell
Baker	Coleman	Irvine	Piper
Lewis	Atlee	Power	Smith
M'Kean	Hubley	Hiester	Snyder
Mifflin	Miller	Lower	Findley
Robinson	Slegle	Lincoln	Todd
Gibbons	Reed	Groscop	Addison
T. Ross	Tyson	Gehr	Hoge
Boyd	Dill	Rhoads	Redick

NAYS.

Mr. J. Ross	Mr. M'Lene	Mr. Graydon	Mr. Henderson
Smilie	Matthews	Pickering	Gibson
Gallatin	Coates		46

So it was determined in the negative.

The twenty-third section of the first article of the proposed constitution being under the consideration of this committee, viz.

Sect. XXI. All bills for raising revenue shall originate in the house of representatives; but the senate may propose or concur with amendments, as in other bills.

On the question, Will the committee adopt the same as the twenty-first section of the said article?

The yeas and nays being called by Mr. Edwards, were as follow, viz.

YEAS.

Mr. Wilson	Mr. Hubley	Mr. Groscop	Mr. Redick
Roberts	Breckbill	Gehr	J. Ross
M'Kean	Miller	Sitgreaves	Smilie
Gray	Slegle	Arndt	M'Lene
Hare	Reed	Rhoads	Matthews
Stout	Tyson	Powell	Morris
Gibbons	Dill	Piper	Gloninger
T. Ross	Whitchill	Smith	Brown
Boyd	Irvine	Snyder	Graydon
Hand	Power	Findley	Henderson
Coleman	Hiester	Todd	Gibson
Graff	Lower	Addison	Sellers
Atlee	Lincoln	Hoge	Graham 52

NAYS.

Mr. Baker	Mr. Robinson	Mr. Gallatin	Mr. Shoemaker
Mifflin	Edwards	Coates	Pickering 8

So it was determined in the affirmative.

The twenty-fourth section of the first article of the said proposed constitution being under consideration, the same was adopted as the twenty-second section of the said article, viz.

Sect. XXII. No money shall be drawn from the treasury, but in consequence of appropriations made by law.

The committee then rose in order to report further progress in the business referred to them, and request leave to sit again.

WEDNESDAY, January 13, 1790. A M.

The twenty-fifth section of the first article of the proposed constitution, reported by the committee of nine, being under the consideration of this committee,

A motion was made by Mr. Sitgreaves, seconded by Mr. Hoge, to strike out the words "three fifths," and in lieu thereof to insert, in the respective places, the words "a majority of the whole number."

It was then moved by Mr. Findley, seconded by Mr. Gallatin, to adjourn the debates on the twenty-fifth section now under consideration, as well as the twenty-sixth section of the same article, in order to

43

take into consideration the second article of the said proposed constitution.

Which was carried in the affirmative, and thereupon the first section of the second article of the said proposed constitution being under consideration, viz.

The supreme executive power of this commonwealth shall be vested in a governor.

It was moved by Mr. Findley, seconded by Mr. Addison, to add after the word " governor," the words "and council."

On the question, Will the committee agree to the amendment ?

The yeas and nays being called by Mr. Thomas Ross, were as follow, viz.

YEAS.

Mr. Boyd	Mr. Lincoln	Mr. Todd	Mr. Smilie
Whitehill	Gehr	Addison	Gallatin
Power	Powell	·Hoge	M'Lene
Hiester	Piper	Redick	Matthews
Lower	Findley	J. Ross	Beale 20

NAYS.

Mr. Wilson	Mr. Stout	Mr. Reed	Mr. Morris
Baker	Gibbons	Tyson .	Coates
Roberts	T. Ross	Pedan	Shoemaker
Lewis	Hand	, Dill	Gloninger
M'Kean	Coleman	Irvine	Brown
Mifflin	Graff	Groscop	Graydon
Gray	Atlee	Sitgreaves	·Pickering
Robinson	Hubley	Arndt	Henderson
Hare	Breckbill .	Smith	Gibson
Edwards	Miller	Snyder	Sellers
Barclay	Slegle		42

So it was determined in the negative, and the original section adopted as follows, viz.

Section I. The supreme executive power of this commonwealth shall be vested in a governor.

The committee then rose in order to report, that they had made further progress in the business referred to them, and request leave to sit again.

THURSDAY, January 14, 1790. *A. M.*

The second section of the second article of the proposed constitution being under the consideration of this committee.

It was moved by Mr. Addison, seconded by Mr. Matthews, to post-pone the consideration of the said section in order to resume the consideration of the tenth section, proposed by Mr. Wilson, seconded by Mr. M'Lene, and postponed on the ninth day of January, instant.

Which was carried in the affirmative.

And the said tenth section being then under the consideration of this committee, viz. " Until the enumeration before mentioned shall be made the number of senators shall be   " as well as the motion made by Mr. Sitgreaves, seconded by Mr. Addison, to fill the blank with the words " twenty-three."

It was then moved by Mr. Wilson, seconded by Mr. Tyson, to fill the blank with the word " eighteen."

A motion was made by Mr. Lewis, seconded by Mr. Wilson, to adjourn the debates on the several amendments proposed to the said tenth section in order to re-consider the fourth section of the first article of the said proposed constitution.

Whereupon, on motion of Mr. James Ross, seconded by Mr. Addison, to resume the consideration of the twenty-fifth section of the first article of the proposed constitution, with the amendments postponed yesterday.

It was determined in the affirmative, and the said twenty-fifth section being under consideration.

The motion made by Mr. Sitgreaves, seconded by Mr. Hoge, recurring, viz. To strike out the words " three-fifths," and in lieu thereof to insert, in their respective places, the words "a majority of the whole number."

On the question, Will the committee agree to the said amendment?

The yeas and nays being called by Mr. Sitgreaves, were as follow, viz.

YEAS.

Mr. Whitehill	Mr. Lincoln	Mr. Piper	Mr. Hoge
Power	Groscop	Todd	Smilie
Lower	Sitgreaves	Addison	Matthews 12

NAYS.

Mr. Wilson	Mr. Gibbons	Mr. Dill	Mr. M'Lene
Baker	T. Ross	Irvine	Morris
Roberts	Boyd	Gehr	Coates
Lewis	Hand	Arndt	Shoemaker
M'Kean	Coleman	Rhoads	Gloninger
Mifflin	Graff	Powel	Graydon
Gray	Atlee	Smith	Pickering
Robinson	Hubley	Snyder	Henderson
Hare	Breckbill	Findley	Gibson
Edwards	Miller	Redick	Beale
Jenks	Slegle	J. Ross	Sellers
Barclay	Reed	Gallatin	Graham
Stout	Tyson		50

So it was determined in the negative.

It was then moved by Mr. Wilson, seconded by Mr. James Ross, to strike out the words " three-fifths," and in lieu thereof to insert, in the respective places, the words " two-thirds."

On the question, Will the committee agree to the same?

The yeas and nays being called by Mr. Wilson, were as follow, viz.

YEAS.

Mr. Wilson	Mr. Robinson	Mr. T. Ross	Mr. Miller
Baker	Hare	Hand	Slegle
Roberts	Edwards	Coleman	Tyson
Lewis	Jenks	Graff	Pedan
M'Kean	Barclay	Atlee	Sitgreaves
Mifflin	Stout	Hubley	Arndt
Gray	Gibbons	Breckbill	Rhoads

YEAS.

Mr. Piper	Mr. Gallatin	Mr. Pickering	Mr. Sellers
Snyder	Morris	Gibson	Graham
J. Ross	Coates		30

NAYS.

Mr. Boyd	Mr. Lincoln	Mr. Todd	Mr. Matthews
Reed	Groscop	Addison	Shoemaker
Dill	Gehr	Hoge	Gloninger
Whitehill	Powell	Redick	Graydon
Irvine	Smith	Smilie	Henderson
Power	Findley	M'Lene	Beale
Lower			25

So it was determined in the affirmative, and the amendment adopted.

A motion was then made by Mr. Lewis, seconded by Mr. Edwards, to strike out the word " not" before the words " be a law," and to add the following, viz. " unless sent back within three days after their next meeting." Which was carried in the affirmative.

And the said twenty-fifth section, with the several amendments, adopted as the twenty third section of the said proposed constitution, as follows, viz.

Sect. XXIII. Every bill, which shall have passed the house of representatives and the senate, shall before it become a law, be presented to the governor. If he approve, he shall sign it; but if he shall not approve it, he shall return it, with his objections, to that house in which it shall have originated, who shall enter the objections at large upon their journal, and proceed to re-consider it. If, after such re-consideration, two-thirds of that house shall agree to pass the bill, it shall be sent, together with the objections, to the other house, by which it shall likewise be re-considered, and if approved by two-thirds of that house it shall become a law. But in all such cases, the votes of both houses shall be determined by yeas and nays, and the names of the persons voting for and against the bill shall be entered on the journals of each house respectively. If any bill shall not be returned by the governor within ten days (Sundays excepted) after it shall have been presented to him, the same shall be a law in like manner as if he had signed it; unless the general assembly, by their adjournment, prevent its return, in which case it shall be a law, unless sent back within three days after their next meeting.

The twenty-sixth section of the first article of the proposed constitution being under consideration, it was unanimously agreed to strike out the words " three-fifths," and in lieu thereof to insert " two-thirds."

On the question, Will the committee adopt the said section as amended, as the twenty-fourth section of the first article of the said proposed constitution?

The yeas and nays being called by Mr. Shoemaker, were as follow viz.

YEAS.

Mr. Baker	Mr. Mifflin	Mr. Hare	Mr. Stout
Lewis	Gray	Jenks	Gibbons
M'Kean	Robinson	Barclay	Boyd

YEAS.

Mr. Hand   Mr. Slegle   Mr. Arndt   Mr. Pickering
Coleman   Reed   Rhoads   Henderson
Graff   Tyson   Snyder   Gibson
Atlee   Pedan   Hoge   Sellers
Hubley   Dill   Redick   Graham
Miller   Sitgreaves   J. Ross   35

NAYS.

Mr. Wilson   Mr. Power   Mr. Smith   Mr. Matthews
Roberts   Hiester   Findley   Morris
Edwards   Lower   Todd   Coates
T. Ross   Groscop   Addison   Shoemaker
Breckbill   Gehr   Smilie   Gloninger
Whitehill   Powell   Gallatin   Beale
Irvine   Piper   M'Lene   27

So it was determined in the affirmative, and the said section adopted as follows, viz.

Sect. XXIV. Every order, resolution or vote, to which the concurrence of the senate and house of representatives may be necessary (except on a question of adjournment) shall be presented to the governor, and before the same shall take effect, be approved by him; or, being disapproved by him, shall be re-passed by two-thirds of the senate and house of representatives, according to the rules and limitations prescribed in case of a bill.

Whereupon, on motion of Mr. James Ross, seconded by Mr. M'Lene, Ordered, that the secretary procure two copies of the several sections of the first article of the said proposed constitution to be printed for the use of each member.

The committee then rose in order to report, that they had made further progress in the business referred to them, and ask leave to sit again.

FRIDAY. January 15, 1790, A. M.

The second section of the second article of the proposed constitution, postponed yesterday, recurring, viz.

He shall hold his office during the term of three years; and shall be chosen on the   Tuesday of October in every third year, by the citizens throughout the commonwealth, at the places where they shall respectively vote for representatives.

It was, on motion of Mr. Hand, unanimously agreed to fill the blank in the said section with the word "second."

A motion was then made by Mr. Sitgreaves, seconded by Mr. Edwards, to add the following words to the said section, viz. "But if it should so happen that no person should have a majority of all the votes given at any election for governor, or if any two or more persons should be highest and equal in votes, in such case the general assembly shall by joint ballot of both houses, elect one of those two who shall be highest in votes, at such election, to be governor for the ensuing three years."

It was moved by Mr. Addison, seconded by Mr. Gallatin, to strike out of Mr. Sitgreaves' amendment the whole preceding the words "if any two or more." Which was carried in the affirmative.

A motion was then made by Mr. James Ross, seconded by Mr. Addison, to strike out the word "ballot," contained in the said amendment proposed by Mr. Sitgreaves, and in lieu thereof to insert the word "vote."

On the question, Will the committee agree to strike out the word " ballot" for the aforesaid purpose?

The yeas and nays being called by Mr. Wilson, were as follow, viz.

YEAS.

Mr. Wilson	Mr. Boyd	Mr. Irvine	Mr. Redick
Baker	Hand	Power	J. Ross
Roberts	Coleman	Hiester	Gallatin
M'Kean	Atlee	Groscop	Matthews
Mifflin	Hubley	Gehr	Morris
Gray	Breckbill	Rhoads	Brown
Robinson	Miller	Piper	Graydon
Jenks	Slegle	Smith	Pickering
Barclay	Reed	Snyder	Henderson
Stout	Tyson	Findley	Gibson
Gibbons	Pedan	Addison	Sellers
T. Ross	Dill	Hoge	Graham 48

NAYS.

Mr. Lewis	Mr. Whitehill	Mr. Arndt	Mr. M'Lene
Hare	Lower	Powell	Coates
Edwards	Lincoln	Todd	Shoemaker
Graff	Sitgreaves	Smilie	Gloninger 16

So it was carried in the affirmative, and the said second section adopted as follows, viz.

Sect. II. He shall hold his office during the term of three years; and shall be chosen on the second Tuesday of October in every third year, by the citizens throughout the commonwealth, at the places where they shall respectively vote for representatives: But if any two or more persons should be highest and equal in votes at any election for governor, in such case the general assembly shall, by joint vote, elect one of them to be governor for the ensuing three years.

The third section of the second article of the said proposed constitution being under consideration, viz.

He shall not be capable of holding his office longer than nine years successively; nor shall he be capable of being elected again till three years after the nine successive years shall have expired.

It was moved by Mr. M'Lene, seconded by Mr. Redick, to strike out the words " nine years successively," and in lieu thereof to insert the following, viz. " six years in any term of nine years."

A motion was then made by Mr. Robinson, seconded by Mr. Graydon, to strike out the word " nine," and in lieu thereof to insert the word "twelve." Which was determined in the negative.

The question being taken on the motion made by Mr. M'Lene, seconded by Mr. Redick, it was determined in the negative.

A motion was then made by Mr. Robinson, seconded by Mr. Smilie, to amend the said third section of the second article of the proposed constitution so as to read as follows, viz.

He shall not be capable of holding his office longer than nine years in any term of twelve years.

On the question, Will the committee agree to the same?
The yeas and nays being called by Mr. Wilson, were as follow, viz

YEAS.

Mr. Mifflin	Mr. Miller	Mr. Groscop	Mr. J. Ross
Robinson	Slegle	Gehr	Smilie
Hare	Reed	Rhoads	Gallatin
Edwards	Tyson	Powell	M'Lene
Jenks	Pedan	Piper	Matthews
Barclay	Dill	Smith	Morris
Stout	Whitehill	Snyder	Coates
Gibbons	Irvine	Findley	Shoemaker
T. Ross	Power	Todd	Gloninger
Boyd	Hiester	Addison	Brown
Hand	Lower	Hoge	Henderson
Coleman	Lincoln	Redick	Gibson
Breckbill			49

NAYS.

Mr. Wilson	Mr. M'Kean	Mr. Hubley	Mr. Pickering
Baker	Gray	Sitgreaves	Sellers
Roberts	Graff	Arndt	Graham
Lewis	Atlee	Graydon	15

So it was carried in the affirmative.

The committee then rose, reported progress and asked leave to sit again.

SATURDAY, January 16, 1790. *A. M.*

The fourth section of the second article of the proposed constitution, reported by the committee of nine, being under consideration.

A motion was made by Mr. Hand, seconded by Mr. James Ross to amend the same so as to read as follows, viz.

Sect. IV. He must be, at least, thirty years of age; and must have been a citizen and inhabitant of this state seven years next before his election. Provided, That no person absent on public business of this state, or of the United States, shall thereby be disqualified.

On the question, Will the committee agree to the section as amended? It was carried in the affirmative.

The fifth section of the said article being under consideration, a motion was made by Mr. James Ross, seconded by Mr. Edwards, to amend the said section so as to read as follows, viz.

Sect. V. No person shall be capable of exercising the office of governor who at the same time, shall be a member of congress, or hold any other office under this state, or any office under the United States.

On the question, Will the committee agree to the said section as amended?

It was carried in the affirmative.

The sixth section of the second article of the said proposed constitution being under the consideration of this committee, the same was adopted as follows, viz.

Sect. VI The governor shall, at stated times, receive for his services a compensation, which shall neither be increased nor diminished during the period for which he shall have been elected.

The seventh section of the said article being under consideration, the same was unanimously adopted as follows, viz.

Sect. VII. He shall be commander in chief of the army and navy of this commonwealth and of the militia, except when they shall be called into the actual service of the United States.

The eighth section of the said article being then under consideration, viz.

He shall appoint the chancellor, judges, prothonotaries, clerks, and all other officers of this commonwealth, whose offices are established by this constitution, or shall be established by law, and whose appointments are not herein otherwise provided for; but no person shall be appointed to an office within any county, who shall not have resided therein one year next before his appointment.

It was moved by Mr. Edwards, seconded by Mr. Brown, to strike out the words "the chancellor, judges, prothonotaries, clerks, and," and the word "other" before the word "officers."

Which was carried in the affirmative, and the section, as amended, agreed to.

A motion was then made by Mr. James Ross, seconded by Mr. Hoge, to add the following words to the said section, viz. *No member of congress from this state, nor any person holding or exercising any office of trust or profit under the United States, shall, at the same time, hold and exercise any office whatever in the state.*

Whereupon, On motion of Mr. Smilie, seconded by Mr. Edwards, Ordered, that the debates on the said eighth section be adjourned until Tuesday next.

The ninth section of the said article being under consideration, the same was adopted as follows, viz.

Sect. IX. The governor shall commission all the officers of this commonwealth.

A motion was made by Mr. Wilson, seconded by Mr. Thomas Ross, to insert the following as the tenth section of the said proposed constitution, viz.

Sect. X. He shall have power to remit fines, and grant reprieves and pardons for crimes and offences, except in cases of impeachment.

It was then moved by Mr. Sitgreaves, seconded by Mr. Boyd, to insert before the word "impeachment" the words "treason and."

Which was determined in the negative.

And the said section adopted.

The tenth section of the proposed constitution, as reported by the committee of nine, being under consideration, the same was adopted as the eleventh section of the second article, viz.

Sect. XI. He may require the opinion, in writing, of the officers in each of the executive departments upon any subject relating to the duties of their respective offices.

The eleventh section of the proposed constitution, reported by the committee of nine, being under consideration, the same was adopted as the twelfth section of the second article, viz.

Sect. XII. He shall, from time to time, give to the general assembly information of the state of the commonwealth, and recommend to their consideration such measures as he shall judge necessary or expedient.

The twelfth section of the second article of the proposed constitution being under consideration,

It was moved by Mr. Addison, seconded by Mr. Gallatin, to amend the same so as to read as follows, viz.

He may, on extraordinary occasions, convene the general assembly, and in case of disagreement between the two houses with respect to the time of adjournment, he may adjourn them to such time as he shall think proper.

A motion was made by Mr Sitgreaves, seconded by Mr. M'Lene, to add the following words to the said section, viz. "not exceeding ninety days."

A motion was then made by Mr. Lewis, seconded by Mr. Henderson, to insert, in lieu of the words "ninety days," the words "four months."

Which was carried in the affirmative.

And the said section adopted as the thirteenth section of the said second article, as follows, viz.

Sect. XIII. He may, on extaordinary occasions, convene the general assembly, and in case of disagreement between the two houses with respect to the time of adjournment, he may adjourn them to such time as he shall think proper, not exceeding four months.

The thirteenth section of the second article of the said proposed constitution being under consideration, the same was adopted as the fourteenth section, as follows, viz.

Sect. XIV. He shall take care that the laws be faithfully executed.

The fourteenth section of the said article being under consideration, the same was, on motion of Mr. Pickering, seconded by Mr. Wilson, adopted as follows, viz.

Sect. XV. In case of the death or resignation of the governor, or of his removal from office, it shall devolve on the speaker of the senate until the next annual election of representatives, when another governor shall be chosen in the manner hereinbefore mentioned.

The fifteenth section of the said article of the said proposed constitution being under consideration, viz.

The state treasurer shall be appointed in the manner prescribed by the twenty-fourth section of the first article of this constitution : All other officers in the treasury department, election officers, officers relating to the poor and highways, constables and other township officers shall be appointed in such manner as shall be directed by law.

It was moved by Smilie, seconded by Mr. Lewis, to amend the first sentence of the said section so as to read as follows, viz. "the state treasurer shall be appointed by the joint vote of both houses."

Which was carried in the affirmative.

The following amendment was then moved by Mr. Hubley, seconded by Mr. Pickering, to add after the word "appointed" the word "annually."

Which was carried in the affirmative.

A motion was made by Mr. Lewis, seconded by Mr. Findley, to adjourn the debates on the second clause of the fifteenth section or the second article.

Which was determined in the affirmative.

It was then moved by Mr. Findley, seconded by Mr. Redick, to insert the following as the seventeenth section of the second article of the said proposed constitution, viz.

A secretary shall be elected by the joint vote of both houses of the general assembly and be commissioned by the governor, he shall coun-

tersign all commissions signed by the governor, and all orders drawn
by him on the treasury of the state for monies appropriated, as well as
tavern and marriage licenses; he shall keep fair records of the proceedings of the supreme executive department, to be laid before either house of assembly when called for, and shall attend the governor
or eithea house when required.

Ordered, that the consideration of the said motion be adjourned.

The first section of the third article of the said proposed constitution
being under consideration, viz.

In elections by the citizens, every freeman of the age of twenty-one
years having resided in the state two years next before the days of the
elections respectively, and paid taxes within that time, shall enjoy the
rights of an elector. The sons of freeholders of the age aforesaid, shall
be entitled to vote though they have not paid taxes.

A motion was then made by Mr. Wilson, seconded by Mr. Tyson, to
strike out the word "two," and in lieu thereof to insert the word "one."

On the question, Will the committee agree to the same?

The yeas and nays being called by Mr. Wilson, were as follow,
viz.

YEAS.

Mr. Wilson	Mr. Tyson	Mr. Todd	Mr. Shoemaker
Baker	Pedan	Hoge	Gloninger
Lewis	Power	Redick	Pickering
Gibbons	Powell		14

NAYS.

Mr. Roberts	Mr. Hand	Mr. Hiester	Mr. Addison
M'Kean	Coleman	Lower	J. Ross
Mifflin	Graff	Lincoln	Smilie
Gray	Atlee	Groscop	Gallatin
Robinson	Hubley	Gehr	M'Lene
Hare	Breckbill	Sitgreaves	Matthews
Edwards	Miller	Arndt	Coates
Jenks	Slegle	Rhoads	Brown
Barclay	Reed	Piper	Henderson
Stout	Dill	Smith	Gibson
T. Ross	Whitehill	Snyder	Sellers
Boyd	Irvine	Findley	Graham 48

So it was determined in the negative.

It was moved by Mr. Sitgreaves, seconded by Mr. M'Lene, to insert after the word "paid" the words "public, state or county."

A motion was made by Mr. Pickering, seconded by Mr. Lewis, to postpone the said amendment in order to introduce the following, viz. to
insert after the words "respectively, and paid," the words "a state or
county tax within that time, which tax shall have been assessed upon
him at least six months before the election," and to strike out the word
"taxes" after the words "and paid."

Which was carried in the affirmative.

A motion was made by Mr. Redick, seconded by Mr. Power, to insert before the words "the sons" the words "freeholders qualified as
aforesaid."

A motion was then made by Mr. Gallatin, seconded by Mr. Hoge,
to strike out the words "the sons of freeholders of the age aforesaid,"

and in lieu thereof to insert the following, viz. "all those who are natives, or have resided ten years in the state, and have attained the age of twenty-one years.

The committee then rose in order to report further progress and ask leave to sit again.

MONDAY, January 18, 1790. *P. M.*

The first section of the third article of the proposed constitution, together with the several amendments made thereto, being under consideration,

It was moved by Mr. Sitgreaves, seconded by Mr. Arndt, to amend the said section, by adding, after the word "electors," the words "provided that natural born citizens of this commonwealth, shall be entitled to vote although they shall not have resided within the state two years next before the election."

A motion was made by Mr. Findley, seconded by Mr. Redick, to adjourn the debates on the amendments proposed, as well as the remainder of the said section.

Which was carried in the affirmative.

The second section of the third article of the said proposed constitution, being under consideration, the same was adopted as follows, viz.

Sect. II. All elections shall be by ballot, except those by persons in their representative or public capacities, which shall be *viva voce*.

The third section of the third article of the proposed constitution, being under consideration, viz.

If elections are not properly attended ; attendance on them shall be enforced by law.

It was then moved by Mr. Lewis, seconded by Mr. Pickering, to amend the same so as to read as follows, viz.

Attendance upon elections shall be enforced by law.

A motion was then made by Mr. Sitgreaves, seconded by Mr. Lincoln, to strike out the word "shall," and in lieu thereof insert the word "may."

The committee then rose in order to report, that they had made further progress in the business referred to them, and ask leave to sit again.

TUESDAY, January 19, 1790. *A. M.*

Agreeably to the order of the day, the committee resumed the consideration of the amendment, moved by Mr. James Ross, seconded by Mr. Hoge, on the sixteenth day of January, instant, to the eighth section of the second article of the constitution, reported by the committee of nine, viz.

No member of congress from this state nor any person holding or exercising any office of trust or profit under the United States, shall, at the same time, hold and exercise any office whatever in this state.

It was moved by Mr. James Ross, seconded by Mr. Hoge, to insert after the word "whatever," the words "otherwise than in the militia."

On the question, Will the committee agree to the same ?

The yeas and nays being called by Mr. Wilson, were as follow, viz.

YEAS.

Mr. Mifflin	Mr. Atlee	Mr. Gehr	Mr. J. Ross
Robinson	Breckbill	Rhoads	Smilie
Hare	Miller	Powell	Gallatin
Edwards	Reed	Piper	M'Lene
Barclay	Tyson	Smith	Mathews
Stout	Pedan	Snyder	Morris
Gibbons	Dill	Findley	Coates
Bull	Whitehill	Todd	Gloninger
T. Ross	Power	Addison	Brown
Boyd	Hiester	Hoge	Gibson
Hand	Lincoln	Redick	Beale
Coleman	Groscop		46

NAYS.

Mr. Wilson	Mr. Gray	Mr. Slegle	Mr. Graydon
Baker	Ogden	Sitgreaves	Pickering
Roberts	Jenks	Arndt	Henderson
Lewis	Graff	Potts	Sellers
M'Kean	Hubley	Shoemaker	19

So it was carried in the affirmative.

And the eighth section of the second article of the proposed constitution adopted as follows, viz.

Sect. VIII. He shall appoint all officers of this commonwealth, whose offices are established by this constitution or shall be established by law, and whose appointments are not herein otherwise provided for; but no person shall be appointed to an office within any county who shall not have resided therein one year next before his appointment. No member of congress from this state, nor any person holding or exercising any office of trust or profit under the United States, shall, at the same time, hold and exercise any office whatever, otherwise than in the militia, in this state.

The motion made by Mr. Findley, seconded by Mr. Redick, the sixteenth day of January, instant, relative to the appointment of a secretary, recurring.

It was, on motion of Mr. Wilson, seconded by Mr. Addison, Ordered, that the debates on the said motion be adjourned.

A motion was made by Mr. Pickering, seconded by Mr. Lewis, in the following words, viz.

Any candidate applying for an office in the appointment of the governor, or the legislature, shall make his application only in writing; every application otherwise made, either by the candidate himself, or any other person for him at his request, shall be deemed a disqualification of such candidate for the office requested.

It was unanimously agreed that the debates on the said motion be adjourned·

A motion was made by Mr. Sitgreaves, seconded by Mr. Arndt, in the following words, viz.

The judges and inspectors or other officers, who are or shall be authorised by law to hold elections and receive votes at the different places of election throughout the commonwealth, shall, at every election for governor, carefully seal up the tickets, tally lists and lists of voters as heretofore, and deposit the same with the clerk of the peace of the

proper county, and the judges and inspectors or other officers aforesaid shall, in such manner as is, or shall be established by law, meet
together in their respective counties, and certify under their hands
and seals, the persons who shall be voted for in the said county for
governor, and the number of votes for each person, in words at length
and not in figures only, which certificates shall, as soon as may be,
be transmitted, sealed, to the seat of government of the state, directed
to the speaker of the senate. The speaker of the senate shall, in the
presence of the senate and house of representatives open all the certificates. The votes shall then be counted; the person having the greatest number of votes shall be declared governor.

It was then, on motion, Ordered, that the debates on the said motion be adjourned.

The third section of the third article of the proposed constitution
recurring, together with the amendments, viz. the motion made by
Mr Lewis and Mr. Pickering, yesterday, that the said section read as
follows: "Attendance on elections shall be enforced by law," and
the motion made by Mr Sitgreaves, seconded by Mr. Lincoln, to
strike out the word " shall" and in lieu thereof to insert the word
"may."

On the question, "Will the committee agree to strike out the
word "shall" and insert the word "may?"
It was carried in the affirmative.

And on the question, Will the committee agree to the said third
section, as amended ?

The yeas and nays being called by Mr. Thomas Ross, were as follow, viz.

YEAS.

Mr. Wilson	Mr. Hubley	Mr. Arndt	Mr. Redick
Baker	Reed	Powell	Smilie
Lewis	Dill	Piper	Matthews
Robinson	Whitehill	Findley	Shoemaker
Hare	Power	Addison	Graydon
Hand	Lincoln	Hoge	Pickering 24

NAYS.

Mr. Roberts	Mr. T. Ross	Mr. Hiester	Mr. M'Lene
M'Kean	Boyd	Groscop	Morris
Mifflin	Coleman	Gehr	Potts
Gray	Graff	Sitgreaves	Coates
Edwards	Atlee	Rhoads	Gloninger
Ogden	Breckbill	Smith	Brown
Jenks	Miller	Snyder	Henderson
Barclay	Slegle	Todd	Gibson
Stout	Tyson	J. Ross	Beale
Gibbons	Pedan	Gallatin	Sellers
Bull			41

So it was determined in the negative.

The committee then rose in order to report, that they had made
further progress in the business referred to them, and ask leave to sit
again,

WEDNESDAY, January 20, 1790. A. M.

A motion was made by Mr. Addison, seconded by Mr. Smilie, to introduce the following as the third section of the third article of the proposed constitution, viz.

Sect. III Electors shall be priviledged from arrest in all cases except treason, felony and breach of the peace during their attendance on elections and in going to and returning from the same.

On the question, Will the committee agree to the same?

It was carried in the affirmative.

The first section of the fourth article of the proposed constitution being under consideration, the same was adopted as follows, viz.

Sect. I. The house of representatives shall have the sole power of impeachment.

The second section of the said article being under consideration, viz.

All impeachments shall be tried before the senate, and the chancellor of the commonwealth shall preside therein; when sitting for that purpose the senate shall be on oath or affirmation : No person shall be convicted without the concurrence of two-thirds of the members present.

It was moved by Mr. M'Lene, seconded by Mr. Sitgreaves, to strike out the words "and the chancellor of the commonwealth shall preside therein," and in lieu thereof to insert "who shall take to their assistance, for advice only, the judges of the supreme court."

Whereupon, On motion, Ordered, that the word "senate" before the word "shall" be struck out, and the word "senators" be inserted in lieu thereof, and that the further debates on the said section be abjourned.

The third section of the said fourth article being under consideration, the same was adopted as follows, viz.

Sect. III. Judgment in cases of impeachment shall not extend further than to removal from office, and disqualification to hold any office of honor, trust or profit under this commonwealth ; but the party convicted shall nevertheless be liable to indictment, trial, judgment and punishment according to law.

The first section of the fifth article of the constitution, reported by the committee of nine, being under consideration.

It was moved by Mr. Thomas Ross, seconded by Mr. Boyd, to amend the same so as to read as follows, viz.

The judicial power of this commonwealth shall be vested in a supreme court, in a court of oyer and terminer and general jail delivery hereinafter mentioned; in a court of common pleas, orphans' court, registers's court and court of quarter sessions for each county; and in such other courts as the legislature may, from time to time, establish: But no special commission of oyer and terminer or jail delivery shall be issued.

A motion was then made by Sitgreaves, seconded by Mr. Barclay, to postpone the consideration of the whole of the said fifth article, in order to introduce the following as a substitute, viz.

ARTICLE V.

Sect. I. The judicial power of this commonwealth shall be vested in a supreme court, the jurisdiction of which shall extend over the whole state, in a court of common pleas, orphans' court, registers' court and court of quarter sessions for each county, in justices of the peace, and in such other courts as may be established by the legislature hereafter.

Sect. II. The judges of the supreme court, and the presidents of of the several courts of common pleas shall be commissioned and hold their offices during good behaviour: But the governor may remove any of them on the address of two-thirds of each branch of the legislature.

Sect. III. The judges of the supreme court shall at stated times receive, for their services, a compensation honorable and adequate, which shall not be diminished during their continuance in office.

Sect. IV. The judges of the supreme court shall, by virtue of their offices, be justices of oyer and terminer and general jail delivery for the whole state: But no special commission of oyer and terminer and general jail delivery shall, at any time, be issued.

Sect. V. The state shall, by law, be divided into circuits, any of which shall include not more than   nor fewer than   counties, A president shall be appointed for the courts of common pleas and quarter sessions in each circuit, and shall receive an adequate compensation for his services, to be raised by a tax on process, or in such other manner as the legislature may provide.

Sect. VI. The judges of the courts of common pleas shall have the like powers with the judges of the supreme court to issue writs of certiorari to the justices of the peace within the several counties respectively, and to cause their proceedings to be brought before them and the like right and justice to be done.

Sect. VII. The supreme court and the several courts of common pleas, beside the powers usually exercised by such courts, shall have the powers of a court of chancery, so far as relates to the perpetuating testimony, obtaining evidence from places not within this state, the care of the persons and estates of those who are *non compotes mentis*, compelling the execution of trusts and the specific performance of agreements, issuing injunctions for the prevention of waste, obliging parties to interplead in proper cases and to make answer upon oath or affirmation respecting matters merely within their own knowledge, and in such other cases as the future legislature may direct. Provided that, if at any future period a court of chancery should be, by law, established within this commonwealth, from thenceforth the extraordinary powers hereby given to the supreme court and courts of common pleas shall cease and determine, except as to the obtaining evidence from places not within this state.

Sect. VIII. A competent number of justices of the peace shall be appointed in each county for the conservation of the peace, and to facilitate the administration of justice in controversies of small value; which justices shall be commissioned for   years, they behaving themselves well. The president of the courts of common pleas and quarter sessions in each circuit, shall be a justice of the peace within that circuit.

Sect. IX. A register's office for the probate of wills and granting letters of administration, and an office for recording of deeds, shall be kept in each county.

Sect. X. The judges of the supreme court shall appoint commissioners of bail in every county of the state, except those in which they shall respectively reside.

Sect. XI. Prothonotaries, clerks of the peace and orphans' courts, recorders of deeds, registers of wills, and sheriffs, shall keep their offices in the county town of the county in which they respectively shall be officers.

Sect. XII. The style of all process shall be *the commonwealth of Pennsylvania*: All prosecutions shall be carried on in the name and by the authority of the commonwealth of Pennsylvania, and shall conclude *against the peace and dignity of the same.*

On the question, Will the committee agree to the postponement for the aforesaid purpose?

It was determined in the negative.

The first section of the fifth article, with the amendment proposed by Mr. Thomas Ross, recurring.

After some debate thereon, the committee rose in order to report, further progress in the business referred to them, and request leave to sit again.

THURSDAY, January 21, 1790. A. M.

The first section of the fifth article of the constitution, reported by the committee of nine, together with the amendment proposed yesterday by Mr. Thomas Ross and Mr. Boyd, recurring.

A motion was made by Mr. Smilie, seconded by Mr. Matthews, to amend the said first section so as to read as follows, viz.

The judicial powers of this commonwealth shall be vested in a supreme court, and in such other courts as the legislature may, from time to time, ordain and establish.

And after considerable debate, the committee rose in order to report, that they had made further progress in the business referred to them, and request leave to sit again,

FRIDAY, January 22, 1790, A. M

The first section of the fifth article of the constitution reported by the committee of nine, together with the amendments proposed by Mr. J. Ross and Mr. Smilie, on the twentieth and twenty-first of January instant, recurring.

A motion was made by Mr. Ogden, seconded by Mr. Lewis, to postpone the said amendments in order to amend the said fifth section so as to read as follows, viz.

The judicial power of this commonwealth shall be vested in a high court of chancery (provided that the said court shall not take cognizance of any cause, matter or thing for which there shall be a specific, adequate and complete remedy in the courts of common law, and at all times subject to such laws as may hereafter be enacted by the legislature of this commonwealth, respecting the jurisdiction of said court) and a supreme court, the jurisdiction of each of which shall extend over the state; in the courts of chancery and of oyer and terminer and general jail delivery hereinafter mentioned; in a court of common pleas, orphans' court, register's court, and court of quarter sessions for each county, and in such other courts as the legislature may from time to time, establish. But no special commission of oyer and terminer or jail delivery shall be issued.

On the question, Will the committee agree to the postponement for the aforesaid purpose ?

It was determind in the negative.

Whereupon, the motion of Mr. Thomas Ross, made on the twentieth of January, instant, being under consideration.

On the question, Will the committee agree to the same.

The yeas and nays being called by Mr. Edwards, were as follow, viz.

YEAS.

Mr. Roberts	Mr. Tyson	Mr Rhoads	Mr. M'Lene
Mifflin	Pedan	Powell	Matthews
Edwards	Dill	Piper	Morris
Bull	Whitehill	Snyder	Coates
T. Ross	Power	Findley	Shoemaker
Boyd	Hiester	Todd	Gloninger
Hand	Lincoln	Addison	Brown
Coleman	Groscop	Redick	Pickering
Breckbill	Gehr	Smilie	Gibson
Miller	Sitgreaves	Gallatin	Beale
Reed	Arndt		42

NAYS.

Mr. Wilson	Mr. Hare	Mr. Graff	Mr. J. Ross
Baker	Ogden	Atlee	Potts
Lewis	Jenks	Hubley	Graydon
M'Kean	Barclay	Smith	Henderson
Gray	Stout	Hoge	Sellers
Robinson			21

So it was carried in the affirmative.

The committee then rose in order to report, that they had made further progress in the business referred to them, and request leave to sit again.

SATURDAY, January 23, 1790. A. M.

The first section of the fifth article of the proposed constitution, as amended, recurring viz.

The judicial power of this commonwealth shall be vested in a supreme court, the jurisdiction of which shall extend over the state; in courts of oyer and terminer and general jail delivery hereinafter mentioned; in a court of common pleas, orphans' court, register's court and court of quarter sessions for each county, and in such other courts as the legislature may, from time to time, establish. But no special commission of oyer and terminer or jail delivery shall be issued.

It was then moved by Mr. Sitgreaves, seconded by Mr. Shoemaker, to postpone the first, second, third and fourth sections of the said article.

Which was carried in the affirmative.

A motion was then made by Mr. Smilie, seconded by Mr. M'Lene, to postpone the consideration of the whole of the said fifth article, in order to introduce the following as a substitute, viz.

45

The judicial power of this commonwealth shall be vested in a supreme court, which shall have jurisdiction throughout the state, in the courts of oyer and terminer and general jail delivery, and in a court of common pleas, an orphans' court, court of sessions of the peace, and register's court in each county ; and the justices of the peace of the several counties shall have right to decide concerning small debts and demands.

The judges of the supreme court, four at least in number, as the legislature shall direct, shall be appointed and commissioned by the governor for and during their good behaviour respectively ; and shall receive a compensation which shall neither be increased nor diminished during their continuance in office; provided that the governor may remove any of them on the address of two-thirds of each branch of the legislature.

There shall be judges not exceeding five in each county, appointed and commissioned by the governor, who shall hold the court of common pleas, who shall also compose the orphans' court and the court of register of wills of the county.

The supreme court and the several courts of common pleas shall, beside the powers heretofore usually exercised by the said courts, have the power of a court of chancery, so far as relates to the perpetuating of testimony, obtaining evidence from places not within the state, and the care of the persons and estates of those who be *non compotes mentis*, and such other powers as may be found necessary by future general assemblies, not inconsistent with the constitution.

Courts of quarter sessions of the peace shall be holden by the justices of the peace of each county respectively.

The legislature shall have power to establish all such other courts as shall be found necessary.

On the question, Will the committee agree to the postponement for the aforesaid purpose ?

The yeas and nays being called by Mr. Smilie, were as follow, viz.

YEAS.

Mr. Smilie	Mr. M'Lene	Mr. Gloninger	Mr. Brown

NAYS.

Mr. Wilson	Mr. Bull	Mr. Whitehill	Mr. Hoge
Baker	T. Ross	Power	Redick
Roberts	Boyd	Lincoln	J. Ross
Lewis	Hand	Groscop	Gallatin
M'Kean	Coleman	Gehr	Matthews
Mifflin	Graff	Sitgreaves	Potts
Gray	Atlee	Arndt	Coates
Robinson	Hubley	Rhoads	Shoemaker
Hare	Breckbill	Powell	Graydon
Edwards	Miller	Piper	Pickering
Ogden	Slegle	Smith	Henderson
Jenks	Reed	Snyder	Gibson
Barclay	Tyson	Findley	Beale
Stout	Pedan	Todd	Sellers
Gibbons	Dill	Addison	59

So it was determined in the negative.

The fifth section of the fifth article of the constitution reported by the committee of nine, being under consideration,

A motion was made by Mr. Wilson, seconded by Mr. Miller, to fill the first blank with the word "six," and the second blank with the word "three."

Which was carried in the affirmative.

It was then moved by Mr. Sitgreaves, seconded by Mr. Smilie, to postpone the said section in order to introduce the following in lieu thereof, viz.

The several courts of common pleas, for the present, shall be established in the following manner : The governor shall appoint and commission a number of judges in each county, not less than   nor exceeding   who, during their continuance in office, shall reside within such county. The state shall, by law, be divided into circuits, any of which shall not include more than six, nor fewer than three counties : A president shall be appointed for the several courts in each circuit, who, during his continuance in office, shall reside within such circuit. Such president and judges, or any three of them, shall be the judges who shall compose the respective courts of common pleas.

On the question, Will the committee agree to the postponement for the aforesaid purpose? The yeas and nays being called by Mr. Ogden, were as follow, viz.

YEAS.

Mr. Edwards	Mr. Coleman	Mr. Groscop	Mr. Todd
Ogden	Hubley	Gehr	Smilie
Jenks	Breckbill	Sitgreaves	M'Lene
Barclay	Slegle	Arndt	Matthews
Stout	Reed	Rhoads	Coates
Gibbons	Pedan	Powell	Shoemaker
Bull	Dill	Piper	Gloninger
T. Ross	Whitehill	Snyder	Brown
Boyd	Power	Findley	Beale
Hand	Lincoln		38

NAYS.

Mr. Wilson	Mr. Gray	Mr. Smith	Mr. Potts
Baker	Robinson	Addison	Graydon
Roberts	Hare	Hoge	Pickering
Lewis	Graff	Redick	Henderson
M'Kean	Atlee	J. Ross	Gibson
Mifflin	Miller	Gallatin	Sellers 24

So it was carried in the affirmative.

And the said section, as amended being under consideration, it was moved by Mr. Sitgreaves, seconded by Mr. M'Lene, to fill the blanks with the words "three" and "five."

A motion was then made by Mr. Lewis, seconded by Mr. Addison, to strike out the words "a number of judges in each county, not less than   nor exceeding   " and in lieu thereof, to insert "four judges in each county."

Which was determined in the negative.

Whereupon, On the question, Will the committee agree to the amendment proposed by Mr. Sitgreaves and Mr. M'Lene, viz. "to fill the blanks with the words 'three' and 'five' ?"

It was carried in the affirmative to fill the first blank with the word "three."

A motion was then made by Mr. Gallatin, seconded by Mr. Edwards, to fill the second blank with the word "four."

Which was carried in the affirmative.

It was moved by Mr. Edwards, seconded by Mr. Lewis, to strike out, after the words "or any," the word "three," and in lieu thereof, to insert the word "two."

Which was carried in the affirmative.

A motion was then made by Mr. Addison, seconded by Mr. M'Lene, to add the following words to the said section, viz.

And any one of them may, in the absence of the others, open and adjourn the court from day to day.

Which was determined in the negative.

And thereupon, the said fifth section of the fifth article adopted as follows, viz

Section V. The several courts of common pleas, for the present, shall be established in the following manner: The governor shall appoint a number of judges in each county, not less than three nor exceeding four, who, during their continuance in office, shall reside within such county. The state shall, by law, be divided into circuits, any of which shall not include more than six, nor fewer than three counties. A president shall be appointed for the several courts in each circuit, who, during his continuance in office, shall reside within such circuit. Such president, or any two of them, shall be the judges who shall compose the respective courts of common pleas.

The committee then rose in order to report, That they had made further progress in the business referred to them, and request leave to sit again.

MONDAY, January 25, 1790. P. M.

The first section of the fifth article of the constitution reported by the committee of nine, with the amendments, recurring,

A motion was made by Mr. Sitgreaves, seconded by Mr. Hare, to postpone the further consideration thereof, in order to take up the sixth section of the said article, viz.

The judges of the courts of common pleas respectively, during their continuance in office shall, the president being one of them, be justices of oyer and terminer and general jail delivery, for the trial of capital and other offenders, for each of the counties within the said circuits respectively; But they shall not hold a court of oyer and terminer and general jail delivery, in any county, when the judges of the supreme court, or some of them, shall be sitting in the same county.

Which was carried in the affirmative.

And the said sixth section being under consideration, it was moved by Mr. Findley, seconded by Mr. Edwards, to postpone the consideration of the said sixth section.

Which was determined in the negative.

A motion was made by Mr. Smith, seconded by Mr. Wilson, to strike out, after the words "common pleas," the word "respectively," and insert, in lieu thereof, "in each county;" and to strike out the words "for each of the counties within the said circuits respectively."

Which was carried in the affirmative.

A motion was then made by Mr. Smith, seconded by Mr. Bull, to strike out the words "during their continuance in office."

Which was carried in the affirmative.

A motion was made by Mr. Sitgreaves, seconded by Mr. Potts, to add the following after the words "each county," "or any two of them, the president being one."

Which was determined in the affirmative.

It was moved by Mr. Findley, seconded by Mr. Piper, to amend the said section so as to read as follows, viz.

Section VI. The judges of the courts of common pleas in each county, or any two of them, the president being one, shall be justices of oyer and terminer and general jail delivery, for the trial of capital and other offenders; but they shall not hold a court of oyer and terminer and general jail delivery in any county, when the judges of the supreme court, or some of them, shall be sitting in the same county. But the parties accused, as well as the commonwealth, may remove the indictment and proceedings into the supreme court at any time before trial.

On the question, Will the committee agree to the same? The yeas and nays being called by Mr. Findley, were as follow, viz.

YEAS.

Mr. Baker	Mr. Hand	Mr. Lincoln	Mr. Todd
Roberts	Coleman	Groscop	Addison
M'Kean	Graff	Gehr	Hoge
Mifflin	Hubley	Arndt	Gloninger
Gray	Breckbill	Rhoads	Brown
Barclay	Miller	Powell	Graydon
Stout	Reed	Piper	Pickering
Gibbons	Pedan	Smith	Henderson
Bull	D	Snyder	Gibson
T. Ross	Power	Findley	Sellers
Boyd			41

NAYS.

Mr. Wilson	Mr. Atlee	Mr. Smilie	Mr. Morris
Robinson	Slegle	Gallatin	Potts
Hare	Whitehill	M'Lene	Coates
Edwards	Sitgreaves	Matthews	15

So it was carried in the affirmative, and the section, as amended, adopted.

The seventh section of the fifth article of the proposed constitution being under consideration,

It was moved by Mr. Addison, seconded by Mr. Sitgreaves, to amend the same so as to read as follows, viz.

The judges of the courts of common pleas, or any two of them, shall compose the courts of quarter sessions, orphans' courts and register's courts for their respective counties.

The committee then rose in order to report, That they had made further progress in the business referred to them, and request leave to sit again.

TUESDAY, January 26, 1790. A. M.

The seventh section of the fifth article of the proposed constitution, together with the amendment proposed yesterday by Mr. Addison, seconded by Mr. Sitgreaves, recurring,

A motion was made by Mr. M'Lene, seconded by Mr. Edwards, to strike out the words "quarter sessions" from the said amendment.

It was then moved by Mr. Ogden, seconded by Mr. Stout, to postpone the said section, with the several amendments, in order to take into consideration the eleventh section of the said fifth article.

Which was determined in the negative.

Whereupon, the motion made by Mr. M'Lene, seconded by Mr. Edwards, to strike out the words "quarter sessions," recurring,

On the question, Will the committee agree to the same? The yeas and nays being called by Mr. Wilson, were as follow, viz.

YEAS.

Mr. Edwards	Mr. Lincoln	Mr. Findley	Mr. Shoemaker
Pedan	Groscop	Smilie	Gloninger
Dill	Gehr	M'Lene	Barclay
Whitehill	Piper	Matthews	Beale
Power	Snyder	Coates	19

NAYS.

Mr. Wilson	Mr. Boyd	Mr. Sitgreaves	Mr. J. Ross
Baker	Hand	Arndt	Gallatin
Lewis	Coleman	Rhoads	Morris
Mifflin	Graff	Powell	Potts
Robinson	Hubley	Smith	Brown
Hare	Breckbill	Todd	Graydon
Ogden	Miller	Addison	Pickering
Jenks	Slegle	Hoge	Henderson
Stout	Reed	Redick	Gibson
Bull			87

So it was determined in the negative.

Mr. Addison and Mr. Sitgreaves withdrew their motion made yesterday. Whereupon,

The seventh section recurring, a motion was made by Mr. Smith seconded by Mr. Henderson, to postpone the consideration thereof in order to introduce the following as a substitute, viz.

The judges of the court of common pleas shall compose the courts of quarter sessions and orphans' court in their respective counties, any two of whom shall be a quorum; and the register of wills, together with the said judges, or any two of them, shall compose the register's court in the respective counties.

On the question, Will the committee agree to the postponement? It was carried in the affirmative.

A motion was then made by Mr. Ogden, seconded by Mr. Morris, to add the following words to the substitute proposed by Mr. Smith, seconded by Mr. Henderson, viz.

The justices of the peace shall sit in conjunction with the judges of the common pleas and form the court of quarter sessions.

On the question, Will the committee agree to the same? The yeas and nays being called by Mr. Ogden, were as follow, viz.

YEAS.

Mr. Edwards	Mr. Pedan	Mr. Groscop	Mr. M'Lene»
Ogden	Dill	Gehr	Morris
Jenks	Whitehill	Piper	Shoemaker
Barclay	Lincoln	Smilie	Gloninger
Stout			17

NAYS.

Mr. Wilson	Mr. Graff	Mr. Rhoads	Mr. Gallatin
Baker	Hubley	Powell	Matthews
Lewis	Breckbill	Smith	Potts
Mifflin	Miller	Snyder	Coates
Robinson	Slegle	Findley	Brown
Hare	Reed	Todd	Graydon
Bull	Tyson	Addison	Pickering
Boyd	Power	Hoge	Henderson
Hand	Sitgreaves	Redick	Gibson
Coleman	Arndt	J. Ross	Beale 40

So it was determined in the negative.

And the substitute proposed by Mr. Smith, seconded by Mr. Henderson, adopted as the seventh section of the fifth article of the said proposed constitution.

The eighth section of the said fifth article being then under consideration, the same was unanimously adopted as follows, viz.

Section VIII. The judges of the courts of common pleas shall have the like powers with the judges of the supreme court to issue writs of certiorari to the justices of the peace within the several counties respectively, and to cause their proceedings to be brought before them, and the like right and justice to be done.

The ninth section of the said fifth article being under consideration, a motion was made by Mr. Sitgreaves, seconded by Mr. Wilson, to amend the same so as to read as follows, viz

Section IX. The president of the court of each circuit shall be conservator of the peace within such circuit; and the judges of the common pleas shall be conservators of the peace within their respective counties.

On the question, Will the committee agree to the same?

It was carried in the affirmative, and the said ninth section, as amended, adopted.

The committee rose in order to report, That they had made further progress in the business referred to them, and request leave to sit again.

WEDNESDAY, January 27, 1790. A. M.

The tenth section of the fifth article of the constitution reported by the committee of nine being under consideration—

On the question, Will the committee agree to the same?

It was determined in the negative.

The eleventh section of the fifth article of the said proposed constitution coming under consideration—

It was moved by Mr. Redick, seconded by Mr. Hoge, to postpone the consideration of the said section, in order to introduce the following in lieu thereof, viz,

The governor shall appoint and commission a competent number of justices of the peace in convenient districts, to be fixed in such manner as shall be, by law, directed. They shall be commissioned for   years, and may be removed for misconduct upon the address of the legislature.

After some debate a division of the question was called for, And on the question, Will the committee agree to the first part thereof? The yeas and nays being called by Mr. Sitgreaves, were as follow, viz.

YEAS.

Mr. Wilson	Mr. Bull	Mr. Tyson	Mr. Hoge
Roberts	T. Ross	Dill	Redick
Mifflin	Hand	Sitgreaves	J. Ross
Gray	Coleman	Arndt	Potts
Edwards	Graff	Rhoads	Graydon
Ogden	Hubley	Powell	Pickering
Jenks	Breckbill	Smith	Henderson
Barclay	Miller	Snyder	Gibson
Stout	Slegle	Addison	Sellers
Gibbons			37

NAYS.

Mr. Baker	Mr. Power	Mr. Findley	Mr. Matthews
Robinson	Lincoln	Todd	Coates
Boyd	Groscop	Smilie	Shoemaker
Reed	Gehr	Gallatin	Gloninger
Pedan	Piper	M'Lene	Brown
Whitehill			21

So it was carried in the affirmative.

The second part of the said section being under consideration, viz. They shall be commissioned for   years, and may be removed for misconduct, upon the address of the legislature.

It was moved by Mr. Findley, seconded by Mr. Todd, to strike out the words "for   years," and to insert, in lieu thereof, "during good behaviour."

A motion was then made by Mr. Edwards, seconded by Mr. Gallatin, to add, after the word "legislature," the following, viz. "but shall not take or receive fees or perquisites of any kind."

Which was determined in the negative.

The amendment moved by Mr. Findley, seconded by Mr. Todd, recurring, viz. to strike out the words "for   years," and in lieu thereof to insert "during good behaviour."

On the question, Will the committee agree to the same? The yeas and nays being called by Mr. Wilson, were as follow, viz.

YEAS.

Mr. Wilson	Mr. Jenks	Mr. Coleman	Mr. Tyson
Baker	Barclay	Graff	Pedan
Roberts	Stout	Hubley	Dill
Lewis	Bull	Breckbill	Whitehill
Gray	T. Ross	Miller	Power
Robinson	Boyd	Slegle	Lincoln
Ogden	Hand	Reed	Groscop

YEAS.

Mr. Gehr	Mr. Todd	Mr. M'Lene	Mr. Brown
Arndt	Addison	Matthews	Graydon
Rhoads	Hoge	Morris	Pickering
Powell	J. Ross	Potts	Henderson
Smith	Smilie	Coates	Gibson
Findley	Gallatin	Shoemaker	Sellers 52

NAYS.

Mr. Edwards	Mr. Sitgreaves	Mr. Snyder	Mr. Gloninger
Gibbons	Piper	Redick	7

So it was carried in the affirmative.

A motion was made by Mr. Miller, seconded by Mr Pickering, to strike out the word " misconduct."

It was then moved by Mr. Sitgreaves, seconded by Mr. James Ross, to add after the word " legislature," the words " or upon the conviction of any crime."

A motion was made by Mr. Findley, seconded by Mr Smilie, to strike out the word "may," and in lieu thereof to insert the word "shall."

Which was determined in the negative.

It was then moved by Mr. Addison, seconded by Mr. Hoge, to strike out the words "and may be removed for misconduct upon the address of the legislature," and in lieu thereof to insert the following: " But may be removed on conviction of misbehaviour in office or any infamous crime, or on the address of both houses of the legislature."

Which was carried in the affirmative, and the second part of the said section agreed to.

Whereupon, on the question, Will the committee adopt the said section as amended, to be inserted as the tenth section of the said proposed constitution, viz. The governor shall appoint and commission a competent number of justices of the peace in convenient districts, to be fixed in such manner as shall be by law directed. They shall be commissioned during good behaviour: But may be removed on conviction for misbehaviour in office or any infamous crime, or on the address of both houses of the legislature ?

It was determined in the affirmative.

The twelfth section of the fifth article of the proposed constitution being under consideration, the same was adopted as the eleventh section, viz.

Sect. XI. A register's office for the probate of wills and granting letters of administration, and an office for the recording of deeds shall be kept in each county.

The thirteenth section of the fifth article of the said proposed constitution being under consideration.

A motion was made by Mr. Smith, seconded by Mr. Addison, to amend the same so as to read as follows, viz.

Sect. XII. Prothonotaries, clerks of the peace and orphans' courts, recorders of deeds, registers of wills and sheriffs, shall keep their offices in the county town of the county in which they respectively shall be officers.

Which was carried in the affirmative, and adopted as the twelfth section of the said article.

The fourteenth section of the fifth article of the said proposed constitution being under consideration, the same was adopted as the thirteenth section of the said article, as follows viz.

Sect. XIII. The style of all process shall be *The commonwealth of Pennsylvania*: All prosecutions shall be carried on in the name and by the authority of the commonwealth of Pennsylvania, and shall conclude *Against the peace and dignity of the same.*

The committee then rose in order to report, that they had made further progress in the business referred to them, and request leave to sit again.

THURSDAY, January 28, 1790. *A. M.*

The fifth section of the first article of the proposed constitution, as amended, recurring, viz.

The judicial power of this commonwealth shall be vested in a supreme court, the jurisdiction of which shall extend over the state; in the courts of oyer and terminer and general jail delivery, hereinafter mentioned; in a court of common pleas, orphans' court, register's court and court of quarter sessions for each county, and in such other courts as the legislature may, from time to time establish. But no special commission of oyer and terminer or general jail delivery shall be issued.

A motion was made by Mr. Wilson, seconded by Mr. Smith, to amend the first section so as to read as follows, viz.

The judicial power of this commonwealth shall be vested in a supreme court, in the courts of oyer and terminer and general jail delivery, in a court of common pleas, orphan's court, register's court and court of quarter sessions for each county, in justices of the peace, and in such other courts as the legislature may from time to time establish.

It was moved by Mr. M'Kean, seconded by Mr. Wilson, to insert the words "of law and equity" after the words " other courts."

Which was carried in the affirmative.

And the section proposed by Mr. Wilson, together with the amendment of Mr. M'Kean, adopted as the first section of the said fifth article.

The second section of the said fifth article recurring, it was moved by Mr. Smith, seconded by Mr. M'Kean, to amend the said section so as to read as follows, viz.

The judges of the supreme court and the several courts of common pleas shall be commissioned and hold their offices during good behaviour: But the governor may remove any of them on the address of two-thirds of each branch of the legislature. The judges of the supreme court and the presidents of the several courts of common pleas shall at stated times, receive for their services an adequate compensation, which shall not be diminished during their continuance in office.

A motion was made by Mr. Smilie, seconded by Mr. Stout, to insert the words "increased or" before the word "diminished."

And the yeas and nays being called by Mr. Smilie were as follow, viz.

YEAS.

Mr. Stout	Mr. Smilie	Mr. M'Lene	Mr. Beale
Piper	Gallatin		

NAYS.

Mr. Wilson	Mr. Boyd	Mr. Power	Mr. Redick
Baker	Hand	Lincoln	J. Ross
Roberts	Coleman	Groscop	Matthews
M'Kean	Graff	Gehr	Morris
Mifflin	Atlee	Sitgreaves	Potts
Gray	Hubley	Arndt	Coates
Robinson	Breckbill	Rhoads	Shoemaker
Hare	Miller	Powell	Gloninger
Edwards	Slegle	Smith	Brown
Ogden	Reed	Snyder	Graydon
Jenks	Tyson	Findley	Pickering
Barclay	Pedan	Todd	Henderson
Gibbons	Dill	Addison	Gibson
Bull	Whitehill	Hoge	Sellers
T. Ross			19

So it was determined in the negative.

It was moved by Mr. James Ross, seconded by Mr. Gallatin, to add the following words to the said section, viz. " But they shall hold no other office of profit in this commonwealth."

Which was carried in the affirmative, and the said section as amended, adopted as follows, viz.

Sect. II. The judges of the supreme court and the judges of the several courts of common pleas shall be commissioned and hold their offices during good behaviour: But the governor may remove any of them on the address of two-thirds of each branch of the legislature. The judges of the supreme court and the president of the several courts of common pleas shall, at stated times, receive for their services an adequate compensation, which shall not be diminished during their continuance in office: But they shall hold no other office of profit within this commonwealth.

The third section of the fifth article of the said proposed constitution being under consideration.

On the question, Will the committee agree to the same?

It was unanimously determined in the negative.

A motion was then made by Mr. Sitgreaves, seconded by Mr. Wilson, to introduce the following in the place of the said third section, viz.

The jurisdiction of the supreme court shall extend over the whole state, the judges of the same court shall, by virtue of their office, be justices of oyer and terminer and general jail delivery in the several counties. No special commission of oyer and terminer and general jail delivery shall be issued.

On the question, Will the committee adopt the said section?

It was carried in the affirmative,

The fourth section of the fifth article of the said proposed constitution being under consideration,

It was moved by Mr. Smilie, seconded by Mr. M'Lene, to postpone the consideration of the said section in order to introduce the following, in lieu thereof, viz,

The supreme court and the several courts of common pleas shall, beside the powers heretofore exercised by said court, have the powers of a court of chancery, so far as relates to the perpetuating of testimoney, obtaining evidence from places not within the state, and the care of the persons and estates of those who be *non compotes mentis,* and such other powers as may be found necessary by future general assemblies, not inconsistent with this constitution.

A motion was then made by Mr. Addison, seconded by Mr. Gallatin, to postpone the motion made by Mr. Smilie, in order to introduce the following in lieu thereof, viz.

The supreme court and the several courts of common pleas of this commonwealth, beside the powers usually exercised by such courts, shall have the powers of a court of chancery, so far as relates to the perpetuating testimony, obtaining evidence from places not within the state, and a discovery of truth by the oath of the parties and the production of their books and papers, the care of the persons and estates of those who are *non compotes mentis,* the repealing letters patent, to preventing waste and vexatious suits, to obliging proper persons to interplead, and to giving adequate and specific relief in cases of agreements, frauds, trusts, powers and accidents. The legislature may, from time to time, regulate the exercise of the powers hereby given, and may vest in the several courts such other powers as may be necessary and not inconsistent with this constitution.

The committee then rose in order to report, That they had made further progress in the business referred to them, and ask leave to sit again.

FRIDAY, January 29, 1790. A. M.

Mr. Addison withdrew his motion of the twenty-eighth instant.

The motion made yesterday by Mr. Smilie, seconded by Mr. M'-Lene, recurring.

A motion was made by Mr. Pickering, seconded by Mr. Miller, to postpone the fourth section of the fifth article, together with the amendment, proposed by Mr. Smilie, in order to introduce the following, viz.

The supreme court and the several courts of common pleas, beside their usual powers, shall have the powers of courts of equity, to give relief in those cases in which there would be a failure of justice by an adherence to the rules of the common law, but in all cases in equity, proof by witnesses where their personal attendance may reasonably be required, and the mode of proceeding in all other respects shall be conformed, as far as may be, to the usual practice of the supreme court and court of common pleas as courts of common law.

On the question, Will the committee agree to the postponement for the aforesaid purpose?

It was determined in the negative.

A motion was then made by Mr. Smith, seconded by Mr. Redick, to strike out all the words contained in the motion made yesterday by Mr Smilie, after the words *"non compotes mentis,"* and in lieu thereof to insert the following, viz.

And the legislature shall, as soon as conveniently may be after their first meeting under this constitution, vest in the said courts such other powers to grant relief in equity in all cases to which common law proceedings are not competent, and shall regulate the exercise thereof, and from time to time enlarge, diminish or vest the same in such other courts as they shall judge necessary for the due administration of justice.

It was moved by Mr. Addison, seconded by Mr. M'Kean, to insert after the words "within the state," the following, viz. "And from parties to suits by their examination on oath or affirmation, and the production of their books and papers."

On the question, Will the committee agree to the said amendment? The yeas and nays being called by Mr. Thomas Ross, were as follow, viz.

YEAS.

Mr. Baker	Mr. Hubley	Mr. Addison	Mr. Henderson
M'Kean	Rhoads	Pickeriug	Sellers
Atlee			9

NAYS.

Mr. Roberts	Mr. Hand	Mr. Groscop	Mr. Smilie
Mifflin	Coleman	Gehr	Gallatin
Gray	Graff	Sitgreaves	M'Lene
Robinson	Breckbill	Arndt	Matthews
Hare	Miller	Powell	Morris
Edwards	Slegle	Piper	Potts
Ogden	Reed	Smith	Coates
Jenks	Tyson	Snyder	Shoemaker
Barclay	Pedan	Findley	Gloninger
Stout	Dill	Todd	Brown
Gibbons	Whitehill	Hoge	Graydon
Bull	Power	Redick	Gibson
T. Ross	Lincoln	J. Ross	Beale
Boyd			53

So it was determined in the negative, and the said fourth section as amended, unanimously adopted as follows, viz.

Sect. IV. The supreme court and the several courts of common pleas shall, besides the powers heretofore exercised by the said courts, have the power of a court of chancery, so far as relates to the perpetuating of testimony, obtaining evidence from places not within the state, and the care of the persons and estates of those who are *non compotes mentis*: And the legislature shall, as soon as conveniently may be, after their first sitting under this constitution, vest in the said courts such other powers to grant relief in equity in all cases to which common law proceedings are not competent, and shall regulate the exercise thereof, and from time to time enlarge, diminish or vest the same in such other courts as they shall judge necessary for the due administration of justice.

Whereupon, on motion of of Mr. Sitgreaves, seconded by Mr. Ogden.

Ordered, That the said section be placed as the sixth section of the said fifth article.

The first section of the sixth article of the proposed constitution being under consideration, viz.

Sheriffs and coroners shall, at the places of the election of representatives, be chosen for three yea·; by the citizens of each county respectively; two persons shall be chosen for each office, one of whom for each shall be commissioned by the governor; no person shall continue in the office of sheriff more than three years successively."

A motion was made by Mr. Hubley, seconded by Mr. Coleman, to strike out the words "for three years," and in lieu thereof to insert the word " annually."

On the question, Will the committee agree to the same?

The yeas and nays being called by Mr. Hubley, were as follow, viz.

YEAS.

Mr. Baker	Mr. Breckbill	Mr. Groscop	Mr. Matthews
Gray	Tyson	Gehr	Morris
Jenks	Pedan	Arndt	Coates
Stout	Dill	Powell	Shoemaker
Coleman	Whitehill	Piper	Gloninger
Graff	Power	Smilie	Beale
Hubley	Lincoln	M'Lene	27

NAYS.

Mr. Roberts	Mr. T. Ross	Smith	Mr. Gallatin
Lewis	Boyd	Snyder	Potts
M'Kean	Hand	Findley	Brown
Mifflin	Atlee	Todd	Graydon
Robinson	Miller	Addison	Pickering
Hare	Slegle	Hoge	Henderson
Edwards	Reed	Redick	Gibson
Ogden	Sitgreaves	J. Ross	Sellers
Gibbons	Rhoads		34

So it was determined in the negative.

A motion was made be Mr. Sitgreaves, seconded by Mr. Smith, to strike out the word " successively," and in lieu thereof to insert the words " in any term of nine years "

It was moved by Mr. Addison, seconded by Mr. Miller, to insert the words " in any term of six years."

It was then unanimously agreed to strike out the word "successively."

On the question, Will the committee agree to insert the words " in any term of nine years"?

The yeas and nays being called by Mr. Sitgreaves, were as follow, viz.

YEAS.

Mr. Robinson	Mr. Whitehill	Mr. Powell	Mr. Redick
Hare	Power	Piper	Morris '
Edwards	Sitgreaves	Smith	Graydon
Graff	Arndt	Findley	15

NAYS.

Mr. Baker	Mr. Stout	Mr. Miller	Mr. Rhoads
Roberts	Gibbons	Slegle	Snyder
Lewis	T. Ross	Reed	Todd
M'Kean	Boyd	Tyson	Addison
Mifflin	Hand	Pedan	Hoge
Gray	Coleman	Dill	J. Ross
Ogden	Atlee	Lincoln	Smilie
Jenks	Hubley	Groscop	Gallatin
Barclay	Breckbill	Gehr	M'Lene

NAYS.

Mr. Mathews   Mr. Shoemaker   Mr. Pickering   Mr. Beale
    Potts   Gloninge   Henderson   Sellers
    Coates   Brown   Gibson   47

So it was determined in the negative.

On the question, Will the committee agree to insert the words " in any term of six years?

It was carried in the affirmative, and the said section as amended adopted as follows, viz.

Sect. I. Sheriffs and coroners shall, at the places of the election of representatives, be chosen for three years, by the citizens of each county respectively; two persons shall be chosen for each office, one of whom for each shall be commissioned by the governor; no person shall exercise the office of sheriff more than three years in any term of six years.

The second section of the sixth article of the said proposed constitution being under consideration, the same was adopted as follows, viz.

Sect. II. The freemen of this commonwealth shall be armed and disciplined for its defence: The militia officers shall be appointed in such manner, and for such time, as shall be, by law, directed.

On motion, ordered, that two copies of the fifth and sixth articles of the said proposed constitution be printed for the use of each member.

The seventh article being then under consideration, viz.

All debts contracted and engagements entered into before the establishment of this constitution shall be as valid against the commonwealth under this constitution, as they have been heretofore.

It was moved by Mr. Lewis, seconded by Mr. M'Lene, to strike out the words " against the commonwealth under this constitution."

Which was carried in the affirmative.

It was then moved by Mr. Pickering, seconded by Mr. M'Kean, to prefix the following words to the said article, viz. " That there may be no doubt relative to the force of former engagements, it is declared, that."

Whereupon, on motion of Mr. Lewis, seconded by Mr. M'Kean, ordered, that the debates on the said article be adjourned.

On motion of Mr. Ogden, seconded by Mr. Edwards,

Resolved, unanimously, that the thanks of this committee be given to the honorable Mr. M'Kean for his able and impartial conduct while chairman thereof.

The committee then rose in order to report, That they had made further progress in the business referred to them, and request leave to sit again.

SATURDAY, January 30, 1790. A. M.

The following note was received, addressed to the chairman, from the honorable Mr. M'Kean, viz.

Permit me, sir, to acknowledge the grateful sense I entertain of the favorable opinion expressed by this honorable committee respecting my conduct while in the chair, and to assure them, as it shall always be my study to merit, so it will afford me the sincerest pleasure to obtain, their approbation.

The seventh article recurring, together with the several amendments.

A motion was made by Mr. Addison, seconded by Mr. Henderson, to reconsider the first section of the sixth article of the said proposed constitution adopted yesterday in order to strike out the words "for three years," and to insert after the word "governor," the following, viz. They shall hold their offices for three years, and until a successor be duly qualified. But no person shall be twice chosen or appointed as sheriff in any term of six years.

On the question, "Will the committee agree to re-consider for the aforesaid purpose?" It was determined in the affirmative.

And the said section adopted as follows, viz.

Section 1. Sheriffs and coroners shall, at the places of the election of representatives, be chosen by the citizens of each country respectively; two persons shall be chosen for each office, one of whom for each shall be commissioned by the governor; they shall hold their offices for three years, and until a successor be duly qualified. But no person shall be twice chosen or appointed as sheriff in any term of six years.

A motion was made by Mr. Addison, seconded by Mr. Graydon, to introduce the following as the second section of the said sixth article, viz.

In case of the resignation, death, or removal from office of the sheriff or coroner of any county, the governor may appoint a successor to hold his office until one of two persons who shall be elected at the ensuing general election, shall be duly appointed.

It was then moved by Mr. Thomas Ross, seconded by Mr. Gibbons, to postpone the consideration of the motion made by Mr. Addison, seconded by Mr. Graydon, in order to introduce the following in lieu thereof, viz.

The general assembly shall make provision for supplying vacancies in the offices of sheriffs or coroners, occasioned by death, resignation or disqualification.

On the question, "Will the committee agree to the postponement for the aforesaid purpose?" It was determined in the negative.

The seventh article of the said proposed constitution again recurring, it was, on motion of Mr. Findley, seconded by Mr. Ogden, ordered, That the debates thereon be postponed.

The first section of the eighth article of the proposed constitution being under consideration, viz.

A school or schools shall be established in each county for the instruction of youth, and the state shall pay to the masters such salaries as shall enable them to teach at low prices.

It was moved by Mr. M'Kean, seconded by Mr. Findley, to add the following words to the said section, viz. "and the poor gratis."

A motion was then made by Mr. Pickering, seconded by Mr. Sitgreaves, to postpone the consideration of the said first section, with the amendment proposed by Mr. M'Kean, in order to introduce the following in lieu of the first and second sections of the said eighth article, viz.

Knowledge generally diffused among the people being essential to the preservation of their rights, it shall be the duty of the legislature to provide for the instruction of children and youth, by the establishment of such schools in the several counties throughout the commonwealth. And the arts, sciences and all useful learning shall be further promoted in one or more universities.

On the question, Will the committee agree to the postponement for the aforesaid purpose? It was determined in the negative.

The first section of the said eighth article recurring, together with the amendment proposed by Mr. M'Kean, On the question, Will the committee agree to the same? It was determined in the negative.

The second section of the said eighth article being under consideration, viz.

The arts, sciences, and all useful learning shall be promoted in one or more universities.

On the question, "Will the committee agree to the same?" It was determined in the negative.

The third section of the said eighth article being then under consideration, It was, on motion of Mr. Smilie, seconded by Mr. Gallatin, ordered, that the further consideration thereof be postponed.

The committee then resumed the consideration of the fifteenth section of the second article of the said proposed constitution, postponed on the sixteenth of January, viz.

The state treasurer shall be appointed annually, by the joint vote of both "houses" all subordinate officers in the treasury department, election officers, officers relating to the poor and high-ways, constables "and other" township officers shall be appointed in such manner as shall be directed by law.

It was moved by Mr. M·Lene, seconded by Mr. Shoemaker, to amend the said section by adding after the words "and other," the following: "county and," which was determined in the negative.

A motion was then made by Mr. Pickering, seconded by Mr. Ogden, to amend the said section by striking out the remainder after the word "houses," and in lieu thereof to insert the following, viz. All other officers in the treasury department, election officers, officers relating to taxes, to the poor and highways, constables and other township officers shall be appointed in such manner as is or shall be directed by law. Which was carried in the affirmative, and the said section adopted as follows, viz.

Section XV. The state treasurer shall be appointed annually by the joint vote of both houses: All other officers in the treasury department, election officers, officers relating to taxes, to the poor and highways, constables and other township officers shall be appointed in such manner as is or shall be directed by law.

The second section of the fourth article being under consideration, it was moved by Mr. Pickering, seconded by Mr. Sitgreaves, to strike out the word "before," and insert in lieu the word "by," which was carried in the affirmative, and the words "the chancellor of the commonwealth shall preside therein" unanimously agreed to be struck out.

And thereupon the said section was adopted as follows, viz.

Section II. All impeachments shall be tried by the senate. When sitting for that purpose the senators shall be on oath or affirmation: No person shall be convicted without the concurrence of two thirds of the members present.

A motion was made by Mr. Redick, seconded by Mr. M'Lene, to re-consider the third section of the said fourth article, in order to insert after the word "commonwealth," the words "for such term as the senators shall determine." Which was determined in the negative.

The first section of the third article being under consideration. A motion was made by Mr. Addison, seconded by Mr. Smilie, to postpone the debates on the said section until Tuesday next. Which was determined in the affirmative.

It was moved by Mr Addison, seconded by Mr. Miller, to re-consider the second and third sections of the second article of the proposed constitution, in order to introduce the following in lieu thereof, viz.

Section II. The governor shall be chosen on the second Tuesday of October, *when occasion shall require*, by the citizens throughout the state, at the places where they shall respectively vote for representatives. Returns of election for governor shall be made to the general assembly, and when two or more are equal and highest in votes, the general assembly shall, by joint vote of both houses, choose one of them to be governor for the ensuing three years. In case of contested elections, the same shall be judged of and determined by a committee to be selected from both houses of the legislature, in such manner as shall be by law directed. *During the trial of contested elections*, the speaker of the *senate* shall exercise the office of governor.

Section III. The governor shall hold his office during the term of three years, from the first Tuesday of December next ensuing his election, and shall not be capable of holding his office longer than nine years in any term of twelve years.

The committee then rose in order to report, that they had made further progress in the business referred to them, and request leave to sit again.

MONDAY, February 1, 1790. A. M.

The motion made by Mr. Addison, January 30, to re-consider the second and third sections of the second article of the proposed constitution, recurring.

On the question, Will the committee agree to re-consider in order to take into consideration the sections proposed to be inserted in lieu of the said second and third sections? It was determined in the affirmative, and the said sections moved by Mr. Addison being under consideration, viz.

Section II. The governor shall be chosen on the second Tuesday of October, *when occasion shall require*, by the citizens throughout the commonwealth, at the places where they shall respectively vote for representatives. Returns of election for governor shall be made to the general assembly, and when two or more are equal and highest in votes, the general assembly shall, by joint vote of both houses, choose one of them to be governor for the ensuing year. In case of contested elections, the same shall be judged of and determined by a committee to be selected from both houses of the legislature, in such manner as shall be by law directed. *During the trial of contested elections*, the speaker of the *senate* shall exercise the office of governor.

Section III. The governor shall hold his office during the term of three years, from the first Tuesday of December next ensuing his election, and shall not be capable of holding his office longer then nine years in any term of twelve years.

It was moved by Mr. Pickering, seconded by Mr. M'Kean, to strike out, in the second section, the words " when occasion shall require." Which was carried in the affirmative.

A motion was then made by Mr. Pickering, seconded by Mr. M'Kean, to amend the said section so as to read as follows, viz.

Section II. The governor shall be chosen on the second Tuesday of October by the citizens throughout the commonwealth, at the places where they shall respectively vote for representatives. The returns of every election for governor shall be transmitted to the seat of government, directed to the speaker of the senate, who shall open and publish the same in the presence of both houses of the legislature. The person having the highest number of votes shall be governor; but if it should so happen that any two or more shall be equal and highest in votes, the general assembly shall choose one of them for governor by the joint vote of both houses. Which was determined in the affirmative.

It was moved by Mr. Sitgreaves, seconded by Mr. Smith, to insert in the said second section, after the words " during the trial of contested elections," the words "the governor of the last year or," and after the word "senate" the following, "as the case may be." Which was determined in the negative, and the section, with the amendment proposed by Mr. Pickering, seconded by Mr. M'Kean, adopted.

The third section of the second article, proposed by Mr. Addison, being under consideration, it was moved by Mr. M'Kean, seconded by Mr. Sellers, to strike out the word "first," and to insert in lieu thereof the word "third." Which was carried in the affirmative, and the said section, as amended, adopted.

A motion was made by Mr. Pickering, seconded by Mr. Smilie, to re-consider the fifteenth section of the second article of the proposed constitution, viz.

In case of the death or resignation of the Governor, or of his removal from office, it shall devolve on the speaker of the senate until the next annual election of representatives, when another governor shall be chosen in the manner herein before mentioned.

On the question, Will the committee agree to re-consider the said section? It was determined in the affirmative.

A motion was made by Mr. Pickering, seconded by Mr. M'Kean, to add the following words to the said section, viz. " And until such newly elected governor shall be duly qualified and commence the exercise of his office." Which was carried in the affirmative, and the said third section, as amended, adopted.

Mr. Findley then called for his motion made the sixteenth day of January last, respecting the appointment of a secretary, and the same being under consideration, it was moved by Mr. M'Kean, seconded by Mr. Findley, to amend the same so as to read as follows, viz.

A secretary shall be commissioned by the governor. He shall countersign all commissions signed by the governor, and all orders drawn by him on the treasury of the state for monies appropriated, as well as tavern and marriage licences. He shall keep fair journals of the proceedings of the supreme executive department, to be laid before either house of the assembly when called for, and shall attend the official orders of the governor, or either house when required. Which was carried in the affirmative.

It was then moved by Mr. M'Lene, seconded by Mr. M'Kean, to insert after the words " a secretary shall be," the words " appointed and " Which was determined in the affirmative.

A motion was then made by Mr. Gray, seconded by Mr. Henderson, to postpone the debates on the said section. Which was determined in the negative.

It was then moved by Mr. Sitgreaves, seconded by Mr. Findley, to amend the said third section so as to read as follows, viz.

A secretary shall be appointed and commissioned by the governor. He shall be keeper of the seals of the state, and shall, under the direction of a committee of both branches of the legislature, affix the seal to the laws when the same shall be enacted. He shall countersign and register all commissions signed by the governor, and all orders drawn by him for monies appropriated, as well as marriage, tavern and other licences. He shall have the custody of all public acts, official documents and state papers which shall be addressed, or belong, to the legislative and executive departments, to be laid before the governor or either house when called for. He shall attend the governor or either house when required, and shall perform all such other duties as shall be enjoined him by future acts of the legislature.

It was moved by Mr. M'Kean, seconded by Mr. Pickering. to insert after the word " commissions," the words " charters of pardon, and patents for land." Which was carried in the affirmative.

A motion was made by Mr. M'Kean, seconded by Mr. Pickering, to strike out the words " and register," and the words " and all orders drawn by him for monies appropriated." Which was carried in the affirmative.

It was thereupon moved by Mr. Smith, seconded by Mr. Brown, to strike out the words " legislative and." Which was determined in the affirmative.

The section, as amended, being then under consideration, viz.

Section XVII. A secretary shall be appointed and commissioned by the governor. He shall be keeper of the seals of the state, and shall, under the direction of a committee of both branches of the legislature, affix the seal to the laws when the same shall be enacted. He shall countersign all commissions, charters of pardon, and patents for land, signed by the governor, as well as marriage. tavern and other licences. He shall have the custody of all public acts, official documents and state papers which shall be addressed, or belong to the executive department, to be laid before the governor or either house when called for. He shall attend the governor or either house when required, and shall perform all such other duties as shall be enjoined him by future acts of the legislature.

On the question, " Will the committee agree to the same ?" The yeas and nays being called by Mr. Smith, were as follow, viz.

YEAS.

Mr. Roberts	Mr. Lincoln	Mr. Hoge	Mr. Morris
M'Kean	Gehr	Redick	Coates
Mifflin	Rhoads	J. Ross	Gloninger
Atlee	Powell	Smilie	Brown
Sleagle	Piper	Gallatin	Graydon
Pedan	Findley	M'Lene	Pickering
Whitehill	Todd	Matthews	Beale—30.
Heister	Addison		

NAYS.

Mr. Baker	Mr. Gibbons	Mr. Miller	Mr. Smith
Gray	T. Ross	Reed	Snyder
Robinson,	Boyd	Tyson	Power
Hare	Hand	Dill	Henderson
Jenks	Graff	Sitgreaves	Gibson
Barclay	Breckbill	Arndt	Sellers—25.
Stout			

So it was determined in the affirmative, and adopted as the seventeenth section of the second article of the proposed constitution.

A motion was made by Mr. Gallatin, seconded by Mr. Smilie, as follows, viz.

The state shall be divided into districts for the purpose of electing members of the house of representatives of the United States, in such manner that the citizens of each district shall be entitled to elect not more than   representatives: And the number of representatives to be elected by the state, shall be apportioned between the said districts in proportion to the number of taxable inhabitants contained in each.

It was then moved by Mr. Gallatin, seconded by Mr. Smilie, to adjourn the debates on the said motion.

Whereupon, on motion, the committee rose in order to report, that they had made further progress in the business referred to them, and request leave to sit again.

TUESDAY, February 2, 1790. A. M.

The first section of the third article of the proposed constitution,, together with the amendments postponed on the eighteenth of January last, being under consideration, a motion was made by Mr. M'Kean, seconded by Mr. M'Lene, to postpone the said section, with the amendments. in order to introduce the following, in lieu thereof, viz.

Every male *citizen* being twenty-one years *of age*, who *has resided* in the state two years next before the days of election, and paid state or county taxes within that time, which shall have been assessed at least six months before the said election, or *having a freehold estate within the city or county of the annual income of three pounds, or any estate of the value of fifty pounds, though he may not have paid taxes, shall enjoy the right of an elector ;* and every male person, of the age aforesaid, who shall have been born in any of the United States, and resided in this state for one year next before the election, having either of the qualifications aforesaid, shall also be entitled to the right of an elector.

It was moved by Mr. Lewis, seconded by Mr. Smilie, to strike out, from the said proposed amendment, the words *or having a freehold estate within the city or county of the annual income of three pounds, or any estate of the value of fifty pounds. though he may not have paid taxes.* Which was determined in the affirmative.

A motion was then made by Mr. Addison, seconded by Mr. Gallatin, to strike out the word "citizen" and the words "has resided," and, in lieu of the former, to insert "inhabitant," and of the latter, the words "has been a resident citizen " Which was determined in the affirmative, and thereupon agreed to strike out the remainder of the said section after the words "shall enjoy the right of an elector."

It was moved by Mr. Pickering, seconded by Mr. M'Kean, to insert after the words " of age," the following: " who is a native of the United States, and has resided one year in this state, and every other male inhabitant." Which was determined in the negative.

On the question, Will the committee agree to the section as amended ? It was determined in the negative.

The committee then resumed the consideration of the said section as reported by the committee of nine, together with the amendments postponed on the eighteenth of January last, viz.

In elections by the citizens, every freeman of the age of twenty one years, having resided in the state two years next before the days of election respectively, and paid public state or county taxes within that time, which tax shall have been assessed upon him at least six months before the election, shall enjoy the right of an elector. The sons of freeholders of the age aforesaid, shall be entitled to vote, though they have not paid taxes.

A motion was made by Mr. Sitgreaves, seconded by Mr. Smith, to amend the second clause of the said section, so as to read as follows, viz.

The sons of freeholders, qualified as aforesaid, between the ages of twenty-one and twenty-two years, shall be entitled to vote although they have not paid taxes. Which was determined in the negative.

On the question, Will the committee agree to the latter part of the said section ? It was determined in the negative, and the first part, as amended, adopted as the first section of the third article of the said proposed constitution, as follows, viz.

Section I. In elections by the citizens every freeman of the age of twenty-one years, having resided in the state two years next before the days of election respectively, and paid public state or county taxes within that time, which tax shall have been assessed upon him at least six months before the election, shall enjoy the right of an elector.

The motion made yesterday by Mr. Gallatin, seconded by Mr. Smilie, to divide the state into districts for the purpose of electing members of the house of representatives of the United States, being withdrawn, the committee proceeded to take into consideration the bill of rights, being the ninth article of the proposed constitution reported by the committee of nine, and the first section being under debate the same was adopted as follows, viz.

Section I. That all men are born equally free and independent, and have certain inherent and indefeasible rights, among which are those of enjoying and defending life and liberty, of acquiring, possessing and protecting property and reputation, and of pursuing their own happiness.

The second section of the said ninth article, or bill of rights, being under consideration, viz.

That all power being originally *vested* in, is derived from the people, and all free governments originate from their will, are founded on their authority, and instituted for their common peace, safety and happiness ; *and for the advancement thereof*, they have, at all times, an unalienable *and indefeasible right* to alter, reform or abolish their government, in such manner as they may think proper.

It was moved by Mr. M'Lene, seconded by Mr. Graydon, to strike out the word *vested*, and, in lieu thereof, to insert the word *inherent.* Which was determined in the negative.

A motion was made by Mr. M'Kean, seconded by Mr. Sitgreaves, to strike out the words "and for the advancement thereof," and, in lieu thereof, to insert the following, viz. "And when the form thereof shall become destructive of these ends"

On the question, Will the committee agree to strike out for the aforesaid purpose? The yeas and nays being called by Mr. Sitgreaves, were as follow, viz.

YEAS.

Mr. Baker Mr. M'Kean Mr. Sitgreaves Mr. Hoge—4.

NAYS.

Mr. Roberts	Mr. Graff	Mr. Mawhorter	Mr. Matthews
Lewis	Atlee	Arndt	Morris
Mifflin	Breckbill	Rhoads	Potts
Gray	Miller	Powell	Coates
Robinson	Slegle	Smith	Shoemaker
Hare	Reed	Snyder	Gloninger
Ogden	Tyson	Findley	Brown
Jenks	Pedan	Todd	Graydon
Barclay	Dill	Addison	Pickering
Stout	Whitehill	Redick	Henderson
Gibbons	Power	J. Ross	Gibson
T. Ross	Heister	Smilie	Beale
Boyd	Lincoln	Gallatin	Sellers—55.
Hand	Gehr	M'Lene	

So it was determined in the negative.

It was then moved by Mr. M'Kean, seconded by Mr. Roberts, to insert, after the words "and indefeasible right," the words "in a peaceable and orderly way."

On the question, Will the committee agree to the same? The yeas and nays being called by Mr. Roberts, were as follow, viz.

YEAS.

Mr. Roberts	Mr. Jenks	Mr. Atlee	Mr. Sitgreaves
M'Kean	Stout	Breckbill	Shoemaker-9
Ogden			

NAYS.

Mr. Baker	Mr. Slegle	Mr. Powell	Mr. Matthews
Lewis	Reed	Piper	Morris
Mifflin	Tyson	Smith	Potts
Gray	Pedan	Snyder	Coates
Robinson	Dill	Findley	Gloninger
Hare	Whitehill	Todd	Brown
Barclay	Power	Addison	Graydon
Gibbons	Heister	Hoge	Pickering
T. Ross	Lincoln	Redick	Henderson
Boyd	Gehr	J. Ross	Gibson
Hand	Mawhorter	Smilie	Beale
Graff	Arndt	Gallatin	Sellers—51.
Miller	Rhoads	M'Lene	

So it was determined in the negative, and the said second section adopted as reported by the committee of nine.

The committee then rose in order to report, that they had made further progress in the business referred to them, and request leave to sit again.

WEDNESDAY, February 3, 1790. A. M.

The third section of the bill of rights being under consideration, viz.

That all men have a natural and indefeasible right to worship Almighty God according to the dictates of their own consciences, and that no man *ought or* of right *can* be compelled to attend any religious worship, or to erect or support any place of public worship, or to maintain any ministry, against his free will and consent; and that no human authority can controul or interfere with the rights of conscience in any case whatever; nor shall any preference ever be given, by law, to any religious establishments or modes of worship.

It was moved by Mr. Pickering, seconded by Mr. Smith, to strike out the words "ought or," and to transpose the word "can" before the words "of right." Which was carried in the affirmative, and the said section, as amended, adopted.

The fourth section of the said bill of rights being under consideration, viz.

That no person *who acknowledges the being of a God, and a future state of rewards and punishments*, shall, on account of his religious sentiments, be disqualified to hold any office or place of trust or profit under this commonwealth.

It was moved by Mr. Robinson, seconded by Mr. Graydon, to strike out the words "and a future state of rewards and punishments."

A motion was then made by Mr. Robinson, seconded by Mr. Sitgreaves, to strike out the words "who acknowledges the being of a God, and a future state of rewards and punishments."

On the question, Will the committee agree to strike out the words?" The yeas and nays being called by Mr. Brown, were as follow, viz.

YEAS.

Mr. Robinson	Mr. Hoge	Mr. Gallatin	Mr. Pickering
Hare	Redick	Potts	Henderson
Ogden	J. Ross	Graydon	Sellers—13.
Sitgreaves			

NAYS.

Mr. Baker	Mr. Boyd	Mr. Power	Mr. Todd
Roberts	Hand	Heister	Addison
Lewis	Graff	Lincoln	Smilie
M'Kean	Atlee	Gehr	M'Lene
Mifflin	Breckbill	Mawhorter	Matthews
Gray	Miller	Arndt	Coates
Jenks	Slegle	Rhoads	Shoemaker
Barclay	Reed	Powell	Gloninger
Stout	Tyson	Piper	Brown
Gibbons	Pedan	Smith	Gibson
Bull	Dill	Snyder	Beale—47.
T. Ross	Whitehill	Findley	

So it was determined in the negative.

It was then moved by Mr. Pickering, seconded by Mr. Ogden, to adjourn the debates on the said fourth section in order to introduce the following in lieu thereof, viz.

That the members of the legislature and all executive and judicial officers shall be bound by oath or affirmation to support the constitution of this state: But no religious test shall ever be required as a qualification to any office or public trust under this state.

On the question, Will the committee agree to the postponement for the aforesaid purpose? It was determined in the negative, and the said fourth section, as reported by the committee of nine, adopted.

The fifth section of the said bill of rights being under consideration, viz.

That elections shall be free and equal.

It was moved by Mr. Pickering, seconded by Mr. Shoemaker, to strike out the words "and equal." Which was determined in the negative.

A motion was then made by Mr. M'Kean, seconded by Mr. Tyson, to add the following words to the said section, viz. " to every person entitled to vote." Which was determined in the negative.

It was moved by Mr. Gallatin, seconded by Mr. Smilie, to add the following words to the said fifth section, viz. And that all freemen, having a sufficient common interest in, and attachment to, the community, be entitled to vote. Which was determined in the negative, and the section adopted as reported by the committee of nine.

The sixth section of the said bill of rights being under consideration, viz.

That trial by jury shall be as heretofore, and the right thereof shall remain inviolate.

On the question, Will the committee adopt the same? It was determined in the affirmative.

The seventh section of the said bill of rights being under consideration, viz.

The printing presses shall be free to every person who undertakes to examine the proceedings of the legislature or any branch of government, and no law shall ever be made restraining the right thereof. The free communication of thoughts and opinions is one of the most invaluable rights of man, and every citizen may freely speak, write and print, being responsible for the abuse of that liberty.

A motion was made by Mr. Pickering, seconded by Mr. M'Kean, to strike out the word "most" contained in the said section. Which was determined in the affirmative

It was then moved by Mr. Thomas Ross, seconded by Mr. Boyd, to amend the said section by adding the following words · And in case of indictments for libels the truth of the accusation may be pleaded in bar of the bill.

A motion was made by Mr. Findley, seconded by Mr. Hare, to postpone the said section, with the amendment. Which was determined in the negative.

Mr. T. Ross then withdrew his motion to amend the said section.

It was then moved by Mr. Smith, seconded by Mr. Findley, to insert the words "on any subject" after the word "print," and to add the following words to the said seventh section, viz. Upon indictment for the publication of papers investigating the conduct of individuals in their public capacity, or of those applying or canvassing for office,

48

the truth of the facts may be given in evidence in justification upon the general issue.

Whereupon, on motion of Mr. Findley, seconded by Mr. Addison, Ordered, That the said section, together with the amendments, be postponed.

The eighth section of the said bill of rights being under consideration, the same was adopted as follows, viz

That the people shall be secure in their persons, houses, papers and possessions against unreasonable searches and seizures, and no warrant shall issue to search any place, or to seize any person or things, but on probable cause, supported by oath or affirmation, and describing them as nearly as may be.

The ninth section of the said bill of rights being under consideration, viz.

That in all *criminal prosecutions* the accused hath a right to be heard by himself and his counsel; to demand the cause and nature of the accusation; to meet the witnesses face to face; to have compulsory process for obtaining witnesses in his favor, and a speedy public trial by an impartial jury of the *vicinage;* nor can he be compelled to give evidence against himself; nor can any man be deprived of his life, liberty or property but by the judgment of his peers or the law of the land.

A motion was made by Mr. Gallatin, seconded by Mr. Smilie, to insert, after the word "vicinage," the following, viz. " Without the unanimous consent of which jury he cannot be found guilty."

On the question, Will the committee agree to insert the same? It was determined in the negative.

It was then moved by Mr. M'Kean, seconded by Mr. Edwards, to strike out the word " criminal." and to insert, after the word " prosecutions." the following, viz. " by indictment." Which was determined in the affirmative, and the said ninth section, as amended, adopted.

The tenth section of the said bill of rights being under consideration, the same was adopted as follows, viz.

That no person shall be proceeded against by information for any indictable offence, except in cases arising in the land or naval forces, or in the militia when in actual service in time of war or public danger; nor shall any person, for the same offence, be twice put into jeopardy of life or limb; nor shall any man's property be taken, or applied to public use, without the consent of his representatives, and on just compensation being made.

The eleventh section of the said bill of rights being under consideration, the same was adopted as follows, viz.

That all courts shall be open, and every freeman for an injury done him in his lands, goods, person or reputation, shall have remedy by the due course of the law, and right and justice administered to him without sale, denial or delay.

The twelfth section of the said bill of rights being under consideration, the same was adopted as follows, viz.

That no power of suspending laws, or the execution thereof, shall be exercised, unless by the legislature or by the authority thereof.

The thirteenth section of the said bill of rights being under consideration, the same was adopted as follows, viz.

That excessive bail shall not be required, nor excessive fines imposed, or cruel punishments inflicted.

The fourteenth section of the said bill of rights being under consideration, the same was adopted as follows, viz.

That all prisoners shall be bailable by sufficient sureties, unless for capital offences, when the proof is evident or the presumption great, and the privilege of the writ of habeas corpus shall not be suspended unless when, in cases of rebellion or invasion, the public safety may require it.

The fifteenth section of the said bill of rights being under consideration, the same was adopted as follows, viz.

That the person of a debtor, where there is not a strong presumption of fraud, shall not be continued in prison after delivering up all his estate for the benefit of his creditors, in such manner as shall be prescribed by law.

The sixteenth section of the said bill of rights being under consideration, the same was adopted as follows, viz.

That no *ex post facto* law, or law impairing contracts shall be made.

A motion was made by Mr. Smith, seconded by Mr. Henderson, to insert, as the 17th section of the said bill of rights, the following, viz.

That religious societies and corporate bodies shall be protected in their rights, immunities and estates.

The committee rose in order to report, that they had made further progress in the business referred to them, and request leave to sit again.

THURSDAY, *February* 4, 1790. *A. M.*

The motion made yesterday by Mr. Smith, to be inserted as the seventeenth section of the bill of rights, being withdrawn.

A motion was made by Mr. Smith, seconded by Mr. Sitgreaves, to insert the following, as the seventeenth section of the said bill of rights, viz.

That religious societies or bodies of men united or incorporated for the advancement of religion and learning, or for other pious and charitable purposes, shall be protected in the enjoyment of their just privileges, immunities and estates.

It was moved by Mr. Lewis, seconded by Mr. M'Kean, to adjourn the debates on the said motion, in order to introduce the following, viz.

That the rights, immunities and estates of religious societies and corporate bodies shall be as valid under this constitution as they have heretofore been.

A motion was made by Mr. M'Kean, seconded by Mr. Pickering, to adjourn the debates on the several propositions before the committee.

On the question, Will the committee agree to the same? The yeas and nays being called by Mr. Sitgreaves, were as follow, viz.

YEAS.

Mr. Baker	Mr. Graff	Mr. Gehr	Mr. Matthews
Lewis	Atlee	Mawhorter	Morris
M'Kean	Breckbill	Rhoads	Potts
Mifflin	Miller	Powell	Coates
Gray	Slegle	Piper	Shoemaker
Robinson	Reed	Findley	Gloninger
Ogden	Tyson	Todd	Brown
Jenks	Pedan	Addison	Graydon
Barclay	Dill	Hoge	Pickering
Stout	Whitehill	J. Ross	Henderson
Bull	Heister	Smilie	Gibson
Boyd	Lower	M'Lene	Sellers—50
Hand	Lincoln		

NAYS.

Mr. Roberts	Mr. Power	Mr. Smith	Mr. Redick
Gibbons	Sitgreaves	Snyder	Gallatin—10
T. Ross	Arndt		

So it was determine l in the affirmative, and the debates adjourned.

The seventeenth section of the said bill of rights, as reported by the committee of nine, coming under consideration, the same was adopted as follows, viz.

That no person shall be attainted of treason or felony by the legislature.

The eighteenth section of the said bill of rights being under consideration, viz.

That no attainder shall work corruption of blood, or forfeiture of *real* estate, *except during the life of the offender.*

A motion was made by Mr. Addison, seconded by Mr. Gallatin, to add the following words to the said section, viz.

The estates of such persons as destroy their own lives shall go to their representatives as in the case of natural death; and if any person shall be killed by casualty or accident there shall be no forfeiture by reason thereof. Which was carried in the affirmative.

It was then moved by Mr. Ogden, seconded by Mr. Power, to strike out the word "real" before the word "estate," and the words "during the life of the offender," and to insert the words "to the commonwealth" after the word "estate." Which was carried in the affirmative, and the said eighteenth section, with the amendments, adopted as follows, viz.

That no attainder shall work corruption of blood or forfeiture of estate to the commonwealth; the estates of such persons as shall destroy their own lives shall go to their representatives as in the case of natural death. And if any person shall be killed by casualty or accident there shall be no forfeiture by reason thereof.

The nineteenth section of the said bill of rights being under consideration, a motion was made by Mr. Roberts, seconded by Mr. Shoemaker, to insert the following in lieu thereof, viz.

That the citizens have a right to assemble together in a peaceable manner to consult for their common good and apply to those invested with the powers of government for redress of grievances or other proper purposes, by petition, address or remonstrance. Which was determined in the affirmative.

The twentieth section of the said bill of rights being under consideration, it was moved by Mr. Pickering, seconded by Mr. M·Kean, to amend the same so as to read as follows, viz.

That the right of the citizens to bear arms in defence of themselves and the state shall not be questioned; but those who conscientiously scruple to bear arms shall not be compellable to do so, but shall pay an equivalent for personal service. Which was carried in the affirmative, and the said sectio as amended, adopted.

The twenty-first section of the said bill of rights being under consideration, the same was adopted as follows, viz.

That no standing army shall, in time of peace, be kept up without the consent of the legislature, and the military shall, in all cases and at all times, be kept in strict subordination to the civil power.

The twenty-second section of the said bill of rights being under consideration, the same was adopted as follows, viz.

That no soldier shall, in time of peace, be quartered in any house without the consent of the owner, nor in time of war, but in a manner to be prescribed by law.

The twenty-third section of the said bill of rights being under consideration, viz.

That the legislature shall at no *time* create any office the appointment to which shall be for a longer term than during good behaviour.

It was moved by Mr. Gallatin, seconded by Mr. Smilie, to insert, after the word "time," the following, viz. "grant any title of nobility or hereditary distinction, nor." Which was carried in the affirmative, and the said section, as amended, adopted.

A motion was then made by Mr. M'Lene, seconded by Mr. Henderson, to insert the following as the twenty-fourth section of the said bill of rights, viz.

That perpetuities and monopolies are contrary to the nature of a republican government, and ought not to exist.

On the question, " Will the committee agree to the same?" The yeas and nays being called by Mr. Lewis, were as follow, viz.

YEAS.

Mr. Boyd	Mr. Piper	Mr. Addison	Mr. M'Lene
Whitehill	Findley	Smilie	Matthews
Lower	Todd	Gallatin	Henderson
			12.

NAYS.

Mr. Baker	Mr. Gibbons	Mr. Pedan	Mr. J. Ross
Roberts	Bull	Dill	Morris
Lewis	T. Ross	Power	Potts
M'Kean	Hand	Gehr	Coates
Mifflin	Graff	Sitgreaves	Shoemaker
Gray	Atlee	Arndt	Gloninger
Robinson	Breckbill	Powell	Brown
Ogden	Miller	Smith	Graydon
Jenks	Slegle	Snyder	Pickering
Barclay	Reed	Hoge	Gibson
Stout	Tyson	Redick	Sellers—44.

So it was determined in the negative.

A motion was then made by Mr. Pickering, seconded by Mr. Redick, to insert the following as the twenty-fourth section of the said bill of rights, viz.

That estates-tail, being repugnant to the principles of republican government, shall not be supported ; but tenants in tail shall be deemed the absolute owners thereof, in fee simple.

On the question, Will the committee agree to the same ? The yeas and nays being called by Mr. Lewis, were as follow, viz.

YEAS.

Mr. Robinson	Mr. Addison	Mr. Redick	Mr. Pickering–4.

NAYS.

Mr. Baker	Mr. Hand	Mr. Lincoln	Mr. Gallatin
Roberts	Atlee	Gehr	M'Lene
Lewis	Breckbill	Sitgreaves	Matthews
M'Kean	Miller	Arndt	Morris
Mifflin	Slegle	Powell	Potts
Gray	Reed	Piper	Coates
Ogden	Tyson	Smith	Shoemaker
Jenks	Pedan	Snyder	Gloninger
Barclay	Dill	Findley	Brown
Stout	Whitehill	Todd	Graydon
Gibbons	Power	Hoge	Henderson
Ball	Heister	J. Ross	Gibson
T. Ross	Lower	Smilie	Sellers—53.
Boyd			

So it was determined in the negative.

The twenty-fourth section of the bill of rights, as reported by the committee of nine, being under consideration, viz.

That emigration from the state shall not be prohibited.

It was moved by Mr. M'Kean, seconded by Mr. Lewis, to add the following words to the said section, viz. "Unless in time of war." Which was determined in the negative, and the original section adopted.

The twenty-fifth section of the said bill of rights being under consideration. the same was adopted as follows, viz.

To guard against transgressions of the high powers which we have delegated, WE DECLARE. that every thing in this article expressed is excepted out of the general powers of legislation, and shall for ever remain inviolate.

A motion was made by Mr. M'Kean, seconded by Mr. Smith, to re-consider the eighteenth section of the bill of rights, in order to strike out the words " to their representatives." Which was determined in the affirmative, and the said section, as amended adopted.

The committee then rose in order to report, that they had made further progress in the business referred to them, and request leave to sit again.

FRIDAY, February 5, 1790, A. M.

The committee resumed the consideration of the seventh section of the bill of rights, with the amendments adjourned the third instant, and the amendment, moved by Mr. Smith, seconded by Mr. Findley, being under consideration.

On the question, Will the committee agree to the same? The yeas and nays being called by Mr. Smilie, were as follow, viz.

YEAS.

Mr. Wilson	Mr. Pedan	Mr. Powell	Mr. Smilie
Mifflin	Dill	Piper	Gallatin
Robinson	Whitehill	Smith	M'Lene
Hare	Power	Snyder	Matthews
Jenks	Hiester	Findley	Coates
Barclay	Lower	Todd	Shoemaker
Boyd	Lincoln	Addison	Gloninger
Hand	Groscop	Hoge	Brown
Breckbill	Gehr	Redick	Pickering
Reed	Mawhorter	J. Ross	Beale 41.
Tyson			

NAYS.

Mr. Baker	Mr. Bull	Mr. Slegle	Mr. Potts
Roberts	T. Ross	Sitgreaves	Graydon
M'Kean	Graff	Arndt	Henderson
Gray	Atlee	Rhoads	Gibson
Ogden	Miller	Morris	Sellers 21.
Stout			

So it was determined in the affirmative, and the amendment adopted.
A motion was then made by Mr. Miller, seconded by Mr. Morris, to adjourn the debates on the said seventh section, together with the amendments, in order to introduce the following, in lieu thereof, viz.

That no law shall ever be made abridging the freedom of speech or the press.

On the question, " Will the committee agree to the adjournment for the aforesaid purpose?" The yeas and nays being called by Mr. T. Ross, were as follow, viz.

YEAS.

Mr. Baker	Mr. Stout	Mr. Slegle	Mr. Morris
Roberts	Bull	Reed	Potts
Lewis	T. Ross	Tyson	Pickering
M'Kean	Graff	Sitgreaves	Henderson
Gray	Atlee	Arndt	Gibson
Ogden	Miller	Rhoads	Sellers
Jenks			25.

NAYS.

Mr. Robinson	Mr. Power	Mr. Smith	Mr. Gallatin
Hare	Heister	Snyder	M'Lene
Barclay	Lower	Findley	Matthews
Boyd	Lincoln	Todd	Coates
Hand	Groscop,	Addison	Shoemaker
Breckbill	Gehr	Hoge	Gloninger
Pedan	Mawhorter	Redick	Brown
Dill	Powell	J. Ross	Beale 35.
Whitehill	Piper	Smilie	

So it was determined in the negative, and thereupon, the said seventh section, as amended, adopted as follows, viz.

That the printing presses shall be free to every person who undertakes to examine the proceedings of the legislature or any branch of government, and no law shall ever be made restraining the right thereof. The free communication of thoughts and opinions is one of the invaluable rights of man, and every citizen may freely speak, write, and print on any subject, being responsible for the abuse of that liberty. But upon indictments for the publication of papers investigating the conduct of individuals in their public capacity, or of those applying or canvassing for office, the truth of the facts may be given in evidence in justification upon the general issue.

On motion of Mr. Lewis, seconded by Mr. Findley, the following was adopted as the preamble to the said proposed constitution, viz.

We, the people of Pennsylvania, having by our representatives freely chosen and in convention met, altered and amended the constitution of this commonwealth, do ordain and establish as follows.

And the said constitution being then read, the same was unanimously adopted.

[For the constitution as reported by the committee of the whole see, page 296 of this volume.]

On motion of Mr. Pickering, seconded by Mr. Ogden,

Resolved, unanimously. That the thanks of this committee be given to general Hand, for his able and impartial conduct while chairman thereof.

The committee, having compleated the business referred to them, rose in order to report the said plan of government to the convention.

PART. V.

The act of the 28th March, 1825, for ascertaining the opinion of the people of this commonwealth, relative to the call of a convention.

Section 1. *Be it enacted by the Senate and House of Representatives of the commonwealth of Pennsylvania in general assembly met, and it is hereby enacted by the authority of the same,* That it shall be the duty of each of the inspectors of votes for the several townships, wards and districts in this commonwealth, at the next general election, to receive tickets from the citizens thereof, qualified to vote at such general elections, and to deposit them in a proper box or boxes, to be for that purpose provided by the proper officers, which tickets shall be labelled with the word "Convention," and within, the words "*For* a Convention," or "*Against* a Convention," and folded, delivered and received in the usual manner.

Sect. 2. *And be it further enacted by the authority aforesaid,* That the said election shall, in all respects, be conducted as the general elections in this commonwealth are now conducted; and it shall be the duty of the return judges of the respective counties thereof, first having carefully ascertained the number of votes given for or against the calling of a convention, to make out duplicate returns thereof, expressed in words at length and not in figures only, one of which returns, so made out, shall be lodged in the prothonotary's office of the proper county, and the other sealed and directed to the speaker of the Senate, which shall be, by one of the said judges, delivered to the sheriff, with the other returns required by law to be transmitted to the secretary of the commonwealth, whose duty it shall be to transmit the same therewith; and the speaker of the Senate shall open and publish the same, in the presence of the members of the two houses of the legislature, on the second Tuesday of December next.

JOEL B. SUTHERLAND, *Speaker*
of the House of Representatives.
THOMAS BURNSIDE,
Speaker of the Senate.

APPROVED—The twenty-eighth day of March, one thousand eight hundred and twenty-five.

J. ANDW. SHULZE.

Lightning Source UK Ltd.
Milton Keynes UK
UKHW021414051118
331796UK00015B/1222/P